PHYSIATRIC PROCEDURES

in Clinical Practice

PHYSIATRIC PROCEDURES

in Clinical Practice

Edited by
TED A. LENNARD, MD
Clinical Assistant Professor
Department of Physical Medicine
  and Rehabilitation
University of Arkansas for Medical Sciences
Little Rock, Arkansas
Springfield Physical Medicine
  and Rehabilitation , P.C.
Springfield, Missouri

HANLEY & BELFUS, INC./ Philadelphia
MOSBY/ St. Louis • Baltimore • Boston • Carlsbad • Chicago • London
Madrid • Naples • New York • Philadelphia • Sydney • Tokyo • Toronto

Publisher: HANLEY & BELFUS, INC.
                  210 S. 13th Street
                  Philadelphia, PA 19107
                  (215) 546-7293
                  FAX (215) 790-9330

North American and worldwide sales and distribution:

                  MOSBY
                  11830 Westline Industrial Drive
                  St. Louis, MO 63146

In Canada: Times Mirror Professional Publishing, Ltd.
                  130 Flaska Drive
                  Markham, Ontario L6G 1B8
                  Canada

Library of Congress Cataloging-in-Publication Data

Physiatric procedures in clinical practice / [edited by] Ted A. Lennard.
        p.   cm.
     Includes bibliographical references and index.
     ISBN 1-56053-069-3
     1. Medicine, Physical.   1. Medical rehabilitation.   I. Lennard, Ted A., 1961–   .
     [DNLM: 1. Physical Medicine—methods.   2. Rehabilitation.   WB 460 P578 1994]
     RM700.P46   1994
     617'.03—dc20
     DNLM/DLC
     for Library of Congress   94-39824
                                                                                        CIP

PHYSIATRIC PROCEDURES IN CLINICAL PRACTICE   ISBN 1-56053-069-3

Last digit is the print number : 9 8 7 6 5 4 3 2 1

DEDICATION

To my wife Suzanne

CONTENTS

CONTRIBUTORS

RUSSELL R. BOND, Jr., D.O.
Clinical Assistant Professor, Department of Physical Medicine and Rehabilitation, University of Missouri, Columbia, Missouri; Rehabilitation Medical Director, Cox Health Systems, Springfield, Missouri

D. WAYNE BROOKS, M.D.
Northwest Arkansas Rehabilitation Hospital, Fayetteville, Arkansas

SUSAN J. DREYER, M.D.
Clinical Assistant Professor, Department of Physical Medicine and Rehabilitation, Emory University School of Medicine, Atlanta, Georgia

PAUL DREYFUSS, M.D.
Clinical Assistant Professor, Department of Rehabilitation Medicine, University of Texas Health Science Center, San Antonio, Texas; Neuroskeletal Center, Tyler, Texas

FRANK J. E. FALCO, M.D.
Active Staff, West Paces Medical Center, Smyrna, Georgia

ANDREW A. FISCHER, M.D., Ph.D
Associate Clinical Professor, Department of Rehabilitation Medicine, Mt. Sinai School of Medicine, New York, New York; Chief, Physical Medicine and Rehabilitation, Veterans Affairs Medical Center, Bronx, New York

JOSEPH D. FORTIN, D.O.
Medical Director, Rehabilitation Hospital of Fort Wayne, Fort Wayne, Indiana

STEVE R. GEIRINGER, M.D.
Associate Professor, Department of Physical Medicine and Rehabilitation, Wayne State University; Medical Director of Outpatient Services and Electrodiagnostic Services, Rehabilitation Institute of Michigan, Detroit, Michigan

RICHARD P. GRAY, M.D.
Associate Professor, Department of Physical Medicine and Rehabilitation, University of Arkansas for Medical Sciences; Staff Physician, John C. McClelland Veterans Affairs Medical Center, Little Rock, Arkansas

BARBARA A. HELLER, D.O., P.T.
Elmhurst Memorial Hospital, Central DuPage Hospital, Oak Park Hospital, Westlake Hospital, Edwards Hospital, Elmhurst, Illinois

PHALA A. HELM, M.D.
Professor and Chairman, Department of Physical Medicine & Rehabilitation, University of Texas Southwestern Medical Center, Dallas, Texas

STANLEY A. HERRING, M.D.
Clinical Associate Professor, Department of Rehabilitation Medicine and Department of Orthopaedics, University of Washington School of Medicine, Seattle, Washington

BRYAN D. KAPLANSKY, M.D.
Staff, Parkview Hospital, Fort Wayne, Indiana

FRANCIS P. LAGATTUTA, M.D.
Clinical Assistant Professor, Department of Orthopedics, Section of Rehabilitation Medicine, Loyola University School of Medicine, Chicago, Illinois

MATHEW H. M. LEE, M.D., M.P.H., FACP
Medical Director, Rusk Institute of Rehabilitation Medicine, New York University Medical Center; Chairman and Professor, Department of Rehabilitation Medicine, New York University College of Medicine; Clinical Professor of Surgical Sciences, New York University College of Dentistry; Executive Vice President, American College of Acupuncture, Inc., New York, New York; President, American Academy of Acupuncture, Inc., Middlebury, Connecticut

TED A. LENNARD, M.D.
Clinical Assistant Professor, Department of Physical Medicine and Rehabilitation, University of Arkansas for Medical Sciences, Little Rock, Arkansas; Springfield Physical Medicine & Rehabilitation, P.C., Springfield, Missouri

JONATHAN P. LESTER, M.D.
Clinical Assistant Professor, Department of Physical Medicine and Rehabilitation, Emory University School of Medicine, Atlanta, Georgia

SUNG J. LIAO, M.D., D.P.H., FACP
Clinical Professor of Surgical Sciences, New York University College of Dentistry; Formerly, Clinical Associate Professor of Rehabilitation Medicine, New York University College of Medicine; Chairman, American College of Acupuncture, Inc., New York, New York; Secretary, American Academy of Acupuncture, Inc., Middlebury, Connecticut

DENNIS M. LOX, M.D.
Medical Director, Florida Spine and Sports Medicine Center, Clearwater, Florida

DENNIS J. MATTHEWS, M.D.
Chairman and Medical Director, The Children's Hospital Rehabilitation Center, Denver, Colorado

CHARLES C. MAULDIN, M.D.
Springfield Physical Medicine & Rehabilitation, P.C., Springfield, Missouri

DAVID L. NASH, M.D.
Assistant Professor, Department of Physical Medicine and Rehabilitation, Mayo Medical School, Rochester, Minnesota

DAVID F. NEALE, M.D.
Assistant Professor, Department of Physical Medicine and Rehabilitation, University of Arkansas for Medical Sciences; Medical Director, Foot-at-Risk (P.A.C.T.) Clinic, John C. McClelland Veterans Affairs Medical Center, Little Rock, Arkansas

JOHN P. OBERMILLER, M.D.
Assistant Clinical Professor, Department of Physical Medicine and Rehabilitation, University of Texas Health Science Center, San Antonio, Texas

NICHOLAS K. OLSEN, D.O.
Sports Medicine Fellow, Department of Physical Medicine and Rehabilitation , Northwestern University Medical School, Chicago, Illinois

INDER PERKASH, M.D.
Professor, Department of Urology and of Physical Medicine and Rehabilitation, and Paralyzed Veterans of America Professor of Spinal Cord Injury Medicine, Stanford University School of Medicine; Chief, Spinal Cord Injury Service, Department of Veterans Affairs Medical Center, Palo Alto, California

JOEL M. PRESS, M.D.
Clinical Assistant Professor, Department of Physical Medicine and Rehabilitation, Northwestern University Medical School; Medical Director, Center for Spine, Sports, and Occupational Rehabilitation, Rehabilitation Institute of Chicago, Chicago, Illinois

K. DEAN REEVES, M.D.
Assistant Professor, Department of Physical Medicine and Rehabilitation, University of Kansas School of Medicine; Medical Director, Bethany Rehabilitation Center, Kansas City, Kansas

ROBERT G. SCHWARTZ, M.D.
Piedmont Physical Medicine & Rehabilitation, P.A., Greenville, South Carolina

DANIEL Y. SHIN, M.D.
Associate Clinical Professor, Department of Orthopedics, University of Southern California School of Medicine, Los Angeles, California; Director, Rehab West Medical Group, and Medical Director, Acute Physical Rehabilitation Center, Downey Community Hospitals Foundation; Director, Neuromuscular Diagnostics Laboratory, Rancho Los Amigos Medical Center, Downey, California

RANDALL D. SMITH, M.D.
Clinical Assistant Professor, Department of Physical Medicine and Rehabilitation, University of Missouri School of Medicine, Columbia, Missouri; Chief, Department of Rehabilitation Medicine, VA Medical Center, Columbia, Missouri

THOMAS SOWELL, M.S.
Speech Pathologist, John C. McClelland Veterans Affairs Medical Center; Instructor, Department of Physical Medicine and Rehabilitation, University of Arkansas for Medical Sciences, Little Rock, Arkansas

VIKKI A. STEFANS, M.D.
Associate Professor, Department of Pediatrics and of Physical Medicine and Rehabilitation, University of Arkansas for Medical Sciences, Little Rock, Arkansas

ROBERT E. WINDSOR, M.D.
Clinical Assistant Professor, Department of Physical Medicine and Rehabilitation, Emory University School of Medicine, Atlanta, Georgia

JEFFREY L. WOODWARD, M.D., M.S.
Springfield Physical Medicine & Rehabilitation, P.C. Springfield, Missouri

JEFFREY L. YOUNG, M.D.
Assistant Professor, Department of Physical Medicine and Rehabilitation, Northwestern University Medical School; Director, Spine and Sports Fellowship, Rehabilitation Institute of Chicago, Chicago, Illinois

PREFACE

The management of pain and many disabling functional disorders can be facilitated by select physiatric procedures. The majority of these procedures are also performed by other specialists. This book is unique, however, in that it is written from a physiatric perspective.

As the first comprehensive physiatric procedure textbook, two goals of the book are worth mentioning: first, to recognize the various types of procedures commonly performed by the physiatrist and, secondly, to provide a standard reference for the clinician by providing practical tips on procedural care, including patient selection, indications, techniques, complications, and follow-up care. Reviews of regional anatomy are also discussed when pertinent. It should be clearly stated that this book is not intended to replace direct supervised residency training, but to supplement it. It may also serve as a useful guide to those who are unfamiliar with physiatric care. Electrodiagnostic procedures and testing were purposefully omitted because of their complexity and the excellent references currently available.

This book is divided into three sections. The initial 13 chapters present a diverse combination of needle procedures for relief of pain as well as non-needle procedures performed on the rehabilitation patient. Chapters 14–18 discuss the clinical indications and techniques for peripheral nerve blocks, and the final chapters, 19–27, emphasize spinal procedures.

Physiatric Procedures in Clinical Practice was made possible by a large supporting cast. I would like to thank the librarians at Cox Health Care Systems in Springfield, Missouri, for the hours spent on literature searches for many of the contributors. Charles Beasley, Radiation Safety Officer for St. John's Hospital in Springfield, Missouri, deserves special recognition for the work he put into the radiation section in the first chapter, "Fundamentals of Procedural Care." My sincere thanks also go to transcriptionists Karen Maddox and Judy Davis, photographers Gail Lurvey and Dan Cunningham, in Springfield, Missouri, speech pathologist Deb Brown, and to my wife, Suzanne, for her support as well as her grammatical proofing. Finally, I would like to thank each of the contributors who willingly shared both their time and expertise on their respective procedures while still investing countless hours in their own practices.

Ted A. Lennard, M.D.

Chapter 1

FUNDAMENTALS OF PROCEDURAL CARE

TED A. LENNARD, M.D.

Physiatric procedures are a useful adjunct in managing pain and functional problems. The physiatrist, as a diagnostician, can derive valuable information from the results of these procedures and from patient responses. This information can be invaluable in directing future treatment. Knowledge of the fundamentals of procedural care is essential to novices and experienced physicians who provide such treatment in order to reduce complications, eliminate unnecessary procedures, and maximize patient recovery.

The patient work-up should commence with a detailed history and a physical examination that focuses on the body part involved. Historical emphasis on the duration of symptoms, previous attempts at procedures, and pending litigation should be well documented. Signs of symptom magnification and malingering should be noted.[5] A thorough functional, social, and psychological history should be included. A comparison of historical and physical findings with available imaging studies is essential to complete the evaluation. During the evaluation period, diagnostic procedures can be useful in providing valuable insight into the patient's pain generator, anatomic defect, threshold for pain, and psychological response to treatment.

Once a provisional diagnosis is made, treatment objectives should be outlined. Conservative, non-procedural-oriented treatment should be undertaken initially if symptoms are not disabling. This treatment should include correction of underlying biomechanical disorders, activity modification in the workplace, technique changes in athletes, and flexibility and strengthening programs. Concomitant psychological disorders also should be treated. Upon deciding to proceed with a therapeutic procedure, the physician should be certain it is performed within the context of a well-designed rehabilitation program.

This chapter discusses a wide variety of basic topics pertinent to the fundamentals of procedures, including general technique, common procedural complications, common drugs used, radiation concepts, and informed consent.

GENERAL PROCEDURE TECHNIQUES

Positioning and Relaxation

Positioning the patient for comfort and physician accessibility is an important step in good technique. Multiple pillows, foam plinths, and pads can be used to increase the patient's tolerance on hard procedure tables, provide some degree of relaxation, and optimize positioning. This is especially important for the patient with cardiac or pulmonary compromise. For the physician, chairs and procedure tables of proper height prevent fatigue during lengthy procedures and improve manual dexterity.

Constant communication with the patient, including explanations of approaching procedural steps, helps reduce anxiety. Inappropriate conversation with assisting medical personnel should be avoided, thereby confirming the physician's total attention to the patient. The patient's gown should fit properly, enhancing relaxation and comfort. If these techniques do not lead to relaxation, oral or parenteral sedation should be provided.

Skin Preparation

Because skin cannot be sterilized without damage, the goal of antiseptics is to remove transient and pathogenic microorganisms while reducing resident flora to a low level.[94] These agents should be safe, rapid-acting, inexpensive, and effective on a broad spectrum of organisms.[70,94] Multiple agents, including iodophors (Betadine), hexachlorophene (pHisoHex), chlorhexidine (Hibiclens, Hibitane) and alcohols, are commercially available and accomplish these desired goals.[29,88,94] Chlorhexidine compounds are believed by many to be superior to most agents.[64,94,96,107] Clinically, the most commonly used agents are alcohol and iodine, with the latter being superior for skin decontamination.[21] Application of 70% isopropyl alcohol destroys 90% of the cutaneous bacteria in 2 minutes, but the usual single wipe without waiting produces, at most, a 75% reduction in cutaneous bacteria.[94]

Skin regions with hair should not alter one's method of skin decontamination. Hair removal by shaving increases wound infection rate and is contraindicated.[3,9,95] If absolutely necessary, clipping hair[67,82] or applying depilatory creams[95] can be safe. The overall risk of wound infection with most physiatric procedures is low and mostly depends on the technique that the practitioner employs during the procedure.

Needle Insertion and Local Anesthesia

Steps should be taken to make all procedures as pain-free as possible. The liberal use of local anesthetics in adequate concentrations will promote this goal while minimizing repeat needlesticks. Small-diameter needles, 28–30 gauge, are initially used to anesthetize the skin and subcutaneous tissue. Distracting the skin with one's fingers while slowly advancing the needle helps to reduce pain. The tip of the needle can be placed in the subcutaneous fat and, upon injection, less pain is noted than with intradermal injections because of the distensibility of fat. Rapid infusion of medication, especially with large volumes, causes tissue distention and results in pain. Lidocaine[4,71,89,100] and bupivacaine[19] buffered with 8.4% sodium bicarbonate causes less pain than plain anesthetics and is equally efficacious. A 1:10 to 1:20 ratio of sodium bicarbonate to anesthetics can be used. Morris et al. found that, when injected, subcutaneous procaine and lidocaine were the least painful anesthetics.[75,76] Only etidocaine was found to be more painful than bupivacaine.

Other preparations used to reduce pain with initial needle injections include topical anesthetics (eutectic mixtures of local anesthetics, or EMLA),[110] vapocoolant sprays, and preheated local anesthetics.[11] If the patient is intolerant of or allergic to anesthetic agents, 0.9% intradermal saline or dilute antihistamines such as diphenhydramine (Benadryl) in 10–25-mg/ml injections can be used as alternatives[69]; however, they are often considered painful, especially when injected intradermally.

Prior to injecting anesthetics, one should aspirate to prevent inadvertent injection into vascular structures. Small-gauge needles are unreliable when aspirating for blood. Needles of 25 gauge or larger rotated in two planes are necessary for this purpose. Continual movement of the needle tip makes injection into a vessel also less likely. Slow, fractionated dosing is recommended while monitoring the patient for early signs of anesthetic toxicity.

Precautions

Good technique not only reduces the risk of wound infection, but also lowers the rate of viral transmission between patient and physician. Physicians who perform exposure-prone procedures should know their human immunodeficiency virus (HIV) and hepatitis B virus (HBV) antibody status. The risk to the patient of contracting the HIV virus from a seropositive surgeon during a procedure ranges from 1 in 42,000 to 1 in 420,000; the risk of contracting fatal HBV infection from an HBeAG-positive surgeon during a procedure ranges from 1 in 76,000 to 1 in 1.4 million.[63] Universal precautions should be understood and include the use of gloves, protective eyewear, masks (optional), and gowns (optional). Recapping used needles should be avoided and is seldom necessary.

COMMON COMPLICATIONS

The range of complications with physiatric procedures extend from transient and insignificant to serious and life-threatening. The physiatrist who chooses to perform these procedures should be well educated and experienced in recognizing and treating a wide range of potential complications. Advanced training in airway management and cardiac/respiratory resuscitation according to advanced cardiac life support (ACLS) protocols is essential.[17,32] Resuscitation equipment, including a cardiac monitor, defibrillator, laryngoscope, endotracheal tubes, oxygen, suction capabilities, and emergency drugs, should be readily available. Many complications are drug related, especially when anesthetics are given (Table 1-1), but also may be related to the procedure itself.

Inherent to most needle procedures is transient postinjection soreness, local tissue bleeding, and minor swelling. These symptoms are usually alleviated with ice, analgesics, and limitation of activity, and they rarely need more aggressive treatment. Bleeding complications can be minimized when a good medical history is taken, including recent intake of medication. Aspirin should be discontinued 7–10 days prior to elective epidural procedures. The effect of aspirin on platelets is irreversible and persists for the life of the platelet (7–10 days); therefore, prolonged bleeding may occur many days after the drug is discontinued.[65] Antiplatelet and anticoagulant drugs are contraindications to needle procedures in the epidural space and other highly vascular areas. Many of these areas are inaccessible to direct external pressure and, with hematoma formation, could potentially compromise organ systems and disrupt both neuronal and vascular function.

Other less common complications include infection and seizures. Seizures are possible with toxic

TABLE 1-1. Differential Diagnosis of Local Anesthetic Reactions

Etiology	Major Clinical Features	Comments
Local anesthetic toxicity Intravascular injection Relative overdose	Immediate convulsion and/or cardiac toxicity Onset in 5 to 15 minutes of irritability, progressing to convulsions	Injection into vertebral or a carotid artery may cause convulsion after administration of small dose
Reaction to vasoconstrictor	Tachycardia, hypertension, headache, apprehension	May vary with vasopressor used
Vasovagal reaction	Rapid onset Bradycardia Hypotension Pallor, faintness	Rapidly reversible with elevation of legs
Allergy Immediate Delayed	Anaphylaxis (↓ BP, bronchospasm, edema) Urticaria	Allergy to amides extremely rare Cross-allergy possible, for example, with preservatives in local anesthetics and food
High spinal or epidural block	Gradual onset Bradycardia* Hypotension Possible respiratory arrest	May lose consciousness with total spinal block and onset of cardiorespiratory effects more rapid than with high epidural or with subdural block
Concurrent medical episode (e.g., asthma attack, myocardial infarct)	May mimic local anesthetic reaction	Medical history important

* Sympathetic block above T4 adds cardiovascular nerve blockade to the vasodilatation seen with blockade below T4; total spinal block may have rapid onset.

(From Covino BG: Clinical pharmacology of local anesthetic agents. In Cousin MJ, Bridenbaugh PO (eds): Neural Blockade in Clinical Anesthesia and Management of Pain, 2nd ed. Philadelphia, J.B. Lippincott, 1988, p 134; with permission.)

levels of injected drugs, usually anesthetics, or from the rapid absorption of anesthetics given in therapeutic doses. Medications that lower the seizure threshold should be recognized and include tricyclic antidepressants, central nervous system (CNS) stimulants, antipsychotic agents, phenothiazine derivatives, and monoamine oxidase (MAO) inhibitors. Sedation with benzodiazepines or barbiturates offers modest protection against seizures by raising the seizure threshold for a few minutes if the agents are given before the procedure starts.

Vasovagal Responses

Vasovagal syncope, or fainting, is a combination of arteriolar dilatation (vaso) and inappropriate cardiac slowing (vagal), resulting in hypotension with loss of consciousness.[1,108] Vasovagal response may occur during any type of procedure in the patient or in other personnel or family members who are present in the room. It is usually a response to relative or absolute loss of blood but may be attributed to strong emotions.[92,108] It is more common in people who are slender and young[28] and is rare in the elderly.[53,62] Twenty percent of normal individuals lose consciousness at some time in their lives.[1] Venodilator drugs,[24,44,91] recent exhaustive exercise, relative dehydration, hypoglycemia, and aortic stenosis are predisposing factors.[108] Adequate hydration prior to the procedure can often prevent this problem.

One should diagnose a vasovagal response when performing a procedure on a patient who has a concomitant drop in pulse and blood pressure. Premonitory symptoms such as sweating, nausea, pallor, and feeling faint are common. Initial treatment is aimed at restoring normal blood pressure and pulse with cold towel stimulation, gentle facial slapping, positioning in a Trendelenburg position, or using smelling salts such as ammonia. Simply removing the painful stimuli often alleviates the symptoms. If these simple maneuvers are unsuccessful, airway maintenance with supplemental oxygen and cardiac monitoring may become necessary. Atropine can be given to restore the pulse to normal. If the patient remains hypotensive, intravenous hydration and vasopressors may be required to restore the blood pressure to normal. Injections administered with the patient in the prone or supine position may prevent vasovagal reactions and falls.

Allergic Reactions

Any drug can potentially cause allergic reactions. Reactions can range from simple skin lesions to bronchospasms and cardiopulmonary arrest. Common skin manifestations include urticaria, pruritus, and angioedema. These symptoms are easily diagnosed and can sometimes be treated with oral or parenteral antihistamines, but they often require epinephrine, especially angioedema.

Although not as common, gastrointestinal manifestations of allergic reactions can be alarming. Common symptoms include nausea, vomiting, abdominal cramps, and diarrhea. Treatment is directed toward proper hydration in conjunction with use of antihistamines, antiemetics, or antidiarrheal agents. The type of allergic reaction causing the most concern is the life-threatening anaphylactic response that occurs within seconds after drug delivery. This response quickly causes respiratory distress, often followed by vascular collapse. The patient may initially complain of hoarseness or a "lump" in the throat, which may suggest early laryngeal edema and airway obstruction. This may progress to the hallmark of anaphylactic reactions—bronchospasms manifested by audible wheezing, which quickly leads to respiratory distress. Airway maintenance is necessary, often with intubation, while epinephrine is given.

DRUGS

Anesthetic Agents

Local anesthetics have a wide range of clinical applications and are safe and effective when used judiciously. This margin of safety and effectiveness often depends upon the practitioner's knowledge of an anesthetic's physicochemical properties, chemical configuration, and biologic effects. A brief discussion of these concepts follows, although in-depth texts are available to the interested reader.[101]

The mechanism of action of local anesthetics is not entirely understood, but is believed to reversibly block nerve transmission by inhibiting ion flux through sodium channels of the axon.[7,48,51,81,101] As a result, the action potential does not reach threshold and nerve transmission ceases, resulting in anesthesia. The speed of onset, depth, and duration of this anesthesia are based on multiple factors, including characteristics of the nerve, anesthetic dosage, tissue site injected, and structure of the anesthetic molecule.

Characteristics of the Nerve

The effect of local anesthetics on nerve fibers often depends on physical characteristics of the nerve. For example, many believe that fibers within peripheral nerves (Table 1–2) are often blocked according to a nerve's diameter, degree of myelination, fascicular arrangement, and conduction velocity. Although controversial, this concept proposes that the smaller B and unmyelinated C fibers are blocked initially, followed by blockage of the small type A delta fibers. This would result in blockade of pain and temperature transmission initially and, later, of proprioception, touch, and

TABLE 1-2. Components of a Peripheral Nerve

	Diameter (micrometers)		Conduction Velocity (meters/sec)	Function
A Fibers		Myelinated		
alpha	12–20		70–120	Motor
beta	5–12		30–70	Touch/pressure
gamma	5–12		30–70	Proprioception
delta	1–4		12–30	Pain/temperature
B Fibers	2	Myelinated	12–15	Preganglionic autonomic/ sympathetic
C Fibers	<1	Non-myelinated	1–2	Pain/temperature Pressure/touch

motor function. Theoretically, this effect can be altered by the dosage, concentration, and type of anesthetic injected.

Tissue Site Injected

Once injected, anesthetics are transported within the body by simple mechanical bulk flow, diffusion, and vascular transport. The location of injection, especially in highly vascular areas, affects the drug's absorption, duration of action, and toxicity. Highly vascular regions of the body (oral mucosa, intercostal region, epidural space) should be injected with caution because small concentrations of anesthetics can result in rapid absorption, leading to elevated plasma concentrations and toxicity.

Anesthetic Structure

Anesthetics consist of two rings, a hydrophilic and lipophilic entity, linked by either an ester or amide bond. The hydrophilic entity facilitates transportation of the anesthetic in extracellular fluids. Once delivered to neural tissue, the lipophilic entity aids in transport into the neural structure by imparting lipid solubility to the molecule. If structural alterations are made to enhance lipid solubility, faster diffusion of the anesthetic molecule through the nerve cell membrane occurs that results in increased potency and duration of action. This duration of action can also be affected by changing a molecule's affinity for proteins. Generally, the higher degree of binding to tissue and plasma proteins, the longer duration of action.

The ester or amide linkage between the hydrophilic and lipophilic rings imparts unique characteristics to the anesthetic molecule. This linkage defines the two distinct classes of anesthetic agents, esters and amides (Table 1-3).

Ester Anesthetics.   Ester anesthetics are hydrolyzed rapidly by the plasma enzyme cholinesterase, resulting in short half-lives of the anesthetics, which subsequently reduce the risk of systemic toxicity. The metabolites, including paraaminobenzoic

TABLE 1-3. Comparison of Commonly Used Anesthetics[27,81,115]

	Onset (Min)	Duration* (Min)	Equivalent Concentration	Toxicity†	Lipid Solubility	Protein Binding
Esters						
Procaine (Novocain)	5	30–60	2	7	1	5
Chloroprocaine	6–12	30–60	2	8	1	2
Tetracaine (Pontocaine)	15	175	0.25	1	80	85
Amides						
Lidocaine (Xylocaine, lignocaine)	0.5–1	100	1	5	4	65
Bupivacaine (Marcaine, Sensorcaine)	5	120–240	0.25	2	30	95
Mepivacaine (Carbocaine, Isocaine)	3–5	100	1	4	1	75
Etidocaine (Duranest)	5	120–240	0.25	3	140	95
Prilocaine (Citanest)	1–2	100	1	6	1.5	55

*Varies with route of administration.
† Approximate ranks among the anesthetics listed.

acid (PABA), are secreted mainly unchanged in the urine and have a small but possible allergic potential.

Amide Anesthetics. Amide anesthetics, by comparison, are hydrolyzyed by liver microsomal enzymes to inactive products and excreted by the kidney. Up to 30% of these agents can be excreted unchanged in the urine. Toxicity from the amide group is more common in patients with diminished hepatic blood flow, i.e., congestive heart failure or hepatic enzyme dysfunction, or in those taking beta blockers.[51] The incidence of allergies to amides is very low and, in general, amide anesthetics are felt to be safer than ester anesthetics.

Although usually combined separately, a mixture of amide and ester anesthetics ("supercaine"— mepivacaine and tetracaine) can be desirable at times. This combination provides an intermediate duration of action (5–7 hours) while staggering peak plasma levels, therefore reducing toxicity.[112]

Complications

Toxicity from local anesthetics is usually dose related and additive[81] but often results from rapid absorption from the injection site or from inadvertent vascular injection. Peak plasma concentration occurs within 5–25 minutes, depending on the route of administration. Toxic effects are primarily manifested in two organ systems: the central nervous system (Table 1-4) and cardiovascular system (Table 1-5). The CNS effects are additive when CNS depressants are given concurrently.

Vasoconstrictor Agents

Vasoconstrictors are occasionally added to anesthetics to reduce local tissue bleeding, although the current trend is to omit these additives. The vascular constriction also decreases anesthetic absorption, therefore prolonging anesthesia while

reducing toxicity. This allows lower concentrations and smaller volumes of local anesthetics to be injected.

Although norepinephrine (Levofed), levonordefrin (NeoCobefrin), and phenylephrine (Neo-Synephrine) can be used, the most commonly used vasoconstrictor is epinephrine in concentrations of 1:100,000 (1 mg/100 ml) to 1:200,000 (1 mg/200 ml). Lower concentrations of 1:500,000 (1 mg/500 ml) also can be used. Adverse complications from epinephrine include increased injection pain, increased wound infection, and the potential for tissue necrosis primarily in the digits, ears, nose and penis.[76,106] Systemic doses affect central nervous system function and can produce symptoms such as anxiety, tremors, dizziness, and headaches. As expected, cardiovascular complications include hypertension, chest pain, tachycardia, palpatations, and arrhythmias. Patients taking beta blockers, tricyclic antidepressants, MAO inhibitors, and phenothiazines should be given epinephrine

TABLE 1-4. Central Nervous System Complications from Toxic Doses of Anesthetics

Anxiety	Hallucinations
Circumoral/tongue numbness	Muscular twitching/
Metallic taste in mouth	tremors
Visual and auditory	Drowsiness
disturbances	Unconsciousness
Nausea	Seizures
Nystagmus	Coma
Dizziness	Respiratory arrest
Slurred speech	Cardiovascular depression

TABLE 1-5. Cardiovascular Complications from Toxic Doses of Anesthetics

Peripheral vasodilation	Bradycardia
Myocardial depression	Arrhythmias
Angina	Cardiac arrest

TABLE 1-6. Comparison of Commonly Used Glucocorticoid Steroids[23,37,39,41,42,50,80]

Agent	Anti-inflammatory Potency*	Salt Retention Property	Plasma Half Life (Min)	Duration	Equivalent Oral Dose (mg)
Hydrocortisone (Cortisol)	1	2+	90	S	20
Cortisone	0.8	2+	30	S	25
Prednisone	4–5	1+	60	I	5
Prednisolone	4–5	1+	200	I	5
Methylprednisolone (Medrol, Depo-Medrol)	5	0	180	I	4
Triamcinolone (Aristocort, Kenalog)	5	0	300	I	4
Betamethasone (Celestone)	25–35	0	100–300	L	0.6
Dexamethasone (Decadron)	25–30	0	100–300	L	0.75

*Relative to hydrocortisone.
[†] S = short, I = intermediate, L = long.

with caution to prevent alterations in blood pressure or pulse.

Corticosteroids

Corticosteroids produced by the adrenal cortex can be classified as salt-retaining (mineralocorticoids), androgenic/estrogenic, and antiinflammatory (glucocorticoids). Of these three corticosteroids, the glucocorticoid class is commonly used in physiatry for the treatment of painful inflammatory disorders. The major glucocorticoid produced in humans is cortisol (hydrocortisone). Cortisol and other synthetic glucocorticoids possess varying degrees of antiinflammatory and sodium-retaining properties (Table 1-6).

Glucocorticoids exert their action by binding to specific intracellular receptors upon entering target cells, altering gene expression, thereby regulating many cellular processes and affecting many organ systems.[13,39] The antiinflammatory effect of glucocorticoids is due to its immunosuppressive action on leukocyte function and availability.[22,55] A single dose of corticosteroids results in a 70% reduction in circulating lymphocytes and a 90% reduction in monocytes.[33] Glucocorticoids that are highly water soluble are rapidly absorbed but quickly metabolized, therefore exhibiting a short duration of action. The duration of action of these drugs is extended by reducing their water solubility. Once injected, glucocorticoids are metabolized in the liver and excreted in the urine. The pharmacokinetics of these drugs is complex, and the interested reader is referred to detailed sources.[39,42,55]

Complications

Glucocorticoid-related complications are common but difficult to predict regardless of their route of administration, medical condition of the patient, or a practitioner's understanding of the drug's pharmacokinetics. Generally, high doses and long-term intake of glucocorticoids precipitate many of their known side effects. Because of their site of metabolism and excretion, caution is needed when these drugs are given to patients with liver and renal diseases. Another important factor is concomitant drug intake. Nonsteroidal antiinflammatory drugs, oral contraceptives, and other exogenous estrogens increase the potency of glucocorticoids, while phenobarbital, phenytoin, carbamazepine, and rifampin decrease their potency[42]; thus, dosages should be altered accordingly.

Local side effects of glucocorticoids common to percutaneous injections include skin, subcutaneous, and periarticular atrophy and alterations in skin pigmentation. This effect can be reduced if the injecting needle is flushed with saline or anesthetic prior to it exit or if a new, separate needle is used to puncture the skin, especially in dark-skinned patients. Reports of tendon and cartilage attrition, crystal-induced arthritis, benign facial flushing, and pericapsular calcification are found in the literature.[40]

Widespread systemic complications with glucocorticoid use are well documented and known to involve almost every organ system.[23,37,55] Fluid and electrolyte disorders (especially in patients with congestive heart failure), gastrointestinal upset (peptic ulcer disease and bleeding), bone demineralization, and impaired glucose tolerance are some of the more common problems. In patients with diabetes, transient glucose elevation often occurs, requiring routine glucose monitoring following these injections.[10] Other less commonly recognized side effects include CNS changes with mood swings, increase in appetite, and nervousness. One of the most serious side effects of glucocorticoids is adrenal cortical insufficiency resulting from suppression of the hypothalamic-pituitary-adrenal axis, usually associated with chronic high doses. This results in the inability to respond to stressful situations, such as infections or surgery.

Nonionic Contrast Dyes

With most fluoroscopic spine and peripheral joint procedures, nonionic water-soluble iodine-based contrast agents such as iohexol (Omnipaque) or iopamidol (Isovue) are used in doses of 240 or 300 mg. In comparison to their less expensive ionic counterparts, they are less irritating and allergenic. Following injection, nonionic agents quicky dissipate from the site of injection, and 90% is eliminated by renal excretion within 24 hours. No significant biotransformation or metabolism occurs. Common side effects include headaches, nausea, vomiting, and CNS disturbances.

Additives

Many different anesthetic and glucocorticoid additives are useful for increasing injectate volume or acting as a preservative. Sterile saline or hypotonic water solutions are additives that have dilutional properties without the added risk of toxic or allergic reactions. When given for intradermal anesthesia, injection pain does not increase.[111] Other additives such as paraben compounds (methylparaben) are antibacterial preservatives often found in many multidose vials. Methylparaben does not cause additional injection pain but does have a well-documented potential for allergic reactions.[2,93,111] Other additives include bisulphite, dextrans, potassium, sodium bicarbonate, and carbon dioxide.

Neurolytic Agents

The ideal neurolytic drug for treatment of pain would selectively destroy the fibers responsible for transmitting pain, mainly A-delta and C fibers, while sparing motor fibers. For treatment of spasticity, the main goal is almost the opposite, destruction of motor axons and preservation of sensory fibers. Unfortunately, this degree of selectivity does not currently exist in neurolytic drugs. Neurolytic agents available today nonselectively destroy all neural fiber types. Of the various neurolytic drugs in existence, the most widely used is phenol.

Phenol

Phenol (carbolic acid) has many clinical applications. In addition to its anesthetic action, bactericidal and fungicidal properties have been well established at concentrations greater than 1.3%.[45,72] Because of its neurolytic properties, phenol has been used extensively to treat spasticity and intractable pain problems.[59,113] Phenol was originally used for the treatment of spasticity by Kelly and Nathan.[56,78] When injected around a motor nerve, phenol can be used to selectively reduce hypertonicity. Intrathecal phenol, although less specific, may be used in selected cases to manage spasticity from spinal cord origin but has limited application in traumatic brain injury (TBI). When used to manage intractable pain disorders, phenol denervates pain-provoking structures either by percutaneous or intrathecal routes. Although Mayer first injected phenol into the thecal space for treatment of intractable cancer pain, this technique has since undergone rapid advances.[68] Peripheral vascular disorders also have been treated with phenol by denervating sympathetic perivascular and paravertebral fibers.[8,31,52,87]

Mechanism of Action

Phenol denatures protein, causing nerve destruction, denervation, muscle atrophy, and necrosis.[43] Histologically, no selective fiber destruction can be demonstrated, which suggests that both alpha and gamma fiber damage is involved.[36,43,72] Electromyographic studies demonstrate denervation potentials as early as 3 weeks following phenol blocks.[15] The length of the clinical response—reduction in spasticity or pain—ranges from 2 months to 2 years regardless of the underlying disorder.[43,72] The temporal response variation results from multiple factors. These include patient selection, completeness of block, and concentration of phenol injected. Higher phenol concentrations are associated with greater tissue destruction, with peak effect noted 2 weeks after administration. Long-term differences in results, however, have not been observed with a 2 or 3% solution,[72] and an optimal concentration has not been established. Reinnervation of muscle and return of spasticity or pain may be slowed by resultant endoneural fibrosis. This damage obstructs axonal growth and results in a prolonged clinical response. In patients who have a permanent response, the result may be the effect of nerve infarction or vascular thrombosis. The "reversible" properties of phenol are felt to be secondary to wallerian degeneration and regeneration. The latter tends to parallel the peripheral nerve crush regeneration rates of 1.5 ± 0.1 mm per day as described by Sunderland.[102]

Aqueous solutions are more effective than those mixed with glycerin or lipids, but glycerin is often used to make phenol more water-soluble.[45] When added to glycerin, phenol diffuses slowly into the tissue, allowing localized tissue fixation. Phenol is soluble in water at room temperature in a mix of one part phenol to 15 parts water. Phenol is available in an 89% solution and must be diluted to achieve the desired concentration. It is commonly mixed with equal parts glycerin and then added to normal saline. This mixture is injected through a syringe disk for final sterilization. Once injected, phenol is conjugated in the liver and 80% is excreted by the kidneys.[34,45]

Complications

Phenol is safe and effective when used judiciously and with meticulous technique. However, complications may occur and patients should be closely monitored. Although the initial phenol injection is usually painless due to its anesthetic properties, one common problem is postinjection soreness, which may be attributed to local tissue necrosis and inflammation.[36] Postinjection soreness usually subsides within 24 hours and is treated prophylactically with ice packs and analgesics. If phenol is injected subcutaneously or remains in contact with the skin, erythema, skin necrosis, and sloughing with resulting skin discoloration may occur.[45] The needle should be flushed with saline or anesthetic prior to withdrawal to eliminate any "tract" of phenol, thereby reducing these skin problems. A risk of chemical conjunctivitis is present if the physician's and/or patient's eyes are not protected from phenol splatter.

Paresthesias and/or dysesthesias from mixed somatic nerve blocks with phenol have been reported. The incidence ranges from 0–23% with 2.0–5.0% phenol, although all cases resolved by 3 months.[25,26,46,54,57-59,74,83,84,86,98] Many of these temporary sensory complaints actually may be the result of an incomplete block[83,86] rather than phenol-induced dysesthesias. This is supported by the fact that repeat injections will often alleviate residual symptoms. A partial block may result from poor needle placement, inadequate volume, or insufficient concentration of phenol. Phenol's anesthetic properties may also give the physician a false sense of having performed a complete block.[34] Open surgical selective motor branch injections have been developed to prevent these temporary sensory dysesthesias[16,36,54,73,103,104] but carry the routine risks of surgery and anesthesia.

Systemic complications from phenol are usually the result of inadvertant vascular injection or central blockade.[6,49,104,105] The cardiovascular and central nervous systems are especially sensitive to phenol.[79,104] Cardiac dysrhythmias and venous thrombosis have been reported.[66,77] CNS symptoms include tremors and convulsions, followed by respiratory depression. Hypotension can occur secondary to central vasomotor depression with concomitant myocardial and peripheral vascular toxicity. Spinal cord and cortical infarcts have also been reported with cervical intrathecal phenol.[105] Intrathecal phenol may alter bladder and bowel function; destroy sensation, rendering the skin more prone to injury; and place the patient at risk for meningitis or arachnoiditis.

Therapeutic doses to prevent these undesirable systemic complications and thus provide a margin of safety have not been well established. The toxic dose in adults may be as low as 8 gm,[34] although death has been reported after ingestion of 1 gm in an adult.[30] One can usually give up to 100 mg without much concern for toxic effects. The maximum advisable total dose injected within a 24-hour period, however, is 1 gm. Because of its route of metabolism, phenol should be avoided in patients with liver disease.

Other Neurolytic Agents

Ethyl alcohol, propylene glycol,[20] ammonium compounds, chlorocresol, glycerol, cold saline, and hypo/hypertonic solutions have all been used for chemical neurolysis, although their efficacy is not as well studied as that of phenol. These agents nonselectively destroy nerve fiber types, similar to phenol.

Transient burning sensation in muscle is common after alcohol injection and often necessitates a concomitant injection of local anesthetic.[18] Muscle biopsy studies 4–6 weeks following alcohol injections have revealed round cell infiltration but no fibrosis.[18]

RADIATION CONCEPTS

Fluoroscopy-guided procedures are routinely used and considered essential for many physiatric procedures. These include many joint and bursae injections, precision needle placement in spine procedures, swallowing studies, and urologic evaluations. Because of the widespread use of fluoroscopy in physiatry, the basic concepts of radiation need to be understood. This section discusses basic concepts, including common terminology, factors affecting radiation exposure, and common radiation exposure with fluoroscopic procedures.

Terminology

Radiation is the process of emission of radiant energy in the form of waves or particles. When radiation produces ions as it passes through matter, the result is known as ionizing radiation, or x-rays. X-rays create electrically charged particles by liberating orbital electrons from the atoms with which they interact. These electrically charged particles have the potential to cause biologic damage by recombining disadvantageously. When an object or body is subjected to ionizing radiation, the total amount is known as exposure, whose unit of measurement is the roentgen (rem = roentgen equivalent man) or milliroentgen (mrem). Exposure is a property of the photons within the ionizing radiation, mainly their ability to ionize air. If the ionizing radiation (x-rays) exposed to a body interacts with the atoms of the material it contacts, energy is transferred from the x-rays to these atoms. This transference of energy is called absorption, and the amount of energy absorbed is referred to as the absorbed dose. Its unit of measurement is the gray (Gy) or, formerly, rad (radiation absorbed dose). The amount of radiation absorbed depends on many factors, including tissue characteristics and, primarily, type and depth. For example, bone absorbs more ionizing radiation than soft tissue. The higher the absorbed dose, the greater likelihood of cellular alterations resulting in biological damage (Fig. 1–1). However, it is the concept of absorption that allows tissue differentiation and, thus, diagnostic capabilities.

Factors Affecting Radiation Exposure

Simply stated, the less radiation to which a body is exposed, the less that is absorbed by the tissue; therefore the need to minimize exposure is justified. The most obvious way to avoid exposure is to spend as little time in the vicinity of radiation as possible. When avoidance is not possible, three effective means of protection from ionizing radiation exists: time, distance, and shielding.

The length of time the physician and patient are exposed to radiation largely depends on the fluoroscopy habits of the physician. Equipment features such as pulsed fluoroscopy, hold-and-store image capabilities, and collimation often shape many of these habits. A radiation technologist can implement many of these equipment alterations as well as control the output of radiation.

The distance between the primary source of the x-ray and the body is of primary importance and should be maximized when possible. A rough estimate of the physician's exposure at a distance of 1 meter from the x-ray tube is 1/1000th of the patient's exposure. Therefore, the position of the physician's body, including hands, should be closely monitored and the physician kept at a maximum distance at all times.[12] The use of extension tubing helps to accomplish this task.

The liberal use of strategically placed lead shielding also reduces radiation exposure. Use of sliding lead panels or drapes between the physician and both the patient and x-ray tube is recommended. Lead aprons, gloves, glasses, and neck and thyroid shields are commercially available in varying sizes. The International Commission on Radiological Protection (ICRP) recommends that shields have a lead equivalent of 0.25 mm or more. Such shielding can decrease radiation exposure by 90% to critical body areas (gonads, eyes, body organs).[61] Protective flexible lead gloves may reduce some exposure without sacrificing dexterity skills.[109] Large, nonflexible gloves are too bulky for use in most psysiatric procedures and are not commonly used.

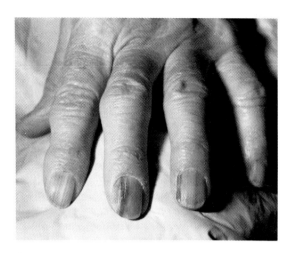

FIGURE 1–1. Fingers of an 83-year-old general practitioner who set fractures under fluoroscopy for 35 years. Note the changes in the nails. A basal cell carcinoma was earlier resected from a proximal phalynx.

Occupational monitoring of cumulative radiation exposure can also be accomplished with personal monitoring devices, such as dosimeters (film badges). These devices are usually mailed to central locations on a regular basis where radiation exposure is recorded.

Common Radiation Exposure

Radiation exposure to the physician and patient during most physiatric procedures is estimated in Table 1-7. These exposure levels are based on reasonable estimates but vary based on multiple equipment and physiologic factors. The physician, however, should become familiar with his or her own unit as well as the maximum permissible doses (MPD). The MPD of radiation varies depending on the body part that is exposed. The extremities

TABLE 1-7. Radiation Exposure Comparison

Procedure/Activity	Exposure	Body Part
Natural background	100–200 mrem/yr	Total body
Lumbar epidural with fluoroscopy—patient	2.5 rem/30 sec	Lumbar region
Lumbar epidural with fluoroscopy—physician	2.5 mrem*/30 sec	Total body
Swallowing videofluoroscopy (patient)	3 mrem/min†	Face/Neck
Posteroanterior chest x-ray	10–30 mrem	Chest
CT scan of head	3–5 rem	Head

*Exposure estimated without shielded protection and at a distance of approximately 1 meter.
† Data collected by Charles Beasley, Radiation Safety Officer, St. John's Regional Hospital, Springfield, MO, based on operation at 85 kVp/0.2 mA.

can be exposed to far greater levels of radiation than critical body areas such as the gonads, eyes, and organs. For example, the MPD to both skin and the extremities is 50 rem/year, the lens of the eye 15 rem/year, and trunk only 5 rem/year.

INFORMED CONSENT

The physiatrist should perform office and hospital procedures only after the patient provides informed consent. Informed consent is an autonomous action by a patient authorizing medical personnel to initiate a treatment plan.[35] This consent is a fundamental right of patients and is a prerequisite to medical treatment decisions.[99] A decision to obtain informed consent for specific procedures depends on both the risk involved to the patient and the general community standard.[35] Open communication between doctor and patient regarding this subject not only provides legal protection, but also helps in establishing a good doctor-patient relationship, which may alleviate later disputes. This discussion cannot be delegated. If a nonemergent procedure is performed in a competent patient without this process, the physician could be guilty of battery or a consent-related malpractice claim.[14]

The key elements of informed consent include (1) disclosure of information, (2) comprehension of the information by a competent patient, and (3) decision making free of coersion.[99]

Disclosure of Information

Disclosure of information is the first step in the informed consent process and allows patients to make a knowledgeable choice about their health care. It is the physicians' responsibility to provide this information without patient solicitation.[114] Information should include a description of the diagnosis, proposed treatment with possible alternatives, technical details of the procedure, risks, and benefits.[47] The amount of information provided is based on what a "reasonable" physician would supply to satisfy a "reasonable" patient's expectation. The definition of reasonable is controversial in this context but is usually based on the community standard for competent physicians and patients.[38] Patients also may have the right to know facts about their physician's health. Recent court decisions have required surgeons to disclose alcoholism and positive HIV status during informed consent for procedures.[97] This leads one to believe that overdisclosure of information is preferable to underdisclosure.

Comprehension of Information

Comprehension of information provided to a competent patient is the second step in the process

of informed consent. Ideally, a discussion of the procedure should take place several days prior to the procedure in a quiet room with a competent patient and his or her family members. One should avoid the use of complex medical terms during this discussion. Herz et al.[47] found in one group of patients that patients retained only 43.5% of the information discussed in this setting. Six weeks after this disclosure and subsequent procedure, retention of information dropped to 38.4%. Patients tend to retain information that supports the decision to have a procedure and suppress information that is anxiety-provoking, such as risks.[47,85,90] As expected, information recall is especially poor among patients who have a below average IQ, have impaired cognitive function, are elderly, and are in pain.[60]

Decision Making

The last step in obtaining informed consent is allowing the patient to make a decision based on the information provided free of coercion. The patient should be given ample time for this decision without being pressured by any medical personnel. Time at home with informed family members works best.

The Consent Form

Once the patient's informed consent has been obtained, a consent form usually should be signed. It may not be the standard of care in a given community to obtain a signed consent form for a trigger point injection, local anesthetic infiltration, or a peripheral nerve block. The process of informed consent should be distinguished from the act of signing a consent form. A consent form is the written documentation of the patient's consent to a procedure. It does not, however, provide proof that the consent was properly informed.[99] In fact, the majority of patients do not read consent forms before signing.[60] Most of these forms provided by the hospital are standard documents written to protect the hospital and are seldom tailored to the procedures performed by physiatrists.

CONCLUSION

Proper application of procedures fosters good patient care, providing safety to both the physician and patient. The patient's safety is directly dependent upon the physician's technical skills, knowledge of drug pharmacology, and ability to recognize and treat potential complications, including cardiac and respiratory emergencies. Once a procedure is complete, it should be integrated into a well-designed comprehensive rehabilitation program directed by the physiatrist.

REFERENCES

1. Abi-Samra F, Maloney JD, Fouda-Tarazi FM, et al: The usefulness of head-up tilt testing and hemodynamic investigations in the workup of syncope of unknown origin. PACE 11:1202-1214, 1988.
2. Aeling JL, Nuss DD: Systemic eczematous "contact-type" dermatitis medicamentosa caused by parabens [Letter to the editor]. Arch Dermatol 10:640, 1974.
3. Alexander JW, Fischer JE, Boyajian M, et al: The influence of hair-removal methods on wound infections. Arch Surg 118:347-352, 1983.
4. Bartfield JM, Ford DT, Homer PJ: Buffered versus plain lidocaine for digital nerve blocks. Ann Emerg Med 22:74-77, 1993.
5. Becker GE: Red Flags. American Back Society Newsletter, Oakland, CA, 1991, p 23.
6. Benzon HT: Convulsions secondary to intravascular phenol: A hazard of celiac plexus block. Anesth Analg 58:150-151, 1979.
7. Berde C: Toxicity of local anesthetics in infants and children. J Pediatr 122:14-20, 1993.
8. Binet A: Valeur de la sympathectomic chemique en gynecologie. Gynecol Obstet 27:393-415, 1933.
9. Bird BJ, et al: Extensive pre-operative shaving: A costly exercise. N Z Med J 97:727-729, 1984.
10. Black DM, Filak AT: Hyperglycemia with non-insulin-dependent diabetes following intraarticular steroid injection. J Fam Pract 28:462-463, 1989.
11. Bloom LH, Scheie HG, Yanoff M: The warming of local anesthetic agents to decrease discomfort. Ophthalmic Surg 15:603, 1984.
12. Boone JM, Levin DC: Radiation exposure to angiographers under different fluoroscopic imaging conditions. Radiology 180:861-865, 1991.
13. Boumpas DT, Paliogianni F, Anastassiou ED, et al: Glucocorticosteroid action on the immune system: Molecular and cellular aspects. Clin Exp Rheumatol 9:413-423, 1991.
14. Bowyer EA, Paulson L: Informed consent allegations affect all specialties. Risk Management Foundation Forum 7:3-6, 1986.
15. Brattstrom M, Moritz U, Svantesson G: Electromyographic studies of peripheral nerve block with phenol. Scand J Rehabil Med. 2:17-22, 1970.
16. Braun RM, Hoffer MM, Mooney V, et al: Phenol nerve block in the treatment of acquired spastic hemiplegia in the upper limb. Am J Bone Joint Surg 55:580-585, 1973.
17. Braunwald E, Isselbacher KJ, Petersdorf RG, et al (eds): Harrison's Principles of Internal Medicine, 11th ed. New York, McGraw HIll, 1987.
18. Carpenter EB, Seitz DG: Intramuscular alcohol as an aid in management of spastic cerebral palsy. Dev Med Child Neurol 22:497-501, 1980.
19. Cheney PR, Molzen G, Tandberg D: The effect of pH buffering on reducing the pain associated with subcutaneous infiltration of bupivacaine. Am J Emerg Med 9:147-178, 1991.
20. Chino N, Awad E, Kottke FJ: Pathology of propylene glycol administered by perineural and intramuscular injection in rats. Arch Phys Med Rehabil 55:33-38, 1974.
21. Choudhuri M, McQueen R, et al: Efficiency of skin sterilization for a venipuncture with the use of commercially available alcohol or iodine pads. Am J Infect Control 18:82-85, 1990.
22. Claman HN: Glucocorticosteroids I: Anti-inflammatory mechanisms. Hosp Pract 123-134, 1983.
23. Claman HN: Glucocorticosteroids II: The clinical responses. Hosp Pract 143-151, 1983.
24. Come PC, Bertram P: Nitroglycerin-induced severe hypotension and bradycardia in patients with acute myocardial infarction. Circulation 54:624-628, 1976.
25. Copp EP, Harris R, Keenan J: Peripheral nerve block and motor point block with phenol in the management of spasticity. Proc R Soc Med 63:17-18, 1970.
26. Copp EP, Keenan J: Phenol nerve and motor point block in spasticity. Rheumatol Phys Med 11:287-292, 1972.
27. Covino BG: Clinical pharmacology of local anesthetic agents. In Cousins MJ, Bridenbaugh PO (eds): Neural Blockade in Clinical Anesthesia and Management of Pain, 2nd ed. Philadelphia, JB Lippincott, 1988, pp 111-144.
28. Dambrink JHA, Imholz BPM, Karemaker JM, et al: Circulatory adaptation to orthostatic stress in healthy 10-14 year old children investigated in a general practice. Clin Sci 81:51-58, 1991.
29. Davies J, Babb JR, Ayliffe GAJ, et al: Disinfection of the skin of the abdomen. Br J Surg 65:855-858, 1978.
30. Deichmann WB, Keplinger ML: Phenols and phenolic compounds. In Patty FA (ed): Industrial Hygiene and Toxicology. New York, Interscience Publishers, 1963, pp 1363-1375.
31. Doppler K: Die sympathikodiaphtherese (chemische sympathikusausschaltung) an der anteria femoralis. Med Klin 22:1954-1956, 1926.
32. Emergency Cardiac Care Committee and Subcommittee, American Heart Association: Guidelines for Cardiopulmonary Resuscitation and Emergency Cardiac Care. JAMA 268:2171-2302, 1992.
33. Fauci AS, Dale DC: The effect of in vivo hydrocortisone on subpopulations of human lymphocytes. J Clin Invest 53:240-246, 1974.
34. Felsenthal G: Pharmacology of phenol in peripheral nerve blocks: A review. Arch Phys Med Rehabil 55:13-16, 1974.
35. Finkelstein D, Smith MK, Faden R: Informed consent and medical ethics. Arch Ophthalmol 111:324-326, 1993.
36. Garland DE, Lucie RS, Waters RL: Current uses of open phenol nerve block for adult acquired spasticity. Clin Orthop Rel Res 165:217-222, 1982.
37. George E, Kirwan JR: Corticosteroid therapy in rheumatoid arthritis. Baillieres Clin Rheumatol 4:621-646, 1990.
38. Gold JA: Informed consent. Arch Ophthalmol 111:321-323, 1993.
39. Goldfien A: Adrenocorticosteroids and adrenocortical antagonists. In Katzung BG (ed): Basic and Clinical Pharmacology, 2nd ed. Los Altos, CA, Lange Medical Publishers, 1984, pp 453-465.
40. Gottlieb NL, Riskin WG: Complications of local corticosteroid injections. JAMA 243:1547-1548, 1980.
41. Gray RG, Gottlieb NL: Intra-articular corticosteroids, basic science and pathology. Clin Orthop Rel Res 177:235-263, 1983.
42. Gustavson LE, Benet LZ: Pharmacokinetics of natural and synthetic glucocorticoids. In Anderson DC, Winter JSD (eds): Adrenal Cortex. London, Butterworth, 1985, pp 235-281.
43. Halpern D: Histologic studies in animals after intramuscular neurolysis with phenol. Arch Phys Med Rehabil 58:438-443, 1977.
44. Hargreaves AD, Muir AL: Lack of variation in venous tone potentiates vasovagal syncope. Br Heart J 67:486-490, 1992.
45. Harvey SC: Antiseptics and disinfectants; fungicides; ectoparasiticides. In Gilman AG, Goodman LS, Gilman A (eds): Goodman and Gilman's The Pharmacological Basics of Therapeutics, 6th ed. New York, Macmillan Publishing, 1980, p 967.
46. Helweg-Larson J, Jacobsen E: Treatment of spasticity in cerebral palsy by means of phenol nerve block of peripheral nerves. Dan Med Bull 16:20-25, 1969.

47. Herz DA, Looman JE, Lewis SK: Informed consent: Is it a myth? Neurosurgery 30:453–458, 1992.
48. Hille B: The common mode of action of three agents that decrease the transient change in sodium permeability in nerves. Nature 210:1220–1222, 1966.
49. Holland AJC, Yousseff M: A complication of subarachnoid phenol blockade. Anesthesia 34:260–262, 1979.
50. Holland EG, Taylor AT: Glucocorticoids in clinical practice. J Fam Pract 32:512–519, 1991.
51. Hondeghem LM, Miller RD: Local anesthetics. In Katzung BG (ed): Basic and Clinical Pharmacology, 2nd ed. Los Altos, CA, Lange Medical Publications, 1984, pp 293–298.
52. Hughes-Davies DI, Rechman LR: Clinical lumbar sympathectomy. Anesthesia 31:1068, 1970.
53. Imholz BPM, Dambrink JHA, Karemaker JM, et al: Orthostatic circulatory control in the elderly evaluated by non-invasive continuous blood pressure measurement. Clin Sci 79:73–79, 1990.
54. Katz JK, Knott LW, Feldman MD: Peripheral nerve injections with phenol in the management of spastic patients. Arch Phys Med Rehabil 48:97–99, 1967.
55. Kehrl JH, Fauci AS: The clinical use of glucocorticoids. Ann Allergy 50:2–10, 1983.
56. Kelly RE, Gautier-Smith PC: Intrathecal phenol in the treatment of reflex spasms and spasticity. Lancet 2:1102–1105, 1959.
57. Khalili AA: Physiatric management of spasticity by phenol nerve and motor point block. In Ruskin AP (ed): Current Therapy in Physiatry. Philadelphia, Saunders, 1984, pp 464–474.
58. Khalili AA, Betts HB: Peripheral nerve block with phenol in the management of spasticity. JAMA 200:1155–1157, 1967.
59. Khalili AA, Harmel MH, Forster S, et al: Management of spasticity by selective peripheral nerve block with dilute phenol solutions in clinical rehabilitation. Arch Phys Med Rehabil 45:513–519, 1964.
60. Lavelle-Jones C, Byrne DJ, Rice P, et al: Factors affecting quality of informed consent. BMJ 306:885–890, 1993.
61. Larimore E (Radiation Consultants): Personal communication, 1994.
62. Lipsitz LA, Marks ER, Koestner J, et al: Reduced susceptibility to syncope during postural tilt in old age. Arch Intern Med 149:2709–2712, 1989.
63. Lo B, Steinbrook R: Health care workers infected with the human immunodeficiency virus. JAMA 267:1100–1105, 1992.
64. Lowbury EJL, Lilly HA: Use of 4% chlorhexidine detergent solution (hibiscrub) and other methods of skin disinfection. BMJ 1:510–515, 1973.
65. Macdonald R: Aspirin and extradural blocks [editorial I]. Br J Anaesth 66:1–3, 1991.
66. Macek C: Venous thrombosis results from some phenol injections. JAMA 249:1807, 1983.
67. Mackenzie I: Preoperative skin preparation and surgical outcome. J Hosp Infect 11:27–32, 1988.
68. Maher RM: Relief of pain in incurable cancer. Lancet 1:18–20, 1955.
69. Mark LC: Avoiding the pain of venipuncture [Letter to the editor]. N Engl J Med 294:614, 1976.
70. Masterson BJ: Skin preparation. Clin Obstet Gynecol 31:736–743, 1988.
71. McKay W, Morris R, Mushlin P: Sodium bicarbonate attenuates pain on skin infiltration with lidocaine, with or without epinephrine. Anesth Analg 66:572–574, 1987.
72. Mooney V, Frykman G, McLamb J: Current status of intraneural phenol injections. Clin Orthop 63:122–131, 1969.
73. Moore TJ, Anderson RB: The use of open phenol blocks to the motor branches of the tibial nerve in adult acquired spasticity. Foot Ankle 11:219–221, 1991.
74. Moritz U: Phenol block of peripheral nerves. Scand J Rehabil Med 5:160–163, 1973.
75. Morris R, McKay W, Mushlin P: Comparison of pain associated with intradermal and subcutaneous infiltration with various local anesthetic solutions. Anesth Analg 66:1180–1182, 1987.
76. Morris RW, Whish DKM: A controlled trial of pain on skin infiltration with local anaesthetics. Anaesth Intensive Care 12:113–114, 1984.
77. Morrison JE, Matthews D, Washington R, et al: Phenol motor point blocks in children: Plasma concentrations and cardiac dysrhythmias. Anesthesiology 75:359–362, 1992.
78. Nathan PW: Intrathecal phenol to relieve spasticity in paraplegia. Lancet 2:1099–1102, 1959.
79. Nour-Eldin F: Preliminary report: Uptake of phenol by vascular and brain tissue. Microvasc Res 2:224–225, 1970.
80. Olin BR (ed): Adrenal cortical steroids. In Drug Facts and Comparisons. St. Louis, Facts and Comparisons, 1993, pp 465–466.
81. Olin BR (ed): Local Anesthetics. In Drug Facts and Comparisons. St. Louis, Facts and Comparisons, 1993, pp 2654–2665.
82. Olsen MM, MacCallum J, McQuarrie DG: Preoperative hair removal with clippers does not increase infection rate in clean surgical wounds. Surg Gynecol Obstet 162:181–182, 1986.
83. Petrillo C, Chu D, Davis S: Phenol block of the tibial nerve in the hemiplegic patient. Orthopedics 3:871–874, 1980.
84. Petrillo C, Knoploch S:Phenol block of the tibial nerve for spasticity: A long term followup study. Int Disabil Studies 10:97–100, 1988.
85. Priluck IA, Robertson DM, Buettner H: What patients recall of the preoperative discussion after retinal detachment surgery. Am J Ophthalmol 87:620–623, 1979.
86. Reeves DK, Baker A: Mixed somatic peripheral phenol nerve block for painful or intractable spasticity: A review of 30 years of use. Am J Pain Manage 2:205–210, 1992.
87. Reid W, Watt JK, Gray TG: Phenol injections of the sympathetic chain. Br J Surg 57:45–50, 1970.
88. Ritter MA, French MLV, Eitzen HE, et al: The antimicrobial effectiveness of operative-site preparative agents. J Bone Joint Surg 62A:826–828, 1990.
89. Roberts JR: Local anesthetics: Injection techniques. Emerg Med News 9–16, March 1992.
90. Robinson G, Merav A: Informed consent: Recall by patients tested postoperatively. Annals Thorac Surg 22:209–212, 1976.
91. Rosoff MH, Cohen MV: Profound bradycardia after amyl nitrite in patients with a tendency to vasovagal episodes. Br Heart J 55:97–100, 1986.
92. Sander-Jensen K, Mehlsen J, Secher NH, et al: Progressive central hypovolemia in man—resulting in a vasovagal syncope? Haemodynamic and endocrine variables during venous tourniquets of the thigh. Clin Physiol 7:231–242, 1987.
93. Schorr WF: Paraben Allergy. JAMA 204:107–110, 1968.
94. Sebben JE: Surgical antiseptics. J Am Acad Dermatol 9:759–765, 1983.
95. Seropian R, Reynolds BM: Wound infections after preoperative depilatory versus razor preparation. Am J Surg 121:251–254, 1971.
96. Smylie HG, Logie JRC, Smith G: From Phisohex to Hibiscrub. BMJ 4:586–589, 1973.
97. Spielman B: Expanding the boundaries of informed consent: Disclosing alcoholism and HIV status to patients. Am J Med 93:216–218, 1992.

98. Spira R: Management of spasticity in cerebral palsied children by peripheral nerve block with phenol. Develop Med Child Neurol 13:164–173, 1971.

99. Sprung CL, Winick BJ: Informed consent in theory and practice: Legal and medical perspectives on the informed consent doctrine and a proposed reconceptualization. Crit Care Med 17:1346–1354, 1989.

100. Stewart JH, Chinn SE, Cole GW, et al: Neutralized lidocaine with epinephrine for local anesthesia—II. J Dermatol Surg Oncol 16:842–845, 1990.

101. Strichartz GR: Neural physiology and local anesthetic action. In Cousins MJ, Bridenbaugh PO (eds): Neural Bockade in Clinical Anesthesia and Management of Pain, 2nd ed. Philadelphia, JB Lippincott, 1988, pp 25–45.

102. Sunderland S: Nerves and nerve injuries. Baltimore, Williams & Wilkins, 1978.

103. Superville-Sovak B, Rasminsky M, Finlayson MH: Complications of phenol neurolysis. Arch Neurol 32:226–228, 1975.

104. Swerdlow M: Complications of neurolytic neural blockade. In Cousins MJ, Bridenbaugh PO, (eds): Neural Blockade in Clinical Anesthesia and Management of Pain, 2nd ed. New York, JB Lippincott, 1988, pp 719–735.

105. Totoki T, Kato T, Nomoto Y, et al: Anterior spinal artery syndrome—A complication of cervical intrathecal phenol injections. Pain 6:99–104, 1979.

106. Tran DT, Miller SH, Buck D, et al: Potentiation of infection by epinephrine. Plast Reconstr Surg 76:933–934, 1985.

107. Tunevall TG: Procedures and experiences with preoperative skin preparation in Sweden. J Hosp Infect 11:11–14, 1988.

108. van Lieshout JJ, Wieling W, Karemaker JM, et al: The vasovagal response. Clin Sci 81:575–586, 1991.

109. Vehmas T: Finger doses during interventional radiology: The value of flexible protective gloves. Fortschr Rontgenstr 154:555–559, 1991.

110. Waldman SD: Eutectic mixture of local anesthetic (EMLA). Pain Digest 3:104–109, 1993.

111. Wightman MA, Vaughan RW: Comparison of compounds used for intradermal anesthesia. Anesthesiology 45:687–689, 1976.

112. Winnie A: Clinical considerations of importance for successful brachial plexus anesthesia. Clinical Dialogues on Regional Anesthesia 2:1–4, 1992.

113. Wood KM: The use of phenol as a neurolytic agent: A review. Pain 5:205–229, 1978.

114. Wu WC, Pearlman RA: Consent in medical decision making: The role of communication. J Geriatr Intern Med 3:9–14, 1988.

115. Young ER, MacKenzie TA: The pharmacology of local anesthetics—A review of the literature. J Can Dent Assoc 58:34–42, 1992.

Chapter 2

PERIPHERAL JOINT INJECTIONS

JOHN P. OBERMILLER, M.D.
DENNIS LOX, M.D.

Intraarticular injections are but one of the clinician's many tools for the treatment of musculoskeletal disorders. Injection should be considered an adjunct to the overall treatment plan—never the sole component of therapy. Injections may be used diagnostically as well as therapeutically and are generally "safe" when used judiciously by a skilled practitioner.

The introduction of hydrocortisone in 1951 advanced the idea for local intraarticular injections. Much of the anecdotal evidence that "steroid" injections are harmful has been found over the ensuing 43 years to be untrue. Although a number of studies have been performed, it has not yet been proved that intraarticular corticosteroids actually destroy joints unless used in an indiscriminate manner.[4] Isolated reports disclose articular surface damage from corticosteroid therapy[1]; in others, concomitant or antecedent facts were likely to have contributed to osteonecrosis or periarticular problems.[2,5,12,18,22] These reports are disputed, and the deleterious effects of corticosteroids used under accepted guidelines are believed to be more transient.[4] The use of corticosteroids in combatting inflammatory conditions and painful arthritic conditions has, in fact, proved beneficial in some studies.[4,14]

Nevertheless, every practitioner must be mindful that complications and serious problems may arise with intraarticular injections. Thus, a basic knowledge of the pharmacokinetics of corticosteroids[6] is paramount along with awareness of the signs of any potential side effects. Of course, the specific anatomy of the joint injected must be well understood. But perhaps most basically, the physician must be able to determine which patients and at what point in their treatment they are most likely to benefit from intraarticular injections. This chapter examines specific aspects of peripheral joint injections and describes their use in common joints.

INDICATIONS FOR INTRAARTICULAR STEROIDS

Understanding the rationale for the use of corticosteroids in intraarticular spaces is of primary importance. The most common use of corticosteroids in the peripheral joints is in patients with rheumatoid arthritis. These drugs are used specifically to reduce inflammation and provide relief from pain attributable to synovitis and conditions associated with rheumatoid arthritis. Corticosteroids also may be very useful in providing pain relief in long-standing osteoarthritic joints. The restoration of joint motion in conditions of adhesive capsulitis is yet another common use. Aspiration of synovial fluid for pain relief and laboratory evaluation of the synovial fluid as well as arthrography for the evaluation of joints are common diagnostic tools that facilitate the rehabilitation of painful joints.

Basically, the physician should consider the use of corticosteroid injections in the peripheral joints when comprehensive therapy, including physical therapy, nonsteroidal antiinflammatory drugs (NSAIDs), analgesics, and other physical modalities, fail.

DRUGS: ACTION, SELECTION, DOSAGE

Corticosteroids produce significant antiinflammatory effects. Numerous long-acting corticosteroid ester preparations are available. The most widely used corticosteroids include triamcinolone acetonide (Kenalog), triamcinolone hexacetonide (Aristospan), betamethasone sodium phosphate and betamethasone acetate (Celestone Soluspan), methylprednisolone acetate (Depo-Medrol), and dexamethasone acetate (Decadron-LA).[12] These compounds were developed to reduce undesirable hormonal side effects with less rapid dissipation from the joint. None of these corticosteroid derivatives appears to have any superiority over another; however, triamcinolone hexacetonide is the least water-soluble preparation and thus provides the longest duration of effectiveness within the peripheral joint space.[3]

Systemic absorption after peripheral joint injection occurs within 2–3 weeks. Improvement of inflammatory processes remote from the injection site demonstrates that intraarticular corticosteroids exert a systemic effect.

The practitioner's choice of a drug should be based upon the intended purpose for injecting the peripheral joint. For example, for long-term suppression of an inflammatory process such as rheumatoid arthritis, the long-acting triamcinolone hexacetonide would be preferable. If the patient's condition requires faster reduction of symptoms but also a long-acting medicine, the betamethasone phosphate and acetate preparation (Celestone Soluspan) would be preferable. The short onset from the phosphate preparation and the long duration from the acetate preparation make this a desirable choice. For more rapid onset of therapy, the shorter-acting methylprednisolone acetate (Depo-Medrol) would be the drug of choice.

Estimated dosages for the peripheral joints are widely variable and usually depend on the size of the joint. The larger joints, such as the knee and shoulder, respond well to a 40-mg dose of methylprednisolone acetate or the equivalent of another agent. The smaller joints, such as the elbow and ankle, respond to a 20- to 30-mg dose of methylprednisolone acetate or the equivalent. Even smaller joints, such as the acromioclavicular and sternoclavicular joints, respond to a 10- to 20-mg dose of methylprednisolone acetate or the equivalent.

The number of injections per joint is also widely variable. Commonly, joints that are injected for the purpose of reducing inflammation in rheumatoid arthritis will be injected many times over the course of the disease process. These multiple injections have been shown to cause interference with normal cartilage protein synthesis.[12] However, it has also been demonstrated that patients with long-standing rheumatoid arthritis who do not receive intraarticular corticosteroid injections have joint disuse and decreased function much sooner than those who receive the injections.[10] For the purposes of pain reduction in osteoarthritis as well as an adjunct in the mobilization of the treatment of adhesive capsulitis, injections at the rate of one per 4–6 weeks for a maximum of three injections is the most commonly accepted regimen. This regimen, of course, is subject to the patient's response to his or her overall treatment plan, of which the intraarticular corticosteroid injection is but one part.

It is usual practice to combine the corticosteroid medications with an anesthetic substance, such as procaine (Novacain) or lidocaine (Xylocaine) or the equivalent. The combined use of corticosteroids and anesthetic agents provides a larger volume of injectable material with which to bathe the joint more adequately. The added effect of analgesia is also desirable for patient comfort and for a more immediate response to treatment. Thus, the patient may obtain immediate pain relief and provide valuable feedback with which to help determine the overall rehabilitation plan. The usual anesthetic injected is lidocaine, 1% without epinephrine, with which the practitioner can provide a preliminary skin wheal and a control test before proceeding with the deeper injection. Bupivacaine (Marcaine, Sensorcaine), 0.25% or 0.5%, is also useful in providing a longer-acting analgesic effect for the patient. Use of the longer-acting bupivacaine, of course, depends on patient compliance, as the patient may "feel cured" and proceed to use the anesthetized joint indiscriminately. The dosages of lidocaine and bupivacaine also vary widely with the size of the joint. Usually, the smaller joints such as the acromioclavicular, sternoclavicular, and elbow joints would take 1–2 cc of 1% lidocaine combined with the corticosteroid. The glenohumeral, knee, and hip joints would take 2–4 cc of anesthetic agent. Bupivacaine is often preferable for nonweightbearing joints such as the shoulder, elbow, acromioclavicular, and sternoclavicular joints, so long as these joints can be somewhat immobilized for several hours. Likewise, lidocaine is the drug of choice for injections in the weight-bearing joints such as the knee because its duration is much shorter and, thus, the joint is subject to less postinjection trauma by the seemingly compliant patient.

CONTRAINDICATIONS AND COMPLICATIONS

The clinician must be acutely sensitive to contraindications and complications of intraarticular corticosteroid therapy. Some of the most obvious contraindications include infection of the joint or of the skin overlying the joint. A patient with generalized infection also should be considered an unsuitable candidate for corticosteroid injection. Injection of corticosteroids may render a joint susceptible to hematogenous seeding from more distant skin lesions. Thus, the overall health of the patient must be assessed before considering the use of intraarticular corticosteroids.[9] Other obvious contraindications include hypersensitivity to any of the anesthetic preparations or the corticosteroids themselves. When hypersensitivity to a medication is suspected, a simple test dose should be given at the site of injection by raising a skin wheal with the indicated anesthetic and allowing time to determine any adverse effects.

Patients receiving intraarticular injections in the presence of anticoagulants would be susceptible to serious bleeding. Determination of prothrombin time is necessary before injection therapy in these patients.

Patients with a recent injury to the joint such as a ligamentous destruction or bony destruction of the underlying joint should not be subjected to corticosteroid therapy. Instead, aspiration of the joint may be indicated if there is a relatively large inflammatory effusion.[23] Soft tissue or bony tumors at or near the underlying joint would also be a major contraindication to corticosteroid injections.

Even small doses of corticosteroids with intraarticular injections may trigger episodes of hyperglycemia, glycosuria, and even electrolyte imbalance in patients with diabetes; caution must be exercised in these situations.[11]

Although rare, infections can be a serious complication.[19] Usually, such infections can be avoided by using an aseptic technique (discussed later in this chapter).[29] Infections may be quite subtle in patients with long-standing rheumatoid arthritis as well as in those receiving immunosuppressive agents; the most common organism is *Staphylococcus aureus*.[27,30] One must also use caution in geriatric patients and those with debilitating diseases.

Hypercorticism from systemic corticosteroid therapy may be a complication if the patient receives multiple intraarticular injections in succession or if the patient is receiving concomitant oral cortisone therapy. Corticosteroid arthropathy with avascular necrosis also has been reported[14] but is rare and has not been noted to occur after single corticosteroid injections. Joint capsule calcification is also a potential complication of multiple intraarticular corticosteroid injections.[13]

Depigmentation and subcutaneous fat necrosis occasionally occur. The depigmentation is cosmetically unacceptable, especially in darker-skinned individuals in whom is can be quite noticeable. Fat necrosis usually is not a complication in superficial joints that have minimal amounts of overlying fat tissue. Using a small amount of lidocaine to flush the needle in order to avoid leaving a needle tract of corticosteroid suspension will help to minimize this complication.

A common complication in patients with rheumatoid arthritis who are receiving corticosteroid injections in the joints is "postinjection flare" (the joint appears inflamed or even infected), which tends to subside spontaneously in 24–72 hours.[8]

TECHNIQUES FOR INTRAARTICULAR INJECTIONS

Once the clinician has established that a peripheral joint needs to be injected or aspirated, the specific preparation for the injection is essentially the same for all joints. Thorough understanding of the underlying anatomy is important in order to accomplish a painless injection. The optimal site for injection of the joint usually is the extensor surface at a point where the synovium is closest to the skin. Approaching the joint from the extensor surfaces allows the injection to be as remote as possible from any major arteries, veins, and nerves.[14] When the site of injection has been determined, it can be marked with the needle hub or a retracted ballpoint pin by pressing the skin to produce a temporary indentation to mark the point of entry. The skin is then prepared by cleansing a generous area with a detergent or cleaner such as an iodine-based surgical scrub. This area is then painted with an antiseptic solution and allowed to dry. Aseptic technique is always advised, including the wearing of sterile gloves so that the area to be injected may be continually palpated and the anatomy appreciated throughout the procedure. A small skin wheal may then be raised using 1% lidocaine with no epinephrine (or an equivalent anesthetic agent). A 27-gauge skin needle approximately 0.75–1.0 inch long is used with approximately 1 cc of anesthetic agent. For joints distended with fluid or in which the joint is particularly close to the surface of the skin such as the acromioclavicular and sternoclavicular joints, the raising of a skin wheal or pre-anesthesia is usually not necessary. If a patient is particularly apprehensive about the injection procedure, one of the vapo-coolant sprays such as dichlorotetrafluoroethane or ethyl chloride may provide adequate anesthesia.

After the skin wheal is raised, a 25- or 22-gauge needle approximately 1.5 inches long may be used to introduce the injectate. The needle is then slid gently into the joint, with the clinician avoiding a strong thrusting motion. Just before beginning the actual injection, the practitioner should aspirate to assure there is no return of blood. After ascertaining the needle's position in the joint space, the injectable material should be introduced using slow, steady pressure on the plunger.

If the joint is to be aspirated before introduction of a corticosteroid, the same technique is used in preparation; however, a large needle may be introduced, such as a 20- or even an 18-gauge needle. Again, slow, steady pressure is used when the needle is introduced into the joint. The aspirate is then withdrawn with the practitioner gently pulling the plunger on the syringe with the dominant hand, holding the syringe barrel steady with the nondominant hand. If it is suspected that not all of the aspirate has been obtained from the joint, the needle tip may be moved around within the joint, and the joint itself may be "milked," using steady pressure with the opposite hand on the joint itself by kneading the skin toward the site of aspiration. After all of the available fluid is aspirated, the needle may be left in place with the syringe removed. A separate syringe may then be attached to the aspirating needle, and the injectate may then be introduced into the joint itself. Again, a slow, gentle introduction of the injectable material is desired.

If resistance is met during the time of the injection, the needle should be readjusted so that there is no resistance. Any time the needle is readjusted, the plunger on the syringe should be withdrawn to assure that the needle tip does not pierce a blood vessel.

After the drug or drugs have been injected, the needle is withdrawn and mild pressure is applied with a sterile gauze pad to prevent bleeding. Whenever the injected material includes corticosteroids, a slight amount of lidocaine may be used to clear the needle before withdrawal. As mentioned earlier, this technique prevents leaving a steroid tract through the adipose tissue and skin, which may cause depigmentation or subcutaneous necrosis.

Psychological care of the patient is important to the success of these injections. Throughout the procedure, the patient must be coaxed to achieve muscle relaxation and reassured of the importance of the procedure. It is likewise important that the patient be reminded of the practitioner's skill with and knowledge of the procedure. After the procedure, the patient should be assessed carefully to be sure that he or she is not exhibiting a vasovagal response and that appropriate measures are taken to prevent any secondary harm, e.g., falling as a result of transient hypotension.

UPPER EXTREMITY JOINTS

Glenohumeral Joint

The glenohumeral joint is subject to multiple traumatic and pathologic problems more frequently than any other joint except the knee. The anatomy of the shoulder must be well understood for a relatively painless injection to be achieved. In entering the subacromial space in the shoulder, there is little anterior space for placement of the needle. A lateral or posterior approach may be more desirable.[7]

When injecting the shoulder for problems such as bicipital tendinitis, the anterior approach is necessary (Fig. 2-1). The patient is placed in a sitting position, and the anterior portion of the shoulder is prepared aseptically and, if desired, a cutaneous wheal is raised medial to the head of the humerus and just inferior to the tip of the coracoid process. It is useful to have obese patients lie supine with the forearm across the abdomen. In this position, the shoulder may be passively rotated internally and externally to identify the head of the humerus. The coracoid process is then easily palpated. The injection is thus directed in the anteroposterior plane just lateral to the coracoid process. The needle is advanced into the groove between the medial aspect of the humeral head and the glenoid. No resistance should be felt to the advancement of the needle.

The lateral approach to injection of the shoulder is sometimes useful when treating supraspinatus tendinitis (*see* Fig. 2-1).[7] The patient is placed in a sitting position with the arm relaxed in the lap, which increases the subacromial space. The lateralmost point of the shoulder is palpated and

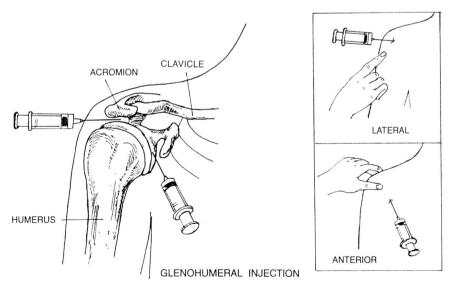

CLAVICLE
ACROMION
LATERAL
HUMERUS
ANTERIOR
GLENOHUMERAL INJECTION

FIGURE 2-1. Approximate surface anatomy (inserts) and internal anatomic sites for injection of the glenohumeral joint laterally and anteriorly.

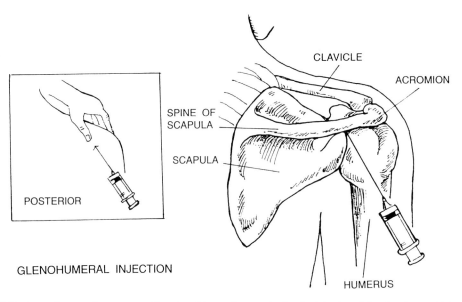

GLENOHUMERAL INJECTION

FIGURE 2-2. Approximate surface anatomy (insert) and internal anatomic sites for injection of the glenohumeral joint posteriorly.

the needle prepared for insertion below the acromion. After aseptic preparation, the needle is directed almost perpendicularly to the skin surface, with a slight upward angle. The space is then easily entered, and no resistance should be felt with advancement of the needle.

The posterior approach to the shoulder is popular for conditions such as adhesive capsulitis as well as synovitis or chronic osteoarthritis (Fig. 2-2). The posterior approach also allows the practitioner to be out of the patient's vision, thus reducing any apprehension. The patient is placed in the sitting position with his or her arm in the lap, which allows internal rotation of the shoulder and adduction of the arm. The skin is prepared aseptically, and the site of injection is palpated. The site of injection is just under the posteroinferior border of the posterolateral angle of the acromion. It is useful for the practitioner to palpate the patient's coracoid process in the anterior portion of the shoulder with the index finger. This is the point at which the needle is "aimed." The needle is then inserted approximately 1 inch below the posterolateral acromion process and directed from the posterolateral portion of the shoulder to the anteromedial portion of the shoulder toward the coracoid process. If resistance is encountered, the needle may be withdrawn slightly and angled upward. The needle will then be in the upper recess of the shoulder joint away from the head of the humerus.

Acromioclavicular Joint

The acromioclavicular joint is small and superficial (Fig. 2-3). It is occasionally swollen and usually tender during palpation when inflamed. This joint

can be injected easily using a 25-gauge needle with the patient sitting or supine and the shoulder propped on a pillow. Usually, injections into this joint are for chronic pain such as occurs in shoulder separations that have not responded to noninvasive treatment.

Many times, the joint is injected for diagnostic purposes to delineate the source of pain in the shoulder and, therefore, corticosteroids are not used. However, with chronic pain that does not subside after a trial of anesthetics (such as lidocaine), corticosteroids may be used.

The joint is prepared aseptically, as described earlier. The joint is easily palpated by locating the tip of the distal clavicle and injecting either from a superior angle or an anterosuperior angle into the joint space. In a degenerative joint, many times the needle will not pass easily into the joint, which then needs to be probed gently so that the needle can be advanced just to the proximal margin of the joint's surface. It is usually not necessary to penetrate the joint any deeper.

Sternoclavicular Joint

The sternoclavicular joint is easily located just lateral to the notch of the sternum (Fig. 2-4). Many times the sternoclavicular joint is slightly dislocated, thus providing a source of pain and making it easily palpable because the proximal clavicle may be slightly elevated in relationship to the sternum. This joint is small and may be difficult to inject unless a 25- or 27-gauge needle is used. Great care should be taken that these injections into the sternoclavicular area are done superficially because immediately posterior to the sternoclavicular joint are the brachiocephalic veins.

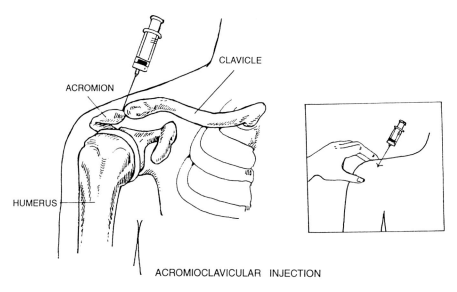

FIGURE 2-3. Approximate surface anatomy (insert) and internal anatomic sites for injection of the acromioclavicular (AC) joint.

Elbow

The elbow region is usually subject to periarticular problems, including lateral epicondylitis and medial epicondylitis; however, in this chapter, attention is directed to the joint space itself. Aspiration for problems such as synovitis in patients with rheumatoid arthritis as well as arthrography of the joint for delineation of multiple pathologic processes, including loose bodies, are the initial approaches to treatment.[17] Once it is determined that an intraarticular injection is needed, the practitioner must remember that the extensor surfaces of the joint are the safest places to avoid vessels and nerves. Thus, the injection should be directed to

the posterolateral portion of the elbow or to the posterior portion of the elbow (Fig. 2-5). These approaches will allow the practitioner to enter the humeroulnar joint, the true elbow joint.

The patient is placed with the elbow positioned between 50–90° of flexion. The posterior and/or lateral skin surfaces are prepared aseptically. For the posterolateral approach, the lateral epicondyle area and the posterior olecranon area are palpated. The groove between the olecranon below and the lateral epicondyle of the humerus is located. The needle is then directed proximally toward the head of the radius and medially into the elbow joint. Again, no resistance should be felt when the needle enters the joint. Aspiration or injection of the joint

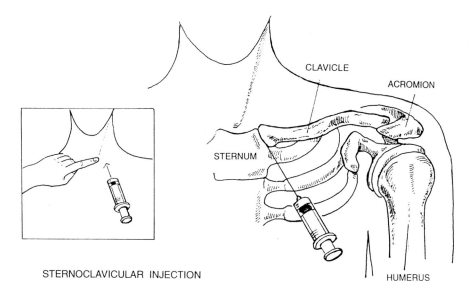

FIGURE 2-4. Approximate surface anatomy (insert) and internal anatomic sites for injection of the sternoclavicular joint.

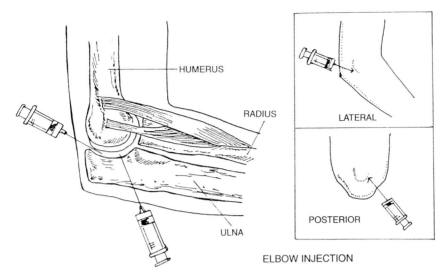

FIGURE 2-5. Approximate surface anatomy (inserts) and internal anatomic sites for injection of the elbow laterally and posteriorly.

may then be undertaken. The posterior approach to the elbow is relatively simple. The posterior olecranon is palpated with the lateral olecranon groove located just posterior to the lateral epicondyle. The needle is then inserted above the superior aspect of and lateral to the olecranon. It is advanced into the joint and, again, no resistance should be felt.

Wrist

Many of the small joints of the wrist have interconnecting synovial spaces, thus making it possible to provide relief to the entire joint complex with one

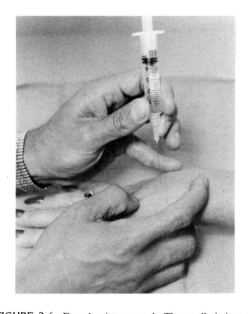

FIGURE 2-6. Dorsal wrist approach. The needle is inserted medial to the extensor pollicis longus tendon.

injection. The wrist may be infiltrated by several methods.[20,28,31] The route of entry may be influenced by the site of inflammation or desired anatomic area. The preferred method is the dorsal approach, which may be facilitated with slight flexion of the hand. This can be easily accomplished by flexing the hand over a rolled towel. The point of entry (Figs. 2-6 and 2-7) is just medial to the extensor pollicis longus tendon in the distal aspect of the midpoint of the radius and ulna. This can be easily palpated as a depression between the radius and the scaphoid and lunate bones. The needle is placed perpendicular to the skin and inserted 1–2 cm lateral to the extensor pollicis longus tendon.[28] Optional approaches to the wrist include the ulnar or the dorsal snuffbox approach. With the ulnar approach, the injection is made just distal to the lateral ulnar margin in a palpable gap between the border of the distal ulna and the carpal bones (Fig. 2-8). A third approach is the dorsal aspect just medial to the anatomic snuffbox between the radius and carpal bones (Fig. 2-9). Anesthetic and corticosteroid preparations may diffuse throughout the joint and is facilitated by range-of-motion exercises following injection.[24,25] The approach used should be based on the area of maximal point tenderness or site of inflammation and specific anatomic structures underlying the region to be infiltrated, such as the scapholunate ligaments or the triangular fibrocartilaginous complex. Caution should be taken in order to arrive at an accurate diagnosis when treating a chronic condition. An underlying wrist injury with unremarkable initial radiographs may cause scapholunate dissociation, carpal instability, or avascular necrosis. These disorders should be considered in the differential diagnosis during conservative management.

Intercarpal Joints

Injection into the intercarpal joints such as the triquetrolunate space can be accomplished by palpating the borders of the carpal bone. Palpation is easier to perform when the joint is swollen and fluctuant.[31] Fluoroscopic guidance may be necessary for precise location.

Carpometacarpal Joint

The first carpometacarpal joint or trapeziometacarpal joint is a frequent source of pain in osteoarthritis and in occupations or sports that subject the patient to undue stress. The joint may be infiltrated or aspirated from the dorsal aspect of the radial side of the carpometacarpal joint (Figs. 2-10 and 2-11) by holding the thumb in slight flexion and palpating for the point of maximal tenderness.[15,20,33] When injecting the carpometacarpal joint, care should be taken to avoid the radial artery and the extensor pollicis tendon.[32] To avoid the radial artery, the needle should be placed toward the dorsal side of the extensor pollicis brevis tendon.

Interphalangeal Joints

The proximal and distal interphalangeal joints are most frequently affected by arthritic processes. The proximal interphalangeal joint is frequently affected in rheumatoid arthritis.[27,31] These smaller joints require a small-gauge needle (25- or 27-gauge) to facilitate entry. A vapo-coolant spray may be used for superficial skin anesthesia with or without a superficial skin wheal to diminish the pain on initial infiltration; infiltration of these smaller joints is painful.[20] Because the joint space is very small, the tip of the needle must be advanced gently into the intraarticular capsule. The joint will accommodate only a small amount of fluid, usually less than

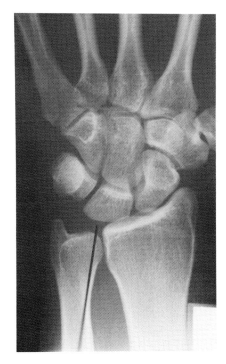

FIGURE 2-7. Anteroposterior x-ray of the wrist demonstrating proper needle placement into the wrist joint using a dorsal approach.

2 cc, and overdistention should be avoided. Pericapsular and subcutaneous injections have been known to provide some beneficial effect when direct joint infiltration could not be obtained, presumably by transport of the corticosteroids to inflamed capsule and synovium.[32] The proximal and distal interphalangeal joints are infiltrated by palpating the borders of the joint and advancing a fine needle, preferably with a small syringe (2 ml) to facilitate fine motor control (Fig. 2-12). Splinting the affected joint may allow resolution of an inflammatory response.[16,21,26]

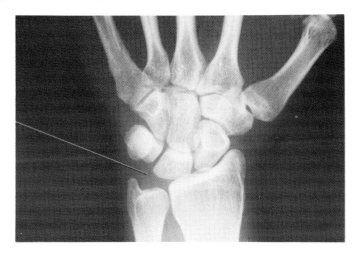

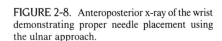

FIGURE 2-8. Anteroposterior x-ray of the wrist demonstrating proper needle placement using the ulnar approach.

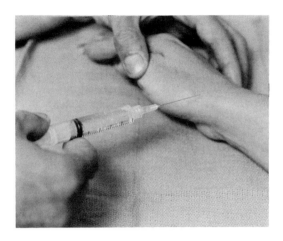

FIGURE 2-9. Needle placement adjacent to the anatomical snuffbox between the radius and carpal bones.

LOWER EXTREMITIES

Hip Joint

The hip joint is often difficult to infiltrate or aspirate due to its depth and the surrounding tissue. Fluoroscopic guidance with injection of contrast material is often necessary to confirm proper needle placement. This joint may be infiltrated by an anterior or lateral approach (Fig. 2-13). The anterior approach is preferred.[28,31] With the anterior approach, the patient is in the supine position with the lower extremity externally rotated. The length of the needle will depend on the patient's size. The anatomic landmarks for the anterior approach are 2 cm distal to the anterior superior iliac spine and 3 cm lateral to the palpated femoral artery at a level corresponding to the superior margins of the greater trochanter. After superficial anesthesia is administered, the needle is advanced at an angle 60° posteromedially through the tough capsular ligaments,

advanced to bone, and slightly withdrawn. This technique places the tip of the needle directly into the joint, and aspiration or injection may be performed. This approach is much simpler using fluoroscopic guidance to direct the needle posteromedially into the joint; once the capsular ligaments have been penetrated, contrast medium will confirm proper needle placement. Depending on the integrity of the joint, 2–4 cc of anesthetic and corticosteroid suspension may be introduced.

The lateral approach is performed by palpating the greater trochanter of the femur, which may be facilitated by externally rotating the lower extremity. Superficial anesthesia may be used and, again, depending on the size of the patient, the appropriate-length needle is selected. A 3- to 4-inch needle is usually sufficient; however, in large patients, longer needles may be necessary. Just anterior to the greater trochanter, the needle is advanced and walked medially along the neck of the femur until the joint is reached. Aspiration may be obtained, but is more difficult with the lateral approach. The amount of fluid that may be introduced may be limited, depending upon the integrity of the joint. Avascular necrosis is a potential complication of corticosteroid injection to the hip. However, no recent cases have been reported in the literature as a direct result of this procedure.

Knee

The knee is the most commonly aspirated and injected joint in the body. It contains the largest synovial space and demonstrates the most visible and palpable effusion (when present). A patient is usually most comfortable lying supine with sufficient pillows. The knee is prepared using an aseptic technique. If a large effusion is present, whether medially or laterally, the site of entry should be over the maximal expansion of the effusion in order to cause the least discomfort during the procedure.

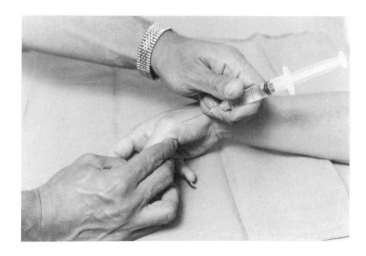

FIGURE 2-10. Needle placement into the carpometacarpal joint.

For injections in which a large effusion is not present, the lateral, medial, suprapatellar, or anterior approach may be used (Fig. 2-14). Before injecting or aspirating the knee, the patella should be grasped between the examiner's thumb and forefinger and rocked gently from side to side to ensure that the patient's muscles are relaxed.

The medial approach to the knee is simple. First, the practitioner puts a small amount of lateral pressure on the patella, pushing it slightly medially and displacing it somewhat to increase the gap between the patella and the femur medially. The needle is then introduced about midway between the superior and inferior pole of the patella medial to the patella and midway between the medial border of the patella and the femur. A preinjection skin wheal may be raised with an anesthetic agent, or the skin itself may be anesthetized with a vapo-coolant spray for patient comfort. As the needle is introduced into the joint space, the needle should be aspirated progressively. If no aspirate is obtained, the corticosteroid can be injected. Before withdrawal of the needle, the needle tract again should be flushed with a small amount of anesthetic.

The lateral approach to the knee is also simple. With the patient supine, the knee is fully extended or placed in slight flexion. The patella is slightly displaced laterally to increase the gap between the patella and femur laterally. The skin may then be anesthetized with 1% lidocaine. The needle is introduced halfway between the superior pole of the patella and the midline of the patella lateral and inferior to the patella. As the needle is introduced, aspiration is performed until the needle is into the joint. The joint can then be aspirated or injected.

If a large effusion is present, the suprapatellar approach may be used. This does not have any specific advantage over the lateral approach unless the effusion is expanding the suprapatellar bursa.

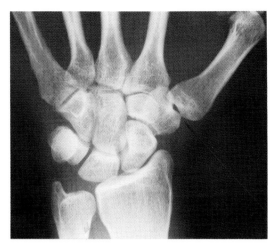

FIGURE 2-11. Anteroposterior x-ray of the hand demonstrating needle placement into the first carpometacarpal joint.

The needle is introduced at the point of maximal expansion of the effusion, and the joint is then aspirated. This approach is usually not as good as the lateral approach if the knee is to be injected only and not aspirated. It is much easier to enter the joint space with the medial or lateral approach.

On occasion, an anterior approach to the knee may be desired if a patient cannot fully extend the knee. In these cases, the patient may be sitting or supine with the knee flexed to 90°. The needle is inserted just inferior to the inferior patellar pole either from the lateral or medial side of the patellar tendon. The needle is then advanced parallel to the tibial plateau until the joint space is entered. It is more difficult to aspirate a knee effusion when using this approach.[23] Moreover, the risk of puncturing the articular cartilage is much higher, as is the risk to the infrapatellar fat pad. Occasionally, the knee is approached anteriorly by inserting the needle directly through the patellar tendon. This approach has no merit because it increases

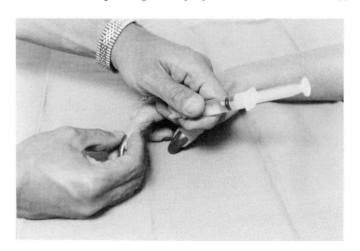

FIGURE 2-12. Needle placement into the interphalangeal joint.

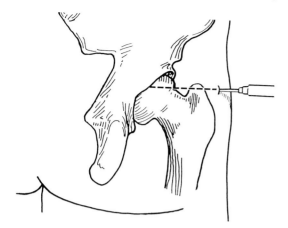

FIGURE 2-13. Lateral arthrocentesis and injection of the hip joint.

discomfort to the patient and may cause bleeding in the patellar ligament.

Other conditions affecting the knee that may warrant injection of corticosteroid include prepatellar bursitis, iliotibial band syndrome, anserine bursitis, and others. These injections are not intraarticular and will therefore be discussed elsewhere.

Ankle Mortise

The ankle joint is not commonly injected; however, it may be subject to osteoarthritis, rheumatoid arthritis, or chronic pain resulting from instability.

An anterior medial or anterior lateral approach may be used, depending on the location of pain or pathologic process (Fig. 2-15). For the medial approach, a slight depression is felt between the extensor hallucis longus tendon laterally and tibialis anterior tendon medially on the inferior border of the tibia superiorly and the talus inferiorly. The needle is then directd slightly laterally and perpendicular to the tibial joint surface. The talus has a superior curve, and the needle may need to be angled slightly superiorly to avoid contact with the talar joint surface.

The lateral approach is useful in situations in which pathologic processes in the ankle appear to be most prominent either at the talofibular joint or the tibiotalar joint. Here, the foot is placed in moderate plantar flexion. The area enclosed by the tibia superiorly, the talus inferiorly, and the fibular head laterally is palpated. The extensor tendons of the toes should be medial to the injection site. The needle is then inserted from an anterolateral position and is directed toward the posterior edge of the medial malleolus. If the joint surface is encountered, the physician should direct the needle slightly upward, remembering that the talar dome arches superiorly.

Subtalar Joint

Occasionally, the subtalar joint is the site of a pathologic process. The easiest approach to this

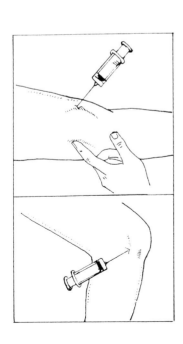

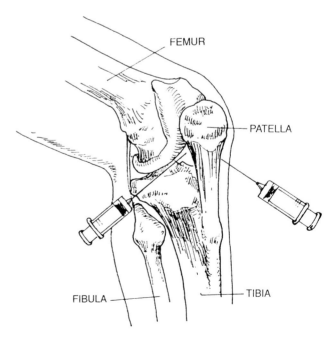

KNEE INJECTION

FIGURE 2-14. Approximate surface anatomy (inserts) and internal anatomic sites for injection of the knee.

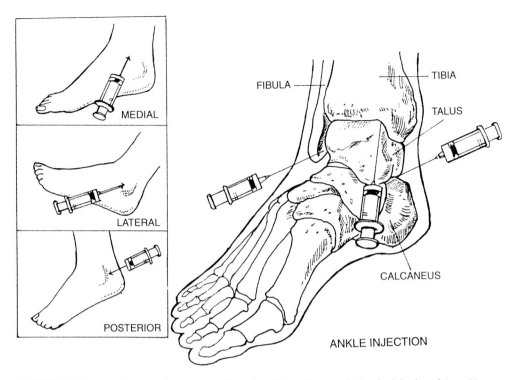

FIGURE 2-15. Approximate surface anatomy (inserts) and internal anatomic sites for injection of the ankle.

joint is to have the patient lie prone with his or her feet extending over the end of the examination table. This allows the ankle to be in the neutral position. The posterior and lateral portions of the ankle are then prepared aseptically. The site of entry for the injection is along a line drawn from the most prominent portion of the distal fibula posterior to the Achilles tendon. This line should be parallel to the plantar aspect of the foot with the foot in neutral position; halfway between the prominent aspect of the lateral malleolus and the Achilles tendon, the needle is inserted and directed toward a point inferior and medial to the medial malleolus.

Intertarsal Joints

Injection of the tarsal joints may be accomplished similarly to injection of the carpal joints. Palpation of the bony landmarks is obtained, and the needle is inserted between the tarsal bones to the desired depth,[32] and aspiration is accomplished if necessary. Fluoroscopic needle guidance simplifies this procedure and ascertains precise needle placement.

FIGURE 2-16. Dorsal approach to the first metatarsophalangeal joint.

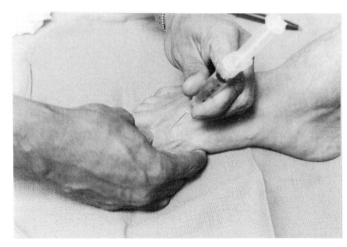

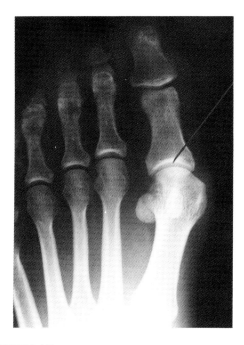

FIGURE 2-17. Anteroposterior x-ray of the foot demonstrating proper needle placement into the first metatarsophalangeal joint.

Metatarsophalangeal Joints

The metatarsophalangeal joints are most frequently infiltrated with a dorsal approach (Figs. 2-16, 2-17).[31] This approach is carried out by palpating the metatarsophalangeal margins with plantar flexion of the toe in order to facilitate insertion of the needle. The needle is then advanced into the joint. The first metatarsophalangeal joint is frequently affected by arthritic conditions and gout. When a swollen joint is encountered, infiltration and aspiration may be easier with a swollen capsule.

CONCLUSIONS

The peripheral joints are not difficult to inject. With practice, the clinician can become quite adept at entering these joints with ease, providing an effective addition to the management of peripheral joint problems. After the joints are injected, they should not be subjected to intensive exercise or motion for several days. This period of relative rest helps to promote the retention of the corticosteroid in the joint, allowing longer contact with the joint surface and delaying absorption of the drug systemically.[23]

REFERENCES

1. Adelberg JS, Smith GH: Corticosteroid-induced avascular necrosis of the talus. J Foot Surg 30:66–69, 1991.
2. Alarcon-Segovia D, Ward LE: Marked destructive changes occurring in osteoarthritic finger joints after intra-articular injection of corticosteroids. Arthritis Rheum 9:443–449, 1966.
3. Bain LS, Balch HW, Wetherly JMR, et al: Intra-articular triamcinolone hexacetonide: Double-blind comparison with methylprednisolone. Br J Clin Pract 26:559–561, 1972.
4. Balch HW, Gibson JMC, El Ghobarey AF, et al: Repeated corticosteroid injections into knee joints. Rheumatol Rehabil 16:137–140, 1977.
5. Behrens F, Shepherd N, Mitchel N: Alterations of rabbit articular cartilage by intra-articular injection of glucocorticoids. J Bone Joint Surg 57A:1157, 71–73, 1975.
6. Castles JJ: Clinical pharmacology of glucocorticoids. In McCarty DJ, Hollander JL (eds): Arthritis and Allied Conditions, 12th ed. Philadelphia, Lea & Febiger, 1993, pp 665–682.
7. Doherty M, Hazleman BL, Hutton CW, et al: Rheumatology Examination and Injection Techniques. Philadelphia, W.B. Saunders, 1992.
8. Gordon GV, Schumacher HR: Electron microscopic study fo depot corticosteroid crystals with clinical studies after intra-articular injection. J Rheumatol 6:7–14, 1979.
9. Gowans J, Granieri P: Septic arthritis: Its relations to intra-articular injections of hydrocortisone acetate. N Engl J Med 261:502, 1959.
10. Gray RG, Gottlieb NL: Intra-articular corticosteroids: An updated assessment. Clin Orthop 177:235–263, 1983.
11. Gray RG, Gottlieb NL: Rheumatic disorders associated with diabetes mellitus: Literature review. Semin Arthritis Rheum 6:19–34, 1976.
12. Gray RG, Tenenbaum J, Gottlieb NL: Local corticosteroid injection treatment in rheumatic disorders. Semin Arthritis Rheum 10:231–245, 1981.
13. Hardin JG Jr: Controlled study of the long-term effects of "total hand" injection. Arthritis Rheum 22:619, 1979.
14. Hollander JL: Intrasynovial corticosteroid therapy in arthritis. Maryland State Med J 19:62–66, 1972.
15. Hollander JL: Joint problems in the elderly: How to help patients cope. Postgrad Med 21:209–311, 1988.
16. Howard LD, Pratt ER, Punnell S: The use of compound L (hydrocortisone) in operative and nonoperative conditions of the hand. J Bone Joint Surg 35A:994–1002, 1953.
17. Hudson TM: Elbow arthrography. Radiol Clin North Am 19:227–240, 1981.
18. Jalava S: Periarticular calcification after intra-articular triamcinolone hexacetonide. Scand J Rheumatol 9:190–192, 1980.
19. Kothari T, Reyes MP, Brooks N, et al: Pseudomonas capacia septic arthritis due to intra-articular injections of methylprednisolone. Can Med Assoc J 116:1230–1235, 1977.
20. Leversee JH: Aspiration of joint and soft tissue injections. Prim Care 13:572–599, 1986.
21. Marks M, Gunther SF: Efficacy of cortisone injection in treatment of trigger fingers and thumbs. J Hand Surg 14A:722–727, 1989.
22. McCarty DJ, McCarthy G, Garrera G: Intra-articular corticosteroids possibly leading to local osteonecrosis and marrow fat-induced synovitis. J Rheumatol 18:1091–1094, 1991.
23. Neustadt DH: Intra-articular corticosteroids and other agents: Aspiration techniques. In Katz W: The Diagnosis and Management of Rheumatic Diseases, 2nd ed. Philadelphia, J.B. Lippincott, 1988, pp 812–825.
24. Neustadt DH: Local corticosteroid injection therapy and soft tissue rheumatic conditions of hand and wrist and rheumatism. J Arthritis Rheum 34:923–926, 1991.
25. Owen DF: Intra-articular and soft tissue aspiration injection. Clin Rheumatol Pract Mar–May:52–63, 1986.

26. Pavno P, Anderson HJ, Simonson O: A long-term follow up of the effects of repeated corticosteroid injections for stenosing tenosynovitis. J Hand Surg 14B:242–243, 1989.

27. Pfenninger JL: Injections of joints and soft tissue: Part I. General guidelines. Am Fam Physician 44:1196–1202, 1991.

28. Pfenninger JL: Injections of joints and soft tissues: Part II. Guidelines for specific joints. Am Fam Physician 44:1690–1701, 1991.

29. Stanley D, Connolly WB: Iatrogenic injections injuries of the hand and upper limb. J Hand Surg 17B:442–446, 1992.

30. Stefanich RJ: Intra-articular corticosteroids in treatment of osteoarthritis. Orthop Rev 15:65–71, 1986.

31. Steinbrocker O, Neustadt DH: Aspiration Injection Therapy in Arthritis and Musculoskeletal Disorders: Handbook on Technique and Management. Hagerstown, MD, Harper & Row, 1972.

32. Taweepoe P, Frame JD: Acute ischemia of the hand by accidental radial infusion of Depo-Medrol. J Hand Surg 15:118–120, 1990.

33. Wilke WS, Tuggle CJ: Optimal techniques for intra-articular and peri-articular joint injections. Mod Med 56:58–72, 1988.

34. Zuckerman JD, Neislan RJ, Rothberg M: Injections for joint and soft tissue disorders: When and how to use them. Geriatrics 4:45–52, 55, 1990.

Chapter 3

TRIGGER POINT INJECTION

ANDREW A. FISCHER, M.D., Ph.D.

TRIGGER AND TENDER POINTS: A FREQUENT CAUSE OF PAIN IN MANY CONDITIONS

Trigger points (TrPs) are small, exquisitely tender areas in various soft tissues, including muscles, ligaments, periosteum, tendons, and pericapsular areas. These points may radiate pain into a specific distant area called a "reference pain zone."[1,10–13,15–18] The referred pain may be present at rest. The pain may also occur on activation of the TrP by local pressure, piercing by an injection needle, or activity of the involved muscle (particularly its overuse). TrPs located in muscles are called myofascial because they also may involve the fascia. In addition to the focal tenderness, they are characterized by the presence of a taut band[15–18] that is sensitive to pressure, which indicates sensitization of the nerve endings within. The hard resistance to palpation and needle penetration is interpreted as evidence that a group of the affected muscle fibers is constantly contracted. Later, approximately 6–8 weeks after an injury, the resistance to the needle usually becomes very hard. This is characteristic of fibrotic (scar) tissues, which fail to react to conservative therapy. Since there are no definitive histologic studies of TrPs at different stages, it may be assumed that the damaged tissue has healed by a scar.

Trigger point injections (TIs) represent specific techniques for the alleviation of pain caused by the trigger area. Optimally, TIs are aimed at mechanically breaking up the entire abnormal tissue that causes pain. The most frequent findings related to pain are tender spots (TSs), a term reserved for point tenderness without radiating pain. TSs are frequently located within taut bands that have characteristics identical to TrPs. TIs have the same effect, indications, and limitations in both TSs and TrPs. Therefore, the rest of this chapter uses the expression "TrPs" for both tender spots and TrPs, since the technique of injection in both cases is

identical: directed at the point of maximum tenderness and taut bands.

Commonly, tender spots and some TrPs represent local tissue damage that causes inflammation and irritation that can be diagnosed by increased sensitivity to pressure. Figures 3-1 and 3-2 illustrate a possible concept of pathologic changes. This hypothesis may explain clinical findings in acute and chronic injury and the effect of needling. Conceptually, the TSs or TrP at the chronic stage can be thought of as a pocket of fibrotic tissue that contains sensitizing agents that are the products of tissue damage. These substances cause sensitization of the entrapped nerve fibers. This sensitization increases the nerve's reactivity so that a lower pressure produces pain. The sensitivity of the nerve ending can be quantified by measurement of "pressure pain threshold" (tenderness) using a dolorimeter (algometer).[4–7,12]

The needling, even without infiltration by anesthetic instantaneously abolishes the pain, tenderness, and fibrotic type of resistance. Such effect of dry needling can be best explained by breaking up a fibrotic pocket that has entrapped the nerve endings along with sensitizing substances. This allows the entering blood flow to wash away the sensitizing substances. This concept may explain the effect of the TIs but has not been substantiated by histologic studies. Needling also may interrupt neuromuscular mechanisms involved in TrP activity.

Figure 3-2 and Table 3-1 illustrate physical findings over TrPs and taut bands before, during, and after injection combined with needling.

TrPs and TSs are the immediate cause of pain in a variety of conditions, including sports- or work-related injuries, sprains, strains, pinched nerves, disc disease, and arthritis or muscle tension related to nonphysiologic posture or stress. Headaches are also frequently caused by TrPs. Certain hormonal disorders such as thyroid or estrogen deficiencies are frequent causes and perpetuators of widespread TrPs.

1. ACUTE STAGE

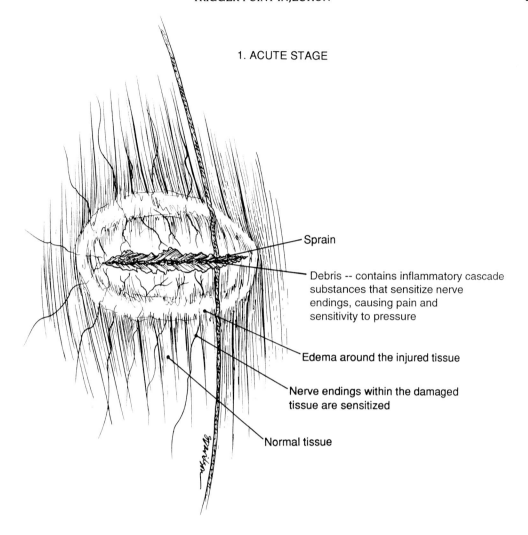

Sprain

Debris -- contains inflammatory cascade
substances that sensitize nerve
endings, causing pain and
sensitivity to pressure

Edema around the injured tissue

Nerve endings within the damaged
tissue are sensitized

Normal tissue

FIGURE 3-1. Conceptual illustration of pathologic changes in acute tissue injury that causes focal tenderness with pain. *(Figure continued on following page.)*

TRIGGER POINT INJECTIONS: THE MOST EFFECTIVE TREATMENT

Needling represents the most effective treatment of trigger points, TSs, and acute or chronic soft tissue injuries. Injection of a local anesthetic (usually lidocaine) is combined with a special needling technique to break up the abnormal tissue that causes the pain. The critical factor in TIs is not the injected substance but rather the mechanical disruption of the abnormal tissue and interruption of the TrP mechanism if one has developed.[8,9] Intensive stimulation also may contribute to the prolonged relief of pain by TrP injections.[14] The fact that the symptoms originated in the treated TrP is confirmed by observing whether the pain is reproduced by pressure upon the trigger area or relieved after TrP injection.[2] The injections are followed by a specific program of physical therapy and exercises. Once

fibrotic tissue (scar) has formed in the damaged tissue, the most effective way to break it up is through needling: the repetitive insertion and withdrawal of the injection needle in the affected area.

Local anesthetics, such as 1% lidocaine or 0.5% procaine, provide temporary relief, lasting about 45 minutes. The long-term relief from pain is achieved by the needling, which mechanically breaks up the abnormal tissue. The number of injections needed depends on the number of TrPs present.

One or two areas are usually injected during each treatment visit. Injections may be given two or three times a week for acute pain; once per week or once every 2 weeks is usually adequate as pain relief is being achieved. Each trigger point requires at least one injection. In large TrPs, however, injection may be limited to one segment per visit, depending on the patient's tolerance. Sufficient tissue must be left around the needled areas for proper healing to

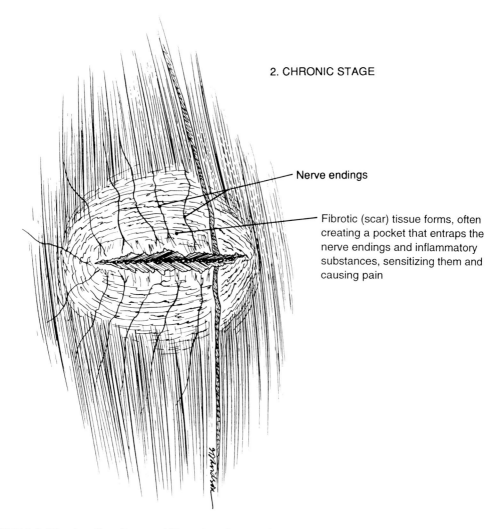

2. CHRONIC STAGE

Nerve endings

Fibrotic (scar) tissue forms, often
creating a pocket that entraps the
nerve endings and inflammatory
substances, sensitizing them and
causing pain

FIGURE 3-1 *(Continued).*   Conceptual illustration of pathologic changes in chronic tissue injury that causes focal tenderness
with pain.

(Figure continued on following page.)

occur. Without proper treatment, TrPs have the
tendency to spread to additional muscles, causing
flareup of pain.

The injection technique used for TrPs (combination of needling with infiltration) is effective in
alleviating pain and restoring function in focal
tenderness. The procedure is effective regardless of
the underlying pathology and whether or not the
pain is referred or limited to the tender area. Sprains
and strains of muscles, ligaments, soft tissue injuries,
inflammation, injuries of pericapsular tissues, and
bursitis are the most common conditions that improve dramatically after needling combined with
injection of local anesthetic. In osteoarthritis, a
ligament tear is frequently the main cause of pain.
These conditions in the chronic stage also respond
well to injections, combining mechanical needling
without the use of corticosteroids. TrPs caused by
endocrine dysfunction (especially thyroid or estrogen

deficiency), fibromyalgia, psychological tension, or
ischemia caused by muscle spasm also may be treated
effectively by TIs. Often psychological tension and
muscle spasm may not be alleviated without eliminating TrPs, which prevent relaxation of the muscle.
Inability to relax tight muscles produces more TrPs,
and a vicious cycle ensures. Lacking a better name,
the injections for all of the above conditions are
called "TIs," since the technique is identical.

The main contraindications for TIs include bleeding disorders, local infection, anticoagulant therapy,
certain psychiatric conditions (anxiety, paranoia,
schizophrenia), and inability to rest the injected
body part following the procedure. Depression is
not a contraindication for TIs. On the contrary,
relief from chronic pain frequently improves depression profoundly. Unless the conditions that
caused the TrPs and perpetuating factors are diagnosed and treated, the TrPs will recur.

3. EFFECT OF NEEDLING-INJECTION

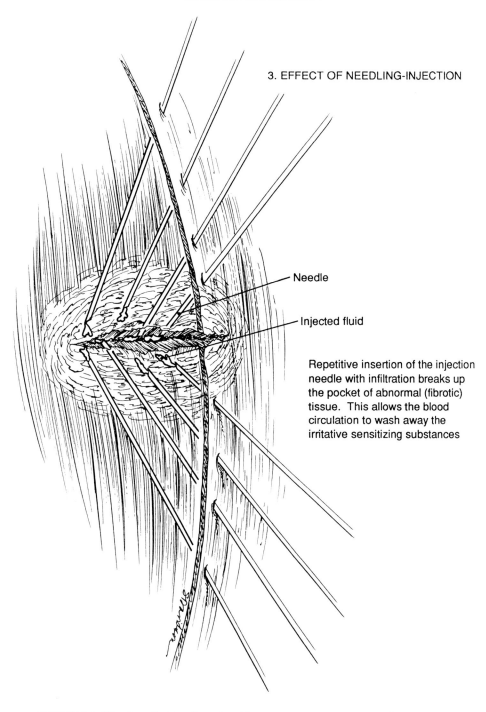

Needle

Injected fluid

Repetitive insertion of the injection
needle with infiltration breaks up
the pocket of abnormal (fibrotic)
tissue. This allows the blood
circulation to wash away the
irritative sensitizing substances

FIGURE 3-1 *(Continued)*. The effect of needling that breaks up the abnormal tissue is also shown.

Three commonly employed trigger point injection techniques include needling combined with infiltration, technique of Travell and Simons, and injection of corticosteroids.

1. **Needling combined with infiltration** is the most effective technique of TI in the author's experience. Infiltration with a local anesthetic such as 1% lidocaine or 0.5% procaine is combined with needling. After withdrawal of the needle to the subcutaneous level, repetitive insertion and redirection of the needle are required to cover the entire abnormal (painful) area with as few skin penetrations as possible.

2. **Technique of J. Travell and D.G. Simons.**[17,18] A small amount of 0.5% procaine is injected into the TrP in order to desensitize the most tender spot.

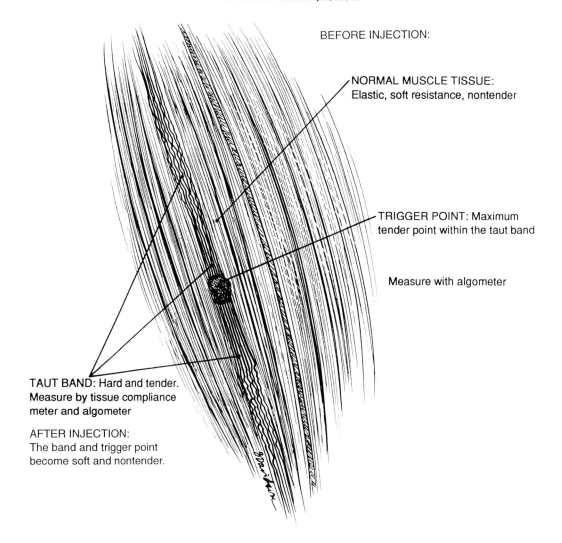

BEFORE INJECTION:

NORMAL MUSCLE TISSUE:
Elastic, soft resistance, nontender

TRIGGER POINT: Maximum
tender point within the taut band

Measure with algometer

TAUT BAND: Hard and tender.
Measure by tissue compliance
meter and algometer

AFTER INJECTION:
The band and trigger point
become soft and nontender.

FIGURE 3-2. Physical findings over a trigger point and taut band before, during, and after trigger point injection with needling.

This approach limits the needling and injection of 0.5 procaine to the most tender spots. The goal is to inactivate the neuromuscular TrP mechanism. The needling progresses in millimeters rather than centimeters, as described later.

3. **Steroid injection.** A 1.5-inch thin needle, usually 25-gauge, is used. Corticosteroids are combined with a small amount (1–3 ml) of local anesthetic, usually lidocaine. Corticosteroids are not necessary for myofascial TrP treatment. Precise needling, which breaks up the abnormal tissue, is more effective. In fact, corticosteroids may induce local myopathy. However, corticosteroids may be useful in the treatment of conditions involving passive tissues, such as bursitis, tendinitis, epicondylitis, or ligament sprain. The disadvantages of corticosteroid injections into ligaments and tendons include loosening and incomplete healing. This may make the injected structures more susceptible to reinjury. Also, the number of injections

is limited to three to five, leaving numerous TrPs untreated.

TECHNIQUE

The purpose of the injection is to break up the abnormal, sensitized, tender tissue mechanically by needling. Injection of any fluid adds to the mechanical effect of the procedure. Usually 1% lidocaine is optimal. In case of allergy to the "caine" group, saline is satisfactory. The anesthetic also blocks pain and the irritation resulting from tissue damaged by the needle.

The needle should be sufficiently long in order to reach deeper than the trigger point. The diameter of the needle should be large enough to facilitate mechanical disruption of the abnormal tissue areas. A 22- to 25-gauge needle is usually sufficient. The total amount of 1% lidocaine injected ranges from 1–12 ml. Commonly, an extensive area has to be

TABLE 3-1. Physical Findings Before, During, and After Trigger Point Injections

Before Injection	During Injection	After Injection
Normal muscle tissue		
Elastic soft resistance; nontender	Minimal resistance to needle progression; no pain	Normal tissue findings
Taut band		
Hard and tender. Measure tissue compliance and algometry. Local twitch response can be elicited on snapping.	Penetration of the needle causes pain and encounters hard resistance as in fibrotic tissue (particularly in chronic TrP). Local twitch response occurs when the needle enters the hyperirritable fibers.	The hard and tender areas on palpation become nontender. Pressure pain sensitivity (algometry) becomes normal immediately. Soreness from injection resolves in 3–5 days. Local twitch response can no longer be elicited. Hyperirritability resolves.
Trigger point		
Maximum tender point within the taut band.	Maximum pain on needle penetration with hard resistance as in the taut band.	Trigger point sensitivity to pressure disappears. Hard consistency becomes normal, similar to improvement in taut bands.
Measure with algometer.		Confirm decreased tenderness with algometry.

infiltrated, which ranges from 3–25 cm long and 2–10 cm wide. The size of the infiltration depends on the extent of the trigger point and on the length of the affected muscle fibers. At each stop of the needle's penetration, no more than 0.1 or 0.2 ml should be injected. Larger volumes can damage the muscle, negating any benefit.

PROCEDURE

1. Ask the patient to point out with one finger the area of most intense pain. If this pain is diffuse and corresponds to a trigger point's reference zone(s), locate the TrP causing the symptoms.[10,15,17,18] Palpate the muscle or ligament[10] that has a corresponding reference zone. Position the patient to allow proper access to the painful area.

2. Palpate the point of maximum tenderness. Mark it by impression of a fingernail. Palpate around to find the entire taut and tender band, which may reach from the origin to the insertion of the muscle, and mark it with fingernail impressions. Presence of abnormal tenderness (pressure pain sensitivity) can be confirmed quantitatively by a pressure algometer.[4–7, 12] Figure 3-3 shows the pressure algometer measuring pressure pain sensitivity (tenderness) of a trigger point.

3. Explain the procedure to the patient.

4. Measure the pressure pain threshold with the dolorimeter (algometer).

5. Clean the skin with betadine or alcohol. Use surgical gloves.

6. Spray with ethyl-chloride to frost. If the patient does not like the vapocoolant, pinch the skin in the area of injection and immediately insert the needle. Because the pinching distracts and occupies the sensory pathways, the patient does not feel the needle.

7. Needle the entire area where increased fibrotic type of resistance is present, including the entire taut band. Explore with the needle beyond the border of the trigger point and the taut band. Inject only a small amount (0.2–0.5 ml) each time you stop the needle penetration. It is of great importance always to aspirate at each needle stop before the injection, especially when the neck or upper body is treated. Terminate the injection if blood is aspirated.

Proceed with the needle insertions through the taut band. Stop in 1–2 cm increments and, again, deposit only a small amount of anesthetic (0.1–0.2 ml) at each stop. When you reach the normal muscle below the taut band, the pain and hard resistance to the needle cease. Deposit a smaller amount in the normal tissue and then withdraw the

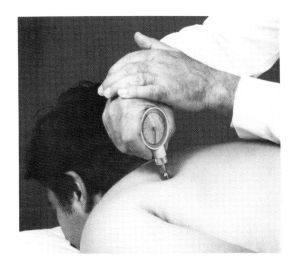

FIGURE 3-3. A dolorimeter is used for quantification of pressure pain sensitivity. Diagnosis of abnormal tenderness can be confirmed and treatment results quantified.

needle to the subcutaneous level. Make sure that the needle is out of the muscle when you change the direction of the needle; otherwise, you will cut the tissue. Redirect the needle tip within the subcutaneous tissue along the plane of the taut band. Enter the band in distances 1–3 cm from the previous infiltration. The distance to the next insertion depends on the size of the muscle and the taut band. Proceed similarly until you needle and infiltrate the entire taut band. Depending on the patient's tolerance, about 10 local infiltrations can be performed in one session, covering one large TrP and its taut band. If the patient becomes annoyed or the planned amount of anesthetic has been exhausted, terminate the injection. If necessary, the remaining parts of the taut band can be injected in the following session, usually 1 week later.

Immediately following an effective injection, the tenderness of the TrP and the taut band, as well as the associated increased consistency of the surrounding tissue, disappear or diminish substantially. Results can be documented by dolorimeter and tissue compliance meter. Figure 3-4 shows the tissue compliance meter, its rubber tip being pressed into the examined tissue. The depth of penetration per unit of force expresses compliance. Taut bands, muscle spasm, and tension, and their reaction to treatment can be documented objectively and quantitatively.[6]

Special attention should be directed to injecting the myotendon junction as well as the origin and the insertion of the involved muscle(s). Injection is usually particularly painful at these sites. Techniques of injection in specific muscles have been described,[12,17,18] and it is highly recommended that these textbooks are consulted before a novice starts TIs.

8. Compress the injected site for about 2 minutes to prevent bleeding. Cover with a Band-Aid.

9. If the needling was effective, the pressure threshold increases by 3 kg/cm^2.

POSTINJECTION CARE

Postinjection care includes the following steps:

1. Promote hemostasis by pressure.

2. Encourage active slow movement of the injected muscle to its full range; repeat three times.

3. Heat locally.

4. Use physiotherapy consisting of hot packs and electric stimulation using sinusoid surging current (adjust volume to induce strong contractions that are not too painful). Use vapocoolant spray to inactivate remaining painful areas. This step is followed by limbering and stretching exercises. Three such sessions of physiotherapy are necessary for each injection for best results, preferably the days following the procedure.

5. If soreness is excessive, give ibuprofen or acetaminophen.

6. Prescribe limbering exercises and/or passive stretching to be performed by the patient every 2 hours. Limbering exercises have been proved effective in preventing the recurrence of low back pain.[3] Experience shows that this applies to all types of muscle pain.

7. Advise the patient to avoid heavy use of the injected muscle such as walking or driving long distances after lower body injections and to avoid sports after upper body injections.

Pressure algometers and tissue compliance meters are distributed by Pain Diagnostics and Treatment Inc., 233 East Shore Road, Suite 108, Great Neck, NY 11023.

Acknowledgment. D.G. Simons, MD, clarified several points in this article. The author expresses deep appreciation for the exceptional amount of time and effort Dr. Simons devoted to this work.

REFERENCES

1. Bonica JJ: The Management of Pain. Philadelphia, Lea & Febiger, 1990.
2. Bonica JJ: Management of myofascial pain syndromes in general practice. JAMA 164:732–738, 1957.
3. Deyo RA: Conservative therapy for low back pain. JAMA 250:1057–1062, 1983.
4. Fischer AA: Diagnosis and management of chronic pain in physical medicine and rehabilitation. In Ruskin AP (ed): Current Therapy in Physiatry. Philadelphia, W.B. Saunders, 1984, pp 123–145.
5. Fischer AA: Pressure threshold measurement for diagnosis of myofascial pain and evaluation of treatment results. Clin J Pain 2:207–214, 1987.

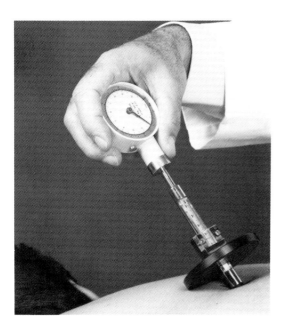

FIGURE 3-4. A tissue compliance meter measures soft tissue consistency.

6. Fischer AA: Documentation of myofascial trigger points. Arch Phys Med Rehabil 69:286–291, 1988.

7. Fischer AA: Application of pressure algometry in manual medicine. J Man Med 5:145–150, 1990.

8. Frost FA, Jessen B, Siggaard-Andersen J: A controlled, double-blind comparison of mepivacaine injection versus saline injection for myofascial pain. Lancet 1:499–500, 1980.

9. Garvey TA, Marks MR, Wiesel SW: A prospective, randomized, double-blind evaluation of trigger-point injection therapy for low-back pain. Spine 14:962–964, 1989.

10. Hackett GS: Ligament and Tendon Relaxation Treated by Prolotherapy. 3rd ed. Springfield, IL, Charles C Thomas, 1958.

11. Kraus HL: Clinical Treatment of Back and Neck Pain. New York, McGraw-Hill, 1970.

12. Kraus H: Diagnosis and Treatment of Muscle Pain. Lombard, IL, Quintessence Publishing, 1988.

13. Kraus H, Fischer AA: Diagnosis and treatment of myofascial pain. Mt Sinai J Med 58:235–239, 1991.

14. Melzack R: Prolonged relief of pain by brief, intense transcutaneous somatic stimulation. Pain 1:357–373, 1975.

15. Simons DG: Myofascial pain syndromes due to trigger points. In Goodgold J (ed): Rehabilitation Medicine. St. Louis, Mosby, 1988, pp 686–723.

16. Simons DG: Muscular pain syndromes. In Fricton JR, Awad, EA (eds): Advances in Pain Research and Therapy. New York, Raven, 1990, pp 1–41.

17. Travell JG, Simons DG: Myofascial Pain and Dysfunction. The Trigger Point Manual, Vol 1. Baltimore, Williams & Wilkins, 1983.

18. Travell JG, Simons DG: Myofascial Pain and Dysfunction. The Trigger Point Manual. The Lower Extremities, Vol 2. Baltimore, Williams & Wilkins, 1992.

Chapter 4

BURSAL INJECTIONS

NICHOLAS K. OLSEN, D.O.
JOEL M. PRESS, M.D.
JEFFREY L. YOUNG, M.D.

Bursitis accounts for a large number of disorders seen in a physiatric practice that focuses on musculoskeletal dysfunction. Inflamed bursae often respond to conservative treatments offered by the comprehensive physical medicine and rehabilitation team. In patients who fail to respond to traditional approaches, a soft tissue injection into the bursa can serve as a useful diagnostic and therapeutic adjunct to therapy.

Bursae function to reduce irritation at friction-prone areas between muscles, tendon, skin, and bone. They are composed of synovial-like tissue that forms a fluid-filled sac and are usually located adjacent to joints. Inflammation may occur during repetitive activities as a result of poor body mechanics or from direct trauma. An accurate diagnosis can be made by taking a thorough history that explores the occupational and recreational activities of patients. Correction of improper biomechanics is essential to avoid chronic irritation to the involved bursa.

After the history is obtained, the physical examination will reveal focal tenderness during palpation of the area overlying the bursa. If the patient presents following an episode of acute trauma, fracture or ligamentous instability of the joint should be ruled out. More commonly, patients present with bursal irritation from chronic overload. The physical examination should include a survey of other joints to rule out a systemic process. Skin overlying the area of tenderness should be inspected for evidence of penetrating trauma. The patient may have intense pain upon palpation of the affected area and an increase in skin temperature. In fact, skin warmth at the bursa may be the most sensitive indicator of a septic (versus nonseptic) bursa.[15] Any fluid obtained by aspiration should undergo microscopic examination to screen for increased leukocytes, bacteria on the Gram stain,

or crystals. Additional laboratory studies of the serum may demonstrate an elevated erythroctye sedimentation rate or leukocytosis. The septic bursa should be treated with an appropriate antibiotic following aspiration. Operative incision and drainage may be necessary for effective treatment.[7,20] Contraindications to bursal injection with corticosteroids include cellulitis, generalized infection, and coagulation disorders.

Bursal injections serve both diagnostic and therapeutic roles. An initial bursal injection with local anesthetic alone can provide important information, leading to the correct diagnosis. The patient should be examined just prior to and after administration of an anesthetic. When a septic bursa has been ruled out, a small amount of corticosteroid is introduced into the inflamed bursa to provide long-term relief and promote patient participation in a comprehensive treatment program. Following the injection, the patient should be instructed as to how to avoid aggravating the condition. A physical therapist may be consulted for soft tissue mobilization and development of a stretching and strengthening program, or the clinician may prefer to provide a well-directed home program during the initial visit. Ice may be a useful adjunct during the initial phases of treatment, and nonsteroidal anti-inflammatory drugs (NSAIDs) may provide additional relief. Each of these options should be individualized for the clinical situation, and none of these should be used, especially bursal injections, as the primary form of therapy. Follow-up should be scheduled within the first few weeks, and the program should be tailored to the patient as symptoms subside.

This chapter describes the basic approach to injection of many of the bursae encountered in clinical practice. Although the rehabilitation program

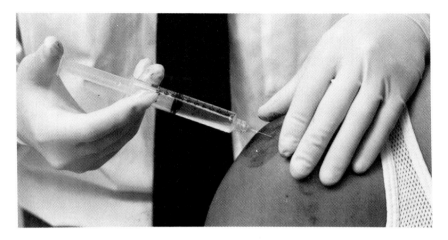

FIGURE 4-1. The subacromial bursa is injected from a posterolateral approach.

for each bursa has not been detailed in order to allow for closer attention to procedural techniques, it is essential to employ a comprehensive rehabilitation program for each patient.

SUBACROMIAL (SUBDELTOID) BURSITIS

The subacromial bursa rests on the supraspinatus tendon and is covered by the acromion, the coracoacromial ligament, and the deltoid. This is the most commonly affected bursa of the shoulder, with inflammation usually occurring secondary to rotator cuff tendinitis or shoulder impingement syndrome. In pure subacromial bursitis, the impingement signs may be absent, and the inflamed bursa may limit full passive induction due to compression at the near end range.[9] However, subacromial bursitis may coexist with impingement syndrome or rotator cuff syndrome. Determining the cause of shoulder pain may be difficult, and a diagnostic injection into the bursa can narrow the field of possibilities. A diagnostic injection helps to identify weakness and loss of range of motion secondary to pain from deficits due to neurologic injury. The patient should be thoroughly examined prior to the administration of local anesthetic and then reexamined 5–10 minutes after injection. After the injection, the patient may be less guarded and more cooperative during the physical exam, yielding further diagnostic information.

Although an anterior, posterior, or lateral approach may be used, the posterolateral approach is usually easier to palpate. Sterile technique is used to cleanse the skin with povidone-iodine. The bursa is entered from the posterolateral angle of the acromion (Figs. 4-1 and 4-2).[19] A mixture of 3–5 ml of 1% or 2% lidocaine hydrochloride and 3–5 ml of 0.5% bupivacaine hydrochloride is injected into the bursa after a 25-gauge, 1.5-inch needle is introduced

approximately 1 inch.[1] In our experience, an inflamed subacromial bursa accepts a total volume of 4–6 ml. Following the injection, a reduction of pain with improved strength supports the diagnoses of shoulder impingement, supraspinatus tendinitis, and subdeltoid bursitis. Patients who respond with greater than 50% relief are good candidates for an immediate follow-up injection with 1 ml of betamethasone sodium phosphate.[1] Subacromial bursography is helpful when the initial blind injection is unsuccessful or in a patient whose diagnosis is unclear. A normal bursogram casts doubt on a diagnosis of subacromial impingement.[10]

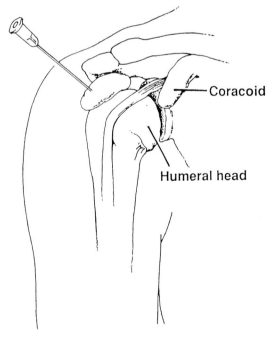

FIGURE 4-2. Schematic diagram of a subacromial bursa injection. (Adapted from Vander Slam TJ: Atlas of Bedside Procedures. Boston, Little, Brown, 1988, with permission.)

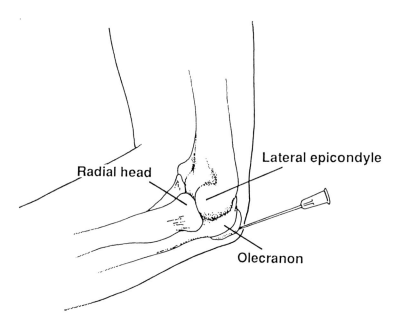

FIGURE 4-3. Approach for olecranon bursae aspiration and injection. (Adapted from Vander Slam TJ: Atlas of Bedside Procedures. Boston, Little, Brown, 1988, with permission.)

OLECRANON BURSITIS (DRAFTSMAN'S ELBOW)

The olecranon bursa is located subcutaneously and protects the proximal ulna where the olecranon is often subjected to trauma. Inflammation of this bursa is commonly seen in rheumatologic disorders. Aspiration of the bursa should always precede injection and may be helpful to ensure proper location of the needle, as the wall of the bursa is often thickened and fibrotic from chronic irritation. Gout may be seen at the olecranon, and any aspirated bursal fluid should undergo microscopic examination for crystals. Treatment is usually successful with aspiration of the bursa using a larger needle (187 gauge), because the fluid is likely to be gelatinous. The needle enters the skin perpendicular to the central swelling while the clinician withdraws on the syringe (Fig. 4-3).[19] The procedure is followed by application of a compressive dressing, and the patient is instructed to protect the elbow from further trauma. Persistent cases may benefit from a low-dose corticosteroid injection. Rarely, surgical excision or arthroscopic bursectomy is warranted after failure of conservative measures.

TROCHANTERIC BURSITIS

The trochanteric bursa lies beneath the tendon of the gluteus maximus and posterolateral to the trochanter. Trochanteric bursitis is common in elderly persons and manifests as pain in the lateral thigh during ambulation. Patients may describe a pseudoradicular pattern with the pain extending down the lateral aspect of the lower extremity and into the buttock. The symptoms can be elicited by placing the lower extremity in eternal rotation and abduction. Direct palpation or deep pressure applied posterior and superior to the trochanter will reproduce the pain.[14] The patient should be examined for limitations in flexibility at the long restrictors of the hip (tensor fascia lata, hamstrings, and rectus femoris). If the history and physical exam are consistent with bursitis, a corticosteroid combined with anesthetic agent is delivered via a 3.5-inch, 22-gauge needle directed at the point of maximal tenderness overlying the greater trochanter (Fig. 4-4).[11] Persistent hip pain despite injection therapy and comprehensive rehabilitation should alert the physician to other sources of pain, including the lumbar spine, hip joint, and distal joints in the lower extremity.[2,18]

ILIOPECTINEAL BURSITIS (ILIOPSOAS)

The iliopectineal bursa, the largest bursa near the hip joint, is located anterior to the hip capsule and covered by the iliopsoas. Inflammation of this bursa is not particularly common but may be functionally limiting because it causes the patient to avoid extension of the lower extremity during the gait cycle. Bursitis in this area may cause referral of the pain to the anterior thigh following the distribution of the femoral nerve. Patients hold

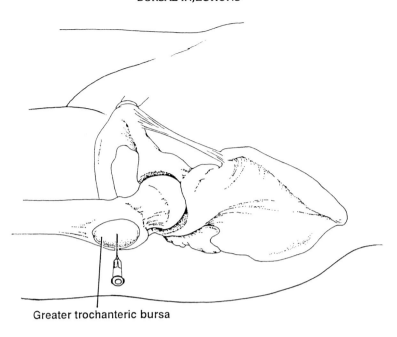

Greater trochanteric bursa

FIGURE 4-4. Greater trochanteric bursal injection. (Adapted from Vander Slam TJ: Atlas of Bedside Procedures. Boston, Little, Brown, 1988, with permission.)

the lower extremity in external rotation with the hip in flexion to relieve pressure on the inflamed bursa. The examiner may elicit symptoms by passively extending the patient's hip in either a supine or prone position. Injection under fluoroscopic guidance is useful for both diagnosis and treatment.[14] Once needle placement is confirmed, a mixture of anesthetic and corticosteroid is injected through a 3.5-inch spinal needle.

ISCHIAL BURSITIS (TAILOR'S OR WEAVER'S BOTTOM)

The ischial bursa lies between the ischial tuberosity and the gluteus maximus. The examiner's index of suspicion must be high because ischial bursitis—so-called tailor's or weaver's bottom— is not common. Classically, ischial bursitis occurs from friction or from the trauma of prolonged sitting on a hard surface. It may occur in adolescent runners, often in conjunction with ischial apophysitis. Pain is aggravated during uphill running.[12] The pain is distributed down the posterior aspect of the thigh and occurs with activation of the hamstring muscles. Initial treatment addresses modification of the patient's activity, including a decrease in the duration and frequency of running for the athlete. If an alternative to running includes cycling, the patient should be advised to avoid the use of toe clips, which increase activation of the hamstrings. When the etiology is related to

prolonged sitting, the patient's workstation should be modified to allow activities to be conducted in a standing position, and a cushion should be used during sitting. Ice and NSAIDs are helpful in controlling symptoms. Adolescent athletes may require a radiologic series to screen for callus formation secondary to ischial apophysitis, if the pain does not resolve with conservative measures. Persistent pain may benefit from injection as an adjunct to rest, ice, and NSAIDs. The patient lies on his or her side with the knee fully flexed to relax the hamstrings. A 3-inch, 22-gauge needle is held in a horizontal position and directed toward the point of maximal tenderness overlying the ischial tuberosity.

The injection of contrast dye into the bursa under fluoroscopy may be necessary to demonstrate a bursogram. This verifies needle placement and avoids unnecessary repeat injections.

ANSERINE BURSITIS

The anserine bursa separates the three conjoined tendons of the pes anserinus (semitendinosus, sartorius, and gracilis muscles) from the medial collateral ligament and the tibia. It is one of the most common bursa affected in the lower extremity. Anserine bursitis is commonly seen in women with heavy thighs and osteoarthritis of the knees. The bursa may also become inflamed as the result of direct trauma in athletes, especially soccer players.[12] Patients report pain inferior to the anteromedial surface of the knee with ascension of stairs. Moving the patient's knee in flexion and extension while internally rotating the leg will reproduce the symptoms during the physical exam. The palpatory exam will localize the pain to the anserine bursa. The injection is easy and quite effective in reducing inflammatory symptoms. After sterile preparation, the knee is fully extended, and a 1- to 1.5-inch, 22-gauge needle is directed at the point of maximal tenderness (Fig. 4-5) to deliver a 1- to 3-ml combination of anesthetic and corticosteroid. The patient should enter a rehabilitation program, and the athlete at risk for repetitive trauma may benefit from padded protection about the knee.

TIBIAL COLLATERAL LIGAMENT BURSITIS

The tibial collateral ligament (TCL) bursa, referred to as the "no name, no fame"[15] bursa, is located between the deep and superficial aspects of the tibial collateral ligament. The bursa does not adhere to the medial meniscus, and it appears to reduce friction between the superficial layer of the TCL and the medial meniscus. TCL bursitis should be considered in any patient with medial joint line tenderness. Kerlan reports it as accounting for 5% of knee complaints in an orthopedic setting over a 3-year period.[6] Physical examination will not show evidence of new ligamentous or capsular instability. Treatment consists of a local

injection of lidocaine and 1 ml of triamcinolone (40 mg/ml)[6] directed perpendicularly to the medial joint line at the point of maximal tenderness (Fig. 4-6).

PREPATELLAR BURSITIS (HOUSEMAID'S KNEE)

Prepatellar bursitis, often called housemaid's knee, is often the result of frequent kneeling that produces swelling and effusion of the subcutaneous bursa at the anterior surface of the patella. The patient rarely complains of pain unless direct pressure is applied to the bursa. The area is easily entered with a needle at the middle to superior pole of the patella. Repeat injections may be required since the bursa is often multiloculated. Occupational adjustments should include patient education, avoidance of kneeling, and the use of knee pads when pressure must be applied to the patella.

RETROCALCANEAL (SUBTENDINOUS) BURSITIS

The retrocalcaneal bursa lies between the posterior surface of the calcaneus and the tendon of the triceps surae. Inflammation of the bursa may occur with overtraining such as early assumption of increased mileage in a runner, or an ill-fitting shoe resulting in pressure from a restricting heel counter. Discomfort occurs when the examiner places the

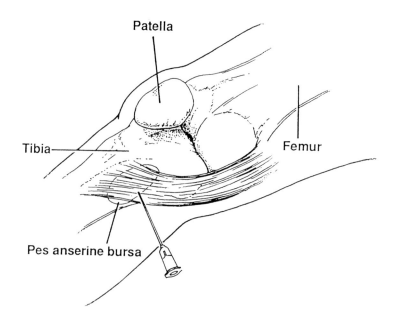

FIGURE 4-5. Anserine bursal injection. (Adapted from Vander Slam TJ: Atlas of Bedside Procedures. Boston, Little, Brown, 1988, with permission.)

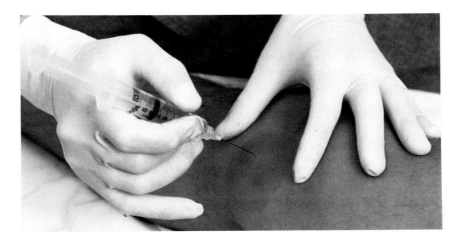

FIGURE 4-6. Approach for tibial collateral bursa.

thumb and index finger on the anterior edges of the Achilles tendon and applies pressure. Modification of footwear is an important first step, and symptoms should be controlled with ice and anti-inflammatory medications. As the pain is controlled, the patient should stretch the triceps surae complex daily to avoid recurrence. Injections into the bursa are considered only after the above measures have been pursued. A 20- to 22-gauge needle should be inserted where the bursa demonstrates the greatest distention, often on the lateral aspect of the heel, and is then advanced with an anterior angle of 15–20° to avoid instilling corticosteroid into the Achilles tendon, which weakens the structure and increases the risk of tendon rupture.

SUBCUTANEOUS (ACHILLES) BURSITIS

Subcutaneous bursitis, also known as Achilles bursitis, affects the bursa that lies subcutaneous to the posterior surface of the tendon. Midline swelling develops where the upper edge of the heel counter comes in contact with the heel cord. Subcutaneous bursitis is common in women who wear high-heeled shoes that apply direct pressure on the bursa. The mainstay of treatment is to change the patient's shoes. Ice and anti-inflammatory medications help provide symptomatic relief. Injection of the bursa is usually not necessary, but if symptoms persist, injection should be pursued. Care should be given to avoid the Achilles tendon.

CALCANEAL BURSITIS

Calcaneal bursitis often develops in elderly patients with a calcified spur that subjects the bursa to trauma after prolonged walking or running. Evaluation of the footwear may reveal poor

shock-absorbing capacity. Injection into the point of maximal tenderness may have both diagnostic and therapeutic value. Selection of an appropriate walking or running shoe and the use of a heel cup are beneficial. Athletes should be encouraged to change running shoes every 200–300 miles because mid-sole breakdown occurs after this amount of wear.[21]

PHARMACOLOGIC AGENTS FOR BURSAL INJECTION

A number of local anesthetics are available for bursal injections, and clinicians should be familiar with their pharmacologic properties. Concentrations of 0.5–1% lidocaine or 0.25–0.5% bupivacaine are appropriate for bursal injection. Bach describes the benefits of using a combination of lidocaine hydrochloride and bupivacaine hydrochloride in subacromial space injections to obtain an early onset of action with prolonged anesthesia.[1]

Corticosteroids are widely available and very effective in alleviating bursal inflammation. Corticosteroids with an intermediate- or long-acting duration are suitable for treatment of bursitis. Triamcinolone acetonide (10 mg/ml and 40 mg/ml) is a commonly used intermediate-acting agent with a half life of 24–36 hours. Betamethasone is a longer-acting corticosteroid with a half-life of 36–72 hours and a relative anti-inflammatory potency five times greater than that of triamcinolone.[3] The dosage is adjusted to the size of the bursa, and the lowest effective dose should be delivered to the bursa. Clinicians may want to avoid corticosteroid injection acutely (the first 7 days after an initial injury) because corticosteroids theoretically inhibit the healing process.[13] About 14–21 days after injury, glucocorticoids can control the inflammation and

TABLE 4-1. Guidelines for Bursal Injections

Bursae*	Anesthetic Volume† (ml)	Corticosteroid Volume (ml)	Needle Length (20–22 gauge)‡
Subacromial	4.0–6.0	0.5–1.0	1.5″
Trochanteric	4.5–9.0	1.5–1.0	1.5–3.5″
Iliopectineal	4.0–4.5	0.5–1.0	3.5″
Ischial	2.5–4.0	0.5–1.0	3.5″
Anserine	2.5–4.5	0.25–0.5	1.5″
Prepatellar§		0.5–1.0	1.5″

*Fluoroscopic guidance may be necessary to increase accuracy of bursa injection. A bursogram may be a useful tool, increasing the diagnostic and therapeutic value of injections.

† The volume refers to the capacity of the bursa, and the clinician should select a corticosteroid concentration appropriate for the bursal volume.

‡ The clinician may prefer an 18-gauge needle initially for aspiration if gelatinous fluid is anticipated and then change to a finer gauge for instillation of pharmacologic agents.

§ The prepatellar bursa is often multiloculated, and its capacity may vary.

edema of the proliferative phase. The Achilles and patellar tendons should be avoided because direct injections into the tendon can place the patient at risk for rupture.[13]

The clinician must be careful to select a combination of medications within recommended volumes to avoid further injury to the bursae. Table 4-1 may be used as a guideline for selecting the type and volume of corticosteroid and anesthetic to be administered.

CONCLUSIONS

Bursal injections provide a useful diagnostic and therapeutic approach within a comprehensive rehabilitation program. The clinician should have a strong foundation in anatomy and must be familiar with the pharmacologic agents injected. Many of the bursae discussed can be difficult to localize,

leading the physician to question the diagnosis and thus reducing the effectiveness of the treatment program. As the medication is delivered, palpation can be used as an aid to verify instillation of the medication into a superficial bursa, such as the pes anserine. Bursae that are located deep to soft tissue structures, such as the iliopectineal bursa, may require additional guidance with fluoroscopic imaging to ensure delivery of the anesthetic and corticosteroid to the bursa. Fluoroscopic guidance with injection of contrast medium into the bursa increases the diagnostic and therapeutic yield and avoids unnecessary repeat injections due to an inaccurately placed needle. Injection therapy and pain relief are not endpoints of a comprehensive rehabilitation program. Underlying biomechanical deficits and muscle strength and flexibility imbalances must be aggressively sought and corrected so that further injury may be prevented.

REFERENCES

1. Bach BR, Bush-Joseph C: Subacromial space injections: A tool for evaluating shoulder pain. Phys Sportsmed 2:93–98, 1992.
2. Collée G, Dijkmans BAC, Vandenbroucke JD, et al: Greater trochanteric pain syndrome (trochanteric bursitis) in low back pain. Scand J Rheumatol 20:262–266, 1991.
3. Covino BG, Scott DB: Handbook of Epidural Anesthesia and Analgesia. Orlando, FL, Grune & Stratton, 1985.
4. Hemler DE, Ward WK, Karstetter KW, et al: Saphenous nerve entrapment caused by pes anserine bursitis mimicking stress fracture of the tibia. Arch Phys Med Rehabil 72:336–337, 1991.
5. Kelley WN, Harris ED, Ruddy S, et al (eds): Textbook of Rheumatology, 2nd ed. Philadelphia, W.B. Saunders, 1993.
6. Kerlan RK, Glousman RE: Tibial collateral ligament bursitis. Am J Sports Med 16:344–346, 1988.
7. Kerr BR: Prepatellar and olecranon arthroscopic bursectomy. Clin Sports Med 12:137–142, 1993.
8. Lee JK, Yao L: Tibial collateral ligament bursa: MR imaging. Radiology 178:855–857, 1991.
9. Magee DJ: Orthopedic Physical Assessment. Philadelphia, W.B. Saunders, 1992.
10. Nicholas JA, Hershman EB: The Upper Extremity in Sports Medicine. St. Louis, Mosby, 1990, pp 124–125.
11. Rasmussen KJ, Farro N: Trochanteric bursitis: Treatment by corticosteroid injection. Scand J Rheumatol 14:417–420, 1985.
12. Reid DC: Sports Injury Assessment and Rehabilitation. New York, Churchill Livingstone, 1992.
13. Saal JA: General principles and guidelines for rehabilitation of the injured athlete. Phys Med Rehabil State Art Rev 1:527–528, 1987.
14. Schumacher RH: Primer on the Rheumatic Diseases. Atlanta, Arthritis Foundation, 1988.
15. Smith DL, McAfee JH, Lucas LM, et al: Septic and nonseptic olecranon bursitis: Utilization of the surface temperature probe in the early differentiation of septic and nonseptic case. Arch Intern Med 149:1581–1585, 1989.

16. Stuttle FA: The no-name, no-fame bursa. Clin Orthop 15:197–199, 1959.

17. Swezey RL: Pseudo-radiculopathy in subacute trochanteric bursitis of the subgluteus maximum bursa. Arch Phys Med Rehabil 57:387–390, 1976.

18. Traycoff RB: "Pseudotrochanteric bursitis": The differential diagnosis of lateral hip pain. J Rheumatol 18:1810–1812, 1991.

19. Vander Slam TJ: Atlas of Bedside Procedures. Boston, Little, Brown, 1988.

20. Waters D, Kasser J: Infection of the infrapatellar bursa. J Bone Joint Surg 72:1095–1096, 1990.

21. Young JL, Press JH: Rehabilitation of running injuries. In Buschbacher RH, Braddom RL (eds): Sports Medicine and Rehabilitation: A Sport-Specific Approach. Philadelphia, Hanley & Belfus, 1994, pp 123–124.

Chapter 5

TENDON SHEATH AND INSERTION INJECTIONS

STEVE R. GEIRINGER, M.D.

ANATOMY AND PHYSIOLOGY

Tendons are impressively strong structures that link muscles to bone. They function to transmit the force of muscular contraction to a bone, thereby moving a joint or helping to immobilize a body part (as in making a fist). Their microscopic organization is thoroughly described elsewhere.[6,27,30,33] The organizational unit in a tendon is the collagen fibril, which together form fascicles, which as a group compose the tendon itself.[30] Some tendons, especially long ones, are guided and lubricated along their paths by sheaths (Fig. 5-1), e.g., biceps brachii, extensor pollicis brevis, and abductor pollicis longus.

A prototypical muscle consists of the muscle belly centrally, two musculotendinous junctions, and tendinous insertions into bone at the points of anatomic origin and insertion. Some muscles, such as the extensor carpi radialis longus and brevis at the elbow, insert directly into bone, an arrangement that might be more susceptible to injury.[5]

Much is known about a tendon's response to laceration and operative repair[20] even though this is a clinical situation that is not frequently encountered. Less is understood about the more common and clinically relevant overuse tendinitis. A tendon, along with its sheath if present, will undergo a typical inflammatory response to either acute or chronic overuse injury, followed by a regenerative repair process.[4,20] The distinction between an overload type of acute injury and a chronic overuse mechanism will aid in successful rehabilitation of tendinitis.[10]

CORTICOSTEROID INJECTIONS

Cortisone and its derivatives are known to reduce or prevent inflammation. Numerous corticosteroid preparations are available for local injection.[15] The injectable corticosteroids are suspensions of insoluble particles, and, therefore, the anti-inflammatory effect is profound only where the material is deposited.[7] It is the ability of corticosteroids to control inflammation that makes them a valuable adjunct in treating tendon injuries, as they do not alter the underlying process that leads to inflammation.[15]

Contraindications, Complications, and Side Effects

The lack of a specific diagnosis is the single largest contraindication to a local corticosteroid injection. If the diagnosis is clear, and the anti-inflammatory effect of a corticosteroid might facilitate the rehabilitation process, injection can be considered.[15]

Repeated injections to the same area are to be avoided, particularly into joints. Alterations in articular cartilage have been documented with repeated administration,[21] possibly resulting in joint damage, and ligaments may be weakened.[26] A widely recognized complication of steroid injection is tendon rupture, a negative outcome that seems to be decreasing in frequency because it is now well recognized. Achilles and other tendon ruptures have been reported,[11,14,16,31,32] and deposition of injected material directly into any tendon substance is contraindicated. One report links the effect of repeated steroid injections to rupture of the plantar fascia.[19]

Some experimental findings have suggested that corticosteroid administration led to smaller and weaker tendons as a side effect.[13] A more common side effect is subcutaneous atrophy, especially at the knee and lateral elbow and more frequently with the use of triamcinolone.[15] Theoretically, atrophy of the specialized fat pads of the heel following steroid injection for plantar fasciitis could lead to a significant disability in an athlete because of the

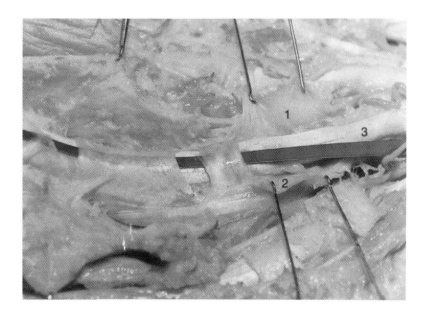

FIGURE 5-1. Gross specimen demonstrating a flexor tendon (3) within its sheath (metal rod inserted). Ulnar vertical paratendinous septum (1) and everted radial vertical paratendinous septum (2). (From Zancolli EA, Cozzi EP (eds): Atlas of Surgical Anatomy of the Hand. New York, Churchill Livingstone, 1992, p 357; with permission.)

loss of cushioning effect, although this has not been reported.

Indications

Diagnosis. Corticosteroid or local anesthetic injections should not be used routinely in arriving at diagnoses pertinent to the musculoskeletal system. The range of physical examination techniques used by the physiatrist is described elsewhere[10] and, in most cases, will suffice at pinpointing the specific cause of pain. The distinction between the conditions of subacromial bursitis and rotator cuff tendinitis can be clarified with injection,[15] but even in that circumstance, the physical examination and subsequent rehabilitation program deservedly receive most of the attention.

Treatment. In most instances, the literature supports an adjunctive, not primary, role for injections in the treatment of tendon and tendon sheath injuries.[15,31] When the doctor and patient decide to proceed with injection, the control of inflammation that is obtained should be used to advantage in facilitating the prescribed rehabilitation program rather than being considered treatment unto itself. The area of exception to this generalization is the wrist and hand, to be discussed in detail later.

Typically, because of the documented side effects and complications, a limit of about three corticosteroid injections in a given area is considered judicious for an injury. This limit is particularly important for intra-articular injections, and, as mentioned previously, corticosteroid should not be injected directly into the substance of a tendon.

Upper Extremity Injections

Cyriax[7] has provided detailed descriptions of soft tissue injection techniques; therefore, these descriptions will not be repeated here.

In the hand, the literature (reviewed for this chapter from 1989 forward) supports the use of corticosteroid injection as a primary treatment for stenosing flexor tenosynovitis, known as trigger thumb or trigger digit.[2,9,17,18,22,24,28] In this setting, injection has been shown to be as effective as operative release of the tendon sheath and to have fewer complications.[17] As with other soft tissue injections, a physiatrist treating trigger finger with instillation of corticosteroid needs to maintain technical expertise by performing this procedure at least several times yearly.

Stenosing tenosynovitis of the first dorsal wrist compartment is also known as de Quervain syndrome. This compartment typically transmits the tendons of both the abductor pollicis longus (APL) and extensor pollicis brevis (EPB). Anatomic studies have demonstrated, though, that multiple APL slips are common, as are two subcompartments.[23] Interestingly, while one or more injections are usually successful in treating de Quervain syndrome nonoperatively,[3,12,34] patients requiring subsequent operative release have been found to have two subcompartments in greater than expected frequency.[12,34] Trigger digit and de Quervain syndrome,

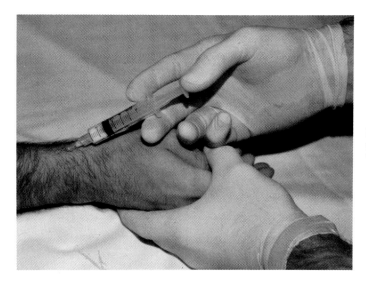

FIGURE 5-2. Injection technique for first dorsal compartment stenosing tenosynovitis (de Quervain syndrome).

therefore, are usually treated successfully nonoperatively, and corticosteroid injection is the primary component of the management (Fig. 5-2).

The use of corticosteroid injection for lateral epicondylitis (tennis elbow) appears widespread, although carefully controlled studies to confirm its efficacy are lacking in the recent literature. One prospective investigation found that corticosteroid injection was more effective in controlling symptoms 8 weeks after injury than anesthetic alone, but the benefit disappeared by 24 weeks.[29] This may be explained by the finding that the histology of tennis

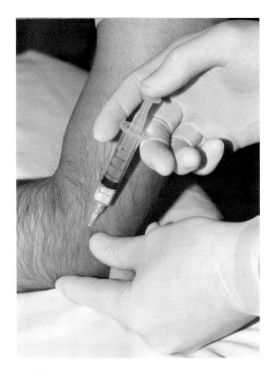

FIGURE 5-3. Injection technique for lateral epicondylitis.

elbow is noninflammatory.[25] A retrospective chart review found that injection alone was effective in 91% of patients within 1 week, but was associated with a 51% recurrence after 3 months. A standard physical therapy regimen led to improvement in only 74% initially, but the recurrence rate dropped to 5%.[8] In the typical clinical setting, of course, injection(s) and physical therapy are often combined, along with careful consideration of the intrinsic and extrinsic biomechanical factors that may be contributing (Fig. 5-3).[10]

No recent studies have examined the use of corticosteroid injections in the treatment of biceps brachii tendinitis. In this area, care should be taken to deposit the corticosteroid suspension so as to bathe the tendon sheath rather than to deposit it into the body of the tendon itself (Fig. 5-4). Additionally, heavy lifting or vigorous exercise of the arm should be restricted for 48–72 hours following injection.

Corticosteroid injection has been found to be effective for rotator cuff tendinitis, at least for the first several weeks. In one study, injection was superior to placebo and to oral anti-inflammatory medication over the course of 4 weeks.[1] No more than three injections are recommended,[15] and the technique itself is detailed elsewhere.[7] After corticosteroid injection for treatment of rotator cuff tendinitis, heavy lifting and excessive overhead work are to be avoided for at least 2 days.

Lower Extremity Injections

The literature since 1988 contains few references to corticosteroid injections of the lower extremity for tendon or tendon sheath injuries. No well-controlled trials were found. In this area, therefore, as in much of musculoskeletal medicine, the practitioner must rely on anecdotal evidence and trial and error when choosing a course of treatment.

Although it is not a true tendinitis, plantar fasciitis is commonly treated with corticosteroid injections (Fig. 5-5). If used, they must be considered complementary to a complete rehabilitation program that includes flexibility training and correction of any contributing intrinsic or extrinsic biomechanical factors.[15] As mentioned, if lipoatrophy occurs in the fat pad of the heel secondary to corticosteroid deposition, true disability in the active individual could result. Cosmesis is less of a problem because of the location.

Most physicians are aware of possible tendon rupture if corticosteroid is injected directly into the Achilles tendon. On the other hand, the Achilles sheath can be injected,[7] often with a good therapeutic result. Here, too, this procedure must be considered an adjunct to a more wide-ranging rehabilitation effort.

Iliotibial band tendinitis, refractory to other measures, sometimes responds to corticosteroid injection. The material is placed around the insertion of the iliotibial band at the proximal, lateral tibia, or, depending on the site of symptoms, where it passes over the prominence of the lateral femoral condyle.[15] Careful attention to flexibility is crucial when treating this syndrome.

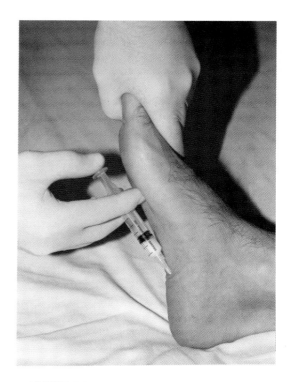

FIGURE 5-5. Injection technique for plantar fasciitis.

The quadriceps (infrapatellar) tendon can be injected for cases of tendinitis,[7] although because this is a weightbearing structure, many practitioners avoid this procedure for fear of rupture.

SUMMARY

In most cases of tendinitis or tenosynovitis of the upper or lower extremity, corticosteroid injection for control of inflammation should be considered, at most, as a supplement to an individualized, well-designed physiatric rehabilitation program. Notable exceptions are trigger digit or thumb, in which corticosteroids are a successful primary intervention, and, to a lesser extent, de Quervain syndrome. The physiatrist using corticosteroid injections must perform them often enough to maintain technical expertise. Three injections for any given injured area is considered a conservative maximum. Subcutaneous atrophy is a common side effect, and the known complication of tendon rupture speaks strongly against injection of corticosteroid directly into the substance of tendons.

REFERENCES

1. Adebajo AO, Nash P, Hazleman BL: A prospective double blind dummy placebo controlled study comparing triamcinolone hexacetonide injection with oral diclofenac 50 mg tds in patients with rotator cuff tendinitis. J Rheumatol 17:1207–1210, 1990.

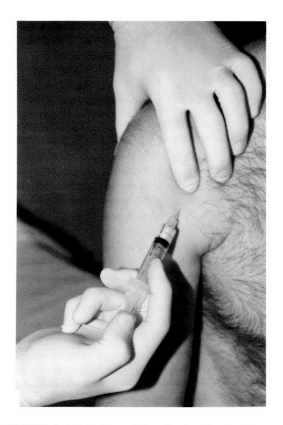

FIGURE 5-4. Injection technique for long head of biceps brachii.

2. Anderson B, Kaye S: Treatment of flexor tenosynovitis of the hand ("trigger finger") with corticosteroids: A prospective study of the response to local injection. Arch Intern Med 151:153–156, 1991.

3. Anderson BC, Manthey R, Brouns MC: Treatment of de Quervain's tenosynovitis with corticosteroids: A prospective study of the response to local injection. Arthritis Rheum 34:793–798, 1991.

4. Badalamente MA, Sampson SP, Dowd A: The cellular pathobiology of cumulative trauma disorders/entrapment syndromes: Trigger finger, de Quervain's disease and carpal tunnel syndrome. Transactions of the Orthopedic Research Society 17:677, 1992.

5. Cooper RR, Misol S: Tendons and ligament insertion: J Bone Joint Surg 52A:1–20, 1970.

6. Curwin S, Stanish WD: Tendinitis: Its Etiology and Treatment. Lexington, Collamore Press, 1984.

7. Cyriax J: Textbook of Orthopaedic Medicine, Vol. 2. Treatment by Manipulation Massage and Injection. London, Ballière Tindall, 1980.

8. Dijs H, Mortier G, Driessens M, et al: A retrospective study of the conservative treatment of tennis elbow. Acta Belg Med Phys 13:73–77, 1990.

9. Fauno P, Anderson HJ, Simonsen O: A long-term follow-up of the effect of repeated corticosteroid injections for stenosing tenovaginitis. J Hand Surg 14A:242–243, 1989.

10. Geiringer SR, Bowyer BL, Press JM: Sports medicine. The physiatric approach. Arch Phys Med Rehabil 74:S428–S432, 1993.

11. Halpern AA, Horowitz BG, Nagel DA: Tendon ruptures associated with corticosteroid therapy. West J Med 127:378–432, 1993.

12. Harvey FJ, Harvey PM, Horsley MV: de Quervain's disease: Surgical or nonsurgical treatment. J Hand Surg 15A:83–87, 1990.

13. Kapetanos J: The effects of the local corticosteroids on the healing and biomechanical properties of the partially injured tendon. Clin Orthop 163:160–179, 1982.

14. Kennedy JC, Baxter-Willis R: The effects of local steroid injections on tendons: A biochemical and microscopic correlative study. Am J Sports Med 4:11–18, 1976.

15. Kerlan RK, Glousman RE: Injections and techniques in athletic medicine. Clin Sports Med 8:541–560, 1989.

16. Kleinman M, Gross A: Achilles tendon rupture following steroid injection. J Bone Joint Surg 65A:1345–1347, 1983.

17. Kraemer BA, Young VL, Arfken C: Stenosing flexor tenosynovitis. South Med J 83:806–811, 1990.

18. Lambert MA, Morton RJ, Sloan JP: Controlled study of the use of local steroid injection in the treatment of trigger finger and thumb. J Hand Surg 17A:69–70, 1992.

19. Leach R, Jones R, Silva T: Rupture of the plantar fascia in athletes. J Bone Joint Surg 60A:537–559, 1978.

20. Leadbetter WB: Cell-matrix response in tendon injury. Clin Sports Med 11:533–578, 1992.

21. Mankin H, Conger K: The acute effects of intra-articular hydrocortisone on articular cartilage in rabbits. J Bone Joint Surg 48A:1383–1388, 1966.

22. Marks MR, Gunther SF: Efficacy of cortisone injection in treatment of trigger fingers and thumbs. J Hand Surg 14A:722–727, 1989.

23. Minamikawa Y, Peimer CA, Cox WL, et al: de Quervain's syndrome: Surgical and anatomical studies of the fibro-osseous canal. Orthopedics 14:545–549, 1991.

24. Newport ML, Lane LB, Stuchin SA: Treatment of trigger finger by steroid injection. J Hand Surg 15A:748–750, 1990.

25. Nirschl RP: Elbow tendinosis/tennis elbow. Clin Sports Med 11:851–870, 1992.

26. Noyes F, Grood E, Nussbaum N: Effect of intra-articular corticosteroids on ligament properties. Clin Orthop 123:197–209, 1977.

27. O'Brien M: Functional anatomy and physiology of tendons. Clin Sports Med 11:505–520, 1992.

28. Panaytopoulos E, Fortis AP, Armoni A, et al: Trigger digit: The needle or the knife? J Hand Surg 17A:239–240, 1992.

29. Price R, Sinclair H, Heinrich I, et al: Local injection treatment of tennis elbow—hydrocortisone, triamcinolone and lignocaine compared. Br J Rheumatol 30:39–44, 1991.

30. Reid DC: Connective tissue healing and classification of ligament and tendon pathology. In Reid DC (ed): Sports Injury Assessment and Rehabilitation. New York, Churchill Livingstone, 1992, pp 65–83.

31. Saal JA: General principles and guidelines for rehabilitation of the injured athlete. Phys Med Rehabil State Art Rev 1:527–528, 1987.

32. Sweetham R: Corticosteroid arthropathy and tendon rupture. J Bone Joint Surg 51B:397–398, 1969.

33. Warwick R, Williams PL: Gray's Anatomy, 36th ed. Edinburgh, Churchill Livingstone, 1980.

34. Witt J, Pess G, Gelberman RH: Treatment of de Quervain tenosynovitis: A prospective study of the results of injection of steroids and immobilization in a sprint. J Bone Joint Surg 73A:219–222, 1991.

Chapter 6

ACUPUNCTURE FOR PAIN MANAGEMENT

MATHEW H. M. LEE, M.D., M.P.H., FACP
SUNG J. LIAO, M.D., D.P.H., FACP

Acupuncture is a therapeutic procedure that involves the insertion of small-gauge needles into strategic points of the body. It has been an essential part of traditional Chinese medicine but only became popular in the United States in 1971 when James Reston's article, "Now, About My Operation in Peking," appeared in the *New York Times*.[70] This article reported his experience with acupuncture for treatment of his postappendectomy complications. Also in 1971, after visiting China, two American physicians reported in the *Journal of the American Medical Association* their observations on the use of acupuncture for analgesia in surgical procedures.[17] At that time, acupuncture was highly controversial among American physicians. This controversy exists today and originates from a poor understanding of this alien concept, its use by inexperienced practitioners, and its unwarranted claims of cures, especially in the early 1970s.

Acupuncture has been used by the Chinese for nearly every type of disease, from dysentery to epilepsy. The limitation of its use to painful conditions, especially when all other treatment fails, is a frequent practice among Western physicians. Despite the other potential applications of acupuncture, this chapter focuses on its usefulness in pain management. The interested reader is referred to other texts for more information on acupuncture.[39,46,57a]

TRADITIONAL THEORY OF ACUPUNCTURE

Acupuncture is a product of the Chinese culture with indigenous concepts that are often difficult to explain to the Western physician. Its holistic and problem-oriented approach is built on a mixture of philosophy, environmental and emotional factors, alchemy, quasi-science of anatomy and physiology, and chronobiology.

Three centuries ago, many schools of philosophic ideas flourished in China,[25] including the *yin-yang* idea. The Yin-Yang concept defines *yin* and *yang*

as opposing binary forces of nature, each capable of complementing and supporting the other. *Yin* is represented as the female, night, darkness, negativity—whereas *yang* is represented as the male, day, light, positivity. Human health is thought to exist between the balance of these two forces. For example, when *yin* and *yang* are in balance, an individual is considered to be in a healthy and pain-controlled state. However, when *yin* and *yang* are out of balance, turmoil occurs and results in human sickness and pain.

Another concept fundamental to the theory of traditional acupuncture is *Qi*, the "spirit of life." Qi can be thought of as a primordial matter that circulates freely along meridians within the human body, often following circadian rhythms. These meridians are interconnecting channels each thought to be associated with an internal organ. Each meridian and its associated organ are considered either *yin* or *yang*. According to tradition, for good health these meridians have to be patent, and Qi can circulate freely. Any stagnation of Qi would result in illness, suffering, and pain. By inserting needles at the proper acupoints, such stagnation is released and Qi can flow freely again. This results in human wellness and pain relief.

MECHANISMS OF ACUPUNCTURE ANALGESIA

Advances in our knowledge of acupuncture analgesia have occurred over the last 25 years. Although its mode of action remains partly elusive, two mechanisms have emerged—neurophysiologic and neuropharmacologic mechanisms that will be described briefly below. Its effect on the autonomic nervous system also will be discussed.

Neurophysiologic Mechanism

A neurophysiologic mechanism for acupuncture analgesia appears to involve the sensory receptors at the acupoint. These receptors and their groups 2 and 3, small myelinated muscle afferent fibers of the peripheral nerves, are involved in transmitting this analgesic effect.[11,60,71] This analgesic effect is bilaterally represented and transmitted segmentally.[5,11,12] The *De Qi* response (needling sensation) from acupuncture is transmitted along the extralemniscal system in the lateral funiculus of the spinal cord. It extends proximally to the reticular formation, periaqueductal gray, and the thalamus.[5,12] The reticular formation appears to play a major role in the analgesic effect evoked at the distant acupoints in humans.[2,55] Noxious stimuli routinely generate evoked potentials transmitted to the sensory cortex that can be blocked by acupuncture at appropriate acupoints.[44,60]

A temporal latency seems to exist between the initiation of acupuncture and the appearance of analgesia. For example, the induction time for a tonsillectomy ranges from 20–30 minutes, but dental extraction surgeries can take as little as 5 minutes. This analgesic effect may last several days and appears to be cumulative.[48] Many researchers have noted similar findings in animals.[60,65,72,78]

Neuropharmacologic Mechanism

A neuropharmacologic or humoral mechanism of acupuncture analgesia was first discovered in the early 1970s. Chinese researchers demonstrated that the analgesic effect of acupuncture could be transmitted between animals. Through a cross-circulation technique[62] or through infusion of cerebral ventricular fluid,[69] transmission of this analgesic effect was noted from an acupuncture-treated donor animal to the nontreated recipient animal. In addition, atropine weakened the analgesic effect and reserpine enhanced the effect.[69] Among these neuropharmacologic mechanisms, two systems exist, opioid and nonopioid.

The Opioid System

Pomeranz et al.[9,64] reported three important observations from animal experiments regarding involvement of the opioid system in acupuncture analgesia: (1) analgesia could not be produced from sham acupuncture; (2) the analgesic effect could be eliminated by the ablation of the pituitary gland; and (3) acupuncture analgesia could be eliminated by naloxone. Naloxone's effect was demonstrated by a reduction in the number of acupuncture-evoked electric discharges at the layer 5 cells in the dorsal horn of a cat's spinal cord. Its blocking effect was dose-dependent and also affected by dexamethasone and 2% saline. Other reports indicate that naloxone partially blocks the analgesic effect of acupuncture in dental pain.[53]

The adrenal and pituitary glands were found to have a mutually reversing influence on acupuncture analgesia.[75,76] Because naloxone is a morphine antagonist, the results of the above-cited and other similar reports imply that the animal body must produce an endogenous substance with the properties of morphine. Thus, the word "endorphin" has been used for the group of natural neurochemicals involved in analgesia. The analgesic potency of acupuncture can be enhanced by the degradation of met-enkephalin, by d-phenylalanine, d-leucine, or bacitracin, or by the inhibition of endorphins.[18,19]

The endogenous opioid system is activated by high-intensity, low-frequency (2–4 Hz) electroacupuncture,[8] acupuncture at distant acupoints,[53] and even pain itself.[53] The low-frequency, high-intensity electroacupuncture tends to result in slow-onset, long-lasting, and cumulative analgesia. This effect often can be abolished by naloxone.

Some animals and humans are genetically deficient in opiate receptors. In these cases, acupuncture is ineffective in pain relief.[64]

The Nonopioid System

Nonopioid systems also seem to play an important role in acupuncture analgesia. Serotonin, acetylcholine,[67] atropine,[60,67] L-tryptophan,[34] norepinephrine,[31] Ca^{++} and Mg^{++} ions,[32] glutamine, and the gamma-aminobutyric acid system[14] have often been implicated in acupuncture analgesia. Opioid and nonopioid systems often interact with each other. For example, both serotonin and endorphin were released by electroacupuncture in rats. However, when one of them was reduced by its antagonists, the other was increased.[32,49,57] Monoamine inhibitors, with interference of the tryptaminergic mechanism, also appear to be involved.[22,32,54]

The nonopioid (such as serotoninergic) system is activated by low-intensity, high-frequency electroacupuncture[8] and by acupuncture at local acupoints.[6] This low-intensity, high-frequency electroacupuncture tends to induce a rapid-onset, short-lasting, and noncumulative analgesia that can be inhibited by unusually large doses of naloxone.

Autonomic Nervous System

Acupuncture appears to involve the autonomic nervous system as manifested by changes in skin temperature. An increase in skin temperature has been observed with thermography in both the treated body part and the contralateral and untreated corresponding part.[20–22,37,38] A nonsegmental, long-lasting warming (sympatholytic) effect of a craniocaudal gradient in the temperature distribution also has been demonstrated. Other studies have indicated that stimulation of the Zusanli acupoint (ST 36) of the affected leg of a stroke patient induced slight temperature increases of the normal leg and a marked increase of temperature in both hands.[47]

Such temperature increases appear to correlate with the pain relief obtained with acupuncture.[47] These observations may also help to explain the therapeutic effectiveness of the "distant acupoints" and the "opposite acupoints" due at least to a partial involvement of the autonomic nervous system.

ACUPOINTS

In *Neijing Suwen* (Yellow Emperor's Classic of Internal Medicine Book of Common Questions, compiled probably in the second century B.C.)[46] it was declared, "Let the tender loci (on the meridians) be acupoints." At that time, only a few acupoints had names. The acupoints seem to correlate well with Western medicine's trigger points. Ling[79] in 1834 and Griffin et al.[28] in 1843 observed a relationship between tender points and visceral diseases. Weihe later reported his discovery of 195 tender loci in relation to visceral diseases.[52] A correlation between Weihe's points and Chinese acupuncture points were later observed.[16,23] Lee and Liao[39] have since reported that about 80% of the acupoints coincide with trigger points. Melzack, Stillwell, and Fox[56] also demonstrated "a remarkably high degree (71%) of correspondence" between trigger points and acupoints. They commented that "this close correlation suggests that trigger points and acupuncture points for pain, though discovered independently and labeled differently, represent the same phenomenon and can be explained in terms of the underlying neural mechanism." In addition to the acupoints on the meridians (or meridian acupoints), Sun Simiao in the seventh century found that tender loci outside the meridian system also had therapeutic effects. He called them *A shi Xue*, or Ouch Acupoints.

About 361 meridian acupoints are scattered throughout the body, including those on the scalp, face, palm of the hand, and sole of the foot. In addition there are about 1,600 extra-meridian odd acupoints and new acupoints.

It is beyond the scope of this chapter to list even the commonly used acupoints (which number about 100–200). To illustrate the clinical application of acupuncture, the six *zhong* (premier or, literally, summary) acupoints are listed. Each of these acupoints functions as a "summary" of the therapeutic effectiveness of a meridian for a particular area or system of the body. They are basic acupoints that can be used to treat common problems found in clinical practice. A description of each follows in suitable detail so the reader can easily localize them.

1. Zusanli Acupoint (the 36th acupoint on the Stomach Meridian, St 36 or S 36)

The Zusanli acupoint (Fig. 6-1) is used for diseases of the gastrointestinal system, including abdominal pain. It also plays an important role in the enhancement of the immune system. This acupoint can be localized by placing the thumb of the clinician's right hand in the front of the patient's left leg, just below the tibial tubercle. The interphalangeal joint of the thumb is positioned across the tibial crest. This acupoint is located at the tip of the thumb on the anterolateral aspect of the leg. The thumb of the left hand can be used to locate this acupoint on the right leg in a similar manner. The Zusanli acupoint correlates well with the motor point of the anterior tibialis muscle.

2. Weizhong Acupoint (the 40th acupoint on the Urinary Bladder Meridian, UB 40 or B 40)

The Weizhong acupoint (Fig. 6-2) is used for treatment of low back pain, lower extremity weakness, and spasms of the gastrocnemius muscle. This acupoint is located at the midpoint of the transverse popliteal crease in the posterior aspect of the knee superficial to the tibial nerve and artery.

3. Lieque Acupoint (the 7th acupoint on the Lung Meridian, L 7)

The Lieque acupoint (Fig. 6-3) is used for disorders of the head and neck, including headaches,

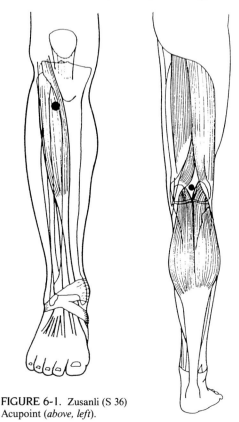

FIGURE 6-1. Zusanli (S 36) Acupoint (*above, left*).

FIGURE 6-2. Weizhong (UB 40) Acupoint (*above, right*).

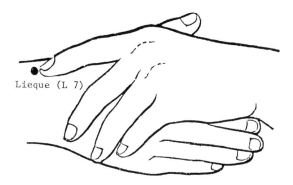

FIGURE 6-3. Lieque (L 7) Acupoint.

neck pain, and stiffness. It also may be used for periarticular soft tissue diseases of wrist. The Lieque acupoint is located on the radial styloid process, between the tendons of the brachioradialis and the abductor pollicis longus muscles.

4. Hegu Acupoint (the 4th acupoint on the Large Intestine Meridian, LI 4)

The Hegu acupoint (Fig. 6-4) is used to treat pain of the face and oropharynx. It can generate analgesia for tonsillectomies, thyroidectomies, and dental surgery. It is also one of the important acupoints to control headaches. This acupoint can be located in the middle of the first interdigital space between the metacarpi of the thumb and the index finger. The motor point of the first dorsal interosseus muscle coincides with this acupoint.

5. Neiguang Acupoint (the 6th acupoint on the Pericardium Meridian, P 6)

The Neiguang acupoint (Fig. 6-5) is used to treat diseases of the chest and heart, carpal tunnel syndrome, nausea and vomiting, hiccups, and motion sickness. It can be located on the anterior surface of the distal forearm about two and a half fingerbreadths proximal to the midpoint of the volar transverse carpal crease. The acupoint is between the flexor carpi radialis muscle and the palmaris longus tendon superficial to the median nerve.

6. Sanyinjiao Acupoint (the 6th acupoint on the Spleen Meridian, Sp 6)

The Sanyinjiao acupoint (Fig. 6-6) is used to treat diseases of the pelvic region, i.e., the urogenital system, especially pain control with premenstrual syndrome. This acupoint can be located on the inner aspect of the lower leg, about four fingerbreadths proximal to the tip of the medial malleolus, between the posterior border of the tibia and the

soleus muscle. The flexor digitorum longus muscle lies deep to this acupoint.

TECHNIQUE

Acupuncture needles are solid and made of stainless steel. They vary in size and length, ranging from 1.25–5 cm with diameters of 0.30–0.33 mm or 28–30 gauge. Japanese traditional practitioners use much thinner needles, often 34–36 gauge. These thinner needles are placed in a guiding tube to assist with insertion. After the acupuncture needle is inserted, it may be twirled or pushed and pulled, gently or vigorously. Because of the fine caliber of modern acupuncture needles, treatments are usually not painful. In fact, many patients are surprised to find no needle mark.

RESPONSES

At the insertion of the needle, the patient may feel a pricking sensation. When the needle reaches the proper acupoint, the patient may feel soreness, tingling, numbness, warmth, or an expanding sensation of the needle. This is known as the De Qi response. This response confirms that the needle is at the proper acupoint and, therefore, causes its therapeutic effect. The depth of needle placement

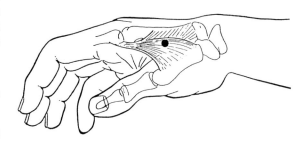

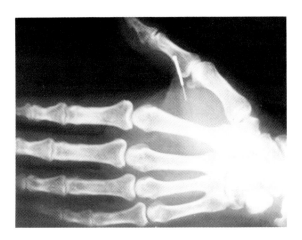

FIGURE 6-4. Hegu (LI 4) Acupoint. *A, drawing, above; B, radiograph, below.*

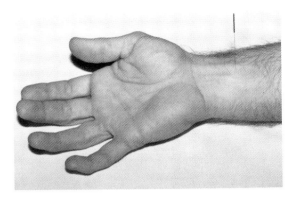

FIGURE 6-5. Neiguang (P 6) Acupoint.

is guided by the anatomic makeup of the acupoint and the De Qi response at the time the needle is inserted.

During the first acupuncture treatment, it is not unusual for some patients to be tense and anxious. Acupuncture may induce a tranquilizing and sedating effect, which allows many patients to relax. During treatment, many patients feel drowsy and often fall asleep. After treatment, the involved limb may feel heavy, especially if the shoulder or hip was treated. However, it is difficult to predict which patients will respond in this manner.

On the other hand, some patients feel energized and elated as they experience a sense of "well-being" for the first time in many years after suffering from a chronic painful condition. This type of response has not been reported in the literature to the best of our knowledge. Properly designed statistical clinical investigations are necessary to better understand the therapeutic outcome of acupuncture.

DURATION AND FREQUENCY OF TREATMENT

The duration and frequency of acupuncture treatment vary based on the clinical diagnosis and the patient's response to treatment. No fixed number of treatments is recommended for any specific diagnosis. Several treatment sessions usually are required to achieve therapeutic goals and determine efficacy. Fewer than 5% of patients with pain problems will have a dramatic improvement after one or two sessions of treatment; the vast majority require five to ten treatments. If improvement is not observed after 15 treatments, acupuncture should probably be discontinued. However, more than 15 treatments can be justified if the treatment has proved beneficial. When patients experience partial pain relief after multiple treatment sessions, discontinuing treatment may be advantageous in order to evaluate any changes. A decision then can be made whether to resume acupuncture.

The optimal frequency of acupuncture treatment is not well established but depends on the patient's clinical status and response to treatment. Daily treatments are common in China, where health care is inexpensive. In our practice, treatment is usually given one to three times weekly at the outset and slowly tapered over the following weeks. In animal experiments, the analgesic effect of acupuncture usually lasts 48 hours. An additional acupuncture treatment after the 48th hour boosts such analgesic effect to a higher level. It is also possible that the body may need 1 or 2 days between treatments to prepare for and respond to the next treatment. As the patient's condition improves, treatment can be quickly tapered and discontinued.

Many patients with chronic pain do not respond to short series of acupuncture treatment immediately. These patients may notice a subtle reduction of pain 1 to 4 weeks after treatment, thereby implicating a delayed response.

RISKS, COMPLICATIONS, AND CONTRAINDICATIONS TO ACUPUNCTURE

Acupuncture has minimal risk, if any, when used correctly and the clinician has a good understanding of acupoint anatomy. However, as for other medical procedures, complications can arise. Transmittable diseases such as hepatitis B,[36] local infection of the ears after auricular acupuncture,[35] and septicemia[10] have been reported. The advent of disposable sterile needles has made these complications less likely. Proper sterile techniques are mandatory.

When acupuncture is successful in reducing pain, many patients have a tendency to overexert themselves, thus risking an aggravation of the original problem. For this reason, patients are instructed to

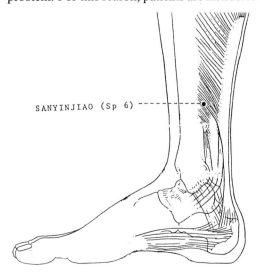

SANYINJIAO (Sp 6)

FIGURE 6-6. Sanyinjiao (Sp 6) Acupoint.

avoid strenuous activity for two days or so following treatment.

Other less common complications include the unintentional induction of labor in pregnant women and pneumothorax and hemothorax when treatment occurs around the chest wall.[4] Sensitivity to nickel, a component of stainless steel of which the acupuncture needle is composed, is rare but does occasionally occur. Five patients with such sensitivities have been seen by the authors during their more than 20-years practice of acupuncture.

The number of painful conditions potentially amenable to acupuncture is unlimited. Its duration of effect is often quite long enough to advance a well-designed rehabilitation program. The literature contains numerous case reports on the effectiveness of acupuncture in the management of acute and chronic pain.[46]

Lee and Yang's review[41] recommended acupuncture as an alternative treatment for arthritis due to its analgesic and anti-inflammatory effects. The pituitary gland's release of beta-lipoprotein, the precursor of adrenocorticotropic hormone and beta-endorphins,[29] increase of blood cortisol level by acupuncture,[7] and inhibition of exudate reaction[73] may explain these antiinflammatory effects.

In 1987, Peng[61] reported a double-blind study of the long-term therapeutic effects of electroacupuncture for chronic neck and shoulder pain. Twenty-four of 37 patients (65%) experienced long-term improvement. Liao[42] treated chronic neck pain with acupuncture in 195 patients who had failed to respond to traditional medical management; 46% experienced improvement after an average of five sessions of treatment. In patients with low back pain, acupuncture is less likely to reduce pain in patients who have had previous surgery.[46]

Acupuncture has been reported to control the pain from headaches,[46] postherpetic neuralgia,[46] epicondylitis,[3] fractured ribs,[46] healed surgical scars,[43] malignancies, phantom limb,[46] trigeminal neuralgia,[45] temporomandibular disorders,[66] foot disorders,[46] and premenstrual syndrome.

SURGICAL ANALGESIA WITH ACUPUNCTURE

Acupuncture may be used to induce analgesia at surgery, especially in patients allergic to anesthetics. In the early 1970s, acupuncture analgesia was used in China for such procedures as lobectomy or pneumonectomy in patients with tuberculosis, thyroidectomy, cesarean section, and appendectomy. In 1972, Liao successfully performed acupuncture analgesia for a tonsillectomy in a 21-year-old man who was allergic to most anesthetics.[48] In 1973,[40] Lee et al. reported on acupuncture analgesia for dental procedures in 20 patients. Each patient experienced successful gingival analgesia before the

surgery, and 16 patients had no pain during the surgical procedure.

Anesthesia with acupuncture has been used for childbirth. Certain acupoints tend to induce dilation of the cervix and contraction of the pregnant uterus. Thus, acupuncture may be used to induce labor and provide excellent analgesia for childbirth. It is recommended that other analgesics be readily available if acupuncture analgesia is inadequate.[46]

CONCLUSION

Acupuncture can be used effectively to treat acute and chronic pain in many cases, thereby improving the function of patients by relieving their pain. Acupuncture is not a "cure-all." Although recent advances have enlightened many about the mechanism of acupuncture action, additional well-controlled, double-blind clinical studies are necessary to better elucidate this mechanism as well as treatment outcomes.

REFERENCES

1. Bache F, trans: Memoir on Acupuncture, Embracing a Series of Cases, Drawn up under the Inspection of M. Julius Cloquet, by M. Morand, Doctor of Medicine. Paris, 1825. Philadelphia, Robert Desilver, 1825.
2. Bowsher D: Role of the reticular formation in response to noxious stimulation. Pain 2:361–378, 1976.
3. Brattberg G: Acupuncture therapy for tennis elbow. Pain 16:285–288, 1983.
4. Carron H, Epstein BS, Grand B: Complications of acupuncture. JAMA 228:1552–1554, 1984.
5. Chang HT: Integrative action of thalamus in the process of acupuncture for analgesia. Sci China [B] 16:25–60, 1973.
6. Chapman CR, Benedictti C: Analgesia following TENS and its partial reversal by a narcotic antagonist. Life Sci 21:1645–1648, 1977.
7. Cheng R, McKibbin L, Roy B, et al: Electroacupuncture elevates blood cortisol levels in naive horses: Sham treatment has no effect. Int J Neurosci 10:95–97, 1980.
8. Cheng R, Pomeranz B: Electroacupuncture analgesia could be mediated by at least two pain-relieving mechanisms: Endorphin and non-endorphin systems. Life Sci 25:1957–1962, 1979.
9. Cheng R, Pomeranz B, Yu G: Dexamethasone partially reduces and 2% saline treatment abolishes electroacupuncture analgesia: These findings implicate pituitary endorphins. Life Sci 24:1481–1486, 1979.
10. Cheng TO: Acupuncture needles as a cause of bacterial endocarditis. BMJ 287:689, 1983.
11. Chiang CY, Chiang CT, Chu HC, et al: Peripheral afferent pathway for acupuncture analgesia. Sci China [B] 16:210–217, 1973.
12. Chiang CY, Liu JY, Chu TH, et al: Studies of spinal ascending pathways for effect of acupuncture analgesia in rabbits. Sci China [B] 18:651–658, 1975.
13. Christian HA (ed): The Osler's Principles and Practice of Medicine, 14th ed. New York, Appleton-Century, 1944.
14. Chu CC, Zong YY, Gong ME, et al: Effect of electroacupuncture analgesia on free amino acid content in the brain of the mice. Kexue Tongbao 24:45–46, 1979 (in Chinese).
15. Chu LY: Electroacupuncture. Xian, Shaanxi People's Publishers, 1957.

16. de la Fuye R: Traite d'Acupuncture. Paris, L Francis, 1947.
17. Dimond EG: Acupuncture anesthesia. Western Medicine and Chinese traditional medicine. JAMA 218:1558–1563, 1971.
18. Ehrenpreis S: Analgesic properties of enkephalinase inhibitors: Animal and human studies. Prog Clin Biol Res 192:363–370, 1985.
19. Ehrenpreis S: Potentiation of acupuncture analgesia by inhibition of endorphin degradation. Acupunct Electrother Res Int J 8:319, 1983.
20. Ernst M, Lee MHM: Sympathetic effects of manual and electrical acupuncture of the Tsusanli knee point: Compared with the Hoku hand point sympathetic effects. Exp Neurol 94:1–10, 1986.
21. Ernst M, Lee MHM: Sympathetic vasomotor changes induced by manual and electrical acupuncture of the Hoku point visualized by thermography. Pain 21:25–33, 1985.
22. Ernst M, Lee MHM, Dworkin B, et al: Pain perception decrement produced through repeated stimulation. Pain 26:221–231, 1986.
23. Ferreyrolles M, de Morant GS: Coincidences existant entre certains points de Weihe et certains points d'acupuncture Chinoise. l'Homéopathie Francoise, 1929.
24. Frost FA, Jessen B, Siggaard-Anderson J: A controlled, double-blind comparison of mepivacaine injection versus saline injection for myofascial pain. Lancet 1:499–501, 1980.
25. Fung YL: A Short History of Chinese Philosophy. New York, The Free Press, 1948.
26. Goldstein A, Hilgard ER: Failure of the opiate antagonist naloxone to modify hypnotic analgesia. Proc Natl Acad Sci 72:2041–2043, 1975.
27. Greenfield ME: Acupuncture as a rehabilitation modality in chronic low back pain syndrome [Master's thesis]. New Haven, CT, Department of Epidemiology and Public Health, Yale University, 1977.
28. Griffin W, Griffin D: Medical and Physiological Problems, Being Chiefly Researches for Correct Principles of Treatment in Disputed Points of Medical Practice. London, Sherwood, Gilbert and Piper, 1843.
29. Guillemin R: Beta-lipoprotein and endorphins: Implications of current knowledge. Hosp Pract 13:53–60, 1978.
30. Gunn CC: Treating Myofascial Pain: Intramuscular Stimulation (IMS) for Myofascial Pain Syndromes of Neuropathic Origin. Seattle, University of Washington School of Medicine, 1989.
31. Han JS, Ren MF, Tang J, et al: The role of central catecholamines in acupuncture analgesia. Chin Med J 92:793–800, 1979.
32. Han JS, Terenius L: Neurochemical basis of acupuncture analgesia. Ann Rev Pharmacol Toxicol 22:193–220, 1982.
33. Head H: On the disturbances of sensation with especial reference to the pain of visceral disease. Part III. Pain in diseases of heart and lungs. Brain 19:153–276, 1986.
34. Jenkins C: On L-tryptophan. Acupuncture News 10:3, 1982.
35. Jones HS: Case records. Auricular complications of acupuncture. J Laryngol Otol 99:1143–1145, 1985.
36. Kent GP, Brondum J, Keenlyside RA, et al: A large outbreak of acupuncture-associated hepatitis B. Am J Epidemiol 127:591–598, 1988.
37. Lee MHM, Ernst M: Clinical and research observations on acupuncture analgesia and thermography. Presented at Duesseldorfer Akupunktur Symposium, July 31, 1987.
38. Lee MHM, Ernst M: The sympatholytic effect of acupuncture as evidenced by thermography: A preliminary report. Orthop Rev 12:67–72, 1983.
39. Lee MHM, Liao SJ: Acupuncture in physiatry. In Kotke FJ, Lehmann JF (eds): Krusen's Handbook of Physical Medicine and Rehabilitation, 4th ed. Philadelphia, W.B. Saunders, 1990, pp 402–432.
40. Lee MHM, Teng P, Zaretsky HH, Rubin M: Acupuncture anesthesia in dentistry. N Y State Dent J 39:299–301, 1973.
41. Lee MHM, Yang WGF: The possible usefulness of acupuncture in rheumatic disease. Clin Rheumatol 3:237–247, 1985.
42. Liao SJ: Acupuncture in cervical spondylosis [Abstract]. Acupunct Electrother Res Int J 1:226, 1975–76.
43. Liao SJ: Acupuncture treatment for skin diseases, including psoriasis, acne, painful surgical scars, etc [Abstract]. Acupunct Electrother Res Int J 11:281, 1986.
44. Liao SJ: Unpublished data, 1975.
45. Liao SJ: Use of acupuncture for relief of head pain. Presented at American Dental Association 118th Annual Session. Miami Beach, FL, October 10, 1977.
46. Liao SJ, Lee MHM, Ng LKY: Principles and Practice of Contemporary Acupuncture. New York, Marcel Dekker, 1994.
47. Liao SJ, Liao MK: Acupuncture and tele-electronic infrared thermography. Acupunct Electrother Res Int J 10:41–66, 1985.
48. Liao SJ, Merriman H: Hegu (LI4) acupoint to generate analgesia for tonsillectomy in an adult. Unpublished data, December 12, 1972.
49. Li SJ, Tang J, Han JS: The implication of central serotonin in electroacupuncture tolerance in rats. Sci China [B] 25:620–629, 1982.
50. Liao SJ, Wen KK: Patients' hypnotizability and their response to acupuncture treatments for pain relief. A preliminary statistical study. Am J Acupunct 4:263–268, 1976.
51. Licht S: History of electrodiagnosis. In Licht S (ed): Electrodiagnosis and Electromyography, 3rd ed. New Haven, CT, Elizabeth Licht, 1971, pp 6–7.
52. Lu GD, Needham J: Celestial Lancets. A History and Rationale of Acupuncture and Moxa. New York, Cambridge University Press, 1980.
53. Mayer DJ, Price DD, Rafii A: Antagonism of acupuncture hypalgesia in man by the narcotic antagonist naloxone. Brain Res 121:368–372, 1977.
54. McLennan H, Gilfillan K, Heap Y: Some pharmacological observations on the analgesia induced by acupuncture in rabbits. Pain 3:229–238, 1977.
55. Melzack R, Melinkoff RF: Analgesia produced by brain stimulation: Evidence of a prolonged onset period. Exp Neurol 43:369–374, 1974.
56. Melzack R, Stillwell DM, Fox EJ: Trigger points and acupuncture points for pain correlation and implications. Pain 3:3–23, 1977.
57. Ng LKY, Thoa NB, Dothitt TC, et al: Decrease in brain neurotransmitters and elevation of foot shock-induced pain threshold following repeated electrostimulation of putative acupuncture loci in rats. Am J Chin Med 2:236–237, 1974.
57a. Ng LKY, Liao SJ: Acupuncture: Traditional and scientific perspectives. In Weiner RS (ed): Innovations of Pain Management: A Practical Guide for Clinicians, vol. 3, chapter 31. Orlando, FL, Paul M. Deutsch Press, 1992, pp 31.1–31.59.
58. Nogier PFM: Treatise of Auriculotherapy. Paris, Maisonneuve, 1972.
59. Osler W: The Principles and Practice of Medicine. New York, Appleton and Co., 1892.
60. Peking Acupuncture Anesthesia Coordinating Group: Preliminary study on the mechanism of acupuncture anesthesia. Sci China [B] 16:447–456, 1973.
61. Peng ATC, Behar S, Yue SJ: Long term therapeutic effects of electroacupuncture for chronic neck and shoulder pain—a double-blind study. Acupunct Electrother Res Int J 12:37–44, 1987.
62. People's Republic of China: Acupuncture Anesthesia [movies], 1973.
63. Pomeranz B: Scientific basis of acupuncture. In Stux G, Pomeranz B (eds): Acupuncture: Textbook and Atlas. Berlin, Springer-Verlag, 1987, pp 1–34.

64. Pomeranz B, Cheng R, Law P: Acupuncture reduces electrophysiological and behavioral responses to noxious stimuli: Pituitary is implicated. Exp Neurol 54:172–178, 1977.
65. Pomeranz B, Chiu D: Naloxone blockade of acupuncture analgesia. Endorphin implicated. Life Sci 79:1757–1762, 1976.
66. Raustia AM: Diagnosis and treatment of temporomandibular joint dysfunction. Proc Finn Dent Soc 82(suppl X):1–41, 1986.
67. Ren MF, Tu ZP, Han JS: The effect of hemicholine, choline, eserine, and atropine on acupuncture analgesia in rats. In Advances in Acupuncture and Acupuncture Anesthesia. Beijing, People's Publishing House, 1980, pp 439–440.
68. Renton J: Observations on acupuncturation. Edinburgh Med J 34:100, 1830.
69. Research Group of Acupuncture Anesthesia, Peking Medical College, Peking: The role of some neurotransmitters of brain in finger-acupuncture analgesia. Sci China [B] 17:112–113, 1974.
70. Reston J: Now, about my operation in Peking. The New York Times, July 26, 1971.
71. Section on Acupuncture Analgesia of the Second Laboratory of Shanghai Institute of Physiology: Knowing the mechanism of acupuncture anesthesia in practice. Kexue Tongbao (Scientia) 23:342–347, 1976.
72. Shanghai Institute of Physiology: Electric response to nocuous stimulation and its inhibition in nucleus centralis lateralis of thalamus in rabbits. Chin Med J 131:135, 1973.
73. Sin YM: Acupuncture and inflammation. Int J Chin Med 1:15–20, 1984.
74. Spiegel H: Hypnosis: An adjunct to psychotherapy. In Freedman AM, Kaplan HI, Sadock BJ (eds): Comprehensive Textbook of Psychiatry, 2nd ed. Baltimore, Williams & Wilkins, 1975.
75. Tang J, Han JS: Changes in the morphine-like activity in the rat brain and pituitary gland during electroacupuncture analgesia. J Beijing Med Coll 3:150–152, 1978.
76. Tang J, Wang Y, Yang XD, et al: The pituitary opioids in electroacupuncture analgesia in the rat. J Beijing Med Coll 13:202–204, 1981.
77. Travell J: Office Hours: Day and Night. The Autobiography of Janet Travell, M.D. New York, World Publishing, 1968.
78. Vierck CJ Jr, Lineberry CG, Lee PK, et al: Prolonged hypalgesia following "acupuncture" in monkeys. Life Sci 15:1277–1289, 1984.
79. Wallnoefer H, von Rottauscher A; Palmedo M, trans: Chinese Folk Medicine. New York, Bell, 1965.

Chapter 7

TECHNIQUE OF PROLOTHERAPY

K. DEAN REEVES, M.D.

Proliferation therapy, or prolotherapy, is the intraligamentous and intratendinous injection of solutions that induce the proliferation of new cells. These new cells strengthen incompetent tendon and ligaments,[17] thereby promoting joint stability and reducing pain. The alternative term—TILT (trigger injection of ligament and tendon) therapy—can also be used to describe this treatment.

Hippocrates first used cautery to irritate tissue and promote wound healing. The first recorded use of a chemical irritant to promote healing in acute injuries was by Pare't, a French surgeon in the 1500s. At that time, the term "sclerotherapy" was used because fibrous tissue developed resembling scar tissue. Hackett, in 1939, began using a local irritant to start the healing cascade in linearly oriented connective tissue in the presence of chronic pain.[17] Hackett coined the term prolotherapy, short for proliferation therapy, because the term sclerotherapy implied scar formation. With the agents he and subsequent physicians have used, no scar development has been demonstrated, probably because injections are now given in linear connective tissue. This linear pull of tendons and ligaments probably provides orientation feedback to newly formed cells.

MECHANISM OF ACTION

To understand the mechanism of action of proliferation therapy, one needs a good understanding of myofascial pain and trigger points (see chapter 3). Myofascial pain syndrome is one of the most common disorders seen in chronic pain clinics.[12] This disorder is associated with trigger points, popularized by Travell and Simon.[48] Trigger points are believed to occur not only in the fascia and tendons of muscles, but also in joint capsules and ligaments.[48] Many investigators have described referred pain from these tendinoligamentous structures.[9,13,17,31,35,36,47,49] Deeper somatic structures such as periosteum and periosteal attachments of tendons and ligaments are pain generators and have very low pain thresholds.[2] Inman and Saunders reported stimulating periosteum and eliciting severe referred pain to muscles or bony prominences in reproducible patterns.[28] The distribution of specific referred pain patterns from tendon and ligament attachments has been described in the most detail by Hackett.[15-21]

Tendons and ligaments are semielastic tissues, and, as such, may be stretched or weakened with chronic or acute injury. Tendon or ligament laxity or weakness is proposed to cause chronic nociception via inadequate skeletal support, intermittent stretch of fixed-length sensory fibers, or development of myofascial trigger points.[19,41] The solution that is injected includes a combination of anesthetic and proliferant. The anesthetic agent affects the "trigger" of the pain cycle, and the proliferant strengthens the injected ligament or tendon and reduces painful nociception.[5,34,42]

When injected, proliferants such as simple dextrose solution are thought to create irritation by an osmotic gradient. Cells in the area lose water and desiccate to the point of an injury response. The goal of proliferation therapy is to restore normal connective tissue length and strength in the affected area, thereby restoring adequate skeletal support and eliminating sources of myofascial trigger perpetuation.[1]

NORMAL TENDON AND LIGAMENT HEALING

The normal tissue healing cascade and the timing of its various stages is complex and well-described in other sources.[6] Within hours of an injury to ligaments and tendons, monocytes are found at the site of injury, and fibroblasts appear within 48 hours. Procollagen is deposited within 1 week and aligns with the tendon or ligament structure over several weeks. Six weeks after an injury, maturation of collagen from procollagen occurs, ultimately resulting

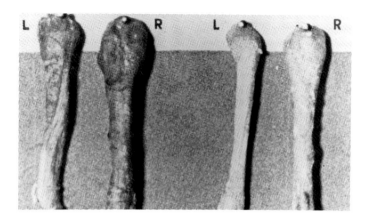

FIGURE 7-1. Rabbit tendons 9 and 12 months after injection with proliferant; controls (L), treated (R). (From Hackett GS, Hemwall GA, Montgomery GA: Ligament and Tendon Relaxation Treated by Prolotherapy, 5th ed. Oak Park, IL, Gustav A. Hemwall, 1992, p 96; with permission.)

in improvement of tensile strength and thickness of the affected ligament or tendon. As a result of cross-band maturation, the area previously elongated by injury shortens to approach its normal length. Increase in tissue strength begins to plateau 8 weeks after injury but may increase up to 6 months. Without further fibroblast activity and collagen deposition the healing cascade ends.

ANIMAL AND HUMAN STUDIES

Hackett injected sylnasol, a sodium salt fatty acid and an early proliferant, into tendons of rabbits.[17] Biopsy 48 hours after injection demonstrated lymphocytic infiltration and 2 weeks later demonstrated fibroblastic proliferation with a 40%

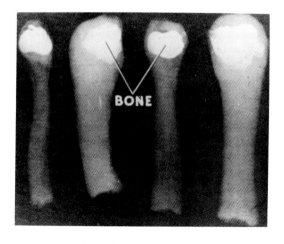

FIGURE 7-2. Paired radiographs of tendon-to-bone attachment of rabbit tendons 1 and 3 months after injection of proliferant. Controls are on the left side of each pair, treated tendons on the right. (From Hackett GS, Hemwall GA, Montgomery GA: Ligament and Tendon Relaxation Treated by Prolotherapy, 5th ed. Oak Park, IL, Gustav A. Hemwall, 1992, p 96; with permission.)

increase in diameter (Fig. 7-1). An x-ray of the bone-to-tendon junction showed a similar increase in size of the tendino-osseous junction (Fig. 7-2). Similar studies of medial collateral ligaments in rabbits with the proliferant sodium morrhuate demonstrated 40% increases in mass, thickness, and strength by 42 days.[37] Other researchers have demonstrated marked inflammatory reactions when 12.5% dextrose solution was injected into rat muscle (Figs. 7-3, 7-4).[4]

In human studies, Klein et al. injected lumbosacral ligaments, including the sacroiliac, with proliferant solution (15% dextrose, 1.25% phenol, and 12.5% glycerin) weekly for 6 weeks. Pre- and posttreatment biopsy demonstrated an average increase in collagen fiber diameter of 0.55 to 0.88 μm.[33]

Ongley et al. injected the ends of collateral and cruciate ligaments of knees that had substantial ligamentous laxity as measured by a computerized knee analysis device.[8,24,43] The ligaments were injected with a proliferant solution (12.5% dextrose, 1.25% phenol, 12.5% glycerin, and 0.25% lidocaine) at 2-week intervals on four occasions. Statistically significant reduction in ligamentous laxity was demonstrated at 9 months with corresponding pain reduction.

Hackett reported an 82% success rate in the treatment of chronic spine pain in 1,816 patients treated during a 20-year period.[19,20] Coplans demonstrated similar results, with an 80% reduction of chronic back pain lasting greater than 2 years using prolotherapy.[7] Others have reported similar results even with placebo comparisons.[10,14,25,26,29,30,34,39,40,42,46]

APPROACHES TO PROLOTHERAPY

There are two general approaches to proliferation therapy (Table 7-1). The first, known as the Hackett method, is based on the approach of George Hackett

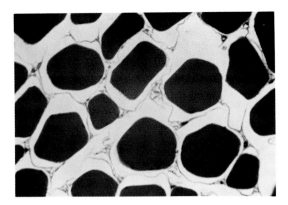

FIGURE 7-3. Photograph of a cross-section of rat muscle prior to proliferant injection, stained with hematoxylin and eosin (Courtesy of Gale Borden, MD).

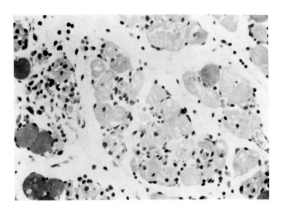

FIGURE 7-4. Photograph of a cross-section of rat muscle 48 hours after injection with the proliferant, 12.5% dextrose in 0.5% lidocaine, stained with hemotoxylin and eosin (Courtesy of Gale Borden, MD).

and subsequent refinements made primarily by Hemwall and Montgomery.[15-23] The second method, popularized by Dorman, Ongley, and others, [10,42] is called the West Coast method, because it was popularized by physicians in that region. The comparisons in Table 7-1 come through direct observation of techniques used by Hemwall, Montgomery, Ongley, and subsequent personal experience.

The technique section that follows is best described as the Hackett method. Dextrose is sufficient as a proliferant in the great majority of cases. It is relatively harmless to tissue and eliminates all concern of even temporary neurolysis from an accidental overconcentration of proliferant. Phenol and sodium morrhuate can be used in cases in which some improvement is seen but a stronger proliferant action needed. Discomfort after injection of phenol and sodium morrhuate is substantially more with the corresponding increase in inflammation, especially if the injection is not performed accurately.

The Hackett method is emphasized for teaching purposes since, unlike the West Coast method, it does not require manipulation. It is generally performed more slowly, making it more comfortable for the patient. Consequently, it is better tolerated. Although the frequency of injection can be more often, injections are routinely given every 6–12 weeks. In comparison to the West Coast method, the Hackett method avoids rigorous postinjection exercises in the involved body part.

GENERAL PRINCIPLES AND TECHNIQUE

The general principles and technique of proliferation therapy encompass several concepts important to most procedures. These concepts, discussed below, include proper patient selection, timing, identification of injection sites, technique, proliferant solution, postprocedure care, and complications.

Patient Selection

Identifying patients who may benefit from prolotherapy is necessary for good outcomes. Generally, patients with ligamentous insufficiency or laxity are good candidates for this treatment. Traditionally, laxity has been determined by physical examination with forced joint motion, i.e., drawer testing, or with stress radiographs. Subtle signs of possible ligamentous insufficiency include popping, cracking, or grinding sensations in joint regions that may result from friction secondary to improper movement without adequate ligament support. Other signs may include recurrent joint dislocation, benefit from wearing a supporting brace, or numbness and pain radiating in nondermatomal patterns with normal neurologic examination. Patients who receive temporary benefit from spinal manipulation also may respond favorably to proliferation therapy. This treatment appears to reduce or eliminate the feeling that "something is out of place." If the patient does not show signs of improvement after two treatment sessions, the diagnosis must be reevaluated or the technique altered.

TABLE 7-1. Comparison of Prolotherapy Approaches

	Hackett Method	West Coast Method
Proliferant used	Dextrose almost exclusively	Phenol or sodium morrhuate
Manipulation	Not required	Usually
Needle size	Smaller bore	Larger bore
Sedation	Anesthetic gun/gel plus IV	Minimal
Frequency of treatment	Every 6–12 weeks	Weekly
Exercise recommendations	Gentle activity	Fast resumption

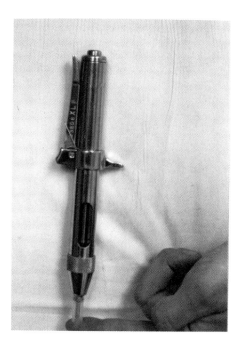

FIGURE 7-5. Anesthetic gun commonly used in prolotherapy.

Timing

Before undergoing proliferation therapy, a patient should have completed other more conventional forms of treatment. These include oral medications, physical modalities, and stretching and exercise. If the patient has evidence of an inflammatory disorder, injections of corticosteroids may be preferable. Proliferation therapy should be used in the context of a well-designed rehabilitation program. The timing of prolotherapy in patients with chronic pain is variable and often based on the patient's accessibility to this form of treatment. Some physicians, however, treat acute pain with prolotherapy to reduce or eliminate pain in order to allow a more rapid return to functional activities. In acute injuries, including postoperative cases, treatment is usually not initiated for 8 weeks. This time delay allows the natural healing cascade to take place.

Identifying Injection Sites

Using the fingertip, palpation should occur in potential pain referral sources for the patient's clinical complaints. A knowledge of ligament and tendon referral patterns is essential to determine the sites of injection. The objective presence of twitch contractions can often be elicited with cross-fiber palpation over the tendon or ligament in question, as well as reproduction of the patient's pain pattern. Once these specific areas are identified, the skin is marked. Trigger points from muscle are usually not marked since they are considered secondary. Once

located, the skin over these sites is anesthesized with an anesthetic gun (Fig 7-5) or with anesthetic cream. However, some authors have noted minor pigmentation changes in the skin from the air gun, and its use probably should be avoided in cosmetically important areas.[10]

Injection Technique

Before initiating proliferation therapy, all nonsteroidal antiinflammatory drugs (NSAIDs) should be discontinued, usually 3 days prior to treatment. Immediately prior to treatment, prophylactic antinausea medication such as hydroxyzine pamoate (Vistaril) can be provided. If necessary, sedation, often in the form of intravenous meperedine (Demerol) is given. Oxygen saturation values in the 90s and predrawn Narcan are recommended.

During injection, the needle tip is advanced into the ligament or tendon attachment site. This requires an excellent knowledge of ligamentous anatomy in order to avoid inadvertent needle puncture. One rule of treatment is that the injection is given only when the needle tip touches bone. The only exception to this rule is with intra-articular injections. Small volumes, only 0.5–0.75 ml (and less if strong proliferants are used) are injected at each site. Too much proliferant injected at one site may provoke more inflammation than desired.

Proliferant Solution

The most common proliferant is made with 4 ml of 50% dextrose, 2 ml of 2% xylocaine., and 6 ml of bacteriostatic water. Both xylocaine and water should be free of methylparaben. Two milliliters of sodium morrhuate can substitute for bacteriostatic water to make a more inflammatory solution. One percent phenol also can be prepared. The latter two proliferants should rarely be used and, then, only by an experienced physician and not at the lumbosacral junction in midline.

Another commonly used proliferant is Ongley's solution. Also known as P25G, this solution contains 2.5% phenol, 25% glucose, 25% glycerin, and pyrogen-free water. The solution is diluted 50% with 0.5% lidocaine prior to injection. However, accuracy and completeness of injection are more critical factors than the type of proliferant used. In addition, this solution and proliferants should be changed weekly and refrigerated.

Postprocedure Care

After the procedure, patients generally can be discharged to the care of a responsible driver when they can walk without dizziness. Analgesics are provided, but NSAIDs should be avoided for at least 10 days. Application of ice or heat in combination with slow gentle stretching is recommended, and activities should be gentle for 2–4 days. Repetitive motion and impact aerobics should be avoided if possible. Supports in the form of splints and braces may be provided.

Complications

Proliferation therapy is considered safe when it is used judiciously. The most common complication is an exacerbation of pain that lasts 2–7 days following the injection session. If pain persists beyond this time, residual ligament or tendon trigger points may be present. A superimposed inflammatory process also may be present.

Phlebitis of the vein used for intravenous sedation can occur. Infection and allergic reactions have not been reported in the literature. However, fish allergy should be questioned before use of sodium morrhuate.

Other complications are specific to the injected body part and are usually a result of improper needle placement. Injections around the thorax can lead to pneumothorax, but it is rare.[38] Injection into the vertebral artery is rare and safe if 0.5 ml or less of standard solution is used.[3] Five cases of neurologic impairment from spinal cord irritation from subdural injection above the sacrum have been reported since 1955 and were attributed to very strong proliferants.[27,32,45] Among current proliferants, phenol has significant risk resulting from an error in concentration.[44]

SELECTED CONDITIONS AMENABLE TO PROLIFERATION THERAPY

Many painful conditions are amenable to proliferation therapy. Common problems such as back, neck, and extremity pain presenting with signs of ligament instability or referred pain from tendinous or ligamentous trigger points are likely to do well with this treatment. Patients with atypical, noncardiac, noninflammatory chest pain or fibromyalgia also have been treated. The following section offers general tips to the novice prolotherapist on approaches to several common clinical problems. It is assumed that a complete physical exam has been performed and that no definite indication for surgery is present. The interested reader is referred to more detailed texts on ligament and tendon anatomy as well as injection techniques.[10,22] Common general injection locations are reviewed in Tables 7-2 and 7-3.

Neck and Upper Extremity Injection Techniques

Neck and upper extremity pain is often treated by proliferation therapy if the pain generator originates from cervical ligamentous structures. An understanding of common trigger point referral patterns from these cervical structures is helpful (Fig. 7-6). Many cases of upper extremity pain resembling thoracic outlet syndrome or pseudo–reflex sympathetic dystrophy may be a result of cervical ligamentous pathology. This also may affect the

TABLE 7-2. Common Sites of Injection for the Upper Body (Regions of Pain)

Referral Source Examples	Head	Head and Neck	Neck	Top of Shoulder	Shoulder	Elbow	Arm	Upper Back
Semispinalis capitis	■	■						
Splenius capitis	■	■						
Rectus capitis	■	■						
TMJ capsule/ligaments	■	■						
Cervical intertransverse ligaments		■	■	■	■		■	
Cervical facet ligaments		■	■	■	■		■	
Anterior/posterior tubercles		■	■	■	■		■	■
Posterior superior trapezius		■	■	■	■			
Costotransverse ligaments			■	■	■		■	■
Longissimus thoracis			■	■	■		■	■
Iliocostalis thoracis			■	■	■		■	■
Shoulder capsule				■	■		■	
Biceps					■		■	
Subscapularis					■		■	
Pectoralis					■		■	
Deltoid					■		■	
Infraspinatus					■		■	
Teres major					■		■	
Teres minor					■		■	
Common extensors						■	■	
Common flexors						■	■	

TABLE 7-3. Common Sites of Injection for the Lower Body (Regions of Pain)

Referral Source Examples	Back	Back and Leg	Buttock	Thigh	Knee	Calf/Shin	Ankles	Heel	Arch	Toes
Facet ligaments	■	■	■	■		■				
Lumbar intertransverse ligaments	■	■	■	■		■				
Sacroiliac ligament/joint	■	■	■	■		■	■	■	■	■
Iliolumbar ligament	■	■	■	■						
Gluteal insertions			■	■		■				
Sacrospinous ligament			■	■		■	■			
Deep articular ligaments, hip			■	■		■	■	■	■	■
External rotators, hip			■	■						
Distal knee adductors				■	■					
Distal hamstrings				■	■	■				
Knee capsule				■						
Distal vastus medialis			■	■						
Anterior tibialis					■					
Peronei					■					
Talofibular ligament						■				
Calcaneofibular ligament						■				
Tibionavicular ligament						■				
Tibiotalar ligament						■				
Tibiocalcaneal ligament						■				
Achilles tendon							■			
Calcaneonavicular ligament								■		
Calcaneocuboid ligament								■		
Long plantar ligament								■		
Tarsometatarsal ligaments									■	

posterior cervical sympathetic outflow, resulting in the Barré-Lieou syndrome.[11,23] In addition, many tension and migraine headaches unresponsive to medication and other traditional treatments may be treated with injections into the cervical structures. Common cervical structures thought to be involved include the intertransverse and facet ligaments, scalene attachments, occipital insertions, and posterior superior trapezius attachments.

With the posterior portion of the cervical region exposed, potential injection sites are marked on the skin. The C2 spinous process is easily palpable as the most superior midline bone. To inject the intertransversarii and facet ligaments, the needle is introduced posteriorly, usually 1 to 1½ inches in depth, directed slightly inferiorly until the posterior surface of the cervical laminae is contacted. Several rows on multiple cervical segments are usually injected (Fig. 7-7).

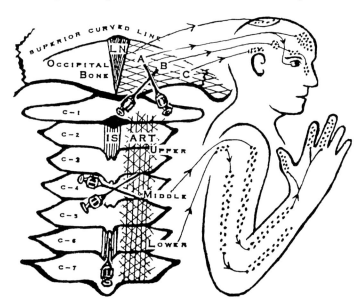

FIGURE 7-6. Common referral patterns of cervical structures. Forehead, eye (A); temple, eyebrow, nose (B); above ear (C); interspinus ligaments (IS), and articular ligaments (ART). (From Hackett GS, Hemwall GA, Montgomery GA: Ligament and Tendon Relaxation Treated by Prolotherapy, 5th ed. Oak Park, IL, Gustav A. Hemwall, 1992, p 70; with permission.)

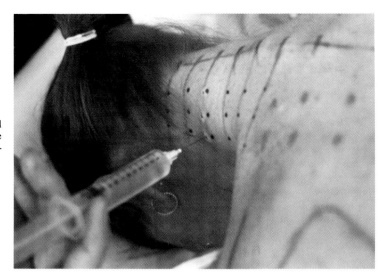

FIGURE 7-7. Injection of posterior cervical ligamentous structures. Note the multiple marks on the skin in preparation for additional injections.

If suboccipital tenderness is present, the insertion sites of the trapezius, semispinalis capitus, splenius capitus, and suboccipital triangle muscles can be injected (Fig. 7-8). For the skull insertions, two rows of injections are usually necessary. The most inferior injection site is directed superiorly from the C2 spinous process toward the rectus capitus muscle. The needle should remain ¾ inches from the midline to avoid dural puncture. A higher row of injections can be directed toward tender areas of the insertion sites of the trapezius and capiti muscles, usually with a 1-inch needle.

An anterolateral approach is often necessary to inject scalene attachments from C2–C6 (Fig. 7-9). Recall that the C1 vertebra is palpable immediately anterior and inferior to the mastoid process. The

second cervical tubercles are located 1½ fingerbreadths (FB) below the C1 vertebrae. The C6 tubercles correspond to a point three FB above the clavicle. Injections with this approach usually require a 1-inch needle and may require administration in two rows depending on the extent of pain when palpating the anterior or posterior tubercles.

Complications from injections into the deep cervical structures appear obvious. These include cervical nerve irritation with temporary paresthesia, or vertebral artery injection, so caution is advised.

Shoulder Girdle Injection Techniques

Pain originating from the muscles and ligaments of the shoulder girdle, as in other locations,

FIGURE 7-8. Common tender sites in the occipital and cervical region that often require injection. (From Hackett GS, Hemwall GA, Montgomery GA: Ligament and Tendon Relaxation Treated by Prolotherapy, 5th ed. Oak Park, IL, Gustav A. Hemwall, 1992, p 143; with permission.)

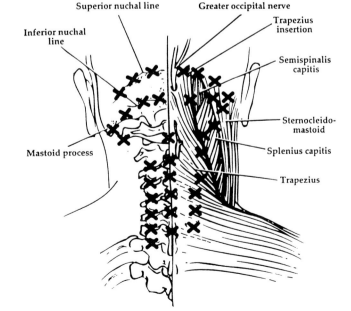

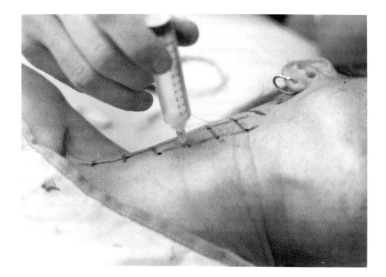

FIGURE 7-9. Cervical spine injection technique from a lateral approach.

can be complex. Commonly, injections are required into the attachment sites of the infraspinatus, teres minor, and teres major muscles. These attachments are injected over four or five vertical rows. The initial row of injections contacts the lateral edge of the scapula (Fig. 7-10). The subscapularis, coracobrachialis, and pectoral insertions are often injected to treat recalcitrant cases of bicipital tendonitis, and they are easy to perform (Fig. 7-11). The subscapularis and pectoralis major insertion sites are injected with the anterior shoulder exposed and the humerus externally rotated. This accesses the attachment sites of these two muscles. Injection is given in two to three rows over the proximal 3–4 inches of the anterior humerus. Coracobrachialis and pectoralis minor insertions are injected vertically. Origins of pectoralis major muscle, sternocostal, and sternoclavicular ligaments also may be injected along the edge of the sternum.

Forearm Injection Techniques

Proliferation treatment of medial and lateral epicondylitis usually begins after other treatments fail—corticosteroid injections, activity modification, therapy—or if cases are recurrent. In some chronic cases, debridement surgery becomes necessary for this condition. However, this surgery closely parallels the effect of proliferation therapy. Surgery often consists of debriding bone and reattaching muscles, a proliferation-inducing and tendon-shortening procedure.

In cases of lateral epicondylitis, the common forearm extensor attachments are injected. Frequently, the primary "triggers" to inject are located up to ¾ inch from the epicondyle. With the forearm supinated, injections are performed from the superior to inferior ridge of the lateral epicondyle (Fig. 7-12), extending down to the radial head. If the forearm is not fully supinated, attachment sites may not be accessible to the needle.

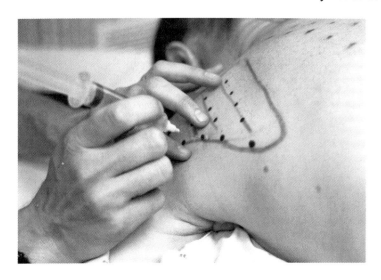

FIGURE 7-10. Injections to the scapular muscle attachments. Note that the needle tip is on the axillary border of the scapula.

Back and Lower Extremity Injection Techniques

Acute and chronic back, hip, buttock, and lower extremity pain can often be attributable to referred pain from trigger points within ligament or tendon structures around the sacrum or lumbar spine. Failed back syndrome from surgery may be in part due to instability of ligament and tendon structures, thus resulting in greater pain. Chronic pain from osteoporotic fractures can be in part due to traumatic laxity of spinal ligaments with pain from the facet and costotransverse ligaments or longissimus muscle attachments. Referred lower extremity pain unexplained by nerve root pathology may represent a disorder of the numerous ligament and tendon insertions in the lumbar, sacral, and pelvic regions (Figs. 7-13, 7-14), including the sacroiliac (SI), iliolumbar (IL), costotransverse, intertransverse, supraspinous, sacrospinous, and sacrotuberous ligaments. SI joint referral is similar to the SI ligament pattern depicted.

As in other locations, prior to performing injections into the lumbar spine, gluteal region, and hips, thorough palpation is necessary to identify abnormal ligaments that appear to be painful. Recall that the posterior superior iliac spine (PSIS) is at the S2 level and the iliac crest corresponds to the L4 level. These landmarks are helpful in identifying posterior lumbar and sacral ligaments prior to initiating the numerous injections often required (Fig. 7-15).

The IL ligament can be injected immediately adjacent to the iliac crest. After palpating the top of the iliac crest, the needle is inserted above the crest, then retracted and reinserted in order to inject in several rows moving medially and inferiorly.

In the posterior sacrum, multiple ligaments and muscular attachments are potential pain generators. To approach this broad area, injections are directed inferiorly from above the iliac crest and medial to the crest down onto the IL and SI ligament insertions and then along the top of the sacrum. The needle is often inserted lateral to the PSIS with injection rows fanning out as needed to cover the broad gluteus muscle insertion and inferior SI ligament. Attachments of the gemelli, obturator internus, piriformis, and gluteal muscles at the posterolateral femoral trochanter also can be injected (Fig. 7-16). These attachments are injected in three rows, with the most medial row located ¾ inch off the midline of the posterior thigh.

The intertransverse ligaments within the lumbar spine have characteristic referral patterns (see Fig. 7-13). Each of these ligaments can be injected with a 25-gauge, 2-inch needle, longer in obese patients. For the L4 transverse process, the needle is inserted ¾ inch superior to the iliac crest and 2 inches lateral to the midline. The needle is advanced until it contacts the transverse process. This same technique

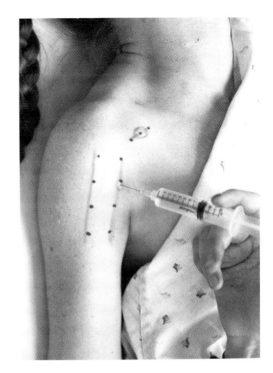

FIGURE 7-11. Injections into the anterior arm deep into the atachment sites of the pectoralis major, coracobrachialis, and the subscapularis muscles.

is used in the upper lumbar segments, usually up to L1 in most cases (Fig. 7-17). If the facet ligaments require injection, they can be reached ¼ inch superior and medial to this transverse process row.

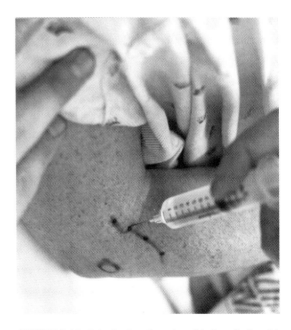

FIGURE 7-12. Injection into the region of the lateral epicondyle where the forearm extensor mass attaches.

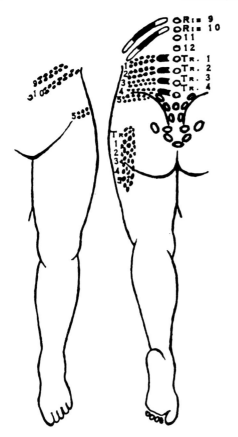

FIGURE 7-13. Common referral patterns of the iliocostalis and transverse process structures. (From Hackett GS, Hemwall GA, Montgomery GA: Ligament and Tendon Relaxation Treated by Prolotherapy, 5th ed. Oak Park, IL, Gustav A. Hemwall, 1992, p 36; with permission.)

The SI joint is usually injected along with the SI ligaments. Entry of the needle to aim toward the broadest opening of the joint is ½ inch off midline and ½ inch below the top of the iliac crest. The needle is directed inferolaterally and redirected as needed until the SI joint is entered. A volume of 4–6 ml of standard solution is injected.

Leg Injection

The knee capsule is often injected inferomedially with 6 ml of 25% dextrose. The thigh adductors and vastus medialis insertions are injected from a semicircle about the medial condyle of the femur and the hamstring insertions from several rows oriented vertically below the knee articular line (Fig. 7-18).

Injection of the calcaneofibular and talofibular ligaments is performed by palpating about the lateral malleolus anteriorly and inferiorly, injecting at tender origins. The lateral talocalcaneal ligament or intercarpal ligaments may be painful to palpation and merit injection. Injection of the medial ankle is similar, with palpation revealing tenderness in the tibionavicular, tibiotalar, and tibiocalcaneal portion.

Note for foot injection that the anterior medial malleolus is about even with the calcaneal insertion of the spring ligament with short plantar ligament insertion medial to this. Navicular and cuboid insertions of these ligaments can be injected more distally to this, and long plantar ligament nearer midline and closer to calcaneal prominence (Fig. 7-19). To inject tarsometatarsal ligaments, palpate the metatarsal head by dorsiflexing the toe and inject directly over the head.

Interscapular Injections

Interscapular injections are given, depending on palpable tenderness, over the costotransverse or facet ligaments. A short needle can be used and rib palpated between the fingers to minimize risk (Fig. 7-20).

Temporomandibular Joint Injection Techniques

Treatment of temporomandibular joint (TMJ) pain with proliferation therapy is directed at the joint capsule and supportive tendons and ligaments internal to the joint. The objective is to strengthen these structures by thickening and tightening the ligaments, thus providing joint stability and less pain.

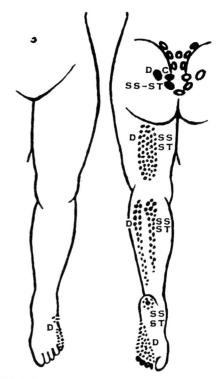

FIGURE 7-14. Common referral patterns of the sacroiliac, sacrospinous, and sacrotuberous ligaments. (From Hackett GS, Hemwall GA, Montgomery GA: Ligament and Tendon Relaxation Treated by Prolotherapy, 5th ed. Oak Park, IL, Gustav A. Hemwall, 1992, p 32; with permission.)

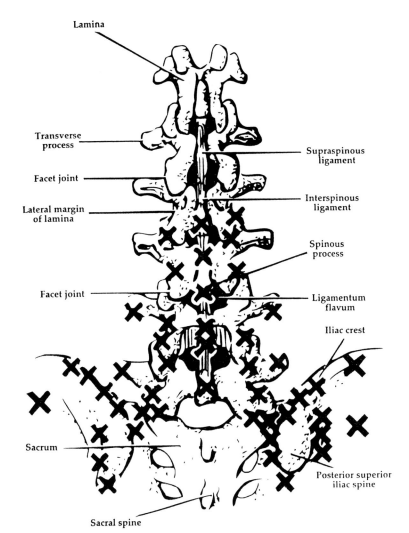

FIGURE 7-15. Common sites of injection in the lumbar spine. (From Hackett GS, Hemwall GA, Montgomery GA: Ligament and Tendon Relaxation Treated by Prolotherapy, 5th ed. Oak Park, IL, Gustav A. Hemwall, 1992, p 181; with permission.)

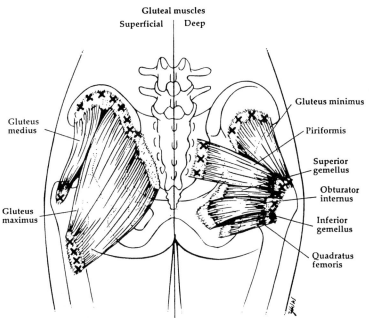

FIGURE 7-16. Common sites of tenderness at the attachments of the gluteus medius and minimus muscles and the smaller hip rotator muscles. (From Hackett GS, Hemwall GA, Montgomery GA: Ligament and Tendon Relaxation Treated by Prolotherapy, 5th ed. Oak Park, IL, Gustav A. Hemwall, 1992, p 226; with permission.)

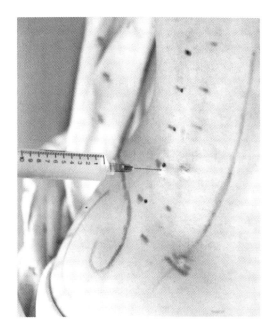

FIGURE 7-17. Injection technique for the intertransverse process ligaments.

FIGURE 7-18. Inferomedial injection of the knee. Note lines over adductor insertions and hamstring insertions.

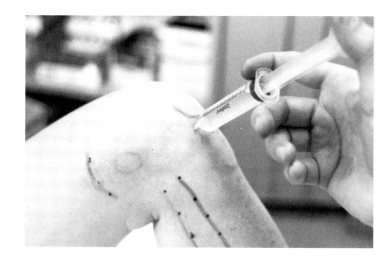

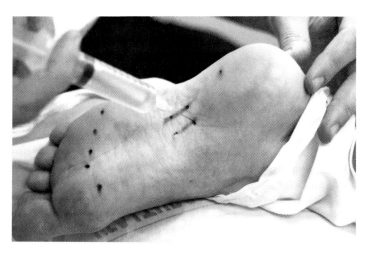

FIGURE 7-19. Injection of the spring ligament. Note marks over plantar, spring, and tarsometatarsal ligaments.

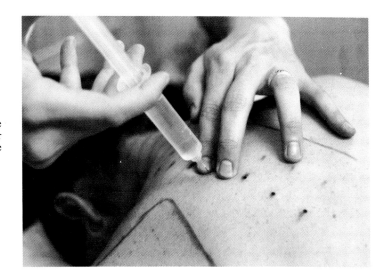

FIGURE 7-20. Injection of costotransverse ligaments. Note marks over entry points for facet ligaments. For facet ligaments, the needle is directed inferomedially for safety.

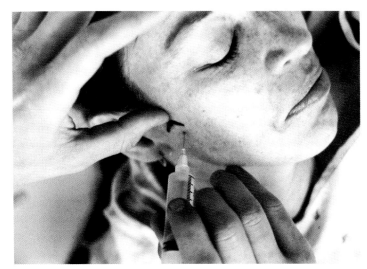

FIGURE 7-21. Needle placement for the closed-mouth approach when injecting for temporomandibular joint disorders.

With the patient's mouth closed and teeth not clenched (closed-mouth approach), the physician palpates the zygomatic arch adjacent to the condylar process of the mandible with a finger of the injecting hand. A 1¼-inch, 27-gauge needle is inserted ½ inch inferior to the apex of this palpable structure, felt as a semicircle (Fig. 7-21). The needle is directed approximately 10° posteriorly and 40° superiorly. As the needle penetrates the joint capsule, the patient often experiences a twitch contraction and burning sensation in the facial region. The needle is advanced about 1 to 1¼ inches, and ¾ ml of 25% dextrose solution is injected.

CONCLUSION

Proliferation therapy is a nontraditional but often useful technique in the treatment of pain from trigger points within ligaments and tendons. It also may be used to treat both subtle and prominent ligamentous laxity in nonsurgical candidates who have associated pain. A key concept of proliferation therapy is that the time period of active healing of semielastic tissue after injury is limited and that resumption of a healing cascade sequence is initiated with injection of a simple osmotic irritant. Animal studies demonstrate an increase in tendon and ligament girth and strength after proliferant injection. Human studies demonstrate similar structural results, and blind studies indicate corresponding pain reduction. Technical difficulty and the meticulous nature of the procedure make prolotherapy difficult to incorporate in the usual outpatient practice except for the more focal pain conditions.

REFERENCES

1. Banks AR: A rationale for prolotherapy. J Orthop Med (UK) 13:54–59, 1991.
2. Bonica JJ: Anatomic and physiologic basis of nociception and pain. In Bonica JJ (ed): The Management of Pain, 2nd ed. Philadelphia, Lea & Febiger, 1990, pp 28–94.

3. Bonica JJ, Buckley FP: Regional analgesia with local anesthetics. In Bonica JJ (ed): The Management of Pain, 2nd ed. Philadelphia, Lea & Febiger, 1990, pp 1883–1966.
4. Borden AG: Some investigational aspects of prolotherapy in animals and man. Presented at the 11th Annual Clinical Symposium of the Prolotherapy Association, June 16, 1968, San Francisco.
5. Byrn C, Olsson I, Falkheden L, et al: Subcutaneous sterile water injections for chronic neck and shoulder pain following whiplash injuries. Lancet 341:449–452, 1993.
6. Clark RAF, Henson PM: The Molecular and Cellular Biology of Wound Repair. New York, Plenum Press, 1988.
7. Coplans CW: The conservative treatment of low back pain. In Helfet AJ, Gruebel L (eds): The Conservative Treatment of Low Back Pain. Philadelphia, J.B. Lippincott, 1978, pp 145–183.
8. Daniel DM, Malcolm LL, Losse G, et al: Instrument measurement of anterior laxity of the knee. J Bone Joint Surg 67A:720–725, 1985.
9. de Valera E, Laffery H: Lower abdominal and pelvic pain in women. In Bonica JJ, Albe Fessard D (eds): Advances in Pain Research and Therapy, Vol 1. New York, Raven Press, 1976, pp 925–936.
10. Dorman TA, Ravin TH: Diagnosis and Injection Techniques in Orthopedic Medicine. Baltimore, Williams & Wilkins, 1991.
11. Gayral L, Neuwirth E: Oto-neuro-ophthalmologic manifestations of cervical origin: Posterior cervical sympathetic syndrome of Barré-Lieou. NY State J Med 54:1920–1926, 1954.
12. Gerwin RD: The Clinical Assessment of Myofascial Pain. In Turk DC, Melzack R (eds): Handbook of Pain Assessment. New York, Guilford Press, 1992, p 61.
13. Gorrell RL: Troublesome ankle disorders and what to do about them. Consultant 16:64–69, 1976.
14. Grieve EFM: Mechanical dysfunction of the sacroiliac joint. Int Rehabil Med 5:46–52, 1983.
15. Hackett GS: Joint stabilization through induced ligament sclerosis. Ohio State Med J 49:877–884, 1953.
16. Hackett GS: Shearing injury to the sacroiliac joint. J Int Coll Surg 22:631–642, 1954.
17. Hackett GS: Ligament and tendon relaxation treated by prolotherapy, 3rd ed. Springfield, IL, Charles C Thomas, 1956.
18. Reference deleted.
19. Hackett GS: Prolotherapy in whiplash and low back pain. Postgrad Med 27:214–219, 1960.
20. Hackett GS: Prolotherapy for sciatica from weak pelvic ligaments and bone dystrophy. Clin Med 8:2301–2316, 1961.
21. Hackett GS, Huang TC, Raftery A: Prolotherapy for headache. Headache 2:20–28, 1962.
22. Hackett GS, Hemwall GA, Montgomery GA: Ligament and Tendon Relaxation Treated by Prolotherapy, 5th ed. Oak Park, IL, Gustav A Hemwall, 1992.
23. Hemwall G: Barré-Lieou syndrome. J Orthop Med (UK) 11:79–81, 1989.
24. Highgenboten CL: The reliability of the Genucom knee analysis system. Presented at the Second European Congress of Knee Surgery and Arthroscopy, Basel, Switzerland, September 29, 1986.
25. Hirschberg GG, Froetscher L, Naeim F: Iliolumbar syndrome as a common cause of low back pain: Diagnosis and prognosis. Arch Phys Med Rehabil 60:516–519, 1979.
26. Hirschberg GG, Williams KA, Byrd JG: Medical Management of Iliocostal Pain. Geriatrics 47:62–68, 1992.
27. Hunt WE, Baird WC: Complications following injections of sclerosing agent to precipitate fibro-osseous proliferation. J Neurosurg 18:461–465, 1961.
28. Inman VT, Saunders JB: Referred pain from skeletal structures. J Nerv Ment Dis 99:660–667, 1944.
29. Kayfetz DO: Occipito-cervical (whiplash) injuries treated by prolotherapy. Med Trial Tech Q June:9–29, 1963.
30. Kayfetz DO, Blumenthal LS, Hackett GS, et al: Whiplash injury and other ligamentous headache—Its management with prolotherapy. Headache 3:1–8, 1963.
31. Kelgren JH: Observations on referred pain arising from muscle. Clin Sci 3:280–281, 1975.
32. Keplinger JE, Bucy PC: Paraplegia from treatment with sclerosing agents. JAMA 173(12):113–115, 1960.
33. Klein RG, Dorman TA, Johnson CE: Proliferant injections for low back pain: Histologic changes of injected ligaments and objective measurements of lumbar spine mobility before and after treatment. J Neurol Orthop Med Surg 10:141–144, 1989.
34. Klein RG, Bjorn CE, DeLong B, et al: A randomized double-blind trial of dextrose-glycerine-phenol injections for chronic low back pain. J Spinal Disord 6:23–33, 1993.
35. Kraus H: Clinical Treatment of Back and Neck Pain. New York, McGraw-Hill, 1970.
36. Leriche R: Des effetes de l'anesthesia a la novocaine des ligaments et des insertions tendineuses per-articulaires dans certaines maladies articularies et dans vices de position fonctionnels des articulations. Gazette des Hopitaux 103:1294, 1930.
37. Liu YK, Tipton CM, Mathes RD, et al: An in-situ study of the influence of a sclerosing solution in rabbit medial collateral ligaments and its junction strength. Connect Tissue Res 11:95–102, 1983.
38. Montgomery GA: Complications of prolotherapy. Presented at Prolotherapy Teaching Seminar (George S. Hackett Foundation), Watersmeet, MI, October 29–November 1, 1993.
39. Myers A: Prolotherapy treatment of low back pain and sciatica. Bull Hosp Joint Dis 22:48–55, 1961.
40. Naeim F, Froetscher L, Hirschberg GG: Treatment of the chronic iliolumbar syndrome by infiltration of the iliolumbar ligament. West J Med 136:372–374, 1982.
41. O'Donoghue DH: Principles in the management of specific injuries. In O'Donoghue DH (ed): Treatment of Injuries to Athletes, 4th ed. Philadelphia, W.B. Saunders, 1984, pp 39–91.
42. Ongley MJ, Dorman TA, Klein RG, et al: A new approach to the treatment of chronic low back pain. Lancet 2:143–146, 1987.
43. Ongley MJ, Dorman TA, Esk BC, et al: Ligament instability of knees: A new approach to treatment. Man Med 3:152–154, 1988.
44. Reeves KD, Baker A: Mixed somatic peripheral phenol nerve block for painful or intractable spasticity: A review of 30 years of use. Am J Pain Manage 2:205–210, 1992.
45. Schneider RC, Liss L: Fatality after injection of sclerosing agent to precipitate fibro-osseous proliferation. JAMA 170:1768–1772, 1959.
46. Schultz LW: Twenty years experience in treating hypermobility of the temporomandibular joints. Am J Surg 92:925–928, 1956.
47. Travell J: Pain mechanisms in connective tissue. In Ragan C (ed): Connective Tissues: Transactions of the Second Conference. New York, Josiah Macy Jr Foundation, 1952, pp 96–111.
48. Travell JG, Simons DG (eds): Myofascial Pain and Dysfunction: The Trigger Point Manual. Baltimore, Williams & Wilkins, 1983.
49. Weiser HI: Semimembranosus insertion syndrome: A treatable and frequent cause of persistent knee pain. Arch Phys Med Rehabil 60:317–319, 1979.

Chapter 8

WOUND MANAGEMENT PROCEDURES FOR DECUBITUS AND NEUROPATHIC ULCERS

DAVID F. NEALE, M.D.
PHALA A. HELM, M.D.

PERSPECTIVE AND HISTORY

Wound management has by tradition and rich historical precedent been the purview of the surgeon and, in antiquity, the battlefield surgeon. The fundamental principles of wound care that evolved through the centuries by clinical observation and trial and error were the "dividend of the tragedy of war."[28] Unfortunately, they were often discovered only to be forgotten, rediscovered, and relearned by succeeding generations of war surgeons.

The enduring methods of wound treatment generally support the biologic dictum that "the good physician is truly 'nature's servant.'"[28] As the Swiss physician Paracelsus (1493–1541) stated: "The surgeon should know that not he but Nature is the healer."[26] Ambrose Paré (?1510–1590), the great military barber-surgeon, revolutionized the treatment of wounds in the 16th century by abandoning the use of cautery (with "scalding oyle") in favor of simple dressings[36] that protected rather than perturbed the wound. He humbly stated in his famous aphorism:

Je le pansay, Dieu le guarit![28] (I dress him, God heals him!)

Good physicians are still "nature's servant" insofar as their modern wound management is an extension of the lessons and methods of their predecessors that have as the central goal the optimization of the milieu in which protected natural healing can take place. In this regard we find ourselves on a continuum with the best efforts of the battlefield surgeons. The enduring Halstedian principles of atraumatic tissue handling, careful hemostasis, and appropriate irrigation of the wound enhance healing and prevent infection.[15]

Future scientific inquiry and practice will no doubt hone the ability to improve the milieu of the wound by identifying for correction the many impediments to healing and the few overlooked enhancements to healing. One such enhancement discovered (or perhaps rediscovered) in 1962 was the benefit of a moist wound environment. This was noted in Winter's work with experimental wounds treated with occlusive dressings versus air drying.[39,40] He proved that drying of the wound surface with scab formation impeded healing. Thus began the "dressing revolution" that continues today.

ULCER DEBRIDEMENT

An appreciation of local anatomy, the depth of necrosis, the presence or absence of infection, and the patient's level of nutrition and immune competence are all critical to outcome. In general, if the skin wound is large, if it exceeds full thickness dermal destruction with necrosis of subcutaneous or deeper tissues (stage 3 or greater pressure ulcer), if it is associated with vascular insufficiency or bony deformity, or if a flap or graft is likely to be needed, it is in the patient's and physiatrist's best interest to obtain appropriate, early surgical consultation for initial debridement.

Wound management implies a process. The first step in that process is protection from the localized pressure that causes the ulceration and further tissue damage.[9] Correction, where possible, of deficiency factors that influence wound healing must accompany the process. Systemic factors such as malnutrition, vitamin deficiency, anemia, hypoxemia, decreased circulating volume, and vascular insufficiency must be addressed.[2,9]

FIGURE 8-1. Peeled navel orange used for debridement simulation and practice. Goal: a clean, unbroken membrane (From Razor BR, Martin LK: Validating sharp wound debridement. J ET Nurs 18(3):107, 1991, with permission.)

The second step is debridement. Debridement is "the removal of foreign material and devitalized or contaminated tissue from or adjacent to a traumatic or infected lesion until surrounding healthy tissue is exposed."[6] Sharp debridement of an ulcer may be *selective* in that only devitalized tissue is excised, or it may be *nonselective*, as in the case of total surgical excision of both devitalized and adjacent viable tissue prior to closure or grafting.[41] Selective debridement is well within the purview of the physiatrist or his or her trained designee. It is particularly effective in the treatment of infected ulcers, because only nonviable, necrotic tissue is removed, thereby decreasing the bacterial contamination while hastening the removal of physical blocks to healing. When done sequentially on consecutive days, the ulcer can be rendered "clean" in a short time unless tissue damage is ongoing (e.g., as a result of pressure) or systemic host deficiency factors have not been corrected.

Undebrided devitalized tissue enhances infection by acting as a culture medium for bacterial growth.

TABLE 8-1. Instruments for Sharp Wound Debridement

Gloves
Adson forceps with teeth
No. 3 scalpel handle with No. 10 and No. 15 blades
Two mosquito clamps
Silver nitrate sticks
Absorbable gelatin film (Surgical or Gelfoam)
Gauze sponges
Curved iris scissors
Normal saline solution
Sterile towels

From Razor BR, Martin LK: Validating sharp wound debridement. J ET Nurs 18:107, 1991, with permission.

In addition, devitalized tissue inhibits leukocyte phagocystosis of bacteria and their subsequent destruction.[11] The bacteria present are protected from systemic or topically applied antimicrobials by avascular necrotic tissue. This allows infection to persist and may encourage the development of resistance to such antimicrobials.

The physical effect of devitalized material includes mechanical obstruction of wound contraction and a surface barrier to eventual reepithelialization from the wound perimeter. Epithelial cells require a moist environment in which to migrate. The presence of a dry eschar or necrotic debris forces these cells to burrow beneath such material, significantly delaying the healing process. Wound contraction by myelofibroblastic activity in and around the healing ulcer serves to shorten the healing process by reducing the size of the defect. This contraction is prevented by a hard eschar.[41]

Partial surgical debridement is usually painless and associated with minimal if any blood loss when performed properly and carefully. As with any psychomotor task, skill and confidence are acquired with practice and experience. A useful practice task described by Davis[5] closely simulates actual wound and burn debridement if necrotic tissue is of a less adherent type. This simulation involves peeling a navel orange of all skin down to its thin pulp membrane without the leakage of any juice (Fig. 8-1).

Debridement Procedure: Decubitus Ulcer

The procedure of debridement is easily divided into three parts: preparation, debridement, and dressing.

Preparation

1. Time. For the initial debridement, morning allows better coordination of nursing issues and support systems as well as the convenience of an afternoon wound check.

2. Obtain the patient's informed consent for initial debridement to remove dead and/or infected tissues from the wound. Determine any allergies.

3. Supplies (see Table 8-1). These and other instruments are often in a minor surgery tray. A minor debridement tray can be arranged through the hospital's central sterile supply in order to provide only what is desired. Other disposable supplies should be ordered if they are not routinely available. They include povidone-iodine solution, normal saline irrigation solution, local anesthetic of choice (the author prefers 1% or 2% lidocaine without epinephrine), sterile gloves, glasses or goggles (optional), gown, silver nitrate sticks, Gelfoam (optional), and dressing supplies.

4. Arrange for an assistant familiar with sterile technique to retrieve additional supplies.

5. Position the patient comfortably on an adjustable-height bed or plinth.

6. Cleanse the wound area and surrounding area with povidone-iodine solution and gauze sponges. Work from center outward in spirals, discarding sponges between spirals.

7. An adjustable local light source is recommended. If a gooseneck exam light is used, the bulb should be positioned no closer than 18 inches to the patient's skin.

8. Set up a sterile impermeable barrier on a mobile bedside table, and set up a sterile field with instruments, supplies, and a basin of normal saline.

9. Drape the ulcer site with sterile towels, leaving the ulcer exposed. Simple cloth surgical towels work best, though paper, adhesive-stripped, windowed drapes are available.

10. Wipe povidone-iodine solution from the exposed ulcer and skin with a saline-moistened gauze sponge or alcohol swabs.

11. If the site is inflamed and tender and not of neuropathic etiology, it may be necessary to infiltrate a local anesthetic in the skin edge of the dermatome proximal to the ulcer at this point. Lidocaine 2% without epinephrine injected subdermally via a 25-gauge 1½-inch needle will give 2–4 hours of anesthetic time.

Debridement

12. Using toothed Adson forceps, pick up the edge of the eschar and develop a plane using the curved iris scissors by spreading the points and snipping. Traction on the freed eschar or any other tissue freed from the wound should always be perpendicular to the plane of the wound. This affords not only the best visibility of the wound, but the best chance of staying within the chosen tissue plane without inadvertently cutting into a deeper plane. In this manner the devitalized tissue of the ulcer can be removed in sequential layers. Adipose subcutaneous tissue, when necrotic, is gray in color and has little, if any, tensile strength and must be picked from the wound. Curved mosquito hemostats are useful in this procedure.

Hemostasis

13. Occasionally (more often when using a scalpel) viable tissue will be entered and capillary or small vessel bleeding will occur. Usually this can be controlled with gentle pressure and a moist saline sponge, which has the added benefit of wicking away the blood before it stains nearby tissues pink. This unwanted staining of otherwise obviously necrotic tissue is the reason one should start debridement at the lowest point and work up whenever possible. In this way any bleeding flows away

from the work area. If small vessel bleeding or capillary ooze persists, a silver nitrate stick lightly touched to the area is usually sufficient. Persistent venous bleeders respond to Gelfoam and pressure for 5 minutes. A defiant arteriolar bleeder will occasionally require a suture ligature.

14. Keep the wound moist. Do not allow it to dry out. A moist saline gauze should cover as much of the debrided ulcer bed and viable tissue as possible. This protects the tissue and, on removal, helps locate any unnoticed bleeding.

15. Remember, this is a process of debridement, not an event. If the clinician or the patient gets tired, it is best to stop and resume the process at a later time.

Dressing

16. Dressings and dressing orders should aid in the debridement effort. Coarse mesh gauze—wet to moist with normal saline—loosely packed into every corner of the ulcer deficit and covered with a sterile absorbent dressing should be changed every eight hours.

17. Lastly, a procedure note should reflect what was done. For example: "Partial surgical debridement of necrotic eschar and tissue from (type of wound and location)." The note should record the position of the patient, the prep solution and sterile drapes, the type of any local anesthetic and the amount used, the condition of the ulcer before and after debridement, any bleeding encountered and how it was controlled, the estimated tissue layer depth of necrosis identified, estimated stage of necrosis, and any complications.

Delayed Debridement

Partial surgical debridement often can be delayed advantageously in the case of an intact dry eschar over a decubitus lesion so long as there are no signs or symptoms of infection. The skin eschar here eventually should be removed but acts as a temporary biologic dressing while pressure relief and host deficiency factors are addressed. Within 3–5 days the inflammatory phase of wound healing may become evident at the wound as leukocytes and macrophages collect in the viable interface. Often the eschar edges will "lift" from the surrounding well-vascularized, viable tissue as this wound healing inflammation progresses. The lift gives a palpable mobile sensation and denotes an opportune time to initiate sharp partial surgical debridement prior to actual separation or the development of infection at the eschar borders. It should be noted that the differentiation of a stage 3 ucler, which involves only subcutaneous fat, from a stage 4 ulcer extending into muscle or bone is difficult to assess beneath intact eschar. Generally, a knowledge of local anatomy, the history and condition of the patient, and the size of the surface involvement are the only clues. The area at the surface usually underrepresents the area of necrosis at maximum depth, and, therefore, the total volume of necrosis. If a deep stage 3 or stage 4 ulcer is clinically suspected, consultation for initial debridement in a formal surgical setting is indicated.

Debridement Exceptions

Specialized tissues that perform important physical functions such as nerves, tendons, and fascia may be left undebrided. Though devitalized, such fibrous tissues can often be rendered surgically clean by local debridement and irrigation. With the granulation process, they act as transplant grafts of correct length and ideal location and are recellularized. (Fig. 8-4A).[27]

Another exception is black eschar attached to underlying bone, such as a posterior heel or sacral decubitus. As long as bacterial growth beneath it is minimized, it serves as a temporary biologic dressing.[41]

Underlying Osteomyelitis

Longstanding or chronically draining decubitus ulcers frequently overlie osteomyelitis. Plain radiographs are frequently diagnostic. If normal, they serve as a baseline for later comparison since radiographic changes often lag up to 4 weeks behind acute bone infection.[37]

The triple phase technetium 99m bone scan, when negative, rules out bone involvement at the 90% sensitivity level.[37] When positive, infectious etiologies can be differentiated at the 80–90% sensitivity level from noninfectious inflammatory processes by the addition of an indium 111 or a technetium 99m (Ceretec) labeled leukocyte scan. The spatial resolution of the latter can be enhanced by single photon emission computed tomography (SPECT) reconstruction to aid in the detection and localization of infected tissues.

When osteomyelitis is absent but the overlying tissue condition warrants debridement, all viable tissues or a thin layer of necrotic tissue and periosteum should be left in place over intact cortical bone. In the interest of preventing bacterial invasion, this remaining thin necrotic tissue over bone can be kept moist while its bacterial contamination is reduced by local treatment with topical antimicrobials such as silver sulfadiazine.

Ulcer Dressings

In the remainder of the ulcer, daily sequential partial surgical debridement and mechanical

wet-to-dry saline dressing debridement of the surrounding necrosis will reduce the bacterial growth and encourage the formation of granulation tissue.[3] Normal saline wet-to-dry dressings with coarse mesh gauze will debride nonselectively both residual necrotic debris *and* some surface granulation tissue while retarding epithelialization. It is, however, the dressing of choice for initial management of necrotic wounds. The frequently used solutions of 1% povidone-iodine, 0.25% acetic acid, 3% hydrogen peroxide, and 0.5% sodium hypochlorite (Dakins) have useful antimicrobial activity in heavily infected ulcers but should be discontinued in favor of saline as soon as possible due to their proven cytotoxic effects on fibroblasts.[20]

Once the bulk of necrotic tissue and debris have been removed by sequential, partial surgical debridements and wet-to-dry dressing, underlying granulation tissue should be visible in parts or all of the wound. The establishment of this granulation bed and its confluent spread in the wound are the goals of all subsequent efforts until healing occurs. Healing may be achieved by secondary intention: that is, by filling in of the defect by granulation tissue (so-called proud flesh), contraction of the defect by myofibroblasts and reepithilialization from the periphery, or by a formal surgical intervention such as secondary closure or a grafting procedure. The spreading granulation tissue enhances autolytic debridement of the remaining necrotic debris by bringing to the wound polymorphonuclear leukocytes and macrophages. The breakdown of fibrin, protein, mucopolysaccharides, glycoproteins, glycolipids, DNA, and RNA is performed by the enzymes of these cells, which add their activity to that of bacterial enzymes present in the ulcer fluid.[41]

Autolytic debridement requires a moist environment in which to occur. The thin-film, polymeric dressings are useful in noninfected superficial wounds to retain moisture and autolytic activity while allowing visualization of the wound. In deeper wounds, the moisture-retentive and absorptive properties of hydrocolloid dressings aid in debridement by increasing tissue fluid flow across the wound and, in the case of DuoDERM (ConvaTec, Princeton, NJ), providing fibrinolytic activity.[23] Both the thin, oxygen-permeable, polymeric films and the hydrocolloids change the wound environment beneficially by lowering the pH of wound fluid (more so with hydrocolloids) and by reducing the partial pressure of oxygen (PO_2). Low oxygen tension has been shown to enhance fibroblast growth and macrophage production of angiogenesis factors in vitro and is now felt to enhance the healing process in clean wounds.[34] While small amounts of necrotic tissue are still present, occlusive dressings should be changed once or twice a day to allow additional selective debridement and to monitor the wound for signs of infection. Such wounds are always colonized, but infection, as evidenced by the signs of tissue invasion (pain, erythema of peripheral skin, induration, tenderness, change in volume and character of wound exudate, or fever), should prompt the temporary suspension of occlusive, moisture-retentive dressings. Appropriate bacteriologic studies, antibiotic coverage, and a return to wet-to-dry or wet-to-moist dressings suffice until the infection is controlled. Selective debridement should continue as tenderness permits since this removes necrotic nutrients from the wound and hastens resumption of moisture retentive dressings.

DIABETIC FOOT CARE

Levin and others[7,10,19] have advocated the management of the diabetic foot by a clinic-based, multidisciplinary team that is dedicated to limb preservation and salvage. In centers where multidisciplinary teams exist, the rate of amputations in diabetic persons has decreased by 50–85%.[7,14] Unfortunately, such centers have been slow to develop.[12] Although members from all disciplines of the team do not have to be physically present, the availability of immediate, in-clinic consultation facilitates cross-education of the team, prevents fragmentation of care, and improves salvage rates for patients at risk for limb loss.

The outpatient management of the diabetic foot entails patient education[1]; physical examination for deformity, intrinsic foot and distal limb strength, level of protective sensation,[16,33] skin temperature, condition, and hair pattern; vascular assessment by pulses and Doppler ultrasound[35,42]; wound management and closure of neuropathic ulcers; and assessment and provision of protective footwear. Also, nail and callus trimming is essential in the diabetic patient. In many instances, patients cannot and should not attempt these procedures because their vision, sensation, and dexterity are impaired.

Nail Reduction

The diabetic patient's toenails, if normal, should be trimmed straight across to avoid ingrowth at the distal margins. The toenails often grow slowly due to impaired circulation and become thickened by fungal infections (onychomycosis).[17] If neglected, such nails may curve plantarly over fungal debris and form so-called ram's horn nails that are prone to avulsion or subungual bleeding and infection. Lateral curving may threaten adjacent toes with ulceration.[25]

Normal nails and thickened nails that have been softened by hydrotherapy can be safely reduced with plier type toenail nippers without risk of shatter or splitting (Fig. 8-2A).

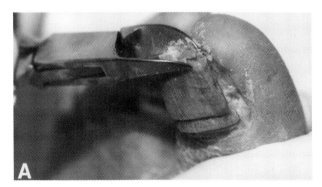

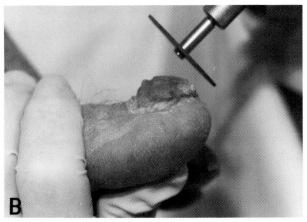

FIGURE 8-2. *A*, Normal to moderately thickened nails can be cut correctly with toenail nippers. *B*, Hypertrophic and "ram's horn" nails are best reduced and smoothed with a high-speed emery disc. Goggles and mask are recommended.

Thickened hypertrophic nails are best reduced and smoothed with a high-speed, rotary tool (Dremel) fitted with a small emery disc (Fig. 8-2B). In this way, the nail and its subungual debris can be carefully shaped and reduced as well as smoothed to prevent shoe trauma or snagging on clothing and bedding.

Callus Trimming

The sentinel sign of the diabetic foot at risk for neuropathic ulceration is the plantar callus. Loss of protective sensation allows repetitive high-pressure stress during ambulation without the normal shift of weight to protect the skin from damage.[4] Structural deformities such as hammer toes, bunions, and Charcot joints predispose the foot to the development of areas of high pressure. The dermis responds initially with hyperkeratosis at the site of pressure. The callus thus formed becomes a "rock in the shoe." If the callus is kept trimmed, plantar pressures are reduced.[43] Continued hyperkeratosis and the subsequent increased local concentration of pressure lead to dermal necrosis and the telltale darkening of the callus by blood known as a preulcer (Fig. 8-3A).

Prophylactic trimming of nonulcerated callus is easily accomplished with either a #10 scalpel or a single-edged razor blade. Care must be taken not to enter the vascular dermis but to remove only enough epidermal callus by serial tangential cuts to restore a supple surface.

Foot Grades

A classification of diabetic foot lesions has been described by Wagner based on clinical progression.[35]

It is useful in determining treatment for six grades of foot lesions.

Grade 0: Intact skin. Bony deformity and/or keratotic skin thickenings may be present.
Grade 1: Superficial ulcer. Full thickness skin or nail loss.
Grade 2: Deep ulcer. Penetrates subcutaneous fat down to tendon, ligament, joint capsule, or bone.
Grade 3: Ulcer with deep infection of tendon sheath, joint, bone, or abscess of deep tissues.
Grade 4: Gangrene of a portion of the foot requiring local amputation or possibly Syme's amputation.
Grade 5: Gangrene of foot sufficient to prevent surgical salvage. Amputation below knee or higher required.

Care for Neuropathic Grades 1 and 2 Ulcers

If a preulcer callus is removed, the bed of a true neuropathic ulcer is usually exposed (Fig 8-3B). This bed, though necrotic, is usually clean and will heal if protected from further pressure. The ulcer must be probed to determine any undermining or sinus tracts. The ulcer must then be pared of its overlying and/or surrounding callus and debrided of its necrotic tissues.

A general principle for this debridement in Wagner grade 1 and 2 neuropathic ulcers is that the ulcer should be as wide as it is deep. This allows adequate drainage and prevents premature, superficial

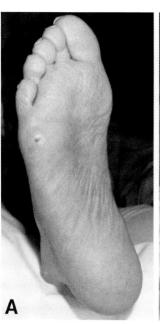 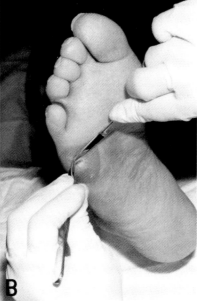

FIGURE 8-3. *A,* "Preulcer": telltale darkening beneath plantar callus at lateral metatarsal head. *B,* Unroofing callus exposes clean, neuropathic ulcer bed. Probing revealed no undermined edge or sinus tract.

A **B**

FIGURE 8-4. *A,* Attenuated plantar fascia exposed and left intact after incision and drainage of abscess at site of grade 3 chronic medial ulcer in Charcot deformed foot. Osteomyelitis was ruled out. Granulation is enveloping fascia. *B,* Irrigation and debridement and culture-specific antibiotics, followed by hydrotherapy, sequential local debridement, and serial total contact casting using resulted in progressive closure.

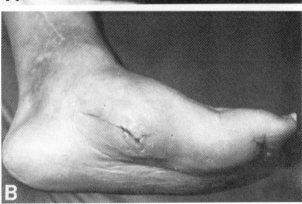

healing.[4] Sequential paring of the "ring callus" that often develops around healing ulcers reduces pressure and shear at the ulcer rim and allows wound contracture to hasten closure.

Clean or granulating neuropathic superficial (Wagner grade 1) and deep (Wagner grade 2) ulcers without infection can usually be successfully treated with total contact walking casts on an outpatient basis. High rates of healing (72–90%) in 6 weeks or less have been reported.[4,13,24] Deep ulcers with tendon or joint sepsis, deep abscess, or osteomyelitis (Wagner grade 3) require hospitalization with antibiotics and appropriate surgical treatment. Once successfully treated and effectively rendered grade 1 or 2, the ulcer and surgical wound can be treated with total contact casts to aid healing (Fig. 8-4).[24]

Localized gangrene of the toes, forefoot, or heel (Wagner grade 4) requires hospitalization with local amputation and often vascular reconstruction. Gangrene of the entire foot (Wagner grade 5) requires major amputation above the ankle.[35]

Infected Grades 1 and 2 Ulcers

Patients frequently present with an open, infected superficial or deep (grade 1 or 2) neuropathic ulcer. If the clinical examination reveals cellulitis, admission for elevation, intravenous antibiotics, and a search for deep, limb-threatening infection or osteomyelitis is indicated. In the absence of cellulitis,

when probing reveals a sinus tract into joint, abscess, or bone, or when an x-ray reveals joint or bone involvement, the lesion is grade 3, and admission is also indicated.

Locally infected Wagner grade 1 and 2 lesions without cellulitis can be managed in the outpatient setting. These ulcers should be cleansed with hydrotherapy to reduce soluble debris and bacterial load and begun on sequential, partial surgical debridement to reduce adherent, necrotic tissue. Initial dressings of normal saline or dilute 10:1 saline:povidone-iodine wet-to-dry coarse mesh gauze changed three times daily will aid debridement.

Depending on the clinical setting, empirical antibiotics are often required. Adequate cultures to retrieve both aerobic and anaerobic organisms should be attempted prior to antibiotic treatment. Surface swab cultures are notoriously inaccurate,[32,38] and tissue aspirates may miss the pathogen[21]; however, deep biopsy cultures are not always indicated or available in grades 1 and 2 lesions. A curettage specimen culture obtained from the ulcer base and edges has been shown to correlate better with deep tissue biopsy and to be more sensitive for anaerobes and gram-negative bacilli.[21,31] The technique of collection involves surface decontamination of superifical colonizers with saline-soaked gauze, povidone-iodine or isopropyl alcohol pads, irrigation, and collection of tissue scrapings from the ulcer base and edges.

Acute and superficially infected ulcers tend to contain one or two aerobic, gram-positive cocci (frequently staphylococci or streptococci) species per infection and respond to either oral cephalexin or clindamycin. Detection of aerobic, gram-negative bacilli (frequently *Proteus, Klebsiella-Enterobacter,* or *Pseudomonas* species and *Escherichia coli*) require a change to broader coverage with agents such as trimethoprim-sulfamethoxazole, amoxicillin-clavulanate or ciprofloxacin. Detection of obligate anaerobes, foul odor, or polymicrobial cultures suggest addition of metronidazole and consideration of inpatient management for deeper infection.

An adequate discussion of the microbiology and antimicrobial therapy of diabetic limb infections is beyond the scope of this chapter. The reader is referred to a recent review article on this subject by Lipsky et al.[22]

The patient should elevate the affected limb at home at bed rest to reduce edema while the infection comes under control. Wet-to-moist saline dressings three times a day, preferably applied by a family member, and diligent nonweightbearing via crutches, walker, or a wheelchair is essential. The wound is checked and debrided as necessary—initially every 2 or 3 days until it is clean and the local signs of infection are resolving. Antibiotics are usually needed for only 1 or 2 weeks.[21] However, continued swelling, excessive drainage, pain, or deterioration of the wound should prompt review of the antibiotic coverage and additional studies to rule out osteomyelitis or abscess.

When the ulcer is clean and edema resolved (often at the first or second follow-up visit), ambulatory care via total contact casting may be initiated. It the patient is not a candidate for casting due to conditions such as ataxia, blindness, fragile skin, morbid obesity, or claustrophobia, then nonweightbearing mobility, dressing changes, and local wound care with foot protection in a molded Plastizote shoe or "healing sandal" are continued until healing occurs.

Total Contact Casting Technique

High rates of healing have been achieved by casting Wagner grades 1 and 2 neuropathic ulcers. This is probably due to the ability of the total contact cast to redistribute high pressures over the entire surface of the insensate foot while significantly reducing and controlling edema in the foot. This aids tissue fluid exchange and tends to localize infection. The plaster cast permits drainage to be absorbed from the wound while it maintains a moisture-retentive environment around the healing site. Lastly, it protects the foot from trauma, limits noncompliance, and allows weightbearing. Once healed, the patient is fitted with a custom-molded,

rockered sandal for partial weightbearing until the skin toughens over the ulcer site. Alternatively, the patient may be placed directly into definitive extra-depth shoes with total contact molded insoles so long as he or she is limited to 1–2 hours of weightbearing a day initially for the first week with frequent foot checks the second week.

The classic technique of prone total contact cast application has been described by Coleman, Brand, and Birke of the National Hansens Disease Center, Carville, Louisiana.[4] A slight variation in the technique is presented here, which allows immediate weightbearing, custom rocker molding, and level leg length. The addition of Webril cast padding allows safer removal of this fiberglass-reinforced cast with the cast saw.

Supplies

1. Fine mesh gauze or Xeroform gauze
2. Thin 2″ × 2″ or 4″ × 4″ gauze dressing
3. 1″ paper tape
4. 1 oz package (gas) sterilized lamb's wool or low-density ½″ adhesive backed foam (Sci-Foam by Next Generation, Rancho, CA)
5. 3″ stockinette sewn or folded over at toe and rolled into "donut"
6. Orthopedic felt ⅛″–¼″ thick (option: adhesive-backed), cut and beveled into 2½″-diameter maleolar pads and a 2″-wide tibial crest to dorsal arch pad
7. Two 3″ rolls of Webril cotton cast padding
8. Rockerbottom cast shoe
9. Plaster cast materials: three 3″ rolls, fast setting; three 4″ rolls, fast setting; two 5″ × 30″, five-thickness splints
10. Fiberglass casting tape: one 3″ roll; one 4″ roll
11. Bucket of cold water
12. Vinyl or latex gloves

Total Contact Cast Procedure

Preparation

1. Apply in the early morning following overnight elevation to ensure as little edema as possible in the foot and leg. Some centers use Ace wrapping or pneumatic pumping to reduce edema prior to casting
2. Prepare the wound with diluted povidone-iodine solution and rinse.
3. Remove all necrotic ulcer tissue and surrounding callus. Excessive granulation tissue can be reduced with a silver nitrate swab and rinsed with saline.

Application

Step 1. The patient is positioned prone with the knee flexed 90° and the ankle at neutral. Pillows

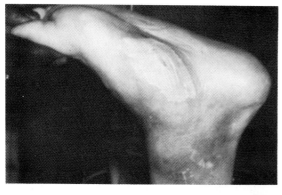
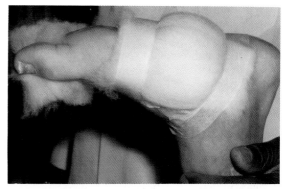
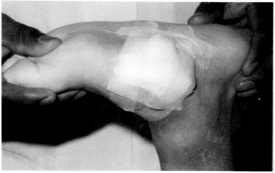

FIGURE 8-5

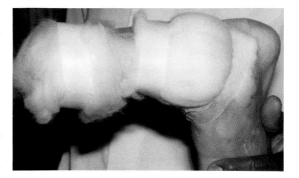

FIGURE 8-6

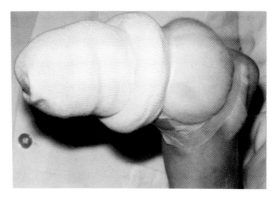

FIGURE 8-7

beneath the shoulders and hips improve comfort. Obese or breathless patients may be casted in the sitting position.

Step 2. The dressing of choice is applied and secured with paper tape at edges (Fig. 8-5).

Step 3. Lamb's wool is placed over the dressing, between the toes, and around the toes and secured with paper tape. This prevents maceration of toes and wound by wicking moisture away and into the cast. Alternate toe protection can be substituted here with low-density ½″ adhesive-backed foam (Sci-Foam) folded over the stockinette cut to form a toe cap. Interdigital wicks of lamb's wool or thin cotton wisps are still required (Fig. 8-6).

Step 4. A snug-fitting stockinette sewn or folded at toe is rolled over the foot and leg to the tibial tubercle (Fig. 8-7).

Step 5. Beveled pads of orthopedic felt are taped over the maleoli, tibial crest, and dorsum of instep (Fig. 8-8).

Step 6. A single layer of overlapping 3″ Webril cotton cast padding is applied snugly from toe cap to just below the tibial tubercle (Fig. 8-9).

Step 7. An inner shell of plaster is applied using a 3″ roll for foot and ankle and a 4″ roll for ankle and leg (Fig. 8-10).

Step 8. In quick succession five-ply 5″ × 30″ plaster splints are applied from the calf around the toe cap and mediolaterally across the ankle stirrup

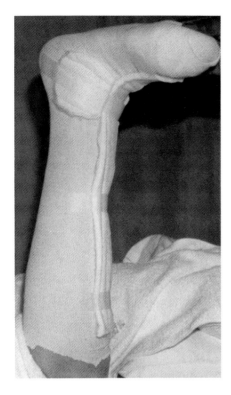

FIGURE 8-8

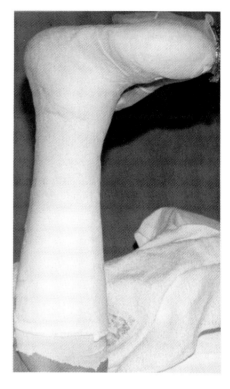

FIGURE 8-10

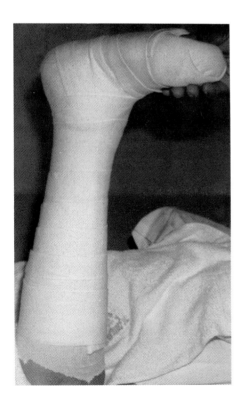

FIGURE 8-9

and molded to the inner shell while ankle position is held. Cast is allowed to set (Fig. 8-11).

Step 9. Rocker bottom, sole height, and ankle position correction is adjusted with fan-folded layers of 3″ plaster roll (Fig. 8-12).

Step 10. Reinforcing layers of fiberglass cast tape are applied in sitting position (Fig. 8-13).

Step 11. A cast shoe is applied and the patient allowed to bear weight (Fig. 8-14).

Step 12. The patient is given written instructions for cast care and to return for signs of cast loosening, softening, excessive drainage or symptoms of pain, fever, or lymphadenopathy.

Step 13. The first cast is changed after 2 or 3 days due to rapid loss of edema. Subsequent casts are changed at 1- to 3-week intervals, depending on ulcer condition and experience.

Skills Acquisition and Resources

The development of debridement, casting, and wound management skills can best be achieved by practice under experienced individuals. Most wound care specialists and multidisciplinary diabetic foot clinics welcome interest in their work and are eager to pass on their expertise to interested clinicians, nurses, and therapists. An excellent three-day course on comprehensive management of insensitive feet

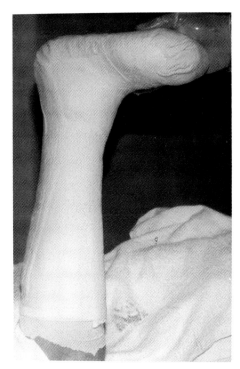
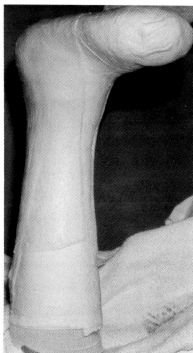

FIGURE 8-11

is given biannually by the US Public Health Service's Gillis W. Long Hansen's Disease Center, Carville, Louisiana. Resources and information regarding continuing medical education courses are available through the American Diabetes Association. Additionally, several texts give excellent instruction and guidance on the entire breadth and the intricacies of successful care of the diabetic foot.[8,18,30]

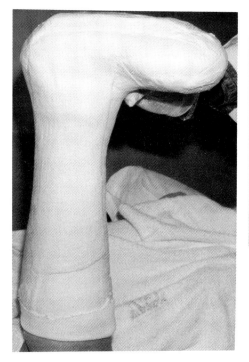
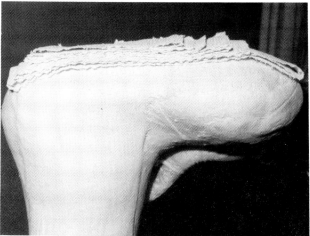

FIGURE 8-12

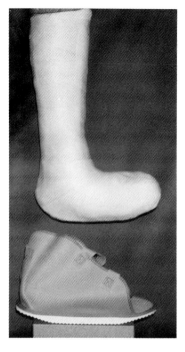

FIGURE 8-13

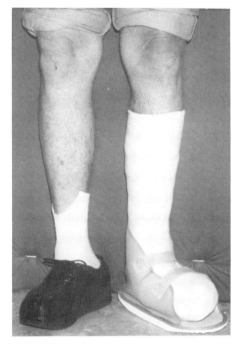

FIGURE 8-14

REFERENCES

1. Assal JP, Muhlhauser I, Pernet A, et al: Patient education as the basis for diabetic foot care in clinical practice. Diabetologia 28:602–613, 1985.
2. Carrico TJ, Mehrhof AI Jr, Cohen IK: Biology of wound healing. Surg Clin North Am 64:721–733, 1984.
3. Coche W Jr, White RR IV, Lynch DJ, et al: Wound Care. New York, Churchill Livingstone, 1986.
4. Coleman WC, Brand PW, Birke JA: The total contact cast. A therapy for plantar ulceration on insensitive feet. J Am Podiatr Med Assoc 74:548–552, 1984.
5. Davis JT: Enhancing wound debridement skills through simulated practice. Phys Ther 66:1723–1724, 1986.
6. Dorland's Illustrated Medical Dictionary, 25th ed. Philadelphia, W.B. Saunders, 1979.
7. Edmonds ME, Blundell MP, Morris ME, et al: Improved survival of the diabetic foot: The role of a specialised foot clinic. Q J Med 601:763–771, 1986.
8. Frykberg RG (ed): The High Risk Foot in Diabetes Mellitus. New York, Churchill Livingstone, 1991.
9. Goode PS, Allman RM: The prevention and management of pressure ulcers. Med Clin North Am 73:1511:1524, 1989.
10. Grunfeld C: Diabetic foot ulcers: Etiology, treatment, and prevention. Arch Intern Med 37:123, 1991.
11. Haury B, Rodeheaver G, Vensko J, et al: Debridement: An essential component of traumatic wound care. Am J Surg 135:238–242, 1978.
12. Helm PA, Kowalski MD: Rehabilitation. In Levin ME, O'Neal LW, Bowker JH (eds): The Diabetic Foot, 5th ed. St. Louis, Mosby, 1993.
13. Helm PA, Walker SC, Pullium G: Total contact casting in diabetic patients with neuropathic foot ulcerations. Arch Phys Med Rehabil 65:691–693, 1984.
14. Hobgood E: Conservative therapy of foot abnormalities, infections, and vascular insufficiency. In Davidson JK (ed): Clinical Diabetes Mellitus. New York, Thieme, 1986.
15. Hochberg J, Murray GF: Principles of operative surgery. In Sabiston D (ed): Textbook of Surgery, 14th ed. Philadelphia, W.B. Saunders, 1991.
16. Holewski JJ, Moss KM, Stess RM, et al: Prevalence of foot pathology and lower extremity complications in a diabetic outpatient clinic. J Rehabil Res Dev 26:35–44, 1989.
17. Jacobs RL, Karmody AM: Office care and the insensitive foot. Foot Ankle 2:230–237, 1982.
18. Levin ME, O'Neal LW, Bowker JH (eds): The Diabetic Foot, 5th ed. St. Louis, Mosby, 1993.
19. Levin ME: Pathogenesis and management of diabetic foot lesions. In Levin ME, O'Neal LW, Bowker JH (eds): The Diabetic Foot, 5th ed. St. Louis, Mosby, 1993.
20. Lineaweaver W, Howard R, Soucy D, et al: Topical antimicrobial toxicity. Arch Surg 120:267–270, 1985.
21. Lipsky BA, Pecoraro RE, Larson SA, et al: Outpatient management of uncomplicated lower-extremity infections in diabetic patients. Arch Intern Med 150:790–797, 1990.
22. Lipsky BA, Pecoraro RE, Wheat LJ: The diabetic foot: Soft tissue and bone infection. Infect Dis Clin North Am 4:409–432, 1990.
23. Lydon MJ, Hutchinson JJ, Rippon M, et al: Dissolution of wound coagulum and promotion of granulation tissue under DuoDERM. Wounds 1:95–106, 1989.
24. Myerson M, Papa J, Katulle E, et al: The total-contact cast for management of neuropathic plantar ulceration of the foot. J Bone Joint Surg 74A:261–269, 1992.
25. O'Neal LW: Surgical pathology of the foot and clinicopathologic correlations. In Levin ME, O'Neal LW, Bowker JH (eds): The Diabetic Foot, 5th ed. St. Louis, Mosby, 1993.
26. Paracelsus: Gross Chirurgie, 1536.
27. Peacock EE Jr: Wound Repair, 3rd ed. Philadelphia, W.B. Saunders, 1984.

28. Peterson CG: Perspectives in Surgery. Philadelphia, Lea & Febiger, 1972.
29. Razor BR, Martin LK: Validating sharp wound debridement. J ET Nurs 18:105–110, 1991.
30. Sammarco GJ (ed): The Foot in Diabetes. Philadelphia, Lea & Febiger, 1991.
31. Sapico FL, Witte JL, Canawati HN, et al: The infected foot of the diabetic patient: Quantitative microbiology and analysis of clinical features. Rev Infect Dis 6:S171–S176, 1984.
32. Sharp CS, Bessman AN, Wagner FW Jr, et al: Microbiology of superficial and deep tissue in infected diabetic gangrene. Surg Gynecol Obstet 149:217–219, 1979.
33. Sosenko JM, Kato M, Soto R, et al: Comparison of quantitative sensory-threshold measures for their association with ulceration in diabetic patients. Diabetes Care 13:1057–1061, 1990.
34. Varghese MC, Balin AK, Carter DM, et al: Local environment of chronic wounds under synthetic dressings. Arch Dermatol 122:52–57, 1986.
35. Wagner WF Jr: The treatment of the diabetic foot. Compr Ther 10(4):29–38, 1984.
36. Walton J, Beeson PB, Scott RB (eds): Oxford Companion to Medicine, Vol 2. Birmingham, AL, Gryphon Editions, 1988.
37. Wegener WA, Alavi A: Diagnostic imaging of musculoskeletal infection. Orthop Clin North Am 22:401–418, 1991.
38. Wheat LJ, Allen SD, Henry M, et al: Diabetic foot infections: Bacteriologic analysis. Arch Intern Med 146:1935–1940, 1986.
39. Winter GD: Formation of the scab and the rate of epithelialization of superficial wounds in the skin of the young domestic pig. Nature 193:293–294, 1962.
40. Winter GD, Scales JT: Effects of air drying and dressings on the surface of a wound. Nature 197:91–92, 1963.
41. Witkowski JA, Parish LC: Debridement of cutaneous ulcers: Medical and surgical aspects. Clin Dermatol 9:585–591, 1992.
42. Yao ST, Hobbs JT, Irvine WT: Ankle systolic pressure measurements in arterial disease affecting the lower extremities. Br J Surg 56:676–679, 1969.
43. Young MJ, Cavanaugh PR, Thomas G, et al: The effects of callus removal on dynamic plantar foot pressures in diabetic patients. Diabet Med 9:55–57, 1992.

Chapter 9

BOTULINUM TOXIN INJECTIONS

ROBERT G. SCHWARTZ, M.D.

The popularity of botulinum toxin injections has evolved partly due to botulinum's unique properties as well as its proven efficacy, especially in difficult medical conditions involving neuromuscular abnormalities. This chapter discusses the properties of botulinum, its mechanisms of action, and clinical uses. A comparison of botulinum injections to traditional phenol motor point blocks is also provided, along with a description of the actual technique of botulinum toxin injections.

Botulinum, a toxin produced by *Clostridium botulinum*, an anaerobic organism responsible for food poisoning (botulism), was first discovered in 1897. Since that time, seven immunologically distinct toxins have been identified (types A-G). Only types A, B, and E have been linked to cases of botulism in humans, and an antitoxin is available for each of these types. In the United States, type A is found primarily west of the Mississippi River; type B, east of the Mississippi River, and type E is usually found in shellfish. Types C, D, F, and G are less prevalent.

PROPERTIES OF BOTULINUM TOXIN TYPE A

Botulinum toxin type A (botulinum toxin) is one of the most lethal biologic toxins. Its neurotoxic component has a molecular weight of 150,000. However, the toxin forms a complex with nontoxic proteins and hemagglutinin, creating a much larger molecule.

Cultures of *Clostridium botulinum* are established in a fermenter, grown and harvested by acidification and centrifugation, and further purified and processed for commercial use. Currently, in the United States, botulinum toxin type A is marketed by Allergan Pharmaceuticals in a freeze-dried form known as Botox. Dissolved in normal saline, Botox is clear and odorless. It is harvested from broth culture and purified and microfiltered, resulting in a crystallized toxin that is complexed with nontoxic proteins.[6,12,18,26]

Botulinum toxin for clinical use is supplied in a highly purified freeze-dried and lyophilized state. It must be stored at –5°C and diluted with normal cellulin without preservative before its use. Once reconstituted, it remains effective for about 4 hours at room temperature. Studies are in progress to determine whether reconstituted toxin may be refrozen for later use. It is an expensive agent (about $285 a vial, and two vials are needed for standard treatment of torticollis), and the ability to save unused reconstituted toxin for future use would result in significant cost savings.

The standard method of measuring the potency of commercially available toxin in the United States is derived from a mouse assay. In this assay, one unit of botulinum toxin (mouse unit) is the amount that kills 50% of a 18–20 female Swiss-Webster mice (average weight, 400 gm) (lethal dose [LD_{50}]). The toxin available in the United Kingdom (Dysport) is much more potent than what is available in the United States. One nanogram of the British toxin contains 40 mouse units, whereas 1 nanogram of the American toxin contains 2.5 mouse units. The lethal dose for humans, projected from primate experiments, is approximately 2700 mouse units.

The dosages used in human therapeutic applications are roughly proportional to the mass of the muscle being injected and are much lower than the estimated LD_{50}. Clinical resistance to the effect of subsequent injections of botulinum toxin has been demonstrated in some patients after repeat treatment. This resistance also has been correlated with the presence of antibodies to botulinum toxin detected with bioassays. A cumbersome in vivo mouse neutralization assay has been used to detect serum antibodies to botulinum toxin. The presence of neutralizing (blocking) antibodies is suggested if the mice remain healthy after the injection of both serum and botulinum toxin. When unprotected mice die, a negative assay results. Enzyme-linked immunosorbent assays for the detection of antibodies have been developed, but the specificity and

84

clinical correlation with resistance to treatment of botulinum toxin have not been demonstrated.[22]

In human studies of adult patients injected with 250–400 units of toxin, no systemic side effects have been reported. Single doses of greater than 500 units have produced mild, transient systemic symptoms. No cumulative effects of repeated botulinum injections have been noted locally or in distant muscles. Motor function and electromyographic measurements returned to preinjection levels 12–24 weeks after injection. No evidence seems to suggest chronic denervation following repeat Botox injections. Once Botox has altered the neuromuscular junctions, sprouting of the motor axons occurs, reinnervating the muscle fiber. Clinically significant muscular weakness is noted 1–3 days after intramuscular botulinum injections. The localized weakness usually lasts 6–28 weeks and varies with the site of botulinum toxin injection. Terminal neural axon sprouting occurs with reinnervation of the muscle fibers and return of muscular contractions in 6–12 weeks. It is believed that botulinum toxin does not cross the normal blood-brain barrier. Radionuclide labeling has shown that toxin diffuses approximately 4 cm per injection site. The advantage of such a large diffusion area is that the medication does not have to be placed exactly at the neuromuscular junction. Electromyographic guidance is preferred in order to ascertain that the proper muscle is being injected. However, crisp, clean motor units generated by this muscle demonstrate that needle placement is close enough to obtain the desired effect. As a result of this feature, the desired neurolytic effect can be achieved much more rapidly than with the use of other materials such as phenol or alcohol.

MECHANISM OF ACTION

Botulinum toxin exerts its paralytic action by rapidly and strongly binding to presynaptic cholinergic nerve terminals. It becomes internalized and ultimately inhibits the exocytosis of the acetylcholine by decreasing the frequency of acetylcholine release (Figs. 9-1 and 9-2). The treatment of muscle with botulinum toxin results in an accelerated loss of junctional acetylcholine receptors. The speed of axon destruction depends on the volume of toxin exposure, but generally occurs within 72 hours. This results in a blockade of neural transmission at the motor endplate, caused by inhibition of acetylcholine release from nerve endings and by interference of the uptake of cytoplasmic acetylcholine. A reduction in miniature endplate potentials occurs within a few hours after the injection of botulinum toxin. The muscle becomes functionally denervated, atrophies, and develops extrajunctional acetylcholine receptors. The effects of botulinum injection are not immediate but depend on the supply of acetylcholine from the presynaptic nerve terminal being exhausted via spontaneous release of acetylcholine. Within 2 days after muscle exposure to the toxin, the axon terminal begins to sprout, and the proliferating branches form contacts on the adjacent muscle fibers.

Although it is likely that the clinical effect of botulinum toxin primarily is due to its action at the neuromuscular junction, the toxin can enter into the central nervous system after peripheral administration. It is believed to be transported to the spinal cord by retrograde axonal transport and later can be detected in the appropriate segment of the spinal cord. Intraspinal transfers evidenced by the

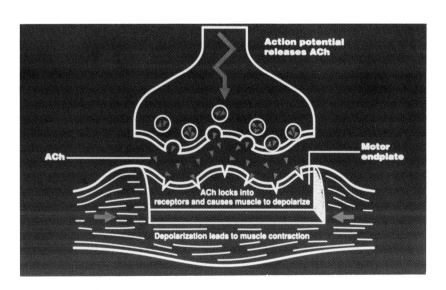

FIGURE 9-1. Normal neuromuscular transmission. (From Allergan, Inc., Irvine, CA, with permission.)

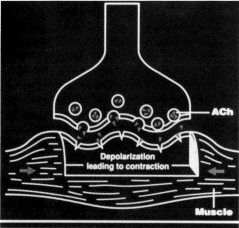

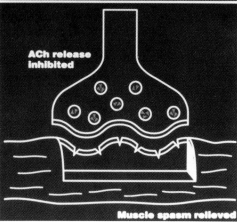

FIGURE 9-2. Action of Botox on the neuromuscular junction. Botox inhibits the release of acetylcholine from nerve endings and interferes with the uptake of cytoplasmic acetylcholine (From Allergan, Inc., Irvine, CA, with permission.)

subsequent appearance of botulinum toxin in the contralateral half segment are believed to occur. In the cord, the toxin appears to block recurrent inhibition mediated by the Renshaw cells.

Other data confirm distant effects of botulinum toxin on neuromuscular transmission and autonomic function. Botulinum toxin injection was found to induce and increase the mean jitter values above normal limits in patients who underwent two sessions of treatment. The onset of these changes has been reported by Garner et al. to occur 3–13 days after injection.[14] In the second session, the dosage of botulinum injection was doubled from that of the usual dosage. An increase of fiber density was recorded on single fiber studies 6 weeks after the treatment. In addition, cardiovascular reflexes showed mild abnormalities in 4 of 5 patients, although they remained asymptomatic. However, in one individual, borderline postural hypotension was indicated by a fall of 20 mmHg in systolic blood pressure during standing. In the autonomic

nervous system, botulinum toxin blocks ganglionic nerve endings, preganglionic sympathetic nerve endings, and postganglionic sympathetic nerve endings in which acetylcholine has been transmitted. A partial antagonistic action and motor response has also been demonstrated in some adrenergic and nonadrenergic atropine-resistant autonomic neuromuscular sites. The effect of botulinum toxin on distant sites is dose-dependent. An additional mechanism of spread to distant sites is presumed to be vascular after local administration.[14,16]

BOTULINUM INJECTIONS VERSUS PHENOL MOTOR POINT BLOCKS

When phenol motor point blocks are used to control a spastic muscle, an electrical stimulator is used as a constant current generator, working at a frequency of approximately 2 pulses per second (see chapter 14). The intensity of current is set at approximately 1 mA, and the duration is varied from 0.1–0.2 ms. Typically, a 5% aqueous phenol solution is injected. However, 2% and 3% solutions also have been advocated. In most centers, it is easy to obtain phenol in its clinical useful form.[4,13,25] The amount of phenol solution required for an effective motor point block ranges from 0.5–5 ml per site. Typically, one to three sites per muscle group are injected.

With phenol blocks, a direct current stimulator and a 22-gauge 2- or 3-inch insulated spinal needle are used to accurately locate the nerve fiber neuromuscular junction. The technique used with a phenol motor point block causes it to become a time-consuming and often painful procedure. Precise localization of motor points with a surface stimulator is commonly performed but is often difficult. Also, because of the cost of phenol, judicious selection of injection sites is important. Because of practicalities involving this procedure, its frequency of use has diminished in the clinical setting.

Botulinum toxin injections have been received favorably by physicians over phenol motor point blocks. The procedure can be carried out with a typical electromyography machine and does not require exact needle placement in the neuromuscular junction. In fact, rather than targeting the nerve in the neuromuscular junction, as with phenol motor point blocks, botulinum injection is directed toward the muscle belly as the target itself.

As in the case of phenol motor point blocks, the Teflon-coated monopolar cannula is used for botulinum injection. A surface electrode is sufficient for a reference and ground. With botulinum toxin, depending on the site that is to be injected, the size of the cannula varies. In small ocular muscles, a 25-gauge, 1-inch cannula is used; for larger muscles such as the trapezius, a 26-gauge, 1- or 1½-inch cannula.

Although patients may complain of pain after botulinum injection—as they do with phenol—the amount of pain experienced with botulinum injection is no different than that from standard electromyographic examinations.

CLINICAL USES

Botulinum toxin has been found to have value in the treatment of various neurologic and ophthalmologic disorders. It is approved by the FDA as a therapeutic agent in patients with strabismus, blepharospasm, hemifacial spasm, and other facial nerve disorders. It has been endorsed by the National Institutes of Health, American Academy of Neurology, and the American Medical Association's Department of Drug Divisions in Toxicology for peripheral and central nervous system disorders where hypertonic spastic conditions exist (Fig. 9-3).[23]

SPECIFIC INDICATIONS

Extraocular Disorders

Botulinum toxin was first used to weaken extraocular muscles. The toxin was later introduced for the treatment of strabismus as an alternative to conventional incisional surgery. Follow-up studies up to 5 years after the injection revealed that 85% of the patients available for reassessment had satisfactory improvement of their condition. Side effects, including presbyopia and secondary vertical deviations, are usually transient and do not result in concomitant amblyopia. Strabismus, lateral rectus palsy, and nystagmus have all been treated with botulinum toxin injections.

Dysphonia

The American Academy of Otolaryngology–Head and Neck Surgery has made a statement of the clinical usefulness of botulinum toxin for the treatment of spasmodic dysphonia. In this condition, patients present with a choked and constrained voice pattern with break in vocalization. The original dystonia has been characterized as a slowly developing voice disorder with increasing vocal fatigue, spastic constriction of the throat muscles, and pain around the larynx. Patients sound as if they are trying to talk while being choked. The voice strain and voice arrest are believed to derive from hyperadduction of the true and false vocal cords; however, 10% of patients will present with the abductor form. In this form of phonation, the cord will have spasmodic motion of the posterior cricoarytenoid muscles as well as several other of the original muscles.

Botulinum injection also represents an alternative to recurrent laryngeal nerve resection when return of dysphonia from continued vocal cord paralysis occurs despite previous nerve resection.

Facial Disorders

Other disorders that have been treated in the cranial region with botulinum toxin include oral mandibular dystonia, meige syndrome, and hemifacial spasm. These conditions involve various muscles in the face, either alone or in association with ocular findings.

In the treatment of blepharospasm (Fig. 9-4), hemifacial spasm, meige syndrome and the oral mandibular dystonias, various studies have documented relief of spasm ranging from 85–94%. The duration of a spasm-free interval as well as the incidence of ptosis, diplopia, or facial weakness is dose dependent. When an additional 20–25 units are injected into each muscle, there is a marked increase in the incidence of side effects but only a small increase in the duration of spasm-free intervals. Spasm-free intervals range from 3–5 months, and the effect is reproducible with reinjection. For patients with oral mandibular findings alone, the success rate has been lower (47%); however, this technique remains the best treatment for this condition. Generally, spasms diminish only as long as the muscles are clinically weak, because uninjected muscles remain strong and exhibit spasms.[2,5,15,20,24,29]

Cervical Dystonia

Botulinum injection is frequently used in patients with cervical dystonia (spasmodic torticollis). In this condition, the involved neck muscles cause a pattern of repetitive, clonic (spasmodic), and tonic (sustained) head movement. Abnormal posture of the head as a result of twisting (torticollis), tilting one's shoulder (lateral collis), flexing (antrocollis), or extending (retrocollis) the neck is usually present (Table 9-1). The majority of patients with cervical dystonia have a combination of these abnormal postures. Approximately one-third of patients with cervical dystonia have involvement of a contiguous body part, such as the oral mandibular region, shoulder, and arm.

The efficacy and safety of botulinum toxin in the treatment of cervical dystonia have been demonstrated in several controlled and open studies. A total of 61–92% of patients have reported improvement after the injection of botulinum toxin. Furthermore, 93% had marked relief of neck pain. The average length between the injection and onset of improvement (and muscle atrophy) was 1 week, and the average duration of maximal improvement was 3½ months. The total duration of improvement, however, was about 6 weeks longer. Most patients required injection every 3 months. Some patients received benefit for only weeks and others for as many as 4–5 months.

Complications with injections for cervical dystonia include dysphagia, neck weakness, nausea, generalized malaise, and pain. The pain is the most frequent side effect secondary to the local injection. The pain is more severe in individuals in whom botulinum toxin is injected directly into or around a peripheral nerve.

The use of electromyographic assistance during the injections has minimized the likelihood of these side effects (with the exception of weakness). At least one study also has demonstrated that a lower

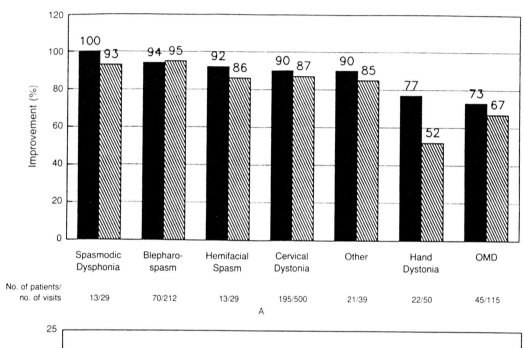

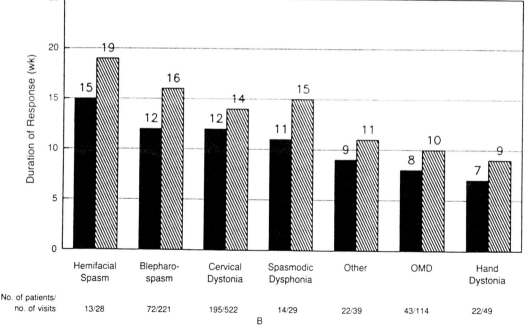

FIGURE 9-3. Effects of treatment with botulinum toxin. Solid bars represent patients who improved; hatched bars represent percentage of treatment sessions at which improvement was made. (From Jankovic J, Brin MF: Therapeutic uses of boutlinum toxin. N Engl J Med 324:1192, 1991, with permission.)

total dosage of botulinum toxin is required and a better clinical effect occurs as a result of an improved ability to effectively identify and treat the deep muscles electromyographically.[10]

Abnormal excessive weakness following injection begins to occur within 3 days. Patients usually report immediate change in strength as well as dystonia after injection. Usually, weakness is maximal 2–3 weeks after injection. Appropriate supportive measures are required for the muscle groups that become weak. Cervical collars are frequently used when the neck musculature is involved, and minor changes in daily diet to prevent aspiration may be required if too high a dosage of toxin is injected in the area of the anterior strap muscles. Typically, these side effects are temporary and resolve over a period of weeks, leaving the desired clinical effect to last for months.[11,20,23]

Focal Dystonias

One of the most rewarding changes associated with botulinum injections can be observed when treating focal dystonias. Focal dystonias, either fixed or task-specific, are often disabling and usually unresponsive to medical therapy. Several groups have noted the efficacy of botulinum toxin in the treatment of occupational cramps and limited task-specific dystonias. Affected muscles are identified clinically and by recording with electromyography from needle electrodes at rest and during performance of tasks that precipitate these abnormal postures. Subjective improvement lasting for 1–4 months has been reported in 82% of patients. The major side effect is transient focal weakness; it has been noted in 53% of patients injected with the toxin.

Writer's cramp is the most common form of focal dystonia in the general population and frequently involves the flexor pollicis longus, flexor digitorum profundus, extensor indicis, extensor hallucis longus, extensor carpi ulnaris, and the flexor carpi radialis muscles. The first dorsal interosseous and abductor digiti minimi are other muscles that are frequently involved (Fig. 9-5).

Focal dystonia of the limbs has been reported in reflex sympathetic dystrophy, musicians with movement disorders, and in overuse syndromes. Equinovarus changes in the foot and involvement in other distal lower extremity muscles also may present as focal dystonias.[7,8,27,30,33,34]

Tremors

Another indication for botulinum toxin injections is tremors (Fig. 9-6). In a study in which 51 treatments were given to patients with disabling tremors classified as dystonic, essential, a combination of dystonic and essential, parkinsonian, peripherally

FIGURE 9-4. Blepharospasm involving lower facial and neck contractions. (Courtesy of David R. Jordan, MD, Ottawa, Ontario, Canada.)

induced, and midbrain, 67% of patients improved with the injection of botulinum. EMG recordings showed decreased amplitude of motor units after treatment with botulinum toxin. The most common side effects were weakness and dysphagia.[22]

Additional Uses

Additional indications for botulinum injections include stroke-related hemiplegia, spinal cord injury, multiple sclerosis, cerebral palsy, and detrusor sphincter dyssynergia. In contrast to focal and segmental dystonias, which are usually idiopathic, the majority of patients with hemidystonia have an identifiable etiology such as head trauma, stroke, arteriovenous malformation, tumor, encephalitis, or other pathology affecting the contralateral basal ganglia.[1,3,28,32]

New uses for botulinum toxin injections include the treatment of painful conditions that result from

TABLE 9-1. Muscles Involved in Cervical Dystonia*

Torticollis	Ipsilateral splenius, contralateral SCM
Head tilt	Ipsilateral SCM, splenius capitis, scalene complex, levator scapulae, posterior vertebrals
Shoulder elevation	Ipsilateral trapezius and levator scapulae
Retrocollis	Splenius capitis, upper trapezius, deep postvertebrals
Anterocollis	SCM, both sets scalene, submental muscles, longus capitis, longus colli

*Special thanks to Mitchell F. Brin, MD, and Judith Blazer at WE MOVE–"Worldwide Education and Awareness for Movement Disorders"–for providing this information.

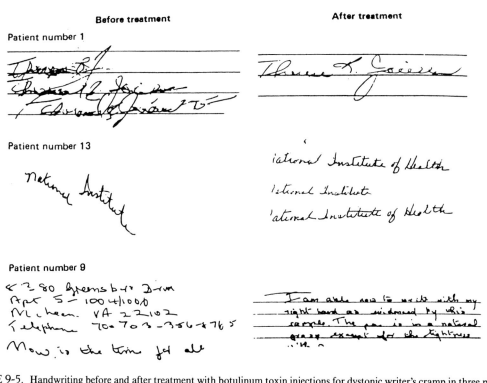

FIGURE 9-5. Handwriting before and after treatment with botulinum toxin injections for dystonic writer's cramp in three patients. (From Cohen L: Treatment of focal dystonias of the hand with botulinum toxin injection. Neurol Neurosurg Psychiatry 52:360, 1989, with permission.)

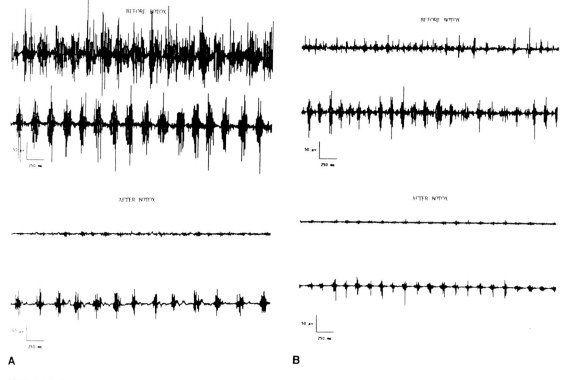

A   B

FIGURE 9-6. Reduction in tremor amplitude after Botox injections into (A) forearm muscles in a patient with postural hand tremor and (B) splenius capitis muscles in a patient with lateral head oscillation. (From Jankovic J, Schwartz K: Botulinum toxin treatment of tremors. Neurology 41:1187, 1991, with permission.)

prolonged muscle spasm and contractures. Other indications are chronic pain especially in the postoperative back, and myofascial pain. Thoracic outlet syndrome associated with spasm of the scalene musculature can be relieved with botulinum injection, which results in significant improvement in peripheral blood flow. Botulinum toxin should be used as a last resort in these patients and require careful patient selection.[19]

Botulinum toxin has been used in children even though the FDA's statement of efficacy applies to individuals no younger than 12. Abnormal tone as a result of cerebral palsy is the most common condition treated. A generalized form of dystonia can occur with childhood onset, as in dystonia musculorum deformans, which also may be treated with botulinum injections.[3,9,17,21,28]

CONTRAINDICATIONS

Botulinum toxin injection is contraindicated in patients receiving aminoglycoside or spectinomycin antibiotics, known sensitivity to botulinum, myasthenic syndrome, myasthenia gravis, motor neuron disease, upper eyelid apraxia, and ptosis. A paucity of data exists regarding the use of botulinum toxin during pregnancy.[1] In one report of nine patients treated during pregnancy (dose unspecified), one gave birth prematurely, but this complication was not thought to be related to the botulinum.

PROCEDURAL DETAILS

Prior to injection with botulinum toxin, patients should be notified of all potential complications. Although these complications may not occur, it is always best to cover every potential effect that could occur, especially weakness. Many clinicians find it useful to photograph or videotape patients before, during, and after treatment with botulinum toxin in order to have a pictorial history of improved function as a result of the treatment. It is also helpful for patients to evaluate their pre- and posttreatment outcomes. Most patients that receive botulinum injections are told beforehand that outcomes are variable. On a statistical basis, an average of 85% of individuals are pleased with the results. As long as patients are notified of potential weakness prior to the injection, they are not particularly disturbed if weakness occurs. Most patients are appreciative for any benefit that results from the botulinum injection therapy. The only true concern becomes how long the effect will last.

While superficial muscles are accessible for injection with a tuberculosis syringe with a 25-gauge, ⅝-inch needle, most practitioners prefer to inject with a monopolar Teflon-coated cannula and identify the muscle electromyographically prior to injection.

With standard reference and ground electrodes, the clinician can use electrodiagnostic equipment that is readily available on the market today. For the smaller facial muscles, a 30-gauge, 1-inch cannula is preferred; for larger muscles, a 26-gauge, 1½-inch cannula. All injections are intramuscular. If alcohol is used to cleanse the skin, it should be allowed to dry because it can deactivate the toxin.

Once the needle is inserted into the muscle, the practitioner looks for the classic dystonic firing of the muscle group involved on EMG. In cases of spastic dystonia associated with hemiplegia or other central nervous system pathology, excessive firing of motor unit action potentials helps to identify the muscle groups involved.

Exact dosages of botulinum toxin for specific diagnoses have not been well established, but general guidelines do exist. It is preferable to underdose an individual with botulinum toxin during the first treatment and repeat the treatment within 30 days should the desired effect not occur. The dosage may be increased proportionately until the desired clinical effect is obtained.

In the eye, 25 units injected into the orbicularis oculi and corrugator muscles is an appropriate starting point. This may be increased up to 75 units per eye, as required, in order to achieve the desired clinical effect. It may take two or three office visits to achieve this effect. A dilution of 5.0 units per 0.1 ml is preferred. To achieve this dose, 2 ml of preservative-free saline are injected into the 100-unit vial of botulinum. Complications with these ocular injections may include tearing, irritation, paralysis, eye opening, and ptosis.

For hemifacial spasms, a 30-gauge needle is used. However, 4 ml of preservative-free saline is added to the 100-unit vial of botulinum to achieve a concentration of 2.5 units per 0.1 ml. Facial weakness can occur with just a few more units over the therapeutic dose, which may be as little as 20 or 25 units. As with all botulinum toxin injections, titration upward until the clinical effect is achieved is advised.

When larger muscles are to be injected, as in cervical dystonia (spasmodic torticollis), a 26-gauge, 1½-inch cannula is used and 2 ml of preservative-free saline is added to a 100-unit vial of botulinum to achieve a 5-unit per 0.1 ml concentration. These muscles typically require a minimum of 35-40 units and as much as 300 units in order to achieve the desired effect. It is not uncommon to use 50–75 units per muscle to achieve a therapeutic response; however, this depends entirely on the patient (Table 9-2). Typically, 200 units per session is the starting therapeutic dose. If the desired effect is not achieved, an additional 100 units is given in 30 days. The Food and Drug Administration does not approve the use of more than 300 units per month. However,

TABLE 9-2. Common Doses of Botox When Injected into Neck Muscles for Cervical Dystonia*

Muscle	Units (U)	Range (U)
SCM	50	15–75
Trapezius	75	50–100
Splenius capitis	75	50–150
Levator scapulae	50	25–100
Semispinalis capitis	75	50–150
Longissimus capitis	75	50–150

*Special thanks to Mitchell F. Brin, MD, and Judith Blazer at WE MOVE–"Worldwide Education and Awareness for Movement Disorders"–for providing this information.

500 units have been given in the clinical setting without ill effect in individual cases.

Important cervical structures to avoid during botulinum injection into the cervical muscles include the brachial plexus, carotid sheath, and greater occipital nerve. The pharynx, esophagus, pleura and apex of the lung also should be avoided. Depending on the site that is being injected, knowledge of regional anatomy that may be affected by such needle placement should be carefully considered.[15,19,20,31]

If individual muscles are being treated that have spastic dystonia, 200 units per muscle may be required to achieve a therapeutic response. It would not be uncommon to begin at 100 units, for example, with the gastrocnemius soleus muscle and increase the dose as needed. In cases of generalized spasticity, it becomes clear that treatment with botulinum toxin injection is difficult, if not impossible. If, however, focal muscle groups can be identified as the primary generator of a diffuse spastic reaction or for cases in which individual muscle groups are explicitly involved in function and hygiene, botulinum injections may be helpful.

Treatments are repeated as necessary and should be individualized among patients. Usually 3 months of clinical benefit can be expected from the botulinum toxin. The duration of benefit is variable, lasting only weeks in some individuals and as long as 5 or 6 months in others. Periodic assessment of function and response should be done for each patient as medically necessary.

It is essential that patients be as relaxed as possible for their injections. This requires proper positioning so that the practitioner can be certain that the muscles that are contracting are not doing so in a normal postural response to their current positioning. This is especially true if one is having difficulty obtaining the classic burst of rhythmic firing pattern seen with dystonia. If individuals do not demonstrate dystonic firing of individual muscles during needle placement, tricks that initiate their dystonia may be sought. Patients frequently can diminish their dystonia through tricks, but they also can initiate dystonia through different body movements or postures. This procedure is always patient-specific and requires explicit knowledge of the patient and his or her particular characteristics.

The presence of family members is not required during the procedure. However, many patients feel more comfortable knowing that someone will drive them home, especially if it is a patient's first botulinum injection.

In patients who have taken nonsteroidal drugs or are taking anticoagulants, the possibility of increased bruising at the injection site should be considered but is not a contraindication to the procedure. It is quite helpful to needle muscles that are not obviously involved from the clinical examination alone. Frequently, the muscles will be firing in a dystonic fashion and should be injected. While some individuals achieve an excellent response when the entire dosage is injected at one site, spreading the dosage among three sites is widely believed to provide a more effective response.

Due to the high cost of the medication, it can be useful to schedule more than one patient at a time for botulinum injections. Any medication left over from one patient can be given to the next. Once the medication has been prepared, it must be used within 4 hours. The vial should not be agitated, and the vacuum-sealed valve should draw the preservative-free saline into it from the prefilled syringe. If this does not occur, the vial should be returned to the manufacturer and not used.

POSTPROCEDURE CARE

Muscle relaxants or acetaminophen may be given to patients after treatment if any discomfort occurs over the ensuring 24–48 hours. Patients rarely require stronger analgesics.

A follow-up appointment in 2–3 weeks after the first time that an individual receives botulinum injection therapy is quite helpful to determine if an adequate dosage was given. A telephone call to the patient 3–4 days after the injection also will help determine if the desired response is likely to occur or if there are adverse side effects as a result of the injection. This approach also results in patient reassurance, which is usually appreciated.

CONCLUSION

Botulinum injection therapy offers the clinician a powerful tool in the treatment of individuals with movement disorders and painful conditions associated with dystonia and hyperactive muscle tone. These injections can dramatically improve patient function and enhance the rehabilitation program for individuals whose impairments are disabling.

When the injections are properly used, the side effects can be minimized and the desired effect achieved in a most gratifying manner for both patient and practitioner.

REFERENCES

1. American Academy of Neurology, Assessment Subcommittee: The clinical usefulness of botulinum toxin A in treating neurologic disorders. Report of the Therapeutics and Technology Assessment Subcommittee, 1990.
2. American Academy of Otolaryngology–Head and Neck Surgery: Physician's statement on the clinical usefulness of botulinum toxin and treatment as Monosphonia, 1990.
3. American Medical Association Drug Evaluations and Subscription, Vol. 3.
4. Awad E: Phenol block for control of hip flexor and adductors spasticity. Arch Phys Med Rehabil 554–557, 1972.
5. Blitzer A: Botulinum toxin injection for the treatment of oral mandibular dystonia. Rhinolaryngology 98:93–97, 1989.
6. Chesleff S: Motive action of botulinum toxin and the effect of drug antagonist. Adv Psychopharmacol 3:35–43, 1979.
7. Cohen L: Treatment of focal dystonias of the hand with botulinum toxin injection. J Neurol Neurosurg Psychiatry 52:355–363, 1989.
8. Cole RA, Cohen LG, Hallett M: Treatment of musician's cramp with botulinum toxin. Med Probl Perform Art 6:137–143, 1991.
9. Cooper F, Riklon R: Dystonia musculorum deformans. American Academy of Physical Medicine and Rehabilitation, p 607.
10. Cormella C: Botulinum toxin injection for spasmodic torticollis: Increased magnitude of benefit with electromyographic assistance. Neuralgia 42:878–882, 1992.
11. Cormella C: Dysphagia after botulinum toxin injections for spasmodic torticollis; radiologic findings. Neuralgia 42:1307–1310, 1992.
12. Drachman DB: Effect of botulinum toxin on speed of skeletal muscle contraction. Am J Physiol 216:1453–1455, 1982.
13. Felsenthal G: Pharmacology of phenol in peripheral nerve blocks: A review. Arch Phys Med Rehabil 55:1, 19xx.
14. Garner CG: Time course of distant effects of local injection of botulinum toxin. Mov Disord 8:33–37, 1993.
15. Geller B: Botulinum toxin therapy and hemifacial spasms: Clinical and electrophysiological studies. Muscle Nerve 716–722, 1989.
16. Girlamda P: Botulinum toxin therapy: Effects of neuromuscular transmission and autonomic nervous systems. J Neurol Neurosurg Psychiatry 55:844–845, 1992.
17. Gormley M: Botulinum toxin disease in children. Presented at the 55th Annual Meeting of the American Academy of Physical Medicine and Rehabilitation, Miami, October 31–November 4, 1993.
18. Holland R: Nerve growth and botulinum toxin plays in muscles. Neural Sci 6:1157–1179, 19xx.
19. Hughes HF: Botulinum toxin in the treatment of post-traumatic thoracic outlet syndrome [poster]. Annual Meeting of the American Academy of Electrodiagnostic Medicine, Ralston, SC, October 1992.
20. Jankovic J: Botulinum toxin for cranial cervical dystonia. Neurology 37:616–663, 1989.
21. Jankovic J: Botulinum toxin therapy for focal dystonia. Med Probl Perform Art 122–124, 1991.
22. Jankovic J: Botulinum toxic treatment of tremors. Neurology 41:1185–1188, 1991.
23. Jankovic J: Therapeutic uses of botulinum toxin. N Engl J Med 324:1186–1194, 1991.
24. Jordan DR, Anderson RL: Essential blepharospasm: Focal Points 1988: Clinical Modules for Ophthalmologists. Vol. 6, Module 6, 1988.
25. Khalili AA: Peripheral nerve block with phenol in the management of spasticity. GM 200:103–105, June 26, 1967. 3–16 Jan 1974.
26. Lange DJ: Distant effects of local injection of botulinum toxin. Muscle Nerve 10:552–555a, 1987.
27. Lockwood E: Reflex sympathetic dystrophy after overuse: The possible relationship with focal dystonia. Med Probl Perform Art 4:114–117, 1989.
28. NIH Consensus Statement: Botulinum toxin. 8:8, 1990.
29. Ophthalmic Procedures Assessment Committee of the American Academy of Ophthalmology: Botulinum toxin therapy of eye muscle disorders, safety and effectiveness. San Francisco, American Academy of Ophthalmology, September, 1989.
30. Riderst J: Writer's cramp with botulinum toxin injections from movement disorders. 6:55–59, 1991.
31. Rivner M: Botulinum injection in training sessions. Department of Neurology, Medical College of Georgia, Augusta, GA.
32. Rome S: Use of botulinum toxin in the treatment of spasticity in large muscles [poster]. Presented at the 54th Annual Meeting of the American Academy of Physical Medicine and Rehabilitation, San Francisco, November 13–17, 1992.
33. Schwartzman R: The movement disorder of reflex sympathetic dystrophy. Neurology 40:57–61, 1990.
34. Yoshimura D: Botulinum toxin therapy for limb dystonias. Neuralgia 627–630, 1992.

Chapter 10

REMOVABLE RIGID DRESSING FOR BELOW-KNEE AMPUTEES

RANDALL SMITH, M.D.
RUSSELL R. BOND, D.O.

The removable rigid dressing (RRD) is an outgrowth of the immediate postsurgical prosthesis and rigid dressing. It has many of the advantages and benefits of its predecessors and can be placed postoperatively by the physiatrist. It also may be removed and replaced by a surgeon who wishes to inspect the wound, or by the patient when bathing and conditioning the skin. The RRD is easily made by a physician or therapist, and the cost of materials is minimal. The physician will find that using the RRD is probably the most convenient way to protect and shape the residual limb before fitting the prosthesis.

The concept of the immediate postsurgical prosthesis was developed by Berlemont in the late 1950s[1] and was introduced by Weise at an international conference in Germany in 1966.[16] Dr. Weise was invited to present his method to physicians in the United States. Subsequently, the concept was accepted by many American physicians interested in amputation surgery. Dr. Ernest Burgess and others have done an excellent job of describing the manufacture of the immediate postsurgical prosthesis and its use in clinical practice.[2,3]

DEVELOPMENT OF THE REMOVABLE RIGID DRESSING

Weise's postsurgical prosthesis is composed of a plaster socket made over the residual limb in the operating room with provisions made for wound drainage, relief of pressure over bony prominences, suspension, and weightbearing. The socket is supracondylar, enabling it to hold the knee in extension. A metal pylon with a prosthetic foot is attached in the operating room a day or so after surgery, when weightbearing begins. Typically, prosthetists are involved in making the immediate postsurgical prosthesis. Considerable skill is required to prevent

injury and to assure that the patient will be comfortable under weightbearing conditions. Many reports have documented the safety and benefits of this procedure.[2,5,7] Benefits include wound healing, comfort, shaping of residual limb, early ambulation, and a positive psychologic outlook with regard to rehabilitation.[3]

Omission of the foot and pylon results in a rigid plaster dressing extending above the knee. This dressing is not easily removable but can be placed by the surgeon in the operating room and replaced on a weekly basis in the clinic or on the ward. The prosthetist is not necessarily required because there is no pylon or foot to align. The dressing can be used when a patient is nonambulatory or when there is concern that weightbearing may injure the residual limb. Cummings evaluated 153 patients fitted with the rigid dressing.[4] He felt that early ambulation and discharge from the hospital were "fringe benefits" for certain capable patients but that the rigid dressing might be most valuable in the elderly, senile, disoriented, or diabetic patient with potential to ambulate. Benefits of wound healing, edema control, protection, and comfort of the residual limb were justification enough to use a rigid dressing for all patients. Mooney et al. reported successful management of below-knee vascular amputees with a thin plaster dressing that was not designed to bear weight but to control edema and prevent knee contracture.[8] A plaster cast with pylon was added later. The interval between surgery and use of the prosthesis was less than 6 weeks in unilateral amputees. Wound healing and eventual level of function were not lowered. Other studies in vascular amputees have clearly demonstrated improved wound healing with nonweightbearing rigid plaster dressing.[9,11]

Regardless of the documented success of postsurgical rigid plaster dressings, many surgeons are

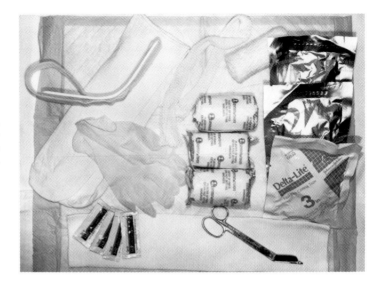

FIGURE 10-1. Materials needed to fabricate the RRD: Supracondylar cuff (*upper left*), one-ply socks (*left*), plaster and fiberglass casting materials (*right*), scissors, gloves, and cast padding.

reluctant to use this device. Physiatrists often find themselves beginning to manage the care of the amputee long before wound healing is complete. Most surgeons have no objection to the application of a rigid dressing at this time provided that it is possible to inspect the wound.

In 1977, Dr. Yeongchi Wu developed a technique for making a below-the-knee rigid dressing that was removable.[17] One of his patients who had fared well with a rigid dressing developed sores on the residual limb after the rigid dressing had been removed and an ace wrap applied.[18] The RRD that resulted was made of plaster and extended just below the knee. It was covered by tubular stockinette that was held in place above the knee by a supracondylar cuff.

This dressing could be made within an hour by a physiatrist or therapist; it provided protection for the wound and the residual limb; it was safe and effective in shaping the residual limb; and it allowed frequent inspection of the wound. It is for these reasons that the RRD has become a particularly useful procedure in the postoperative management of the below-knee amputee.

FABRICATION OF THE REMOVABLE RIGID DRESSING

The materials needed (Fig. 10-1) and a step-by-step technique for making the rigid dressing are outlined in Tables 10-1 and 10-2 and discussed below. Our technique generally follows that of Wu.[17,18] Variations in the technique are presented at the end of this section.

Padding

With the postoperative rigid dressing, the bony prominences are protected with felt padding, but in the RRD, these areas are protected by relief that is provided by placing cotton padding over these areas before applying the plaster. The padding is removed after the plaster dries, leaving the proper relief on the inside of the dressing. The same principle is used to prevent any proximal narrowing of the dressing. If any proximal part of the dressing is smaller in circumference than the more distal portion of the residual limb, the dressing will not be removable. It is almost always necessary to pad the area below the medial tibial flare. Consequently, a bulbous distal end will no longer prevent removal of the rigid dressing.

The cotton padding is placed between two layers of socks—either one-ply stump socks or tube socks. The outer sock adheres to the plaster and is removed with the rigid dressing.

Applying the Plaster

Two 4-inch rolls of fast-set plaster are typically used to make the rigid shell. The plaster is soaked in water and applied gently over the residual limb. Care must be taken to avoid ridges and to avoid

TABLE 10-1. Materials and Equipment

One-ply stump socks or tube socks with the elastic removed, two each

Cotton cast padding

Two rolls of 4-inch fast-set plaster *or*
Two rolls of 2-inch synthetic casting tape

Four-inch tubular stockinette, about 18 inches long *or*
Elastic tubular netting, size 7, 18 inches long

Layers of 3-inch Hexcelite, 12–18 inches long *or*
2- to 3-inch wide casting tape

Bandage scissors
Rubber gloves
Lubricating jelly

TABLE 10-2. Making the Rigid Removable
Dressing Step by Step

Preparation
1. Cover limb with snug-fitting stump sock or tube sock.
2. Place 3–4 layers of cast padding over the fibular head and along the shaft of the tibia. Place extra padding over the distal end of the tibia.
3. Fill the depression below the medial tibial flare and make circumferential warps, if necessary, to produce a more or less conical shape.
4. Roll a stump sock or tube sock over the padding.
5. Pull up on the socks and secure them proximally with tape.

Manufacture
1. Wet the plaster in the package.
2. Roll the plaster circumferentially below the patella anteriorly and below hamstring tendons posteriorly.
3. Roll the plaster in a figure 8 pattern or in back and forth layers to cover the distal end.
4. Trim the outer sock 2 inches above the proximal trim line and fold back over the edge of the plaster; secure this with another wrap of plaster.
5. Mark the midpatellar line.
6. Allow 10 minutes to dry.
7. Remove and inspect inside of the dressing for bumps or ridges. The padding is discarded.

Suspension
1. Soften layers of hexcelite in 71°C water and cut to length. Reheat hexcelite and mold to supracondylar area, protecting the skin with plastic wrap *or*

   Fold three or four layers of 3-inch synthetic casting tape lengthwise to the appropriate length and mold over the supracondylar area as noted in the text.
2. Tie a knot in the bottom of the stockinette or elastic netting, and pull it over the dressing and residual limb to above the knee.
3. Apply the cuff over the stockinette and then fold the stockinette back over the cuff.

Inspection and Training
1. Look for bumps and ridges on the inner surface.
2. Look for reddened areas on the residual limb after 30 minutes and throughout the first day.
3. Ask amputee to demonstrate donning and doffing of the RRD.

compressing the cotton padding. The dressing is extended to just below the patella anteriorly, while posteriorly the trim line needs to be lower, making room for the hamstring tendons during knee flexion.

It is advisable to start at the proximal trim line and wrap distally. Covering the distal end of the residual limb is tricky. Going back and forth over this area and then securing the folded ends of the loops with circumferential wraps works well. One may also cut strips to reinforce the distal end, which is necessary if weightbearing is planned. The one-ply cast sock upon which the plaster was rolled is folded back over the proximal edge of the dressing, trimmed, and secured with more plaster. Ten minutes are allowed for drying. The dressing should be marked anteriorly, in line with the patella so the amputee can properly replace the RRD.

Newer materials such as synthetic casting tape have also been used to make RRDs. The use of these materials and modifications of the basic technique are discussed below.

Suspension

The RRD is suspended by covering the dressing with stockinette. A knot is tied on one end of the stockinette, and the other end is pulled up over the knee. A supracondylar cuff is placed over the stockinette just above the femoral condyles, and the upper end of the stockinette is folded back over the cuff. Elastic tubular netting that is used to secure surgical dressings makes a good substitute for the stockinette and provides some distal pressure on the distal end of the limb.

The cuff is usually made from a thermoplastic material such as hexcelite. Several layers are warmed in a hydroculator and cut in strips approximately 3 inches wide and long enough to fit around the supracondylar area of the thigh but not touch or overlap posteriorly. The cuff is molded with the hands as it cools. Pressure with the palm of the hand just above the medial femoral condyle makes a depression in the cuff that will help to prevent the cuff from slipping distally. Fiberglass cast tape also may be used. In both cases, the edges need trimming to eliminate sharp corners. Traditionally, the cuff is secured by a Velcro closure attached to the cuff between the layers of hexcelite. A band of Velfoam wrapped around the cuff and fastened with Velcro hook material also works well and is simple. Most occupational therapy departments will have the above supplies available (see Table 10-1).

Inspection

Even clinicians experienced in rolling plaster should not expect to make a perfect dressing on the first try. Thus, inspection of the dressing is an important step. The inside should be free of ridges or bumps, especially over bony areas. The dressing should slide on and off easily. It is imperative that the dressing be removed and the skin inspected after 30 minutes of wear and every 2 hours the first day. The amputee must be taught how to don and doff the rigid dressing, then observed to assure independence.

Variations and Modifications

Several clinicians have used synthetic casting tape to make the rigid dressing.[6,14,18] Gandhavadi points out that the porous nature of the casting tape permits good aeration of the residual limb area to prevent buildup of warmth and moisture under the dressing.[6] The light weight makes the dressing easier to suspend and less cumbersome, while the strength of the casting tape makes it suitable for some weightbearing.

When making the rigid dressing with casting tape, two 2-inch rolls will usually suffice. More care needs to be taken, however, to avoid bumps or ridges on the inside of the dressing. These can usually be avoided if the cast tape is applied to the residual limb without wetting it first. The dressing is subsequently moistened and smoothed on the residual limb by rubbing with any type of water-based cream or gel. Surgical lubricating jelly or even electrode gels are usually available and work well.

Smith and Hof have used a rigid dressing made of fiberglass cast tape that covers the end of the residual limb only.[14] It does not extend to the patellar area or even the head of the fibula. It is somewhat simpler to make but still provides protection and shrinkage for the distal end of the limb. Another option by Swanson[15] is the use of below-the-knee polyethylene semirigid dressing, which is usually done by the prosthetist using direct molded techniques. The socket is flexible, and the patient also uses a stump shrinker. The advantages include that it is lighter weight, nonporous and easier to clean when drainage occurs, and comfortable to flex (Fig. 10-2).

USES FOR THE REMOVABLE RIGID DRESSING

Wound Management

The first and foremost obvious use of the RRD is to cover the surgical wound in the operating room. In this case, the wound is covered with a nonabsorbable dressing. The removable rigid dressing is made over a sterile stump sock. The RRD protects the wound, holds soft tissue in place, and prevents edema in much the same way that the nonremovable dressing does. Alternatively, the rigid dressing can be applied at the time of the first cast change when the nonremovable rigid dressing is removed.

Many surgeons, however, do not wish to apply a rigid dressing in the operating room, opting for a traditional soft dressing with which they are familiar. Fortunately, the RRD can provide the benefits of shaping, protecting, and providing comfort to the residual limb, even when applied several days after surgery. As a consequence, the RRD is useful for the clinician in the postoperative management of the patient.

Because the RRD allows examination of the wound, it is well accepted by most surgeons. Its removability also allows physicians and nursing staff to check for pressure ulcers that may arise from improper manufacture or placement of the RRD in a patient with poor sensation.

Almost all patients and staff can learn quickly how to don and doff the RRD and apply the cuff

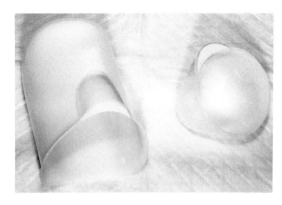

FIGURE 10-2. Two separate removable rigid dressings. Note the differences in length.

suspension (Figs. 10-3, 10-4). The same cannot be said for wrapping with elastic bandages, which, more often than not, are applied incorrectly. Proximal circumferential constriction is common, but even more dangerous is pressure over the tibial crest.[18] Sores may develop within hours in patients who have lost pain sensation.

Protection

The importance of protecting the residual limb cannot be overemphasized. Rarely, an agitated patient will traumatize the residual limb in the early postoperative period. When serious trauma occurs, however, it usually happens after the amputee begins to transfer from bed to chair or after he or she begins to walk. Cases of severe wound dehiscence are common and have been reported in rehabilitation literature.[13] During a fall, there is a reflex extensor response that persists after an amputation.

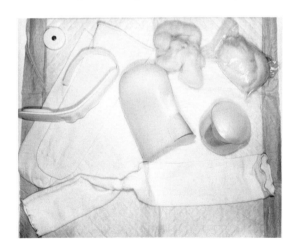

FIGURE 10-3. Materials needed for wearing the removable rigid dressing: stump shrinker (*bottom*), one-ply socks (*left*), supracondylar cuff (*left*), rigid removable dressing (*center*), and lamb's wool (*upper right*).

FIGURE 10-4. Application of the removable rigid dressing.

Unfortunately, this often places the weight of the amputee directly on the end of the residual limb at impact. There have even been cases of amputees getting out of bed in the night and stepping down on the missing limb. A rigid dressing will protect the amputee from this type of trauma, which, in some cases, would have led to surgical revision at a higher level. Thus, it is important that the RRD be worn nearly 24 hours a day and always during transfers and ambulation with crutches. As it turns out, after the surgical wound has healed, the term "removable rigid dressing" has less meaning and amputees will often call the RRD a stump protector.

Shaping

Shaping of the residual limb is an important component of preprosthetic management of the amputee. Postoperatively, residual limbs are edematous from the trauma of surgery and have essentially the same amount of fatty tissue and muscle that was present before the amputation. Over the next several months or years however, the weight-bearing on soft tissues that occurs during prosthetic use causes the fatty tissue to atrophy. Additionally, in most cases, muscles in the residual limb are not used and atrophy along with other tissues. Shrinkage

is quite variable but in some cases limbs may shrink 10 inches in circumference.

During the period of stump shaping, the amputee may require numerous prosthetic sockets, the cost of which is not small. If, however, shrinkage can be maximized and a "mature" shape provided to the residual limb before prosthetic fitting, the first and subsequent prosthetic sockets will fit better and fit longer.

The RRD prevents edema if applied at the time of the amputation and is effective in reducing edema when applied several days postoperatively.[10] By adding stump socks under the RRD, gentle even pressure is maintained on all parts of the residual limb. As a general guideline, one should expect one ply of socks to be added every 1–2 days for the first week or two. After 10 to 15 ply of socks are added, the residual limb will probably no longer be shaped like the RRD and it will be time to remake the dressing. At this point, a reduction in adipose tissue and muscle mass is apparent.

The RRD also may be used along with a stump shrinker such as Compressogrip. The shrinker is applied in its normal fashion and an RRD is simply made over the elastic shrinker. The cotton padding is placed on the shrinker and covered by a stump sock before the plaster is applied. As the residual limb becomes smaller, socks are added over the stump shrinker beneath the RRD as described above. The small ring at the bottom of the elastic shrinker is over soft tissue and causes no problems.

Pressure applied to the bottom of the RRD helps to mobilize edema, which tends to develop distally. Distal pressure may be applied by placing a strap on the bottom of the RRD and pulling proximally with the patient in a seated position or by placing the rigid dressing on a stool while the amputee stands on the sound leg and bears some weight on the rigid dressing.[12,18]

To summarize, the RRD can be very useful in shrinking and shaping the residual limb. Despite the rigid nature of the dressing itself, its use is quite flexible. The RRD can be applied at the time of surgery or later and still be quite effective. It is easily made, so making a new dressing for a better fit is not a problem. Distal pressure and even elastic compression can be incorporated when using the RRD. This makes the dressing quite versatile and effective in shaping the residual limb.

CONCLUSION

Postoperative rigid dressings have been shown to be safe and comfortable for the amputee. They control edema, protect the wound, and shape the residual limb better than other dressings. The RRD provides these benefits but also allows wound inspection and rapid shrinking of the residual limb.

The RRD can be applied at the time of surgery, after the removal of a traditional rigid dressing, or as a first rigid dressing several days after the amputation. It can be made in 30–60 minutes with materials generally found in the hospital, and it is easy for amputees to don and doff. These attributes make the RRD dressing a suitable alternative to the traditional rigid dressing and an improvement over traditional soft dressings. The physiatrist should become familiar with RRD and make its use routine in the care of the below-knee amputee.

REFERENCES

1. Berlemont M, Weber R, Willot JP: Ten years of experience with the immediate application of prosthetic devices to amputees of the lower extremities on the operating table. Prosthet Int 3:8, 1969.
2. Burgess EM, Romano RL: The management of lower extremity amputations using immediate postsurgical prostheses. Clin Orthop 57:137–146, 1968.
3. Burgess EM, Romano RL, Zettl JH: The management of lower extremity amputations surgery. Washington, DC, U.S. Government Printing Office, TR-10-G, 1969.
4. Cummings V: Immediate rigid dressing for amputees: Advantages and misconceptions. N Y State J Med 74:980–983, 1974.
5. Folsom D, King T, Rubin JR: Lower extremity amputation with immediate postoperative prosthetic placement. Am J Surg 164:320–322, 1992.
6. Gandhavadi B: Porous removable rigid dressing for complicated below-knee amputation stumps. Arch Phys Med Rehabil 68:51–53, 1987.
7. Kitowski VJ, Appel MF, Haslam T: Prosthetic fitting immediately after below-knee amputation. South Med J 68:739–742, 1975.
8. Mooney V, Harvey JP, McBride E, Snelson R: Comparison of postoperative stump management: Plaster vs soft dressings. J Bone Joint Surg Am 53A:241–249, 1971.
9. Mooney V, Wagner FW, Waddell J, et al: The below-the-knee amputation for vascular disease. J Bone Joint Surg Am 58A:365–368, 1976.
10. Mueller MJ: Comparison of removable rigid dressings and elastic bandages in preprosthetic management of patients with below-knee amputations. Phys Ther 62:1438–1441, 1982.
11. Nicholas GG, DeMuth WE: Evaluation of the use of the rigid dressing in amputation of the lower extremity. Surg Gynecol Obstet 143:398–400, 1976.
12. Parhad A, Gervais B, Wu Y: Beyond the rigid dressing: Preprosthetic ambulation of the below-knee amputee. Am Correct Ther J 37:66–89, 1983.
13. Richter KJ, Hurvitz EA, Girardot K: Rigid removable dressing in a case of poor wound healing. Arch Phys Med Rehabil 69:128–129, 1988.
14. Smith RD, Hof JJ: Lightweight rigid dressing for below-knee amputations. Arch Phys Med Rehabil 69:793, 1988.
15. Swanson VM: Below-knee polyethylene semi-rigid dressing. J Prosthet Orthot 5:30–35, 1993.
16. Weiss MA, Gielzynski A, Wirski J: Myoplasty-immediate fitting-ambulation. Proceedings of Sessions of the World Commission on Research in Rehabilitation, Tenth World Congress of the International Society, Wiesbaden, Germany, 1966.
17. Wu Y, Keagy RD, Krick H, et al: An innovative removable rigid dressing technique for below-the-knee amputation. J Bone Joint Surg 61A:724–729, 1979.
18. Wu Y, Krick H: Removable rigid dressing for below-knee amputees. Clin Prosthet Orthot 11:33–44, 1987.

Chapter 11

SERIAL CASTING

DAVID L. NASH, M.D.

Serial casting is a technique of contracture treatment that has been successfully used in a number of clinical conditions. One might consider it an aggressive nonoperative form of management that requires an understanding of the pathologic process that is contributing to the contracture development. It also requires a commitment to the close monitoring of the progress and potential side effects of the casting interventions and to the time, resources, and knowledge to apply and remove multiple casts. Because serial casting most often is indicated for patients with many other medical, rehabilitation, and sometimes surgical care issues, the decision to perform serial casting and the implementation of the intervention are usually a team process involving one or more physicians and a physical or occupational therapist. Serial casting is just one of many clinical tools that can be used to manage the effects of spasticity on a joint and prevent or treat a joint contracture. The intent of this chapter is to review the principles and practice of serial casting as it has been applied to patients with spasticity and contractures of upper and lower limb joints.

CONTRACTURES AND SPASTICITY

Contractures result from the shortening of periarticular connective tissue, particularly in muscle, joint capsules, and scars, but if contractures persist they eventually include other soft tissues such as skin, ligaments, tendons, and neurovascular structures. Shortening of these tissues occurs over time if a joint is allowed to remain in a constant position.[19] Perry emphasizes that "contractures must be recognized as an unnecessary complication" and that "the prevention of contractures and deformities must be a deliberate component of the therapeutic program for the patient with prolonged disability such as arthritis, paralysis or severe injury."[16] Spasticity has been defined as a condition associated with a persistent increase in the involuntary reflex activity of a muscle in response to stretch and

often associated with one or more of four features: hypertonia, hyperactive deep tendon reflexes, clonus, and spread of reflex responses beyond the stimulated muscle.[9] Spasticity secondary to a cerebral lesion such as a traumatic brain injury or cerebral palsy[11] often predisposes to flexion contractures of the elbows and equinus and knee flexion contractures in the lower extremities. One study of 75 consecutive hospitalized patients with traumatic head injury found 84% developed at least one clinically significant joint contracture, with contractures of the ankle occurring in 76% and of the elbow in 44% of the patients.[22]

The literature documenting the use and effectiveness of serial casting in conditions associated with spasticity and contracture is fairly limited. Clinical conditions studied include traumatic brain injury and cerebral palsy. The majority of these studies are descriptive—case reports and clinical series of patients without experimental control comparisons.

SERIAL CASTING IN PATIENTS WITH TRAUMATIC BRAIN INJURY

One of the early physical management challenges in patients with severe brain injury is that of pathologic tone management because of its potential to cause permanent contracture and deformity. If not prevented, these contractures and deformities, have the potential to slow the acute and postacute rehabilitation process and interfere with functional recovery. Serial casting has been used in both the acute intensive care setting and the acute and postacute rehabilitation settings primarily to assist patients in regaining lost range of motion. Serial casting also has been used to try to decrease spastic tone[2,3,5] and facilitate gait retraining[23] in patients with traumatic brain injury (TBI).

Spastic equinus foot and ankle posturing and contracture is the most common deformity in TBI patients that may benefit from serial casting.[3] Lower extremity serial casting was used in 21% (42 of 201) of TBI patients admitted to a rehabilitation center following transfer from acute medical care. Thirty-nine of the 42 patients were treated with short leg casts. The mean time from injury to initial casting was about 3 months, with average duration of casting 4–5 weeks and a range of 7–92 days. Some of the casts were applied to assist in managing tone and improving range of motion (ROM). An average ROM gain of about 20° was reported for patients whose casting was designed exclusively for improving ROM.

Serial casting also has been reported to be used effectively in the acute intensive care setting following TBI.[2,5,13] In a series of 10 TBI patients reported by Conine,[5] initial casting was performed 2–14 days following head injury. The patients averaged five casts, requiring a duration of 1 month of serial cast application. The average gain in ROM was 20°; two patients failed to improve and one worsened in spite of casting. Because only limited data were presented, it is difficult to make direct comparisons of the relative effectiveness of early casting[5] with postacute casting,[3] but a crude comparison suggests similar ROM gains and duration of casting treatment.

It is common practice to bivalve the final cast once the desired gains in ROM have been achieved. Imie[13] reported six TBI patients who underwent serial casting with bilateral short leg casts. In order to compare the effects of bivalved casts with non-bivalved casts, one randomly selected serial cast was bivalved in each patient. Imie reported significantly greater improvement in ROM and significantly fewer problems with skin breakdown in the ankles treated with nonbivalved casts.

KNEE AND ELBOW DROPOUT CASTS

Serial casting also has been successfully applied to spastic knee[1,3,4] and elbow[1,3,14] flexion contractures. Because the knee and elbow are more hingelike in their primary plane of motion, dropout casts have been used as an alternative to cylinder style casts for both the elbow and knee.[1,3,14] For a knee flexion contracture, a dropout cast is applied as a cylinder cast and subsequently cut to remove a portion either over the anterior lower leg or the anterior thigh so that the posterior portion acts as a flexion stop. With proper positioning the dropout cast can take advantage of gravity to provide periodic prolonged stretches to the tight flexors. In a similar manner, a long arm cylinder cast is applied to an elbow flexion contracture and cut out to expose the extensor portion of the upper or lower arm. Because some joint motion generally occurs between cast changes, less joint stiffness is observed at the time of cast change. In addition,

some clinicians have combined the dropout casting technique with neuromuscular electrical stimulation (NMES), claiming additive benefits in overcoming flexion contracture by periodically stimulating the extensor muscle groups.[1] In theory, the NMES not only applies an extensor muscle-induced stretch at the joint but may also provide some temporary reflex inhibition of the antagonist spastic flexor muscles.

INHIBITIVE (TONE-REDUCING) CASTS

Short leg casts with special features designed to decrease abnormal tone and therefore improve gait characteristics have been described as an adjunct to neurodevelopmental therapy (NDT) in children with cerebral palsy.[7,20,21] The theory that these casts are helpful is based on the premise that a "balanced secure support under the dynamic arch systems and stable midline forefoot, subtalar, and ankle control" will reduce excessive reflex and tone responses during standing and gait and secondarily allow for more effective neurodevelopmental therapy to train more normal patterns of motor control and mobility.[2] Sussman[20] hypothesized that two primary factors promote balance and mobility gains in therapy with "tone-reducing casts." First, gains may be achieved by inhibiting abnormally strong plantar grasp reflexes by supporting the toes in slight dorsiflexion in the casts. The second factor is based on the theory that the cast provides greater stability at the ankle, which in turn decreases stimulus for excessive reflex motor response. In a study comparing the effects of "tone-reducing" casts with standard short leg walking casts in children with cerebral palsy, Hinderer et al.[10] demonstrated a significantly better stride length with the tone-reducing casts along with other subjective differences. This result suggests that the therapeutic benefits of the casting are not entirely due to providing ankle stability. Another study failed, however, to show any radiologic difference in bony alignment of children with cerebral palsy standing in their "inhibitory casts" compared to standing barefoot. Duncan and Mott[7] emphasize the role of "inhibitive casts" in reducing input to certain reflexogenic areas of the feet that in turn trigger overactive tonic reflexes. Watts found that the primary effect of "inhibitive casting" was to increase dorsiflexion in spastic children; however, the gains were lost after 5 months, even though rigid ankle-foot orthotics were used after the 3 weeks of casting. The critical features and mechanisms of action that seem to make inhibitive casts at least a temporary beneficial adjunct to therapy in spastic children remains unclear. These casts are often used by practitioners not only for the "tone-reducing" qualities, but also to treat equinus contractures with serial casting.

INDICATIONS FOR SERIAL CASTS

Serial casting should be considered when there is a failure to achieve or maintain functional ROM of a peripheral joint such as the ankle, knee, or elbow with traditional ROM and stretching exercises and resting splints. When one identifies the potential for developing significant joint deformity and contracture secondary to severe spasticity that is not responding well to medical and physical measures, serial casting should be considered. In patients with TBI it is generally believed that the earlier the serial casting is initiated, the more effective it will be in restoring functional ROM.[2,3] Serial casting is most effective when the patient is still showing signs of neurologic recovery and when the loss of ROM is primarily due to spasticity rather than other possible factors such as heterotopic ossification, healing fracture, or ligamentous injury.[3]

CONTRAINDICATIONS

The skin must be free from lesions that might worsen or become infected when hidden from view and denied frequent wound care and observation.[3] Serial casts should be avoided in patients with skin that appears particularly vulnerable, such as the very thin skin of individuals who chronically take corticosteroids or the mottled or pale and cool skin of those with severe peripheral vascular disease. Although not well documented in the literature, concern has been expressed by some that serial casting possibly may increase hypertension or intracranial pressures, particularly in acutely injured and agitated TBI patients.[3] It is essential in patients with acute brain injury that the primary physician agree with any plans to perform serial casting. If the limb, particularly an upper extremity limb, is required for monitoring vital signs or administering medications, the priority obviously is medical management, and serial casting must be postponed.[2] ROM limited by acute heterotopic ossification should be treated with ROM exercises rather than immobilization.

GUIDELINES FOR CASTING

Several helpful resources detail preparation for casting and application of the cast itself.[6,8,12,15] One should always consider the indications, contraindications, and potential alternative options before engaging in serial casting. Once it has been decided to recommend serial casting, the clinician needs to explain the procedure, its purpose, and its goals with the patient and family. The local informed consent procedure must be followed. If the patient is agitated when the cast is applied, some type of sedation may be helpful. Sometimes, initial casts can be applied when the patient is under general anesthesia that has been given for another procedure, such as a tracheotomy, gastrostomy, or surgical wound management.

Lower Extremity Serial Casts

The spastic eqinus deformity is the most common deformity to be treated by serial casts. The patient needs to be positioned as comfortably as possible, which is often supine with hips and knees flexed for short leg casting. Some prefer the patient to be prone with the knee flexed 90° or sitting, if tolerated. Gentle stretching and ROM exercises immediately prior to casting help to achieve optimal positioning. When severe spasticity limits even a mild reduction in the equinus posturing, a temporary tibial nerve block with bupivacaine might be considered, or for more prolonged reduction in spasticity, a phenol motor point or tibial nerve block.[17] Depending on the patient's ability to cooperate, one or two assistants will be indispensable during the procedure. The short leg cast is started by applying a stockinette extending from the knee to several inches beyond the toes. Cotton padding is rolled up the leg from the toes to about 2 or 3 cm below the level of the fibular head, and the procedure is repeated to create two layers. Additional foam or felt padding may be added around bony prominences,[6] with the extra padding fixed between layers of cotton roll padding. Before beginning to apply the plaster, it is essential to reassess hindfoot and forefoot alignment. It is more important to correct the hindfoot to subtalar neutral and try to achieve midtarsal neutral alignment before exerting any significant dorsiflexion stretch. If the alignments are difficult to establish and hold, the casting process can be divided into two steps. First, a slipper cast is applied in an attempt to establish some correction toward subtalar and midtarsal neutral. The plaster is allowed to begin to set before a slight amount of dorsiflexion stretch is applied and the plaster extended up the leg.[6] After two or three layers of plaster are appplied, the top and bottom stockinette are trimmed back and rolled back onto the cast and covered with plaster 3-inch by 15-inch splints, leaving exposed the padded rolled stockinette edge at the proximal and distal extremes of the cast. Serial short leg casts are depicted in Figure 11-1.

If ankle plantor flexors and knee flexors are equally affected by spasticity and contracture, a long leg cast can be made to incorporate both the knee and the foot. A cylinder cast extending from just proximal to the ankle up the leg to the proximal thigh can be used for an isolated knee flexion contracture. Dropout casts of the lower extremity can be made by cutting out the anterior thigh or leg portion of a cylinder cast as described.

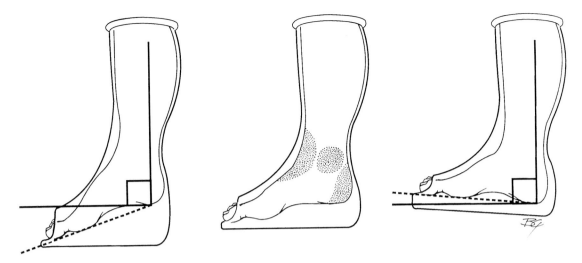

FIGURE 11-1. Serial short leg casts depicting a reduction of plantar flexion contracture of 20° to a final holding cast at 5° of dorsiflexion. Several intermediate casts between the initial and final holding cast may be required to achieve a gradual lengthening of the contracted gastrocsoleus muscle.

Upper Extremity Casts

Elbow flexor spasticity and contracture can be treated with long-arm cylinder casting.[3] The patient is positioned supine, the elbow flexors are stretched, and ROM is provided to the shoulder and hand prior to initiating casting. The arm is positioned in slight abduction with the elbow extended and slightly supinated to the degree that can be comfortably tolerated by the patient and maintained by the individual assisting with the casting. A stockinette is rolled up the arm, covering the wrist to the axilla. Three-inch cotton padding is applied next, winding around the arm from the wrist to the axilla and overlapping the edges. Extra padding is then added around bony prominences, including the olecranon process and the humeral condyles. This is then covered with another layer of cotton padding. A 4-inch plaster roll is moistened and applied over the cotton padding. While the plaster is still wet, it is smoothed and gently molded to the arm's contours while the assistant maintains the relative extension and supination. The proximal and distal ends of the stockinette are rolled back onto the cast and incorporated into the cast by applying moistened 3-inch by 15-inch plaster splints around each end of the cast. While the cast is setting, it is important to maintain the desired positioning without applying any squeezing pressure with the fingers over the cast that would create an undesirable point of increased pressure to the skin beneath the cast.

In some circumstances it may be desirable to incorporate the wrist and hand into the cast to provide prolonged stretch to tight wrist and finger flexors.[3] Short arm casts can be used if the elbow isn't as tight as the wrist and can be maintained with conventional ROM and stretching.

Cast Monitoring and Changes

Following application of the initial cast, fingers or toes distal to the casts are monitored for discoloration. If discoloration suggestive of circulation compromise persists longer than 30 minutes, the cast should be removed and reapplied.[3] The casts should be protected from deforming forces for 24 hours, particularly weight-bearing on a lower extremity plaster cast. Fiberglass casts achieve their full strength more quickly and can tolerate weightbearing shortly after application. The casts are generally changed approximately weekly with a brief period of therapeutic ROM and joint mobilization prior to fabricating the next cast. Casting is continued until the goal ROM has been reached or gains from the casting seem to have reached a plateau. Four or five cast changes are common. The final cast, often referred to as a holding cast, is often left in place 10–14 days and then bivalved so that it can be used as a night splint (Fig. 11-2). If needed, it can be worn on a scheduled basis throughout the day to maintain ROM. There usually is a prolonged need for a positioning aid for the extremity in order to maintain the gains in ROM. A light-weight orthoplast splint or polypropylene orthosis can be fabricated for this purpose.

CONCLUSION

Serial casting is a useful but labor-intensive adjunct to the treatment of clinically and functionally significant spasticity and contracture of the upper and lower extremities. Careful patient selection and clearly defined objective therapeutic goals are essential. Rehabilitation team members with casting skills can clearly contribute significant expertise within the full spectrum of comprehensive rehabilitation services.

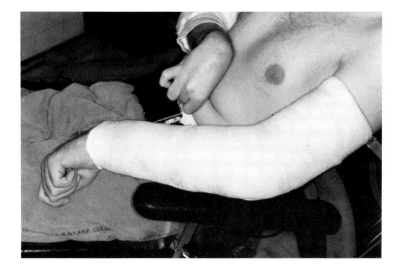

FIGURE 11-2. A 32-year-old man with an old right hemiparesis from a traumatic brain injury as a child suffered a superimposed left hemiparesis from an intracranial hemorrhage as an adult. A spastic elbow flexion contracture of 2 years' duration limited some residual function in the left hand. A phenol musculocutaneous nerve block followed by serial casting reduced the contracture by 50% and helped improve function and ease of care. The photo shows the final holding cast before it was bivalved.

REFERENCES

1. Baker LL, Parker K, Sanderson D: Neuromuscular electrical stimulation for the head injured patient. Phys Ther 63:1967–1974, 1983.
2. Barnard P, et al: Reduction of hypertonicity by early casting in a comatose head-injured individual. Phys Ther 64:1540–1542, 1984.
3. Booth BJ, Doyle M, Montgomery J: Serial casting for the management of spasticity in the head-injured adult. Phys Ther 63:1960–1966, 1983.
4. Cherry DB, Weingand GM: Plaster drop-out casts as a dynamic means to reduce muscle contracture. Phys Ther 61:1601–1603, 1981.
5. Conine TA, et al: Effect of serial casting for the prevention of equinus in patients with acute head injury. Arch Phys Med Rehabil 71:310–312, 1990.
6. Cusick BD: Serial Casts: Their Use in Management of Spasticity-Induced Foot Deformity, revised ed. Tucson, Therapy Skill Builders, 1990, pp 1–105.
7. Duncan WR, Mott DH: Foot reflexes and the use of the "inhibitive cast." Foot Ankle 4:145–148, 1983.
8. Feldman PA: Upper extremity casting and splinting. In Glenn MB, Whyte J (eds): The Practical Management of Spasticity in Children and Adults. Philadelphia, Lea & Febiger, 1990, pp 149–166.
9. Gans BM, Glenn MB: Introduction. In Glenn MB, Whyte J (eds): The Practical Management of Spasticity in Children and Adults. Philadelphia, Lea & Febiger, 1990, p 1.
10. Hinderer KA, et al: Effects of "tone-reducing" vs. standard plaster-casts on gait improvement of children with cerebral palsy. Dev Med Child Neurol 30:370–377, 1988.
11. Hoffer MM, Knoebel RT, Roberts R: Contractures in cerebral palsy. Clin Orthop 219:70–77, 1987.
12. Hylton N: Dynamic casting and orthotics. In Glenn MB, Whyte J (eds): The Practical Management of Spasticity in Children and Adults. Philadelphia, Lea & Febiger, 1990, pp 167–200.
13. Imie PC, Eppinghaus CE, Broughton AC: Efficacy of non-bivalved and bivalved serial casting on head injured patients in intensive care. Phys Ther 66:748, 1986.
14. King TI: Plaster splinting as a means of reducing elbow flexion spasticity: A case study. Am J Occup Ther 36:671–673, 1982.
15. Leahy P: Precasting work sheet—an assessment tool: A clinical report. Phys Ther 68:72–74, 1988.
16. Perry J: Contractures: A historical perspective. Clin Orthop 219:8–14, 1987.
17. Ratcliff R, Kempthorne P: Temporary tibial nerve block: Adjunct to inhibitory plasters in the physiotherapy management of equinus in severely head-injured children. Austr J Physiother 29:119–125, 1983.
18. Ricks NR, Eilert RE: Effects of inhibitory casts and orthoses on bony alignment of foot and ankle during weight-bearing in children with spasticity. Dev Med Child Neurol 35:11–16, 1993.
19. Stolov WC, Thompson SC: Soleus immobilization contracture in the baboon [abstract]. Arch Phys Med Rehabil 60:556, 1979.
20. Sussman MD: Casting as an adjunct to neurodevelopmental therapy for cerebral palsy. Dev Med Child Neurol 25:804–805, 1983.
21. Sussman MD, Cusick B: Preliminary report: The role of short-leg, tone-reducing casts as an adjunct to physical therapy of patients with cerebral palsy. Johns Hopkins Med J 145:112–114, 1979.
22. Yarkony GM, Sahgal V: Contractures, a major complication of craniocerebral trauma. Clin Orthop 219:93–96, 1987.
23. Zachazewski JE, Eberle ED, Jeffries M: Effect of tone-inhibiting casts and orthoses on gait. Phys Ther 62:453–455, 1982.

Chapter 12

PEDIATRIC AND ADULT SWALLOWING VIDEOFLUOROSCOPY

VIKKI STEFANS, M.D.
RICHARD P. GRAY, M.D.
THOMAS SOWELL

Many patients under physiatric care have conditions associated with swallowing disorders. These disorders can be evaluated by swallowing videofluoroscopy (SVF) studies, also known as a modified barium swallow (MBS) examination. The medical interpretation of the results of this procedure, decision making about feeding and swallowing, and the management of these tests can be directed by the physiatrist. Knowledge of the procedure and its limitations is essential for optimal, medically sound, and individualized decision making.

THE DYSPHAGIA TEAM

The most basic "dysphagia team" should include the patient and family, swallowing therapist, physician, nutritionist, and radiologists. When the evaluation and management of dysphagia occur within an inpatient rehabilitation setting, the nurses, aides, or therapists involved in feeding should be included. Involvement of the patient and family is essential because eating is a highly emotional area for all concerned. If full involvement does not occur, disputes about familial rejection of limitations on oral feeding are extremely common.[3] At least one family member should be in the radiology suite during the study. This is especially helpful in pediatric cases because many children will not perform optimally, or at all, with an unfamiliar feeder. Family members can be helped to visualize and therefore appreciate events such as silent aspiration, inadequate mastication, or severe pooling as they occur.

The swallowing therapist is usually a speech pathologist or occupational therapist with additional training in the field of dysphagia. As Logemann noted, there is minimal, if any, specific education regarding dysphagia in most professional schools.[23]

Interdisciplinary collaboration is necessary to optimally evaluate and manage feeding and swallowing problems.

PHASES OF SWALLOWING

An understanding of the anatomy and physiology of swallowing is essential for all professionals involved in the evaluation and management of dysphagia (Fig. 12-1). Many excellent sources are available on this subject.[6,8,9,13,23,24] The swallowing phases include four phases:

1. *The oral preparatory phase* (Fig. 12-2): intake, mastication, and bolus formation.
2. *The oral or voluntary swallowing phase* (Fig. 12.3): control and movement of the bolus into a position to trigger the swallow.
3. *The pharyngeal or reflex swallowing phase* (Figs. 12-4 to 12-7): initiated normally with passage of the bolus at the faucial arch.
4. *The esophageal phase* (Fig. 12-8): passage of the bolus beyond the cricopharyngeus muscle.

The first phase is relatively, although not completely, accessible to evaluation via bedside examination. All phases except the esophageal phase may be influenced by therapeutic or compensatory swallowing techniques.

INDICATIONS FOR VIDEOFLUOROSCOPY

SVF is indicated for most patients with swallowing complaints and many patients without any specific symptoms who are at risk for alterations in swallowing physiology. This procedure often detects conditions that are not obvious during the best clinical or "bedside" evaluation. There is a well-documented existence of silent aspiration in both

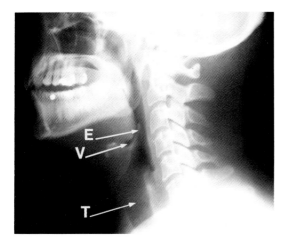

FIGURE 12-1. Lateral x-ray of the cervical spine demonstrating the epiglottis *(E)*, vallecula *(V)*, and trachea *(T)*.

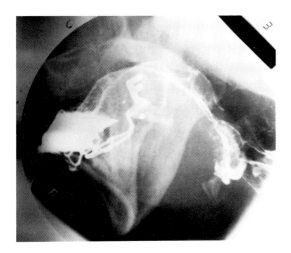

FIGURE 12-2. Bolus formation during the oral preparatory phase.

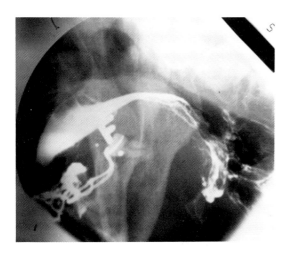

FIGURE 12-3. Advancement of the bolus from the oral swallowing phase.

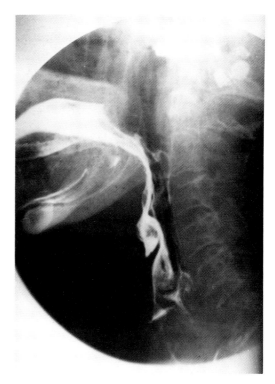

FIGURE 12-4. Movement of the bolus from the oral swallowing phase into the pharyngeal phase.

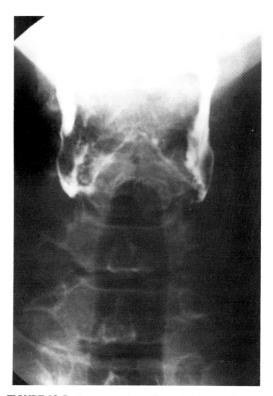

FIGURE 12-5. Posteroanterior radiograph demonstrating movement of the bolus from the oral swallowing phase into the pharyngeal phase.

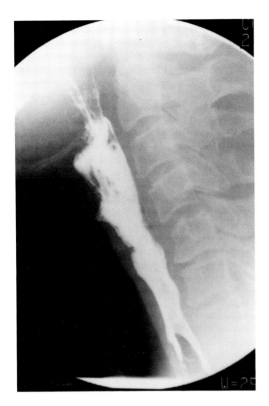

FIGURE 12-6. Lateral view demonstrating the pharyngeal phase of swallowing.

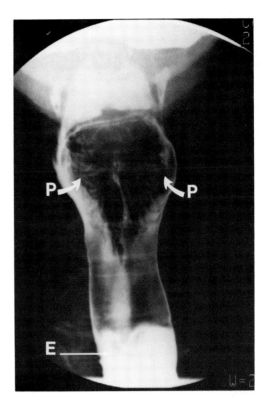

FIGURE 12-7. Posteroanterior radiograph demonstrating the pharyngeal phase of swallowing. Note the asymmetrical filling within the piriform sinuses *(P)* and esophagus *(E)*.

children and adults.[10,34,36] Other procedures may delineate information about oral function and even estimate delay in swallowing and laryngeal evaluation, but no other study can fully define laryngeal closure or relative amounts of pooling in all pharyngeal recesses. Silent aspiration may present as pulmonary diseases, such as repeated pneumonia or episodic wheezing suggestive of primary reactive airway disease. Aspiration without choking or coughing is more common with significant central nervous system impairment but may also occur with other chronic conditions, probably via desensitization of the trachea over time.[27] The presence of a foreign body, i.e., a tracheostomy tube, is sufficient to cause desensitization. Refusal to eat or inadequate oral intake to maintain nutrition or growth in children may be related to dysphagia. In children, dysphagia is most commonly associated with oral motor impairment and/or oral hypersensitivity. Medical conditions known to be associated with dysphagia and specifically discussed in the available literature are listed in Table 12-1.

A common misconception of SVF is that it simply evaluates aspiration, thereby solely determining whether a patient can safely eat and swallow. Instead, this procedure should be used as a tool for elucidating many aspects of an individual's swallowing physiology, such as optimal food consistencies to

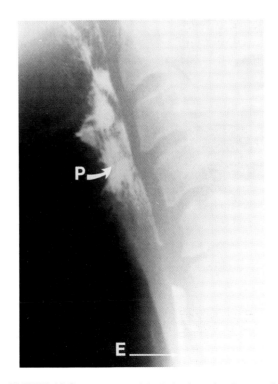

FIGURE 12-8. Movement of the bolus from the pharyngeal *(P)* phase into the esophageal *(E)* phase of swallowing.

TABLE 12-1. Medical Conditions Associated with Dysphagia

Central Nervous System–Static	Neuromuscular Disease
Cerebral palsy	Duchenne muscular dystrophy (late)[15]
Cerebrovascular accident	Myasthenia gravis
Traumatic brain injury	Myotonic dystrophy
Cervical spinal cord injury*	Polymyositis/dermatomyositis
Central Nervous System–Progressive	Anatomic or Gastrointestinal
Amyotrophic lateral sclerosis	Oral and oropharyngeal cancer[†]
CNS tumor	Laryngeal cancer[†]
Dysautonomia	Cleft palate
Dystonia	Tracheoesophageal fistula
Leukodystrophy	Esophageal stricture, tumor, web, or dysmotility
Multiple sclerosis	Cervical spondylosis
Parkinson's disease	Cricopharyngeal spasm
Other degenerative CNS disorders	Gastroesophageal reflux or ulcer disease

*May be mechanical, as for cervical spondylosis.
†May be related to either surgical therapy or radiotherapy.

be used, positioning for optimal swallowing function, length of time to swallow if delayed, need for extra swallows to clear residue, and the effectiveness of maneuvers and techniques designed to compensate for specific swallowing problems.[20] Groeher lists the results of SVF as only one of eight factors to be considered in recommending nonoral feedings. Other factors are altered state of consciousness, medical instability, dependence on ventilatory support, poor mental status, need for supervision, difficulty in positioning for feeding, and risk for inadequate nutrition or hydration.[13]

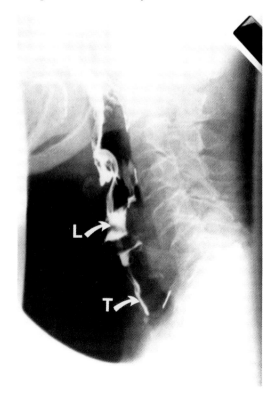

FIGURE 12-9. Lateral radiograph demonstrating laryngeal penetration *(L)* and tracheal aspiration *(T)*.

Although it must not be considered exclusively or in isolation, observed aspiration is an important factor that can be best assessed via videofluoroscopy (Fig. 12-9). Logemann observed that neurologically intact patients with cancer voluntarily discontinued using foods of a specific consistency if they aspirated more than 10%. Penetration into the larynx, which is cleared and does not go below the vocal cords, should be distinguished from even "trace" (less than approximately 10%) aspiration, as it may in some cases require only minimal modification to feeding. Observed aspiration indicates that feeding modification is required to reduce this risk. If 10% aspiration is noted and swallowing modifications are unsuccessful, the involved food consistency should be avoided. The amount of chronic low-level aspiration that will cause permanent lung damage is not known. However, significant pulmonary impairment and death can result from massive aspiration of food, medication, or contrast material,[11] and these adverse complications can occur with repeated lesser aspirations. Long-term aspiration morbidity studies are complicated by the co-occurrence of gastroesophageal reflux. This causes damaging acidic substances to enter the airways during swallowing resulting in various pulmonary disorders.[7,22,29]

EVALUATION OF SWALLOWING

Three steps are necessary when evaluating swallowing function.

1. **Preevaluation.** Usually a swallowing therapist performs a preevaluation that includes a medical history with emphasis on oropharyngeal function. The development of a hypothesis about the patient's swallowing disorder and its realistic management options, rationale, and any modification to the routine study are developed.[23,30,31,36] If indications for a study appear valid, a plan for the SVF can be made. There may be occasions when it may not be

appropriate or necessary to proceed. For example, the patient may not be in optimal medical condition or cannot be properly positioned to participate in the study.

2. **Swallowing Study.** It is important to maintain a structured and sequenced videofluoroscopy procedure that can be kept standardized when needed, especially for research purposes, or allow flexibility for specific individual needs.

3. **Team Decision Making.** A philosophy and procedure for team notification and decision making on the basis of videofluoroscopic results should be outlined, including indications for planning follow-up studies.

PROTOCOLS

Most investigators agree that SVF should follow a protocol using specific consistencies and bolus sizes. For adults, liquid bolus sizes range from one third of a teaspoon (Logemann) to one half teaspoon (Robbins) and up to 30 ml (6 teaspoons) described by Rosenbeck.[31] Logemann's protocols use thin and thick liquids, paste, and solid. Robbins uses only liquid of thin-water consistency, semisolid, and solid, with three swallows. Foods that require chewing usually are not given unless indicated from the results of an oral motor evaluation and medical history. Less than one quarter of a Lorna Doone cookie coated with barium paste is sufficient and will tend to soften and crumble into a paste if held in the oropharynx rather than swallowed. Amounts and types of food selected can be advanced judiciously on subsequent trials during the study.

The rationale for the variety of consistencies is their different characteristics and risks with different types of swallowing pathophysiology. Liquids require little mastication and will pass easily through partially obstructed areas. However, they are more difficult to control and usually present greater anterior bolus loss with poor oral control and greater aspiration risks with impaired neurologic control of the pharyngeal phase. Semisolids or solids may be better controlled but are more likely to stagnate proximal to an anatomic obstruction or in pharyngeal recesses and to obstruct the airway if aspirated.

EQUIPMENT

Equipment required for videofluoroscopy includes 3- or 5-ml syringes, which are used to deliver the measured first bolus to the anterior or anterolateral oral cavity; injections into the posterior oropharynx are contraindicated. Also necessary are containers and utensils for mixing foods with barium to achieve desired consistencies: i.e., normal, "sippee," and cutaway cups; baby bottles

with enlarged nipple holes or a device to make small crosscut incisions to enlarge them as needed for thicker liquids; and some normal and rubber-tipped feeding spoons. Plastic spoons are contraindicated for patients who may exhibit a tonic bite reflex. Patients who can feed themselves may be encouraged to do so and should bring their own familiar or adaptive eating utensils if possible.

Food consistencies can be simulated with barium in many ways. The usual liquid barium is slightly thicker than most thin liquids but can be diluted with one or two parts of water, formula, clear juice, or Kool-Aid. It can be thickened with ice cream, rice cereal, or puree, such as baby food. Cold foods such as ice cream may help to stimulate the swallow reflex. Barium powder can be added to pureed foods or ice cream. Barium "cream" or paste can be mixed with less than an equal part liquid for a paste or semisolid consistency. Solids can be coated with or soaked in barium. Lorna Doone cookies are a traditional choice, but foods of the patient's choice may be used as long as they do not pose a major choking hazard. For instance, avoid popcorn or uncut hot dogs in children younger than 4. A small wire whip or electric mixer is helpful when preparing for the study. Newer, flavored types of barium products are not as chalky or ill-tasting as the older ones that many adults recall, and individual tolerance for these unusual preparations of foodstuffs may vary. Vanilla barium paste with chocolate ice cream seems palatable to most adults.

TECHNIQUE

The following are sample protocols for SVF in adults and children.

Test materials: Thin liquid, thick liquid, paste, solid.

1. The patient is positioned to allow visualization of the oropharynx from a lateral approach under fluoroscopy.

2. The patient's swallow is observed with the following:
- one teaspoon of thin liquid barium
- one teaspoon of thick liquid barium
- one teaspoon of applesauce with barium paste

3. The feeder holds one corner of a cookie coated with barium paste and tells the patient to "bite the corner of this cookie and chew as you normally would until you feel you are ready to swallow."

4. Optional procedures such as the administration of 10- and 33-ml boluses of thin and thick liquid by cup and/or straw are undertaken if more information is desired.

5. Positions may be changed to allow an antero-posterior view. This view is used to assess symmetry of pharyngeal structures during the swallow and to evaluate function of the vocal cords.

6. If the anteroposterior view is used:
- The patient is instructed to tilt the head back or hold the chin up slightly. This position brings the mandible and other structures away from the pharynx and larynx for better visualization.
- The patient is told to say "ah" and prolong it at least twice.
- The patient is given one teaspoon of thick liquid barium.

7. If the patient is unable to protect the airway, additional positioning may be attempted or food consistencies changed, or the study may be terminated, especially if most of a bolus is aspirated. Criteria for terminating a study include the following:
- failure to initiate a swallow
- absence of a cough in response to significant (not just trace) aspiration
- significant amounts of material fill the pharyngeal space and do not pass into the esophagus with multiple dry swallows

Information obtained and conveyed to the treatment team should include the following:

1. Site of difficulty, either oral, pharyngeal, or both.

2. Aspiration, either nasopharyngeal, laryngeal, or both. For laryngeal aspiration, include timing (before, during, or after the swallow) and cause and/or source, i.e., during the swallow due to reduced laryngeal closure, or after the swallow due to reduced pharyngeal peristalsis, reduced laryngeal closure, or material moving back into the pharynx from a Zenker diverticulum.

3. Recommendations and documentation of counseling given to the patient and family.

Ideally, after the study, the whole team should come to a consensus and develop a single report.[14,29] In practice, there may be separate reports from just the swallowing therapist and radiologist.

A careful history should be obtained regarding the administration of liquid medications, especially by syringe. A swallowing study with a barium tablet can clarify whether esophageal spasm or functional stricture creates a risk for localized medication-induced esophagitis.[29] Sedatives such as muscle relaxants and anticonvulsants also may have direct or indirect effects on swallowing coordination beyond simple central nervous system depression. Anticholinergic drugs such as antidepressants and bladder medications may impair esophageal motility. Optimizing treatment of Parkinson's disease or myasthenia gravis can improve swallowing if it improves other aspects of motor function and fatigue.

Based on the complete assessment of swallowing, various passive and active compensatory techniques are available to the swallowing therapist, and the reader is referred to existing texts and manuals for further details on their techniques and indications.[13,23–25,29] Passive techniques include positioning; methods of presentation such as straw, spoon, or a special cup designed to slow the rate of intake; consistencies chosen for ongoing use; supervision or assistance to control the rate and/or mode of intake; and thermal stimulation to facilitate the swallowing reflex. Active strategies include repeated swallows, swallow with effort, supraglottic swallow, and the Mendelssohn maneuver. The latter requires adequate cognition and cooperation by the patient. Oral exercises and swallowing training may improve performance or compensate effectively in the long term.[4,17,26]

Repeat studies are based on the rate of improvement or disease progression. Patients receiving active therapy may wait until the therapist notes some change in oral motor or swallowing function. For example, when a patient at risk for aspirating thin liquids before the swallow regains better oral control and no longer grossly exhibits a delayed swallow, reevaluation may be scheduled. The repeat study may be much more limited and targeted to a specific question in many cases.

POSITIONING DURING VIDEOFLUOROSCOPY

With compensatory techniques, SVF should allow for several swallows of each food consistency in various feeding positions. It is important to test positions that are likely to be used by family members and not just the upright position. Feeders often compensate for a poor oral phase by having a patient recline. Neurodevelopmental therapists often advocate a side-lying position for tone reduction. The upright position with slight cervical flexion is ideal for reducing the risk of aspiration in neurogenic dysphagia. Alternative head positions also need to be evaluated. Some cases in which side lying was preferred because it led to less coughing proved to be associated with an increase in the amount of aspiration when studied radiographically. Aspiration became "more silent" as the child became more relaxed. Circumstances in which supine feeding positions are preferred have been described in other studies.[12,27]

Having proper equipment in the radiology suite may help to achieve optimal positioning for swallowing studies. For children and adults, there are specialized chairs for positioning.[5] It may be possible to use a child's car seat on the platform of an x-ray table in some cases. Often, positioning will have to be improvised, making use of whatever chairs, bolsters, wedges, and straps that are available. A high back or headrest is helpful for a person with limited head and trunk control. Patients who are able to stand for the study may do so if it is convenient. Complete immobilization is neither necessary nor desirable for a successful study and is to be avoided.

CONTRAINDICATIONS

A low level of consciousness, poor cooperation, or inability to follow commands are absolute contraindications to SVF. Infants can be successfully studied as well as some individuals at Rancho Los Amigos level III or higher level of neurologic recovery from coma. The ability to perform voluntary rather than solely passive compensatory maneuvers is limited in these patients.

COMPLICATIONS

Videofluoroscopy is considered a low-risk procedure. Risk of aspiration during the procedure can be minimized by two factors: first, the amount of food used for an initial trial of any consistency is kept small, and second, suction and oxygen equipment should be available. One milliliter of fluid allows adequate visualization of a swallow, especially in a child. Two milliliters is necessary for semisolids. Few individuals have a combination of disordered swallowing physiology, total inability to compensate, and severe medical risks that preclude using even tiny amounts of some consistency of foodstuff orally.

Radiation exposure to the patient and medical personnel should be monitored (see chapter 1). Five minutes of fluoroscopy time is routine and should be achievable by an experienced team.

CONSIDERATIONS IN CHILDREN

There are differences in swallowing physiology and anatomy in children that should be appreciated. It is essential that foods be presented in a developmentally appropriate manner. For example, infants younger than 6 months should receive only thin or thick liquids by bottle. An infant's tongue is relatively larger compared to the total oral cavity, and the hyoid and laryngeal structures are relatively higher. Suckle feeding is the normal pattern for infants and is normally gradually superseded by voluntary chewing and swallow initiation beginning in the second half of the first year and becoming completely adult in pattern by age 3 or 4. The anatomy of infants favors the suckle pattern and, if neurologic maturation does not occur in children and suckling persists, increasing difficulties may occur as the anatomy changes even if neurologic status is not deteriorating. The distinctive features of suckling on videofluoroscopy include repeated stripping action of the tongue before each swallow, which may lead to some vallecular pooling as a normal finding; more frequent swallows; more filling of the esophagus before clearing; and the critical importance of the suck-swallow-breathe coordination cycle. It is essential to assess the effects of fatigue and especially to pay attention to the last swallow before respiration in each cycle since this is where breakdown of coordination and resultant aspiration is most likely.[18,19]

REFERRAL FOR SURGERY

Surgery is usually indicated any time there are recommendations for alternative feeding methods since chronic nasogastric or orogastric tubes have high rates of local tissue trauma and reflux-related complications. Logemann's stated limit for nonsurgical tube feedings is 3 months, with exceptions for a patient who can learn to perform and/or tolerate repeated placement and removal of the tube between meals.[23]

If the swallowing study suggests the individual can tolerate at least small amounts of thickened liquids, total oral nutrition may be possible if eating is functionally a reasonable activity. Adequate intake of calories, protein, and fluid is usually difficult on semisolids alone. The time and effort necessary for eating also must be considered for individual patients. Recommendations based only on SVF occasionally reduce the time and effort involved at mealtime and usually neither increase or decrease it significantly.[12,27] A nutritionist can help to select palatable foods of the desired consistencies with higher caloric density as needed. Foods can be thickened with a commercial product such as Dia-Foods "Thick-It" or by using naturally thicker foods such as nectars instead of juices, or thick milk shakes. Recipe manuals for modified diets are available.[2]

If the SVF is unrevealing, additional studies may be recommended to search for the cause of persistent symptoms. As noted earlier, gastroesophageal reflux may cause respiratory symptoms in the absence of any swallowing disorder. Gastric, duodenal, or esophageal disease may cause painful swallowing. If alternate feeding methods are to be considered, testing should be performed to assess for gastroesophageal reflux, especially in children, for whom an antireflux procedure is frequently indicated at the time of gastrostomy surgery. Some authors report an association of cricopharyngeal dysfunction with reflux. Radionuclide scanning, esophageal pH probe, or endoscopy may be considerd for further evaluation. Computerized tomography or magnetic resonance imaging may be essential to delineate anatomical structures in greater detail than can be appreciated on any dynamic or functional study. Such techniques are essential in diagnosis and management of preoperative or postoperative cases of head and neck cancer.[16,30]

ALTERNATIVE STUDIES

Other methods of assessing the swallow have been used in attempts to be more physiologic and/ or reduce radiation exposure. Cervical auscultation, ultrasound, and endoscopy are the most widely reported. Auscultation may, in selected patients, permit follow-up of timing of velopharyngeal closure and/or triggering of the swallow. It also may provide clues to the occurrence of aspiration if specific sounds can be identified and correlated with swallowing events for the individual.[32] However, gurgling or "wet hoarse" sounds can result from retained pharyngeal or nasopharyngeal material and does not always indicate laryngeal penetration.[21] Ultrasound evaluation has the advantage of being portable to the bedside and, like auscultation, is noninvasive and requires no radiation. The transducer is placed under the chin and may cover a field from tongue tip to epiglottis in a sagittal plane. Larger adults may need to be repositioned slightly. A coronal plane image can capture vocal fold and cord movement. It can definitely supplement bedside evaluation of the oral phase. However, it is limited in delineating the amount and timing of aspiration.[33] Endoscopy, usually with a flexible endoscope inserted from above the nasopharynx, also can provide information without radiation exposure but requires specialized equipment and expertise in operation. Its chief limitation is that, when upper pharyngeal constriction is not severely impaired, the remainder of the swallow is obscured from view. For example, vocal cord movement during breathing or phonation may be seen, but closure during a swallow and the presence of aspiration during or immediately after a swallow generally will not be directly visible.

CONCLUSION

In summary, involvement of the physiatrist in SVF may be of great benefit to individual patients, rehabilitation team, or the dysphagia program. This procedure, when performed well, provides an excellent opportunity to obtain detailed information about swallowing function. Thorough study and understanding of swallowing physiology techniques involved in SVF are essential for the physiatrist to make an optimal contribution to the evaluation and rehabilitation of this most essential human function.

REFERENCES

 1. Beck TJ, Gayler BW: Radiation in video-recorded fluoroscopy. In Jones B, Donner MW (eds): Normal and Abnormal Swallowing: Imaging in Diagnosis and Therapy. New York, Springer-Verlag, 1991.
 2. Campalans NM, VanBiervliet A: Educational materials for the dysphagia diet; development and evaluation. J Am Diet Assoc (Suppl)92:A110, 1992.
 3. Campbell A: Tube feeding: Parental perspective. Exceptional Parent 36–40, April 1988.
 4. Christiansen JR: Development approach to pediatric neurogenic dysphagia. Dysphagia 3:131–134, 1989.
 5. Cox MS, Petty J: A videofluoroscopy chair for the evaluation of dysphagia in patients with severe neuromotor disease. Arch Phys Med Rehabil 72:157–159, 1991.
 6. Cuningham ET, Donner MW, Point SM, et al: Anatomical and physiological overview. In Jones B, Donner MW (eds): Normal and Abnormal Swallowing: Imaging in Diagnosis and Therapy. New York, Springer-Verlag, 1991.
 7. DeVito MA, Wetmore RF, Pransky SM: Laryngeal diversion in the treatment of chronic aspiration in children. Int J Pediatr Otorhinolaryngol 18:139–145, 1989.
 8. Dodds WJ, Stewart ET, Logemann JA: Physiology and radiology of the normal oral and pharyngeal phases of swallowing. Am J Roentgen 154:953–963.
 9. Donner MW, Bosma JF, Robertson DL: Anatomy and physiology of the pharynx. Gastrointest Radiol 10:196–212, 1985.
10. Feinberg MJ, Knebl J, Segall L, et al: Aspiration and the elderly. Dysphagia 5:61–71, 1990.
11. Gray C, Sivaloganathan S, Simpkins KC: Aspiration of high density barium contrast medium causing acute pulmonary inflammation: Report of two fatal cases in elderly women with disordered swallowing. Clin Radiol 40:397–400, 1989.
12. Griggs CA, Jones PM, Lee RE: Videofluoroscopic investigation of feeding disorders of children with multiple handicap. Dev Med Child Neurol 31:303–308, 1989.
13. Groeher M: Dysphagia Diagnosis and Management. Stoneham, MA, Butterworth, 1984.
14. Henson D, White L, Hedburg V: Report writing made easy: Combining radiologist and SLP's swallow study reports [poster]. Annual Meeting of the Arkansas Speech-Hearing-Language Association, October 1993.
15. Jaffe KM, McDonald CM, Haas J, et al: Symptoms of upper gastrointestinal dysfunction in Duchenne muscular dystrophy: Case-control study. Arch Phys Med Rehabil 71:742–744, 1990.
16. Jones B, Donner MW: The tailored examination. In Jones B, Donner MW (eds): Normal and Abnormal Swallowing: Imaging in Diagnosis and Therapy. New York, Springer-Verlag, 1991.
17. Kasprisin AT, Clumeck H, Nino-Murcia M: Efficacy of rehabilitative management of dysphagia. Dysphagia 4:48–52, 1989.
18. Kramer SS: Special swallowing problems in children. Gastrointest Radiol 10:241–250, 1985.
19. Kramer SS: Swallowing in children. In Jones B, Donner MW (eds): Normal and Abnormal Swallowing: Imaging in Diagnosis and Therapy. New York, Springer-Verlag, 1991.
20. Langmore SE, Logemann JA: After the bedside swallowing examination: What next? Am J Speech Lang Pathol 1:13–20, 1991.
21. Linden P, Siebens AA: Dysphagia: Predicting laryngeal penetration. Arch Phys Med Rehabil 64:281–284, 1983.
22. Logemann JA: Evaluation and Treatment of Swallowing Disorders. San Diego, College-Hill, 1983.
24. Logemann JA: Manual for the Videofluorographic Study of Swallowing. London, Taylor & Francis, 1986.
25. Logemann JA: Treatment for aspiration related to dysphagia; an overview. Dysphagia 1:34–38, 1986.
26. Morris SE: Development of oral-motor skills in the neurologically impaired child receiving non-oral feedings. Dysphagia 3:135–154, 1989.

27. Morton RE, Bonas R, Minford J, et al: Videofluoroscopy in the assessment of feeding disorders of children with neurological problems. Dev Med Child Neurol 35:388–395, 1993.

28. Muz J, Mazog RH, Borrero G, et al: Detection and quantification of laryngotracheopulmonary aspiration with scintigraphy. Laryngoscope 97:1180–1185, 1987.

29. Palmer JB, DuChane AS, Donner MW: Role of radiology in the rehabilitation of swallowing. In Jones B, Donner MW (eds): Normal and Abnormal Swallowing: Imaging in Diagnosis and Therapy. New York, Springer-Verlag, 1991.

30. Point SW, Bryan RN, Cunningham ET: Integrated approach to cross-sectional imaging and dysphagia. In Jones B, Donner MW (eds): Normal and Abnormal Swallowing: Imaging in Diagnosis and Therapy. New York, Springer-Verlag, 1991.

31. Robbins J, Sufit R, Rosenbeck J, et al: A modification of the modified barium swallow. Dysphagia 2:83–86, 1987.

32. Smith D, Hamlet S, Jones L: Acoustic technique for determining timing of velopharyngeal closure in swallowing. Dysphagia 5:142–146, 1990.

33. Sonies BC: Ultrasound imaging and swallowing. In Jones B, Donner MW (eds): Normal and Abnormal Swallowing: Imaging in Diagnosis and Therapy. New York, Springer-Verlag, 1991.

34. Splaingard ML, Hutchins B, Chaudhuri G, et al: Aspiration in rehabilitation patients: Videofluoroscopy vs bedside clinical assessment. Arch Phys Med Rehabil 69:637–640, 1988.

35. Zerelli KS, Stefans VA: Pediatric swallowing videofluoroscopy one year follow-up. Dev Med Child Neurol 31:(Suppl 5), 1989.

36. Zerrelli KS, Stefans VA, DiPietro MA: Protocol for the use of videofluoroscopy in pediatric swallowing dysfunction. Am J Occup Ther 44:441–446, 1990.

Chapter 13

UROLOGIC DIAGNOSTIC TESTING

INDER PERKASH, M.D.

Neurologic lesions of the brain, spinal cord, or peripheral nerves invariably lead to voiding dysfunctions. Quite often, there is either partial or complete retention of urine or some degree of incontinence. Intracranial lesions such as head injury, cerebrovascular accident, Alzheimer's disease, and brain tumors can lead to a hyperreflexic bladder that causes patients to void frequently with smaller volumes of urine. However, in the early phase after the injury or following cerebrovascular accident, urine may even be retained. In the rehabilitation of such patients, it is therefore important to evaluate voiding dysfunction so that a management plan can be developed for long-term care.

ANATOMY

The micturition reflex center in the brain has been localized in the pontine mesencephalic reticular formation in the brain stem[2,4] with interconnection to and from the frontal lobe and cortical and other subcortical areas. Efferent axons from the pontine micturition center travel down the spinal cord in the reticulospinal tract to the detrusor motor nuclei located in the sacral 2, 3, and 4 segments in the sacral gray matter. The reticulospinal tracts are in close proximity to the pyramidal tracts in the lateral column of the spinal cord. Sacral 3 and 4 nuclei have major innervation to and from the detrusor muscle through the pelvic parasympathetic nerves. The sacral 2 spinal segment has a major contribution to the external urethral sphincter through pudendal nerves, which arise from S2, S3, and S4 motor nuclei in the sacral cord (conus) as well. The external urethral sphincter surrounds the membranous urethra and also extends up and around the lower part of the prostatic urethra. Thus, there are two sphincters, one at the bladder neck, which is involuntary, and one around the prostatic and membranous urethra, which is essentially voluntary (external striated sphincter).

Lesions

Lesions below the pons produce detrusor sphincter dyssynergia; however, intracranial lesions above the pons only produce detrusor hyperreflexia wherein the bladder empties at a lower volume (a low-threshold detrusor reflex). It has been well established that spinal cord disconnection from the brain with lesions involving pyramidal tracts will lead to loss of voluntary relaxation of the striated urethral sphincter that surrounds the lower part of the prostatic urethra.

In transection of spinal cord, lesions below the pons with detrusor sphincter dyssynergia, urine is usually retained because bladder contraction leads to simultaneous contraction of the external urethral sphincter. Tetraplegics and paraplegics with lesions above T5 also exhibit autonomic dysreflexia, which is associated with detrusor sphincter dyssynergia.[1,6] Voiding is therefore incomplete and often associated with detrusor hyperreflexia and high intravesical pressure. It is known that high, sustained intravesical pressure (more than 40–50 cm of water) can lead to vesicoureteral reflux.[5] The presence of vesicoureteral reflux in patients with spinal cord injury (SCI) is risky because the higher incidence of bladder infection in these patients invariably leads to pyelonephritis and renal stone disease.

The neurogenic bladder resulting from spinal cord lesions (injury, inflammation, etc.) may not empty adequately due to two key factors: lack of adequate voluntary control to contract the bladder and lack of voluntary control to relax the external urethral sphincter. Any attempted voiding is associated with detrusor sphincter dyssynergia. Often, the detrusor muscle is also weak due to either nerve root lesions or overdistention of the bladder.

URODYNAMIC EVALUATION

Urodynamic studies play a vital role in the examination of suspected neurologically impaired

114

patients with known or suspected neuromuscular dysfunction of the bladder. This may be associated with a known definable or unknown neurologic lesion. The urodynamic evaluation is multipurpose: (1) to determine if the neurogenic dysfunction exists, (2) to recognize and define urodynamic abnormalities such as detrusor hyperreflexia, areflexia, and detrusor sphincter dyssynergia (DESD), (3) to determine the maximum voiding pressure, (4) to determine the appropriate therapy based on the patient's disability and motivation for therapy, and (5) to titrate and evaluate drug therapy to improve voiding.

URODYNAMIC TECHNIQUES

Cystometric Examination

Cystometric (CMG) examination involves filling the bladder with air or water at body temperature. It also may be carried out with radiographic contrast in the bladder for both voiding cystogram and cystometrogram or combined cinéfluoroscopic studies. Similar studies also may be performed under ultrasonic control to provide visualization of the dynamic contraction of the bladder while intravesical pressures are being recorded through a small catheter connected to a strain gauge or a simple manometer.

For cystometric studies, a French size 7 or 10 triple-lumen catheter (Fig. 13-1) is used to fill the bladder and simultaneously record the pressure. Prior to filling the bladder, the clinician instructs the patient to relax and tell when he or she has a "feeling" of filling and when he or she has the desire to void. The patient is then instructed to void. A paraplegic or quadriplegic patient cannot stand and void; ambulatory patients are asked to stand and void so that voiding pressures can be determined. In normal persons, the first sensation of fullness is usually perceived when the bladder is filled with 100 ml of fluid; there is a desire to void when the bladder is filled with about 300–400 ml of fluid. During filling of the bladder, the intravesical pressure is usually around 20 cm water; however, if the bladder is fibrosed, this pressure may rise steeply and the bladder is then considerd noncompliant. Maximum voiding pressures on attempted voiding are noted. Postvoid residuals are checked before and after cystometric examination. In patients with neurogenic bladder dysfunction, about 100 ml of postvoid residual is considered acceptable. Cystometric study thus is used to assess bladder sensation, compliance, and maximum voiding pressures.

The International Continence Society has classified the detrusor as either normal, hyperreflexic, or hyporeflexic based on the CMG. The hyperactive disorder is characterized by involuntary detrusor contractions that may be spontaneous or provoked by rapid filling. When involuntary detrusor

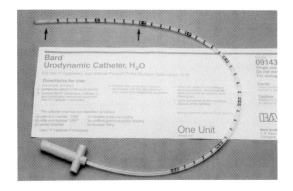

FIGURE 13-1. A triple-lumen catheter (Bard). The arrows indicate two holes, one near the tip for sensing bladder pressure and the other 10 cm from the tip for sensing urethral pressure.

contractions are due to neurologic disorders, the condition is called detrusor hyperreflexia. In the absence of a demonstrable neurological etiology, involuntary detrusor contractions are defined as detrusor instability. The absence of a detrusor contraction, particularly in females, during CMG is not considered to be abnormal unless there are other clinical or urodynamic findings to substantiate the presence of lower motor neuron disease. In patients with spinal cord injury, suprapubic tapping can initiate voiding. It is also important to record blood pressure during the bladder filling, particularly in tetraplegic patients, to find out if patients are prone to autonomic dysreflexia.

An example of a multiple-channel urodynamic study is shown in Figure 13-2. The CMG shows a rise of 50 cm of water in intravesical pressure with the bladder filled to 300 ml. This is a true detrusor pressure because there is very little change in the rectal pressure. Tracings 1 and 6 show that there is a simultaneous reduction in EMG activity with the rise in intravesical pressure (CMG). This indicates the lack of detrusor-sphincter dyssynergia. If seen in normal persons, the sustained rise in the intravesical pressure (tracing 1) would indicate outflow obstruction, either at the bladder neck due to nonrelaxation of the internal urethral sphincter or due to an enlarged prostate. The absence of detrusor sphincter dyssynergia in the patients with spinal cord injury who are taking high-dose baclofen (such as the patient in Figure 13-2) has been observed. Sustained rise in intravesical pressure over 40 cm of water can lead to vesicoureteral reflux.[5] Such patients on intermittent catheterization therefore need anticholinergic drugs to reduce this pressure. Another example of a multichannel study (Fig. 13-3) shows in the top tracing (CMG) pressures of 70–80 cm water with a sustained rise in intravesical pressure associated with marked increase in EMG activity of external urethral sphincter, indicating detrusor sphincter dyssynergia.

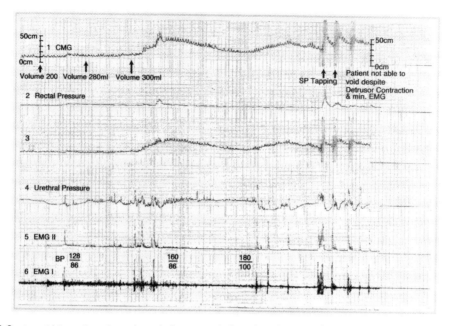

FIGURE 13-2. A multichannel urodynamic study in a tetraplegic patient. It shows simultaneous cystometrogram (CMG) (*top tracing*), rectal pressure (*second tracing*), subtracted pressure (CMG minus rectal pressure) indicating true detrusor pressure (*third tracing*), and urethral pressure (*fourth tracing*). EMG I is a true EMG with motor units and EMG II is an integrated EMG activity of the external urethral sphincter. The CMG (*top tracing*) shows sustained bladder contraction with minimal EMG activity (*sixth tracing*). Even after suprapubic tapping, a minimal increase in EMG activity of the external urethral sphincter is noticed. Reduced EMG activity is explained on the basis of a high-dose Lioresal taken by this spinal cord-injured patient during the study. A rise in blood pressure from 120/86 to 180/100 during bladder filling is indicative of autonomic dysreflexia, which is most often associated with detrusor sphincter dyssynergia. (From Perkash I: Long term urologic management with spinal cord injury. Urol Clin North Am 20:423, 1993, with permission.)

Uroflow (Act of Micturition)

In the able-bodied, the measurement of urinary flow rate is most frequently used as a screening procedure for the diagnosis of bladder outlet obstruction. However, it is not used in patients with spinal cord injury and other neurologic disorders because it is often difficult to evoke a flow rate.

Suprapubic tapping over the bladder region 15–20 times often leads to micturition in patients with spinal cord injury. It is usually intermittent, which does not give an easily measured flow rate. Intermittent flow rate, however, is indicative of the existence of detrusor sphincter dyssynergia, since the dyssynergic urethral sphincter relaxes intermittently. Therefore, patients with spinal cord injury can be evaluated at the bedside: the bladder is first palpated and then suprapubicly tapped to empty it. If, following this procedure, the bladder empties easily with a good stream and without the patient becoming dysreflexic, and no significant rise in blood pressure occurs, chances are that the patient is voiding satisfactorily.

Bladder outlet obstruction due to a bladder neck ledge,[8] enlarged prostate, or detrusor sphincter dyssynergia is associated with a diminished uroflow, but usually with a sustained detrusor contraction and high intravesical pressure (see Figs. 13-2 and

13-3). On the other hand, impaired detrusor contractility is characterized by a diminished flow rate and a low pressure detrusor contraction that is poorly sustained. Even a normal uroflow may not always exclude bladder outlet or sphincteric obstruction in incomplete spinal cord lesions. Therefore, uroflow is not of great clinical value as a single examination.

Electromyography of the External Urethral Sphincter

Simultaneous cystometrographic study and electromyography (EMG) of the external urethral sphincter is important to diagnose detrusor external sphincter dyssynergia. A triple-lumen catheter is used for filling the bladder, and for recording intravesical and intraurethral pressures. Disposable concentric needles (TECA Corp., Pleasantville, NY) with a diameter of 0.46 mm (or 23 gauge) are inserted about 1.5 cm anterior to the anal verge and aimed at the tip of the prostate and guided with the finger in the rectum. The bladder is filled with air or water for cystometric studies. Intra-abdominal pressures are recorded with a rectal balloon, and EMG activity of the external urethral sphincter is monitored simultaneously. In the relaxed state, the normal external sphincter is generally electrically silent with only infrequent low-amplitude motor units (fewer

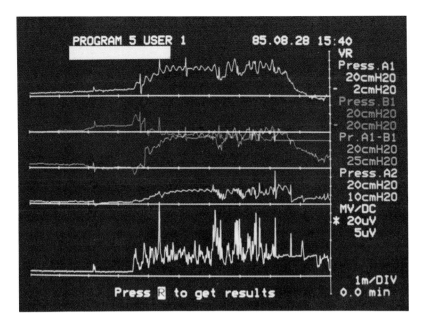

FIGURE 13-3. A simultaneous CMG demonstrating a sustained rise in intravesical pressure (*top tracing*) and increased EMG activity of the external urethral sphincter indicating detrusor-sphincter dyssynergia.

than 200 μv). With progressive bladder filling, there is usually an increase in external urethral sphincter EMG activity and bladder contraction that reaches a maximum just prior to voiding. An increase in EMG activity usually accompanies cough, straining, or movement. The beginning of a voluntary detrusor contraction is marked by relaxation of the external urethral sphincter in a normal person. When this happens, the sphincter EMG becomes electrically silent and the maximum urethral pressure drops dramatically (Fig. 13-4). Sphincter relaxation persists through the detrusor contraction, and, at the end of voiding, electromyographic activity resumes.

Cysto-Uroflowmetry

Multichannel studies use a triple-lumen catheter in the bladder and a rectal catheter to determine rectal pressure, which also indicates abdominal pressure. The bladder is filled with water through one channel. The second channel records pressure through transducers, and the third channel (with a side hole) records urethral pressure. Pressure flow studies can provide bladder pressures (Pves) and corresponding urine flow rates (Qura). True detrusor (Pdet) can be determined by subtracting rectal pressure (Pabd) from bladder pressure (Pves).

FIGURE 13-4. The study shows CMG, rectal pressures, and EMG of the external urethral sphincter in a patient with incomplete spinal cord lesion. This patient had a desire to void at 220 ml (normal around 100 ml). He was able to hold his urine by contracting his external urethral sphincter and was able to relax his sphincter (shown by reduced EMG activity of the external urethral sphincter).

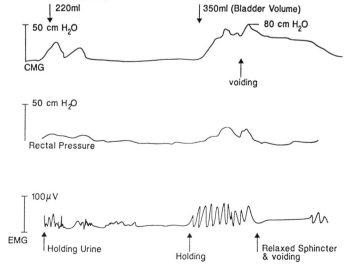

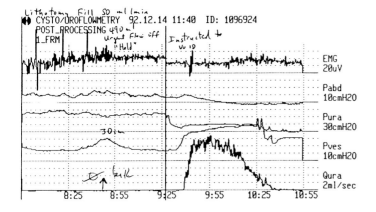

CYSTO/UROFLOWMETRY 92.12.14 11:42 ID: 1096924
POST_PROCESSING

FIGURE 13-5. Multichannel studies and computer-generated results in a patient with urge incontinence. CMG (Pves) shows uninhibited contraction during the filling phase when the patient leaked urine as shown by the small arrow at point 8:55. This action indicates an unstable bladder.

Results of UROFLOWMETRY

Delay Time	0:12	min:sec
Voiding Time	0:55	min:sec
Flow Time	0:55	min:sec
Time to Max Flow	0:16	min:sec
Max Flow Rate	14.9	ml/sec
Average Flow Rate	8.0	ml/sec
Voided Volume	486	ml
Residual Volume	2	ml
Pdet at Max Flow	40	cmH2O

An illustrated study is shown in Figure 13-5 in a woman whose bladder was filled to 490 ml and who had an urgent desire to void and also an uninhibited bladder contraction with intravesical pressure rising to 30 cm of water. When instructed to void, she had a sharp bladder contraction with intravesical pressure (Pdet) rising 40–50 cm of water (illustration) with continued, reduced EMG activity of the external urethral sphincter. This was accompanied by significant voiding and urine flow rate as shown in the lowest tracing (Qura). The results of uroflowmetry are shown in Figure 13-5. The patient voided 486 ml with a residual of 2 ml. Because she had shown uninhibited detrusor contraction during the filling phase, she was given a small dose of anticholinergic to control her uninhibited contraction and leakage of urine.

Urethral Pressure Profilometry

The urethral pressure profile (UPP) represents the lateral closure pressure along the length of the urethra. It is usually studied with a multichannel catheter. Profilometry, with a pull-through technique, provides graphic representation of the lateral pressure along the length of the urethra (Fig. 13-6). Currently, the practiced technique has been adapted from Brown and Wickham.[3] The functional length of the urethra can be measured. These studies are done with an empty bladder. If the bladder contraction occurs other than "Pura-Dif," it is calculated by subtracting bladder pressure (Pves) from Pura to give true urethral pressures (Fig. 13-6). For static UPP, one of the holes meant for sensing the pressure is positioned in the middle of the posterior urethra. A triple-lumen catheter, commonly used for such studies, is shown in Figure 13-1. It has a terminal hole 1 cm from the tip for filling the bladder and another side hole at 10 cm to sense the urethral pressure. Other sophisticated techniques, using a microtransducer mounted at the tip of the urethral catheter, have been used over the more simple and less expensive perfusion catheter systems. These microtransducer catheters are expensive, fragile, and difficult to insert in the male urethra. They also are prone to distortional errors due to the curvature and length of the transducer catheter. While the bladder is gradually filled for CMG, both intravesical and urethral pressures can be simultaneously recorded. In patients with neurologic lesions of the spinal cord, when the bladder contracts, the rise in urethral pressure along with increased EMG activity of the external urethral sphincter is indicative of detrusor sphincter dyssynergia.

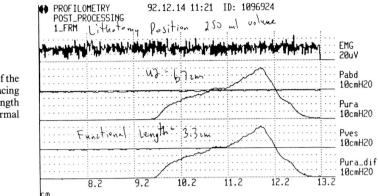

FIGURE 13-6. Urethral pressure profile of the same patient as in Figure 13-5. The upper tracing (Pura) and Pura-dif indicate a functional length of urethra being 3.3 cm, which is within normal limits.

Micturitional Urethral Pressure Profile

Profilometry can be combined with simultaneous voiding. The micturitional urethral pressure profile (MUPP) thus obtained is useful for defining not only the presence of a bladder outlet obstruction but the site of the obstruction as well. The examination is performed by slowly withdrawing the urethral port of the catheter through the urethra during micturition. Normally, the bladder and the entire proximal urethra are approximately isobaric during micturition. When an obstruction exists, there is an immediate drop in pressure distal to the point of obstruction. Unless urethral pressures are monitored and measured with fluoroscopic or ultrasound control, the obstruction could appear to be the bladder neck. Regardless of the recording technique, used alone without visualization, it is impossible to determine the exact site of the anatomic vesical neck. Thus, when the proximal urethra is nonfunctional, the first rise in pressure does not occur at the site of the vesical neck but in the more distal urethra. Consequently, one may conclude erroneously that this finding represents a vesical neck obstruction.

Voiding Cystourethrography and Video-Urodynamics

Measurement of the bladder and urethral pressures and simultaneous fluoroscopic or sonographic visualization are useful for the detection of both anatomical and physiologic abnormalities. In radiographic studies, contrast is used as the infusant. The bladder is catheterized with a triple-lumen urodynamic catheter to simultaneously measure intravesical and urethral pressures. The third lumen is used to fill the bladder. The voiding events on fluoroscopic examination are visualized intermittently, and representative events are recorded on videotape. The bladder is filled until either an involuntary detrusor contraction occurs, the patient is asked to void voluntarily, or leakage of the infusant occurs at the urethral meatus, which gives a leak pressure. Bladder outlet obstruction is characterized by a high voiding pressure and low flow. If obstruction is suspected but the site of the obstruction is not clear, the combination of radiographic visualization and MUPP may provide a definitive answer.

Voiding cystourethrography (VCUG) is useful to help define vesicoureteral reflux presence of the bladder with diverticulae, trabeculation, prostato-ejaculatory reflux, detrusor sphincter dyssynergia (Fig. 13-7), and postvoid residual urine (Fig. 13-8).

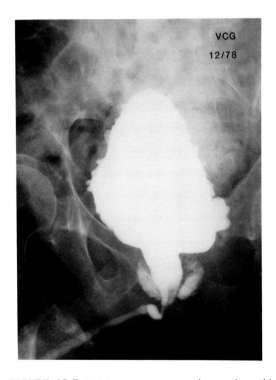

FIGURE 13-7. Voiding cystometrogram in a patient with spinal cord injury shows trabeculated bladder, wide open bladder neck, dilated prostatic urethra, prostato-ejaculatory reflux, and narrow external urethral sphincter, indicating bladder outflow obstruction due to detrusor sphincter dyssynergia.

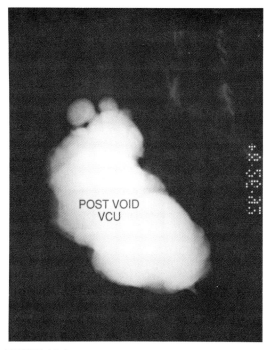

FIGURE 13-8. Post-void film after voiding cystogram shows excessive postvoid residual, trabeculated bladder and voiding multiple bladder diverticula.

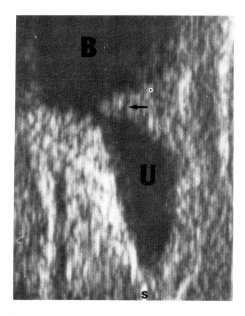

FIGURE 13-10. Transrectal sonographic voiding study showing a bladder neck obstruction (arrow) due to a bladder neck ledge. The bladder is seen as black (B). The prostatic urethra (U) is dilated, and the external sphincter is closed (S).

The site of outflow obstruction at the bladder neck or in the urethra also may be visualized on voiding films. The presence of prostato-ejaculatory reflux, as seen in Figure 13-7, is indicative of obstruction distal to the ejaculatory duct openings in the urethra due to bladder-external urethral sphincter dyssynergia. In Figure 13-7 the external urethral sphincter

is almost closed between the prostate and bulbous urethra. Such patients develop repeated urinary tract infections and epididymo-orchitis. They do not respond well to conservative management with intermittent catheterization. Transurethral sphincterotomy is indicated to prevent recurrent epididymo-orchitis.

Ultrasonography in Urodynamics

Several recent reports have shown encouraging results using ultrasound as an alternative to fluoroscopy for urodynamics.[7,10] Longitudinal real-time imaging of the posterior urethra in a sagittal plane can be achieved during voiding. Using a transrectal linear array sonographic probe, the bladder neck and posterior urethra, including bulbous urethra, can be visualized without the use of dye. Urine itself provides good contrast for sonographic studies. An example of this is shown with a wide open bladder neck, posterior urethra, and bulbous urethra (Fig. 13-9). Bladder neck obstruction is easily visualized on sonography. Secondary bladder neck obstruction due to a ledge in patients with spinal cord injury has been reported.[3] Recognition of this obstruction is important since intermittent catheterization may be difficult in these patients (Fig. 13-10). Sonographic voiding cystourethrogram shows bladder neck obstruction due to a ledge (shown as arrow) posteriorly at the bladder neck. These ledges are believed to be a complication in

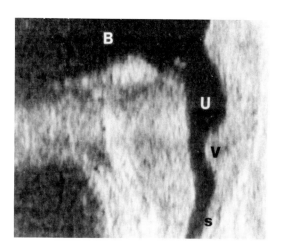

FIGURE 13-9. Sonographic voiding cystogram demonstrating the bladder (B) and wide open bladder neck, prostatic (U) and membranous urethra. Verumontanum (V) is seen prominently in the middle of the posterior urethra. The lower part of the urethra is slightly narrow and is surrounded by external urethral sphincter (S).

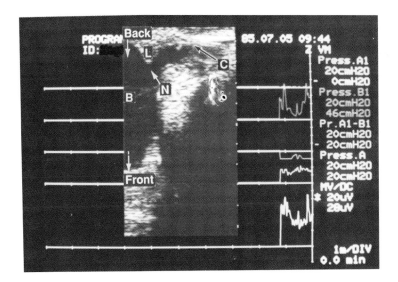

FIGURE 13-11. A multichannel urodynamic study combined with sonography. The bladder *(B)*, bladder neck *(N)*, bladder neck ledge *(L)*, and urethral catheter *(C)* are shown. The bladder neck is wide open, which occurred after the bladder neck was touched with the urethral catheter. (From Perkash I, Wolfe V: Detrusor hyperreflexia and its relationship to posterior bladder neck sensory mechanism in spinal injured patients. Neurourology and Urodynamics 10:125–133, 1991, with permission.)

patients with detrusor-sphincter dyssynergia who are on long-term intermittent catheterization.[7] The presence of a bladder neck ledge invariably leads to difficulty in catheterization with a plain catheter. A coudé tip catheter is more effective for intermittent catheterization.

Combined synchronous, ultrasonographic and urodynamic monitoring is feasible (Fig. 13-11). This study could be done in lieu of a cine radiographic study combined with simultaneous urodynamics. It has been shown that simple insertion of a catheter by touching the bladder neck ledge can result in bladder contraction and wide open bladder neck[8,9] (see Fig. 13-11) with a wide-open bladder neck and posterior urethra. It is therefore important to catheterize such patients carefully[10] and not stimulate the bladder neck to produce bladder neck stimulated cystometrogram.[8] Persistent narrowing of the membranous urethra on ultrasound imaging and elevated detrusor pressure is consistent with DESD in a complete suprasacral spinal cord injury. The main advantage of the sonographic study over cine radiographic studies is the lack of radiation exposure for the patients. However, bladder shape, trabeculation, diverticula, and vesicoureteral reflux are difficult to visualize on sonography alone.

Ultrasonographic Studies of Kidneys

Renal sonography is useful in detecting hydronephrosis of the kidneys with dilated pelvicaliceal system, stones, or other filling defects in the renal pelvis. In following patients with spinal cord injury to detect early hydrophronesis, sonography is noninvasive and eliminates yearly intravenous pyelographic studies that once were used frequently.

Intravenous Pyelography

Intravenous pyelography (IVP) is indicated to rule out stone disease and hydronephrosis and to define anatomic configuration of the pelvicaliceal system. Because routine, once yearly, IVP in patients with spinal cord injury leads to a high dose of radiation exposure, it has been widely replaced with kidney sonographic studies. If a stone is suspected, IVP is necessary for localization and for treatment with extracorporeal shockwave lithotripsy.

Nuclear Scanning of the Kidneys

Radioisotope renography in patients with spinal cord injury has been found to be useful for follow-up screening.[11] The most common abnormality is the delay of isotope excretion. Renal plasma flow is calculated and reduction in flow of 20% or more is felt to be significant in patients with spinal cord injury. This indicates that urodynamic studies are needed to rule out any outflow obstruction at the bladder neck due to ledge, median lobe, or the presence of detrusor sphincter dyssynergia.

SUMMARY

Neurophysiologic dysfunctions of the bladder can best be evaluated by urodynamic studies. If not carried out carefully, however, studies can give erroneous results. Selection of an appropriate size of urodynamic catheter, careful introduction of the catheter without irritating the bladder neck region, and fluid introduction at 37°C (isothermic to body) are important prerequisites to achieve true results. Sonographic studies are much less invasive than the studies using a catheter, dyes, and radiographs, but they do not provide complete information and are therefore useful only as a screening modality.

REFERENCES

1. Bors E, French JD: Management of paroxysmal hypertension following injuries to cervical and upper thoracic segments of the spinal cord. Arch Surg 64:803, 1952.
2. Bradley WE, Timm GW, Scott FB: Innervation of the detrusor muscle and urethra. Urol Clin North Am 1:3, 1974.
3. Brown M, Wickham JEA: The urethral pressure profile. Br J Urol 41:211, 1969.
4. Denny-Brown D, Robertson EG: On the physiology of micturition. Brain 56:149, 1933.
5. McGuire EJ, Woodwide JR, Borden TA, et al: Prognostic value of urodynamic testing in the myelodysplastic patient. J Urol 126:205, 1981.
6. Perkash I: Detrusor-sphincter dyssynergia and dyssynergic responses: Recognition and rationale for early modified transurethral sphincterotomy in complete spinal cord injury lesions. J Urol 120:469, 1978.
7. Perkash I, Friedland GW: Posterior ledge at the bladder neck: The crucial diagnostic role of ultrasonography. Urol Radiol 8:175, 1986.
8. Perkash I, Friedland GW: Transrectal ultrasonography of the lower urinary tract: Evaluation of bladder neck problems. Neurourol Urodynam 299–306, 1986.
9. Perkash I, Wolfe V: Detrusor hyperreflexia and its relationship to posterior bladder neck sensory mechanism in spinal injured patients. Neurourol Urodynam 10:125, 1991.
10. Shapeero G, Friedland GW, Perkash I: Transrectal sonographic voiding cystourethrography: Studies in neuromuscular dysfunction. AJR 141:83, 1983.
11. Tempkin A, Sullivan G, Paldi J, et al: Radioisotope renography in spinal cord injury. J Urol 133:228, 1985.

Chapter 14

BASIC CONCEPTS OF NEURAL BLOCKADE

TED A. LENNARD, M.D.
DANIEL Y. SHIN, M.D.

Percutaneous nerve blocks can be used in a variety of clinical circumstances (Table 14-1). They are easy to perform when one understands the regional anatomy, block technique, indications, and pharmacology of the medication injected. These blocks can provide anesthesia for procedures, as well as rapid diagnostic, prognostic, and therapeutic information when applied in the appropriate clinical setting. The result, either temporary or permanent, promotes a higher level of function when used within the framework of a well-designed rehabilitation program.

NEUROVASCULAR BUNDLE ANATOMY

The neurovascular bundle consists of peripheral nerve fibers wrapped in connective tissue intermingled by a capillary plexus (Fig. 14-1). Three types of connective tissue are present within the peripheral nerve: endoneurium, perineurium, and epineurium. The endoneurium is a delicate, supporting structure located adjacent to individual axons within a fascicle. Individual fascicles are bound by the perineurium, a layer felt to monitor intrafascicular fluid diffusion.[11,17] These fascicles are bound in groups by the outermost layer, the epineurium (Fig. 14-2). This layer contains the vasa nevorum, which divides into arterioles that penetrate the perineurium (Fig. 14-3). Ultimately a network of capillaries reach each fascicle to supply individual axons.

The neurovascular bundle lies well protected usually between muscle or bone. At its most proximal location—the spinal root level—the neurovascular bundle contains motor, sensory, and autonomic fibers. These roots divide into dorsal and ventral rami, the latter of which reconnect to form a plexus of nerves. Ultimately, terminal nerve branches of isolated fiber types—sensory or motor branches—are formed.

NEURAL BLOCK TECHNIQUE: GENERAL CONSIDERATIONS

Several techniques can be used to block a peripheral nerve. Each technique requires a thorough knowledge of both surface and gross anatomy as well as good manual dexterity. When selective motor nerves are blocked, an understanding of kinesiology is helpful.

The two common approaches used to block nerves are the paresthesia technique (PT) and nonparesthesia technique (NPT). PT attempts to purposefully provoke paresthesias of the nerve prior to injection. These paresthesias indicate that the needle is in contact with the nerve and serve as a warning of potential nerve injury. This technique assumes that the patient's sensory pathways are intact and that the patient is able to cooperate fully with the injection. The second approach, NPT, avoids this deliberate probing for paresthesias and relies on anatomic landmarks, but may require greater volumes of medication to achieve the desired block. With NPT the needle tip may not approximate the nerve as closely as PT. As expected, PT is associated with a greater incidence of nerve injury[10,12,15] and should be avoided if possible.

As an alternative technique, a nerve stimulator (Fig. 14-4) can be used to locate and block peripheral nerves. These stimulators are available commercially, although office electrodiagnostic equipment can often suffice. An electrical impulse generated by the stimulator and controlled by a rheostat is transmitted through a needle. The entire shaft of this needle is coated with Teflon except the bevel. The Teflon prevents spread of stimulus into surrounding tissue and directs electrical current to the needle tip. As the needle approaches the nerve, either a motor, sensory, or mixed response can be elicited depending on the fiber types contained within the nerve. The neural response should increase as

TABLE 14-1. Indications for Percutaneous
Nerve Blocks

With local anesthetics
 1. Provides anesthesia for procedures
 2. Differentiates pain problems and helps better understand nociceptive pathways
 3. Serves as a treatment for inflammatory compression neuropathies in combination with corticosteroids
 4. Provides treatment for sympathetic mediated pain syndromes often by breaking the "vicious cycle" involved
 5. Differentiates spasticity from joint contractures
 6. Helps predict the effect of a neurolytic procedure
 7. Allows selective recording in nerve conduction studies[5]
 8. Promotes functional activities in an occupational or physical therapy program
 9. Assists in serial or inhibitory casting

With neurolytic agents (chemical neurolysis)
 10. Facilitates functional goals in the spastic patient: positioning, ambulation, bracing, transfers
 11. Improves caregiver tasks such as hygiene in the spastic patient: perineal, axillary, elbow, or hand regions
 12. Improves self image of the spastic patient by reducing joint deformities and improving cosmesis
 13. May improve residual voluntary muscle control by eliminating unwanted hypertonia in the spastic patient
 14. Reduces pain caused by hypertonia
 15. Provides treatment for specific, intractable pain disorders
 16. Prevents nerve compression injuries in hyperflexed joints, i.e., median nerve at the wrist from wrist flexor spasticity
 17. Prevents skin breakdown by promoting proper seating and positioning

With normal saline
 18. Provides placebo response

the needle tip approaches the nerve. It is desirable to obtain a strong neural response with a low stimulus output, thereby assuring accurate needle placement. This technique is preferred when injecting neurolytic agents for the treatment of spasticity.

One can quickly identify selective motor responses, such as musculocutaneous nerve stimulation causing elbow flexion, and quickly determine the effect of chemical neurolysis after injection.

Regardless of the technique used, the needle tip should remain in the epineural space when solution is injected (Fig. 14-5). Solution should not be injected into the nerve because intraneural injections have a high association with fascicular damage.[3,4] If paresthesias are elicited, the needle should be repositioned before solution is injected. Forceful infection is not recommended, because it may be a sign of injecting into a fixed space such as tendon or adjacent to bone. Intravascular injection can usually be avoided by aspirating for blood in several planes prior to injecting. Slow administration of the drug is advisable to allow detection of early side effects from vascular injection.

Repeat anesthetic injections close to the same nerve within a single office visit should be avoided. Because warning paresthesias may not be present, occult iatrogenic nerve injury may occur.

NERVE INJURIES

Three major factors contribute to nerve injury from injections: trauma, toxicity, and ischemia. Many nerve injection injuries are due to a combination of these factors.[12]

Trauma to the nerve during injection occurs with overly vigorous probing during insertion of the needle. This can directly injure the nerve fascicles. Selander et al. demonstrated a lower risk of nerve fascicle injury using short beveled needles. They also demonstrated that nerve fascicles rolled or slid with needle contact.[12]

FIGURE 14-1. Under magnification, the neurovascular bundle with extrinsic blood vessels and a segmental supplying artery are apparent (*EV*). The linear extrinsic vessels parallel grooves created by adjacent fascicles (*F*). (From Beek AV, Kleinert HE: Peripheral nerve injuries and repair. In Rand R (ed): Microneurosurgery, 3rd ed. St. Louis, Mosby, 1985, p 742, with permission.)

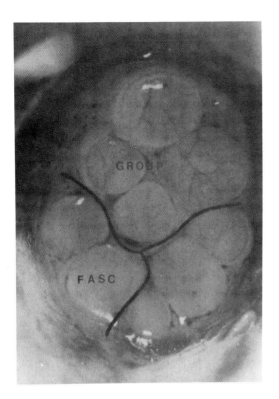

FIGURE 14-2. Under magnification, a cross-section of the median nerve demonstrates individual and groups of fascicles (FASC). Note the connective tissue between each fascicle and surrounding the entire nerve. (From Beek AV, Kleinert HE: Peripheral nerve injuries and repair. In Rand R (ed): Microneurosurgery, 3rd ed. St. Louis, Mosby, 1985, p 742, with permission.)

FIGURE 14-3. Neurovascular bundle demonstrating the entrance of the arterial supply into the epineurium with surrounding connective tissue. (From Zancolli, Cozzi: Nerves of the upper limb. In Zancolli, Cozzi (eds): Atlas of Surgical Anatomy of the Hand. New York, Churchill Livingstone, 1992, p 685, with permission.)

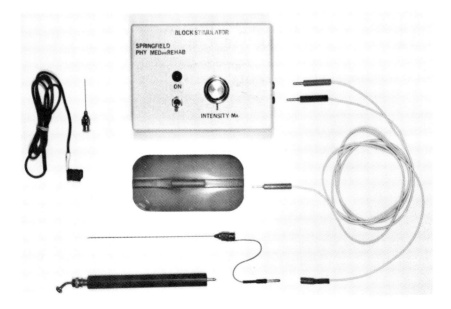

FIGURE 14-4. A constant current stimulator (*top*), surface probing electrode (*bottom left*), and a large surface anode. Teflon-coated, usually 22-gauge, hypodermic needles varying from 37-75 mm in length with exposed tips are commonly used. The needle acts as a cathode. An "alligator" clip with a small Teflon-coated needle is also pictured (*top left*).

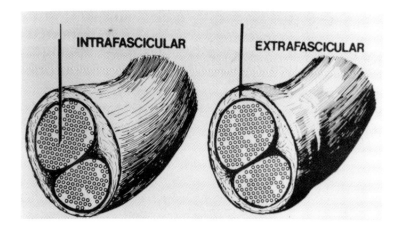

FIGURE 14-5. Needle placement in the intrafascicular space compared to that within the extrafascicular space. (From Gentili F, Hudson A, Kline D, et al: Peripheral nerve injection injury: An experimental injury. Neurosurgery 4:244, 1979, with permission.)

Intraneural injections of solution not only directly injure both myelinated and unmyelinated nerve fibers but also cause a breakdown in blood-nerve barrier function.[3,4] The spread of anesthesia with intraneural injections has been demonstrated and, when near the spine, may cause unexpected spinal anesthesia.[16] Neural compression or stretching may also result from large volumes of solution injected into a fixed space, thereby traumatizing the nerve.

Neurotoxicity can be caused by direct injection of drugs into nervous tissue. Intrafascicular injections of anesthetics cause profound nerve damage. The degree of damage depends on the type and amount of drug injected.[3,4] Ester anesthetics generally demonstrate greater toxicity than amides when injected into the intrafascicular space.[2,9] Extrafascicular injections of anesthetics in routine concentrations rarely cause significant histologic nerve damage or disruption of the blood-nerve barrier but can alter the permeability of the perineurium leading to endoneurial edema.[2,9] The epineurium provides some neuroprotective function during injection, thereby reducing toxicity from medication.

Additives, such as epinephrine, increase the toxicity of the anesthetics when injected intrafascicularly.[1,13] Consequently, if extended duration of anesthesia is desired from a nerve block, a long-acting anesthetic or continuous infusion technique is preferable to the addition of epinephrine.[15]

Mackinnon et al. found that corticosteroid injections into the epineural tissue did not cause nerve damage.[7] When injected into the intrafascicular space, corticosteroids exerted a direct neurotoxic effect with disruption of the blood-nerve barrier, similar to anesthetics. Severe nerve fiber damage was noted with hydrocortisone (Solu-Cortef) and triamcinolone hexacetonide (Aristospan), moderate damage with triamcinolone acetonide (Kenalog) and methylprednisolone (Depo-Medrol), and the least damage with dexamethasone (Decadron) (Fig. 14-6).

Ischemia may result not only from application of a tourniquet or improper positioning of the patient, but also by the nerve block itself if the injection is given into the intrafascicular space. The ischemia results from increased intraneural compartment pressure by the injectate volume, which reduces neural perfusion. This intraneural pressure has been shown experimentally to remain above the blood perfusion pressure for 15 minutes without damage.[16]

GENERAL PRINCIPLES OF NEURAL BLOCKADE

Drugs in isolation or in combinations can be injected to block nerves. The most common mixtures include anesthetic agents in combination with corticosteroids (see chapter 1). When chemical neurolysis is desired, neurolytic drugs are injected. Under the correct clinical circumstance, these neurolytic agents can be successfully used to treat hypertonicity and chronic intractable pain disorders. The following section will briefly discuss the principles behind anesthetic motor and sensory blocks and neurolytic blocks for spasticity and pain.

Anesthetic Blocks

As a result of an anesthetic's reversible properties, nerve blocks can be performed to intentionally paralyze or deactivate specific muscles and/or selectively disrupt sensory pathways. This effect has numerous clinical applications, especially when prior treatment has failed or a diagnosis is unclear. With the exception of anesthesia for surgical procedures, blocks should seldom be the initial treatment of a disorder and always be integrated into a well-planned rehabilitation program.

Motor Blocks

Isolated blocks purely to motor nerves or to motor components of mixed nerves are useful to

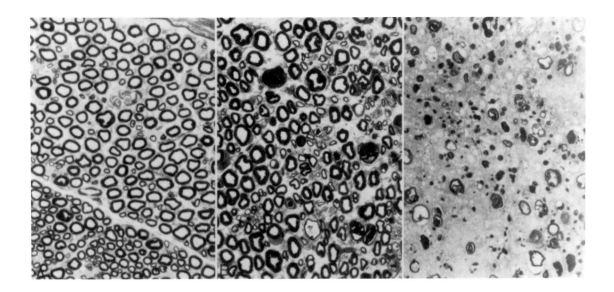

FIGURE 14-6. *Left,* Cross-section of a normal myelinated nerve fiber population within a sciatic nerve (×585). *Center,* cross-section 12 days after intrafascicular injection of dexamethasone (Decadron), demonstrating relatively normal appearance with minimal evidence of nerve fiber injury (× 585). *Right,* cross-section 12 days after intrafascicular injection of triamcinolone hexacetonide (Aristospan), demonstrating severe widespread axonal and myelin degeneration (× 585). (From Mackinnon SE, Hudson AR, Gentili F, et al: Peripheral nerve injection injury with steroid agents. Plast Reconstr Surg 69:482–489, 1982, with permission.)

relax specific muscles. The goal is to promote a better examination or allow defined treatment. For example, multiple trigger points in the trapezius muscle are common in myofascial pain disorders. When conventional treatment fails, a spinal accessory nerve block will render the trapezius muscle flaccid and facilitate gentle stretching. This aids in diminishing these trigger points. It must be remembered, however, that overzealous stretching is not advisable because the muscle is more vulnerable to stretch injury.

Motor blocks also may be useful in differentiating joint contracture from spasticity. For example, if a patient presents with an elbow flexion deformity, a musculocutaneous anesthetic nerve block can be performed. After injection, the patient's elbow is passively extended and any change in range of motion is evaluated. If only minimal improvement in passive elbow extension occurs, one would suspect contracture formation or bony ankylosis as the etiology. However, if full extension is achieved, the elbow flexion deformity is more likely to be related to spasticity. A neurolytic block may then be pursued. The information gained from the previous anesthetic block assists the clinician in predicting the outcome from subsequent chemical neurolysis. In addition, anesthetic peripheral nerve blocks can facilitate serial casting by relaxing spastic muscles. The effect allows placement of casts on extremity joints in the desired joint position.

Sensory Blocks

Anesthetic peripheral nerve blocks are most commonly used to facilitate surgical procedures by blocking sensory pathways. In an office practice setting, anesthetic blocks can be used to assist in the diagnosis of difficult pain problems. When sensory components to nerves are interrupted, expected dermatomal sensory changes can be evaluated and compared with actual "blocked" changes, thereby diagnosing nociceptive pain pathways undetected with conventional testing. For example, a radial sensory neuropathy masked by de Quervain's tenosynovitis may be diagnosed after a radial sensory nerve block. This and other compressive neuropathies such as carpal tunnel syndrome may later require corticosteroid injections.

Patients who malinger or magnify symptoms also may be evaluated using blocks. Response to injections with various concentrations of anesthetic versus placebo can be analyzed and, thus, the patient's reliability determined.

Another way to use sensory blocks is to "reset" the pain generators, especially in cases of sympathetic mediated pain disorders with serial injections. Once a response to painful stimuli is attenuated, the patient can participate in a therapy program that emphasizes functional tasks, joint range of motion, stretching, and skin desensitization. The goal is to gradually eliminate the painful stimulus over time.

Neurolytic Blocks

Spasticity

Hypertonicity due to upper motor neuron dysfunction may be caused by lesions at many levels within the brain and spinal cord. Among patients with traumatic brain injury (TBI), the most severe hypertonicity is found in those with diffuse axonal injury (DAI) or hypoxic–ischemic injury (HII) following cardiopulmonary arrest. Rigidity, spasticity, and dystonia all contribute to joint abnormalities and restricted function. Hypertonicity is usually greatest within the first 6 months of injury. Because this is the period of spontaneous neurologic recovery, one should avoid any permanent surgical procedure intended to control hypertonicity. Without any treatment, disabling musculotendinous contracture and abnormal, dyssynergic patterns of movement occur, further complicating the patient's recovery and outcome. Peripheral nerve blockade may be useful during this interval to assist in the treatment of spasticity.

A large number of patients with TBI and spinal cord injury require localized nerve blocks designed to depress the final common pathway during reorganization and recovery of the central nervous system. If nerve blocks are performed early in the course of rehabilitation, therapy can be facilitated. Noninvasive treatment for spasticity should be maximized prior to proceeding with percutaneous neurolytic blocks. This includes medications, stretching, serial casting, icing, electrical stimulation, and positioning. Any cerebral or spinal cord anomalies, such as hydrocephalus and syringomyelia, should be corrected surgically. Any noxious stimuli, such as urinary tract infection and skin lesion, should be eliminated when possible. Drug-induced movement disorders should be evaluated and, when possible, the offending drug discontinued.

The prognosis for motor return and stage of recovery should be established. The physician must determine if the hypertonicity is generalized or focal. Generalized hypertonicity is usually not responsive to nerve blocks and, unless hygiene is the primary concern, blocks should not be performed. Focal hypertonicity, however, does respond well to nerve blocks. Consistent patterns of hypertonicity need to be established, and treatment should initially be directed toward proximal tone. Any block should affect the most proximal nerve capable of denervating the maximum number of spastic myotomes. All residual voluntary motor function of the affected limb is to be preserved. Phenol generally results in alleviation of spasticity with little decrease of voluntary contraction.[8]

Pain Management

The most common use of neurolytic agents for pain management is to treat intractable cancer pain in patients with a limited life span. This can be done with intrathecal or peripheral nerve injections. An in-depth discussion of this topic is beyond the scope of this chapter. However, a brief discussion about the limited applications of peripheral neurolytic blocks in patients without cancer follows.

If an identifiable pain generator can be located whose nerve does not provide extensive sensation or innervate vital structures such as organs and muscles, a neurolytic block may be considered. All other treatment options must be exhausted first. Injection should be considered as a last resort and given with great caution only by well-qualified clinicians. Anesthetic blocks are used both to confirm the diagnosis and to predict outcomes from the neurolytic injection. For example, anesthetic dorsal ramus medial branch (facet nerve) blocks may be initially performed with reduction of the patient's spine pain being closely monitored over the duration of the anesthetic. If successful, denervation procedures could be performed, i.e., chemical neurolysis. Cryotherapy and radiofrequency are other options for treatment when neurolytic agents are undesirable. Neuromas can also be successfully treated with neurolytic blockade.[6]

CONCLUSION

Any peripheral nerve can be blocked if a physician is familiar with the regional anatomy, indications, and technique. Judicious use of these procedures requires a thorough understanding of the appropriate indications for blockade and the medications to be used. With this understanding, outcomes are maximized while the potential for complications is reduced.

REFERENCES

1. Covino BG: Potential neurotoxicity of local anesthetic agents [editorial]. Can Anaesth Soc J 30:111–116, 1983.
2. Gentili F, Hudson A, Hunter D, et al: Nerve injection injury with local anesthetic agents: A light and electron microscopic, fluorescent microscopic and horseradish peroxidase study. Neurosurgery 6:263–272, 1984.
3. Gentili F, Hudson A, Kline D, et al: Peripheral nerve injection injury: An experimental study. Neurosurgery 4:244–253, 1979.
4. Hudson AR: Nerve injection injuries. Clin Plast Surg 11:27–30, 1984.
5. Kimura J: Electrodiagnosis in Diseases of Nerve and Muscle: Principles and Practice, 2nd ed. Philadelphia, F.A. Davis, 1989.
6. Kirvela O, Nieminen S: Treatment of painful neuromas with neurolytic blockade. Pain 41:161–165, 1990.
7. Mackinnon SE, Hudson AR, Gentili F, et al: Peripheral nerve injection injury with steroid agents. Plast Reconstr Surg 69:482–489, 1982.
8. Moritz U: Phenol block of peripheral nerves. Scand J Rehabil Med 5:160–163, 1973.
9. Myers R, Kalichman M, Reisner L, et al: Neurotoxicity of local anesthetics: Altered perineurial permeability, edema, and nerve fiber injury. Anesthesiology 64:29–35, 1986.

10. Plevak DJ, Linstromberg JW, Danielson DR: Paresthesia vs nonparesthesia: The axillary block. ASA Abstracts, Anesthesiology 59, 1983.
11. Ross MH, Reith EJ: Perineurium: Evidence for contractile elements. Science 165:604–606, 1969.
12. Selander D: Paresthesias or no paresthesias? Nerve complications after neural blockades. Acta Anaesthesiol Belg 39:173–174, 1988.
13. Selander D, Brattsand R, Lundborg G, et al: Local anesthetics: Importance of mode of application, concentration and adrenaline for the appearance of nerve lesions. Acta Anesthesiol Scand 23:127–136, 1979.
14. Selander D, Dhuner K, Lundborg G: Peripheral nerve injury due to injection needles used for regional anesthesia. Acta Anaesthesiol Scand 21:182–188, 1977.
15. Selander D, Edshage S, Wolff T: Parethesiae or no parethesiae? Acta Anaesthesiol Scand 23:27–33, 1979.
16. Selander D, Sjostrand J: Longitudinal spread of intraneurally injected local anesthetics. Acta Anaesthesiol Scand 22:622–634, 1978.
17. Thomas PK, Olsson Y: Microscopic anatomy and function of connective tissue components of peripheral nerve. In Dyck PJ, Thomas PK, Lambert EH, Bunge R (eds): Peripheral Neuropathy, vol 1. Philadelphia, W.B. Saunders, 1984, pp 97–120.

Chapter 15

PROXIMAL UPPER EXTREMITY, TRUNK, AND HEAD BLOCKS

DANIEL Y. SHIN, M.D.
TED A. LENNARD, M.D.

Nerves of the proximal upper extremity, trunk, and head are easily accessible to percutaneous block procedures. Blocks in many of these specific areas carry risks of pneumothorax due to the proximity of the pleural cavity to the regional anatomy. This is especially true with intercostal, suprascapular, thoracodorsal, pectoral, and lower subscapular blocks. Therefore, blocks in this region require the clinician to have a thorough knowledge of shoulder, neck, and chest wall anatomy.

SUPRASCAPULAR NERVE

The suprascapular nerve originates from the superior trunk of the brachial plexus and contains fibers from the fifth and sixth cervical nerve roots. It enters the supraspinous fossa below the transverse scapular ligament after passing obliquely deep to the trapezius and omohyoid muscles. The nerve innervates the supraspinatus muscle and gives branches to the glenohumeral and acromioclavicular joints as well as the conoid, trapezoid, and coracoacromial ligaments. The nerve passes around the spinoglenoid notch to terminate in the infraspinatus muscle. It also carries sympathetic innervation to the joint capsule.

Therapeutic or diagnostic injections can be performed to block the suprascapular nerve. Anesthetic injections with or without corticosteroids can be used to treat suprascapular neuropathies, cancer pain, and postoperative shoulder pain, especially after acromioplasty.[4,8,10] These injections also may be useful to facilitate glenohumeral range of motion in patients with adhesive capsulitis with or without superimposed reflex sympathetic dystrophy.[11]

Suprascapular Nerve Block Technique

Granirer originally described a suprascapular nerve block technique using a posterior approach.

A point is identified on the scapular spine 2 inches from the lateral border of the acromion.[3] The needle is inserted ½ inch superior to this point into the supraspinatus fossa (Fig. 15-1) and is advanced until bone is contacted and then withdrawn several millimeters and angled approximately 15° cephalad.

An alternative posterior approach involves dividing the scapular spine into thirds and dropping a perpendicular line at the junction of the middle and outer third. The scapular notch lies 1–2 cm superior to this point of intersection. The needle is advanced about 2 inches until bone is contacted. The needle can be adjusted until the suprascapular notch is identified, and 8–10 ml of solution can be injected.

An anterior approach described by Wassef can be performed with the patient in the supine or sitting position.[11] The point of entry of the needle is at the anteromedial border of the trapezius muscle where it attaches to the lateral third of the clavicle. The needle is inserted above the clavicle and advanced posteriorly with a slight downward and medial projection.

Pneumothorax is the most serious complication of suprascapular nerve block. In skilled hands, its incidence is reported to be less than 1% from the posterior approach , and it is even less common from the anterior approach.[5]

MEDIAL AND LATERAL PECTORAL NERVES

The medial (MPN) and lateral (LPN) pectoral nerves are small in size and purely motor (Fig. 15-2). MPN is a branch of the medial cord of the brachial plexus that originates from the C8 and T1 spinal roots. This nerve innervates the pectoralis minor muscle (Pmm) and emerges from its inferolateral border to innervate the lower portion of the pectoralis major muscle (PMM). The remaining clavicular head of the PMM is innervated by the LPN. This nerve is a branch of the lateral cord of the brachial plexus originating from the C5, C6, and C7 spinal roots. It emerges from the superior border of the Pmm immediately below the midclavicle prior to innervating the PMM.

The PMM is partly responsible for humeral adduction and internal rotation movements while the Pmm depresses and rotates the scapula. Therefore, in cases of spasticity affecting these muscles, shoulder adduction and internal rotation deformities result. This deformity creates problems with axillary hygiene, upper extremity dressing, positioning, and shoulder pain.

Medial Pectoral Nerve Block Technique

When performing pectoral nerve blocks, accurate anatomical landmarks must be identified on the anterior chest wall. Outlining the borders of the Pmm on the skin is the key to a successful block. This muscle originates from the outer surfaces of the third, fourth, and fifth sternocostal margins and inserts into the coracoid process. The MPN can be located using a surface stimulator at the intersection of the lower border of the Pmm and a perpendicular line drawn from the midclavicle. Once located with surface stimulation, a needle is introduced in a plane parallel to the muscle. To avoid inadvertent intrapleural injection, the needle should not be advanced perpendicular to the chest wall.

Lateral Pectoral Nerve Block Technique

With the lateral pectoral nerve block technique, the LPN becomes exposed at the superior margin of the Pmm. If the same mid-clavicular line described in the MPN block is extended perpendicularly, across the Pmm superiorly, the LPN can be located. Recognizing the Pmm attachment sites is essential for an accurate block. A surface stimulator is useful, and once the nerve is identified, the needle is inserted in a posterior and superior directed angle. As in the MPN block, caution is advised with needle advancement to avoid intrapleural injection. Needle advancement in blocking both the MPN and LPN should not occur in a perpendicular plane to the chest wall. This avoids penetration into the pleural cavity and subsequent pneumothoraces.

THORACODORSAL NERVE

The thoracodorsal nerve originates from the posterior cord of the brachial plexus and is composed

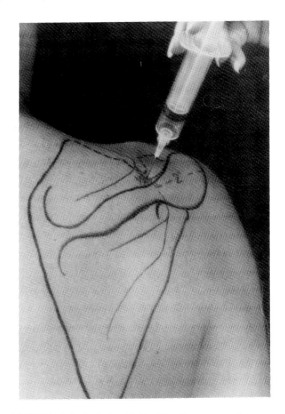

FIGURE 15-1. Technique for blocking the suprascapular nerve. The right scapula is outlined with the course of the nerve. The needle is inserted perpendicular to the skin until bone is reached. It is then withdrawn a few millimeters and tilted 30° cephalad into the supraspinous fossa. (From Torres-Ramos FM, Biundo JJ: Suprascapular neuropathy during progressive resistive exercises in a cardiac rehabilitation program. Arch Phys Med Rehabil 73:1107–1111, 1992, with permission.)

of fibers from the C6, C7, and C8 nerve roots (Fig. 15-3). As it exits the posterior cord, it travels adjacent to the subscapular artery along the posterior wall of the axilla where it terminates into the latissimus dorsi muscle.

The latissimus dorsi muscle is one of the strongest humeral adductors and also assists in humeral internal rotation and extension. A thoracodorsal nerve block is useful to reduce spasticity that results in a shoulder adduction and internal rotation deformity. This block is often used in conjunction with blocks of the pectoral and lower subscapular nerves.

Thoracodorsal Nerve Block Technique

The thoracodorsal nerve can be blocked in the anterior axillary region. A mid-axillary line is drawn that intersects with a perpendicular line 1½ inches above the nipple line (Fig. 15-4). Using a surface stimulator, the nerve is located at the intersection of these lines between the latissimus dorsi and the chest wall. The latissimus dorsi muscle

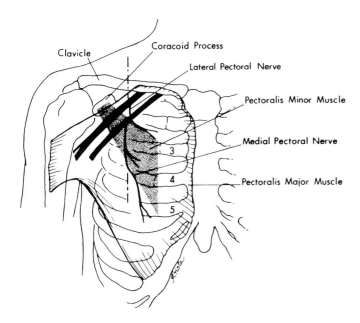

FIGURE 15-2. The medial and lateral pectoral nerve (anterior chest view) originates from the medial and lateral cord of the brachial plexus. Note their exit in the mid-clavicular line.

can be easily separated from the lateral chest wall since the nerve passes between these two structures. The needle is inserted anterior to the latissimus dorsi muscle in a posteriorly directed orientation. Caution is necessary to prevent introduction of the needle into the pleural cavity or into the subscapular artery that travels with the nerve. The nerve may be approached more precisely with the use of a nerve stimulator, watching for strong humeral adduction with current less than 2 mA.

LOWER SUBSCAPULAR NERVE

The lower subscapular nerve (LSN) originates from the posterior cord of the brachial plexus and contains fibers from the C5 and C6 spinal nerves (see Fig. 15-3). The LSN initially enters the axillary portion of the subscapularis muscle and later terminates in the teres major muscle (see Fig. 15-5). This latter muscle primarily acts as an internal rotator and adductor of the humerus. The teres major muscle, in combination with the pectoralis major and latissimus dorsi muscles, is partly responsible for spasticity-induced shoulder adduction deformities.

Lower Subscapular Nerve Block Technique

The LSN can be localized along the axillary border of the scapula at the midpoint between the acromion and the inferior angle of the scapula. The needle is advanced immediately adjacent to the bone and directed parallel to the chest wall in an anterior and lateral direction (Fig. 15-5). The combination

use of both surface and Teflon-coated needle electrodes facilitates this procedure.

MUSCULOCUTANEOUS NERVE

The musculocutaneous nerve (MCN) originates from the lateral cord of the brachial plexus and is composed of fibers from the C5, C6, and C7 spinal nerve roots. It exits the lateral cord just proximal to the origin of the median nerve. The MCN travels obliquely downward and laterally to supply the coracobrachialis, biceps, and brachialis muscles (Fig. 15-6). A small branch often supplies the elbow joint, but the main MCN terminates to supply the skin of the radial surface of the forearm, often extending to the dorsum of the wrist.

Musculocutaneous Nerve Block Technique

The MCN is easily blocked with an axillary approach. A needle is inserted below the tendon of the pectoralis major muscle adjacent to its insertion into the humerus and anterior to the axillary artery. The needle is advanced parallel to the arm and toward the coracoid process. The tip of the needle will first lie in proximity to the median nerve, as noted by a contraction of the wrist and finger flexors when a nerve stimulator is used. With additional needle advancement approximately 1 cm, the needle tip should be near the MCN, confirmed with a visible contraction of the biceps when using a nerve stimulator. The needle should remain anterior to the axillary artery.

An alternative approach can be performed while the humerus is in abduction. The axillary artery is palpated posteriorly, and a needle is inserted perpendicular to the coracobrachialis muscle immediately posterior to the pectoralis major tendon (see Fig. 15-6). The MCN is anterior and lateral to the axillary neurovascular sheath at this location and approximately 2 cm in depth within the coracobrachialis muscle.

In patients with marked internal rotation and adduction deformities of the humerus, normal anatomic landmarks can be difficult to palpate. In this event, inadvertant injection into the axillary artery is possible, although rare. This complication can be avoided by careful palpation of the axillary pulse during advancement of the needle.

INTERCOSTAL NERVE

Intercostal nerves originate as anterior divisions of the first through twelfth thoracic spinal nerves. These paired nerves vary depending on their spinal level, but most divide into four branches. Initially, they communicate with the sympathetic chain by way of a gray rami communicans branch. Three cutaneous branches—lateral, posterior, and anterior—supply sensation to skin and nearby muscles, including the internal and external intercostal muscles. Collectively, the three branches supply sensation to the abdominal and chest wall, including breast tissue in distinct segmental distributions. In the lower thoracic region, intercostal nerves supply motor branches to the abdominal musculature. The intercostal nerves lie in the costal groove on the inferior surface of the rib adjacent to the intercostal artery and vein.

A block of an intercostal nerve can be used to treat the pain of herpes zoster, rib fractures, and intercostal neuropathies. It can be helpful in the diagnosis of unusual abdominal or chest wall pain. In postoperative thoracotomy, physical therapy can be facilitated.

Intercostal Nerve Block Technique

With the patient semiprone or in the lateral decubitus position and the intended block region upward, the lateral mass of the paraspinal muscles is identified. At the intersection of the rib margins and the paraspinal muscles, the lower border of the rib is palpated. Meticulous technique is required to properly locate these rib landmarks. A ¾- to 1-inch, 22- or 25-gauge needle can be inserted over the rib and directed about 20° cephalad. Longer needles may be necessary in obese patients. Once the needle contacts bone, it can be slowly walked off the inferior border of the rib. Manually retracting the skin superiorly prior to needle puncture allows the needle to automatically move inferior once the needle contacts bone. This maneuver reduces needle

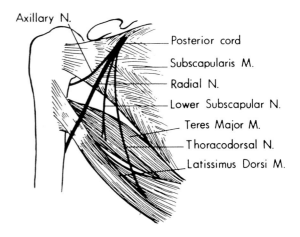

FIGURE 15-3. A posterior view of the posterior cord of the brachial plexus and its branches: axillary, radial, lower subscapular, and the thoracodorsal nerves with the scapula removed.

motion and rotation. Once the lower rib margin is identified, the needle can be advanced 2-3 mm into the subcostal groove (Fig. 15-7). About 3-5 ml of anesthetic is usually injected.

The most common problem with intercostal blocks occurs when an injection is given too superficially. This can be avoided with the correct technique and proper advancement of the needle tip. Vigorous needle advancement or probing should be avoided because of the risk of pneumothorax—the most serious complication with intercostal nerve blocks. Local absorption of anesthetics may cause systemic toxicity and can be potentially serious.

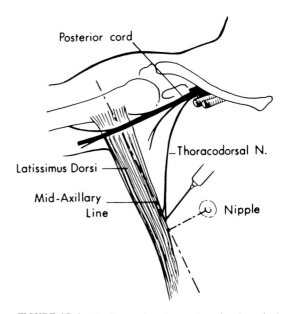

FIGURE 15-4. The thoracodorsal nerve (anterior chest view) takes its origin from the posterior cord of the brachial plexus. Note the needle tip above and lateral to the nipple level.

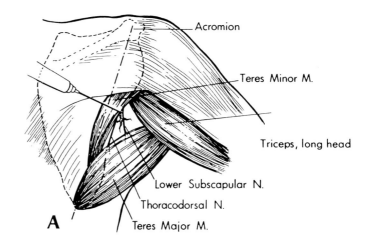

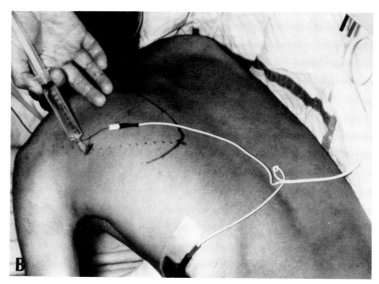

FIGURE 15-5. *A*, The lower subscapular nerve (posterior shoulder view with the scapula shown in dotted lines) is visualized in its relation to thoracodorsal nerve and teres major. *B*, Lower subscapular nerve block technique.

Careful postprocedure monitoring is necessary to detect these complications.

SPINAL ACCESSORY NERVE

The spinal accessory, or eleventh cranial nerve, is composed of two parts: a spinal portion that innervates the trapezius and sternocleidomastoid (SCM) muscles and an accessory portion that joins the vagus nerve. This nerve divides after its exit from the jugular foramen with the spinal portion emerging adjacent to the transverse process of the atlas. This spinal portion reaches the upper SCM muscle, later emerging from its posterior surface at the junction of the superior and middle thirds. It then traverses the posterior cervical triangle to innervate the trapezius muscle about 5 cm above the clavicle. Branches from the C3 and C4 ventral rami also innervate the trapezius muscle while those from the C2 innervate the SCM.

When these nerves are blocked, these muscles relax and can be stretched in disorders such as myofascial pain syndromes and torticollis, thus facilitating physical therapy. An anesthetic block could predict the effect of surgical denervation of the nerve or section through the muscle in cases of torticollis.

Spinal Accessory Nerve Block Technique

The spinal portion of the spinal accessory nerve can be easily blocked anywhere along its course on the posterior cervical triangle. The most common area is immediately posterior to the SCM at the junction of the middle and superior third of the muscle belly. The needle is advanced to the depth of the posterior aspect of the SCM muscle, and 8–10 ml of solution can be injected. Only the trapezius muscle will be affected with this technique, sparing the SCM muscle.

Ramamurthy et al. have described blocking the nerve in the substance of the SCM muscle.[7] A 23-gauge, 2.5-cm needle is introduced 2-3 cm inferior to the tip of the mastoid process and advanced

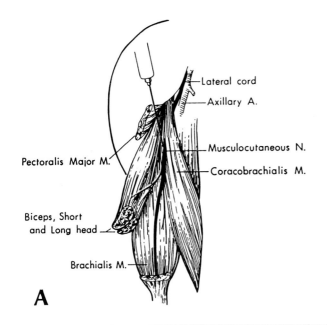

A

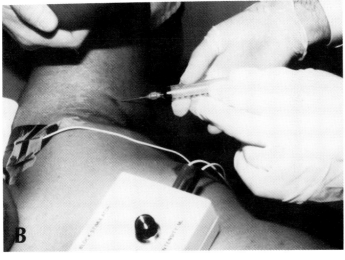

B

FIGURE 15-6. *A*, The musculocutaneous nerve is shown behind the pectoralis major tendon and in the substance of coracobrachialis muscle. *B*, Musculocutaneous nerve block technique.

into the belly of the SCM. About 5–10 ml of anesthetic can be injected. This technique blocks both the SCM and trapezius muscles.

Due to the close proximity of the lesser occipital nerve to the block location when performing the injection within the substance of the SCM, this nerve is often blocked, resulting in numbness behind the ear. One should expect movement changes around the neck for the life of the anesthetic, i.e., inability to turn the neck or elevate the shoulders.

GREATER AND LESSER OCCIPITAL NERVES

The greater occipital nerve (GON) is the largest branch of the C2 dorsal ramus and curves around the border of the obliquus inferior muscle and

crosses deep to the semispinalis capitis. It emerges above the superior nuchal line, about one-third of the way between the occipital protuberance and the mastoid process (Fig. 15-8). It receives communicating branches from the third occipital nerve and may send a branch to the semispinalis capitis muscle. The nerve enters the scalp above the aponeurotic sling between the SCM and trapezius muscles, thereby rendering it safe from trapezius spasm.[1] It ultimately supplies sensation to the skin of the occiput and temporal region, extending across the vertex toward the forehead and into the auricle. The posterior occipital artery accompanies the nerve in the scalp.

The lesser occipital nerve (LON) supplies sensation to the lateral occipital region, including the posterior portion of the ear. This nerve originates from the C2 and C3 ventral rami and emerges

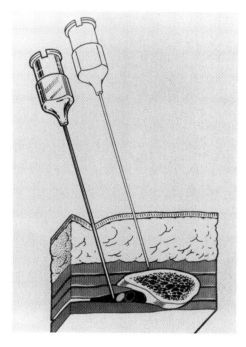

FIGURE 15-7. Needle placement when blocking the intercostal nerve. The needle tip initially contacts the rib and is slowly moved inferior to rest in the subcostal groove. (From Thompson GE, Moore DC: Celiac plexus, intercostal, and minor peripheral blockade. In Cousins MJ, Bridenbaugh PO (eds): Neural Blockade in Clinical Anesthesia and Management of Pain, 2nd ed. Philadelphia, J.B. Lippincott, 1988, p 514, with permission.)

superficially at the posterior border of the upper SCM muscle (see Fig. 15-8).

Primary neuropathies of the GON have been reported but are believed to be rare causes of occipital neuralgia.[12] The pain generator in most cases of occipital neuralgia is believed to be the upper cervical facet joints; therefore, treatment directed at these structures is advocated (see chapter 23). It appears that cervical spine strains such as whiplash injuries would injure the atlantoaxial joints rather than the C2 nerves. Nevertheless, GON blocks can be performed easily at the bedside with very little risk to the patient and can help differentiate various types of headaches.[2,6,9]

Greater Occipital Nerve Block Technique

The patient's occipital protuberance and mastoid process is identified by palpation on the involved side of the skull. An imaginary horizontal line above the base of the skull connecting these two bony landmarks is identified. The greater occipital

nerve lies on the medial third of this line. The posterior occipital artery can be palpated adjacent to this nerve as it traverses the superior nuchal line. Using clean technique, a 25-gauge needle is injected into the subcutaneous tissue down to the occipital bone and slightly withdrawn. The medication is injected in a fan-like manner medially and laterally (see Fig. 15-8). Immediate anesthesia will be noted locally and soon in the nerve's distribution.

Lesser Occipital Nerve Block Technique

Similar to the GON block, the LON can be blocked in the posterior scalp region. The imaginary line described above between the mastoid process and the occipital protuberance can be visualized. The junction of the middle and outer third of this line directly above the superior nuchal line is located. A small 25-gauge needle is advanced down to the bone, and solution is injected. Branches from the GON will also be blocked with this technique.

SUPRAORBITAL NERVE

The supraorbital nerve (SON) originates from the frontal branch of the purely sensory ophthalmic nerve. At the base of the orbit the frontal nerve divides into the supratrochlear and supraorbital branches. The supraorbital branch penetrates the supraorbital foramen where it gives off fibers to the upper eyelid. It ascends through the supraorbital notch where it divides into the medial and lateral terminal branches (Fig. 15-9). These terminal branches innervate the skin of the forehead as far posterior as the occiput. Other branches supply the pericranium of the frontal and parietal bones.

An SON block is useful for anesthesia for procedures involving the upper forehead region. Treatment for tic douloureux and in the differential diagnosis of headaches are other uses.[2]

Supraorbital Nerve Block Technique

With the patient supine and the forehead exposed, the upper border of the orbit is identified. The supraorbital notch is located in the upper orbit adjacent to the brow, usually in a direct line above the pupil. A $\frac{3}{8}$- or $\frac{1}{2}$-inch needle of 25 or 27 gauge in diameter is directed toward the supraorbital notch. Paresthesias from the supraorbital nerve may be encountered during needle advancement, verifying accurate placement. If bone is contacted first, the needle can be directed in a fan-like direction, and 2–4 ml of anesthetic solution is injected.

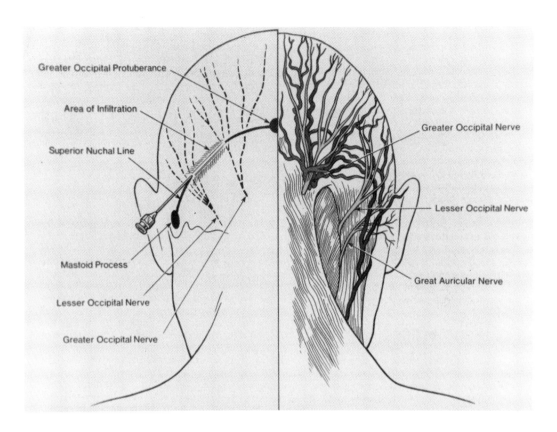

FIGURE 15-8. Posterior view of the occipital region demonstrating the location of the greater and lesser occipital nerves. (From Murphy TM: Somatic blockade of the head and neck. In Cousins MJ, Bridenbaugh PO (eds): Neural Blockade in Clinical Anesthesia and Management of Pain, 2nd ed. Philadelphia, J.B. Lippincott, 1988, p 552, with permission.)

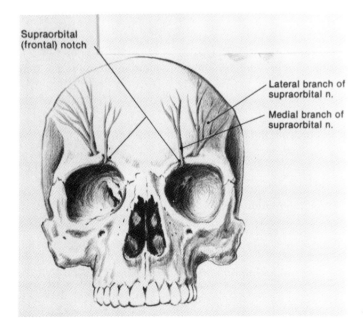

FIGURE 15-9. Anterior drawing of the skull demonstrating the supraorbital notch with the medial and lateral branches of the supraorbital nerve. (From Katz J (ed): Atlas of Regional Anesthesia, 2nd ed. East Norwalk, CT, Appleton & Lange, 1994, p 9, with permission.)

REFERENCES

1. Bogduk N: The anatomy of occipital neuraliga. Clin Exp Neurol 17:167–184, 1981.
2. Bovim G, Sand T: Cervicogenic headache, migraine without aura and tension-type headache: Diagnostic blockade of greater occipital and supra-orbital nerves. Pain 51:43–48, 1992.
3. Granirer LW: A simple technic for suprascapular nerve block. N Y U State J Med 51:1048, 1951.
4. Meyer-Witting M, Foster JMG: Suprascapular nerve block in the management of cancer pain [letter]. Anaesthesia 47:626, 1992.
5. Moore DC: Regional Block, 4th ed. Springfield, IL, Charles C Thomas, 1965, pp 300–303.
6. Plum F: Diagnostic nerve block for headache? [abstract and commentary]. Neurology Alert, 33–34, January 1993.
7. Ramamurthy S, Akkineni S, Winnie A: A simple technic for block of the spinal accessory nerve. Anesth Analg 57:591–593, 1978.
8. Risdall JE, Sharwood-Smith GH: Suprascapular nerve block. New indications and a safer technique [letter]. Anaesthesia 47:626, 1992.
9. Sanchez CA: Nerve blocks for the relief of chronic headaches [abstract]. Reg Anesth 18:45, 1993.
10. Torres-Ramos FM, Biundo JJ: Suprascapular neuropathy during progressive resistive exercises in a cardiac rehabilitation program. Arch Phys Med Rehabil 73:1107–1111, 1992.
11. Wassef MR: Suprascapular nerve block: A new approach for the management of frozen shoulder. Anaesthesia 47:120–124, 1992.
12. Weinberger LM: Cervico-occipital pain and its surgical treatment: The myth of the bony millstones. Am J Surg 135:243–247, 1978.

Chapter 16

ARM, FOREARM, AND HAND BLOCKS

CHARLES C. MAULDIN, M.D.
D. WAYNE BROOKS, M.D.

Arm, forearm, and hand blocks require meticulous technique and can be challenging to those unfamiliar with the regional anatomy. Blocks in this region should be generally performed with small, short bevel needles with the least volume of solution necessary. Surface or needle tip nerve stimulation is often helpful to minimize probing and volume injected, especially with deep injections. One must be familiar with the common anatomic variations[20] of the upper extremity in order to understand the otherwise unexpected result that may be seen with these blocks.

This chapter explains common approaches to arm, forearm, and hand blocks commonly performed in a physiatrist's practice. Volumes indicated in this chapter are for anesthetic solutions alone; volumes of corticosteroids would usually be less.

CUTANEOUS NERVES OF THE FOREARM

Sensation to the forearm is supplied by three nerves: the medial (MACN), lateral (LACN), and posterior (PACN) antebrachial cutaneous nerves. Diagnostic blocks to these nerves are often used because their distributions overlap significantly, interfering with the clinical diagnosis. Neuropathies involving these cutaneous nerves can occur spontaneously or secondary to acute or repetitive injury. Initial conservative management may include injections of these nerves at the site of inflammation with corticosteroid and/or anesthetic solution, which often hastens resolution.[1] Chemical neurolysis may be considered for more permanent relief of painful neuropathy.

Medial Antebrachial Cutaneous Nerve

The MACN carries fibers from the C8 and T1 roots via the medial cord of the brachial plexus. At the junction of the middle and lower third of the medial arm, the nerve exits the deep fascia between the biceps and triceps muscles and is accompanied by the basilic vein. The MACN then divides into its anterior and ulnar branches, ultimately supplying sensation to the medial forearm.

Medial Antebrachial Cutaneous Nerve Block Technique

With the medial arm exposed, mark the midpoint between the biceps tendon and the medial epicondyle at the elbow crease. Insert a needle subcutaneously at a point approximately 5–6 cm superior to the mark along the inferomedial border of the biceps muscle. Inject 2–5 ml of solution with a ⅝-inch, 25- to 27-gauge needle in a fanlike manner anterior to posterior across the path of the nerve. An inadequate block will occur if the injection is given too deep below the brachial facia.

Lateral Antebrachial Cutaneous Nerve

The LACN is derived from the C5 and C6 spinal roots and is the terminal cutaneous branch of the musculocutaneous nerve. At the elbow, the LACN runs under the lateral border of the biceps beneath the deep brachial fascia on top of the brachialis muscle. The nerve courses the antecubital fossa and becomes subcutaneous as it pierces the brachial fascial lateral to the biceps tendon at the elbow crease.[1] The nerve often pierces the brachial fascia 5–10 cm above the elbow crease. Once subcutaneous, it divides into the anterior and posterior branches, supplying sensation to the skin of the lateral forearm.

Lateral Antebrachial Cutaneous Nerve Block Technique

With the elbow extended, mark the intersection of the elbow crease and biceps tendon. Insert the needle subcutaneously just lateral to the mark, and inject 3–5 ml of solution with a 1-inch, 25- to 27-gauge needle. As an alternative, a subcutaneous field block can be performed extending from where the biceps tendon inserts into the radius to approximately two-thirds the distance to the lateral epicondyle.

An inadequate block results if the solution is injected on the wrong side of the brachial fascia. This can easily occur when one considers the exit point variability of the LAC nerve from the brachial fascia. Blocks of this nerve above the elbow crease could be made just deep to the fascia and subcutaneous with the same needle insertion to help ensure that the nerve is infiltrated. Many subcutaneous vessels lie in this area, and care should be taken to avoid intravascular injection.

Posterior Antebrachial Cutaneous Nerve

The PACN originates from the radial nerve at the level of the humeral spiral groove, carrying fibers from the C5–C8 nerve roots. The nerve passes through the brachial fascia about 8 cm above the elbow and descends behind the lateral epicondyle of the humerus, where it often becomes palpable. The PACN supplies sensation to the skin of the posterior forearm, distally to the wrist.

Posterior Antebrachial Cutaneous Nerve Block Technique

With the patient's posterior arm exposed, insert a 2-inch, 25-gauge needle perpendicular to the skin directly over the lateral epicondyle, and infiltration of 3–5 ml is made subcutaneously extending 3–4 cm toward the olecranon.

MEDIAN NERVE

The median nerve innervates the muscles of the forearm flexor group, excluding the flexor carpi ulnaris and ulnar portion of the flexor digitorum profundus. In the hand, the nerve normally supplies the lumbricales to the index and middle fingers and all the muscles of the thenar eminence except for a portion of the flexor pollicis brevis. On the palmar surface, its normal cutaneous innervation includes the medial part of the thenar eminence, the central depressed area of the palm, and the lateral $3\frac{1}{2}$ digits. Dorsally, its distribution of sensation includes the distal phalanges and the nail beds of the lateral $3\frac{1}{2}$ digits.

Median Nerve at the Elbow

The median nerve arises from the union of the medial and lateral cords in the axilla and is supplied by the C5–T1 spinal roots. The nerve leaves the axilla and descends the arm adjacent to the brachial artery. At the elbow, the nerve lies just medial to the brachial artery. This artery divides into its ulnar

and radial branches high in the arm in 15% of people,[20] thereby distorting normal anatomical landmarks. At the flexor crease, the nerve passes midway between the medial epicondyle and the biceps tendon. In the forearm, the nerve innervates the pronator teres muscle prior to passing through its two heads.

Median Nerve Block Technique at the Elbow

With the elbow extended, mark the intersection of the elbow crease and the biceps tendon. Just superior and medial to this mark, palpate the brachial artery. While palpating the artery to avoid intravascular injection, a $1\frac{1}{2}$-inch, 23- to 25–gauge needle is inserted subcutaneously just medial to the artery. Once through the skin, direct the needle slightly lateral and advance it slowly toward the nerve to a depth slightly deeper than the artery. If desired, use a nerve stimulator while observing for wrist and finger flexion to ensure close proximity of the nerve. A median nerve block at the elbow level will affect all of the median innervated muscles and its entire cutaneous distribution.

Median Nerve at the Pronator Teres Muscle

The median nerve can become entrapped as it passes through the two heads of the pronator muscle, causing a neuropathy commonly referred to as the pronator syndrome. This syndrome also may be caused by a thickened lacertus fibrosus, thickened flexor superficialis arch, and by the median nerve passing below the pronator heads.[5,11,19] The symptoms and findings of the pronator syndrome vary and are often vague, with the most consistent finding being tenderness over the pronator muscle.[5,11,19] Any portion of the median nerve can be affected, but the anterior interosseous nerve branch is usually spared.[19]

Median Nerve Block Technique at the Pronator Teres Muscle

At the elbow crease make a mark at the midpoint between the medial epicondyle and the biceps tendon. Insert a $1\frac{1}{2}$-inch, 23- to 25-gauge needle into the pronator teres muscle approximately 2–2.5 cm below the mark or at the point of maximal tenderness in the muscle (Fig. 16-1). Confirm needle placement using a nerve stimulator to provoke contractions of the wrist and finger flexors, and inject 3–5 ml of solution. If using a nerve stimulator, direct stimulation of the pronator teres muscle will occur, erroneously suggesting the needle tip is close to the median nerve. A block at this site can affect all median motor and sensory innervations.

When using corticosteroid solutions for the treatment of pronator syndrome, perform the injection in a fanlike manner, superior to inferior, to improve

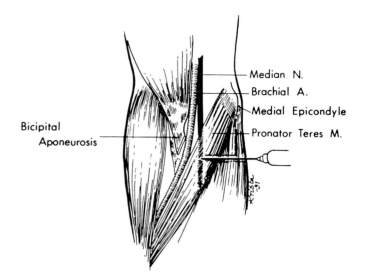

FIGURE 16-1. Median nerve block at the pronator teres muscle. Note the relationship between the nerve and artery above the elbow in reference to blocks at that site.

Bicipital
Aponeurosis

Median N.
Brachial A.
Medial Epicondyle
Pronator Teres M.

the likelihood the solution contacts the area of compression. The proximity of the needle tip to the nerve should be rechecked with the stimulator each time the needle is repositioned.

Anterior Interosseous Nerve

The anterior interosseous nerve (AIN) is the largest branch of the median nerve. In the cubital fossa, the AIN branch arises posteriorly soon after the median nerve passes between the two heads of the pronator teres. It descends on the volar surface of the interosseous membrane along with the anterior interosseous branch of the ulnar artery. Near its origin, the AIN supplies branches to the radial portion of the flexor digitorum profundus (FDP) muscle. Descending toward the wrist, the nerve innervates the flexor pollicis longus (FPL) and pronator quadratus (PQ) muscles and then terminates in articular branches to the wrist and intercarpal joints.

Anterior interosseous nerve syndrome is an entrapment neuropathy that causes weakness in the FDP, FPL, and PQ muscles. Injury to the terminal sensory fibers can cause dull aching volar wrist pain.[6] An extensive list of etiologies of AIN syndrome has been described by Wertsch.[21]

Proximal Anterior Interosseous Nerve Block Technique

With the posterior elbow exposed and the forearm in neutral rotation, mark the skin over the posteromedial aspect of the ulna approximately 5 cm distal to the tip of the olecranon (Fig. 16-2). Insert a 2-inch, 25-gauge needle just medial to the mark at a depth of about 3.5 to 5 cm, directing it toward the biceps tendon insertion at the radius. The needle should be in the AIN innervated portion of the FDP. A nerve stimulator is essential with this technique and once needle position is verified, 3–5 ml of solution can be injected.

Phenol nerve blocks of the AIN for flexor spasticity of the hand should not cause paresthesias. Care has to be taken to avoid accidental injection of the main branch of the median nerve (Fig. 16-3). Stimulation of the main branch of the median nerve

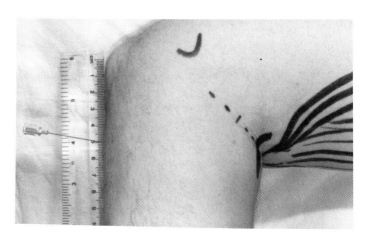

FIGURE 16-2. Needle entry site for proximal anterior interosseous nerve block. The first muscle penetrated is the flexor digitorum profundus.

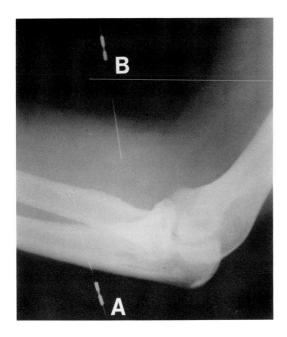

FIGURE 16-3. Radiograph showing the relationship between the anterior interosseous (A) and the median nerve (B). The needle tip is adjacent to the corresponding nerve and was confirmed by nerve stimulation.

at this level would cause flexion of digits 2 through 5, flexion of the wrist, and paresthesias in the median cutaneous distribution, but it would not activate the PQ muscle. As an alternative approach, the main branch of the median nerve could be initially located with a deep injection and the AIN found with gentle needle withdrawal while using a nerve stimulator.

In 30% of people, the AIN will innervate the flexor digitorum superficialis muscle.[19] A Martin-Gruber median-to-ulnar anastomosis usually arises from the AIN,[10,19] and blocks in this situation may affect intrinsic hand muscles, which may not be desired. Because of these abnormalities, temporary blocks with anesthetic agents should be performed prior to any chemical neurolysis.

Distal Anterior Interosseous Nerve Block Technique

With the patient's dorsal forearm exposed, make a mark on the skin at the point between the middle and distal thirds along a line from the olecranon to the radial styloid process. At the mark, insert a 2-inch, 25-gauge needle and advance it until it is between the radius and ulna bones. The needle tip will be in close proximity to the AIN as soon as the interosseous membrane is pierced. Determine proximity by using a nerve stimulator and observing for PQ contraction. The patient may also complain of an aching pain in the volar wrist. If the needle is positioned too deep, the electrical stimulation will

cause thumb flexion; if too superficial, it will cause finger and/or wrist extension. Take care to avoid penetrating the extensor tendons and to avoid injecting into the anterior or posterior interosseous vessels. Inject 5 ml of solution once maximal PQ contraction is obtained. Blocking the distal AIN from a volar approach has been described but can be more difficult due to the increased number of tendons and vessels which may be encountered. A distal AIN block can be useful when evaluating difficult volar wrist pain.

Median Nerve at the Wrist

At the wrist, the median nerve is invested by the ulnar bursa and is accompanied by the tendons of the FPL, FDP, and the flexor digitorum superficialis (FDS) muscles. It travels between but deep to the flexor carpi radialis (FCR) and palmaris longus (PL) tendons. The nerve is usually the most superficial structure coursing beneath the flexor retinaculum in the area referred to as the carpal tunnel.

Median nerve blocks at the wrist are usually indicated for the treatment of carpal tunnel syndrome (CTS), but they also may be used to treat pain in a median nerve distribution within the hand. Conservative treatment of CTS, including corticosteroid injections, splinting, and activity modification, has been used for more than 40 years.[16] In general, CTS that exhibits mild, intermittent signs and symptoms of short duration usually responds well to conservative treatment.[9,14,15] However, advanced cases of CTS—with constant symptoms, weakness, atrophy, and electromyographic evidence of denervation—are unlikely to respond to this form of treatment.[5]

Median Nerve Block Technique at the Wrist

Although the injections are commonly referred to as carpal tunnel injections, solution is actually injected into the ulnar bursa proximal to the carpal tunnel. Many injection techniques have been described for treating CTS.[3,12]

With the patient's forearm supinated, insert a ⅝-inch, 27-gauge needle proximal to the distal wrist crease and ulnar to the PL tendon. About 2–20% of people lack a PL muscle,[20] and in such cases the midpoint between the ulna and radial styloid processes can be used as a reference point. Direct the needle dorsally and angle it 30° distally to a depth of about 1.5 cm or upon contact with a tendon. Confirm placement by moving the needle with gentle passive finger extension. Inject 2 ml of volume slowly, and then use active finger flexion and extension for 1–2 minutes to distribute the solution throughout the ulna bursa[12] (Figs. 16-4 and 16-5). Increased pain during injection is rare and should alert the physician of abnormal needle placement.

An alternative technique involves inserting a 1½-inch, 23-gauge needle 1 cm proximal to the distal wrist crease ulnar to the PL tendon. The needle is angled 45–60° distally and is advanced 1 cm until it pierces the flexor retinaculum. Solution is injected after advancement of the needle an additional 1 ml. With this technique, the injection should occur under the transverse carpal ligament. This technique causes pain and is no more effective than the first technique described.

Local tenderness and superficial hematomas at the injection site are common after carpal tunnel injections. Intraneural corticosteroid injections that cause nerve damage requiring surgical debridement have been reported.[8]

Recurrent Motor Branch of the Median Nerve

The median nerve enters the palm under the flexor retinaculum radial to the PL tendon and gives off the recurrent motor branch just distal to the transverse carpal ligament, though occasionally it pierces through the ligament. Though there are many variations, most commonly the recurrent motor branch innervates the abductor pollicis brevis, opponens pollicis, and the superficial head of the flexor pollicis brevis (Fig. 16-6).

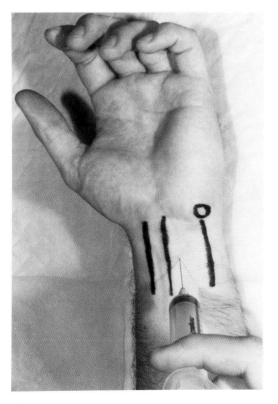

FIGURE 16-4. Preferred method for ulnar bursa injection. Needle puncture is just ulnar to the palmaris longus tendon. The circle is over the pisiform bone.

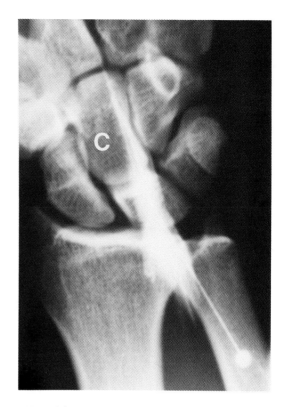

FIGURE 16-5. Radiograph showing free flow of dye as far as the distal capitate bone (C) after ulnar bursa injection of 1.5 ml.

A block of the recurrent motor branch can be used to help evaluate and treat palm-in-hand spasticity. This block can potentially affect other intrinsic hand muscles if the patient has a Riche-Cannieu anastomosis between the recurrent branch of the median and the deep branch of the ulnar nerve or if there are other anatomic variations.

Recurrent Motor Branch Block Technique

With the patient's palm positioned upward, make a mark at the intersection of the radial border of the third metacarpal and Kaplan's cardinal line. This line is parallel to the proximal palmar crease beginning at the apex of the first web space. Use a nerve stimulator to localize the nerve, observing for opposition, abduction, and proximal phalanx flexion movements of the thumb. Slowly insert a 1-inch, 25- to 27-gauge needle, and inject 2 ml of solution.

ULNAR NERVE

The ulnar nerve innervates the majority of intrinsic hand muscles, excluding the median innervated thenar and the two most radial lumbrical muscles. In the forearm, the ulnar nerve supplies the flexor carpi ulnaris and ulnar portion of the flexor digitorum profundus muscles. Its cutaneous distribution is to the ulnar aspect of the distal

FIGURE 16-6. The recurrent thenar branches (*R*) arising from the median nerve (*M*) just distal to the transverse carpal ligament (removed). The proximity of the common digital nerve to the thumb (*CDN*) is of concern in neurolytic blocks. (From Zancolli EA, Cozzi EP: Atlas of Surgical Anatomy of the Hand. New York, Churchill Livingstone, pp 263–325, 1992, with permission.)

forearm, wrist, and hand. In the hand on the volar surface, the ulnar nerve supplies sensation to the ulnar aspect of the palm and the entire fifth and ulnar half of the fourth digits. Dorsally, the nerve supplies sensation to the medial aspect of the hand, the entire fifth finger, the entire fourth finger except for the radial aspect of the distal phalanx, and the ulnar one-half of the middle finger to about the distal interphalangeal joint. There is no site along the nerve where selective blocks of motor branches can be achieved without potentially affecting sensation.

Blocks of the ulnar nerve are used as part of conservative treatment of mild compression or entrapment neuropathies at the elbow and wrist.[15] Acute or subacute compression neuropathies—as seen from trauma to the elbow or to more prolonged compression during a phase of illness or anesthesia— or entrapment at the cubital tunnel or Guyon's canal usually respond well to conservative care.[6a] Chronic ulnar neuropathies and those associated with intrinsic atrophy and denervation on electromyographic studies will not respond well to conservative treatment.

Ulnar Nerve at the Elbow

The ulnar nerve is formed from the C8 and T1 spinal roots and is the major terminal branch of the medial cord of the brachial plexus. At the elbow, the nerve travels between the borders of the triceps and brachialis muscles, soon emerging to lie within the ulnar groove where it becomes palpable. The nerve descends through the cubital tunnel that is formed by the fibroaponeurotic triangular or arcuate ligament, two heads of the flexor carpi ulnaris (FCU), and the medial collateral ligament. An ulnar nerve branch to the FCU muscle runs adjacent to the main nerve in the groove and is rarely involved in neuropathies at the elbow.

Ulnar Nerve Block Technique at the Elbow

With the patient's medial arm and elbow exposed, mark the ulnar nerve between the triceps and brachialis muscle approximately 5 cm above the medial epicondyle (Fig. 16-7). It should be on a line between the epicondyle and the apex of the axilla. Insert a 1-inch, 23- to 25-gauge needle subcutaneously at this point perpendicular to the humerus. If the nerve is not palpable, inject subcutaneous in a fanlike manner across the expected path of the nerve, or use a nerve stimulator and observe for wrist flexion and intrinsic hand movements to assure close proximity to the nerve. In either case, inject 5–8 ml of solution.

An alternative ulnar nerve block can be performed within the ulnar groove. With the patient's posteromedial elbow exposed, palpate and mark the medial epicondyle. While pinching and retracting

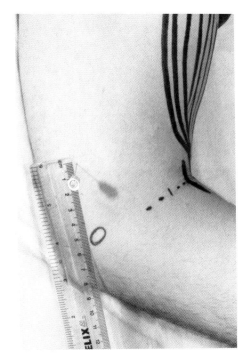

FIGURE 16-7. Ulnar nerve block above the elbow. The circle is over the medial epicondyle.

the redundant skin over the groove, insert the needle at the medial epicondyle, aiming just below and anterior to the tip of the olecranon. As an alternative, one can gently stabilize the nerve between a finger and the olecranon and insert a needle subcutaneously between the finger and the medial epicondyle.

While in the groove, the ulnar nerve is tightly confined, thereby increasing the risk of injury at this site. Injections at this site should be reserved for corticosteroid solutions for treatment of compression neuropathies, both within the groove and cubital tunnel. Injection solution should be limited to less than 5 ml. Limiting the use of anesthetic agents in the groove, which could mask paresthesias, will also reduce the risk of nerve injury.

An ulnar nerve block above the ulnar groove is considered safer than within the groove. In this location, less risk of direct nerve injury by the needle and greater volumes of solutions, including anesthetic agents, can be safely used. Blocks from the ulnar groove and above will affect the entire motor and sensory distribution of the nerve. Since the sensory distribution of the ulnar nerve is at the wrist and hand, anesthetic blocks need not be performed at the elbow unless block of the dorsal ulnar cutaneous nerve distribution is necessary.

Ulnar Nerve at the Wrist

At the wrist, the ulnar nerve lies directly below the tendon of the FCU just proximal to the pisiform bone. At this point, the nerve lies on the ulnar side of and deep to the ulnar artery. The nerve at this level has given off its palmar and dorsal cutaneous branches. As the nerve passes radial to the pisiform, it enters the ulnar tunnel, commonly referred to as Guyon's canal. The borders of this canal are the pisiform bone medially and proximally, and the hook of the hamate bone laterally and distally. The roof is formed by the thickening of the deep forearm fascia and the floor by the thick transverse carpal ligament. Within the canal, the nerve bifurcates into its terminal deep (motor) and the superficial (sensory) branches. The ulnar artery travels through the canal with the nerve. The deep branch supplies the muscles of the hypothenar compartment, the interosseous muscles, the medial two lumbricals, the adductor pollicis, and a portion of the flexor pollicis brevis. The superficial branch supplies the palmaris brevis and digital sensory branches to the fifth finger and the ulnar half of the fourth finger.

Ulnar Nerve Block Technique at the Wrist
Ulnar nerve block at the wrist is more reliable and carries less risks of complications than a block at the elbow. With the volar wrist exposed, palpate

and mark the pisiform bone and FCU tendon. The ulnar nerve can be blocked from either a volar or ulnar approach.

With the volar approach, insert a 1-inch, 25- to 27-gauge needle to either side of the FCU tendon about 1 cm proximal to the pisiform bone. Inject 2–5 ml of solution into the tissue between the tendon and the distal ulna.

With the ulnar approach, introduce a similar size needle subcutaneously at the medial wrist and direct it radially until the needle tip lies under the FCU tendon. Inject 2–5 ml of solution. The needle can be withdrawn and repositioned subcutaneously and an additional 1–2 ml of solution can be injected on the ulnar side and well onto the dorsum of the wrist. This blocks the dorsal cutaneous branch of the ulnar nerve. With the ulnar approach, there is a reduced chance of puncturing the ulnar artery in comparison to the volar approach. However, if the needle is inserted anterior to the neurovascular bundle and thus anterior to the thick fascial layer, the block may be ineffective (Fig. 16-8).

Ulnar Nerve Block Technique at Guyon's Canal
First, palpate and mark the pisiform bone and the hook of the hamate. The motor branch of the nerve may be palpable in the canal between these marks. Insert a 2-inch, 25-gauge needle at the distal wrist crease to the radial side of the pisiform bone and angled sharply distally so that its tip lies just ulnar to the palpable hook of the hamate (Figs. 16-8 and 16-9). Inject 1 ml of solution very slowly. Compression neuropathies in Guyon's canal are infrequent but are seen more often in occupations that require frequent hand tool use and in recreational activities such as biking and golf.[5] Similar to the ulnar nerve in the ulnar groove, the nerve is also in a confined space in Guyon's canal. For this reason, injections into Guyon's canal should be considered primarily for injections of corticosteroid solution for treatment of nerve compression at this site.

RADIAL NERVE

The radial nerve is a terminal branch of the posterior cord of the brachial plexus formed from the C5–C8 spinal roots. The radial nerve innervates the posterior arm and forearm compartment muscles and often the lateral portion of the brachialis muscle.[19] It supplies sensation to the posterior forearm, lateral thenar eminence and dorsum of the hand, and the dorsal aspect of the lateral 2½ fingers. It also supplies articular branches to the elbow and wrist.

Distal radial neuropathies that occur near the origin of the posterior interosseous nerve (PIN), often called radial tunnel or supinator syndrome,

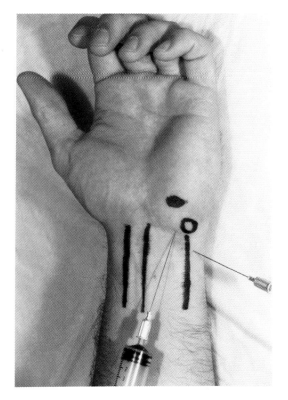

FIGURE 16-8. Approaches for two ulnar nerve blocks. The needle with syringe attached demonstrates the puncture for block at Guyon's canal. The circle is over the pisiform bone and the solid mark over the hook of the hamate. The second needle demonstrates the puncture site for an ulnar nerve block at the wrist, ulnar approach.

and the superficial radial nerve near the wrist have been well described.[5,19] Entrapment of the distal PIN has been reported to cause dorsal wrist pain.[4]

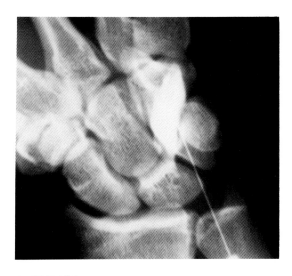

FIGURE 16-9. Radiograph showing dye pattern after injection of 1 ml into Guyon's canal by the technique shown in Figure 16-8.

Initial management of mild radial compression neuropathies should be conservative, which can include corticosteroid injections. Pain relief after a diagnostic nerve block of the proximal PIN has been shown to be a good indicator of a successful outcome from surgical decompression.[17]

Radial Nerve at the Arm

In the arm, the radial nerve pierces the lateral intermuscular septum approximately 10 cm above the elbow crease at the lateral side of the arm where it is prone to injury. It crosses anterior to the lateral epicondyle after lying between the brachialis and brachioradialis muscles. In the arm, the radial nerve supplies motor branches to the brachioradialis and extensor carpi radialis longus muscles. It also gives off the posterior antebrachial cutaneous nerve (PACN).

Radial Nerve Block Technique at the Arm

With the patient's lateral arm exposed, locate the skin over the humerus at the point between the middle and distal one thirds on a line between the lateral epicondyle and the tip of the acromion process. This point lies between the muscle bellies of the biceps and triceps and is located about 15 cm proximal to the tip of the olecranon. Insert a 1-inch, 23- to 25-gauge needle at this point, and advance it until bone is contacted. If a nerve stimulator is used, elbow flexion and wrist extension will be visualized. About 4–7 ml of solution may be injected.

A radial block at the elbow affects all radial innervated muscles except for the elbow extensors. This includes the brachioradialis, extensor carpi radialis longus and brevis, and the muscles innervated by the PIN and all radial sensory innervations.

Radial Nerve at the Elbow

In the cubital fossa, the radial nerve divides into the PIN and the superficial radial nerve between the brachialis and brachioradialis muscles. Prior to this division, motor branches to the brachioradialis (BR) and extensor carpi radialis longus (ECRL) are formed. A motor branch to the extensor carpi radialis brevis (ECRB) arises from the superficial radial nerve in most cases.[19] After giving off branches to the supinator, the PIN passes through the arcade of Frohse between the deep and superficial heads of the supinator muscle where it may become entrapped, referred to as supinator syndrome. The PIN then passes distally along the dorsum of the forearm to terminate in articular branches to the dorsum of the carpus.

Radial Nerve Block Technique at the Elbow

With the patient's anterior elbow exposed, mark a point at the elbow crease between the lateral border of the biceps tendon and the medial border of the BR muscle. The nerve is blocked as it crosses the anterior aspect of the lateral epicondyle close to the humerus (Fig. 16-10). Insert a 2-inch, 23- to 25-gauge needle at the mark and direct it posterior until bone is contacted at the lateral margin of the epicondyle. Withdraw the needle 0.5–1.0 cm and inject approximately 2 ml of solution. Withdraw the needle to the skin and redirect it slightly more medial, and advance it again until bone is contacted. The use of a nerve stimulator will prevent excessive probing and help localize the tip of the needle. Varying degrees of effect will be noted on the BR and ECRL muscles with a radial nerve block at the elbow and in the arm. The PACN should not be affected with either of these two blocks.

Posterior Interosseous
Nerve Block Technique at the Elbow

Locate the most distal point of the insertion of the biceps tendon on the radius, about 2–3 cm below the elbow crease. With the forearm pronated, insert a 2-inch, 25-gauge needle 1 cm lateral to this point just medial to the BR muscle. Using a palpating finger on the posterior aspect of the ulna about 5 cm from the olecranon as a guide, advance the needle to the surface of the ulna. With the use of a nerve stimulator, the PIN can be quickly located by observing for finger extension at a low stimulus intensity. Inject 2–5 ml of solution. This block can be used in suspected cases of supinator syndrome and forearm and wrist spasticity.

Distal Posterior Interosseous Nerve

In the dorsal forearm, the PIN emerges with the posterior interosseous artery in the interval between the deep and superficial muscles of the forearm extensor group. Lying on the dorsal aspect of the interosseous membrane, the nerve courses toward the wrist and passes deep to the extensor pollicis longus muscle. At the wrist, it terminates as a small gangliform enlargement from which branches supply the intercarpal joints.

Distal Posterior Interosseous
Nerve Block Technique

With the patient's distal dorsal forearm exposed, insert a 2-inch, 25-gauge needle 3 cm proximal and 1 cm ulnar to Lister's tubercle. Slowly advance the needle to the depth of the interosseous membrane. Inject solution across the nerve's path.[4] This block can be useful when evaluating difficult pain disorders of the wrist.

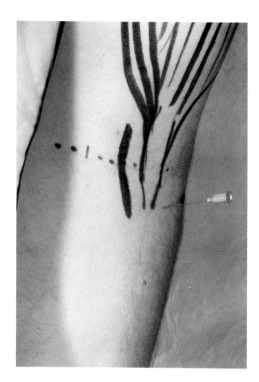

FIGURE 16-10. Radial nerve block at the supinator muscle. Note that the needle entry is between the biceps tendon and the brachioradialis muscle.

Radial Nerve at the Wrist

Radial nerve blocks at the wrist are used to interrupt the terminal cutaneous branches that supply the radial side of the dorsum of the hand and the proximal parts of the radial 3½ digits. Although uncommon, isolated compression neuropathies of the cutaneous branch of the radial nerve, referred to as cheiralgia paresthetica, can occur from acute injury or from prolonged compression, i.e., watchband. Local injection of corticosteroids can be an effective treatment.

The superficial radial nerve descends to the wrist along the lateral side of the forearm behind the BR muscle. The nerve pierces the deep fascia and becomes superficial as it emerges from the posterior border of the BR just proximal to the muscle's insertion. At this location, the nerve is most likely to be injured. Once superficial, it divides into dorsal digital nerves supplying the thenar eminence, dorsum of the first, second, and the radial side of the third digit.

Superficial Radial Nerve Block Technique

With the forearm pronated, locate the anatomic snuffbox and mark its bordering tendons: extensor pollicis longus (EPL) and brevis (EPB). Take a point over the EPL tendon adjacent to the base of the first metacarpal where the nerve is often palpable.

Direct the needle proximally along the tendon as far as the dorsal radial tubercle. Inject 2 ml of solution superficially. Withdraw the needle to the skin and redirect it across the snuffbox just past the EPB tendon, and inject an additional 2–3 ml of solution.

DIGITAL NERVES

Anesthetic digital blocks for minor procedures of the fingers are common. Compression neuropathies of the common digital nerves can occur at the intermetacarpal ligaments and can be treated with digital blocks. Neuropathies of proper digital nerves, sometimes referred to as digitalis paresthética, can be caused by acute or repeated trauma; this condition is commonly known as "bowler's thumb."

The common digital nerves are derived from the median and ulnar nerves and divide in the distal palm into the volar digital nerves to supply the adjacent sides of the fingers, palmar aspect, tip, and nail bed area. These main digital nerves are accompanied by the digital vessels and run on the ventromedial and ventrolateral aspects of each finger beside the flexor tendon sheath. Small dorsal digital nerves derived from the radial and ulnar nerves supply the back of the fingers as far as the distal joint. These run on the dorsomedial and dorsolateral aspect of the fingers.

Digital Nerve Block Technique

Insert a 2-inch, 25-gauge needle at a point on the dorsolateral and dorsomedial aspect of the base of the finger and direct it anteriorly to slide past the base of the phalanx. Advance the needle until noting the resistance of the palmar dermis or the pressure on a "protective" finger placed under the patient's finger and directly opposite the needle path. Inject about 1 ml of solution while withdrawing the needle 2–3 mm to block the volar nerve, and inject 0.5–1 ml just under the point of entry to block the dorsal nerve. The volar digital nerves can also be approached from the sides of the finger, which is more useful for index and little fingers.

An alternative technique is to block the digits from the bifurcation of the common digital nerve at the metacarpal heads. With the fingers widely abducted, insert the needle into the web 2–3 mm dorsal to the junction of the web and palmar skin. Direct the needle straight back toward the hand in line with the extended fingers to a depth of about 1.5 cm, and inject 1–2 ml of solution. Redirection to block the dorsal nerves can easily be performed from the same point of entry.

As an alternative technique, a metacarpal approach can also be performed from the dorsal aspect of the hand. Insert the needle between the bones almost as far as the palmar skin and inject while withdrawing the needle.

A thumb block can be performed by blocking the radial and median nerves at the wrist or with a circumferential infiltration block or "ring block." Another option for the median portion of the block is to inject the common digital nerve to the thumb with a single injection in the palm. With the thumb in palmar abduction, enter the skin in the fascial plane between the flexor pollicis brevis and the adductor pollicis 1–2 cm proximal to the margin of the skin web. Direct a 1-inch, 25- to 27-gauge needle toward the medial margin of the first metacarpal somewhat perpendicular to the skin at the site of entry and gently advance it until its tip rests upon the palmar fascia. Inject 1–2 ml of solution.

These described blocks are for anesthesia. If using corticosteroids, direct the injection at the site of compression or palpable neuroma. The use of epinephrine with digital blocks is not advised.

REFERENCES

1. Bassett FH, et al: Compression of the musculocutaneous nerve at the elbow. J Bone Joint Surg 64A:1050–1052, 1982.
2. Bonica JJ: Causalgia and other reflex sympathetic dystrophies. In Bonica JJ (ed): The Management of Pain. Philadelphia, Lea & Febiger, 1990, pp 220–241.
3. Bridenbaugh LD: The upper extremity: Somatic blockade. In Cousins MJ, Bridenbaugh PO (eds): Neural Blockade in Clinical Anesthesia and Management of Pain, 2nd ed. Philadelphia, J.B. Lippincott, 1988, pp 387–417.
4. Carr D, et al: Distal posterior interosseous nerve syndrome. J Hand Surg 10A:873–878, 1985.
5. Dawson DM, Hallett M, Millender LH (eds): Entrapment Neuropathies, 2nd ed. Boston, Little, Brown & Co., 1990, pp 64–67.
6. Dellon AL, et al: Terminal branch of anterior interosseous nerve as source of wrist pain. J Hand Surg 9:316–322, 1984.
6a. Dellon AL, Hament W, Gittelshon A: Nonoperative management of cubital tunnel syndrome. Neurology 43:1673–1677, 1993.
7. Ditmars DM Jr: Local and regional block anesthesia for the upper extremity. In Kasdan ML (ed): Occupational Hand and Upper Extremity Injury and Diseases. Philadelphia, Hanley & Belfus, 1991, pp 143–153.
8. Frederick HA, et al: Injection injuries to the median and the ulnar nerves at the wrist. J Hand Surg 17A:645–647, 1992.
9. Giannini F: Electrophysiologic evaluation of local steroid injection in carpal tunnel syndrome. Arch Phys Med Rehabil 72:738–742, 1991.
10. Gutman L: AAEM Minimonograph #2: Important anomalous innervations of the extremities. Muscle Nerve 16:339–347, 1993.
11. Hartz CR, et al: The pronator syndrome: Compressive neuropathy of the nerve. J Bone Joint Surg 63A:885–890, 1981.
12. Minamikawa Y, et al: Tenosynovial injection for carpal tunnel syndrome. J Hand Surg 17A:178–181, 1992.
13. Olson IA: The origin of the lateral cutaneous nerve of forearm and its anesthesia for modified brachial plexus block. J Anat 105:381–382, 1969.

14. Özdogan H, et al: The efficacy of local steroid injections in idiopathic carpal tunnel syndrome: A double-blind study. Brit J Rheumatol 23:272–275, 1984.

15. Pechan J, et al: Treatment of cubital tunnel syndrome by means of local administration of corticosteroids: Long-term follow-up. Acta Univ Carol [Med] (Praha) 26:135–140, 1980.

16. Phalen GS: The carpal-tunnel syndrome: Seventeen years experience in diagnosis and treatment of six hundred forty-four hands. J Bone Joint Surg 48A:211–228, 1966.

17. Ritts GD, et al: Radial tunnel syndrome. Clin Orthop 219:201–205, 1987.

18. Rosenbaum RB, Ochoa JL: Nonsurgical treatment of carpal tunnel syndrome. In Rosenbaum RB, Ochoa JL (eds): Carpal Tunnel Syndrome and Other Disorders of the Median Nerve. Boston, Butterworth-Heinmann, 1993, p 251–256.

19. Spinner M: Injuries to the Major Branches of Peripheral Nerves of the Forearm. Philadelphia, W.B. Saunders, 1978, pp 162–192.

20. Tountas CP, Bergman RA: Anatomic Variations of the Upper Extremity. New York, Churchill Livingstone, 1993, pp 211–240.

21. Wertsch JJ: AAEM Case Report #25: Anterior interosseous nerve syndrome. Muscle Nerve 15:977–983, 1992.

Chapter 17

PROXIMAL LOWER EXTREMITY BLOCKS

DANIEL Y. SHIN, M.D.
TED A. LENNARD, M.D.

Lower extremity peripheral nerves can be selectively blocked with a good understanding of lumbar, pelvic, and gluteal anatomy. Their usefulness in practice is directed primarily toward hip and knee spasticity that affects gait patterns, sitting posture, and transfer. As with other nerve blocks, they are also useful in differentiating pain disorders and providing anesthesia for procedures in this region of the body.

SOMATIC LUMBAR NERVE BLOCK

Somatic lumbar nerves can be blocked after their exit from the intervertebral foramen outside the epidural space. This is in contrast to the selective epidural nerve root blocks discussed in chapter 27 that intentionally places medication into the epidural space. These somatic nerves innervate distal myotomes and transmit sensation to large peripheral areas. Therefore, a block at this level would be expected to affect multiple distal structures.

Meelhuysen[9] performed phenol lumbar somatic blocks in an effort to avoid the complications of intrathecal blocks and to yield a selective effect upon spastic hip and knee flexors in paraplegics. Hip flexor spasticity was treated by injecting the L2, L3, and L4 nerves. Knee flexor spasticity was treated by injecting the L5 and S1 nerves. Each nerve was blocked at its emergence from the intervertebral foramen using a nerve stimulator. Of the 31 blocks, 21 yielded partial muscle relaxation with electrical evidence of denervation.

Lumbar somatic nerve blocks are technically more cumbersome than intrathecal procedures, but have the advantage of high selectivity. A single paravertebral nerve block may result in loss of spasticity in several different muscle groups and changes in sensation in the corresponding dermatome.

Technique

The lumbar somatic nerves can be blocked with the patient in the prone or the lateral decubitus position with the intended block side up. The patient's lumbar spinous processes are palpated and marked on the skin. A horizontal line is extended 3 cm lateral from the superior edge of the spinous process. This line corresponds with the transverse process. A needle is directed perpendicular to the skin at the end of this line and advanced until the transverse process is contacted (Fig. 17–1). Once bone is contacted, the needle is slid over the superior surface of the transverse process and advanced an additional 2–4 cm. The lumbar somatic nerve can be blocked at this location with 3–7 ml of solution, depending on the agent injected. If precise diagnostic information is desired, only 1–2 ml of solution may be required.

Alternatives to somatic blocks to control hip flexor spasticity can be performed by blocking the direct innervation to the psoas major muscle. Not only does the femoral nerve innervate this muscle, but also direct spinal branches from the L2 and L3 spinal nerves (Fig. 17–2). These latter nerves can be blocked within the L4 and L5 interspaces. A needle is inserted 1 cm medial to the tip of both the L4 and L5 transverse processes and advanced 1–2 cm (Fig. 17–3). The nerve to the psoas major muscle lies immediately anterior to this point. The L2 and L3 nerve fibers contributing to the femoral nerve pass posterolateral to these nerves to the psoas muscle, and the fibers supplying the obturator nerve are located posteromedially (Fig. 17–4). When using a nerve stimulator, if contraction of the quadriceps muscle is observed during a block of these spinal nerves to the psoas major muscle, the needle should be withdrawn and redirected anteromedially.

Control of hip flexor spasticity originating from the psoas major muscle also may be accomplished by injecting solution directly into the psoas muscle.

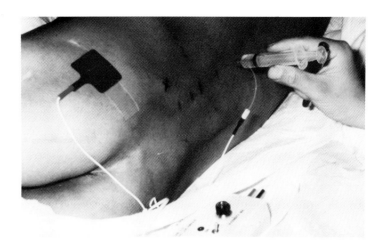

FIGURE 17-1. Lumbar somatic nerve block. The needle is placed approximately 3 cm lateral to the spinous process and advanced about 3 cm anterior to the transverse process.

This technique requires an excellent knowledge of lumbar and pelvic anatomy to avoid inadvertent needle placement into the abdominal peritoneum or adjacent vascular structures. Fluoroscopic or EMG needle guidance may be helpful to determine needle depth to prevent these complications. Koyama et al. performed direct psoas major and minor intramuscular phenol blocks under ultrasonic monitoring in an attempt to reduce x-ray exposure and minimize the risk of organ and vascular injury.[7] Hip range of motion improved in all patients without significant complications. This latter technique is limited to clinicians skilled in echographic anatomy.

Most complications with lumbar somatic nerve blocks, direct psoas nerve blocks, or intramuscular psoas blocks, occur as a result of misplaced needles. If the needle is advanced too deep, inadvertent puncture of major blood vessels may occur, including the aorta on the left side and inferior vena cava on the right. Also, with deep injections or when using large volumes of anesthetics, sympathetic blockade may occur. If the needle is angled too far medially either a transforaminal epidural, paramedian epidural, or subarachnoid block would be possible.

ILIOHYPOGASTRIC AND ILIOINGUINAL NERVE BLOCK

The iliohypogastric and ilioinguinal nerves are branches from the first lumbar nerves. The iliohypogastric nerve emerges from the psoas major muscle and crosses obliquely anterior to the quadratus lumborum muscle. It extends toward the iliac crest where it divides into the iliac and hypogastric branches. The iliac branch supplies sensation to the gluteal region and the hypogastric branch to the hypogastric region.

The ilioinguinal nerve arises from the first lumbar nerve just below the iliohypogastric nerve. It also passes obliquely anterior to the quadratus lumborum

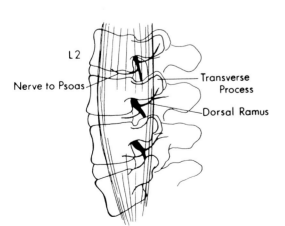

FIGURE 17-2. The direct spinal nerve branches to the psoas major muscle shown at the L2-3 and L3-4 intertransverse space.

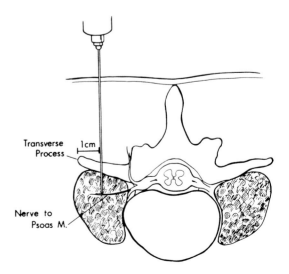

FIGURE 17-3. Needle position and depth when injecting the direct spinal nerve to the psoas major muscle.

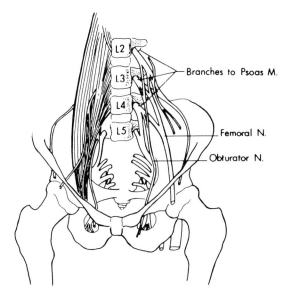

FIGURE 17-4. The lumbar plexus, branches to psoas major, and its relation to the femoral nerve (posterolateral) and the obturator nerve (posteromedial) at the third and fourth lumbar space.

muscle, but also the iliacus muscle. The nerve innervates the internal oblique muscle and later follows the spermatic cord through the external abdominal ring. The ilioinguinal nerve ultimately supplies sensation to the proximal medial thigh, male scrotum, and female labium major.

One of the primary reasons to block these nerves is to differentiate painful conditions of the medial thigh and genital regions. Treatment for primary neuropathies, entrapments, and scarring from lower abdominal surgeries such as herniorrhaphies can be other indications.

Technique

With the patient's anterior pelvis exposed, the bony landmarks of the iliac crest are identified, specifically the anterior superior iliac spine (ASIS). Two cm above the ASIS a needle is injected immediately medial to the iliac crest. The needle is maintained against the iliac bone as it is advanced toward the iliacus muscle and directed medially toward the umbilicus (Fig. 17–5). With the needle tip in this position, both the ilioinguinal and iliohypogastric nerves can usually be blocked. The needle depth varies depending on the patient's size, but averages 3–5 cm.

LATERAL FEMORAL CUTANEOUS NERVE BLOCK

The lateral femoral cutaneous nerve provides sensation to the anterior, lateral, and posterior aspect of the thigh. This purely sensory nerve originates from the L2 and L3 nerve roots. Deep in the pelvis, it emerges from the psoas major muscle where it passes adjacent to the iliacus muscle and posterior to the inguinal ligament near the ASIS. The nerve passes over the sartorius muscle, becomes superficial 12 cm inferior to the ASIS where it terminates into smaller branches that supply the skin of the thigh.

Lateral femoral cutaneous nerve blocks can be performed in suspected cases of neuropathic pain originating from this nerve. In cases of entrapment, i.e., meralgia paresthetica, a mixture of anesthetic and corticosteroids can be injected. As expected, this nerve is commonly blocked in conjunction with other peripheral nerves to provide anesthesia for thigh procedures.

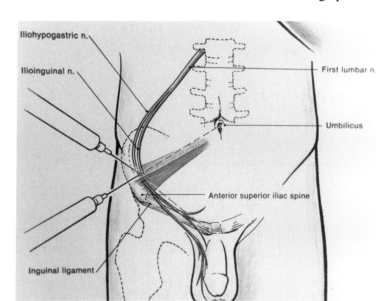

FIGURE 17-5. Needle placement for the iliohypogastric and ilioinguinal nerve blocks. (From Katz J: Atlas of Regional Anesthesia, 2nd ed. East Norwalk, CT, Appleton & Lange, 1994, p 121, with permission.)

Technique

With the patient's anterior pelvis exposed, the ASIS and the inguinal ligament are identified. A needle is placed perpendicular to the skin approximately one inch medial to the ASIS and inferior to the inguinal ligament. The needle is advanced into the soft tissue about 1 inch, but varies depending on the patient's size. At times, paresthesias may be elicited, therefore varifying needle placement. Once needle placement is satisfactory, 5–10 ml of solution can be injected.

OBTURATOR NERVE BLOCK

The obturator nerve originates in the substance of the psoas major muscle from the L2–L4 spinal nerves (see Fig. 17–4). It exits the pelvis through the obturator foramen where it lies adjacent to the obturator vessels. The nerve divides into the anterior and posterior branches at the external obturator muscle. The anterior branch innervates the adductor brevis, gracilis, adductor longus, and in some cases the pectineus muscle (Fig. 17–6). It also gives a branch to the hip joint and supplies sensation to the medial thigh. The posterior branch innervates the external obturator, adductor magnus, and occasionally the adductor brevis muscles. The posterior branch often sends a branch to the knee joint. Both the anterior and posterior branches of the obturator nerve lie almost at the same sagittal plane separated by the adductor brevis muscle. The posterior branch lies at a deeper plane than the anterior branch.

The obturator nerve is frequently blocked in cases of adductor spasticity (Fig. 17–7 and 17–8). This can facilitate perineal hygiene, positioning, and lower extremity dressing. Scissoring gait patterns can also be improved. The block also can be used to differentiate hip and knee pain.

Technique

The main branch of the obturator nerve can be blocked at its exit from the obturator foramen. A block at this level would affect both the anterior and posterior branches. The patient is first placed in the supine position with the hip abducted and externally rotated. Attempts are made to palpate the obturator foramen and nearby bony landmarks, especially the pubic tubercle, ischial tuberosity, and symphysis pubis. Delineating each of these landmarks may be difficult depending on the patient's size and any deforming hip contractures that may be present. After locating the pubic tubercle, the needle is placed in the skin 2 cm below and 2 cm lateral to this bony landmark. The needle is advanced in a slight medial direction until the bony ridge of the pubic bone is contacted. The needle is withdrawn slightly and redirected in a more superior and lateral position until the superior bony border of the obturator foramen is contacted. It is important to "walk" the needle around the superomedial border of the obturator foramen, contacting bone. This gives a good indication of the depth of the obturator nerve and vessels and avoids inadvertent puncture into organs medial and superior to this point, such as the bladder and vagina. Once the needle is in a superior position against bone, it is slowly directed posteriorly and "walked" through the obturator foramen. About 8–12 ml of solution can be injected; however, caution should be exhibited during infusion to avoid vascular injection.

An alternative approach involves blocking the anterior and posterior branches separately, but more distal. This technique can provide a more specific block while reducing the risk of vascular or organ puncture with the more proximal block. The anterior branch can be blocked by inserting a needle on the anterolateral surface of the adductor longus

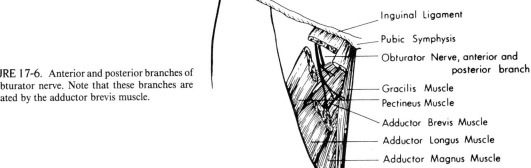

FIGURE 17-6. Anterior and posterior branches of the obturator nerve. Note that these branches are separated by the adductor brevis muscle.

Inguinal Ligament

Pubic Symphysis

Obturator Nerve, anterior and posterior branch

Gracilis Muscle

Pectineus Muscle

Adductor Brevis Muscle

Adductor Longus Muscle

Adductor Magnus Muscle

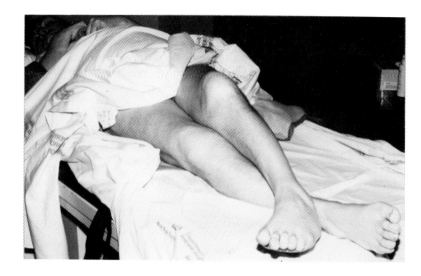

FIGURE 17-7. Adductor spasticity prior to an obturator block causes poor bed positioning and difficult perineal hygiene.

muscle 3–7 cm from the pubic tubercle (Fig. 17–9). The muscle bellies of the adductor longus and brevis can be "gripped" in most patients close to the pubic tubercle, thereby providing an important landmark. The needle is directed posteriorly to the adductor longus muscle and slowly advanced. It is stopped on the posterior surface of the adductor longus muscle to block the anterior branch. About 5–8 ml of anesthetic solution can be injected. The needle can be advanced through the adductor brevis muscle to its posterior border where the posterior branch of the obturator nerve can be blocked. This branch lies between the adductor brevis and adductor magnus muscles. Again, 5–8 ml of anesthetic solution can be injected. The use of a nerve stimulator makes this block quick and simple.

Common pitfalls to both approaches of the obturator block include a misplaced needle secondary to an improper needle angle, especially with the distal block. The majority of patients receiving an obturator block have adductor spasticity resulting in hip adduction and rotation deformities. These deformities distort the normal anatomical relationships and often make this block more challenging while causing frustration to less experienced clinicians.

FEMORAL NERVE BLOCK

The femoral nerve is composed of fibers from the L2, L3, and L4 nerve roots. It enters the anterior thigh posterior to the inguinal ligament and anterior to the iliopsoas muscle. While in the femoral triangle, the nerve lies lateral to the femoral artery and vein. At the level of the inguinal ligament, the nerve divides into two parts: anterior and posterior branches. The anterior branch supplies sensation to the anterior and medial thigh and often a muscular branch to the sartorius muscle. The posterior branch innervates the remaining muscles in the anterior

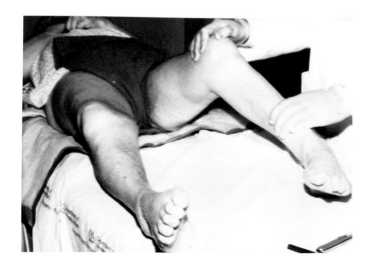

FIGURE 17-8. Marked improvement in bed positioning following bilateral phenol obturator blocks in the same patient as in Figure 17-7.

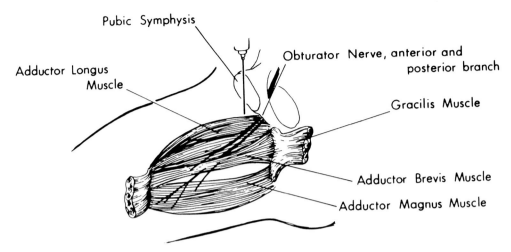

FIGURE 17-9. The obturator nerve at its exit from the obturator foramen. Note the angle of the needle to the hemipelvis.

compartment of the thigh, knee joint, and terminate as the saphenous nerve.

The femoral nerve can be blocked in cases of severe knee extensor spasticity in the nonambulatory patient, which may interfere with sitting. As with other blocks, pain problems in its sensory distribution or anesthetic injections for procedures are other common indications to performing this block.[10]

Technique

The femoral nerve can be easily blocked within the femoral triangle.[6] With the patient supine, the femoral artery is palpated just below the inguinal ligament. This ligament can be visualized by drawing a line connecting the anterosuperior iliac spine and the pubic symphysis. While the second and third digits of the nondominant hand palpate the femoral artery, a needle is slowly advanced perpendicular to the skin in the direction of the femoral nerve immediately lateral to the artery. The needle is advanced through the fascia lata and fascia iliaca, at times causing pain. One can often feel a loss of resistance as the needle advances through these fascial layers. Because an inadequate block occurs if the needle is placed outside of the fascia iliaca, proper depth is essential. If a nerve stimulator is used, one quickly identifies knee extension and hip internal rotation. Up to 15 ml of volume can be injected after careful aspiration is performed.

SCIATIC NERVE BLOCK

The sciatic nerve is composed of the common peroneal and tibial nerves carrying fibers from the L4–S3 nerve roots. This nerve exits the pelvis through the greater sciatic notch just below the

piriformis muscle. It runs in the posterior thigh where it divides into the tibial and common peroneal nerves, usually within the popliteal fossa. The nerve supplies sensation to the posterior thigh, leg, and foot, and motor innervation to the posterior thigh, leg, and foot muscles.

Anesthetic sciatic nerve injections are commonly used to facilitate casting of a spastic ankle or knee flexion contractures. These blocks can be used effectively to control lower extremity spasticity in patients with spinal cord injury,[3] provide anestheseia for lower extremity procedures, or assist with diagnosing lower extremity pain problems, including those at the knee.[10]

Technique

Although a lateral and anterior approach have been described to block the sciatic nerve,[2,5] the posterior approach is the most common. Labat's classical approach places the patient in the lateral decubitus position with the intended block side up.[8] The knee on the intended block side is placed in partial flexion and the heel laid to rest on the contralateral noninvolved extended extremity. Landmarks to identify the sciatic nerve include extending a line between the upper aspect of the greater trochanter of the femur and the posterior superior iliac spine (PSIS). This line should coincide with the upper border of both the piriformis muscle and the sciatic notch. The sciatic nerve is located 3 cm below the midpoint of this line, where the injection site is located.

An alternative method of locating this same injection site includes drawing a line between the greater trochanter of the femur and a point about 2 cm below the sacral hiatus. The midpoint of this line corresponds to the location of the sciatic nerve.

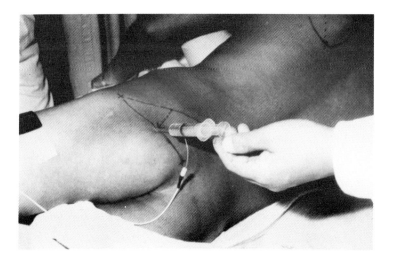

FIGURE 17-10. Landmarks for a sciatic nerve block. The upper line connects the PSIS with the greater trochanter of the femur. The lower line connects the greater trochanter with a point 2 cm below the sacral hiatus.

It should also be the same spot as that located by the first line described above (Fig. 17–10). A long needle, up to 15 cm, is required to reach the sciatic nerve. When using a nerve stimulator, as the needle is advanced, a gluteus maximus muscle contraction will be initially observed. With further advancement of the needle, a knee flexion contraction should be observed as the gluteus maximus muscle contraction diminishes.

Blocking the sciatic nerve within the posterior gluteal region as described above is often difficult due to its depth. Multiple attempts at locating the nerve with frequent needle repositioning are often required. The use of Doppler ultrasound to assist with location of the sciatic nerve has been described to prevent this repeated probing.[4]

INFERIOR GLUTEAL NERVE BLOCK

The inferior gluteal nerve innervates the gluteus maximus muscle, the most powerful hip extensor. The nerve arises from the posterior divisions of the lumbosacral plexus consisting of fibers from the L5, S1, and S2 nerve roots. The nerve parallels the sciatic nerve under the inferior border of the piriformis muscle and turns sharply posterolateral toward the sacrotuberous ligament where it enters the gluteus maximus muscle. In cases of severe hip extensor spasticity that interferes with sitting, this nerve can be blocked.

Technique

To localize the inferior gluteal nerve, a needle is inserted into the center of the gluteus maximus muscle. This center point can be located by outlining

the borders of this quadrilateral shaped muscle. It originates medially from the posterior surface of the sacrum and inserts laterally into the gluteal tuberosity of the femur. The needle is slowly advanced to a depth of about 3 cm, often varying based on the patient's size. When using a nerve stimulator, a strong contraction of the gluteus maximus muscle should be observed. If any contraction is seen in the hamstring muscles, the needle should be withdrawn, indicating that the needle is close to the sciatic nerve.

REFERENCES

1. Gray H: Gray's Anatomy, Descriptive and Surgical. New York, Bounty Books.
2. Guardini R, Waldrom BA, Wallace WA: Sciatic nerve block: A new lateral approach, Acta Anaesthesiol Scand 29:515–519, 1985.
3. Gunduz S, Kalyon TA, Dursun H, et al: Peripheral nerve block with phenol to treat spasticity in spinal cord injured patients. Paraplegia 30:808–811, 1992.
4. Hullander M, Balsara Z, Spillane W, et al: The use of Doppler ultrasound to assist with sciatic nerve blocks. Reg Anesth 16:282–284, 1991.
5. Ichiyanaghi K: Sciatic nerve block: Lateral approach with patient supine. Anesthesiology 20:601–604, 1959.
6. Khoo ST, Brown TK: Femoral nerve block: The anatomical basis for a single injection technique. Anaesth Intens Care 11:40–42, 1983.
7. Koyama H, et al: Phenol block for hip flexor muscle spasticity under ultrasonic monitoring. Arch Phys Med Rehabil 73:1040–1043, 1992.
8. Labat G: Regional Anesthesia. Philadelphia, W.B. Saunders, 1922, pp 289–291.
9. Meelhuysen FE, Halpern D, Quast J: Treatment of flexor spasticity by paravertebral lumbarspinal nerve block. Arch Phys Med Rehabil 49:717–722, 1968.
10. Rooks M, Fleming LL: Evaluation of acute knee injuries with sciatic and femoral nerve blocks. Clin Orthop 179:185–188, 1983.

Chapter 18

LEG, FOOT, AND ANKLE BLOCKS

DENNIS MATTHEWS, M.D.

Lower extremity nerve blocks are used primarily for anesthesia during surgical procedures, especially when general, spinal, or epidural techniques cannot be used. Their use in physiatric practice includes the diagnosis and management of pain syndromes and spasticity.[1,4,17,18] These blocks allow a more active and functional participation in therapies and can assist in orthotic management for gait training and positioning for wheelchair seating evaluations.[1]

TIBIAL AND COMMON PERONEAL NERVES

The tibial and common peroneal nerves originate as a bifurcation of the sciatic nerve, usually high in the popliteal fossa. The tibial nerve consists of fibers from the L4–S3 nerve roots and runs from the apex of the popliteal fossa with the popliteal artery to the distal border of the popliteus muscle. It then passes deep to the arch of the soleus muscle to enter into the deep posterior compartment of the leg. The tibial nerve innervates the posterior compartment muscles of the leg and supplies sensation to the lateral border and sole of the foot.

The common peroneal nerve consists of fibers from the L4–S2 nerve roots and follows the lateral border of the popliteal fossa just deep to the popliteal membrane. It then courses laterally around the neck of the fibula to supply the anterior and lateral compartment muscles of the leg and sensation to the dorsum of the foot and lateral aspect of the leg.

The tibial and common peroneal nerve are usually blocked at the level of the knee. Diagnostic or therapeutic blocks in the popliteal fossa have varying clinical applications.[8,14,39] Local blockade of the tibial and common peroneal nerves produces excellent anesthesia of the lower leg and foot[2,3,13,14,16,19,20,22] and provides good analgesia following surgery below the knee.[15] It can be used as a diagnostic block in children who have toe walking[11] or as an adjunct to physical therapy in children with brain injury and equinus deformities.[12]

Tibial Nerve Block Technique

With the patient in the prone position, the triangular borders of the popliteal fossa are identified. The knee crease corresponds to the base, semimembranosus muscle to the medial border, and the biceps femoris muscle to the lateral border of this triangle. A perpendicular line is extended from the midpoint of the base to the apex of the triangle (Fig. 18-1). The needle is introduced perpendicular to the skin 6–7 cm proximal to the base on this line and 1 cm lateral (Fig. 18-2). The needle should be advanced midway between the skin and the femur or to a depth of approximately 3 cm. The use of a nerve stimulator to provoke a plantar flexion muscle contraction at the ankle can be helpful to better localize this nerve.[25]

Common Peroneal Nerve Block Technique

With the patient's lateral knee and leg exposed, the fibular head is identified (Fig. 18-3). The common peroneal nerve as it crosses the fibula 2–3 cm below the fibular head is palpated. The needle is slowly advanced adjacent to the nerve and small volumes of solution injected, usually fewer than 5 ml. When using a nerve stimulator, contraction of the anterior and lateral compartment muscles of the leg should be observed.

An alternative to the above technique is blocking the common peroneal nerve within the popliteal fossa (see Figs 18-1 and 18-2). Within this fossa, the nerve lies adjacent to the biceps femoris muscle lateral to the tibial nerve. The apex of this fossa is bisected and a needle inserted on the lateral aspect of this division to a depth midway between the skin and femur, usually 0.5 cm below the popliteal membrane.

Complications with tibial and common peroneal blocks are rare. Inadvertant injection into the popliteal artery can be avoided with good technique and careful aspiration after placement of the needle.

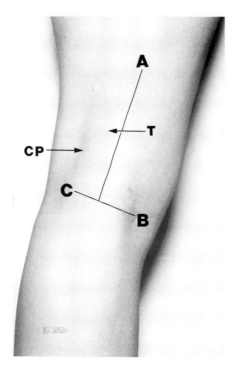

FIGURE 18-1. The borders of the popliteal fossa are outlined (*ABC*) and the surface location of the tibial nerve (*T*) and common peroneal nerve (*CP*) noted.

A pressure neuropathy is possible when injecting around the common peroneal nerve at the fibular head if large volumes of medication are used. Kempthorne and Brown performed 50 blocks in children with no detectable intravascular injections, popliteal hematomas, neuralgias, or persistent sensory changes.[11]

ANKLE BLOCKS

A total ankle block consists of circumferentially blocking five nerves at the level of the ankle that control sensation to the entire foot. Two major nerves, the femoral and sciatic, are represented. These nerves originate from the lumbar and sacral plexus and terminate as the posterior tibial, deep peroneal, sural, saphenous, and superficial peroneal nerves. Simultaneous blocks to each of these nerves are commonly performed to facilitate superficial operations of the foot when a tourniquet is not required. Total ankle blocks are technically difficult because five nerves must be blocked to achieve total anesthesia of the foot. Schurman[21] describes this approach as ideal in producing only minimal immobility of the lower extremity while producing the desired sensory changes. Individual nerves also may be blocked at the ankle to help differentiate painful foot and ankle disorders or cases of neuropathic pain.

POSTERIOR TIBIAL NERVE

The posterior tibial nerve (PTN) originates adjacent to the popliteus muscle and travels with the posterior tibial artery within the posterior compartment of the leg. At the ankle, the nerve passes through the posterior tarsal tunnel at the midpoint between the medial malleolus and calcaneus under the flexor retinaculum. It travels posterior to the posterior tibial artery within the tunnel and divides within 1 cm of the malleolar–calcaneal axis in the majority of feet.[9] The PTN innervates all posterior leg compartment muscles and supplies sensation to the ankle joint, skin of the heel, and inner sole of the foot. The PTN terminates at the medial and lateral plantar nerves that innervate the intrinsic foot muscles and supply sensation to the entire sole of the foot and many of the tarsal and metatarsal joints.

A PTN block is commonly used in podiatric medicine.[7] Tarsal tunnel surgery, removal of soft tissue masses or foreign bodies, and preinjection therapy for painful heel conditions are a few reasons to perform this type of block.

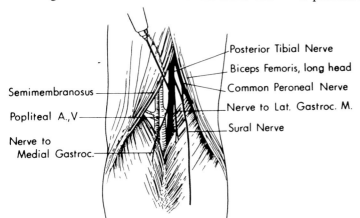

Semimembranosus

Popliteal A., V

Nerve to Medial Gastroc.

Posterior Tibial Nerve

Biceps Femoris, long head

Common Peroneal Nerve

Nerve to Lat. Gastroc. M.

Sural Nerve

FIGURE 18-2. The popliteal fossa with its contents in relation to the posterior tibial and common peroneal nerves. The needle tip is in position to block the posterior tibial nerve.

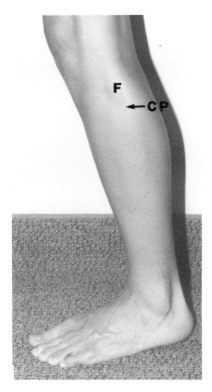

FIGURE 18-3. Lateral view of the leg with surface markings representing the fibular head (F) and common peroneal nerve (CP) well delineated.

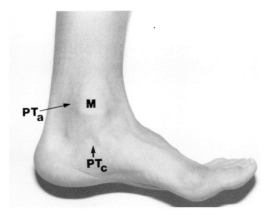

FIGURE 18-4. Medial view of the ankle and foot with surface markings representing the medial malleolus (M), posterior tibial artery (PTa), and sustentaculum tali (PTc) noted.

Bareither et al.[5] identified a range for the PTN bifurcation from 2.8 cm distal to 14.3 cm proximal to the medial malleolus. A PTN block performed lateral to the posterior tibial artery adjacent to the medial malleolus was unsuccessful in 20% of patients. A 96% success rate in blocking the PTN was noted when the injection site was 8 cm proximal to the medial malleolus.

Posterior Tibial Nerve Block Technique

With the patient's medial ankle exposed, the medial malleolus and posterior tibial artery are palpated (Fig. 18-4) at the level of the posterior tarsal tunnel. A needle can be introduced posterior to the posterior tibial artery and directed 45° anteriorly. If nerve stimulation is used, contraction of the intrinsic foot muscles will be observed.

A second approach blocks the PTN proximal to the posterior tarsal tunnel. With the patient supine and the foot elevated and externally rotated, a needle is inserted at the midpoint of a transverse line joining the upper portion of the medial malleolus with the medial edge of the Achilles tendon (Fig. 18-5). The needle is directed anterolaterally until the posterior surface of the tibia is contacted, then withdrawn 2–3 mm before solution is injected.

An alternative approach involves blocking the PTN distal to the posterior tarsal tunnel. With the medial ankle exposed, the borders of the medial malleolus and sustentaculum tali are identified (see Fig. 18-4). A needle is inserted posterior and inferior to the ridge on the sustentaculum tali, immediately below the midpoint of the medial malleolus.[23] The needle is advanced until bone is contacted and withdrawn 2 mm prior to injecting the blocking agent.

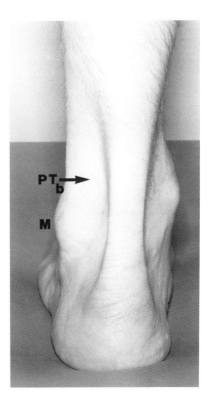

FIGURE 18-5. Posterior view of the ankle with surface markings representing medial malleolus (M) and the block site of the posterior tibial nerve (PTb).

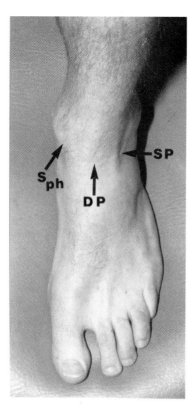

FIGURE 18-6. Anterior view of the foot and ankle depicting the surface locations of the saphenous (*Sph*), deep peroneal (*DP*), and superficial peroneal (*SP*) nerves.

DEEP PERONEAL NERVE

The deep peroneal nerve (DPN) branches from the common peroneal nerve to innervate the muscles of the anterior compartment of the leg (Figs. 18–6 and 18–7). It also innervates the extensor digitorum brevis muscle on the dorsum of the foot and supplies sensation to the ankle, tarsal, and first through fourth metatarsophalangeal joints as well as the dorsal skin between the first and second toes. The DPN lies deep to the extensor retinaculum at the anterior ankle next to the anterior tibial artery, lateral to the extensor hallucis longus (EHL) tendon within the anterior tarsal tunnel.

Deep Peroneal Nerve Block Technique

With the anterior ankle exposed, the midpoint of a line intersecting both the medial and lateral malleoli is identified (see Fig. 18–6). The anterior tibialis tendon and dorsalis pedis artery are palpated over the anterior ankle. A needle can be inserted perpendicular to the skin, just lateral to the artery and advanced 2–4 cm depending on the patient's size (see Fig. 18–7). If the artery is not palpable, the needle is placed lateral to the EHL tendon. The patient is asked to move the great toe as the physician watches

for needle movement, suggesting needle placement into the substance of the EHL tendon. In this case, the needle position is adjusted and solution injected inferior to the extensor retinaculum.

SURAL NERVE

The sural nerve (SN) consists of fibers from the L5 and S1 nerve roots and is formed from branches of the common peroneal and tibial nerves. It arises immediately distal to the popliteal space and descends superficially within the posterior leg in the midline. The SN supplies sensation to the lateral leg and extends distally along the lateral aspect of the ankle, midway between the lateral malleolus and calcaneus, where it supplies sensation to the skin of the lateral aspect of the foot.

Sural Nerve Block Technique

A distal SN block is performed immediately posterior to the lateral malleolus. With the lateral ankle exposed, a needle is inserted midway between the lateral malleolus and calcaneus (Fig. 18–8). The needle is directed toward the posterior surface of the lateral malleolus until bone is contacted. The

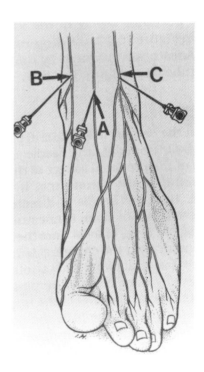

FIGURE 18-7. Anatomic drawing of the ankle and foot depicting block sites and relationships of the deep peroneal nerve (*A*), saphenous nerve (*B*), and the superficial peroneal nerve (*C*). (From Carron H, Korbon GA, Rowlingson JC: Lower extremity blocks. In Carron H, Korbon GA, Rowlingson JC (eds): Regional Anesthesia: Techniques and Clinical Applications. Orlando, FL, Grune & Stratton, 1984, with permission.)

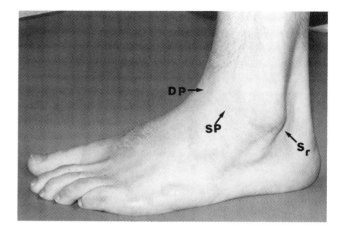

FIGURE 18-8. Lateral view of the foot and ankle depicting the surface locations of the deep peroneal (*DP*), superficial peroneal (*SP*), and sural (*Sr*) nerves.

depth of needle placement varies, but in most patients 4–6 ml of superficially injected solution is adequate.

A proximal SN block can be easily performed in the posterior leg between the skin and the gastrocnemius muscle. The midportion of this muscle is identified and the nerve blocked in the midline 12–16 cm proximal to the upper calcaneous. The needle is advanced to the outer aspect of the gastrocnemius muscle, and 4–7 ml of solution injected.

SAPHENOUS NERVE

The saphenous nerve (SAN) is a purely sensory branch of the femoral nerve derived from the L3 and L4 nerve roots. It runs adjacent to the femoral artery until its superficial exit at the medial knee, where it supplies sensation. The nerve descends in the superficial fascia anterior to the medial malleolus with the great saphenous vein. It ultimately supplies sensation to the medial leg and foot.

Saphenous Nerve Block Technique

With the medial ankle exposed, the medial malleolus at the level of the saphenous vein is identified.[10] The SAN lies immediately medial to the anterior tibialis tendon on the anterior surface of the medial malleolus (see Fig. 18–6). A 25-gauge needle can be inserted at this point and 4–7 ml of solution injected (see Fig. 18–7). Needle depth should remain superficial.

An alternative proximal SAN block can be performed at the knee. A block at this location can be used to treat some cases of medial knee pain attributed to SAN entrapment.[24] With the medial knee exposed, the medial femoral condyle is palpated. Palpation of the SAN is often possible at this location, especially in thin patients. A 23- or 25-gauge needle can be inserted perpendicular to the skin at the level of the medial femoral condyle.

The needle is advanced until the femur is contacted and withdrawn slightly. Injection of 4–8 ml of solution may be required.

SUPERFICIAL PERONEAL NERVE

The superficial peroneal nerve (SPN) branches from the common peroneal nerve to innervate the peroneus longus and brevis muscles of the lateral compartment of the leg. The nerve descends into the leg, where it emerges above the extensor retinaculum, supplying sensation to the skin of the dorsal foot and toes (see Figs. 18–6 and 18–8).

Superficial Peroneal Nerve Block Technique

With the patient supine and the anterior ankle exposed, the anterior tibial artery and lateral malleolus are identified. At the level of the ankle, a needle may be inserted adjacent to the artery but anterior to the extensor retinaculum (see Fig. 18–7). A subcutaneous ridge of anesthetic solution along the skin crease will adequately block the SPN. This ridge will overlay the previously discussed subfascial injection of the deep peroneal nerve.

PLANTAR AND INTERDIGITAL NERVES

The medial and lateral plantar nerves are the terminal branches of the posterior tibial nerve. These nerves innervate the intrinsic foot muscles and ultimately divide into the interdigital nerves that supply sensation to the skin of the toes. Blocks to this region are commonly performed at the level of the metatarsal heads—thus, the name "metatarsal nerve blocks." Metatarsal nerve blocks are designed to deposit solution in a ringlike form around the head of each metatarsal bone. The most common indication for these blocks is to provide anesthesia for bunionectomies and surgical

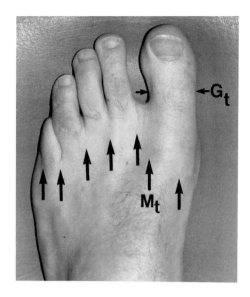

FIGURE 18-9. Dorsal view of the foot depicting the location of metatarsal (*Mt*) blocks (*large arrows*) and great toe (*Gt*) blocks (*small arrows*).

removal of ingrown toenails.[3] Facilitation of digital range of motion and relief of pain from neuromas are other indications.

Metatarsal Nerve Block Technique

From a dorsal approach, a 25-gauge needle is inserted adjacent to the metatarsal head directed toward the sole of the foot. The needle is advanced to the level of the midportion of the metatarsal bone. If all toes need to be anesthetized, each intertarsal space is infiltrated; otherwise, only isolated blocks need to be performed. Separate injections are made on the sides of the first and fifth metatarsals, when indicated. Superficial skin wheals between the metatarsal bones are often necessary to provide greater comfort to the patient before injecting deeper (Fig. 18-9).

For a description of digital nerve blocks, see chapter 16.

SUMMARY

Indications for lower extremity nerve blocks in a physiatrist's practice include pain syndromes and spasticity. These blocks can be used effectively to allow more active and functional participation in therapies. A physician knowledgeable in the regional anatomy, indications, and block technique can safely perform these lower extremity blocks with only rare complications.

REFERENCES

1. Arendzum JH, Van Juijn H, Beckman MK, et al: Diagnostic blocks of the tibial nerve in spastic hemiparesis. Scand J Rehabil Med 24:75–81, 1992.
2. Armitage EN: Regional anesthesia in pediatrics. Clin Anaesthesiol 3:353, 1985.
3. Arthur DS, McNicol LR: Local anesthetic techniques in pediatric surgery. Br J Anaesth 58:760–778, 1986.
4. Awad EA: Injection Techniques for Spasticity. Minneapolis, 1993.
5. Bareither DJ, Genau JM, Massaro JC: Variations in the divisions of the tibial nerve: Application to nerve blocks. J Foot Surg 29:581–583, 1990.
6. Brown TCK, Schulte-Steinberg OH: Neural blockade for pediatric surgery. In Cousins MC, Bridenbaugh PO (eds): Neural Blockage in Clinical Anesthesia and Management of Pain. Philadelphia, J.B. Lippincott, 1988, pp 669–692.
7. Cohen SJ, Roenigk RK: Nerve blocks for cutaneous surgery of the foot. J Dermatol Surg Oncol 17:527–534, 1991.
8. Collins VJ: Fundamentals of Nerve Blocking. Philadelphia, Lea & Febiger, 1960.
9. Dellon AL, Mackinnon SE: Tibial nerve branching in the tarsal tunnel. Arch Neurol 41:645–646, 1984.
10. Gurmarnik S, Hurwitz E: Saphenous and common peroneal nerve block will prevent tourniquet pain in prolonged podiatry procedures. J Foot Surg 30:319, 1991.
11. Kempthorne PM, Brown TC: Nerve blocks around the knee in children. Anesth Intens Care 12:14–17, 1984.
12. Kempthorne PM, Ratcliff RN: Temporary tibial nerve block-adjunct to inhibitory plastics in the physiotherapy management of equinus in severely head-injured children. Aust J Physiother 29:119, 1983.
13. Lofstrom B: Nerve block at the knee. In Illustrated Handbook in Local Anesthesia. Chicago, Year Book, 1969, pp 70–85.
14. McKenzie PJ, Loach AB: Local anesthesia for orthopedic surgery. Br J Anesth 58:779–789, 1986.
15. McNicol LR: Lower limb blocks in children. Anesthesia 41:27, 1986.
16. Moore DC: Regional Blocks. Springfield, IL, Charles C Thomas, 1965.
17. Moore TJ, Anderson RB: The use of open phenol blocks to monitor branches of the tibial nerve in adult-acquired spasticity. Foot Ankle 11:219–221, 1991.
18. Petrillo CR, Knoploch S: Phenol block of the tibial nerve for spasticity: A long-term follow-up study. Int Disabil Stud 10:97–100, 1988.
19. Raj PP: Clinical Practice of Regional Anesthesia. New York, Churchill Livingstone, 1991.
20. Rorie DK, Byer DE, Nelson DO, et al: Assessment of block of the sciatic nerve in the popliteal fossa. Anesth Analg 59:371–376, 1980.
21. Schurman DJ: Ankle block anesthesia for foot surgery. Anesthesia 44:342, 1976.
22. Sparks CJ, Higeleo T: Foot surgery in vanuati: Results of combined tibial, common peroneal, and saphenous nerve blocks in fifty-six adults. Anesth Intens Care 17:336–339, 1989.
23. Wasseff MR: Posterior tibial nerve block. Anesthesia 46:841–844, 1991.
24. Worth RM, Kettelkamp DB, Defalque RJ, et al: Saphenous nerve entrapment: A cause of medial knee pain. Am J Sports Med 12:80–81, 1984.
25. Zahari DT, Englund, Girolamo M: Peripheral nerve block with use of stimulator. J Foot Surg 29:162–163, 1990.

Chapter 19

LUMBAR AND THORACIC DISCOGRAPHY WITH CT AND MRI CORRELATIONS

JOSEPH D. FORTIN, D.O.

There is no sadder or more frequent obituary on the pages of time than "We have always done it this way."

The English Digest

To appreciate the historical controversy surrounding discography is to understand that its inception was a tenuous one, tainted by admonitions, suppositions, and contradictions.

Mixter and Barr were the first to ignite interest in the disc with their 1934 hallmark description of the herniated nucleus pulposus.[55] This mechanical model detailed a lumbar posterolateral prolapse with direct nerve root compression and secondary radiculopathy. The Mixter and Barr precepts became a central model of spine pain that fixated the medical community and diverted attention from other possible causes. Although medical schools continue to propagate the neurocompressive model as the cardinal cause of spine pain, it actually accounts for a relatively small percentage of all patients with axial complaints.[74,84]

In 1938, Steindler and Luck discovered that the injection of procaine into a herniated disc could relieve sciatica.[77] Scientists then queried the existence of an intradiscal pain mechanism.

Roofe's 1940 revelation of annulus fibrosus innervation provided the impetus for conceptualizing the disc as a source of pain independent of a neurocompressive paradigm.[66] A direct clinical link for Roofe's discovery would await nearly a half a century, when Vanharanta et al. demonstrated that only annular fissures extending to the mid to outer annular regions significantly correlated with pain upon provocation injection.[82]

However diaphanous by modern standards, the clinical relevance of annular innervation in Roofe's time was enigmatic. With the combined information available today, which includes the awareness of potent inflammatory mediators within the nucleus

of disrupted discs[70] and low pressure (chemical) activation of annular nociceptors,[24] the need to expand the concept of spine pain beyond a pure mechanical model is obvious. Parenthetically, the rich innervation of the mid to outer layers of the annulus has since been substantiated by four independent investigations[11,36,52,88] using sophisticated staining and magnification techniques.

Four years after Roofe's discovery, Knut Lindblom (1944) demonstrated the presence of radial annular fissures upon injecting cadaveric discs.[48] This fascinating and historically significant observation was manifested as he watched red dye leaking from the injected nucleus into attenuated annular areas. Could disc injections be used to detect annular pathology in patients with low back pain? Lindblom had stumbled upon a potentially powerful diagnostic tool, yet was reticent to clinically apply it, given the warning of Pease.[62] Pease's admonitions were in the form of case reports of disc damage associated with inadvertent disc puncture upon attempted lumbar thecal puncture in children with purulent meningitis.[16] The disc "damage" was most likely iatrogenic discitis. To no surprise, such claims of disc damage, secondary to disc puncture, have never been rigidly validated.[32] Conversely, Lindblom was prompted by Karl Hirsch, as Hirsch noted concordant pain provocation with saline discal distention and no secondary disc "damage" on intraoperative disc injections.[41] Lindblom persevered and later that same year (1948) became a catalyst for future investigations when he reported the nucleographic patterns of 15 discs in 13 patients.[49]

By the early 1960s, the potential for discography to eclipse myelography as the premiere disc imaging study was obvious, and the change seemed imminent. Several large studies had enthusiastically proclaimed the contrast roentgenography study of discs a keen diagnostic tool, superior to myelography in evaluating patients with internal disc problems.[16,30]

However, the pro-discography momentum abruptly shifted following the 1964 and 1968 investigations of Earl Holt.[43] Holt's work remains the bane of earnest discographers to date. Based on his investigations of asymptomatic penitentiary inmates, Holt reported 37% of lumbar disc injections and 100% of cervical disc injections to be false-positive (i.e., erroneously painful). He characterized previous reports of "reproduction of discogenic pain by injection of the responsible disc space" to be "fallacious." Holt sought to demonstrate that a disc that is internally disrupted, or nondemonstrable on myelography, should not be an indication for surgery.

Earl Holt's studies are a reflection of their time—limited by methodology and technology. Unfortunately, Holt's work continues to be cited as an authoritative treatise to discount discography. A recent critical review of Holt's methods found many facets that were either passé by modern standards or of dubious validity.[76] The areas of concern are legion and include the following:

(1) The selection process (volunteer penitentiary inmates).

(2) A high technical failure rate (the inability to successfully inject some discs). This weakness raises several questions. How many injections reported as nuclear were actually annular (see Figure 19-4 in Holt's lumbar study[43])? With the significant percentage of inadvertent annular or peridiscal injections, how many of the reported evoked discogenic pain responses were procedurally induced from misadventure? Specifically, the volunteers may have been provoked from multiple misdirected attempts before the disc was actually cannulated. Conversely, with modern techniques, procedural pain is relatively mild.

(3) Six lumbar injections with normal nucleograms were reported as painful. This finding is not in keeping with the current knowledge of neurophysiologic discogenic pain mechanisms; e.g., nociceptors could not be activated by this mechanism because the annulus was intact and only the mid to outer annulus is innervated.[11,36,52,88]

(4) Holt's studies were stifled by lack of sophisticated technology. In this regard, one of Holt's conciliatory statements was sagacious: "Whether or not cervical discography might be made relevant by a radical change in contrast media and techniques remains speculative." Sodium diatrozoate (Hypaque 50), the contrast agent of Holt's era, is a known neurotoxic agent.[81] Image intensifiers had been developed in the 1950s but their application was limited.[20] Holt was resigned to plain film radiography. Moreover, CT had not been invented; hence, there was no transverse imaging to verify nuclear injections or to substantiate morphologic findings.

In tribute to Earl Holt, his desire to prevent unnecessary, or "knee jerk" surgery, was clear through his pointed commentary. He warned against "over-diagnosis" and basing surgery on technologies that had not been validated by controlled studies.

Curiously, in the same year as Holt's lumbar study, Wiley et al. reported (via 2,517 disc injections) a viable role for discography in the diagnostic evaluation of patients with axial pain and no definite disc prolapse on myelography.[86] Wiley's study was overshadowed by Holt's and, until recent years, the medical community at large seemed impervious to favorable discography reports.

From the 1940s through the 1960s, discography arose within a frustrating void created in the wake of myelography—only to be spurned by misinformation. How does one definitively evaluate patients who have radicular-like symptoms or primary axial pain without an obvious neurocompressive discogenic lesion?

Employing modern techniques, a recent well-controlled prospective study by Walsh et al.[83] refuted Holt's data. Unlike Holt, a provocative discogram was considered positive in Walsh's study only if the disc was roentgenographically abnormal and the patient's pain pattern was reproduced during the administration of the injection. Walsh et al. found discography to be a highly specific and reliable method of distinguishing symptomatic versus asymptomatic discs. The false-positive rate was 0% in Walsh's study versus 26% in Holt's study. Moreover, a host of investigations have disclosed an important application of both cervical and lumbar diagnostic disc injections in prefusion planning.[9,12,25,75,86] Specifically, if the levels selected for fusion are based on discography, the success rate is high. Thus, it now appears that only the obstinate or misinformed would cling to the Holt lineage.

WHEN IS DISCOGRAPHY INDICATED?

According to the 1988 Position Statement on Discography by the Executive Committee of the North American Spine Society[60]: "Discography is indicated in the evaluation of patients with unremitting spinal pain, with or without extremity pain, of greater than 4 months' duration, when the pain has been unresponsive to all appropriate methods of conservative therapy. Before discography, patients should have undergone investigation with other modalities which have failed to explain the source of pain; such modalities should include, but not be limited to, CT scanning, MRI scanning and/or myelography. In these circumstances, discography, especially when followed by CT scanning, may be the only study capable of providing a diagnosis by permitting a precise description of the internal anatomy of a disc and a detailed determination of the integrity of the disc substructures. Additionally, the anatomic observations may be complemented by the critical physiologic induction of pain which is recognized by the patient as similar to or identical with his or her clinical complaint. By including multiple levels in the study, the patient acts as his or her own control for evaluation of the reliability of the pain response."

Other indications for discography include ruling out secondary internal disc disruption or recurrent herniation postoperatively, exploring pseudarthrosis, determining the number of levels to include in a spine fusion, and determining the primary symptom-producing level when chemonucleolysis is contemplated.

In most situations, discography is reserved as a presurgical diagnostic tool. Predicating treatment on a rapidly established diagnosis is the key to successful treatment and to preventing long-term disability from misdiagnosis or improper treatment and recurrence. If a patient has failed an initial trial of aggressive functional restoration, spinal diagnostic injections, including discography, can be extremely effective in pinpointing the pain generators. In this setting, the author has safely employed discography to establish a definitive diagnosis to tailor the course of a rehabilitation program to that specific diagnosis. Moreover, simply validating the patient's pain can, at times, be a potent boost for the healing process. Obviously, the potential for complications should be considered in the decision process before the patient undergoes any spinal injection procedure.

PREPROCEDURAL EVALUATION

Patient education is the most crucial element of the intake evaluation. It serves not only to fulfill requirements of informed consent, but most importantly to allay anxiety and allow the patient to become actively involved in the overall process. The patient is informed of what to expect before, during, and following the procedure. An anatomical model is used to explain the technical aspect of the procedure and to answer questions or concerns accordingly. Screening information obtained from the patient should include history of allergy, recent instrumentation, dental procedures or surgery, and untreated illness or infection. Vital signs are assessed and the patient completes a pain diagram, Dallas Pain Questionnaire,[47] and a baseline visual analog pain scale.

The Dallas Pain Questionnaire affords a basic understanding of how profoundly the patient's condition has affected his or her physical and psychosocial function. This tool can provide a basis for understanding the patient's response to pain, a cardinal element of the study.

The postprocedural visual analog pain scale should be compared with the preprocedural one.

The pain diagram, history (e.g., mechanism of injury), physical examination, and review of imaging studies aid the physician in selecting appropriate levels to study.

TECHNICAL PERFORMANCE OF LUMBAR DISCOGRAPHY

About 3–5 mg of midazolam (Versed) is administered intravenously preprocedurally over 3–5 minutes. The dose is titrated according to the patient's response, which allows an adequate level of sedation (as the patient is responsive and conversive throughout) and prevents the recognized threat of profound respiratory depression associated with benzodiazepines.[38] Nonetheless, immediate ventilatory support must be present.

Most lumbar discs are readily and safely cannulated by a posterior-oblique, extrapedicular approach. This technique, which has been described by Trosier[80] and modified by April,[5] prevents the potential complications associated with thecal puncture from a transdural approach.

Lateral approaches[22,26] render the segmental nerves more vulnerable, as evidenced upon studying the nerve pathway[18,39,65] in relation to the proposed needle trajectories for these techniques. Bowel perforation is another complication associated with the lateral approach.[8] High-resolution, thin-section CT and/or high field strength MR should be studied prior to the procedure to allow the technical performance to accommodate the patient's anatomy.

In general, contraindications to an extrapedicular approach include bilateral severe lateral stenosis, bilateral conjoint nerve root sleeve anomalies, cystic nerve root dilation, and obstructing posterolateral fusion mass and/or instrumentation.

The first task in performing a lumbar diagnostic disc injection is to select the level(s) and side of entry. If an anterior lumbar fusion is proposed for a patient with a L4–5 disc prolapse, the L3–4 and L5–S1 levels also must be studied to exclude the possibility of a symptomatic fissure at an adjacent level. Failure to appreciate this potential scenario may prevent a successful surgical outcome (if all affected levels are not included in the fusion mass).

The side of the patient from which to approach the disc(s) in question must be selected prior to the procedure. A left postero-oblique approach is used for a right posterolateral prolapse, and vice versa, to allow maximal visualization of the lesion following nucleography. The side contralateral to the patient's symptoms is also preferred to prevent needle-induced nociception from conflicting with the provocation response.

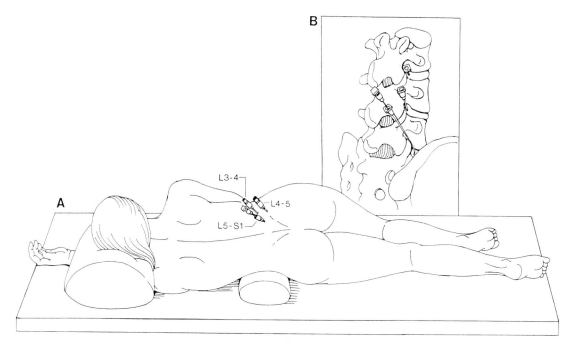

FIGURE 19-1. Technical performance of lumbar disc injection. *A,* Modified Sims' position for lumbar diagnostic disc injection. The arm adjacent to the table is outstretched under a pillow. A figure-of-four position is assumed for the lower extremities. Note the progressive inclination of the needles to the skin surface from L3–4 to L5–S1. *B,* Relationship of needles to anatomical landmarks (superior articular processes and angle of respective interspaces) and to each other from an oblique projection.

(Continued on following page.)

Once the patient is adequately sedated and sterilely prepared and draped, a segmentation count is undertaken with the patient in the prone position. Anomalous lumbosacral junctions or hemivertebrae must be identified and numbered accordingly because these anomalies may lead to surgery at the wrong level.

The lateral view is first obtained using an overhead beam with the patient in a lateral decubitus position. This view provides a "preview" of the patient's lordotic curve to aid the clinician in selecting a needle trajectory angle congruent with the lordosis at each level. The operator's attention is then directed to the subadjacent superior articular process of the disc to be studied. Slowly, the patient is rolled forward from a lateral decubitus position to a modified Sim's or prone-oblique one (Fig. 19-1A). The patient's position is optimal when the superior articular process, subadjacent to the disc space under study, bisects that disc space (Fig. 19-1B). The patient's arm closest to the table should be outstretched overhead and a pillow fashioned between the outstretched arm and the patient's head. The lower extremities are oriented in a near "figure-of-four" (Fig. 19-1A).

With a 25-gauge, 3½-inch spinal needle, a track of local anesthetic (1% lidocaine) is dispersed down to the superior articular process. If 25-gauge needles are to be used for the disc injection, local anesthesia is not necessary because the dysesthetic "sting"

associated with local anesthesia is often more painful than needle-induced nociception.

Lumbar discography often may be accomplished with 25-gauge needles; however, the needle should be selected according to the patient's body habitus (Fig. 19-2). For large, muscular, or tense patients, a 25-gauge needle may not provide enough tensile strength for "steering." A 22-gauge needle will allow ample maneuverability. Six-inch needles are adequately long for most patients, although the author has used 10-inch needles for a few obese patients. Lumbar discs in thin patients may be accessible to the same 3½-inch, 25-gauge needles used for cervical discography.

The spinal needle (under an overhead fluoroscopy tower) is directed through skin, subcutaneous adipose, lumbodorsal fascia and muscle, along the lateral aspect of the tip of the superior articular process, through the annulus, and into the nuclear region. At the lumbosacral junction the sensitive iliotransverse ligament must also be penetrated. Before the needle enters the "spongy" nucleus, it passes through the distinctive "springy" yet coarser annular ligament. Upon piercing of the annulus, the patient will experience an abrupt, unsustained pang of back pain. If the needle deflects off the superior articular process laterally, simply directing the needle tip inward (toward the disc) and the bevel outward will reorient it toward the nucleus.

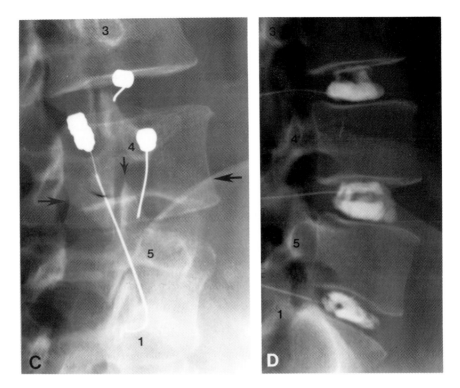

FIGURE 19-1 *(Continued)*. *C,* Preinjection oblique radiograph. Compare this plain film with *A* and *B.* The L4–5 interspace is marked with arrows to identify landmarks for optimal patient position. A bent-needle technique was employed at L5–S1. (3, 4, 5, 1: respective pedicles). *D,* Lateral nucleography. Smooth margins and spherical configurations attest to the integrity of these discs. The needles are in the mid/lower portions of the root canals. *(Continued below.)*

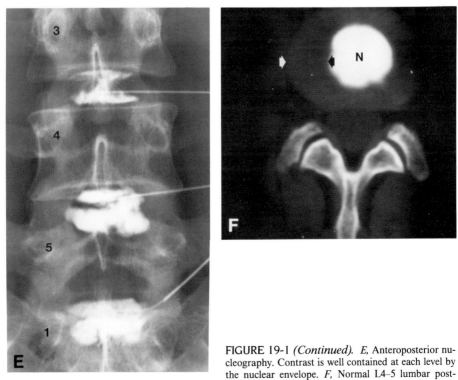

FIGURE 19-1 *(Continued)*. *E,* Anteroposterior nucleography. Contrast is well contained at each level by the nuclear envelope. *F,* Normal L4–5 lumbar post-discography/CT. A classic circular configuration documents contrast medium within the central nuclear zone (n). The strength and integrity of the annular "ligament" is underscored by its thickness *(arrowheads)*.

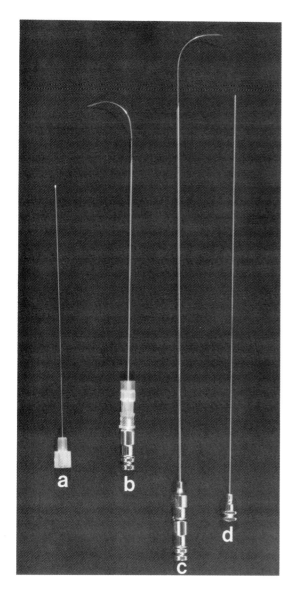

FIGURE 19-2. Primary tools of the discography trade. A 25-gauge 3½-inch spinal needle is routinely used for anesthetic infiltration prior to passing a larger needle and is also used for cervical and thoracic discography (a). A 20-gauge 3½-inch outer trocar/25-gauge 5½-inch inner, bent procedure needle (b). The bend is greater than in c. Conventional set-up for L5–S1 (b). An 18-gauge 6-inch outer trocar/25-gauge 8-inch inner, bent procedure needle (c), a combination necessary for very large or obese patients. A 22-gauge 6-inch spinal needle, the workhorse of lumbar discograpy (d).

As noted, the tip of the superior articular process is a general reference point, but the needle position is adjusted according to the height of the superior articular process in relationship to the segmental nerve root and endplates. The tip of a long, narrow superior articular process may lie dangerously close to the dorsal root ganglion or anterior ramus of the segmental nerve. Conversely, a needle directed along a stubby superior articular process may find its path interrupted by the lower endplate unless adjusted upward. In general, the discography needle should be kept within the lower third of the root canal.[29] A careful preprocedural review of the CT and MRI will allow accurate identification of the pertinent anatomic relationships.

The ease and proficiency by which the L5–S1 disc injection is accomplished is the litmus test of any discographer's skill. The lumbosacral inclination and iliac crest provide a challenge unique to this level. Except in patients with a low intercrestal line, the anatomy of this level necessitates a bent-needle approach. The technique employed has been likened to Laredo's chemonucleolysis technique.[5,45]

Selecting a method and angle of approach for cannulating the L5–S1 disc should ultimately be a function of the "safe window" available for a given trajectory. A "window" is the potential three-dimensional pathway of tissue that would allow a needle to pass from the skin to its target point safely and uninterrupted. The body habitus, iliac crest, lordosis, L5 segmental nerve, and L5 transverse process all must be factored into the trajectory selection.

With the patient in a slight prone-oblique orientation (approximately 25°), a trocar is positioned to act as a guide for advancement of an inner, bent procedure needle (Fig. 19-3). A 3½-inch, 20-gauge outer/5½-inch, 25-gauge inner is the usual combination, except for very large or rotund patients, who may require a 6-inch, 18-gauge outer/8-inch, 22- or 25-gauge inner combination (see Fig. 19-2).

The bony notch between the sacral ala and superior articular process of S1 is the target for the guide (Fig. 19-3A). In the sagittal plane, the percutaneous site must be congruent with the lumbosacral angle and in the axial plane lateral enough to ensure the trocar will direct the bent needle medial (avoiding the L5 segmental nerve). On occasion, bony obstacles such as the iliac crest or L5 transverse process will not allow the operator to select the optimal trajectory. Such predicaments can be assuaged by skill in maneuvering the two-needle system and selecting an appropriate bend for the inner needle. Rolling the patient from side to side under fluoroscopy may help the novice imager gain a three-dimensional appreciation for the optimal "window" commensurate with each patient's anatomy.

Once the trocar has been advanced to the aforementioned notch, its position is observed in the lateral projection relative to the lumbosacral angle and L5 nerve root canal (see Fig. 19-3B). The tip of the trocar should rest at the posterior-inferior border of the lateral canal. Again, the angle of the

needle should be concordant with the lumbosacral inclination.

If the trocar bevel is opened medial toward the disc, it will allow the bent needle to pass accordingly. Two other factors inherent to the bent needle itself act synergistically with the trocar to impart a medial moment on the inner needle: (1) the bend that is oriented toward the disc, and (2) the bevel that faces lateral to allow the tip to move medial upon purchasing soft tissue as the annulus.

Bending the inner needle affords the diagnostician an opportunity to customize the needle shape to the patient's body habitus as well as impart one's personalized flair to the procedure. Commercially bent needles are available. The first consideration is to bend the needle so the bevel faces away from the direction of the bend. Bending approximately 1½ inches from the end of the needle around the thumbnail is rather easy after a limited amount of experience. Running the thumb tangentially along the needle shaft with the index finger under the needle and swiftly arcing the end of the needle back on its shaft can create a gentle, long bend. Once the initial bend is established, applying equal and simultaneous three-point pressure with thumb, index, and middle finger can increase the degree of arc of the bend. The key to a good "bend" is to have

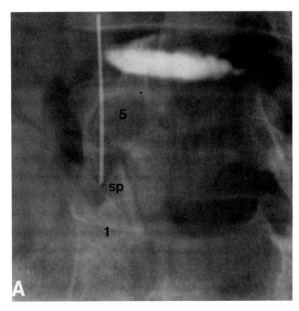
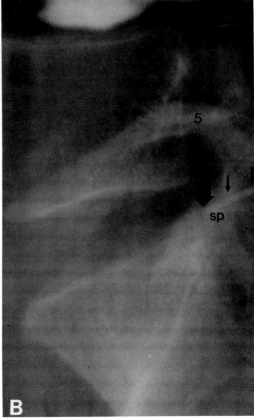

FIGURE 19-3. L5–S1 disc injection technique. *A,* A 20-gauge 3½-inch trocar is in position abutting the S1 superior articular process (5: pedicle of L5, 1: pedicle of S1). *B,* Lateral view demonstrates position of trocar (*arrows*). The trocar is in the inferior aspect of the root canal and advanced to the anterior margin of the S1 superior articular process (*large arrows*).

(Continued on following page.)

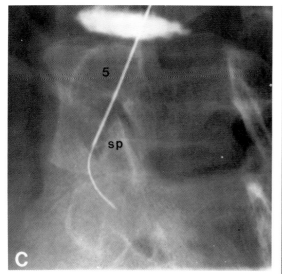

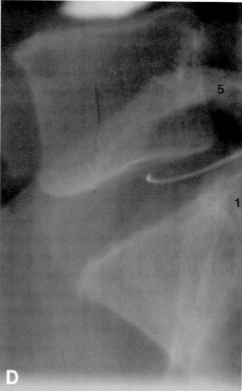

FIGURE 19-3 *(Continued)*. *C*, A 25-gauge 3½-inch, bent spinal needle has been railroaded through the trocar. It was successfully directed around the superior articular process and under the L5 segmental nerve and is in the central nuclear zone. *D*, The bent needle is in the center of the disc space.

(Continued below.)

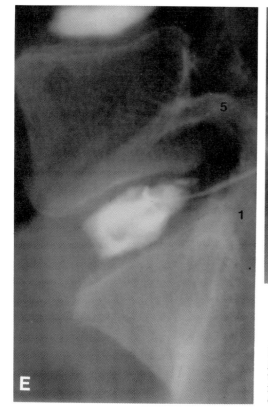

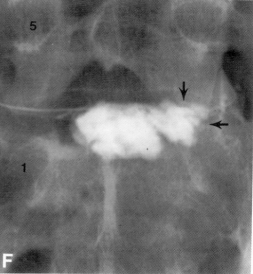

FIGURE 19-3 *(Continued)*. *E*, "Normal" L5–S1 nucleogram in the lateral projection. *F*, L5–S1 nucleogram in anteroposterior projection. There is a slight lateral annular fissure *(arrows)*, which was asymptomatic, to the mid-annulus on the right.

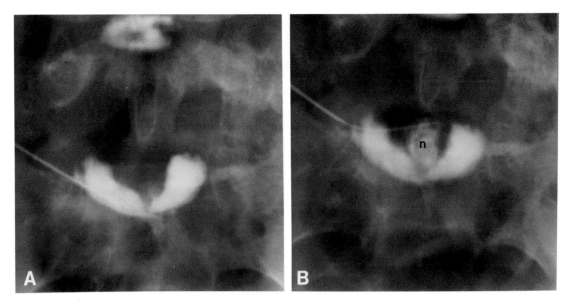

FIGURE 19-4. *A,* An injection into the transitional or innermost annular substance provides hydrodynamic feedback at the syringe stopper, which is deceptively similar to a true nuclear injection. Even the "annulogram" (shown here) as it folds into the spongy nuclear region can be mistaken for a nucleogram. *B,* Following a manipulation of the needle into the nucleus, the nuclear region is filled with contrast medium (n).

a smooth turn and tip in the same plane as the needle shaft (see Fig. 19-2). The degree of bend should be adjusted according to where the trocar tip lies in relation to the central nuclear zone.

With the trocar anchored firmly with one hand, the bent needle is carefully passed through it until resistance is met. The resistance indicates the bent needle has engaged the bevel of the guide. Under an overhead beam, with the patient in a prone-oblique position, the bent needle is advanced so it will "steer" around the S1 superior articular process, pass under the L5 nerve root, and purchase the annulus before turning into the mid-nuclear zone (see Fig. 19-3C). Retracting the guide slightly while advancing the procedure needle may ensure the target point is safely and accurately reached.

The needle position is then assessed in the lateral projection before contrast material is injected (see Fig. 19-3D-F). If the injection is annular, the contrast dispersion pattern should be examined in several planes so the needle position can be adjusted accordingly (Fig. 19-4). Slight needle advancement or retraction and redirecting usually suffices. Rarely, the angle or position of the trocar will need to be altered. Occasionally, the procedure needle loses its bend upon the initial pass, and it must be withdrawn and a new bent needle inserted.

INTERPRETING THE THREE FACETS OF DISCOGRAPHY

There are three cardinal components to a diagnostic disc injection: (1) provocation/analgesia,

(2) discometry, and (3) nucleography. Each facet yields data to be recorded separately yet viewed collectively. For example, an isolated, nonpainful, radial annular fissure may be only as significant as any other incidental imaging finding. Conversely, if this same fissure is associated with an unequivocal pain response, it will need to be treated aggressively to prevent further pain and disability. The provocation aspect is not always the pivotal factor, however. A nonpainful yet dynamically incompetent disc (i.e., discometry yields poor endpoint resistance and the annulus is grossly marred by fissuring) adjacent a proposed fusion level needs to be factored into the surgical decision algorithm if stability is the ultimate goal.

Provocation/Analgesia Assessment

The striking structural information garnered by high-resolution, multiplanar CT and high field strength MR has an allure likened to "trompe l'oeil" artistic works. Yet, this "eye-catching" anatomic information does not obviate the need for physiologic and functional correlation. Accordingly, the marked incidence of false-positive imaging data (albeit myelography, CT or MRI), warrants a need for provocation assessment to ratify whether a structural finding is indeed a physiologic source of pain.[10,42,85] Discography is the sole direct method to distinguish symptomatic versus asymptomatic discs; hence, provocation/analgesia is the sine qua non of diagnostic disc injection.

Provocation (P) is recorded as follows:

P0: No pain response is noted upon injection/distention of the disc with contrast or saline.

P+/−: An equivocal response, vague, uncharacteristic or discordant pain (both by nature and location).

P+: Definite, convincing pain provocation that is familiar to the patient but only reproduces part of the symptom complex.

P++: Exact pain reproduction, concordant with the symptom complex.

Analgesic data is codified with symbology comparable to provocation (denoted R for "response"):

R0: No response to the instillation of anesthetic following a provocation elicitation.

R+/−: A vague, uncertain response. An improvement of 2 or less on a visual analog scale of 0–10 (0 = no pain; 10 = suicidal level of pain).

R+: Symptomatic relief greater than 2 on a visual analog scale of 0–10.

R++: Complete ablation of symptoms.

Analgesic responses should be interpreted relative to the duration of anesthesia. If 1% lidocaine is used for subcutaneous anesthetization, grading is withheld for 1½–2 hours to allow any residual effect to be eliminated. The longer-acting intradiscal agent should continue to act for at least its usual duration.

Occasionally, a patient will have a convincing provocation response, a definite provocation negative control level, and no or temporizing relief with anesthesia. This dilemma occurs most commonly in patients with a chronic condition and significant psychosocial overlay. The author has noted that patients with a high intensity zone in the posterior annulus on MRI[6] and patients with an extremely intense provocation response often complain of heightened symptoms following the procedure. These patients likely have a true physiologic pain generator that may be influenced by poorly understood, remote factors. The role of central neurogenic facilitation or secondary gain in these settings is uncertain. All findings should be carefully and globally considered in the final analysis and discussed openly.

Discometry

Discometry is an estimate of the hydrodynamic competence of a disc. This information is obtained by monitoring resistance at the syringe stopped upon fluid distention of a disc and measuring the volume injected. Although exact measurements in pascals can be obtained by employing a pressure manometer,[24,57,58,61,63,64,83] the amount of annular resistance monitored in a static situation is by no means an accurate reflection of annular performance in daily activities. An intact annulus does, however, have a firm characteristically resilient endpoint, and any experienced discographer is able to distinguish a competent versus grossly incompetent annulus. In fact, an exercise the author recommends to residents is to distend the disc with their eyes closed and the image intensifier off in order to gain an appreciation for this sensation. If the needle tip is inadvertently in the annulus and not in the central nuclear zone, the diagnostician will appreciate a rigid "end feel" without the unmistakable "bounce back" resilience of a nuclear injection. Conversely, if the annulus is disrupted, diminished resistance at the needle hub will be appreciated.

Discographers have long considered the mechanism of pain provocation in discs with poor resilience. "How can such discs be provoked upon dynamic challenge?" "Is it likely that discs that are markedly disrupted and offer little to no resistance are incapable of providing a pain response upon 'distention'?" Paradoxically, Derby et al. found that most discs are provoked at low pressures.[24] They proposed chemical stimulation of attenuated outer annular fibers as the mechanism of pain generation.

Normal lumbar discs accept less than 3.0 ml.[1,28,64,82] Volumetric data should be compared level to level as well as against the norm, since occasionally one encounters an individual with "megadiscs," or a normal lumbar disc accepting 4.0 ml or more contrast.

Nucleography

As the physician instills contrast medium into the disc, a direct contrast view of the internal architecture of the disc is obtained (see Fig. 19-1D,E). Frontal and lateral plain films are routine for both cervical and lumbar disc injections.

In a normal disc contrast should be well contained within the nuclear region and have smooth round margins (see Fig. 19-1D–F). Lumbar nucleograms are spherical (see Fig. 19-1D) They may appear slightly oblong or binucleated; nuclear clefts develop with age. Extravasation of contrast material beyond the central nuclear zone indicates disruption of the annulus (Figs. 19-3F, 19-5, 19-6).

Pierre Erlacher's historic 1952 work was the first to demonstrate a profound correlation between radiographic and cadaveric nuclear contrast/dye dispersal patterns.[28] Erlacher's efforts have been embellished by Sachs et al.[71] (1986), who devised a grading system for nucleographic patterns using postdiscography CT and Vanharanta et al.[82] (1989), who compared each pattern with provocation data. In 1989 Yu devised a grading system of annular

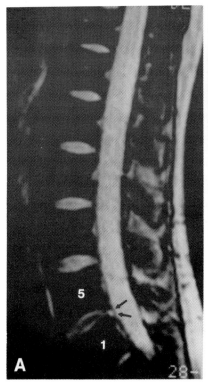

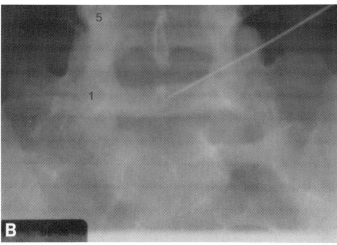

FIGURE 19-5. A 29-year-old rigger presented with refractory low back pain after sustaining a work-related flexion/compression injury. *A,* T2-weighted (2,000/90/90) sagittal image reveals a high intensity zone in the posterior annulus at L5–S1 *(arrows).* The prominent intranuclear cleft is accentuated by desiccation (dark band within the L5–S1 disc). *B,* The patient had a low intracrestal line. Cannulation of the L5–S1 disc did not require a bent needle technique. Note the 6-inch 22-gauge needle in the center of the disc space. The needle inclination is commensurate with Ferguson's lumbosacral angle (5: pedicle of L5; 1: pedicle of S1). *(Continued below.)*

fissures according to cadaveric injection study.[89] Other authors have published their unique nucleographic scoring methods. These systems may all foster communication between physicians but do not obviate the need for accurately detailing the exact relationship of contrast to the nuclear zone, annular regional, and neural elements. The presence of nociceptors within the mid to outer annulus should also be considered when interpreting postdiscography/CT nucleograms (see Fig. 19-1F).

Diagnostic disc injections must be followed by postdiscography CT within 1–3 hours. Postdiscography CT complements the findings of plain film nucleograms.[54,71,82] Moreover, postdiscography CT is more sensitive than MRI for detecting annular fissures (Figs. 19-7 and 19-8)[90] The author and others have disclosed painful radial, annular fissures upon diagnostic disc injections in patients with normal MRI who have electrodiagnostically irrefutable radiculopathy (see Fig. 19-7). Discography also may be applied to resolve conflicting findings among clinical presentation, MR, and CT (see Figs. 19-7, 19-9).

Beyond acquiring postdiscography CT data within the necessary time frame, exercising care and precision in determining CT exam parameters is essential to garner an optimal study. Axial sections of 5 mm from pedicle to pedicle with 3–4 mm table increments suffice for the lumbar spine. Additional selected angled-gantry slices through the L5–S1

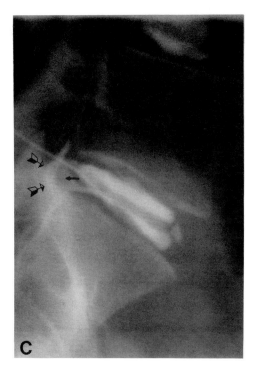

FIGURE 19-5 *(Continued). C,* On this lateral discographic image, contrast extends into the area of the high intensity zone in the posterior annulus *(arrows)* as well as in the epidural region *(arrowheads),* including anterior internal vertebral venous plexus.

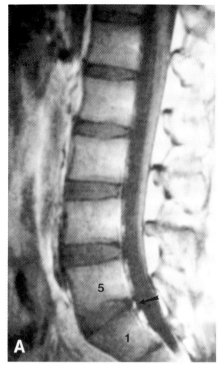

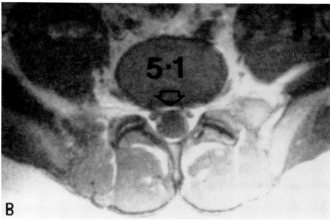

FIGURE 19-6. *A,* T1-weighted (600/20/90) sagittal image (after administration of gadolinium) discloses a subtle area of enhancement in the posterior annulus of L5–S1 *(arrow).* *B,* T1-weighted (1150/40/90) axial MR at L5-S1 (postgadolinium) demonstrates a transverse "rim" of posterior annular enhancement. Could this be an inflammatory outer annular fissure?

(Continued below.)

interspace may improve spatial resolution of the posterior annulus to neural structures.

Bone and soft tissue window and level settings should be individually selected to optimally visualize contrast medium in relation to annular detail, neural elements, and vertebral body margins. Dosimetry (KV, MA, and time of exposure) are likewise customized to the body habitus.

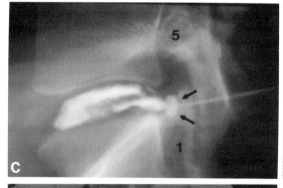

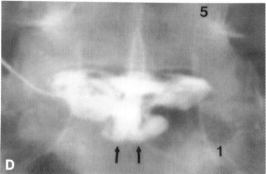

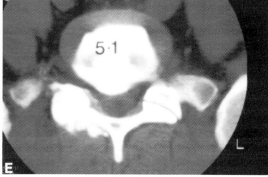

FIGURE 19-6 *(Continued). C,* Lateral plain film nucleogram demonstrates a large concentric outer annular fissure (small prolapse). *D,* Anteroposterior view of the same lesion on plain film nucleography; posteroinferior concentric fissure is demonstrated *(arrows). E,* Postdiscography CT. Compare this image with *B,* the axial MRI section (postgadolinium). The lesion abuts the anterior theca and posteriorly displaces the right S1 nerve root in its entry zone (axillary takeoff point). Parenthetically, contrast from a facet arthrogram is in the right posterior joint and adjacent to the lamina.

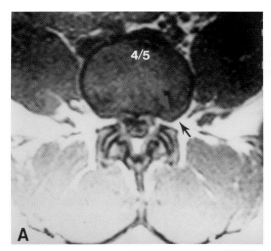

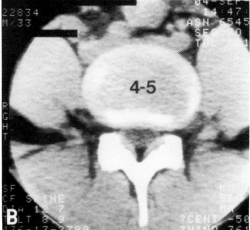

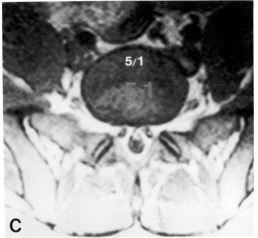

FIGURE 19-7. CT, MRI and postdiscography CT from a 33-year-old off-shore worker who was thrown about the deck during high seas. He presented with a left L5 radiculopathy. The imaging studies were nondiagnostic and confounding. Discography, however, definitely diagnosed the physiologic pain generator and the structural pathology. *A*, Axial T1 (617/16/90) MRI section demonstrates a left posterolateral prolapse at L4-5 (*arrow*). This lesion may abut the L4 anterior ramus (extraforaminally) but does not appear to affect the L5 segmental nerve. *B*, L4–5 axial CT delineates no convincing findings. *C*, L5–S1 axial T1-weighted (617/16/90) MR section is within normal limits.

(*Continued below.*)

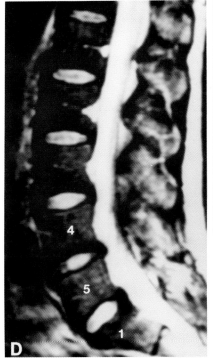

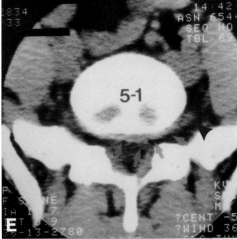

FIGURE 19-7 (*Continued*). *D*, Long T2 sagittal MR (1800/80/80) section provided compelling evidence for intact annuli and normal state of disc hydration. *E*, Axial CT at L5–S1 (soft tissue window setting) demonstrates a broad-based left posterolateral prolapse (*arrows*) that abuts the L5 segmental nerve extraforaminally (*arrowhead*).   (*Continued on following page.*)

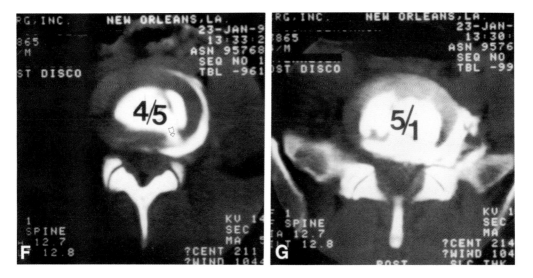

FIGURE 19-7 *(Continued)*. *F,* L4–5 postdiscography discloses a radial fissure *(arrow)* from the central nuclear zone extending into a large circumferential outer annular fissure. *G,* An expansile fissure was revealed at this level that obliterates the left L5–S1 root canal (compare the right canal with the left). This lesion is also contiguous with the L5 epiradicular sheath. Contrast these startling findings with the L5–S1 axial MRI (above). Upon initial injection, the patient's left lower extremity radicular type pain was reproduced and subsequently ablated upon direct intradiscal instillation of bupivacaine.

BEYOND THE DURA MATER

Technically difficult situations can be fulfilling if the skill and ingenuity of the discographer rises to the challenge. However, new techniques or unfamiliar regions should not be explored until the clinician has the necessary skill level and a thorough understanding of the anatomy and potential for complications. Moreover, even the most basic spinal injection procedures should not be attempted without a keen grasp of orthogonal imaging (MR and CT), pathophysiology of pain, and applied spinal biomechanics. Cadaveric dissection to investigate anatomy and the technical performance of fluoroscopically controlled procedures on cadavers forms a solid foundation for accruing new skills. MRI and multiplanar CT provide a segue for mentally "reconstructing" the planar fluoroscopic image into three dimensions.

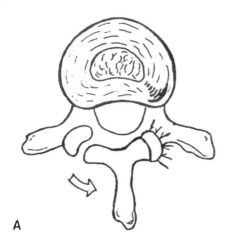

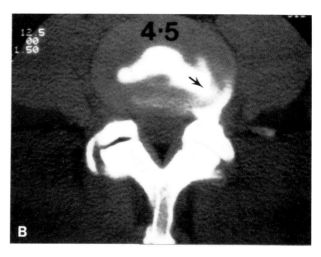

FIGURE 19-8. *A,* The components of a lumbar torsion injury.[29] A series of circumferential annular fissures extend to the outer annulus. There is a distraction/impaction injury to the posterior joints with strain of the capsular ligaments. (From Fortin JD: Enigmatic causes of spine pain in athletes. In Watkins RG (ed): The Spine in Sports, Chicago, Mosby, 1994; with permission.) *B,* Lumbar post discography CT of a torsion injury. The patient, a 40-year-old registered nurse, sustained a work-related slip and fall on the left buttock with her right leg twisted under herself. She complained of aching and stabbing central lumbosacral pain with paresthesias in a left L4 distribution. The same facets of the torsion injury complex illustrated in *A* are noted on this axial scan. A posterolateral radial fissure is indicated by the arrow. The right posterior joint is wider than the left and there is a right capsular calcification owing to distraction/impaction (deformation of the neural arch) as well as severe capsular strain.

Discography Following Posterolateral Fusion

Following posterior lumbar fusion, most patients need a translumbar (interpedicular) approach to the lumbar disc that punctures the theca twice and places the patient at risk for a postprocedure headache. The author has developed a technique for circumventing the dura in some patients with posterolateral fusion/pedicle screw fixation (Fig. 19-10). With this technique the bent inner needle courses *extra*durally through the central canal. Therefore, complications such as cephalgia that are associated with thecal puncture are eliminated.

Thoracolumbar and Thoracic Discography

There is a paucity of information on dorsal diagnostic injection. In 1975, Simmons and Segil may have provided the first description of thoracic discography.[75] They discussed a 42-year-old man suffering from midthoracic pain, radiating on both sides in a band-like fashion with associated T5 hypoesthesia, who experienced reproduction of his symptoms upon injection of the T5-6 disc space. The explanation of their injection technique is accompanied by a radiographic nucleographic figure, suggesting a posterior annular fissure at T5-6.

Thoracic and thoracolumbar discs can be cannulated with a single 3½-inch spinal needle or a bent needle approach but require the utmost circumspection because puncture of the pleura, theca, cord or conus medullaris are potential hazards. Beam hardening from overlying structures, such as the ribs, and a narrower interspace provide added challenges to thoracic discography. Despite possible pitfalls, Schellhas et al. performed 250 thoracic discograms without complication and found thoracic discography safe and effective in evaluating dorsal pain and disc degeneration.[72]

The author approaches thoracic disc injections similar to lumbar discography with a few key anatomic accommodations. If the technician positions the patient so that the superior articular process falls just short of bisecting the interspace and passes the needle posterior to the head of the rib (Fig. 19-11A), the pleura will not be penetrated. An axial MR or CT section of the thorax at the appropriate level(s) can be used as a screening modality to document specific anatomic relationships. If the pleura may be in jeopardy from a direct approach, a bent-needle technique is suggested. The bent-needle technique the author uses is similar to the L5–S1 technique, but the guide is adjusted to the kyphotic angulation of the disc space, and a gentler bend prevents the needle from coursing into the central canal (Fig. 19-11B). Postdorsal discography/CT can be applied to yield the same type of data in the lumbar region (Fig. 19-12); however, thinner

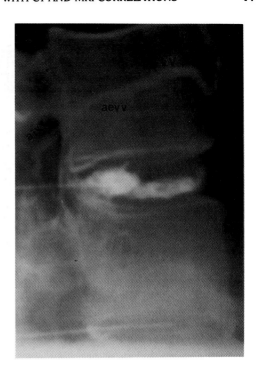

FIGURE 19-9. When Harry Crock first described internal disc disruption syndrome, he alluded to a systemic/immunologic response.[19] Patients with this syndrome often experienced generalized malaise, chronic fatigue, poor appetite, and depression. As revealed on this injection of contrast medium into the disc space, inflammatory contents from a disrupted disc may have direct/immediate communication with the circulatory system. There is rapid clearance of contrast medium into the epidural and lumbar veins upon injection. Could this be one physiologic link between disc disruption and constitutional changes in some patients? Abbreviations: aaiv: portions of anterior internal vertebral venous plexus; aevv: portions of anterior external vertebral venous plexus; LV: lumbar vein; IVC: inferior vena cava.

transaxial sections may be necessary in the mid to upper thoracic regions.

COMPLICATIONS

Strict adherence to a preprocedural screening protocol and impeccable techique in the performance of discography will ensure a low morbidity rate.

Because the intervertebral disc has a large avascular space, its potential to act as a medium for bacterial growth is obvious. Discitis is the most widely recognized complication associated with diagnostic disc injections. However, the incidence is reportedly low, ranging from 0.1–1.3 percent.[19,33,34,51,53,67,86] Isolation of staphylococcal organisms suggest skin surface contaminates play a crucial role, although the isolation of *Escherichia coli* and organisms indigenous to the oropharynx warn the clinician to avoid the bowel (in lumbar injections)[2,34,37] and hypopharynx and esophagus (in cervical injections).[14]

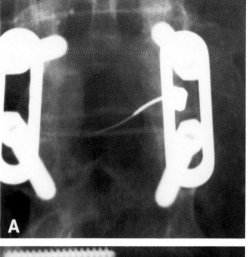
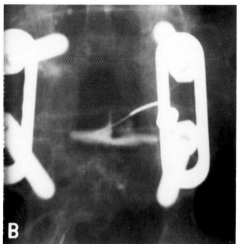
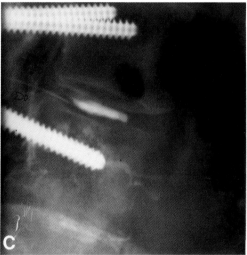

FIGURE 19-10. Circumventing the thecal sac while performing a disc injection at a level with pedicle screw instrumentation and a posterolateral fusion mass. *A*, posteroanterior view. A bent needle has successfully been passed around the outer margin of the central canal (extradurally). Confirmation that the dura had not been violated was evidenced by absence of cerebrospinal fluid when the needle was withdrawn in slow increments with the fluoroscopy table at a 45° (upright) position. *B*, Postinjection posteroanterior nucleogram. *C*, Lateral nucleogram. Epidural venous continuity with the nucleus (*arrows*) indicated a complete annular rent. This level was symptomatic.

The isolation of organisms in patients with discitis has proven to be elusive. It appears in many cases that the offending organism has run its natural course and neovascularization from endplate tributaries have provided rapid immunologic ablation before isolation is customarily attempted.[33,34] Crock has postulated an aseptic or chemical form of discitis.[19] DeSéze also alluded to a chemical discitis that can lead to aseptic necrosis of the disc and secondary intervertebral arthrodesis.[25] De-Haene[23] has proposed that this destructive evolution may be attributed to the concentrated iodine product that DeSéze used. Conversely, Fraser's experimental discitis sheep model provides compelling evidence for a sole infectious etiology.[33] Moreover, a relatively benign and self-limited form of discitis from indolent organisms of low virulence has been alluded to[19] that may allow some organisms and some cases to go undetected.[73] These factors do not obviate the need for an appropriate index of suspicion because sequelae such as epidural and/or retropharyngeal (cervical region) abscesses may occur.[51]

In patients with a dramatic increase in pain and stiffness or a change in the character of symptoms, the procedure can initially be screened with a sedimentation rate. An elevated sedimentation rate should preempt the application of MRI as a definitive diagnostic tool.[31,50,79] Although radionuclide scans are significantly more sensitive than plain roentgenograms,[13,59] MRI is now the goal standard in detection of discitis.[7,56,78] In a comparative experimental rabbit model, MRI was found to be superior to bone scanning, with a 92% sensitivity, 97% specificity, and a 95% overall accuracy.[78]

Because the presenting symptoms of discitis are nonspecific, a patient's premorbid psychiatric history and/or high pain intensity rating may obscure the clinical diagnosis. Hence, the challenge of using screening modalities in a manner that benefits patients through cost containment and establishing or excluding the diagnosis may be disconcerting.

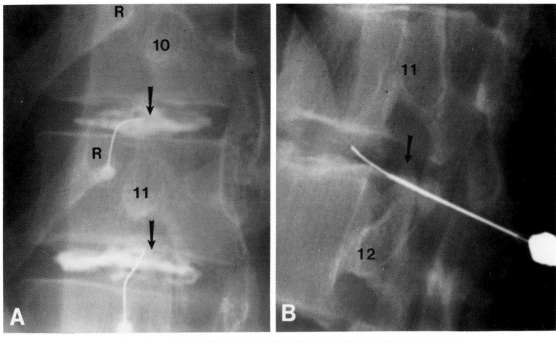

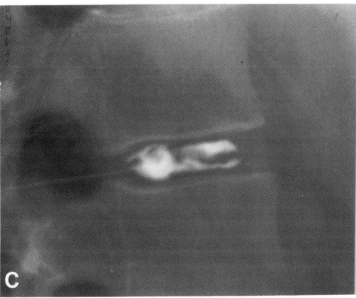

FIGURE 19-11. Thoracolumbar discography. *A*, Oblique view illustrates position of 25-gauge 3½-inch spinal needles in relation to rib heads (r) and tip of superior articular processes (*arrows*). (10: pedicle of T10; 11: pedicle of T11). *B*, Compare this oblique view of a bent needle technique at the thoracolumbar junction to the L5–S1 disc injection technique seen in Figure 19-3. The angulation of the guide corrects for the kyphotic dorsal curve, and the needle bend is gentler than at L5–S1. (11: pedicle of T11; 12: pedicle of T12; arrow: tip of T12 superior articular process.) *C*, Lateral view of a thoracolumbar disc injection provides a view of the typical oblong or elliptical nuclear configuration at this region.

Other complications from discography include neural injury from direct needle trauma (either an impaled segmental nerve root from a misguided lumbar procedure or cord injury from a cervical or thoracic discography needle), pneumothorax from a misguided C7/T1 or thoracic approach, and thecal puncture headache. Postthecal puncture cephalgia or cord injury can occur when a cervical discography needle penetrates to a dangerous depth in the anteroposterior plane. It is also possible to invade the subarachnoid space at L5–S1 if the inner needle is excessively bent or the trocar malpositioned. These complications can be prevented with rigid technique.

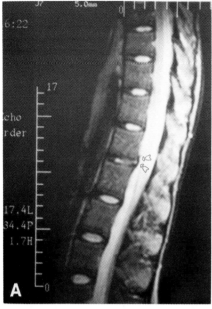
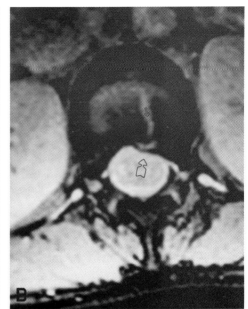
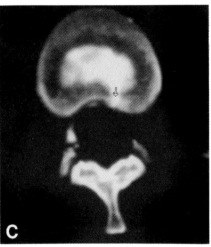

FIGURE 19-12. A 24-year-old patient presented with thoracolumbar pain after having been involved in a rear-end motor vehicle accident. *A,* Note the slight diminution in signal intensity as well as the posterior annular protrusion/small prolapse (*arrows*) at T12-L1 (on this T2-weighted (2,000/90/90) sagittal MRI image). *B,* Gradient echo axial image (650/18/26) through T12–L1 demonstrates a radial fissure (*small arrow*) extending from the central nuclear zone into a mild posterior left paracentral prolapse, which causes slight, angular effacement of the anterior theca (*large arrow*). *C,* Thoracolumbar postdiscography CT. Compare this image with *B.* The same pathology is seen.

POSTPROCEDURE CARE

The patients are attended to in a observation area following the procedure. Vital signs are obtained immediately and, if stable, the patient is transported via gurney or wheelchair to CT, as indicated. Fluids are encouraged immediately, and the patient is provided a meal one hour after the procedure.

Postprocedural instructions include: (1) education on the application of ice to the affected area; (2) information on the usual postprocedural symptoms such as increased local pain, stiffness, and dysphagia (for cervical procedures); and (3) instructions to avoid driving or operating machinery for the remainder of the day; patients are to be accompanied by a responsible driver to and from the procedure site. An instruction sheet is also reviewed that includes the above information and an emergency telephone number to call for any sign of infection (detailed therein), sudden increased pain, sustained progressive increase in pain, or marked change in the character of symptoms.

Narcotic analgesics are dispensed judiciously; a 2-day supply on an as required basis is sufficient. This is often a good opportunity to provide uninformed patients with education concerning the physiology of addiction. Patients can be safely discharged 2 hours following the procedure.

HAS NEW TECHNOLOGY ECLIPSED DISCOGRAPHY?

Controversy surrounding the overall diagnostic efficacy of discography versus other imaging modalities such as MRI and CT is superfluous and belies the awareness necessary to properly apply any given one. Such unfortunate comparisons are perpetuated by reports that draw sweeping conclusions without understanding the fundamental application of the modality in question.

For example, in a 1986 study comparing MRI to discography, Gibson et al.[35] concluded that "MRI was shown to be more accurate than discography in the diagnosis of disc degeneration. It has several major advantages, which should make it the investigation of choice." The authors did not use postdiscography transverse CT imaging to enhance nucleographic findings on plain films even though postdiscography CT scanning was routine in 1986 in many major spine centers.[54,71] If Gibson et al. had used a state-of-the-art protocol, they may have reached an opposite conclusion. Furthermore, the following statement questions the technical expertise used in the study: ". . . the reproduction of symptoms by discography should be one of its main advantages in helping with localization. Unfortunately, this does not seem to be a particularly reliable sign and in a patient under sedation it can be difficult to interpret." Such statements were discredited by the study by Walsh et al.[83] When concluding that a particular modality is the "investigation of choice," one should clearly indicate what clinical scenario(s) should preempt that choice. Obviously, discography is not the study of choice as a screening tool for patients with low back pain. Conversely, discography is indicated for determining if an internally deranged disc is painful in a patient with refractory axial pain who has failed aggressive conservative care. Obviously, the provocation data garnered from a poorly conducted study is meaningless (Fig. 19-13).

Each test should be viewed as an extension of the overall clinical context. The clinician who understands the strengths and weaknesses of each is collectively armed with a powerful diagnostic armamentarium. A well-recognized application of this axiom is the additive benefits of combining CT and myelography.[87]

High resolution multiplanar CT, especially when combined with intrathecal enhancement, can provide an impressive view of the annular contour of the disc as well as its spatial relationship to canals (root and central), neural elements, and posterior joints.[87] Owing to superior osseous resolution, CT conveys the best view of endplates. However, CT provides comparatively little information regarding the internal integrity, biochemical constituency, and state of hydration of the disc. CT subjects the patient to ionizing radiation, and CT/myelography is an invasive procedure with certain morbidity.

High field strength MR is the "Stradivarius" imaging modality—unsurpassed in its depiction of soft tissue anatomy, noninvasive, and without the risk of radiation. Some discs that appear normal

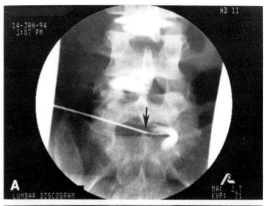

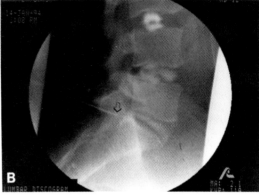

FIGURE 19-13. Lack of experience, poor training, and improper technique all may contribute to the duplicitous reputation of discography. The patient here reportedly was transported via gurney to the emergency department with intractable right leg pain following discography. *A*, Anteroposterior view of an attempted L5–S1 disc injection. The tip of the guide (*arrow*) has been advanced to midline—*well* beyond where it should be (see Figure 19-3). An annular contrast pattern suggests the bent needle has purchased the annulus. *B*, A lateral projection documents the guide position in the central canal (*arrows*). The bent inner needle has been manipulated superomedially to the L5–S1 annulus.

on CT may clearly demonstrate various internal derangements as desiccation, fissuring, and/or inflammation on MRI (see Figs. 19-5 and 19-6). Painful, inflammatory annular fissures may enhance with gadolinium[68] or yield focal high signal on T2 weighted images.[6] The ever expanding applications of MRI and a trend toward greater cost containment has encouraged some centers to forego conventional T2 spin echo sequences. These slow acquisition images are being "replaced" by speedier gradient echo and fast T2 pulses. Equating information regarding the nuclear matrix and annulus from the newer pulse sequences with true spin echo images must be done with caution.[40] For instance, annular signal intensity changes on T2 images that seem to correlate with pain on provocation may not be as conspicuous, or simply appear different, on the modern sequences. Moreover, because studies that

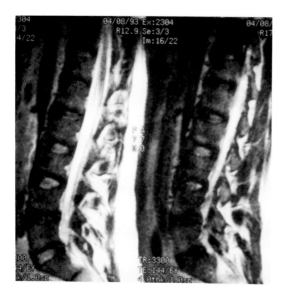

FIGURE 19-14. The right parasagittal portion of the L4–5 disc appears suspicious on these fast T2 weighted sagittal images (TR 3000, TE 144 EF), but despite the signal intensity characteristics of true T2 weighting, it is difficult to discern the state of hydration of the discs. Further confounding this issue is the chemical shift misregistration artifact appearing as dark horizontal bands adjacent to the endplates.

compared diagnostic disc injections to MR used conventional spin echo sequences, the observations from these investigations may not extrapolate to the fast acquisition images (Fig. 19-14).[6,44]

As an imaging modality, discography, when combined with axial CT, surpasses MRI in detecting annular fissures.[90] Discography, however, is an invasive procedure and should be reserved for patients who have unrelenting axial pain, no definite neurocompressive lesion, and who have failed aggressive functional restoration.[3,27,69]

CONCLUSION

Despite the recent exponential growth of noninvasive spinal technology, diagnostic disc injection remains the sole direct method for definitively determining if a disc is a physiologic pain generator.

When indicated and impeccably performed, discography is a safe and powerful complement to the overall clinical context. This diagnostic tool may also enhance information obtained from other imaging modalities or reveal new and otherwise enigmatic findings.

REFERENCES

1. Adams MA, Dolan P, Hutton WC: The stages of disc degeneration as revealed by discograms. J Bone Joint Surg 68B:36–41, 1986.
2. Agre K, Wilson RR, Brim M, et al: Chymodiactin post-marketing surveillance: Demographic and adverse experience data in 29,075 patients. Spine 9:479–485, 1974.
3. Alexander AH: Nonoperative management of herniated nucleus pulposus: Patient selection by the extension sign: Long-term follow-up. Orthop Rev 21:181–188, 1992.
4. Amundsen P: The evolution of contrast media. In Sackett J, Strother C (eds): New Techniques in Myelography. Hagerstown, MD, Harper & Row, 1979, pp 2–5.
5. Aprill CN III: Diagnostic disc injection. In Frymoyer JW (ed): The Adult Spine, Vol. 1. Principles and Practices. New York, Raven Press, 1991, pp 403–442.
6. Aprill C, Bogduk N: High intensity zones in the disc annulus: A sign of painful disc on magnetic resonance imaging. Br J Radiol 65:361–369, 1992.
7. Arrington JA, Murtagh FR, Silbiger ML, et al: Magnetic resonance imaging of post-discogram discitis and osteomyelitis in the lumbar spine: Case report. J Fla Med Assoc 73:192–194, 1986.
8. Benoist M: Positioning alternatives for chemonucleolysis: Current concepts in chemonucleolysis. J R Soc Med 72:47–53, 1984.
9. Blumenthal S, Baker J, Dosett A, Selby DK: The role of anterior lumbar fusion for internal disc disruption. Spine 13:566–569, 1988.
10. Boden SD, Davis DO, Dina TS, et al: Abnormal magnetic resonance scans of the lumbar spine in asymptomatic subjects. J Bone Joint Surg 72A:403–408, 1990.
11. Bogduk N, Tynan W, Wilson AS: The nerve supply to the human lumbar intervertebral discs. J Anat 132:39–56, 1981.
12. Brodsky AE, Binder WF: Lumbar discography. Its value in diagnosis and treatment of lumbar disc lesions. Spine 4:110–120, 1979.
13. Bruschwein DA, Brown ML, McLeod RA: Gallium scintigraphy in the evaluation of disc-space infections. Concise communications. J Nucl Med 21:925–927, 1980.
14. Cloward RB: Cervical discography defended [letter]. JAMA 233:862, 1975.
15. Colhoun E, McCall IW, Williams L, Cassar Pullicino VN: Provocation discography as a guide to planning operations on the spine. J Bone Joint Surg 70B:267–271, 1988.
16. Collis JS Jr, Gardner WJ: Lumbar discography: An analysis of 1,000 cases. J Neurosurg 19:452–461, 1962.
17. Crawshaw C: Needle insertion techniques for chemonucleolysis: Current concepts in chemonucleolysis. J R Soc Med 72:55–59, 1984.
18. Crock H: Normal and pathological anatomy of the lumbar spinal nerve root canals. J Bone Joint Surg 63B:470–490, 1981.
19. Crock H: Practice of Spinal Surgery. New York, Springer-Verlag, 1983.
20. Curry TS, Dowdey JE, Murry RC: Christensen's Physics of Diagnostic Radiology, 4th ed. Philadelphia, Lea & Febiger, 1990, pp 165–166.
21. Dabezies EJ, Murphy CP: Dural puncture using the lateral approach for chemonucleolysis. Spine 10:93–96, 1985.
22. Day PL: Lateral approach for lumbar diskogram and chemonucleolysis. Clin Orthop 67:90–93, 1969.
23. DeHaene R: La discographie. J Belge Radiol 36:131, 1953.
24. Derby R, Kine G, Schwarzer A, et al: Relationship between intradiscal pressure and pain provocation during discography. Proceedings of the Eighth Annual Assembly of the North American Spine Society, San Diego, 1993.
25. DeSeze S, Levernieux J: Les Accidents de la Discographie. Rev Rheum 19:1027–1033, 1952.
26. Edholm P, Fernstrom I, Lindblom K: Extradural lumbar disc puncture. Acta Radiol Scand 6:322–328, 1967.
27. Ellenberg MR, et al: Prospective evaluation of the cause of disc herniations in patients with proven radiculopathy. Arch Phys Med Rehabil 74:3–8, 1993.

28. Erlacher PR: Nucleography. J Bone Joint Surg 34B:204–210, 1952.
29. Farfan HF, Cossette JW, Robertson GH, et al: The effects of torsion of the lumbar intervertebral joints: The role of torsion in the production of disc degeneration. J Bone Joint Surg 52A:468–497, 1970.
30. Feinberg SB: The place of discography in radiology as based on 2320 cases. AJR 92:1275–1281, 1964.
31. Fernand R, Lee CK: Postlaminectomy disc space infection. A review of the literature and a report of three cases. Clin Orthop 209:215–218, 1986.
32. Flanagan MN, Chung B: Roentgenographic changes in 188 patients 10–20 years after discography and chemonucleolysis. Spine 11:444–448, 1986.
33. Fraser RD, Osti OL, Vernon-Roberts B: Discitis following chemonucleolysis: An experimental study. Spine 11:679–687, 1986.
34. Fraser RD, Osti OL, Vernon-Roberts B: Discitis after discography. J Bone Joint Surg 69B:26–35, 1987.
35. Gibson MJ, Buckley J, Mawhinney R, et al: Magnetic resonance imaging and discography in the diagnosis of disc degeneration. J Bone Joint Surg 68B:369–373, 1986.
36. Groen G, Baljet B, Drukker J: The nerves and nerve plexuses of the human vertebral column. Am J Anat 188:282–296, 1990.
37. Guyer RD, Collier R, Stith W, et al: Discitis after discography. Spine 13:1352–1354, 1988.
38. Hall SC, Ovassapian A: Apnea after intravenous diazepam therapy. JAMA 238:1052, 1977.
39. Hasue M, Kunogi J, Konno S, Kikuchi S: Classification by position of dorsal root ganglia in the lumbosacral region. Spine 14:1261–1264, 1989.
40. Hendrick RE, Russ PD, Simon JH: MRI: Principles and Artifacts. New York, Raven Press, 1993, pp 83–89.
41. Hirsch C: An attempt to diagnose level of disc lesion clinically by disc puncture. Acta Orthop Scand 18:131–140, 1948.
42. Hitselberger WE, Whitten R: Abnormal myelograms in asymptomatic patients. J Neurosurg 28:204–206, 1968.
43. Holt EP Jr: The question of lumbar discography. J Bone Joint Surg 50A:720–726, 1968.
44. Horton W, Daftar T: Which disc as visualized by MRI is actually a source of pain? Spine 17:164–171, 1992.
45. Laredo J, Busson J, Wybier M, Bard M: Technique of lumbar chemonucleolysis. In Bard M, Laredo J (eds): Interventional Radiology in Bone and Joint. New York, Springer-Verlag, 1988, pp 101–122.
46. Laun A, Lorenz R, Angnoli AL: Complications of cervical discography. J Neurosurg Sci 25:17–22, 1981.
47. Lawlis GF, Cuencas R, Selby D, et al: The development of the Dallas Pain Questionnaire: An assessment of the impact of spinal pain on behavior. Spine 14:511–515, 1989.
48. Lindblom K: Protrusions of the discs and nerve compression in the lumbar region. Acta Radiol Scand 25:195–212, 1944.
49. Lindblom K: Diagnostic puncture of the intervertebral discs in sciatica. Acta Orthop Scand 17:231–239, 1948.
50. Lindholm TS, Pylkkanen P: Discitis following removal of intervertebral disc. Spine 7:618–622, 1982.
51. Lownie SP, Ferguson GG: Spinal subdural empyema complicating cervical discography. Spine 14:1415–1417, 1989.
52. Malinsky J: The ontogenetic development of nerve terminations in the intervertebral discs of man. Acta Anat 38:96–113, 1959.
53. Milette PC, Melanson D: A reappraisal of lumbar discography. J Assoc Can Radiol 33(11):176–182, 1982.
54. Mital MA, Thompson WC III: Role of discography enhanced by CT scanning in investigation of low back pain with sciatica. Presented at the Meeting of the Federation of Spine Associations. New Orleans, February 19–30, 1986.
55. Mixter WJ, Barr JS: Ruptures of the intervertebral disc with involvement of the spinal canal. N Engl J Med 211:210–215, 1934.
56. Modic MT, Feiglin D, Pirano D, et al: Vertebral osteomyelitis: Assessment using MR. Radiology 157:157–166, 1985.
57. Nachemson A: Lumbar intradiscal pressure. Acta Orthop Scand Suppl 43:1–104, 1960.
58. Nachemson A, Elfstrom G: Intravital dynamic pressure measurement in lumbar discs. Scand J Rehabil Med Suppl 1:1–40, 1970.
59. Norris S, Ehrlich MG, Keim DE, et al: Early diagnosis of disc space infection using Gallium-67. J Nucl Med 19:384–386, 1978.
60. North American Spine Society: Position statement on discography. The executive committee of the North American Spine Society. Spine 13:1343, 1988.
61. Panjabi MM, Brown M, Lindahl S, et al: Intrinsic disc pressure as a measure of integrity of the lumbar spine. Spine 13:913–917, 1988.
62. Pease CN: Injuries to the vertebrae and intervertebral discs following lumbar puncture. Am J Dis Child 49:849–860, 1935.
63. Quinnell RC, Stockdale H: Pressure standardized lumbar discography. Br J Radiol 53:1031–1036, 1980.
64. Quinnell RC, Stockdale HR, Willis DS: Observations of pressures within normal discs in the lumbar spine. Spine 8:166–169, 1983.
65. Rauschning W: Normal and pathologic anatomy of the lumbar root canals. Spine 12:1008–1019, 1987.
66. Roofe PG: Innervation of the annulus fibrosus and posterior longitudinal ligament. Arch Neurol Psychiatry 44:100–103, 1940.
67. Roosen K, Bettag, Fiebach O: Komplikationen der cervikalen diskographie. Rofo Fortgenstr Geb Rontgenstr Neuen Bildgeb Verfahr 122:520–527, 1975.
68. Ross JS, Modic MT, Masaryk TJ: Tears of the annulus fibrosus: Assessment with Gd-DTPA-enhanced MR imaging. AJNR 10:1251–1254, 1989.
69. Saal JA, Saal JS: The nonoperative treatment of herniated nucleus pulposus with radiculopathy: An outcome study. Spine 14:431–437, 1989.
70. Saal JS, et al: High levels of inflammatory phospholipase A_2 activity in lumbar disc herniations. Spine 15:674–678, 1990.
71. Sachs BL, Spivey MA, Vanharharnta H, et al: A clinical grading system of CT/discography for diagnostic value in low back problems. Dallas discogram description: A new classification of CT/discography. Presented at the 1st Annual Meeting of the North American Spine Society. Bolton Landing, NY, July 20–23, 1986.
72. Schellhas KP, Pollei SR: Thoracic disc degeneration: Correlation of MR imaging and discography, Presented at the 8th Annual Assembly of the North American Spine Society. San Diego, July 9–11, 1993.
73. Schofferman L, Schofferman J, Zucherman J, Gunthorpe H: Occult infections causing persistent low-back pain. Spine 14:417–419, 1989.
74. Schwarzer AC, et al: The relative contribution of the disc and zygapophysial joint in chronic low back pain (unpublished data). Clin J Pain, 1994. (in press)
75. Simmons EH, Segil CM: An evaluation of discography in the localization of symptomatic levels in discogenic disease of the spine. Clin Orthop 108:57–69, 1975.
76. Simmons JW, Aprill CN, Dwyer AP, et al: A reassessment of Holt's data on "The question of lumbar discography." Clin Orthop 237:120–124, 1988.
77. Steindler A, Luck J: Differential diagnosis of pain low in the back: Allocation of the source of pain by procaine hydrochloride method. JAMA 110:106–113, 1938.

78. Szypryt E, Hardy J, Hinton C, et al: A comparison between magnetic resonance imaging and scintigraphic bone imaging in the diagnosis of disc space infection in an animal model. Spine 13:1042–1048, 1988.
79. Thibodeau AA: Closed space infection following removal of lumbar intervertebral disc. J Bone Joint Surg 50A:400–410, 1968.
80. Troiser O: Technique de la discographie extra-durale. J Radiol 63:571–578, 1982.
81. Ruohimaa PJ, Melartin E: Neurotoxicity of iothalamates and diatrizoates, II: Historadioautographic study of rat brains with 131-iodine-tagged contrast media. Invest Radiol 5:22–29, 1970.
82. Vanharanta H, Sach BL, Ohnmeiss DD, et al: Pain provocation and disc deterioration by age: A CT/discographic study in a low back pain population. Spine 14:420–423, 1989.
83. Walsh T, Weinstein J, Spratt K, et al: The question of lumbar discography revisited: A controlled prospective study of normal volunteers to determine the false-positive rate. J Bone Joint Surg 72A:1081–1088, 1990.
84. White A, Panjabi M: Clinical Biomechanics of the Spine. Philadelphia, J.B. Lippincott, 1978.
85. Wiesel SW, Tsourmas N, Feffer HL, et al: A study of computer assisted tomography. I. The incidence of positive CAT scans in an asymptomatic group of patients. Spine 9:549–556, 1984.
86. Wiley J, McNab I, Wortzman G: Lumbar discography and its clinical applications. Can J Surg 11:280–289, 1968.
87. Wilmink JT: CT morphology of intrathecal lumbosacral nerve root compression. Am J Neuroradiol 10:233–248, 1989.
88. Yoshizawa H, O'Brien JP, Thomas-Smith W, et al: The neuropathology of intervertebral discs removed for low back pain. J Pathol 132:95–104, 1980.
89. Yu SW, Haughton VM, Sether LA, Wagner M: Comparison of MR and discography in detecting radial tears of the annulus: A post-mortem study. AJNR 10:1077–1081, 1989.
90. Yu SW, Sether LA, Ho PS, et al: Tears of the annulus fibrosus: A correlation between MR and pathologic findings in cadavers. AJNR 9:367–370. 1988.

Chapter 20

CERVICAL DISCOGRAPHY WITH CT AND MRI CORRELATIONS

JOSEPH D. FORTIN, D.O.

Learning is not attained by chance. It must be sought for with ardor and attended to with diligence.

Abigail Adams

The Scandinavian reports surrounding lumbar discography in the late 1940s and early 1950s[19,28,48] invited an opportunity for comparable explorations in other areas of the spine. Working independently in the late 1950s, Smith and Cloward[5,44] developed similar cervical disc injection techniques for evaluating patients with cervicocephalgia and shoulder girdle pain.[5,7,43,44] They found that injection of symptomatic discs could reproduce patients' axial complaints, thereby identifying painful discs or differentiating primary discogenic versus neurogenic pain. To this end, Smith and Cloward used discography to select the proper levels for their cervical fusion techniques, which are still practiced.[6,45]

In the early 1960s several large studies proclaimed the contrast roentgenography study of discs as superior to myelography for evaluating patients with internal disc problems.[10,12] However the pro-discography tide began to turn in 1964. In a study detailed in chapter 19, Earl Holt studied 148 cervical discs with sodium diatrozoate (an irritating contrast medium) in 50 penitentiary inmates.[21] Fluoroscopic guidance was not employed, and the injection technique has been described as suspect in mechanical performance, discometric data and imaging results.[2] Holt concluded that "injections into any cervical disc causes great pain . . ." and "the volume of injectable media is also quite unreliable as an indication of pathology, since 93% of perfectly normal discs allow rapid extravasation."

Although Holt's study discouraged widespread acceptance of cervical discography, many authors have since reported a favorable experience with discography in evaluating patients with chronic cervical syndromes.[1,3,9,16,18,24,30,33,38,40,47] Several studies clearly define a viable role for diagnostic disc injections in selecting symptomatic/deranged levels for a proposed anterior cervical fusion.[36,42,51]

During Holt's era, the disc was not viewed as a primary putative pain source—only secondarily capable of causing pain via neurocompression. Many clinicians since have been reluctant to ascribe symptoms to a disc, however internally disrupted, that is not producing direct pressure on a nerve root. One study of cervical discography noted that pain on injection was indicative of disc abnormality but not diagnostic of protrusion.[25,26] The authors therefore discounted discography in general; one later concluded that induced pain, even if similar to the presenting symptoms, was of no diagnostic value.[25,26]

If the cervical annulus is an innervated ligamentous structure,[4] is it not capable of generating its own pain response when disrupted or strained?

The indications and preprocedural evaluation for cervical discography are comparable to those for lumbar discography and are discussed in detail in chapter 19.

TECHNICAL PERFORMANCE OF DISCOGRAPHY

Cervical Diagnostic Disc Injection

Following sedation, as described in chapter 19, the patient is sterilely prepped and draped in the supine position (Fig. 20-1A).

The author employs a technique similar to that described by Aprill.[2] Under the lateral beam of a C-arm, a segmentation count is taken first. A rule of thumb is to count down from the C2–3 level to at least one disc space below the lowest segment intended for study. Longitudinal, downward traction on the bilateral upper extremities is often necessary to optimally visualize the lower cervical segments because the overlying shoulders cause

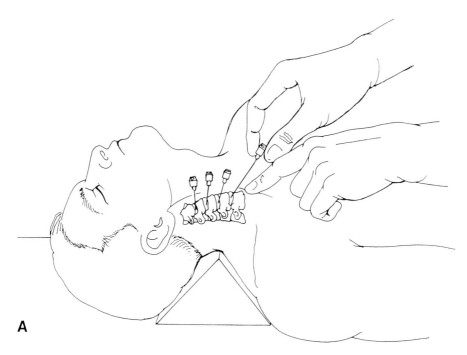

FIGURE 20-1. Cervical disc injection technique. *A,* The patient is positioned supine with the head extended over a triangular pillow. A right anterior approach is employed with the index finger applying pressure to move airway and vessels from the needle pathway. *(Continued below.)*

beam attenuation. This "screening process" allows an estimation of the orientation of each disc space, as the needle must enter at an angle commensurate with the amount of lordosis at the selected level.

The posteroanterior beam from an overhead fluoroscopy tower is then used to visualize the appropriate interspace, and the right uncinate process is identified as a landmark (Fig. 20-1B). The left

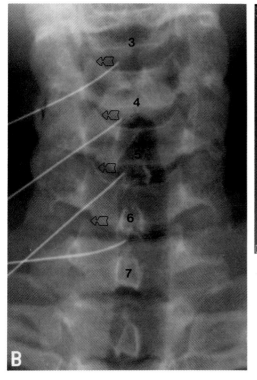

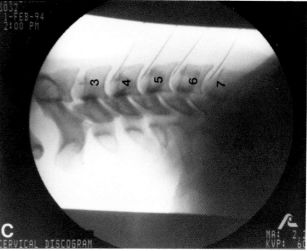

FIGURE 20-1 *(Continued).* *B,* Compare this posteroanterior preinjection spot film with *A* and *D.* Consider the proximity of the needle at each level to its respective uncinate process *(arrows).* There is a gradual progression toward midline, paralleling the sternal head of the sterno-cleidomastoid muscle, from the C3–4 needle to the C6–7 one. All needles except the C6–7 one will need to be advanced to midline prior to injection. *C,* Preinjection lateral view. The inclination of the needles generally follows the cervical lordosis. *(Continued on following page.)*

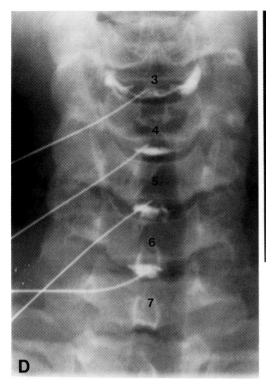

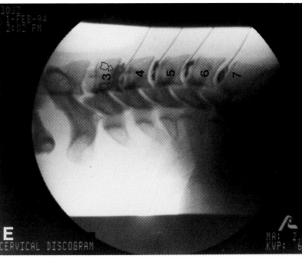

D

FIGURE 20-1 *(Continued)*. *D,* Postinjection posteroanterior projection. All needles have been advanced into the central nuclear zone as evidenced by the nucleograms; compare the needle tip positions with *C.* At C3–4, contrast medium extends into the bilateral uncinate recesses. *E,* Lateral nucleography spot film. Contrast medium is contained within the central nuclear region at each level, except C3–4, where there is some "blushing" of the C3 inferior endplate secondary to uncinate recess extravasation *(arrows)*. *(Continued below.)*

index finger applies firm pressure to divide the great vessels laterally and the laryngeal structures and trachea medially. This maneuver exposes a safe and adequate path for the right anterolateral needle trajectory, providing accessibility to the disc while avoiding the great vessels, larynx, thyroid, and esophagus. The medial border of the sternocleidomastoid muscle is a relative skin surface marker for the needle position at each respective level. At the C2–3 and C3–4 levels the hypopharynx must be avoided with a lateral entry point and the apex of the lung considered at C7–T1 with a medial entry point. A 25-gauge, 3½-inch spinal needle is directed under the posteroanterior beam of an image intensifier into the selected interspace. Occasionally, the tensile strength of a 22-gauge needle is required to circumvent anterior spondylitic ridges or spurs.

The tip of the left index not only applies pressure at the correct site but serves as a marker for percutaneous entry (see Fig. 20-1A). If the needle is directed past the medial aspect of the right uncinate process of the subadjacent vertebrae toward the center of the interspace, it usually finds its way to the central nuclear zone. For depth confirmation, the novice discographer should learn to strike the endplate of the subadjacent vertebrae prior to puncturing the annulus and then slightly withdraw and direct the needle upward into the disc space. Once the skin and subcutaneous tissue is penetrated, the needle will course through the platysma muscle, areolar tissue between the carotid sheath and larynx, the thin

strap-like longus colli muscle, and prevertebral fascia (Fig. 20-2) before purchasing the ligamentous substance of the anterior annulus. Upon piercing of the annulus, the patient will experience an abrupt, unsustained pang of neck and/or shoulder girdle pain.

Relative to its lumbar counterpart, the cervical annulus is meager and the depth of the disc space

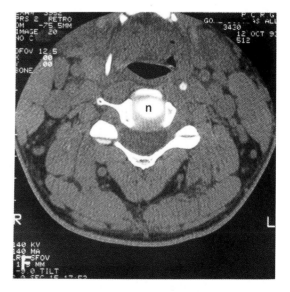

FIGURE 20-1 *(Continued)*. *F,* Postdiscography/CT discloses contrast medium circumscribed in the central nuclear zone (n) and substantiates the integrity of the nuclear envelope.

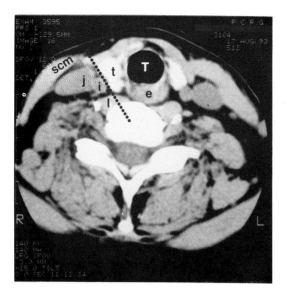

FIGURE 20-2. Axial CT at C6–7, photographed at soft tissue window/level settings, demonstrates the relationship of soft tissue structures to the needle trajectory. Trachea (T), thyroid (t), internal carotid artery (i), internal jugular vein (j), esophagus (e), longus coli muscle (l), sternocleidomastoid muscle (scm).

narrow; therefore, one must proceed with caution when advancing the needle beyond the annulus (Fig. 20-3). The needle depth and height within the disc space is now examined under the lateral beam (Fig. 20-1C) and adjusted accordingly.

Discometry

Recording discometric data during operative intervention, Kambin observed that normal cervical discs held 0.2–0.4 ml of solution while sustaining high intradiscal pressures.[22] Conversely, discs that allowed "posterior escape" of contrast medium accepted greater than 1.5 ml at low, wavering pressures. Herniated or degenerated discs with an intact outer annular capsule held intermediate volumes (0.5–1.5 ml) at sustained, yet intermediate, pressures. In a cadaveric investigation, Saternus discovered that cervical discs that accepted more than 0.5 mm most often demonstrated posterolateral extravasation from the uncinate portions of the annulus.[83]

These studies indicate that cervical discometry yields reproducible information concerning discal hydrodynamic competence. Upon injection, the intact cervical disc holds less than 0.5 ml of solution, at which time a firm endpoint is appreciated.

For complete details on discometry, see chapter 19.

Nucleography

Cervical nucleograms vary widely in configuration. They may appear spherical, disc-shaped, or tubular. As in lumbar discograms, contrast material extravasating beyond the nuclear region indicates annular disruption; however, extension of contrast from the nucleus to the uncinate recesses is common and may simply reflect disc maturation.[20,34,41] Following adolescence, linear annular clefts develop that allow communication between the nucleus and uncinate recesses.[20,41] Uncovertebral recesses are present only in the adults. Curiously, one study demonstrated a slightly higher rate of provocation with flow of contrast material to the joints of Luschka.[35]

Lumbar postdiscography/CT has been widely applied, but technical difficulties have hampered the acceptance of cervical postdiscography/CT.

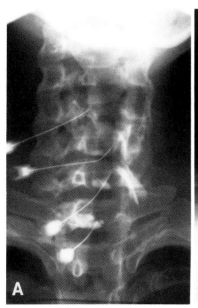
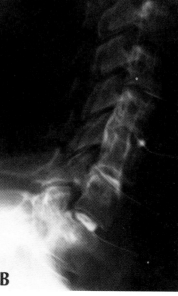

FIGURE 20-3. A 23-year-old college student was diagnosed with C4–5, C5–6, and C6–7 internal disc disruption. Compare these photos with Fig. 20-1. They represent a common misapplication of discography that promotes its unfounded duplicitous reputation. A, Posteroanterior view. The C4–5, C5–6, and C6–7 needles are malpositioned, rendering the study nondiagnostic. Based on this investigation, the above diagnosis is unsubstantiated because the only nuclear injection is at C7–T1. B, Lateral film. Note the annular injection at C5–6 and the bend in the needle, which is likely due to multiple passes. At C6–7 the needle has been inadvertently advanced beyond the posterior annulus into the epidural space. The C7–T1 injection is nuclear.

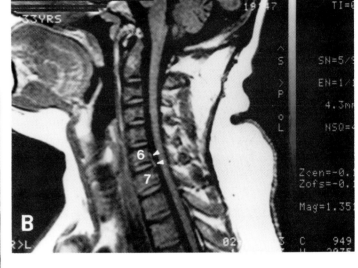

FIGURE 20-4. Imaging studies of a 33-year-old man following a motor vehicle accident, during which he was looking at traffic over his left shoulder when his car was hit in the rear. *A,* T1-weighted (TR 455, TE 28, RF 90°) midline sagittal MR image is within normal limits. *B,* Left parasagittal T1 image (TR 500, TE 16, RF 90°) discloses a small disc extrusion at C6–7 *(arrows).*

(Continued below.)

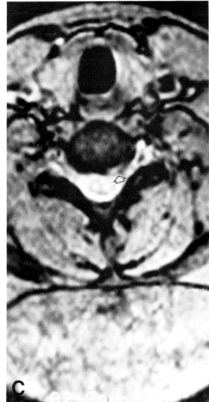

FIGURE 20-4 *(Continued). C,* Same disc lesion *(arrowhead)* seen in *B* on gradient echo axial section (TR 1417, TE 18, RF 30°). *(Continued on following page.)*

Owing to the small amount of contrast material employed and sparse dispersal pattern, transverse imaging of the demure cervical nucleogram is challenging. Fortin has used high-resolution, thin-section CT to garner novel cervical spine imaging information.[14] Fissures, small protrusions, annular attenuation, and nuclear degradation are, at times, indistinct on cervical MRI. Obscuration may occur as slice thickness (3.0–5.0 mm) is wide relative to the cervical nuclear region and long acquisition sequences are susceptible to motion artifact and low signal to noise.

Gradient echo images are prone to magnetic susceptibility and may erroneously create a pseudomyelographic effect. Cervical discography/CT may be employed to visualize pathology that may be confusing, ill-defined or absent on MRI or CT (Fig. 20-4). The postdiscography data is obtained in 1.5-mm

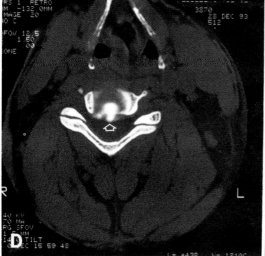
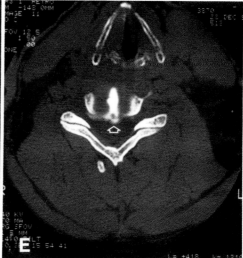
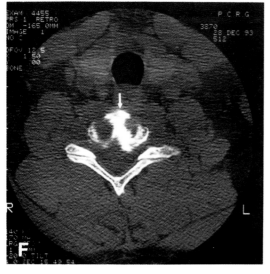

FIGURE 20-4 *(Continued)*. *D,* At C4–5, an asymptomatic posterior radial fissure is revealed on postdiscography/CT *(arrowhead)*. *E,* A radial fissure extends from the central nuclear zone into a concentric outer annular fissure/small prolapse at C5–6. Neither this lesion, which was provocation positive, nor the one seen in *D* was demonstrable on MRI *(arrowhead)*. *F,* C6–7 postdiscography/CT *(arrowhead)*. Compare with *B* and note the anterior circumferential fissuring *(arrow)*

contiguous sections employing a gantry angle commensurate with each interspace (Fig. 20-5).

The author initially employed postdiscography/CT to resolve the dilemma of small prolapse versus pseudoprolapse (i.e., extension of contrast medium into the recesses). If contrast medium extends to the uncinate recesses upon injecting, it may masquerade as a small prolapse on the lateral projection (Fig. 20-6). Orthogonal nucleography rectifies this puzzle. For further details on nucleography, please see chapter 19.

COMPLICATIONS

See chapter 19 for complete details on complications and information on postprocedure care.

Infection of the disc space is the most widely recognized complication associated with the performance of diagnostic disc injections (Fig. 20-7).[9–11,15,17,28,37,50] Yet, like lumbar discography, the incidence is low.

The potential for permanent damage to the disc from puncture and/or distension is speculative. Oddly, Smith and Kim attributed a herniated cervical disc to the performance of discography.[43] In their case report, "A Herniated Cervical Disc Resulting from Discography: An Unusual Complication," the authors provide gradient echo sagittal MRI images that demonstrate that the patient had a disc prolapse prior to the procedure. The prolapse was simply enlarged following the procedure. Additionally, the patient Westergren's sedimentation rate was 55 mm per hour (normal less than 20), increasing to 70 mm per hour, and a white blood cell count was 12,700. To no surprise, a bone scan obtained within 24 hours of the procedure was normal. Two days following the procedure, the patient underwent anterior discectomy/corpectomy with spinal decompression because the patient was experiencing progressive neurologic symptoms. The surgical findings revealed a thickened and edematous posterior

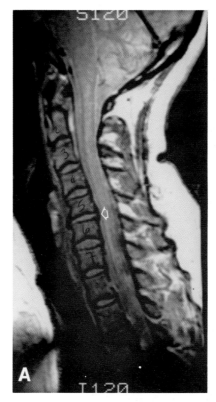
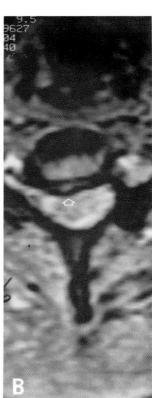

FIGURE 20-5. Imaging studies in a 39-year-old woman following whiplash injury resulting from a motor vehicle accident. *A,* Fast spin echo sagittal MRI with spin density characteristics (TR 3380, TE 17 Ef). A mild, contained prolapse creates a myelographic-like impression at C5–6. *B,* On gradient echo axial section (TR 33, TE 15, RF 5), a right paracentral herniation effaces the right anterolateral subarachnoid space. No cord compression is visualized.
(Continued below.)

longitudinal ligament as well as scattered inflammatory cells and a few white blood cells in the interspace. The clinical presentation and surgical findings are suspicious for an iatrogenically induced chemical or aseptic discitis.[11]

Fernstrom attributed six lumbar disc herniations to discography upon performing more than 1,500 disc injections.[13] He did not have the aid of fluoroscopic guidance nor the ability to validate these findings with transverse imaging. With the exception

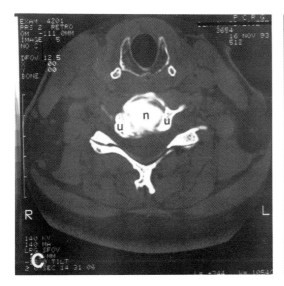
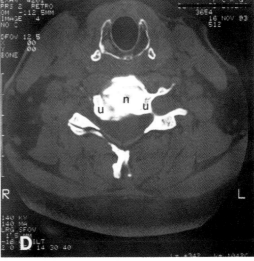

FIGURE 20-5 *(Continued).* *C* and *D,* Thin section (1.5 mm) postdiscography/CT employing a bone algorithm and an angled gantry minimizes partial volume effect and provides optimal resolution of contrast within the disc space. Compare the contrast resolution and edge enhancement with figures 20-3*C* and 20-6*C.* Cervical postdiscography/CT may provide information regarding the annular integrity that is not apparent on MRI. In addition to the above prolapse, these CT films reveal gross nuclear disarray, anterior outer annular circumferential fissuring, and contrast extending into the bilateral uncinate recesses.

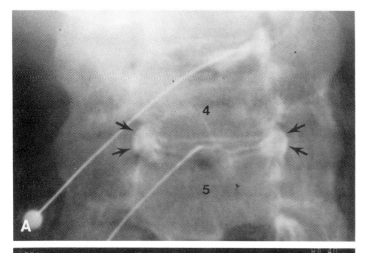

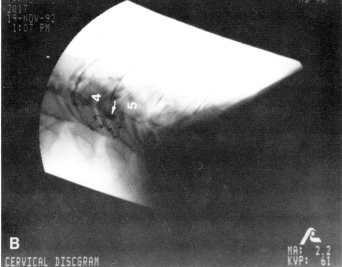

FIGURE 20-6. "Pseudoprolapse." *A*, Contrast in the uncinate recesses creates a bulbous appearance at C4–5 (*arrows*). Incidentally, the needle tip at C3–4 is left of midline. The needle was repositioned following this photograph. *B*, This lateral view suggests a posterior disc prolapse at C4–5 (*arrows*).

(Continued below.)

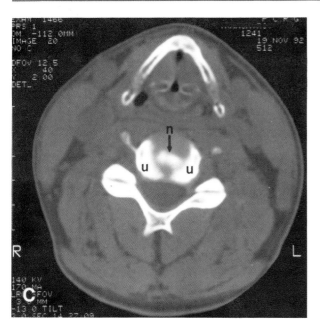

FIGURE 20-6 *(Continued)*. *C*, Postdiscography/CT axial section excludes a posterior prolapse and demonstrated contrast within nucleus (n) and uncinate recesses (u) only. The "pseudoprolapse" on the lateral view was created by contrast within the posterolateral oriented recesses.

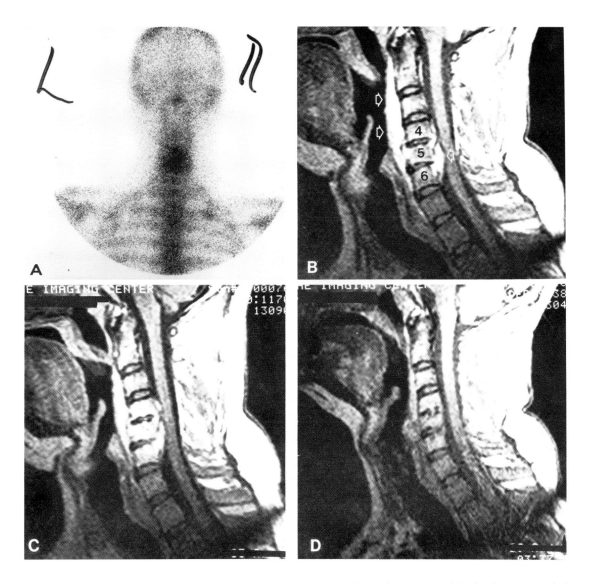

FIGURE 20-7. This patient had a history of crescendo neck and shoulder girdle pain and spasm following four-level cervical discography. White blood cell count and sedimentation rate were markedly elevated (14,000 and 47, respectively). *A,* Radionuclide scan demonstrates abnormal tracer uptake in the mid/lower cervical spine about 2 weeks after the procedure. *B,* Gadolinium-enhanced T1-weighted (TR 500, TE 16, RF 90) sagittal MRI discloses (1) collapse of C4–5 and C5–6 disc space with nascent endplate destructive changes; (2) vertebral body hyperemia, as evidenced by the marrow enhancement (high signal); (3) retropharyngeal and prevertebral abscess; and (4) epidural abscess with cord compression but without intramedullary signal changes. This image was obtained 2 weeks after the procedure. *C,* One week following intravenous full-spectrum antibiotic coverage (no organism was identified), a serial gadolinium-enhanced T1 MRI provides further testimony to a virulent organism. Hyperemic and destructive endplate changes have advanced despite the patient's subjective favorable response to treatment. The abscesses appear unchecked but may reflect a common lag between clinical response and imaging findings. *D,* Four weeks following antibiotic therapy (6 weeks after the procedure), both abscesses have dissipated, hyperemia resolved, and spontaneous arthrodesis of the affected segments is occurring. No further signs of cord compression exist.
(Continued on following page.)

of Smith and Kim's suspect report, no modern studies have related disc damage to the performance of diagnostic disc injections.

CONTRAINDICATIONS

Cervical discography is potentially life threatening when contraindicated. For example, discography in a patient with evidence of cord compression, such as spasticity, weakness, and paresthesias from a massive disc prolapse, has resulted in frank quadriplegia.[27] Discography is contraindicated in patients with central stenosis,[49] myelopathy, neoplasms, infections, infiltrative processes, and relative (borderline) stenosis[49] combined with bilateral root canal stenosis, especially when multiple levels are involved.

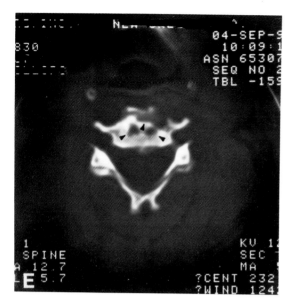

FIGURE 20-7 *(Continued).* E, Two months after the procedure, transaxial CT (bone window/level settings) at C4–5 reveal "moth-eaten" low-density areas in the C4 endplate. An aggressive staphylococcal organism is a likely culprit of these osteolytic remains.

Prima facia imaging studies, which adequately assess spinal stenosis and cord compression, must be examined prior to cervical discography. While MRI is superior in examining the intrinsic substance of the cord, CT affords greater osseous detail and spatial resolution in evaluating stenosis.[23,31] In this setting, MRI is hampered by thicker sections and variable signal intensity in degenerative osseous ridges.[31] With equal or greater accuracy, intrathecal enhanced CT resolves extradural compression from bone or disc material on neural elements, such as theca, cord, or dural pouches.[31]

CONCLUSION

Cervical discography is an important adjunct for definitively diagnosing primary discogenic pain. It should not be used as a screening imaging modality. In fact, cervical diagnostic disc injection should not be performed, even when clinically warranted, until other imaging studies such as high-resolution CT or MRI have been thoroughly studied. Pain provocation is the sine qua non of discography. Additionally, nucleography in the transverse mode may enhance imaging information garnered by CT or MRI.[14]

REFERENCES

1. Altenstein G: Erfahrungen mit der diskographic an hals und lendenwirbelsaule. Z Orthop 102:358–366, 1967.
2. Aprill CN III: Diagnostic disc injection. In Frymoyer JW (ed): The Adult Spine. New York, Raven Press, 1991, pp 403–442.
3. Bettag W, Grote W: Die bedeutung der diskographie fur die behandlung des "zervikalsyndroms." Hippokrates 40:138–141, 1969.
4. Bogduk N, Windsor M, Inglis A: The innervation of the cervical intervertebral discs. Spine 13:2–8, 1988.
5. Cloward RB: Cervical diskography. Technique, indications and use in the diagnosis of ruptured cervical disks. AJR 79:563–574, 1958.
6. Cloward RB: The anterior approach for removal of ruptured cervical disks. J Neurosurg 15:602–617, 1958.
7. Cloward RB: Cervical diskography. A contribution to the etiology and mechanism of neck, shoulder and arm pain. Ann Surg 150:1052–1064, 1959.
8. Cloward RB: Cervical discography. Acta Radiol Suppl (Stockh) 1:675–688, 1963.
9. Cloward RB: Cervical discography defended [letter]. JAMA 233:862, 1975.
10. Collis JS Jr, Gardner WJ: Lumbar discography. An analysis of 1,000 cases. J Neurosurg 19:452–461, 1962.
11. Crock H: Practice of Spinal Surgery. New York, Springer-Verlag, 1983.
12. Feinberg SB: The place of discography in radiology as based on 2,320 cases. AJR 92:1275–1281, 1964.
13. Fernstrom U: A discographical study of ruptured lumbar intervertebral discs. Acta Chir Scand Suppl 258:1–60, 1960.
14. Fortin JD: Cervical nucleography and post discography/CT [unpublished data].
15. Fraser RD: Chymopapain for the treatment of intervertebral disc herniation: The final report of a double blind study. Spine 9:815–818, 1984.
16. Grote W, Wappenschmidt J: Uber technik und indikation zur-zervikalen diskographie. Rofo Fortschr Geb Rontgenstr Neuen Bildgeb Verfahr 106:721–727, 1967.
17. Guyer RD, Collier R, Stith WJ, et al: Discitis after discography. Spine 13:1352–1354, 1988.
18. Hatt MU: Hohenlokalisation der cervicalen discushernie in klinik, elektromyographe (EMG) und myelographie. Dtsch Zeitschr Nervenheilk 197:56–65, 1969.
19. Hirsch C: An attempt to diagnose level of disc lesion clinically by disc puncture. Acta Orthop Scand 18:131–140, 1948.
20. Hirsch C, Schajowicz R, Galante J: Structural changes in the cervical spine: A study on autopsy specimens in different age groups. Acta Orthop Scand Suppl 109:7–77, 1967.
21. Holt EP Jr: Fallacy of cervical discography: Report of 50 cases in normal subjects. JAMA 188:799–801, 1964.
22. Kambin P, Abda S, Kurpicki F: Intradiskal pressure and volume recording: Evaluation of normal and abnormal cervical disks. Clin Orthop 146:144–147, 1980.
23. Karnaze MG, Gado MH, Sartor KJ, Hodges FJ III: Comparison of MR and CT myelography in imaging the cervical and thoracic spine. AJR 150:397–403, 1988.
24. Kikuchi S, Macnab I, Moreau P: Localisation of the level of symptomatic cervical disc degeneration. J Bone Joint Surg 63B:272–277, 1981.
25. Klafta LA Jr, Collis JS Jr: The diagnostic inaccuracy of the pain response in cervical discography. Cleve Clin Q 36:35–39, 1969.
26. Klafta LA Jr, Collis JS Jr: An analysis of cervical discography with surgical verification. J Neurosurg 30:38–41, 1969.
27. Laun A, Lorenz R, Agnoli AL: Complications of cervical discography. J Neurosurg Sci 25:17–22, 1981.
28. Lindblom K: Technique and results of diagnostic disc puncture and injection (discography) in the lumbar region. Acta Orthop Scand 20:315–326, 1951.
29. Lownie SP, Ferguson GG: Spinal subdural empyema complicating cervical discography. Spine 14:1415–1417, 1989.
30. Massare C, Bard M, Tristant H: Cervical discography: Speculation on technique and indications from our own experience. J Radiol 55:395–399, 1974.

31. Modic MT, Masaryk TJ, Mulopulos GP, et al: Cervical radiculopathy: Prospective evaluation with surface coil MR imaging, CT with metrizamide and metrizamide myelography. Radiology 161:753–759, 1986.

32. North American Spine Society: Position statement on discography. The Executive Committee of the North American Spine Society. Spine 13:1343, 1988.

33. Pascaud JL, Mailhes F, Pascaud E, et al: The cervical intervertebral disc: Diagnostic value of cervical discography in degenerative and post-traumatic lesions. Ann Radiol (Paris) 23:455–460, 1980.

34. Payne EE, Spillane JD: The cervical spine. Brain 80:572–596, 1957.

35. Poletti SC, Handal JA: Cervical discography: Morphology versus pain response. Boston, North American Spine Society, July 1992.

36. Riley LH Jr, Robinson RA, Johnson KA, Walker AE: The results of anterior interbody fusion of the cervical spine: Review of 93 consecutive cases. J Neurosurg 30:127–133, 1969.

37. Roosen K, Bettag W, Fiebach O: Komplikationen der cervikalen diskographie. Rofo Fortschr Geb Rontgenstr Neuen Bildgeb Verfahr 122:520–527, 1975.

38. Roth DA: Cervical analgesic discography: A new test for the definitive diagnosis of painful-disk syndrome. JAMA 235:1713–1714, 1976.

39. Saternus KS, Bornscheuer HH: [Comparative radiologic and pathologic-anatomic studies on the value of discography in the diagnosis of acute intervertebral disc injuries in the cervical spine.] Rofo Fortschr Geb Rontgenstr Neuen Bildgeb Verfahr 139:651–657, 1983.

40. Schaerer JP: Anterior cervical disc removal and fusion. Schweiz Arch Neurol Neurochir Psychiatr 102:331–334, 1968.

41. Sherk H, Parke W: Developmental anatomy. In Bailey RW (ed): The Cervical Spine. Philadelphia, J.B. Lippincott, 1983, pp 7–8.

42. Simmons EH, Segil CM: An evaluation of discography in the localization of symptomatic levels in discogenic disease of the spine. Clin Orthop 108:57–69, 1975.

43. Smith GW: The normal cervical diskogram with clinical observations. AJR 81:1006–1010, 1959.

44. Smith GW, Nichols P Jr: Technic for cervical discography. Radiology 68:718–720, 1957.

45. Smith GW, Robinson RA: The treatment of certain cervical spine disorders by anterior removal of the intervertebral disc and interbody fusion. J Bone Joint Surg 40A:607–623, 1958.

46. Smith MD, Kim SS: A herniated cervical disc resulting from discography: An unusual complication. J Spinal Disord 3(4):392–395, 1990.

47. Stuck RM: Cervical discography. AJR 86:975–982, 1961.

48. Unander-Scharin L: Diskografier. Nord Med 57:116, 1957.

49. Verbiest H: Fallacies of the present definition, nomenclature and classification of the stenoses of the lumbar vertebral canal. Spine 1:217–225, 1976.

50. Volgelsang H: Discitis intervertrablis cervicalis nach diskographie. Neurochirurgia 16:80–83, 1973.

51. Whitecloud TS III, Seago RA: Cervical discogenic syndrome: Results of operative intervention in patients with positive discography. Spine 12:313–317, 1987.

Chapter 21

SPINAL CORD STIMULATION IN CHRONIC PAIN

ROBERT WINDSOR, M.D.
FRANK J.E. FALCO, M.D.
SUSAN J. DREYER, M.D.
JONATHAN P. LESTER, M.D.

The long-term results of spinal cord stimulation (SCS) published in the 1970s were disappointing. As with many new devices, problems included poorly designed hardware, inadequate patient selection criteria, and suboptimal surgical technique. The hardware typically consisted of a single- or dual-electrode system that was implanted subdurally. These systems provided a small electrical field and thus were unable to consistently stimulate the spinal cord. In addition, these systems were implanted via laminectomy or laminotomy with the patient under general anesthesia, thus eliminating the possibility of surgeon-patient interaction. Patients were not consistently screened for psychological dysfunction, drug habituation, secondary-gain issues and pain topography that may not be amenable to SCS. All of these factors have considerable impact on the overall efficacy of SCS.

Significant advances in SCS have been made in recent years. The hardware is more durable and more effective. The devices can be implanted percutaneously under fluoroscopic guidance, which allows operator-patient interaction and more accurate positioning of SCS. Two decades of experience have provided improved patient selection criteria. The net result is an improved capacity to control chronic pain. This chapter will discuss the clinical application of SCS, implantation technqiue, follow-up care, and our clinical experience.

PAIN ANATOMY AND PHYSIOLOGY

This chapter serves as an overview to assist the reader in understanding the general application of SCS in the control of chronic pain. The interested reader is directed to outside sources for a more comprehensive analysis of this subject.[4,45]

Pain can originate from stimulation of chemical, mechanical, or thermal receptors found in free nerve endings within injured tissue. This is known as afferent pain, and can occur in ligamentous or muscular injuries of the spine. Pain can also occur from direct injury to the peripheral nerve, which results in burning or shooting pain in the distribution of the affected nerve. This is called peripheral deafferentation (neuropathic) pain and is demonstrated in conditions such as causalgia, reflex sympathetic dystrophy, or radiculopathy. Central deafferent pain appears after injury to the central nervous system structures, such as the thalamus, that are responsible for the transmission of pain.

Peripheral pain signals are transmitted by either thinly myelinated A-δ or unmyelinated C fibers. The A-δ fibers convey discrete, sharp, fast pain at approximately 15 m/sec, whereas the C fibers transmit vague, chronic, burning, slow pain at less than 1 m/sec.

The pain fibers typically enter the spinal cord through the dorsal root and then ascend or descend two to six segments within the dorsolateral fasciculus (Lissauer's tract). The A-δ fibers synapse with the dorsal gray horn neurons located in laminae 1, 2, 5, and 10, whereas the C fibers synapse with dorsal gray horn neurons located in laminae 1, 2, and 5. The majority of fibers then cross to the opposite ventrolateral portion of the spinal cord before ascending in the spinothalamic, spinoreticulothalamic, and spinomesencephalic tracts. The lateral spinothalamic fibers terminate in the thalamic ventralis posterolaterales and posteromedialis nuclei, from which fibers are projected into other areas of the

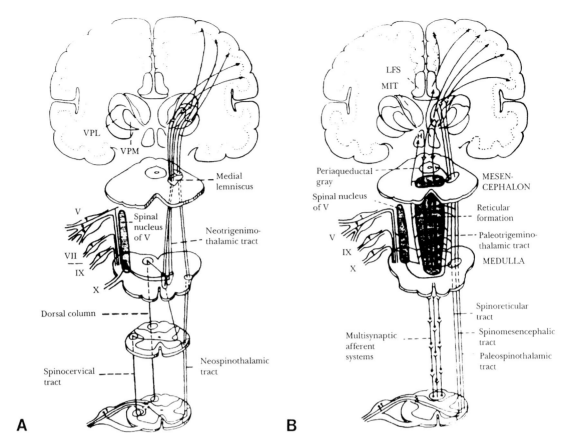

FIGURE 21-1. Neuroanatomic pathway for nociceptive pain transmission in the lateral (A) and medial (B) tracts. (From Bonica JJ: Anatomic and physiologic basis of nociception and pain. In Bonica JJ (ed): The Management of Pain, Vol. 1, 2nd ed. Philadelphia, Lea & Febiger, 1990, p 89, with permission.)

thalamus and to the somatic sensory cortex. The medial spinothalamic, spinoreticulothalamic, and spinomesencephalic tracts end in the reticular activating system within the medulla, pons, midbrain, periaqueductal gray, hypothalamus, and thalamic medial and intralaminar nuclei (Fig. 21-1).

The thalamus plays the primary role for conscious pain perception, and the cortex is involved in interpreting pain quality and locality. The A-δ fibers convey a distinctive, sharp pain, and C fibers conduct a characteristic diffuse, burning, or aching pain. This is likely a reflection of the A-δ fibers terminating at the cortical level versus C fibers, which end diffusely in the brain stem and diencephalon.

In 1965, Melzack and Wall published their "gate control" theory in which they hypothesized that a "gate" system existed for pain modulation located in the dorsal gray horn within the substantia gelatinosa (laminae 2 and 3).[26] They proposed that excess tactile signals traveling along the large myelinated A-β fibers closed the gate, which then inhibited the propagation of pain impulses along the poorly myelinated C fibers (Fig. 21-2).

Although the pain pathway is still not completely understood, researchers have uncovered important parts of the neuronal system. This includes descending inhibitory influences from the brain, which have been shown to suppress transmission of pain.[3,27,33,38] There is also evidence of an endogenous system of opioids that modulate sensory input.[15,39,42]

Today, there is a better awareness that the pain experience is not just physiologic but is also influenced by culture, religion, and psychologial make-up.[10,13,24,25] In order to provide the appropriate treatment, all of these factors must be taken into consideration when evaluating patients.

MECHANISM OF ACTION

Although the exact mechanism for pain control from SCS is not entirely understood, it is believed to result from direct or facilitated inhibition of pain transmission.

The gate control theory motivated Shealy et al. in 1967 to apply SCS as a means to antidromically activate the tactile A-β fibers through dorsal column

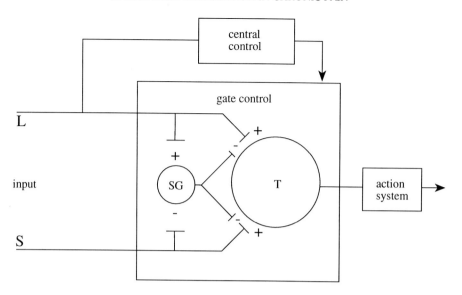

FIGURE 21-2. Melzack and Wall gate-control theory of pain: large-diameter fibers (L), small-diameter fibers (S), substantia gelatinosa (SG), first central transmission cells (T), excitation (+), inhibition (–). (From Melzack R, Wall PD: Pain mechanisms: A new theory. Science 150:975, 1965, with permission.)

stimulation.[40] Shealy reasoned that sustained stimulation of the dorsal columns would keep the gate closed and therefore provide continuous pain relief. While the theoretical model put forth by Melzack and Wall has been shown not to be precisely correct, pain gating or pain control has been shown to exist.

Others believe that pain relief from SCS results from direct inhibition of the pain fibers and not secondary to selective large fiber stimulation.[7] Pain relief may actually occur from blocking the pain pathways in the spinothalamic tracts. This theory has been supported by Hoppenstein, who showed that the posterolateral stimulation of the spinal cord provided effective contralateral pain relief with substantially less current than posterior stimulation.[11]

Some investigators think that the changes in blood flow and skin temperature from spinal cord stimulation may affect nociception at the peripheral level. This postulate is supported in part by data from Marchand et al., who have investigated the effects of SCS on clinical pain using noxious thermal stimuli.[22]

The precise action of pain modulation by SCS is still in debate. A better understanding of the pain system may lead to more effective stimulators and allow for even greater success.

SPINAL CORD STIMULATION SYSTEMS

Only two companies manufacture SCS systems: Neuromed, Inc., (Fort Lauderdale, FL) and Medtronic, Inc. (Minneapolis, MN).

Neuromed produces a quadripolar lead for both temporary and permanent implantation and an eight-channel lead for permanent implantation only. The temporary lead has been designed for trial implantation over a 3- to 7-day period on an outpatient basis. Both leads are designed to be implanted percutaneously; however, this does not preclude them from being implanted via laminotomy. Both four-channel leads have an interelectrode distance of 10 mm, and the eight-channel lead has an interelectrode distance of only 7 mm; 7 mm has been determined to be the optimal distance to provide the greatest stimulation intensity with the least discomfort.[18]

Neuromed has designed three receivers for subcutaneous implantation (Fig. 21-3). One is capable of accepting a single four-channel lead, the second is capable of accepting an eight-channel lead, and a third is capable of accepting two four-channel leads. Neuromed has one rechargeable eight-channel transmitter that has a removable belt clip and an external antenna that communicates with the subcutaneous receiver.

Medtronic also manufactures systems that are implanted by both percutaneous and laminotomy routes. Their trial lead has two electrodes with an interelectrode distance of 40 mm. Their percutaneously implanted four-channel lead has an interelectrode distance of 12 mm. Medtronic's transmitter and receiver are capable of accommodating a single four-electrode lead. Medtronic also has a paddle-type electrode that has been designed for implantation via laminotomy. The transmitter, antenna, and receiver function in a similar manner to that described above for Neuromed.

PATIENT SELECTION CRITERIA

Proper patient selection is essential to the long-term success of an SCS system. As mentioned, poor selection criteria were one of the principal reasons for suboptimal results reported in the 1970s.

An SCS system should be considered for patients who have failed all reasonable conservative care, including appropriate diagnostic, therapeutic, and rehabilitative techniques, and have been given a reasonable period of time to recover, usually longer than 1 year. An ideal patient should be motivated, compliant, and free of drug addictions. A psychological clearance is necessary prior to pursuing an SCS to make certain that there is no occult psychological dysfunction that may adversely affect the outcome of the procedure.

Diagnoses that are general indications for this procedure include failed back surgery syndrome (FBSS), perineural fibrosis, neuropathic pain, reflex sympathetic dystrophy, and causalgia.[2,5,9,16,23] In Europe, SCS is being used for peripheral vascular disease that is not amenable to medical therapy, and excellent results have been reported.[1,12,43] In the United States, peripheral vascular disease is not an FDA-approved indication.

Pain topography also must be considered when contemplating the use of an SCS. In general, extremity pain responds better than axial pain, and the more distal the extremity pain the greater the

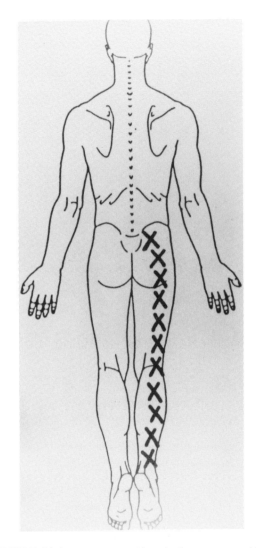

FIGURE 21-4. Ideal topographic pain for treatment with spinal cord stimulation in patients with failed back surgery syndrome.

clinical response (Fig. 21-4). Middle and upper lumbar pain as well as thoracic and chest wall pain are very difficult to adequately control and maintain over the long term. Pain secondary to severe nerve damage is also difficult to treat. Central pain syndromes do not respond to SCS and are best treated with the use of deep brain stimulation.

The use of 3- to 7-day outpatient trials with an SCS system has proved helpful in determining which patients will respond well enough to warrant a permanent implantation. Absolute criteria that must be present for a patient to have a positive trial include tolerance of paresthesia, greater than 50% pain relief, and overall patient satisfaction. Relative requirements for a positive trial include improved functional level, reduced usage of pain medication, and reduced reliance on the health-care system.

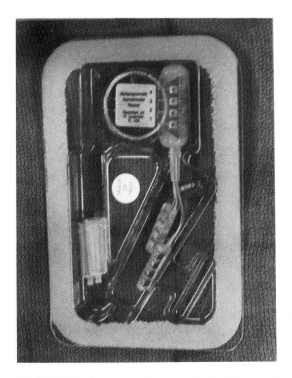

FIGURE 21-3. Neuromed subcutaneous implantable octrode receiver with two four-channel adapters.

Relative contraindications to SCS include psychopathology that may adversely affect the outcome of the procedure, a severe coagulopathy, or a condition that may be adequately treated by other conservative or surgical techniques. Absolute contraindications include severe medical conditions that may adversely affect the safety of the procedure, ongoing systemic infection, or diagnosis that is not adequately treated with SCS.

IMPLANTATION TECHNIQUE

Spinal cord stimulation may be performed by either percutaneous or open approaches. This chapter describes only the percutaneous method, which we use in our practice.

Patients are placed prone on the procedure table in a fluoroscopic suite. Placing a bolster under the bottom of their rib cage is optional. The entire posterior aspect of their torso is cleaned with an antiseptic solution such as Hibiclens or Betadine. Intravenous sedation is optional although it does make patients more comfortable and does not compromise the reliability of the information transferred from the patient to the physician. The procedure must be interactive since proper placement of the electrode is paramount to its success.

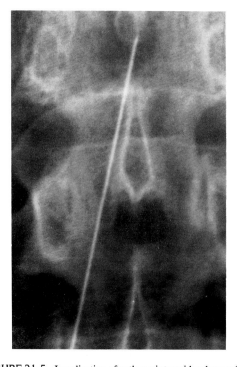

FIGURE 21-5. Localization of pathway into epidural space for percutaneous placement of stimulating electrodes. The epidural needle is advanced in a line that is ipsilateral to the caudal spinous process and directed toward the cephalad portion of the mid-interlaminar space.

The T12-L1 interlaminar space is localized under fluoroscopic visualization as the point of entry into the epidural space. The L1-L2 interlaminar space may be used if the T12-L1 space is determined to be too small for maneuvering with an epidural needle. After choosing which space to enter, the physician must determine the ultimate skin entrance site. Site selection is important because the final resting position of the epidural needle should be no more than 30° off the midline and 45° from the surface of the patient's back.

The skin entrance can be determined by using the following vector method. Under fluoroscopic visualization, a spinal needle should be placed on the patient's back so that it intersects the midline of the interlaminar space. This space is chosen at its cephalad extent and ipsilateral point of the spinous process immediately caudal to the interlaminar space chosen (Fig. 21-5). One should determine whether the patient is large, medium, or small. The approximate skin entrance site for a large, medium, or small patient is 2½, 2, 1½ vertebral bodies, respectively, caudal to the space chosen along the line described above. About 8–10 ml of 1% lidocaine is recommended to make certain that all of the soft tissues posterior to the lamina, periosteum, and ligamentum flavum are well anesthetized prior to insertion of the epidural needle.

The epidural needle is placed into the anesthetized soft tissues and advanced to the ipsilateral, caudal vertebra lamina of the space chosen. Once bony contact has been made, the epidural needle is walked up the lamina in a cephalad and medial direction until the classic loss of resistance is detected, which identifies the epidural space. The lead blank is inserted into the epidural space after no blood or cerebrospinal fluid is aspirated from the needle. The lead is a thin, semirigid metallic rod that is designed to create a narrow tunnel in the epidural space through which the stimulating electrode may be passed.

A variety of techniques may be used to maneuver the lead blank into the proper position after it has been inserted into the epidural space. The first method is simply to rotate the needle bevel clockwise when the needle is placed on the right side of the spine or counterclockwise when the needle is placed on the left side of the spine. Depending on the required stimulation pattern, the lead blank should be advanced until it tracks up the midline or paramidline of the posterior epidural space while the bevel is rotated. The lead blank should be advanced until it lies approximately at the top of the T9 vertebral body. Placing a 45-degree bend on the lead blank approximately 1 cm to its distal aspect and alternately rotating it during insertion may be beneficial if the above technique fails to aid in proper placement of the lead blank. Once the lead blank has been properly placed, it should be moved back and forth in an alternate cephalad-caudal motion to develop the tunnel for the electrode. The lead blank is withdrawn after the tunnel is made.

Next, the spinal cord stimulating electrode should be placed and advanced into the epidural space. The electrode should follow the path of the lead blank with relatively little rotation of the needle bevel. The electrode is removed gently if the electrode does not follow the lead blank path. The electrode is modified by placing a bend approximately 2 cm from the end. With the bend, the electrode is reinserted and should be easier to maneuver into the proper direction if it veers off course. If the needle placement is still incorrect, the physician should place an additional epidural needle and advance a second lead blank along a track that is immediately adjacent to the path that the electrode should follow. This should expedite the proper placement of the electrode.

Stimulation trials should begin after the electrode is placed at the top of the T9 vertebral body (Fig. 21-6) either in the midline or just ipsilateral to midline on the side of pain. The second and third electrodes on a quadripolar electrode should be used initially. The stimulation intensity should be advanced very slowly until the patient indicates that he or she feels something. Stimulation intensity is then increased according to patient tolerance until achieving the desired level of stimulation. The patient should then inform the physician of the stimulation distribution. If the goal is to block pain in the lower back, hips, or lower extremities, there should be no stimulation in the abdomen or inguinal region. Stimulation in either of these areas indicates that the electrode is positioned too high, and it should be pulled down slightly before retesting. The final position of the electrode will provide paresthesia to adequately cover the patient's pain pattern. A lateral fluoroscopic image can be taken to confirm that the electrode has not migrated anterior to the dural sac. Anteroposterior and lateral spot films should be taken at this point for documentation purposes.

To ensure that the lead does not move, the epidural needle is carefully removed under fluoroscopic visualization in patients receiving temporary devices. Betadine ointment is then applied to the lead entry site. The external portion of the lead is then secured to the patient's back with a clear adhesive occlusive dressing such as Tegaderm. Approximately 10 cm of the free lead end is left exposed for attachment to the stimulator.

In patients receiving permanent devices, the receiver is implanted after the spot films are taken. Receiving the dual quadripolar leads with the permanent stimulator, which are introduced through separate epidural needles, is recommended for most patients. This allows for the greatest amount of

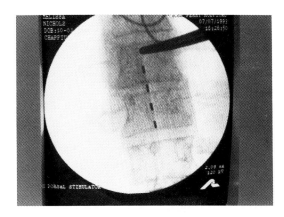

FIGURE 21-6. Epidural location of stimulating electrode at the T9 vertebral body level.

flexibility for pain coverage. The surgeon should make an incision at the epidural needle site to subcutaneously expose the leads. The epidural needles are removed under fluoroscopic visualization to ensure that the lead does not move. The leads are then secured to the supraspinous and/or interspinous ligament with sutures. The remainder of the leads are tunneled subcutaneously to the predesignated hip area, usually just below the iliac crest (belt line), where a pocket for the receiver is made. The leads are connected to the receiver before it is placed into the pocket. The pocket is closed, and the receiver is stimulated using a sterile antenna connected to the transmitter before the patient is taken to the recovery room.

TRANSMITTER PROGRAMMING PARAMETERS

This section discusses the programming of the Neuromed, Inc. systems transmitters (Fig. 21-7). The three parameters that can be adjusted for stimulation are frequency (Hz), pulse width (stimulus duration, μsec), and amplitude (volts). For pain control, the frequency of the transmitter is usually set from 75–125 Hz. Pulse duration can be placed between 50 and 500 μsec. Increasing the pulse duration increases the density of the stimulus, which provides for deeper stimulus penetration into the spinal cord. The amplitude represents the electrical force of the stimulus and varies from 0–10 volts.

Initial stimulation settings are arbitrary and reflect programming experience. The amount of output depends on the size of the patient, which is reflected by the amount of epidural fat, anatomical variations, and the presence or absence of dural scarring. Typical transmitter settings begin with a frequency of 75 Hz and a pulse duration of 100 μsec. The amplitude is slowly increased until paresthesias are felt by the patient. The intensity

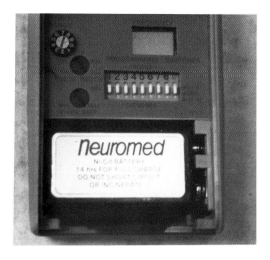

FIGURE 21-7. Control panel for programming the Neuromed octrode transmitter, which is powered by a rechargeable 9-volt battery.

can be increased or decreased by changing any of the three parameters.

In order to generate current from the implanted lead, at least one electrode is made a cathode and another the anode. This allows for current to flow from the anode (positive pole) to the cathode (negative pole), resulting in fiber depolarization. The density and flow of current from the implanted lead can be adjusted depending on which electrodes are selected to represent cathodes and anodes. A cathode and anode close together will generate a small, dense (higher intensity) electrical field, whereas two electrodes spaced far apart will provide a larger but less dense (lower intensity) electrical field. A larger and denser electrical field can be created with a cathode and anode spaced far apart by adding additional anodes to the stimulation scheme, which will increase the density of ion flow to the cathode.

The intensity and distribution of the paresthesias generated by the spinal cord stimulator depend upon the integration of impulse frequency, duration, and force with current density and distribution.

POSTPROCEDURE CARE AND FOLLOW-UP PROTOCOL

The patient who is undergoing a trial SCS routinely recovers for 1 hour following the temporary insertion and is then discharged home. During the recovery period, the SCS programming is fine-tuned, and any questions are answered. The patient is told to keep the SCS area clean and dry. The patient is specifically told not to bathe or shower but to take sponge baths during the trial period. Prophylactic oral antibiotics are provided to help prevent infection. The patient is instructed to avoid excessive

bending or twisting because this may dislodge the trial lead since its only anchoring system is the sterile adhesive dressing. In addition, the patient is told not to alter consumption of medication and to maintain his or her routine activity level. The patient is told to alert the physician in case of any alteration in stimulation pattern, signs of infection, or any other unusual occurrences. The patient typically is seen in the office 5 days following the temporary insertion, at which time the lead is removed and the wound is inspected. The efficacy of the SCS is assessed, and the physician should then determine whether to proceed with a permanent SCS.

The patient undergoing a permanent implantation is brought into the hospital the morning of the procedure. A urinalysis, complete blood count with differential, sedimentation rate, and chest x-ray are obtained. If all laboratory tests are within normal limits, the patient is allowed to proceed with the procedure. The patient is given preoperative intravenous antibiotics and is discharged the following day with a 2-week supply of oral antibiotics. The patient is kept at strict bedrest until discharge to allow time for the epidural adventia to surround the leads, which helps to prevent lead motion or migration.

Upon discharge, the patient is given verbal and written instructions to avoid excessive lifting, twisting, or bending, and to sponge bathe only for 2 weeks. The first postoperative visit is 1 week following the permanent procedure. The wound is checked and the bandage is changed. The second postoperative visit is 2 weeks following the procedure, and the staples (or sutures) are removed. Assuming all is going well, stimulation is begun at the third postoperative visit at 3 weeks. Stimulation generally cannot be effectively performed prior to this time since the pocket incision site is still fragile, and placing the antenna over it to cause stimulation would place the pocket at risk for dehiscence. In addition, there is generally too much edema in the pocket to stimulate effectively. Once stimulation has begun, the SCS programming is fine-tuned and the patient is instructed on its use. The patient is told to notify the physician if there are any problems. Follow-up is monthly for three months and then quarterly.

COMPLICATIONS

There are rarely any serious complications from the percutaneous temporary or permanent procedure of SCS implantation. In one study, one nonfatal pulmonary embolism and one case of paraplegia lasting 3 months occurred.[17] The latter resulted from a laminectomy that was used to place the stimulating lead. Other rare reported complications include sphincter disturbance and gait abnormality.[34]

Most complications from the temporary or permanent devices include formation of scar tissue, poor localization of paresthesias, electrode migration, electrode fracture, electrode dislocation, pain from the electrode, infection, and wound pain.[9,30,44]

In our experience with 82 permanent and temporary spinal cord simulators, we have experienced two in situ infections with permanent devices. One infection resulted from an occult bone stimulator infection from a previous fusion. The second infection occurred 2.5 months after implantation. In both cases, the permanent stimulator units were removed and the patients placed on intravenous antibiotics without further sequelae. We also had three technical failures due to wire fracture within the lead that required replacement. We have had no complications with any of the trial placements.

CLINICAL RESULTS

Original long-term results of pain control from spinal cord stimulation in the late 1960s and 1970s were disappointing. This led to widespread disenchantment regarding SCS use. Poor patient selection, inadequate equipment, and failure to perform implantations with the patient awake accounted for this dismal success rate. The advent of new technology, careful patient selection, temporary stimulator systems, percutaneous implantation, and active feedback from the patient during the procedure have all contributed to the success of spinal cord stimulation over the past 10 years.

The most common SCS application today in North America is in the treatment of failed back surgery syndrome (FBSS). FBSS represents the primary use of SCS in our practice and has provided us with an effective alternative for the treatment of chronic back and lower extremity pain secondary to FBSS.

The largest SCS study incorporates 320 consecutive patients who underwent either temporary or permanent implants at the Johns Hopkins Hospital between 1971 and 1990.[32] This series includes follow-up on 205 patients, the majority of whom had the diagnosis of FBSS. Permanent SCS implants were placed in 171 of these patients. At follow-up (mean interval 7.1 ± 4.5 yrs), 52% of patients had at least 50% continued pain relief, and 58% had a reduction or elimination of analgesic intake. About 54% of patients younger than 65 were working at the time of follow-up; 41% had been working preoperatively.

The percentage of patients having long-term pain relief is similar in the majority of large published SCS series of implants for FBSS. The success rate in most of these studies, which is generally reported as 50% or more pain relief, is approximately 50–60%.[6,16,21,28,35,37] Some studies report success rates as high as 88% and others as low as 37%.[14,41] Although these latter studies differ in implantation technique and screening protocols, the success rate for pain reduction remains generally the same.

More recent published reviews have specifically looked at the effectiveness of SCS in FBSS for pain control, reduction in narcotic usage, function, and work status.[8,19,20,29,30,36] According to these studies, long-term pain reduction (at least 2 years after implantation) can be expected to range from 50–70% in approximately 60% of SCS patients. In 50–90% of individuals, there can be an elimination or decrease in the use of opioids. The return to full employment rate after SCS is low by most accounts, although two studies report a 25–59% return to work.[19,30] The low return-to-work rate reflects the high percentage of unskilled laborers among these patients and the prolonged periods of disability due to pain chronicity. Despite the small change in work status, there is a general increase in function and activities of daily living. The clinical findings in these contemporary investigations have shown significant pain reduction, decreases in narcotic intake, improved function, and return to work for some patients.

We have been placing temporary and permanent SCS devices for the treatment of chronic pain in our practice for 3 years. The majority of patients have had FBSS, but 10 patients were selected for SCS because they were poor candidates for surgery secondary to either multiple medical problems or multilevel disc pathology. A total of 31 men and 26 women ranging in age from 23–66 have undergone the procedure. All but one patient (who was in a motor vehicle accident) represented Workers' Compensation cases. We have implanted 82 devices in 52 patients; 26 patients eventually had permanent stimulators. Among patients receiving permanent devices, the length of time from injury to permanent implantation ranged from 3–12 years (average 6 years). Three patients had multilevel disc disease, one had spinal stenosis, two had causalgia, and the others had FBSS.

All of the patients have experienced subjective pain relief, varying in intensity from 40 to 95%, with the longest follow-up being 2 years. Although only five of our patients returned to work, three quarters experienced improvement in functional activities. The remainder were unchanged. Approximately half decreased their intake of pain medication, but some still take the same medication for chronic neck and upper extremity pain. All individuals continued to use their SCS devices, and all have stated that they would have the procedure again.

Our patients with permanent SCS have had significant pain relief up to 2 years after the implantation. The low return-to-work status that we observed is consistent with the findings of others and s more than likely the result of the subset of individuals receiving these devices. Many of these patients have had one or more surgical procedures to their lumbar spine. All patients were out of work for at least 2 years secondary to chronic pain and disability. Most were previously employed in physically demanding jobs and had a low level of education. These characteristics make it unrealistic to expect a high return-to-work rate regardless of the intervention. Nevertheless, these patients had a significant subjective decrease in pain and most had an increase in function. Achieving pain control rather than return to work is a more realistic expectation in these patients, but it might be reasonable to expect a return to some form of employment if the patients were treated earlier after the initial injuries and if they had a higher level of education. We may find that intensive retraining and education also may improve return-to-work rates.

THE FUTURE

The future of SCS looks promising with the planned technological advances in these devices. Completely contained permanent transmitters without the need for an internal receiver and external transmitter are expected in the near future and would represent a significant cosmetic improvement. A more powerful cellular battery with a longer life will improve effectiveness of the stimulator and increase the time between permanent stimulator replacements. The arrival of patient-interactive computer-controlled stimulation systems in the clinical setting is expected to revolutionize the programming of the SCS devices.[31] Multiple electrode arrays, transmitter frequencies, and transmitter intensities can be tested to find the optimal combination for pain control. We expect the ideal SCS electrode combination and transmitter configuration to be achieved with this system.

REFERENCES

1. Augustinsson LE, Carlsson CA, Holm J, et al: Epidural electrical stimulation in severe limb ischemia. Pain relief, increased blood flow, and possible limb-saving effect. Ann Surg 202:104–110, 1985.
2. Barolat G, Schwartzman R, Woo R: Epidural spinal cord stimulation in the management of reflex sympathetic dystrophy. Stereotact Funct Neurosurg 53:29–39, 1989.
3. Basbaum AL, Fields HL: Endogenous pain control systems: Brain-stem spinal pathways and endorphin circuitry. Ann Rev Neurosci 7:309–315, 1984.
4. Bonica JJ: Anatomic and physiologic basis of nociception and pain. In Bonica JJ (ed): The Management of Pain, Vol. 1, 2nd ed. Philadelphia, Lea & Febiger, 1990, pp 28–94.
5. Broseta J, Roldan P, Gonzalez-Darder V, et al: Chronic epidural dorsal column stimulation in the treatment of causalgic pain. Appl Neurophysiol 45:190–194, 1982.
6. Burton CV: Session on spinal cord stimulation: Safety and clinical efficacy. Neurosurgery 1:164–165, 1977.
7. Campbell JN: Examination of possible mechanisms by which stimulation of the spinal cord in man relieves pain. Appl Neurophysiol 44:181–186, 1981.
8. De La Porte C, Van de Kelft E: Spinal cord stimulation in failed back surgery syndrome. Pain 52:55–61, 1993.
9. Devulder J, De Colvenaer L, Rolly G: Spinal cord stimulation in chronic pain therapy. Clin J Pain 6:51–56, 1990.
10. Fields H: Depression and pain: A neurobiological model. Neuropsychiatry Neuropsychol Behav Neurol 4:83–92, 1991.
11. Hoppenstein R: Percutaneous implantation of chronic spinal cord electrodes for control of intractable pain. Surg Neurol 4:195–198, 1975.
12. Jacobs MJ, Jorning PH, Joshi SR, et al: Epidural spinal cord electrical stimulation improves microvascular blood flow in severe limb ischemia. Ann Surg 207:179–183, 1988.
13. Jensen MP, Turner JA, Romano JM, et al: Coping with chronic pain: A critical review of the literature. Pain 47:249–283, 1991.
14. Kalin MT, Winkelmuller W: Chronic pain after multiple lumbar discectomies—significance of intermittent spinal cord stimulation. Pain 40:S241, 1990.
15. Krieger DT, Martin JB: Brain peptides. N Engl J Med 304:876–885, 1981.
16. Kumar K, Nath R, Wyant GM: Treatment of chronic pain by epidural spinal cord stimulation: 10-year experience. J Neurosurg 75:402–407, 1991.
17. Law JD: Percutaneous spinal cord stimulation for the "failed back surgery syndrome." Pain Management Update 1(1):1–2, 1990.
18. Law JD: Spinal stimulation: Statistical superiority of monophasic stimulation of narrowly separated, longitudinal bipoles having rostral cathodes. Appl Neurophys 46:129–137, 1983.
19. Law JD, Kirkpatrick AF: Update: Spinal cord stimulation. Am J Pain Manage 2(1):34–42, 1992.
20. LeDoux MS, Langford KH: Spinal cord stimulation for the failed back syndrome. Spine 18:191–194, 1993.
21. LeRoy PL: Stimulation of the spinal cord biocompatible electrical current in the human. Appl Neurophysiol 44:187–193, 1981.
22. Marchand S, Bushnell MC, Molina-Negro P, et al: The effects of dorsal column stimulation on measures of clinical and experimental pain in man. Pain 45:249–257, 1991.
23. Meglio M, Cioni B, Rossi GF: Spinal cord stimulation in management of chronic pain: A 9-year experience. J Neurosurg 70:519–524, 1989.
24. Melzack R: Psychological aspects of pain: Implications for neural blockade. In Cousins MJ, Bridenbaugh PO (eds): Neural Blockade in Clinical Anesthesia and Management of Pain, 2nd ed. Philadelphia, J.B. Lippincott, 1989, pp 845–860.
25. Melzack R, Casey KL: Sensory, motivational and central control determinate of pain. In Kenshalo DR (ed): The Skin Senses. Springfield, IL, Charles C Thomas, 1968, pp 423–443.
26. Melzack R, Wall PD: Pain mechanisms: A new theory. Science 150:971–979, 1965.
27. Miletic V, Hoffert MJ, Ruda MA, et al: Serotonergic axonal contacts on identified cat dorsal horn neurons and their correlation with nucleus raphe magnus stimulation. J Comp Neurol 228:129–134, 1984.
28. Nielson KD, Adams JE, Hosobuchi Y: Experience with dorsal column stimulation for relief of chronic intractable pain. Surg Neurol 4:148–152, 1975.
29. North RB, Ewend MG, Lawton MT, et al: Failed back surgery syndrome: 5-year follow-up after spinal cord stimulator implantation. Neurosurg 28:692–699, 1991.
30. North RB, Ewend MG, Lawton MT, et al: Spinal cord stimulation for chronic, intractable pain: Superiority of "multi-channel" devices. Pain 44:119–130, 1991.

31. North RB, Fowler K, Nigrin DJ, et al: Patient-interactive, computer-controlled neurological stimulation system: Clinical efficacy in spinal cord stimulator adjustment. J Neurosurg 76:967–972, 1992.

32. North RB, Kidd DH, Zahurak M: Spinal cord stimulation for chronic, intractable pain: Experience over two decades. Neurosurgery 32:384–394, 1993.

33. Oliveras JL, Redjemi G, Besson JM: Analgesia induced by electrical stimulation of the inferior centralis of the raphe in the cat. Pain 1:139–143, 1975.

34. Pineda A: Complications of dorsal column stimulation. J Neurosurg 48:64–68, 1978.

35. Pineda A: Dorsal column stimulation and its prospects. Surg Neurol 4:157–163, 1975.

36. Racz GB, McCarron RF, Talboys P: Percutaneous dorsal column stimulator for chronic pain control. Spine 14:1–4, 1989.

37. Ray CD, Burton CV, Lifson A: Neurostimulation as used in a large clinical practice. Appl Neurophysiol 45:160–206, 1982.

38. Reynolds DV: Surgery in the rat during electrical analgesia induced by focal brain stimulation. Science 164:444–449, 1969.

39. Ruda MA: Opiates and pain pathways: Demonstration of enkephalin synapses on dorsal horn projection neurons. Science 215:1523–1524, 1982.

40. Shealy CN, Mortimer JT, Reswich JB: Electrical inhibition of pain by dorsal column stimulation. Anesth Analg 46:489–491, 1967.

41. Siegfried J, Lazorthes Y: Long-term follow-up of dorsal column stimulation for chronic pain syndrome after multiple lumbar operations. Appl Neurophysiol 45:201–204, 1982.

42. Snyder SH: Opiate receptors in the brain. N Engl J Med 296:266–271, 1977.

43. Steude U, Abendroth D, Sunder-Plassamann L: Epidural spinal electrical stimulation in the treatment of severe arterial occlusive disease. Acta Neurochir Suppl (Wien) 52:118–120, 1991.

44. Sweet W, Wepsic J: Stimulation of the posterior column of the spinal cord for pain control: Indications, technique and results. Clin Neurosurg 21:278–310, 1974.

45. Yaksh TL: Neurological mechanisms of pain. In Cousins MJ, Bridenbaugh PO (eds): Neural Blockade in Clinical Anesthesia and Management of Pain, 2nd ed. Philadelphia, J.B. Lippincott, 1988, pp 791–844.

Chapter 22

ZYGAPOPHYSEAL JOINT INJECTION TECHNIQUES IN THE SPINAL AXIS

PAUL DREYFUSS, M.D.
FRANCIS P. LAGATTUTA, M.D.
BRYAN KAPLANSKY, M.D.
BARBARA HELLER, D.O.

Injections to diagnose and control pain originating from the zygapophyseal (z) joint should be used as an adjunct to aggressive, conservative spine care. These injections have become an important yet sometimes controversial part of nonsurgical spine care. The value of these injections has been disputed,[17,31,43,44,49] but when appropriately used they can provide both diagnostic information and potentially therapeutic benefit. Fluoroscopically guided contrast enhanced z-joint injection procedures help to specifically evaluate the z-joint as a source of spinal pain.[9,13,18,19,23–25, 28,32,45,46,50,51,55,56,64,66,78,79] These injection procedures also may provide short- and long-term pain relief through the effects of the anesthetic and corticosteroid. Pain relief allows patients to advance through their rehabilitation program more rapidly, which can result in improved patient function.

The lumbar z-joints were first identified as a source of pain in 1911.[37] In 1933, Ghormley coined the term "facet syndrome" referring to the symptom complex associated with pain emanating from these joints.[34] Subsequently, various types of localized, pseudoradicular, and sclerotogenous referred pain have been described from these joints in the lumbar and later in the cervical and thoracic spine.[1,13,26,30,34,41,54,55,79]

Although this chapter reviews the general considerations and indications for z-joint injection techniques (intra-articular or medial branch blocks), it will concentrate on pertinent z-joint anatomy and z-joint block techniques in the cervical, thoracic, and lumbar spine. This chapter will not review or critique the controversial literature related to the potential therapeutic efficacy of these procedures.

GENERAL CONSIDERATIONS AND INDICATIONS

Prior to any z-joint injection, a patient should have a thorough regional spine/extremity physical examination that focuses on the painful spinal segments and any associated secondary sites of dysfunction in the kinetic chain. Plain films should be considered prior to z-joint injections to rule out fractures, infection, or neoplasm. Because there are no pathognomonic findings specific for z-joint mediated pain, further spinal imaging studies (CT, CT/myelography, MRI, bone scans) and other ancillary testing (laboratory and electrodiagnostic testing) may be necessary to help the clinician decide whether other causes such as disc disease, nerve root compression, sacroiliac joint pathology and primary or secondary myofascial syndromes are mimicking z-joint pain. Although no accepted treatment algorithm exists for cervical, thoracic, or lumbar z-joint pain, aggressive conservative care should precede any injection procedure. This conservative care may include oral medication, modalities, traction, instruction in body mechanics, strengthening, flexibility training, specialized manual physical therapy (e.g., direct and indirect articular mobilization techniques, facilitated soft tissue stretching, and positional release) aerobic conditioning, and restoration of optimal movement patterns. The specific details of any therapeutic intervention should be sought rather than assuming "therapy" was delivered as prescribed. Patient compliance should be assessed.

Because the vast majority of z-joint mediated pain appears to be self-limited, the authors advocate z-joint injection procedures only after a minimum of 4 weeks of appropriate, directed conservative care. If pain is inhibiting progress in physical therapy after 4–5 sessions, one may elect for earlier use of z-joint injections, provided adequate time (4 weeks) has elapsed since the onset of presumed z-joint motivated pain.

Z-joint injection procedures are currently the "gold standard" of diagnosing z-joint mediated pain because there is no accepted, proven radiographic, historical, or physical examination findings or combination of findings that are specific for cervical, thoracic, or lumbar z-joint mediated pain. Diagnostically, z-joint injection procedures (intra-articular or medial branch blocks) are useful in confirming a suspected z-joint as either the sole source or as a contributor to a patient's entire pain complex. Either intra-articular or medial branch blocks can be used at the preference of the operator because both approaches are felt to be equally diagnostic.[3,9,22,53] If joint entry is not possible, appropriate medial branch blocks should be performed to block the nerve supply to the suspected painful joint. To obtain diagnostic information and potentially therapeutic benefit, the z-joint should be injected with both anesthetic and corticosteroid. If the procedure is performed only to gain diagnostic information, anesthetic alone should be used. Confirming the z-joint(s) as a significant source of pain allows the patient's rehabilitation program to be more specific. For treatment, intra-articular z-joint injections should not be used in isolation. The analgesic effects of z-joint injections via the anesthetic and/or corticosteroid can be used to facilitate treatment when necessary to advance recovery. Long-term pain relief from intra-articular corticosteroids has been quite variable in open, noncontrolled clinical trials.[13,18,19,23–25,28,46,48,50,51,55,57,66,78,79] Likely, this represents the various selection criteria and heterogeneity of the patient populations studied and the lack of uniformity in postinjection rehabilitation programs, if even prescribed.

Imaging studies provide only anatomic information and cannot independently determine whether a particular structure is painful. Thus, abnormal CT/MRI scans demonstrating disc pathology are not a contraindication to z-joint injection procedures if the clinical evaluation provides sufficient cause to investigate the z-joints.[57,64] Furthermore, absence of degenerative z-joint changes on plain radiographs, CT, or MRI does not contraindicate injection of these joints.[19,22,50,57,64] Also, bone and SPECT scans need not be abnormal to consider the z-joints as putatively painful.[63,71] Pain-inhibited weakness, subjective nondermatomal sensory loss, and extremity complaints should not be contraindications to z-joint injections because these findings can occur with z-joint mediated pain.[32,55]

Prior to z-joint injection procedures, bleeding disorders, infections, drug allergies, and current medications should be noted. There is no consensus concerning the importance of discontinuing non-steroidal anti-inflammatory drugs (NSAIDs) and aspirin prior to z-joint injections. NSAIDs may be stopped 72 hours prior to these injections and aspirin 7–10 days prior. Coumadin should be discontinued 4–6 days prior to the scheduled injection. Preinjection coagulation parameters are rarely necessary except in patients taking anticoagulants.

Patients with diabetes mellitus should be forewarned that there may be an increase in blood sugar after injections of corticosteroids. Appropriate monitoring and treatment should follow the injection. Patients with artificial heart valves and mitral valve prolapse may require antibiotics before and after the procedure, as determined by their surgeon/cardiologist prior to the procedure. Patients taking antibiotics for any active infection should generally not undergo z-joint injection procedures. Patients with fever or a significantly high or low blood pressure should not be injected.

After informed consent is obtained, a precautionary heplock or open intravenous line is recommended for cervical and thoracic injections, although the authors believe this is not routinely required in the lumbar spine. Judicious premedication with sedatives/anxiolytics and not analgesics may be required, especially for cervical and thoracic injections, in order to minimize the risk of patient movement. Blood pressure monitoring is used for all z-joint procedures, although pulse oximetry is generally reserved for cervical and thoracic procedures. Resuscitation equipment should be available, especially for injections performed in proximity to the spinal cord.

Prior to injection, the patient should be examined to find maneuvers or provocative tests that reproduce typical pain. Provocative testing may include manual mobilization, range of motion testing, activities of daily living, and postures felt to stress regional z-joint(s). If the patient does not have pain prior to the scheduled injection, it should be canceled because it will be impossible to make a diagnosis.

All z-joint block procedures should be performed under sterile conditions with the skin appropriately prepped. Fluoroscopic imaging and contrast medium is absolutely necessary to assure proper needle placement and injectant flow. One study on nonfluoroscopically guided ("blind") paravertebral injections concluded that such injections should not be performed without fluoroscopy due to potential complications and the lack of any diagnostic accuracy.[60] After joint entry is perceived with any spinal axis z-joint injection, the minimal amount of contrast necessary to document intra-articular spread and exclude extra-articular spread or venous uptake is instilled (Fig. 22-1)—possibly as little as 0.2–0.3 ml in the cervical and thoracic spine. Continued injection of contrast material will outline the superior

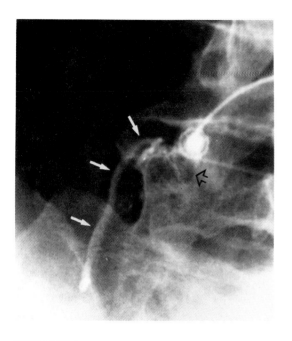

FIGURE 22-1. Anteroposterior radiograph of a L4–5 z-joint injection with venous uptake despite perceived joint entry. The black arrow denotes the inferior aspect of the L4–5 z-joint, and the three white arrows denote venous filling with contrast material.

and inferior capsular recesses that exist in all spinal z-joints. Although a radiographically appealing arthrogram may be obtained, it usually provides little or no additional diagnostic information and only serves to limit the amount of subsequent anesthetic/ corticosteroid that can be injected before reaching joint capacity. Exceptions exist, such as with synovial cysts, which can be visualized by a detailed arthrogram. With a communicating lumbar pars defect, more than 1 ml of contrast medium may need to be injected before spread from one z-joint across the pars defect to an adjoining z-joint can be seen[52,59] (Fig. 22-2). A minimal amount of contrast medium also should be injected at the target location for medial branch blocks in order to exclude venous uptake (even with a negative aspiration) and to assure appropriate initial flow of injectant (Fig. 22-3).

No consensus or available studies exist regarding the appropriate dose or type of corticosteroid injected into the z-joints. These decisions are left to the physician. The most common agents used are methyprednisolone acetate, triamcinolone diacetate, and betamethasone. Most clinicians use a mixture of 25–33% corticosteroid to 66–75% anesthetic for injection into the z-joints.

With all z-joint injections, the injection should cease when a firm capsular endpoint is perceived. If excessive volume is injected or a ventral capsular defect exists, epidural spread can occur, limiting the diagnostic specificity of the block. Throughout the injection and when capsular distension is perceived by the physician, the patient is asked whether concordant pain is reproduced for all or a specific part of the patient's pain pattern. Although pain generally occurs with capsular distention,[26,30] the diagnostic value of this subjective response has yet to be validated.

Because increased risks exist in the cervical and thoracic spine, the injectionist must demonstrate consistent, meticulous fluoroscopically guided needling techniques in the lumbar spine prior to any cervical/thoracic injection. If the injectionist appropriately positions the needle's bevel and concurrently bends the exposed needle while advancing, needle maneuverability is improved. This obviates the need to withdraw the needle and redirect it through additional soft tissues, which may cause a temporary increase in patient discomfort.

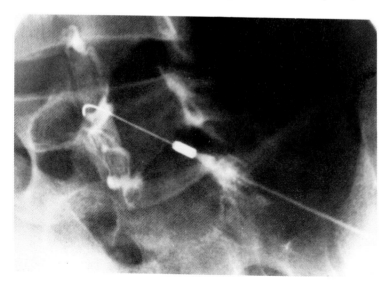

FIGURE 22-2. Oblique radiograph of a L4–5 z-joint injection with contrast demonstrating filling across a pars defect to the ipsilateral L5–S1 z-joint.

Because epidural spread can potentially occur in the cervical and thoracic spine, it is prudent to use the least neurotoxic, nonionic contrast agents, such as Omnipaque and Isovue, in these regions.

One usually begins investigation of suspected painful z-joints based upon clinical evaluation, which may include (1) determining the sites of maximal segmental or direct articular tenderness, (2) mechanical segmental, provocative testing causing concordant pain, (3) determination of "articular restriction" in company with localized soft tissue findings such as facilitated muscle tone,[38] and (4) evaluating for recognized z-joint referral zones.[26,30,54,55] Each clinician relies on a combination of these and other findings to determine at which levels to begin z-joint injections. Although certain levels appear to be more commonly involved regionally (C2–3, C5–6 and L4–5, L5–S1)[13,19,46,57] injections may or may not involve these levels depending upon clinical evaluation.

After the expected onset of anesthesia from a z-joint block, the patient is questioned regarding pain relief. The patient is reexamined with the provocative tests or maneuvers that caused concordant pain prior to the block. Any change in the patient's pain and quality of spinal motion is noted. Depending on the findings after the block(s), further levels above or below the original segment may need to be blocked.

The patient is observed in a well-equipped recovery room for 15–60 minutes depending on the location of the block (cervical blocks require the longest observation), total anesthetic dosage, any procedural complications, and whether sedatives/anxiolytics were administered. The patient should be discharged with a home instruction sheet and a pain diary to fill out over the next 1–2 weeks.

During the ensuing 24–72 hours, some patients may experience an increase in pain that usually abates with Tylenol and application of ice. If fevers, headaches, or neurologic symptoms develop or if unusual pain persists, patients should be promptly evaluated. Typically, physical/manual therapy programs can be reinstituted quickly following the injection. The patient should be reevaluated 1–2 weeks following the procedure.

Controversy exists regarding limitations in the number and frequency of z-joint injections. Most clinicians use no more than three intra-articular corticosteroid injections per year analogous to peripheral joint injections, but no study has determined a "safe" frequency or number of injections. The efficacy of individual blocks should be evaluated; if there is no corticosteroid response to the initial injection, additional corticosteroids should be withheld. Routine "serial" blocks should not be performed.

It is recommended that a different strength anesthetic be used with any second set of z-joint

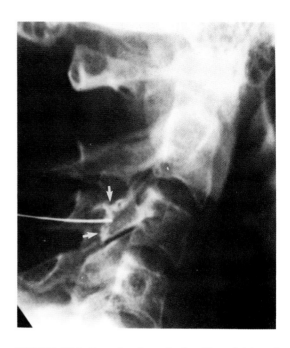

FIGURE 22-3. Lateral radiograph of a C3 medial branch block using a lateral approach. The white arrows denote spread of contrast material along the articular pillar.

blocks (medial branch or true intra-articular) performed on a different day (or better yet, week) than the initial intra-articular block set.[4,22] With this double block paradigm, one can exclude placebo responders without the use of inert agents like saline by assuring the patient has reproducible, physiological responses to different strength anesthetics. The patient should receive adequate pain relief with both sets of blocks, and there should be a longer period of relief with the longer acting anesthetic. For example, there should be longer pain relief with bupivicaine than with lidocaine, with both sets of blocks providing substantial pain relief. This double-block paradigm has been studied and validated to rule out placebo responses that have a 27% incidence in the cervical and a 32–38% incidence in the lumbar spine with single-z-joint block techniques.[5,69,72] A definitive diagnosis of z-joint mediated pain should be made (via successful completion of this double block paradigm) before considering medial branch denervation.[22] Medial branch denervation has been reported with phenol, cryo, or radiofrequency techniques.[33,65,68,73]

Different possibilities exist for the confirmatory second set of blocks. If there was a therapeutic corticosteroid response to the first set of intra-articular injections, two options exist: (1) the second set of injections can be performed with intra-articular corticosteroid alone and concomitant medial branch blocks; immediate pain relief would be due to the medial branch blocks or (2) one could repeat another set of intra-articular z-joint injections with anesthetic and corticosteroid. If no corticosteroid response occurred with the first set of z-joint injections, two options exist for the confirmatory second set of blocks: (1) medial branch blocks or (2) intra-articular injections with anesthetic only.

Excellent, appropriate physiologic relief with the second-block set from either medial branch blocks or intra-articular anesthetic injections with or without corticosteroids would provide confirmatory evidence for z-joint mediated pain. If the patient did not receive long-term relief from the second use of intra-articular corticosteroids with follow-up conservative care, radiofrequency medial branch denervation could be employed without the need for additional confirmatory, diagnostic blocks. This methodology excludes the need for more than two z-joint block procedures before proceeding with radiofrequency medial branch denervation. If medial branch blocks were used to test the confirmatory anesthetic response (either through medial branch blocks alone or medial branch blocks and intra-articular injection of steroids without anesthetic), pain relief following anesthetization of these articular nerves would be studied prior to performing denervation procedures of the same nerves. This avoids relying solely on the results of intra-articular blocks before denervation of the medial branch nerves not previously tested to provide pain relief through anesthetic interruption. Although this argument is theoretically attractive, the use of medial branch blocks to optimally select patients for subsequent medial branch denervation procedures has not been scientifically validated.

CERVICAL ZYGAPOPHYSEAL JOINT INJECTION TECHNIQUES

The cervical z-joints have been shown to be a potential source of pain.[13,25,28,30,66,78] Pain can be referred anywhere from the cranium to the midthoracic spine.[13,30] It was not until 1981 that a z-joint injection technique was first described.[58] Recently, interest has increased in the role of the cervical z-joints in the production of clinical pain syndromes and in the ability to diagnose this entity through selective blocking procedures.[13,25,28,30,42,66,78] A recent report suggests at least 25% of neck pain may be z-joint–mediated without significant combined soft tissue and discogenic pain sources.[1]

Anatomy

The cervical z-joints are paired, diarthrodial synovial joints located between the superior and inferior articular pillars in the posterior cervical column. Cervical z-joints extend from C2–3 to C7–T1. The atlanto-occipital and lateral atlanto-axial synovial joints are not zygapophyseal joints by definition, due to their anterior location. Each z-joint is lined with hyaline cartilage and contains a meniscus.[82] A fibrous joint capsule exists that is richly innervated with both mechanoreceptors and nociceptors.[80,81] The ligamentum flavum covers the internal margin of the joint capsule.[7]

The superior aspect of the joint is the inferior articular process of the more superior vertebral segment and faces forward and downward at 45°. The inferior aspect of the joint is the superior articular process of the more inferior vertebral segment and faces backward and upward at 45° (Fig. 22-4). The inclination of the lower joints is steeper.[29] C2–3 is more oblique in its orientation as a transitional segment, both anatomically and biomechanically.[14] The z-joint's articular surfaces are generally flat with only minimal concavity and convexity.[39]

The joint volume is usually 1 ml or less.[9,30] Both superior and inferior capsular recesses exist with the superior recess adjacent to the neuroforamina and the dorsal root ganglia.

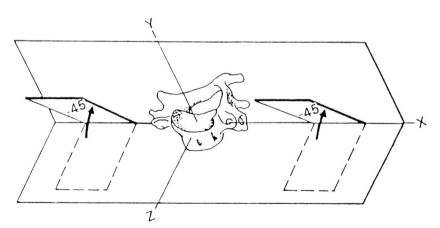

FIGURE 22-4. The plane of the articular facets in a typical cervical z-joint. (From White AW III, Panjabi MM: The basic kinematics of the human spine. Spine 3:12–20, 1978, with permission.)

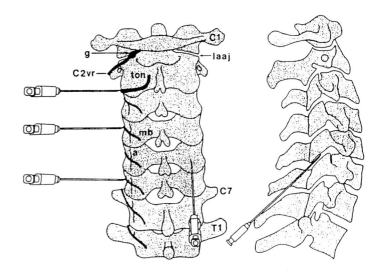

FIGURE 22-5. Proper needle placements for a posterior approach to a third occipital nerve (TON) block, C5–6 intra-articular z-joint injection, and C4 and C6 medial branch blocks. The second cervical ganglia (g), C2 ventral ramus (C2vr) and the lateral atlantoaxial joint (laaj) are noted. (From Bogduk N: Back pain: Zygapophyseal blocks and epidural steroids. In Cousins MJ, Bridenbaugh PO (eds): Neural Blockade in Clinical Anesthesia and Management of Pain, 2nd ed. Philadelphia, J.B. Lippincott, 1988, pp 935–954, with permission.)

Each cervical z-joint from C3–4 to C7–T1 is innervated from the medial branches of the dorsal rami, with each joint supplied from the branch above and below that joint. C2–3 is largely innervated from the third occipital nerve, which is the superficial medial branch of the C3 dorsal ramus. The deep medial branch of the C3 dorsal ramus is referred to as the C3 medial branch proper. Each C3–C7 dorsal ramus crosses the same segment's transverse process and divides into lateral and medial branches. The medial branch curves consistently around the "waist" of the articular pillar of the same numbered vertebrae. The medial branch nerves are bound by fascia and held against the articular pillar. No variation in this location has been reported. The third occipital nerve continues around the lower lateral and dorsal surface of the C2–3 joint embedded in the connective tissue that invests the joint capsule.[8,14]

The anteriorly located vertebral artery ascends through the foramina transversaria of C1–6. It passes directly superior in the neck to the transverse process of the axis, where it then courses upward and laterally to the foramina tranversaria of the atlas.[67] The vertebral artery at C2–7 is located anterior to the z-joints from both a posterior and lateral injection approach.

Third Occipital Nerve Block Techniques

To block the nerve supply to the C2–3 z-joint, the third occipital nerve should be blocked.

Posterior Approach

The target site for blockade of the third occipital nerve is at the posterolateral margin of the C2–3 joint. Because the third occipital nerve is large, it needs to be blocked at three separate sites. Under anteroposterior (AP) imaging, it may be necessary

to move the mandible and teeth so that the joint image is not obscured. A 22- or 25-gauge spinal needle is inserted until the posterolateral aspect of the C2–3 z-joint is reached. The needle is then directed to each of three sites along the posterolateral margin of the joint (Figs. 22-5 and 22-6). The first site is opposite the equator of the joint, the second is at its lower margin, and the third midway between the first and second sites. Adequate blockade of the nerve is achieved using a total of 1.5 ml of anesthetic:

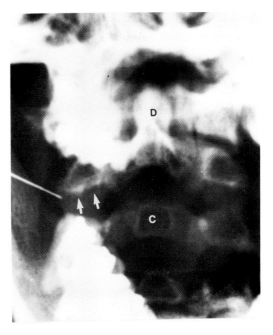

FIGURE 22-6. Open mouth anteroposterior radiograph showing a posterior approach to a third occipital nerve block. The needle tip rests on the posterolateral aspect of the C2–3 z-joint at its equator. The white arrows denote the C2–3 joint line. The dens (D) and the C3 spinous process (C) are noted.

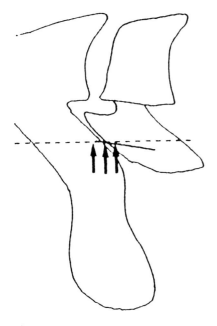

FIGURE 22-7. The target points for a third occipital nerve block using a lateral approach. Three injections are placed along a vertical midline through the C3 articular pillar (*dotted line*). The injections are placed over the joint line (*middle arrow*), immediately above the subchondral plate of the inferior articular facet of C2 (*upper arrow*) and immediately below the subchondral plate of the superior articular facet of C3 (*lower arrow*). (From Barnsley L, Bogduk N: Medial branch blocks are specific for the diagnosis of cervical zygapophyseal joint pain. Reg Anesth 18:343–350, 1993, with permission.)

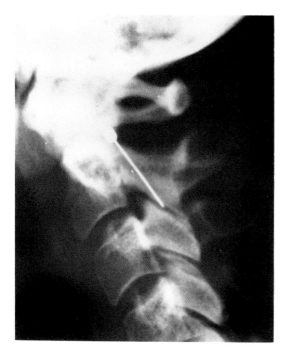

FIGURE 22-8. Lateral radiograph of a lateral approach to a third occipital nerve block. The needle is placed at the middle of three injection sites used for a third occipital nerve block.

0.5 ml of anesthetic is delivered over 30 seconds per site.[14]

Lateral Approach
With the patient in the lateral position, a 22- or 25-gauge spinal needle is inserted toward the target locations for a third occipital nerve block. These target sites are located along a vertical line bisecting the articular pillar of C3. Injections are made directly above the subchondral plate of the C2 inferior articular process, immediately below the subchondral plate of the C3 superior articular process, and midway between these two sites (Figs. 22-7 and 22-8). At each of these three locations, 0.5 ml of anesthetic is injected over 30 seconds.[3]

With a successful third occipital nerve block, a small patch of numbness will occur over the suboccipital area.[4,14]

Cervical Medial Branch Block Techniques

To block the nerve supply to the C3–4 to C7–T1 z-joints, the medial branches above and below the joint should be blocked. For example, to block the C4–5 z-joint's nerve supply, the C4 and C5 medial branches should be blocked.

Posterior Approach
The patient is positioned prone on the x-ray table with the head and chest supported by pillows. The mouth is left free to move. An AP image of the cervical spine will show a scalloped lateral margin. The convexities of this margin represent the z-joints and the concavities the waists of the articular pillars. The C3–C7 medial branches lie at the deepest point in this concavity.

Once the target location is established, the skin is punctured approximately 2 cm lateral to this radiographic point. A 22- or 25-gauge spinal needle is directed ventrally and medially onto the back of the articular pillar just medial to its lateral concavity. Initially, directing the needle to bone assures the needle is not placed too deeply. The needle is then directed laterally until the tip reaches the lateral margin of the waist of the articular pillar. The needle should be felt to barely slip off the bone laterally in a ventral direction. The needle should be directed medially until it rests on bone at the deepest point of the articular pillar's concavity (Figs. 22-5 and 22-9).[9]

For a C8 medial branch block, the needle is first placed onto the transverse process of T1 and then directed until it lies in the concavity formed by the junction of the T1 transverse process and the T1 superior articular process.[9]

Lateral Approach
The patient lies on his or her side and a 22- or 25-gauge spinal needle is inserted toward the centroid

of the projection of the articular pillar, as seen on a true lateral radiograph[3-5] (Figs. 22-3 and 22-10). If necessary, the uppermost articular pillar can be distinguished from the opposite side either by moving the C-arm or rolling the patient. The needle will be seen to travel with the uppermost articular pillar as the two articular pillars separate on the fluoroscopic image.

With both the posterior and lateral medial branch block approaches, 0.5 ml of anesthetic is injected around the nerve once proper needle location is visualized.[3,4] Injections should be performed slowly, at approximately 0.5 ml per 30 seconds, to theoretically prevent excessive diffusion into the local soft tissues.[3] With proper technique, the injectant reaches the target nerve and does not affect any other diagnostically important structures such as the ventral ramus.[3] With accurate needle placement, 0.5 ml adequately diffuses to achieve a successful block.[3]

Intra-articular Cervical Z-joint Injection Techniques

Posterior Approach

With the posterior approach, the patient is placed prone on the x-ray table, and a cushion is placed under the chest to allow for neck flexion. Positioning

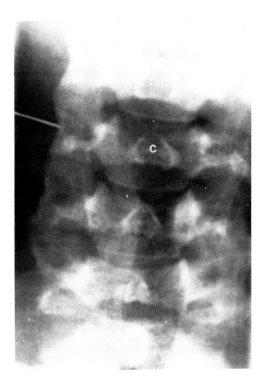

FIGURE 22-9. Anteroposterior radiograph of a posterior approach to a C4 medial branch block. The needle tip rests at the deepest point of the articular pillar's concavity. C denotes the spinous process of C4.

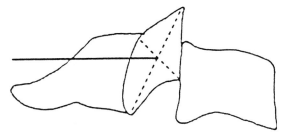

FIGURE 22-10. The target point for C3–7 medial branch blocks using a lateral approach. The target point for injection is the centroid of the articular pillar, as seen in a true lateral view of the cervical spine. The dotted lines intersect at the centroid. (From Barnsley L, Bogduk N: Medial branch blocks are specific for the diagnosis of cervical zygapophyseal joint pain. Reg Anesth 18:343–350, 1993, with permission.)

the patient's head with slight rotation to the opposite side may allow for easier joint penetration. This is recommended by some[65] but not all practitioners.[9] The skin entry point lies approximately two segments below the target joint. It is determined either by directing an imaginary line to the skin along the plane of the joint (as determined by a lateral view) or by directly visualizing the joint via a tangential view of the joint (pillar view) and making a skin mark along the plane of the x-ray beam into the center of the joint lucency.[9] While advancing at approximately a 45-degree angle, one must proceed cautiously to ensure the needle is directed over the articular pillars and not allowed to stray medially toward the interlaminar space or excessively lateral. The needle is advanced until it strikes the articular pillar above or below the target site. Switching to lateral imaging can confirm proper location and assure the needle is not advanced too deeply. The needle is then directed into the joint space, which may require a combination of posterior, pillar, and lateral imaging. The needle should be seen in the joint space laterally and in the midportion of the joint on posterior or pillar imaging (Figs. 22-5, 22-11, and 22-12). Infiltration with contrast medium should confirm intra-articular spread (Figs. 22-13 and 22-14). The joint is injected with a mixture of anesthetic and corticosteroid in a volume not to exceed 1 ml.

Lateral Approach

The lateral approach to the cervical z-joint was first described by Okada[58] and later by Dwyer.[30] Proponents of the lateral versus the posterior approach argue that it is technically less demanding, that a smaller 25- or 26-gauge needle can be used with appropriate operator skill, and that it may be more comfortable because less soft tissue is traversed.

The patient is positioned on the side with the affected target joint uppermost or closest to the fluoroscopic intensifier. It is helpful to pull the

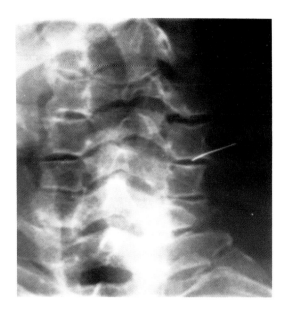

FIGURE 22-11. Pillar view of needle position for a C5-6 z-joint injection using a posterior approach. (Courtesy of Garrett Kine, MD.)

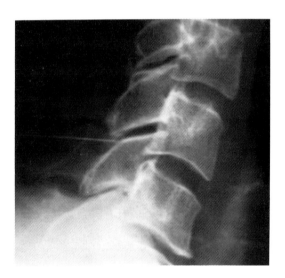

FIGURE 22-12. Lateral radiograph demonstrating needle position for a C5-6 z-joint injection using a posterior approach. (Courtesy of Garrett Kine, MD.)

shoulders down so as not to obscure the joints under fluoroscopy, slightly rotate the plane of the upper torso and shoulders posteriorly, and have the patient's ear lie flat against a pillow in a neutral position. Occasionally, the head may need to be slightly rotated toward the table. Infrequently, slight lateral flexion toward or away from the side being injected is necessary; pillow height can be varied to maximally visualize the joint's silhouette under fluoroscopy (Fig. 22-15).

Straight lateral fluoroscopic imaging visualizes both ipsilateral and contralateral joints at the target level. In order to differentiate the uppermost from the contralateral joints, certain maneuvers are used. A 25- or 26-gauge needle can be inserted toward the z-joints at the target level. The patient is then slightly rolled with the neck and upper torso as one unit. The image of the target joint and needle will then move in the same direction on the fluoroscopic screen as the overlying joint images separate.

Alternatively, the patient remains stationary and the intensifier is rotated so that the ipsilateral and contralateral joints separate on the screen (Fig. 22-16). Depending on the fluoroscopic unit, anterior rotation of the image intensifier can cause

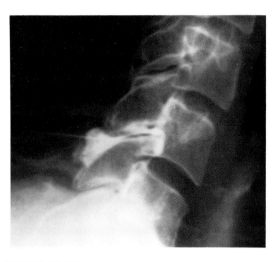

FIGURE 22-13. Lateral radiograph of a C5-6 arthrogram. Needle placement is via a posterior approach. (Courtesy of Garrett Kine, MD.)

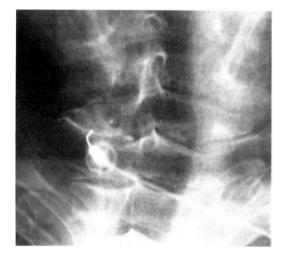

FIGURE 22-14. Anteroposterior radiograph of a C7–T1 arthrogram with needle placement via a posterior approach. Contrast outlines a very thin joint space.

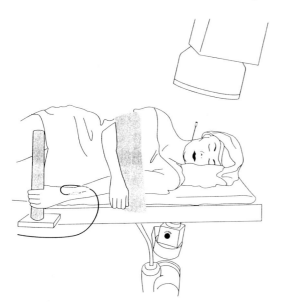

FIGURE 22-15. Patient, needle, and C-arm positioning during a C3–4 z-joint injection using a lateral approach.

the uppermost target joint to move posteriorly on the screen and can be confusing. The movement of the needle in relation to the target joints helps to distinguish the two sides. The relative motion of the uppermost target joint will be greater than the contralateral z-joint because it is closer to the intensifier and the x-ray beams undergo greater dispersion. With a C-arm, better definition of the joint space (increased joint line lucency) can be obtained with a variable amount of cephalad to caudad tilt of the C-arm, depending on the segmental level (Fig. 22-16).

Correct identification of the two sides is absolutely critical to avoid directing the needle toward the contralateral joint potentially through the intervertebral foramina. After the correct joint is clearly identified, the needle is advanced until the superior or inferior articular process is contacted just above or below the joint line. The needle is then directed and advanced through the joint capsule. Typically, the z-joint is more easily entered if one begins slightly superior to the joint and progressively angles the needle inferiorly along the plane of the articular surfaces until the joint is entered. The resistance of the joint capsule can be minimal to negligible. Therefore, switching between lateral and posteroanterior imaging is occasionally required to prevent excessive medial needle placement. Using the lateral approach, the needle remains posterior to the ventral ramus and the vertebral artery.

Due to its unique anatomy, the C2–3 joint is technically more difficult to both visualize and enter. It is not as flat as the more caudal joints, and it tends to be more vertically and medially angulated. Having the patient rotate his or her head downward

to the opposite side may facilitate needle entry. The joint is best entered posterolaterally. Using a lateral approach, after the uppermost and opposite C2–3 articular pillars have been "separated" by the above methods, the C-arm is angled until the joint line is appreciated. At times, because of the more vertical orientation of this joint, the joint line cannot be seen unless the tube is excessively angled such that skin entry along the path of the x-ray beam would begin in the skull. Obviously, this is not feasible. If the joint line cannot be easily visualized laterally or can be visualized only with excessive tube angulation, an oblique visualization is necessary. The needle is advanced down to the articular pillar superior to where the injectionist believes the joint space exists based upon either visualization of the C3–4 joint or of the C2–3 joint space via the previous "excessive" tube angulation. The C-arm is returned to a lateral position and then slowly rotated posteriorly until an oblique joint line is clearly seen (Fig. 22-17). The needle is then guided into the superior aspect of the joint using this view. (Figs. 22-18 and 22-19).

Once joint entry is perceived using a lateral approach, infiltration with contrast medium should

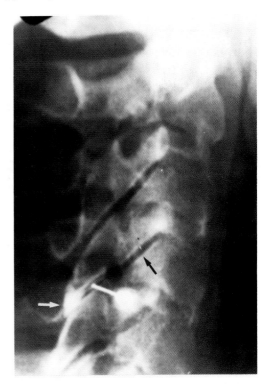

FIGURE 22-16. Lateral radiograph demonstrating needle placement in a midcervical z-joint. A small amount of contrast has been injected (*white arrow*) to assure intra-articular placement. The C-arm has been rotated anteriorly so that the uppermost and contralateral (*black arrow*) joints appear separated. Slight angulation of the C-arm has provided improved definition of the joint line.

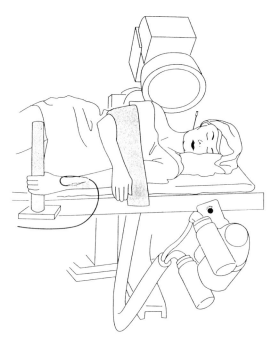

FIGURE 22-17. Patient, needle, and C-arm positioning during a C2–3 z-joint injection using a lateral approach and oblique visualization of the joint.

switching between a posterior and lateral view is necessary, and the needle must be advanced through additional soft tissues, which may divert the path of the needle and necessitate further re-directions. The z-joints are much closer to the skin entry point with a lateral approach. With experience with a lateral approach, an additional AP view to judge depth becomes unnecessary as the operator (1) assesses needle depth by striking the articular pillar, (2) determines minimal joint entry by learning the particular, delicate "feel" of entering the cervical z-joint capsule, and (3) avoids excessive medial needle placement after gaining precision control of the needle.

If volumes greater than 1 ml or forceful rapid injections are used in cervical z-joint injections, the joint capsule may rupture and the injectant spread.[30] In one series, 80% of 142 arthrograms showed that a communicating pathway developed between the z-joint and the interlaminar space, interspinous space, contralateral z-joint, para-extradural space or cervical extradural space when volumes in excess of 1 ml were used.[58] Attempts should be made to avoid extra-articular spread, as this decreases the specificity of the z-joint block.

confirm intra-articular spread (Figs. 22-16, 22-18, 22-19, 22-20, and 22-21). The joint is injected with a mixture of anesthetic and corticosteroid in a volume not to exceed 1 ml.

The posterior approach typically requires more time than the lateral approach for two reasons:

Potential Complications from Cervical Zygapophyseal Joint Injection Techniques

Fewer risks exist with medial branch and third occipital nerve blocks than with intra-articular z-joint blocks. Serious complications from cervical

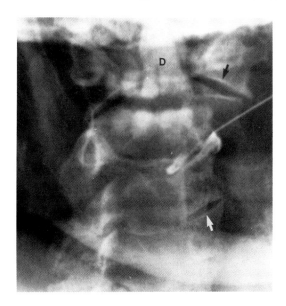

FIGURE 22-18. Oblique radiograph of a C2–3 z-joint arthrogram with needle placement in the superior aspect of the joint. A lateral needle approach was used. The dens (D), lateral atlantoaxial joint (*black arrow*) and C3–4 z-joint (*white arrow*) can be seen.

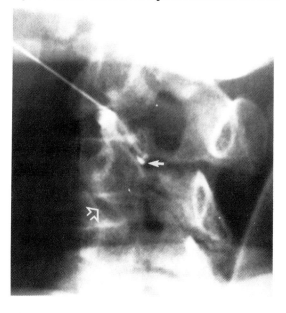

FIGURE 22-19. Oblique radiograph of a C2–3 z-joint arthrogram with needle placement in the superior aspect of the joint. A lateral approach was used. The inferior extent of the joint (*solid white arrow*) and the C3–4 z-joint (*open white arrow*) can be seen.

z-joint block techniques are uncommon when meticulous technique is followed by an experienced physician and the regional anatomy is respected. Minor transient problems such as local postinjection pain and lightheadedness occasionally may occur. At times, ataxia and dizziness due to interruption of the postural tonic-neck reflexes and proprioceptive input to the cervical muscles can occur. This is more common if superfluous anesthetic is used at more proximal segments. This side effect should not outlast the effect of the anesthetic.[9] Excessive volumes or misplaced anesthetics could result in sympathetic blockade. The vertebral artery and ventral ramus is susceptible to injury during a lateral approach if the needle strays anterior to the z-joints. If the vertebral artery is entered and anesthetic is injected, seizures may occur with as little as 1 ml.[21] If air is injected into the vertebral artery, an air embolus may cause severe neurologic sequelae.[61] If overdistention of the z-joints occurs with large volumes, anesthetic leakage into the epidural space may occur with its subsequent effects. Overzealous insertion into the z-joints from a lateral or posterior approach may result in penetration of the epidural or even the subdural or subarachnoid spaces.

THORACIC ZYGAPOPHYSEAL JOINT INJECTION TECHNIQUES

Attention to the thoracic z-joints as a source of pain has greatly lagged behind investigation of the cervical and lumbar counterparts. It was not until 1987 that injection of the thoracic z-joints was reported[79] and only most recently that a detailed description of the technique was outlined.[27] Although cervical and lumbar z-joint–mediated pain appears to be more common, these joints are capable of mediating both local and referred pain.[26] The prevalence of thoracic z-joint–mediated pain is unknown.

Anatomy

The thoracic z-joints are paired diarthrodial joints that extend from C7–T1 to T12–L1. The joint's articular surfaces are inclined 60° from the horizontal to the frontal plane and rotated 20° from the frontal to the sagittal plane in a medial direction (Fig. 22-22). The lateral aspect of the joint is located anterior and the medial aspect is posterior.[29] The superior articular facet is almost flat and faces posterior, superior, and slightly lateral, and the inferior articular facet is oriented in a reciprocal manner. Some variation in the inclination of the joints exists, with the midthoracic joints approximately 60° off the horizontal plane and the upper segments oriented more vertically.

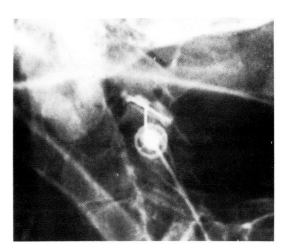

FIGURE 22-20. Lateral radiograph of a C2–3 z-joint arthrogram using a lateral approach. A thin line of contrast is seen in this degenerative, narrowed joint.

The lower thoracic segments show a joint angle that approaches the sagittal plane.[76]

The capsules of the z-joints are attached to the margins of the articular processes. The anterior capsule is formed by the capsular fibers of the ligamentum flavum, and the posterior ligamentous complex blends with the posterior capsule.[77] Intra-articular meniscoid structures have been reported.[38] The joints generally hold a volume of only 0.5–0.6 ml.[26]

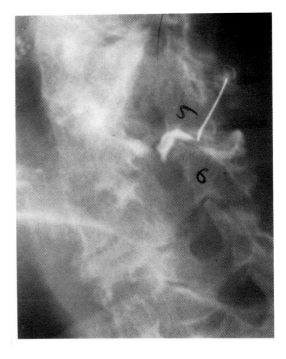

FIGURE 22-21. Lateral radiograph of a C5–6 z-joint arthrogram using a lateral approach. Superior and inferior capsular recesses are easily appreciated.

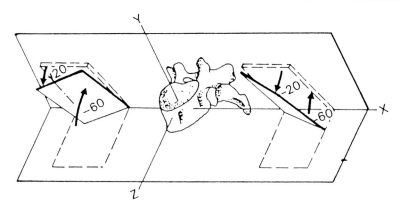

FIGURE 22-22. The plane of the articular facets in a typical thoracic z-joint. (From White AW III, Panjabi MM: The basic kinematics of the human spine. Spine 3:12–20, 1978, with permission.)

A detailed microdissection and histologic study of the human thoracic z-joint and capsule has not been performed. In the primate,[74] the fibrous capsule of the thoracic z-joint has been shown to contain a variety of different sized axons. It seems logical that the human thoracic z-joint capsule is likewise innervated, but this has yet to be shown.

The thoracic z-joints are likely innervated from branches of the posterior rami. Limited human dissections[16] reveal that the thoracic dorsal rami pass posteriorly through an osseoligamentous tunnel bound by the transverse process, the neck of the rib below, the medial border of the superior costotransverse ligament, and the lateral border of the zygapophyseal joint. The nerve then runs laterally through the space formed between the anterior lamella of the superior costotransverse ligament anteriorly, the costolamellar ligament, and the posterior lamella of the superior costotransverse ligament posteriorly. At the end of this space the nerve divides into medial and lateral branches. The medial branch crosses the transverse process obliquely and runs caudomedially between the multifidus and semispinalis muscles. The thoracic medial branch nerve is reported to be consistently related to the subadjacent costotransverse joint at its posteromedial border,[65] as depicted in an illustration generated from these limited dissections.[16] The medial branch divides into three branches, two of which enter the latter two muscles. Articular branches are believed to arise from the medial branch of the dorsal ramus running above and below each joint.[16]

The T1–7 medial branches are musculocutaneous, and the lower thoracic medial branches have a muscular distribution only.[16]

Thoracic Medial Branch Block Technique

Currently, there is no accepted thoracic medial branch block technique; the anatomic studies are preliminary and the definite course of this nerve as it relates to osseous landmarks requires elucidation. Nevertheless, a "thoracic medial branch block" technique has been reported for thoracic medial branch radiofrequency in select patients.[75] The authors state that "a study of the innervation of the thoracic facet joints is still lacking," yet they presume that the target location for thoracic medial branch blocks is at the junction of the superior articular process and the transverse process analogous to the lumbar spine.[75]

Intra-articular Thoracic Z-joint Injection Technique

The patient is positioned prone in the fluoroscopy suite. Initially, AP imaging is used. No rotation should be seen at the levels to be injected. Under intermittent AP imaging, the first joint to be injected is identified and the skin overlying the mid to inferior margin of the pedicle below is marked. For example, if the T5–6 z-joint is to be blocked, the inferior aspect of that z-joint will be located at the superior aspect of the T6 pedicle. For a T5–6 z-joint injection, a skin mark is placed over the mid to inferior portion of the pedicle below (T7) while under AP imaging. A 25-gauge 3½ inch spinal needle is inserted angling up approximately 45–60° off the plane of the back toward the target joint. More proximal segments may require an angle more tangential to the skin. Under intermittent AP imaging, the needle is advanced cephalad toward the superior articular process of T6. The needle should remain on an imaginary vertical line connecting the midportion of the T6 and T7 pedicles. If the needle does not stray medial or lateral to this line, it should be safely over bone. At times, the needle may need to be placed at the medial aspect of the joint where it is more posterior and accessible. The needle should not be placed medial to the most medial aspect of the T6 pedicle on AP imaging or risk entry into the epidural or subarachnoid spaces. After approximately 4–5 cm of needle is inserted or the needle tip is seen to lie at the mid to inferior aspect of the T6 pedicle, the intensifier is rotated away from the side being injected until the outline of the joint is first clearly visible. At times, this may require almost full lateral imaging. Minor rotational

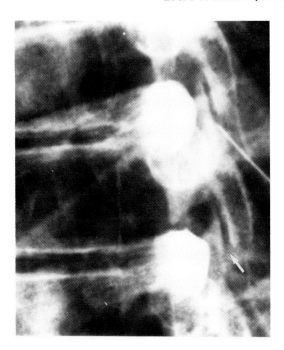

FIGURE 22-23. Near lateral radiograph of needle placement in the inferior aspect of the T6–7 z-joint. The white arrow denotes the target needle location (inferior aspect of the z-joint) for a T7–8 z-joint injection.

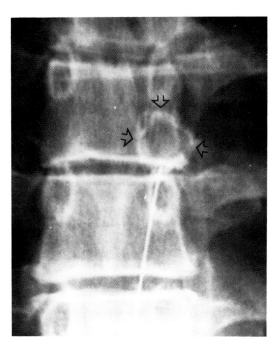

FIGURE 22-24. An anteroposterior radiograph of a T6–7 z-joint arthrogram. The black arrows denote the margins of the joint capsule. The needle tip is in the optimal position in line with the mid-position of the T7 pedicle.

changes to align the x-ray beam with the plane of the joint may be required. On oblique, near lateral imaging, the needle tip should be at or near the inferior aspect of the target joint. The needle is then advanced through the capsule into the inferior aspect of the joint (Fig. 22-23). If upon oblique, near lateral imaging the needle appears that it should but does not contact osseous structures, it should be slightly withdrawn and the intensifier returned to an AP view. The needle should be viewed to assure that it has not wrongly strayed too far medially or laterally. On AP imaging the needle tip should be at the mid to slightly medial aspect of the T6 pedicle and not outside the border of the T6 pedicle (Fig. 22-24). Complications may occur if the needle is quickly advanced and strays from the target location. Once the needle is inserted into the inferior aspect of the joint, a minimal amount of contrast should be injected. The contrast should be seen to fill the joint space and/or the inferior or superior capsular recesses (Figs. 22-24 and 22-25). The total volume injected into the joint generally should not exceed 0.6 ml to prevent rupturing the joint capsule (Fig. 22-26).

Potential Complications

Although some clinicians believe intra-articular thoracic z-joint injections cannot be performed without pleural puncture,[75] complications from thoracic z-joint injections are uncommon when appropriately

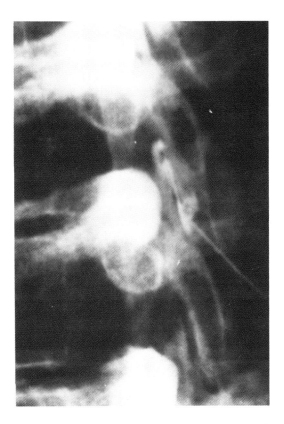

FIGURE 22-25. Near lateral radiograph of a T6–7 z-joint arthrogram. Small superior and inferior capsular recesses are seen.

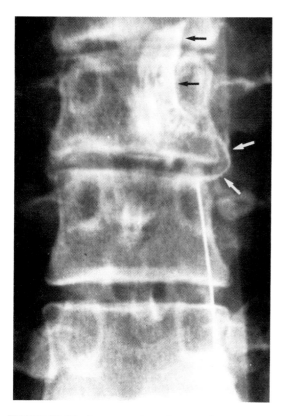

FIGURE 22-26. Anteroposterior radiograph of a T8–9 z-joint injection demonstrating epidural spread when an excessive amount of contrast material was injected. The lateral capsular margin (*white arrows*) and subsequent epidural spread (*black arrows*) are both demonstrated.

performed by skilled injectionists. Most are minor and self-limited such as local postinjection pain or regional muscle spasm. If regional anatomy is not respected or appreciated, misplaced needles theoretically can result in epidural, subarachnoid, or pleural puncture.

LUMBAR ZYGAPOPHYSEAL JOINT INJECTION TECHNIQUES

The lumbar z-joints are well accepted pain generators as evidenced by clinical studies, experimental observations on asymptomatic subjects, and a mass of anatomic and histologic literature supporting the nociceptive ability of these joints. Clinically, lumbar z-joint pathology can cause both local and referred extremity pain. The prevalence of lumbar z-joint pain based upon single diagnostic blocks has been reported to range from 7.7–75%.[17-19, 23,32,40,46,48,50,55–57,62,64] Recent inquiry using a double-block diagnostic paradigm places the prevalence at approximately 15% in chronic low back pain.[70]

Anatomy

The lumbar z-joints are paired synovial joints that vary in shape and orientation.[15] The joints may be flat or curved in a "C" or "J" shape. The average orientation of the L4–5 and L5–S1 z-joints with respect to the sagittal plane is 45° (Fig. 22-27). The more superior joints tend to be oriented in the sagittal plane. The more inferior joints can, at times, be oriented in the frontal plane.

The articular surface is covered with hyaline cartilage, and meniscus structures exist in these joints.[10] The dorsal, superior, and inferior margins of the joint are enclosed by a strong, 1-mm thick fibrous capsule.[20] At the superior and inferior poles of the joint, this capsule creates two subcapsular recesses containing adipose tissue. Anteriorly, the capsule is replaced by the ligamentum flavum. Fascicles of the multifidus muscle attach to the joint capsule, potentially preventing the capsule from being compressed by moving articular surfaces.[15,47] The capsule of the lumbar z-joints is richly innervated with encapsulated, unencapsulated, and free nerve endings.[2,81] Nociceptive nerves have been reported in the joint capsule[35] and substance P-containing nerves have been isolated in the subchondral bone of degenerative lumbar z-joints.[6] The capacity of the lumbar z-joint is approximately 1–2 ml.[36,62]

The lumbar z-joints are innervated by the medial branches of the dorsal rami of L1 through L5.[11,12,15] The L1–4 dorsal rami divide off the spinal nerves and then divide into lateral, intermediate, and medial branches. The fifth dorsal ramus divides

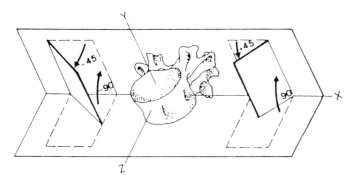

FIGURE 22-27. The plane of the articular facets in a typical lumbar z-joint. (From White AW III, Panjabi MM: The basic kinematics of the human spine. Spine 3:12–20, 1978, with permission.)

into medial and intermediate branches only. The intermediate and lateral branches of the L1–5 dorsal rami enter the erector spinae muscles of the back. Each L1–4 medial branch nerve crosses the base of the superior articular process at its junction with the transverse process. Within 1 cm, the medial branch enters the mammillary–accessory notch under the mammillary–accessory ligament.[22] After exiting this notch, the medial branch supplies articular branches to the z-joint above. It then courses inferiorly across the lamina to supply the interspinous ligament and muscles, the multifidus muscle, and the superior aspect of the z-joint below. The L5 dorsal ramus crosses the ala of the sacrum rather than the transverse process. It then runs in a groove formed by the junction of the sacral ala and the root of the superior articular process of S1. The L5 dorsal ramus divides into medial and intermediate branches at the base of the L5–S1 z-joint. The medial branch wraps around the base of this joint before supplying it and then enters the multifidus. Each L1–4 lumbar medial branch nerve lies across the transverse process of the vertebrae below. For example, the L3 medial branch is located at the junction of the superior articular process and transverse process of L4.[11,12,15]

Lumbar Medial Branch Block Techniques

To block the nerve supply to each lumbar z-joint, two medial branch blocks are necessary due to its dual innervation.[9,22,26a] For example, to anesthetize the nerve supply to the L5–S1 z-joint, one would block the L4 medial branch at the transverse process of L5 and the L5 dorsal ramus at the ala of the sacrum. It has been suggested that a communicating branch from the dorsal ramus of S1 may provide additional supply to the L5–S1 joint and can be blocked just above its exit from the S1 posterior foramina.[22] L4–5 would be blocked by anesthetizing the L3 medial branch at the transverse process of L4 and L4 at the transverse process of L5.

A superior-to-inferior needle approach to medial branch blocks is recommended.[22] The patient is placed prone and a skin mark (and subsequent skin entry) made cephalad and lateral to the target location using AP imaging. Thus, the needle will be directed inferior, medial, and caudad to reach the target location. Theoretically, if an inferior-to-superior needle approach is used, the injected anesthetic may spread toward the spinal nerve root or the sinuvertebral nerve, substantially decreasing the block's specificity.[22] The target location for L1–4 medial branches is at "the dorsal surface of the transverse process just caudal to the most medial end of the superior edge of the transverse process."[12] The nerve should be blocked proximal to the mamilloaccessory ligament and notch.[22] Optimal needle

placement to prevent inadvertent flow toward the neuroforamina is at the mid rather than the superior (proximal) portion of the nerve as it lies in the osseous groove between the superior articular and transverse processes[26] (Figs. 22-29 and 22-30). The target point for the L5 dorsal ramus is in the groove between the ala of the sacrum and the S1 superior articular process[12,22] (Figs. 22-28, 22-29 and 22-31). Optimal needle placement to prevent inadvertent flow toward the L5 or S1 neuroforamina appears to be between the superior and mid positions of the nerve in this osseous groove. Theoretically, if the bevel faces medial rather than superior or inferior it may decrease the chance of partial neuroforaminal spread[26] (Figs. 22-29 and 22-31).

A 22- or 25-gauge spinal needle can be used. From the skin entry point using AP imaging, the needle is advanced toward the back of the root of the transverse process to assure safe needle depth away from the ventral ramus. The needle is then directed to the target location (Fig. 22-29). Switching to an oblique view can be quite helpful for all lumbar medial branch blocks to help guide the needle tip to its target location. In general, for L1–4 medial branch blocks a 25–45-degree angle is necessary, depending on the level, to maximally visualize the osseous landmarks of the "scotty

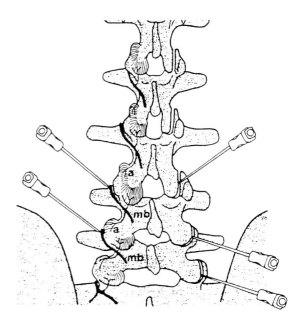

FIGURE 22-28. Needle placement for left L3 and L4 medial branch (mb) blocks in relation to the articular facets (a) and the transverse processes. Although not marked, the location of the L5 dorsal ramus in relation to the ala of the sacrum and the L5–S1 z-joint can be seen. Needles are also placed in the right L3–4, L4–5, and L5–S1 joints. (From Bogduk N: Back pain: Zygapophyseal blocks and epidural steroids. In Cousins MJ, Bridenbaugh PO (eds): Neural Blockade in Clinical Anesthesia and Management of Pain, 2nd ed. Philadelphia, J.B. Lippincott, 1988, pp 935–954, with permission.)

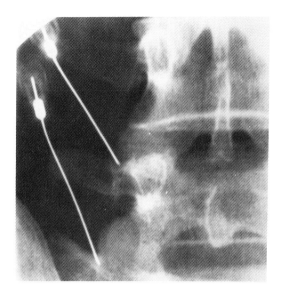

FIGURE 22-29. Anteroposterior radiograph demonstrating needle placement for a L4 medial branch block and a L5 dorsal ramus block.

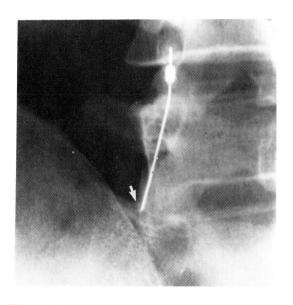

FIGURE 22-31. Slightly oblique radiograph demonstrating needle placement for a L5 dorsal ramus block. The white arrow points to the junction of the sacral ala and the superior articular process of S1.

dog." With needle placement at the mid L1–4 medial branch nerves, the needle tip appears to be in the middle of the "eye" of the scotty dog on the oblique projection (Fig. 22-30).[12,26] Needle placement at the superior (proximal) portion of the medial branch nerve is not recommended owing to a higher incidence of injectant spread toward the neuroforamina.[26a] If the needle is placed at the proximal location of the medial branch nerve as depicted in the figures from Fox and Rizzoli,[33] the needle tip will appear

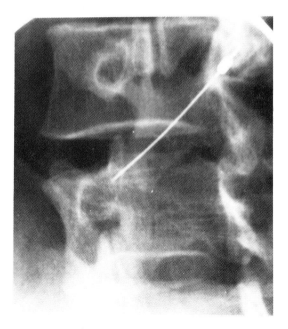

FIGURE 22-30. Oblique radiograph demonstrating needle placement for a L4 medial branch block.

at the superior and lateral portion of the eye of the scotty dog. For a L5 dorsal ramus block, a 10–15° oblique view can be helpful to optimally view the junction of the sacral ala and the superior articular process of S1 (Fig. 22-31).

A direct rather than a superior-to-inferior and lateral-to-medial needle approach may be easier for L5 dorsal rami blocks and provide equal, if not better, injectant spread.[26a]

For L1–4 medial branch blocks and L5 dorsal rami blocks, 0.5 ml of anesthetic should be slowly injected over the target nerve.[22] Injections should be performed slowly at approximately 0.5 ml per 30 seconds to theoretically prevent excessive diffusion into the local soft tissues.

Intra-articular Lumbar Z-joint Injection Techniques

With the patient prone on the fluoroscopy table, pillows are placed under the abdomen to attempt to "open" the z-joints, making needle entry easier. The cephalad lumbar z-joints are more sagittally oriented and can often be visualized on direct AP views. The more inferior z-joints generally require oblique imaging to visualize the joint space. If necessary, either the patient or the C-arm is rotated obliquely until the posterior joint space is first visualized. In curved joints, rotating the C-arm to the point where the joint space is best seen is likely to image the anterior rather than the posterior aspect of the joint where needle entry occurs.[22] Once the joint is visualized, a skin mark is made and in the line of the x-ray beam a needle is directed toward the z-joint. If the superior or inferior articular processes are encountered, safe needle depth can be determined. The needle is then gently repositioned until it is felt to enter the joint space. The posterior joint capsule is relatively firm, and there is a characteristic "feel" when the needle penetrates this capsule. The needle need not be advanced completely into the joint but just a few millimeters past the joint capsule. If the needle is advanced too firmly, it is possible to wedge the needle in the articular cartilage. This may potentially damage the articular cartilage and/or impede the flow of the injectant. At times, anatomically, it is impossible to advance the needle into the posterior joint space. When this occurs, options still remain to obtain intracapsular placement of the injectant. While remaining near the posterior joint margin, the needle can be advanced slightly medially or laterally so that the needle tip penetrates the joint capsule medial to its attachment on the articular processes. This may require slight rotations of the bevel to obtain an arthrogram with contrast injection. The needle can also be directed into either the superior or inferior capsular pockets. The needle should be carefully "walked off" either the superior or inferior aspect of the articular processes into the capsular pockets, but not excessively, or risk overpenetration through these recesses. Upon injection of contrast medium with the above techniques, filling of the entire joint cavity should occur (Figs. 22-32, 22-33, and 22-34).

Occasionally the L4–5 or, more frequently, the L5–S1 z-joint is in or near the frontal plane so that very oblique or lateral imaging is needed to visualize

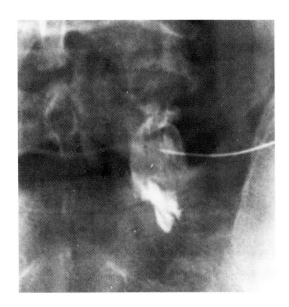

FIGURE 22-33. Anteroposterior radiograph of a L5–S1 z-joint arthrogram. The needle is placed in the mid-portion of the joint.

the joint space. The skin entry point that pertains with the direction of the x-ray beam is then located over the iliac crest, which obstructs use of this approach. If this occurs, a direct posterior approach

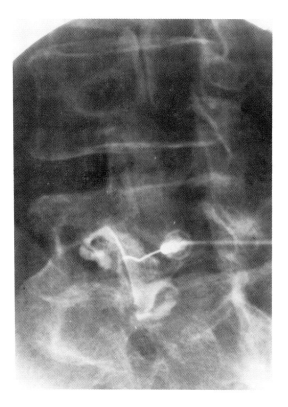

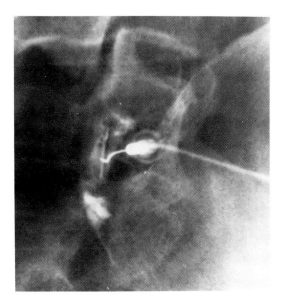

FIGURE 22-32. Oblique radiograph of a L5–S1 z-joint arthrogram. The needle is placed in the mid-portion of the joint.

FIGURE 22-34. Oblique radiograph of a L5–S1 z-joint arthrogram. Superior and inferior capsular recesses are demonstrated.

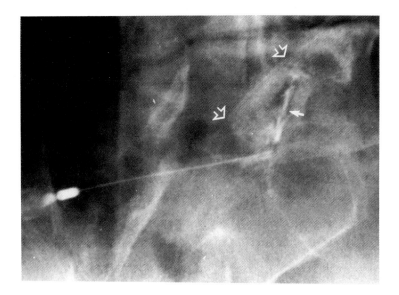

FIGURE 22-35. Near lateral radiograph of a L5–S1 z-joint arthrogram using a direct posterior approach. The needle is placed in the inferior aspect of the joint. Contrast material is seen in the joint (*closed white arrow*), and the margin of the iliac crest is appreciated (*open white arrows*).

can be used. A lateral skin mark is placed pertaining to the inferior aspect of the joint on very oblique or lateral imaging, and the C-arm is then brought back to AP imaging. A horizontal line is drawn perpendicular to the long axis of the spine that intersects this lateral skin mark. On AP imaging, a medial skin mark is placed along this horizontal line or just inferior to it and should also be located lateral to the interlaminar space where the mid-portion of the inferior aspect of the z-joint should exist. Under AP imaging, the needle is inserted directly down or down with a slight superior tilt (if the medial skin mark was placed just inferior to the horizontal line) to the inferior aspect of the joint. The needle should

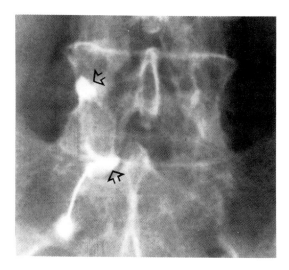

FIGURE 22-36. Anteroposterior radiograph of a L5–S1 z-joint arthrogram using a direct posterior approach. The needle is placed in the inferior capsular recess. Superior and inferior capsular recesses (*open black arrows*) are demonstrated.

not be allowed to stray too far medial into the interlaminar space or too far lateral away from the z-joint. When bone is contacted, the C-arm is rotated until the joint space is seen and the needle is then directed into either the inferior aspect of the joint or the inferior capsular recess. Injection of contrast material will reveal spread throughout the joint space when appropriately placed (Figs. 22-35 and 22-36). If appropriate spread of contrast material does not occur, switching between AP and very oblique or lateral imaging is helpful to guide the needle into the target location.

The lumbar z-joints should generally not be injected with more than 1.5 ml of volume to avoid spread of the injectant posterior to the joint or into the epidural space.[22] If pressure is generated prior to this volume, the injection should cease or risk rupturing the joint capsule and causing extravasation of the injectant.

Potential Complications

Complications from lumbar z-joint block procedures are rare. The majority of problems are self-limited and are usually restricted to increased z-joint pain, and local needle site pain. Thompson reported chemical meningism from penetration of the dural cuff leading to subarachnoid entry with two-level z-joint injections and a one-level medial branch block. Large volumes of injectant were used, and the descriptions of needle placement and contrast flow under fluoroscopic imaging prior to injection was not discussed.[76] With the use of fluoroscopy and contrast in experienced hands, damage to a spinal nerve root or needle placement into the epidural or subarachnoid spaces should not occur.

SUMMARY

The z-joints may be a source of local and referred pain in patients with spinal axis and extremity pain. The definitive diagnosis of z-joint–mediated pain relies on properly performed z-joint block techniques. These techniques maintain an important diagnostic and potentially therapeutic role. They should not be performed in isolation but in the context of other diagnostic and therapeutic methods. Obviously, many questions remain regarding not only the appropriate technical performance of these blocks but their clinical role in the daily practice of spinal medicine. Answers to these questions will be obtained only through future research efforts.

REFERENCES

1. Aprill C, Bogduk N: The prevalence of cervical zygapophyseal joint pain—A first approximation. Spine 17:744–747, 1992.
2. Ashton IK, Ashton BA, Gibson SJ, et al: Morphological basis for back pain: The demonstration of nerve fibers and neuropeptides in the lumbar facet joint capsule but not in the ligamentum flavum. J Orthop Res 10:72–78, 1992.
3. Barnsley L, Bogduk N: Medial branch blocks are specific for the diagnosis of cervical zygapophyseal joint pain. Reg Anesth 18:343–350, 1993.
4. Barnsley L, Lord S, Bogduk N: Comparative local anaesthetic blocks in the diagnosis of cervical zygapophyseal joint pain. Pain 55:99–106, 1993.
5. Barnsley L, Lord S, Walls B, Bogduk N: False-positive rates of cervical zygapophyseal joint blocks. Clin J Pain 9:124–130, 1993.
6. Beaman DN, Graziano GP, Glover RA, et al: Substance P innervation of lumbar spine facet joints. Spine 18:1044–1049, 1993.
7. Bland JH: Anatomy and biomechanics. In Bland JH (ed): Disorders of the Cervical Spine. Philadelphia, W.B. Saunders, 1987, pp 9–63.
8. Bogduk N: The clinical anatomy of the cervical dorsal rami. Spine 7:319–330, 1982.
9. Bogduk N: Back pain: Zygapophyseal joint blocks and epidural steroids. In Cousins MJ, Bridenbaugh PO (eds): Neural Blockade in Clinical Anaesthesia and Pain Management, 2nd ed. Philadelphia, J.B. Lippincott, 1990, pp 935–954.
10. Bogduk N, Engel R: The menisci of the lumbar zygapophyseal joints. A review of their anatomy and clinical significance. Spine 9:454–460, 1984.
11. Bogduk N, Long DM: The anatomy of the "so-called articular nerves" and their relationship to facet denervation in the treatment of low back pain. J Neurosurg 51:172–177, 1979.
12. Bogduk N, Long DM: Percutaneous lumbar medial branch neurotomy: A modification of facet denervation. Spine 5:193–200, 1980.
13. Bogduk N, Marsland A: The cervical zygapophyseal joints as a source of neck pain. Spine 13:610–617, 1988.
14. Bogduk N, Marsland A: On the concept of third occipital headache. J Neurol Neurosurg Psychiatry 49:75–78, 1986.
15. Bogduk N, Twomey LT: Clinical Anatomy of the Lumbar Spine, 2nd ed. New York, Churchill Livingstone, 1991.
16. Bogduk N, Valencia F: Innervation and pain patterns of the thoracic spine. In Grant R (ed): Physical Therapy of the Cervical and Thoracic Spine. Edinburgh, Churchill Livingstone, 1988, pp 27–37.
17. Carette S, Marcoux S, Truchon R, et al: A controlled trial of corticosteroid injections into the facet joints for chronic low back pain. N Engl J Med 325:1002–1007, 1991.
18. Carrera GF: Lumbar facet joint injection in low back pain and sciatica: Preliminary results. Radiology 137:665–667, 1980.
19. Carrera GF, Williams AL: Current concepts in evaluation of the lumbar facet joints. Crit Rev Diagn Imaging 21:85–104, 1984.
20. Cyron BM, Hutton WC: The tensile strength of the capsular ligaments of the apophyseal joints. J Anat 132:145–150, 1981.
21. Derby R: Cervical Injection Procedures (Lecture). In Cervical and Lumbar Spine: State of the Art 1991. San Francisco, 1991.
22. Derby R, Bogduk N, Schwarzer A: Precision percutaneous blocking procedures for localizing spinal pain. Part 1: The posterior lumbar compartment. Pain Digest 3:89–100, 1993.
23. Destouet JM, Gilula LA, Murphy WA, Monsees B: Lumbar facet joint injections: Indication, technique, clinical correlation and preliminary results. Radiology 145:321–325, 1982.
24. Destouet JM, Murphy WA: Lumbar facet block: Indications and technique. Orthop Rev 14:57–65, 1985.
25. Dory MA: Arthrography of the cervical facet joints. Radiology 148:379–382, 1983.
26. Dreyfuss P, Tibiletti C, Dreyer S: Thoracic zygapophyseal joint pain patterns: A study in normal volunteers. Spine 19:807–811, 1994.
26a. Dreyfuss P, Schwarzer AC, Lau P, Bogduk N: The target specificity of lumbar medial branch blocks (unpublished data).
27. Dreyfuss P, Tibiletti C, Dreyer S, Sobel J: Thoracic zygapophyseal joint pain: A review and description of an intra-articular block technique. Pain Digest 4:44–52, 1994.
28. Dussault RG, Nicolet VM: Cervical facet arthrography. J Can Assoc Radiol 36:79–80, 1985.
29. Dvorak J, Dvorak V: Biomechanics and functional examination of the spine. In Dvorak J (ed): Manual Medicine-Diagnostics, 2nd ed. New York, Thieme, 1990, pp 1–34.
30. Dwyer A, Aprill C, Bogduk N: Cervical zygapophyseal joint pain patterns 1: A study in normal volunteers. Spine 15:453–457, 1990.
31. Esses SI, Moro JK: The value of facet blocks in patient selection for lumbar fusion. Spine 18:185–190, 1993.
32. Fairbank JCT, Park WM, McCall IW, O'Brien JP: Apophyseal injection of local anesthetic as a diagnostic aid in primary low-back pain syndromes. Spine 6:598–605, 1981.
33. Fox JL, Rizzoli HV: Identification of radiologic co-ordinates for posterior articular nerve of luschka in the lumbar spine. Surg Neurol 1:343–346, 1973.
34. Ghormley RK: Low back pain with special reference to the articular facets, with presentation of an operative procedure. JAMA 101:1773–1777, 1933.
35. Giles LG, Harvey AR: Immunohistochemical demonstration of nociceptors in the capsule and synovial folds of human zygapophyseal joints. Br J Rheumatol 26:362–364, 1987.
36. Glover JR: Arthrography of the joints of the lumbar vertebral arches. Orthop Clin North Am 8:37–42, 1977.
37. Goldthwaith JE: The lumbosacral articulation: An explanation of many cases of lumbago, sciatica and paraplegia. Boston Med Surg J 164:365–372, 1911.
38. Grieve GP: Common Vertebral Joint Problems, 2nd ed. New York, Churchill Livingstone, 1988.
39. Grieve GP: Applied anatomy-regional. In Grieve GP: Common Vertebral Joint Problems, 2nd ed. New York, Churchill Livingstone, 1988, p 7.
40. Helbig T, Lee CK: The lumbar facet syndrome. Spine 13:61–64, 1988.

41. Hirsch D, Ingelmark B, Miller M: The anatomical basis for low back pain. Acta Orthop Scand 33:1–17, 1963.

42. Hove B, Gyldensted C: Cervical analgesic facet joint arthrography. Neuroradiology 32:456–459, 1990.

43. Jackson RP: The facet syndrome: Myth or reality? Clin Orthop 279:110–121, 1992.

44. Jackson RP, Jacobs RR, Montesano PX: Facet joint injection in low back pain: A prospective statistical study. Spine 13:966–971, 1988.

45. Jeffries B: Facet steroid injections. Spine State Art Rev 2:409–417, 1988.

46. Lau LSW, Littlejohn GO, Miller MH: Clinical evaluation of intra-articular injections for lumbar facet joint pain. Med J Aust 143:563-565, 1985.

47. Lewin T, Moffet B, Viidik A: The morphology of the lumbar synovial intervertebral joints. Acta Morphol Neerlando-Scand 4:299–319, 1962.

48. Lewinnek GE, Warfield CA: Facet joint degeneration as a cause of low back pain. Clin Orthop 213:216–222, 1986.

49. Lilius G, Laasonen EM, Myllynen P, et al: Lumbar facet joint syndrome: A randomised clinical trial. J Bone Joint Surg 71B:681–684, 1989.

50. Lippit AB: The facet joint and its role in spine pain: Management with facet joint injections. Spine 9:746–750, 1984.

51. Lynch MC, Taylor JF: Facet joint injection for low back pain. J Bone Joint Surg 68B: 138–141, 1986.

52. Maldague B, Mathurin P, Malghem J: Facet joint arthrography in lumbar spondylolysis. Radiology 140:29–36, 1981.

53. Marks RC, Houston T: Facet joint injection and facet nerve block—A randomized comparison in 86 patients. Pain 49:325–328, 1992.

54. McCall IW, Park WM, O'Brien JP: Induced pain referral from posterior lumbar elements in normal subjects. Spine 4:441–446, 1979.

55. Mooney V, Robertson J: Facet joint syndrome. Clin Orthop 115:149–156, 1976.

56. Moran R, O'Connell D, Walsh MG: The diagnostic value of facet joint injections. Spine 12:1407–1410, 1986.

57. Murtagh FR: Computed tomography and fluoroscopy guided anaesthesia and steroid injection in facet syndrome. Spine 13:686–689, 1988.

58. Okada K: Studies on the cervical facet joints using arthrography of the cervical facet joint. Nippon Seikeigeka Gakkai Zasshi 55:563–580, 1981.

59. Park WM, McCall IW, Benson D, et al: Spondylarthrography: The demonstration of spondylosis by apophyseal joint arthrography. Clin Radiol 36:427–430, 1985.

60. Purcell-Jones G: Paravertebral somatic nerve block: A clinical, radiographic and computed tomographic study in chronic pain patients. Anesth Analg 68:32–39, 1989.

61. Racz G: Personal communication. Lubbock, Texas.

62. Raymond J, Dumas JM: Intra-articular facet block: Diagnostic tests or therapeutic procedure? Radiology 151:333–336, 1984.

63. Raymond J, Dumas JM, Lisbona R: Nuclear imaging as a screening test for patients referred for intra-articular facet block. J Can Assoc Radiol 35:291–292, 1984.

64. Revel ME, Listrat VM, Chevalier XJ, et al: Facet joint block for low back pain: Identifying predictors of a good response. Arch Phys Med Rehabil 73:824–828, 1992.

65. Rossi V, Pernak J: Low back pain: The facet syndrome. Adv Pain Res Ther 13:231–244, 1990.

66. Roy DF, Fleury J, Fontaine SB, Dussault RG: Clinical evaluation of cervical facet joint infiltration. J Can Assoc Radiol 36:118–120, 1988.

67. Schaeffer JP (ed): Morris' Human Anatomy—A Complete Systematic Treatise. New York, Blankston Company, 1953.

68. Schuster GD: The use of cryoanalgesia in the painful facet syndrome. J Neurol Orthop Surg 3:271–274, 1982.

69. Schwarzer AC, Aprill CN, Derby R, et al: The false positive rate of single diagnostic blocks of the lumbar zygapophyseal joints. Pain (accepted).

70. Schwarzer AC, Aprill CN, Fortin J: The relative contributions of the disc and zygapophyseal joint in chronic low back pain. Spine (accepted).

71. Schwarzer AC, Scott AM, Wang S: The role of bone scintigraphy in chronic low back pain: Comparison of SPECT and planar images and zygapophyseal joint injection. Aust N Z J Med 22:185, 1992.

72. Schwarzer AC, Wang S, Laurent R, et al: The role of the zygapophyseal joint in chronic low back pain. Aust N Z J Med 22:185, 1992.

73. Silvers HR: Lumbar percutaneous facet rhizotomy. Spine 15:36–40, 1990.

74. Stillwell DL: The nerve supply of the vertebral column and its associated structures in the monkey. Anat Rec 125:139–162, 1956.

75. Stolker RJ, Vervest AC, Groen GJ: Percutaneous facet denervation in chronic thoracic spinal pain. Acta Neurochir 122:82–90, 1993.

76. Thompson SJ, Lomax DM, Collett BJ: Chemical meningism after lumbar facet joint block with local anesthetic and steroids. Anaesthesia 46:563–564, 1991.

77. Valencia F: Biomechanics of the thoracic spine. In Grant R (ed): Physical Therapy of the Cervical and Thoracic Spine. New York, Churchill Livingstone, 1988, pp 39–50.

78. Wedel DJ, Wilson PR: Cervical facet arthrography. Reg Anaesth 10:7–11, 1985.

79. Wilson PR: Thoracic facet joint syndrome—a clinical entity? Pain Suppl 4:S87, 1987.

80. Wyke B: Neurology of the cervical spinal joints. Physiotherapy 65:72–75, 1979.

81. Hyke B: Articular neurology—a review. Physiotherapy 58:563–580, 1981.

82. Yu S, Sether L, Haughton VM: Facet joint menisci of the cervical spine: Correlative MR imaging and cryomicrotomy study. Radiology 164:79–82, 1987.

Chapter 23

ATLANTO-OCCIPITAL AND LATERAL ATLANTO-AXIAL JOINT INJECTIONS

PAUL DREYFUSS, M.D.

Head and upper neck pain can be challenging problems to accurately diagnose and treat. Various innervated structures in the upper three cervical segments are capable of causing upper neck pain and referred headaches.[3] These primarily include the suboccipital muscles, C2-3 disc, upper cervical ligaments, C1-3 nerve roots, and the atlanto-occipital (AO), lateral atlanto-axial (AA), and C2-3 synovial joints.[3,5,16] Confirming the diagnosis of painful upper cervical joint dysfunction is optimally performed via selective, fluoroscopically guided intra-articular injection. This chapter specifically addresses the pertinent anatomy, clinical presentation, evaluation, and treatment of the AO and AA synovial joints relating to selective injection of these articulations.

ANATOMY

Atlanto-occipital Joints

The AO articulations are paired synovial joints located between the occipital condyles and the superior articular facets of the atlas. Innervation is from the ventral ramus of C1.[3] The joint is bean-like, with its long axes converging anteriorly and its lateral edges sloped upward. The joint angle, on average, lies 28° from the sagittal plane and 62° from the frontal plane.[15] A loose synovial membrane surrounds the joint with its laxity pronounced at the anterior, posterior, and lateral joint margins.[11] Capsule extensions to the odontoid and transverse ligaments have been described.[24] The AO joint is large with the surface area of the superior facet of C1 ranging from 103.2–277.4 mm^2 and area of the occipital condyle from 109.76–329.0 mm^2.[23] CT evaluation reveals an average joint space of 1 mm.[10]

A thorough understanding of the regional anatomy is required to minimize the risk of piercing critical anatomic structures during injection of these articulations. The vertebral artery initially ascends through the foramina transversaria of C1-C6. It passes vertically through the neck until the transverse process of the axis where it then courses upward and laterally to the foramina transversaria of the atlas. It exits the foramina transversaria, curving backward behind the lateral mass of the atlas along with the ventral ramus of C1. From the lateral mass of C1 it travels cephalad upon the posterior arch of the atlas, curves medially and superiorly, and enters the vertebral canal passing below the posterior AO membrane.[25] The C1 ventral and posterior rami are situated between the posterior arch of C1 and the vertebral artery. The ventral rami then curves forward around the lateral aspect of the atlas to innervate the AO joint.[1]

Thus, directly inferior to the midportion of the posterior aspect the AO joint are the C1 ventral and dorsal rami and the vertebral artery. The C1 ramus and vertebral artery are closer to the posterior aspect of the AO joint at its medial aspect. Posteriorly, the vertebral artery is farthest from the AO joint at the most superior and lateral margin of the joint[25] (Fig. 23-1).

Atlanto-axial Joints

The AA joints are paired synovial articulations formed from the superior articular facet of the axis and the inferior articular facet of the lateral mass of the atlas. The articular surface of the axis is convex, and faces superolaterally, and the articular surface of the atlas is flat or very slightly concave and faces inferomedially.[14,26] The long axis of the joint is oblique and the medial aspect of the joint more ventral. The superior facet of C2 (axis) and the inferior facet of C1 (atlas) slope slightly downward and laterally.[10] There may be an anterior and posterior joint gap of approximately 3.5 mm,[15] but the main articulation is 1 mm wide.[10] The joint

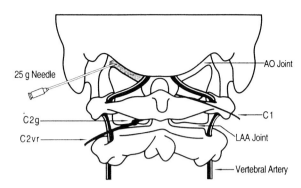

FIGURE 23-1. Placement of a 25-gauge spinal needle into the atlanto-occipital (AO) joint. The relationship of the needle to the C-2 ganglia (C2g), C-2 ventral rami (C2vr), lateral atlanto-axial (LAA) joint, C-1 nerve (C1) and vertebral artery is shown. (From Dreyfuss P, Michaelsen M, Fletcher D: Atlanto-occipital and lateral atlanto-axial joint pain patterns. Spine 19:1125–1131, 1994, with permission.)

capsule is quite lax, which assists in the significant rotation at this joint. Synovial folds exist, which project over the medial aspect of the joint with a 1-5 mm width that tapers laterally.[8,15] The AA joint is innervated from the ventral ramus of C2.[3]

Understanding regional neural and vascular anatomy is important. The C2 nerve roots are intimately related to the posterior aspect of the AA joint. They leave the dural sac medial to the AA joint and travel inferiorly and obliquely across the posterior aspect of the joint. The C2 spinal nerve is short and quickly divides into a ventral and dorsal rami. The ventral ramus passes laterally across the joint and vertebral artery to merge with the cervical plexus. The dorsal ramus passes inferior and posterior. The C2 spinal nerve and rami are bound to the AA joint capsule by investing fascia and are surrounded by

a venous plexus and variable amount of fat.[2,20] Anatomically the C2 ganglion lies opposite the medial half of the AA joint, but from a postero-anterior (PA) radiographic view the ganglion lies opposite the midpoint of the joint's silhouette.[2] Also, from a PA radiographic view the dural sac covers the medial half of the AA joint and the vertebral artery lies just lateral to the lateral margin of the joint.[2]

Upon true lateral imaging of the AA joint, the vertebral artery lies at the middle to posterior aspect of the joint (Figs. 23-2 and 23-3). A study of 558 vertebral angiograms demonstrated no instance in which the vertebral artery was appreciated anterior to the midportion of the joint using pure lateral imaging.[9] However, with rotation of C1-2 the anteroposterior relationship of the vertebral artery to the AA joint changes. For example, with rotation to the right, the left vertebral artery is displaced anterior over the AA joint as viewed laterally. With rotation to the left, the left vertebral artery may be displaced posteriorly.[18]

The internal carotid artery (ICA) passes superiorly in front of the transverse processes of the upper cervical vertebrae, lying upon the rectus capitis

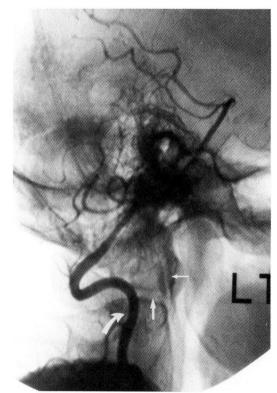

FIGURE 23-3. Lateral radiograph showing a vertebral artery angiogram in relation to the AA joint. The thicker straight arrow points to the target location for needle entry into AA using a lateral approach. The thinner straight arrow points to the atlanto-dental interval, and the curved arrow points to the vertebral artery.

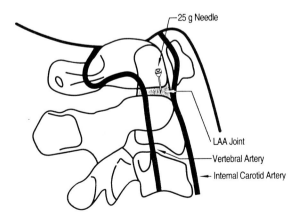

FIGURE 23-2. Placement of a 25-gauge spinal needle into the lateral atlanto-axial (LAA) joint using a lateral approach. The relationship of the needle to the vertebral artery and internal carotid arteries is shown. (From Dreyfuss P, Michaelsen M, Fletcher D: Atlanto-occipital and lateral atlanto-axial joint pain patterns. Spine 19:1125–1131, 1994, with permission.)

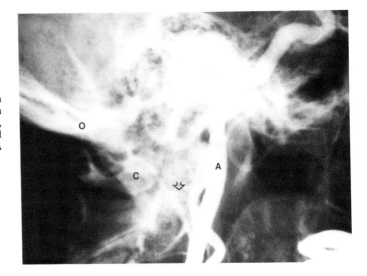

FIGURE 23-4. Lateral radiograph showing an internal and external carotid artery angiogram in relation to the AA joint. O denotes the occiput, C the C-1 segment, and A the internal carotid artery. The arrow points to the center of the AA joint.

anticus major muscle from C1-3 until it enters the carotid foramen in the temporal bone. At C1-2 the ICA is beneath the internal jugular vein, which lies slightly posterior to the ICA. The ICA is separated anteriorly from the external carotid artery (ECA) by the stylopharyngeus muscle, glossopharyngeal nerve, and pharyngeal branch of the vagus nerve.[25] Transverse sectional anatomy reveals that the ICA rests at or anterior to the atlanto-dental space as viewed laterally.[6,21] No studies review the antero-posterior relation of the ICA to the C1-2 interval in a normal or anomalous situation. Thus, this author reviewed 50 pure lateral ICA angiograms performed at a regional medical facility to evaluate athero-sclerotic disease. There was a substantial degree of variation in the anteroposterior position of the ICA. In most instances, the artery was visualized at or anterior to the atlanto-dental interval, but on occasion arterial loops or curves in the ICA brought it to rest at the anterior portion of the AA joint, thus

posterior to the atlanto-dental interval (Fig. 23-4). In no instance was the ICA at the mid or posterior portion of the AA joint. The occipital artery was seen on multiple occasions to cross the anterior to midlateral silhouette of the AA joint after it branched posteriorly from the ECA (Fig. 23-5). Rarely, loops in the ECA were seen to cross the anterior aspect of the AA joint just posterior to the atlanto-dental interval. Furthermore, sectional anatomy reveals additional nonarterial structures located directly lateral to the AA joint that include the external and internal carotid veins, parotid gland, superior cervical ganglion, hypoglossal nerve, and cranial nerves 9–11.[6,21] Interestingly, sectional anatomy from a posterior approach reveals that the only structures encountered upon advancement to the AA joint are regional muscles and the C2 ganglia and nerves. On the posterior aspect of the AA joint, the dura extends laterally to the joint's mid-portion and the spinal cord is located at its most disto-medial aspect.[6,21]

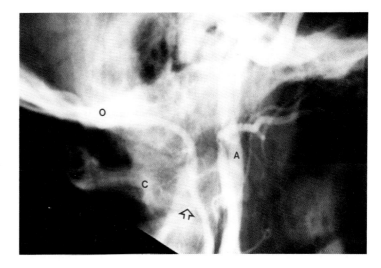

FIGURE 23-5. Lateral radiograph showing an internal and external carotid artery and occipital artery angiograms in relation to the AA joint. O denotes the occiput and C the C-1 segment. The arrow points to the junction of the anterior two-thirds and posterior third of the AA joint. Note the occipital artery crossing the midportion of the AA joint.

OA LEFT

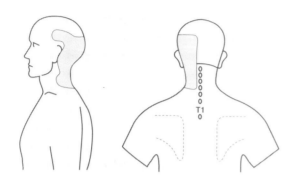

FIGURE 23-6. Composite referred pain map for the atlanto-occipital joint. (From Dreyfuss P, Michaelsen M, Fletcher D: Atlanto-occipital and lateral atlanto-axial joint pain patterns. Spine 19:1125–1131, 1994, with permission.)

CLINICAL PRESENTATION

Patients with AO pain as presumptively diagnosed by a detailed manual examination with subsequent relief from manipulation complain primarily of unilateral suboccipital pain. Pain may spread toward the frontal area slightly anterior to the vertex. Laterally, referred pain approaches but does not include the ear. Rarely, the whole hemicranium or supraorbital regions are involved.[19] Recently, an experimental referral map was produced for the AO joint[13] (Fig. 23-6). This study involved the selective injection of the AO joint with lothalamate meglumine (Conray) under fluoroscopy in five patients. With capsular distension, the predominant referral pattern was suboccipital pain, although occipital and temporal pain that approached but did not include the vertex was seen. In one patient,

C1-2 RIGHT

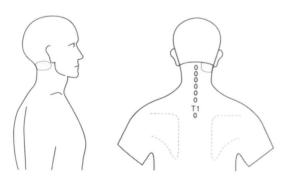

FIGURE 23-7. Composite referred pain map for the lateral atlanto-axial joint. (From Dreyfuss P, Michaelsen M, Fletcher D: Atlanto-occipital and lateral atlanto-axial joint pain patterns. Spine 19:1125–1131, 1994, with permission.)

inferior pain occurred as distal as C5. In another, isolated temporal pain occurred.[13]

Patients with symptomatic AA joints complain primarily of pain localized to the retromastoid, suboccipital, postauricular, or the C1-2 segment lateral and posterolaterally.[17,27] An experimental referral map also has been generated from fluoroscopically guided intra-articular injection of asymptomatic AA joints[13] (Fig. 23-7). With capsular distention, the referral zone was well localized to the C1-2 segment laterally and posterolaterally.[13]

Cervical stiffness, a tired neck, headache, restricted movement, and a constant or intermittent ache are common complaints of patients with AO or AA joint dysfunction. Episodic pain may occur and is greatly influenced by external mechanical factors. Unusual complaints such as visual disturbances, dizziness, nausea, tongue numbness, and a variety of autonomic complaints have also been attributed to the AO and AA joints.[3,5,22]

INDICATIONS FOR AO OR AA JOINT INJECTION

Diagnostic and potentially therapeutic blockade of the AO and AA joints is still relatively uncommon. Precise indications are not uniformly accepted; in general, therapeutic injection should only be considered after all other conservative options have been adequately performed. Treatment options may include physical, manual, or occupational therapy or pharmacologic, psychological, or ergonomic intervention. Although an algorithm for the treatment of cervical facet pain exists,[12] there is no universally accepted treatment approach to AO or AA joint pain. A comprehensive approach that addresses both the mechanical and potentially inflammatory abnormalities in the articulations and soft tissues is desired. Most clinicians use conservative care for at least 4–6 weeks before considering diagnostic/therapeutic AO or AA joint injections.

Because no accepted radiographic, laboratory or clinical examination method is available to precisely diagnose AO or AA joint pain, AO and AA joint injections can be an important diagnostic tool in determining the patient's pain generator.

If less aggressive conservative care fails, the joints to be blocked are determined by clinical history and physical examination. Pain relief after diagnostic injection with local anesthetic confirms that joint's role in the patient's pain complex. Therapeutic injection of these joints usually includes both local anesthetic and a corticosteroid preparation. After successful injection, a period of significant pain relief may occur that will allow for additional therapeutic interventions so that the goals of normalizing soft tissue length and strength relationships, articulatory motion, and mechanics can occur. With this, optional function can be restored, and pain should occur unless confounding factors exist.

INJECTION TECHNIQUES

Sparse information exists regarding the injection of these joints. Although reports of AO injections exist,[7] the exact technique has not been described. A posterior approach to the AA joint has been described[4]; however, a lateral approach to the AA joint was not reported in English until 1994.[13]

AO and AA joint injections hold significant risks and require both excellent hand-eye coordination and substantial experience in spinal injections. A thorough understanding of the regional anatomy and ability to diagnose and treat potential complications is imperative. Blood pressure, pulse, and oxygen saturation monitoring should be used with these injections. Full resuscitation equipment with appropriate pharmacologic agents should be available with intravenous access established prior to the procedure. Light sedation without narcotics is usually provided to minimize inadvertent movement. The skin overlying the appropriate joint should be sterilely prepared and draped. These injections cannot be performed with any insurance of safety unless fluoroscopy is used. Written informed consent must be obtained prior to sedation.

AO Joint Injection

The patient is placed in the lateral decubitus position with the painful side up. The C-arm is positioned perpendicular to the fluoroscopy table. The head is then rotated toward the table approximately 30° and slightly flexed while the trunk

FIGURE 23-8. Positioning of the patient for an AO joint injection. The dashed line illustrates the cleft formed between the mastoid process and the occipital prominens. The needle is inserted in the ideal location.

position is not altered. The mastoid process and occipital prominens are located through palpation and marked with a sterile pen. The cleft, which is located medial to the mastoid process, lateral to the occipital prominens and inferior to the occipital brim, is palpated and marked (Fig. 23-8). At this cleft, a metallic marker is placed and stabilized, or a skin mark is made with a sterile pen. The patient's head is rotated back and forth and adjusted in flexion and extension until the tip of the metal marker or skin mark (as determined by a metal pointer) is seen to lie over the most superior, lateral, and posterior aspect of the AO joint line (target location) unobscured by the occipital brim (Fig. 23-9). At this superior, lateral, and posterior aspect of the AO joint, the vertebral artery is furthest away from the joint (see Fig. 23-1). A lidocaine skin wheal

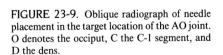

FIGURE 23-9. Oblique radiograph of needle placement in the target location of the AO joint. O denotes the occiput, C the C-1 segment, and D the dens.

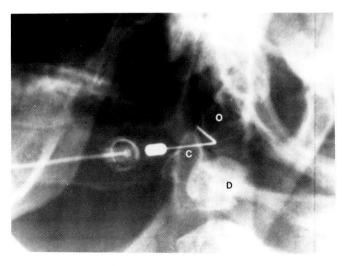

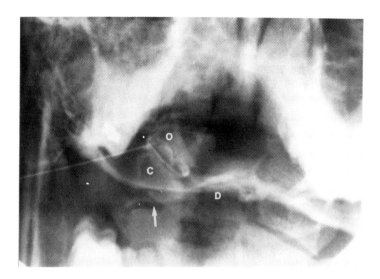

FIGURE 23-10. AP radiograph of an AO joint arthrogram. O denotes the occiput C the C-1 segment, and D the dens. The arrow points to the AA joint. (From Dreyfuss P, Michaelsen M, Fletcher D: Atlanto-occipital and lateral atlanto-axial joint pain patterns. Spine 19:1125–1131, 1994, with permission.)

is raised. At times, skin entry may need to be slightly inferior to the target point to avoid contact with the occipital brim. Under intermittent fluoroscopy, a 25-gauge, 3.5-inch spinal needle is carefully guided toward the target location in the AO joint. Using this oblique view the needle is inserted until osseous contact is made or substantial needle advancement (approximately 3–5 cm) has occurred

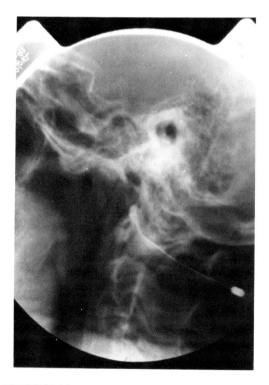

FIGURE 23-11. Lateral radiograph of an AO joint arthrogram. (From Dreyfuss P, Michaelsen M, Fletcher D: Atlanto-occipital and lateral atlanto-axial joint pain patterns. Spine 19:1125–1131, 1994, with permission.)

without osseous contact. The C-arm is positioned to obtain an open mouth anteroposterior (AP) view while the patient's head position is unchanged. With the AP view the needle should be seen just lateral and inferior to the superior and lateral aspect of the AO joint. The needle should then be slowly advanced to enter the most lateral and superior aspect of the AO joint on this AP view (see Fig. 23-1). If on the AP view it appears that the needle should have made osseous contact but did not, the needle may have strayed too far lateral or medial and the C-arm should be repositioned in the oblique view to reguide the needle to the target location. Alternating from an oblique to an open-mouth AP view when adequate depth is obtained greatly assists the injectionist in placement of the needle within the joint while decreasing potential complications. If the needle strays too far medial or inferior, risk of vertebral artery or spinal canal puncture occurs. If the needle strays too far lateral and anterior, there is risk of contact with other neurovascular structures. Once joint entry and negative aspiration is achieved, nonionic water-soluble contrast medium is injected under fluoroscopy to confirm intra-articular placement (Figs. 23-10, 23-11, and 23-12). If any soft tissue or vascular spread of contrast medium occurs, the needle should be repositioned. The quantity of contrast material injected is limited to that necessary to confirm joint entry, which is usually less than 0.3 ml. At times, minimal contrast material may cause pain. An equal mixture of 0.5% bupivacaine, 1.5% lidocaine, and betamethasone (6 mg/ml) is injected. Two-inch tubing between the syringe and needle facilitates injection without needle movement. Injection should cease either when capsular distension and pressurization occurs or when a maximum of 1–1.2 ml has been injected.[13] Any pain provocation on injection and whether this

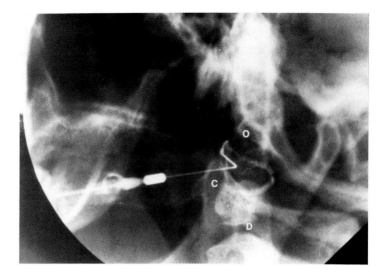

FIGURE 23-12. Oblique radiograph of an AO joint arthrogram. O denotes the occiput, C the C-1 segment, and D the dens. (From Dreyfuss P, Michaelsen M, Fletcher D: Atlanto-occipital and lateral atlanto-axial joint pain patterns. Spine 19:1125–1131, 1994, with permission.)

pain is concordant to the patient's typical pain is noted. The patient may feel no sensation/pain, or the evoked discomfort will be unlike the usual pain or location of pain. Evoked discomfort can be significant and exactly concordant in some before the anesthestic takes effect in a symptomatic joint. Evoked referral patterns are recorded. The needle is removed, the skin is cleansed, and the patient is transferred to the recovery room.

AA Joint Injection

The AA joint may be injected through either a lateral or posterior approach; however, the posterior approach is preferable because far fewer vascular and neural structures are situated between the skin and the joint's surface. One should be proficient in both techniques because the occasional patient cannot tolerate a posterior approach to the joint, thus necessitating a lateral approach.

Posterior Approach

The patient is placed in a prone position without any rotation of the neck. A pillow is placed under the sternum or forehead for comfort and access to the airway. The C-arm and neck are moved cephalad to caudad until the silhouette of the AA joint can be visualized using anteroposterior (AP) imaging. Imaging preferably occurs with the head and neck in a neutral position. Repositioning and movement of the C-arm may be required so that the occiput, mandible, teeth, and any metallic dental work does not obstruct the AA joint's silhouette. A puncture point is selected slightly superior to the joint line and at a point on the skin that overlies the junction of the medial two-thirds and lateral third of the joint's silhouette. Placement at this point is the target location for needle entry into

the posterior aspect of the AA joint. After skin anesthesia is achieved, a 25-gauge spinal needle is inserted slowly through the posterior musculature toward the target location (Fig. 23-13). The needle should not stray toward the mid-portion of the joint, or the C2 ganglion may be irritated. Because this ganglion may lie on the inferior surface of the joint, beginning slightly superior to the joint line may help to avoid irritation to this structure. Advancement of the needle toward the medial half of the joint's silhouette may be complicated by dural and/or spinal cord puncture, and if the needle strays lateral to the joint margin contact may be made with the vertebral artery.[3] With appropriate needle placement, only skin, subcutaneous tissue, and the posterior cervical muscles are contacted before entry into the joint. Once the osseous borders of the joint are contacted or adequate depth is perceived, a lateral view should be obtained to confirm true needle depth. Using alternative AP and lateral imaging allows accurate insertion of the needle into the joint space. The minimum volume of nonionic contrast medium is injected to confirm intra-articular placement without venous, soft tissue, nerve sheath, epidural, or intrathecal spread (Figs. 23-14 and 23-15). Following this, the joint is injected with an equal mixture of 1.5% lidocaine, 0.5% bupivacaine, and betamethasone (6 mg/ml) via 2-inch tubing between the syringe and needle hub, which facilitates injection without needle movement. Injection should cease when either capsular distension and pressurization occurs or a maximum of 1 ml has been injected. The patient is questioned regarding pain reproduction and concordance of these responses to his or her usual pain pattern. The needle is removed, the skin is cleansed, and the patient is transferred to the recovery room.

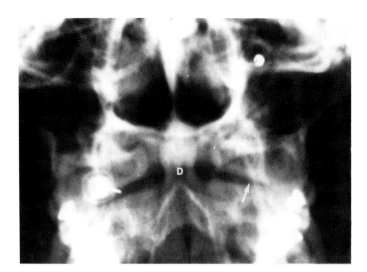

FIGURE 23-13. PA radiograph of needle placement just slightly medial to the target location of the AA joint using a posterior approach. D denotes the dens, and the arrow points to the target location for needle entry into the contralateral AA joint.

Lateral Approach

The patient is placed in a pure lateral decubitus position so that the C2–3 segments are perfectly aligned under the image intensifier with absolutely no cervical rotation. The side to be injected is placed superior. The C-arm is angled in a cephalad-to-caudad or caudad-to-cephalad manner until the AA joint lucency becomes maximally visualized. A skin mark corresponding to the junction of the anterior third and posterior two-thirds of the joint line (target location) is placed. The joint line is defined from the junction of the articular facets posteriorly to the atlanto-dental line anteriorly. A skin wheal is raised with 1.5% lidocaine prior to insertion of a 25- or, preferably, 26-gauge 3.5-inch spinal needle slowly toward the target location (Figs. 23-2, 23-3, and 23-16). The needle should not be allowed to stray anterior or posterior from the target point while advancing. Prior to joint entry the needle should be directed toward the superior or inferior osseous aspect of the joint to assure proper depth. After osseous contact is made, an open mouth AP view is used to guide the needle into the joint cavity. If adequate depth is perceived and the needle has not contacted osseous structures, switching from a pure lateral to an open mouth AP view can be very helpful to guide the needle toward the target location. Because there may be variations in the locations of the vertebral artery, ICA, ECA, or its branches, injection of this joint and needle advancement should be performed slowly and cautiously. With a slow needle advancement and a gentle touch on the needle hub, arterial pulsations can generally be felt when the needle abuts an arterial structure. If arterial contact is made, the needle can be gently repositioned or the procedure aborted. Once joint entry is perceived as felt through the needle hub, nonionic contrast medium is injected to confirm intra-articular spread (Figs. 23-17 and 23-18). At times, the AA joint

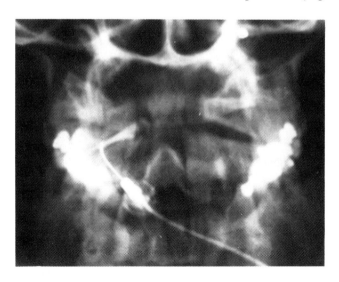

FIGURE 23-14. PA radiograph of an AA arthrogram using a posterior approach wiht the needle at the target location.

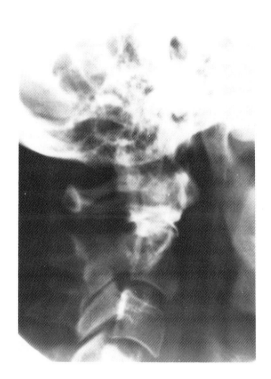

FIGURE 23-15. Lateral radiograph of an AA arthrogram using a posterior approach.

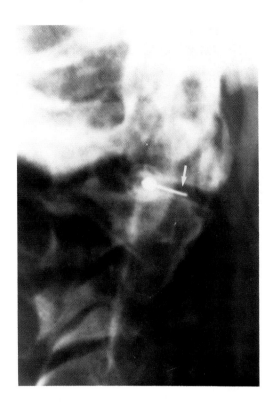

FIGURE 23-16. Lateral radiograph showing needle placement just slightly anterior to the target location of the AA joint using a lateral approach. The arrow points to the target location for needle entry.

capsule may be very loose and the needle may need to be advanced farther into the joint itself to prevent the needle from slipping back outside the joint capsule. The needle should not require placement beyond the mid-portion of the joint to obtain an adequate arthrogram. Occasionally a normal variant occurs in which contrast material flows from one AA joint cross the median atlanto-dental articulation to the contralateral AA joint with only a unilateral injection (Fig. 23-19). Once intra-articular spread is noted, the joint is injected with no more than 1.0 ml of an equal mixture of 1.5% lidocaine, 0.5% bupivacaine, and betamethasone (6 mg/ml). If firm capsular pressure is perceived before 1.0 ml is instilled, the injection should cease to prevent capsular rupture. With injection, the patient is questioned about evoked pain and the concordance of these responses. The needle is removed, the skin is cleansed, and the patient is transferred to the recovery room.

Recovery after any of the above three injections requires observation for 40 minutes with intermittent neurologic, blood pressure, pulse, and oxygen saturation determinations. The local anesthetics should be effective about 20 minutes after the procedure. The patient is encouraged to move the head freely to determine the degree of pain relief. The response to injection is followed over the next 2 weeks by a pain diary that the

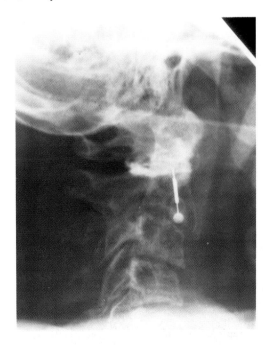

FIGURE 23-17. Lateral radiograph showing an AA joint arthrogram using a lateral approach. Needle placement is slightly posterior to the target location. (From Dreyfuss P, Michaelsen M, Fletcher D: Atlanto-occipital and lateral atlanto-axial joint pain patterns. Spine 19:1125–1131, 1994, with permission.)

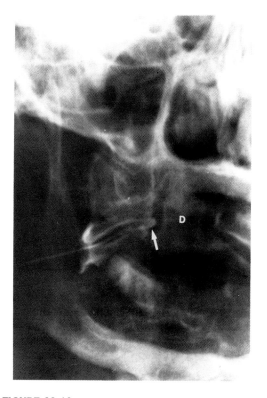

FIGURE 23-18. AP radiograph showing an AA arthrogram using a lateral approach. D denotes the dens, and the arrow points to contrast material filling the medial joint capsule. (From Dreyfuss P, Michaelsen M, Fletcher D: Atlanto-occipital and lateral atlanto-axial joint pain patterns. Spine 19:1125–1131, 1994, with permission.)

patient brings to his or her follow-up appointment in 2 weeks.

Potential Risks

Potential risks associated with these injections include, but are not limited to, exacerbation of usual pain, bleeding, infection, venous or arterial penetration, C1-2 nerve root irritation, and epidural or intrathecal spread of the injectant. If injection occurs into the vascular system and particulant matter is injected, seizures and other central neurologic events may occur. Epidural or intrathecal spread may result in partial blockade of the upper cervical cord function with the potential for respiratory compromise. This can be minimized by avoiding overzealous injection of anesthetic or inappropriate placement of the needle. To date, no respiratory depression or any other serious complication has been reported with upper cervical joint injections. If soft tissue spread occurs using a lateral approach to the AA joint, temporary anesthetization of the lower cranial nerves (9–11) and upper cervical sympathetic system may occur. A systemic or local reaction to any injected agent can occur.

Follow-up After Injection

On the day of the injection, the patient is excused from work and not allowed to drive or operate machinery. Occasionally, there may be an increase in the level of usual pain in the first few days after the injection. If this occurs, ice rather than heat should be placed over the injection site. This abates and the corticosteroids usually exert their effect in about 3 days. The patient should avoid any increase in activity in the next week. Thereafter, activity can be increased slowly. Physical therapy and/or manual therapy usually is reinstituted 2 days after the injection. No literature exists regarding the long-term clinical response to injection of these joints. The author has noted relief spanning from 100% relief on a permanent basis (more than 1 year) to brief relief lasting the duration of the anesthetic only.

If the injection was effective but the results short-lived, one may wish to reinject if at least 3 weeks have passed. One may wish to alter treatment directly after the injection in hopes of obtaining a longer lasting effect by including physical and/or manual therapy immediately after the patient recovers and while the anesthetic is still effective. This may be the only time the patient can tolerate such therapy to establish normal motion in the articulations and/or soft tissues. The author recommends upper cervical injections not be performed more

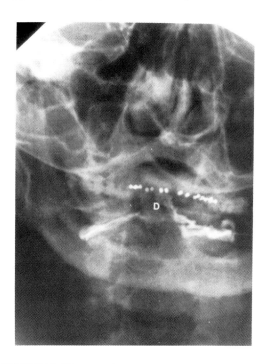

FIGURE 23-19. AP radiograph of a normal anatomic variant. Contrast is filling the contralateral AA joint across the median atlanto-dental interval from a unilateral AA joint injection using a lateral approach. D denotes the dens.

than 3 times a year even though no literature exists that addresses the safety or efficacy of repeated cervical facet injections. If all conservative options have failed but the patient has obtained excellent temporary relief with AO or AA joint injections on at least two occasions to exclude false positive responders, one other treatment option is surgical fusion. Surgical fusion possesses much higher risks to the patient than injection of these joints, and the success of arthrodesis of the AO or AA articulations for pain likewise has not been studied well.

REFERENCES

1. Bogduk N: The clinical anatomy of the cervical dorsal rami. Spine 7:319–330, 1982.
2. Bogduk N: Local anesthetic blocks of the second cervical ganglia: A technique with application in occipital headache. Cephalgia 1:41–50, 1981.
3. Bogduk N: Cervical causes of headache and dizziness. In Griefe GP (ed): Modern Manual Therapy of the Vertebral Column. New York, Churchill Livingstone, 1987, pp 289–302.
4. Bogduk N: Back pain: Zygapophyseal blocks and epidural steroids. In Cousins MJ, Bridenbaugh PO (eds): Neural Blockade in Clinical Anesthesia and Management of Pain, 2nd ed. Philadelphia, J.B. Lippincott, 1988, pp 935–954.
5. Bogduk N, Corrigan B, Kelly P, et al: Cervical headache. Med J Aust 143:202–207, 1985.
6. Bergman RA, Afifi AK, Jew JY, Reimann PC: Atlas of Human Anatomy in Cross Section. Munich, Urban & Schwarzenberg, 1991.
7. Busch E, Wilson PR: Atlanto-occipital and atlanto-axial injections in the treatment of headache and neck pain. Reg Anesth 14(S2):45, 1989.
8. Chang H, Found EM, Clark CR, et al: Meniscus-like synovial fold in the atlantoaxial (C1-C2) joint. J Spinal Disord 5:227–231, 1992.
9. Cox TCS, Stevens JM, Kendall BE: Vascular anatomy in the suboccipital region and lateral cervical puncture. Br J Radiol 54:572–575, 1981.
10. Daniels DL, Williams AL, Haughton VM: Computed tomography of the articulation and ligaments of the occipito-atlantoaxial region. Radiology 146:709–716, 1983.
11. Dirheimer Y, Ramsheyi A, Reolon M: Positive arthrography of the craniocervical joints. Neuroradiology 12:257–260, 1977.
12. Dreyfuss P: Cervical facet pain. In Ramamurthy S, Rogers JN (eds): Decision Making in Pain Management. St. Louis, Mosby, 1993, pp 96–99.
13. Dreyfuss P, Michaelsen M, Fletcher D: Atlanto-occipital and lateral atlanto-axial joint pain patterns. Spine 19:1125–1131, 1994.
14. Duckworth J: Anatomy of the suboccipital region. In Vernon H (ed): Upper Cervical Syndrome: Chiropractic Diagnosis and Treatment. Baltimore, Williams & Wilkins, 1988, p 7.
15. Dvorak J, Dvorak V: Biomechanics and functional examination of the spine. In Dvorak J, Dvorak V: Manual Medicine-Diagnostics, 2nd ed. New York, Thieme, 1990, pp 8–19.
16. Edmeads J: The cervical spine and headache. Neurology 38:1874–1878, 1988.
17. Ehni G, Benner B: Occipital neuralgia and the C1-2 arthrosis syndrome. J Neurosurg 61:961–965, 1984.
18. Fielding JW: Cineroentgenography of the normal cervical spine. J Bone Joint Surg 39A:1280–1288, 1957.
19. Grieve GP: Common patterns of clinical presentation. In Grieve GP (ed): Common Vertebral Joint Problems. New York, Churchill Livingstone, 1981, pp 206–208.
20. Ho PSP, Yu S, Sether L, et al: MR and cryomicrotomy of C1 and C2 roots. AJNR 9:829–831, 1988.
21. Koritke JG, Sick H: Atlas of Sectional Human Anatomy, 2nd ed. Munich, Urban & Schwarzenberg, 1988.
22. Lance JW, Anthony MS: Neck-tongue syndrome on sudden turning of the head. J Neurol Neurosurg Psychiatry 43:97–101, 1980.
23. Mysorekar VR, Nandedkar AN: Surface area of the atlanto-occipital articulations. Acta Anat 126:223–225, 1986.
24. Poirier P, Charpy A, Nicolas A: Traite d'anatomie humanine. Tome 1, Arthrologie. Paris, Masson, 1926.
25. Schaeffer JP (ed): Morris' Human Anatomy—A Complete Systematic Treatise. New York, Blankiston, 1953.
26. Schafer RC, Faye LJ: The cervical spine. In Schafer RC, Faye LJ: Motion, Palpation and Chiropractic Technic—Principles of Dynamic Chiropractic. Huntington Beach, CA, The Motion Palpation Institute, 1990, pp 77–139.
27. Star MJ, Curd JG, Thorne RP: Atlantoaxial lateral mass osteoarthritis: A frequently overlooked cause of severe occipitocervical pain. Spine 17:S71–S76, 1992.

Chapter 24

FACET JOINT NERVE ABLATION

ROBERT E. WINDSOR, M.D.
SUSAN J. DREYER, M.D.

Facet or zygapophyseal (z) joint nerve ablation (FJNA), also known as facet denervation and facet rhizotomy, is used to treat chronic posterior element pain unresponsive to more conservative measures. Facet joint nerve ablation involves the interruption of the facet joint nerve (medial articular branch of the posterior primary ramus). The procedure was originally described in 1971 by Rees,[18] who percutaneously inserted a long knife into the paravertebral muscles and claimed a success rate of 99.8% in 1,000 patients. In 1976, King and Lager demonstrated that the knife used by Rees was too short to reach the facet joint nerve.[11] They suggested that his results must have been on the basis of a myofasciotomy. In 1972, Shealy attempted to repeat Rees' results and only achieved a success rate of 50% in 29 patients.[21] Subsequently, Shealy described the modern percutaneous radiofrequency technique of FJNA.[22]

The literature regarding lumbar FJNA reveals that most authors divide their results into categories 1 (nonoperated back), 2 (previous surgery without fusion), and 3 (previous fusion). Combined results indicate that good to excellent results will occur in 60–80% of patients in category 1, 30–60% in category 2, and only 30% in category 3.[1,5,9,12–14,16,19,20,22,23] This is consistent with our experience. Results for cervical FJNA are believed to be similar, but additional research is needed.

Currently, FJNA is not widely used, and although this procedure remains controversial, numerous studies have reported its efficacy in the treatment of chronic posterior element pain.

INDICATIONS

Facet joint nerve ablation is indicated in patients with chronic, recalcitrant pain of cervical or lumbar facet joint origin. Clinically, facet joint pain is difficult to evaluate but may be suspected when axial pain is greater than extremity pain, extremity pain is in a vague distribution, there are no

neurologic changes, and pain is greatest with extension.[3,6–8,10,15,19] Because this pain complex may be mimicked by other conditions, facet joint pain should be confirmed by diagnostic anesthetic facet joint nerve blocks (FJNB). If FJNB do not substantially relieve the pain complex for at least the life of the local anesthetic, other sources of pain should be considered.

To be a candidate for an FJNA, a patient must have undergone at least one previous successful anesthetic FJNB. (See chapter 22 for details of the procedure.) Immediately prior to FJNB, the patient is asked to rank the intensity of the various components of his or her pain by selecting a number on a linear scale of 0–10. Following FJNB, the patient is instructed (1) to fill out the pain diary as accurately as possible by assigning a number value to the pain every 15 minutes for 8 hours following the procedure, (2) to call if he or she has any questions or concerns, and (3) not to apply ice to the back or take pain medication for the next 4–6 hours because this may alter the accuracy of the pain diary. Patients should be kept relatively "blinded" to the expected duration of action of the local anesthetic in order to minimize the placebo response.

The patient is seen in the clinic within 1 week for evaluation of the pain diary. A pain score dropping greater than 50% for at least 4 hours is reasonably good evidence that the pain is primarily mediated via the previously blocked facet joint nerves. If sedation is used, the first 45 minutes of the pain diary is disregarded, which eliminates any pain relief that may occur secondary to use of short-acting benzodiazepine. Failure of pain to decrease substantially is fairly good evidence that the pain is not primarily mediated via the facet joint nerves.

PROTOCOL

For a patient to be considered for an FJNA, the clinical presentation must be consistent with

238

primarily facet joint pain; the injury should be at least 6 months old and unresponsive to at least 3 months of aggressive manual and conditioning physical therapy; and the pain must still be interfering with daily function.

A variety of conditions other than facet dysfunction present with predominantly cervical or lumbar axial pain and vague referred extremity pain. Potential etiologies may exist in isolation or in combination. Often, patients may have both anterior and posterior element pain due to dysfunction or injury of the entire vertebral segment. Other patients experience pain from both posterior element and sacroiliac joint involvement. In these cases as well as in pure facet dysfunction, patients may derive at least some benefit from an FJNA. In short, additional sources of pain should not thwart FJNA as long as facet joint pain has been adequately relieved by FJNB.

A number of factors should be considered when planning an FJNA. Psychopathology, litigation, and other secondary gain issues may adversely affect the outcome of FJNA but are not absolute contraindications.[14] A patient with medical problems such as severe cardiac or pulmonary dysfunction, coagulopathy, or other bleeding disorders should be evaluated by an appropriate specialist prior to undergoing FJNA; however, very few medical conditions exclude a patient from FJNA.

LUMBAR FACET JOINT NERVE ABLATION TECHNIQUE

Once the decision has been made to proceed with an FJNA, informed consent is obtained and the patient is prepped, draped, and positioned as described for the anesthetic facet joint nerve block (see chapter 22). The patient's vital signs are evaluated. Local anesthesia is achieved with 1% lidocaine or 0.5% bupivacaine. Under fluoroscopy, the radiofrequency (RF) probe (Ray probe, Sluyter probe, Radionics, Inc., Burlington, MA) is angled down to the lateral border of the superior articular process at a 30–60° cephalad tilt. It is placed at the superior portion of the base of the dorsal aspect of the transverse process so that as much of the distal probe is in contact with the target nerve as possible.[2,4] This is important since the zone of coagulation is in a spheroid configuration between 2 × 2 mm and 6 × 6 mm in size, depending on the type of probe used (Fig. 24-1).[4,17] Thus, since the long axis of the probe is in contact with the facet joint nerve, as much nerve may be ablated as possible.[4] If the probe is placed in a perpendicular position to the nerve, only a short segment of the nerve will be ablated. As with the needle in FJNB, the probe placement should be reconfirmed with both AP and oblique visualization if proper placement is in doubt.

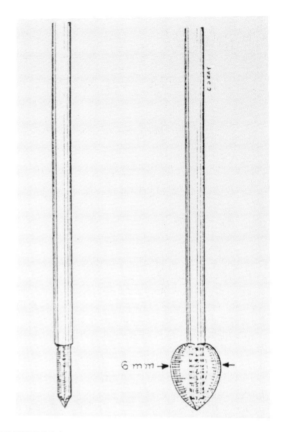

FIGURE 24-1. Zone of coagulation from radiofrequency ablation probe. (From Ray CD: Percutaneous radio-frequency facet nerve blocks: Treatment of the mechanical low back syndrome [monograph]. Burlington, MA, Radionics Inc., 1982, with permission.)

For the L5 facet joint nerve, the probe must be directed to the junction of the lateral border of the S1 superior articular process and the sacral ala. In addition to this site, Ray suggests that the L5–S1 facet joint receive significant innervation from the S1 nerve root (Figs. 24-2 and 24-3).[17] As a result, the probe should be placed at the inferior margin of the L5–S1 facet capsule and the superior edge of the posterior S1 foramen.

After the probe tip has been properly positioned, a test stimulation should be performed by stimulating via the probe with 1–1.5 V and 10–15 W of electricity for 30 seconds. If the probe is too near the segmental nerve, the patient will feel an electrical stimulus in the distribution of the nerve and the position of the probe must be reevaluated and corrected. Once the probe has been properly placed and the test stimulation is negative, the probe is heated to and maintained at 75–80° C for 90 seconds.[17]

CERVICAL FACET JOINT NERVE ABLATION

If a cervical FJNB temporarily relieves greater than 50% of the patient's pain and the decision has

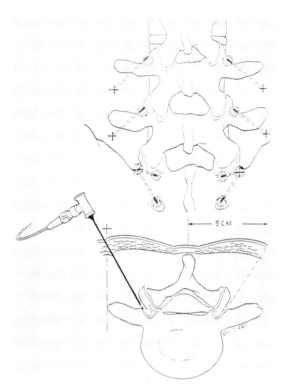

FIGURE 24-2. Proper location for needle/probe to block/ablate lumbar facet nerves and S1 nerve root contribution to L5–S1 facet joints. (From Ray CD: Percutaneous radio-frequency facet nerve blocks: Treatment of the mechanical low back syndrome [monograph]. Burlington, MA, Radionics Inc., 1982, with permission.)

been made to proceed with an FJNA, the same protocol as described for the lumbar region is followed. The patient's vital signs are monitored before, during, and following the procedure. An intravenous line is started, and the patient is transported to a fluoroscopy suite and placed prone and prepped and draped in a sterile fashion. Intravenous sedation

is optional but recommended to minimize the patient's anxiety and movement.

For treatment of the C4–C8 facet joint nerves, the cervical spine is slightly flexed so that the "waist" of the vertebrae is best seen. If the C2 or C3 facet nerves are being treated, the cervical spine should be kept in a neutral posture with the mouth wide open to optimize visualization. The probe is directed down to the lamina of the vertebra at the same level as the inferior articular process of the targeted facet joint until bone is contacted. The probe is then "walked" laterally toward the waist until it begins to slip off the lateral border of the vertebra (Fig. 24-4). At this point, a rubbery resistance may be detected as the probe enters the mamillary ligament. The probe must not be advanced more than 1–2 mm anterior to this point to avoid contact with the segmental nerve or vertebral artery. The probe is held in place and a test stimulation is performed. If no radicular sensation is created, the probe temperature is raised and maintained at 75–80° C for 60 seconds.[24,25] This procedure is

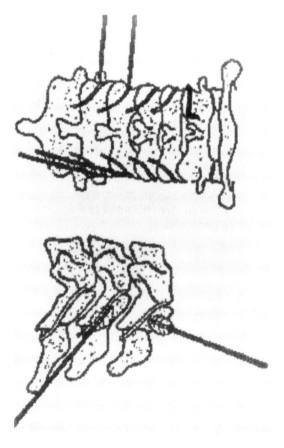

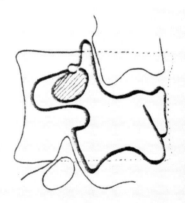

FIGURE 24-3. Placement of needle/probe to block/ablate lumbar facet joint nerve with oblique projection of lumbar spine. (From Ray CD: Percutaneous radio-frequency facet nerve blocks: Treatment of the mechanical low back syndrome [monograph]. Burlington, MA, Radionics Inc., 1982, with permission.)

FIGURE 24-4. Radiofrequency ablation probe placement for cervical facet joint nerves. (From Bogduk N, Macintosh J, Marsland AP: Technical limitations to the efficacy of radiofrequency neurotomy for spinal pain. Neurosurgery 20:529–535, 1987, with permission.)

repeated at the level above to ensure adequate ablation of the descending innervation.[24,25]

POSTPROCEDURE CARE

Following an FJNA, ice is applied directly to the skin over the procedure site for 20–30 minutes every hour for the first day and 3–4 times daily for the next 3–4 days. Patients are instructed to avoid heating modalities for the first 7–10 days. Postprocedure pain may last about 3 weeks, but 7–10 days is more common. Patients are prescribed appropriate pain medication for 7–10 days.

The patient is instructed to avoid showering for the first 24 hours following the procedure, but sponge bathing is acceptable. Patients are also advised to restrict physical activity to a sedentary level for the first 3 or 4 days to help limit soft tissue bleeding and pain. Following this, physical activities should be limited only by pain unless the patient is taking narcotics.

CONCLUSION

Cervical and lumbar FJNA is not a panacea. Instead, FJNA should be viewed as an additional treatment tool for chronic axial pain of predominantly facet joint etiology. It may not affect the long-term outcome of facet joint pain but does appear to provide pain relief in many patients.

Because pain relief appears to deteriorate over 6–9 months in some patients, FJNA may need to be repeated. Previous FJNA procedures do not appear to alter the efficacy of additional procedures. Percutaneous FJNA appears to be a safe, effective treatment for chronic cervical and lumbar facet joint pain. Additional controlled studies are needed to further evaluate the efficacy of this procedure in producing pain relief.

REFERENCES

1. Anderson K, Mosdal C, Vaernet K: Percutaneous radio frequency facet joint denervation in low back and extremity pain. Acta Neurochir 87:48–51, 1987.
2. Bogduk N, Long D: Percutaneous lumbar medial branch neurotomy. Spine 5:193–200, 1980.
3. Bogduk N, Marsland A: The cervical zygapophyseal joints as a source of neck pain. Spine 13:610–617, 1988.
4. Bogduk N, Macintosh J, Marsland A: Technical limitations to the efficacy of radio frequency neurotomy for spinal pain. Neurosurgery 20:529–535, 1987.
5. Burton C: Percutaneous radio frequency facet denervation. Appl Neurophysiol 39:80–86, 1977.
6. Dwyer A, Aprill C, Bogduk N: Cervical zygapophyseal joint pain pattern 1: A study in normal volunteers. Spine 15:453–457, 1990.
7. Ghormley R: Low back pain with special reference to the articular facets with presentation of an operative procedure. JAMA 101:1773, 1933.
8. Helbig T, Lee C: The lumbar facet syndrome. Spine 13:61–64, 1988.
9. Ignelzi R, Cummings T: A statistical analysis of percutaneous radio frequency lesions in the treatment of chronic low back pain and sciatica. Pain 8:181–187, 1980.
10. Jackson R, Jacobs R, Montesano P: Facet joint injections in low back pain. Spine 13:967–971, 1988.
11. King J, Lagger R: Sciatica viewed as a referred pain syndrome. Surg Neurol 5:46–50, 1976.
12. Lazorthes Y, Verdie J, Lagarrigue J: Thermocoagulation percutanee des nerfs rachidiens a visee analgesique. Neurochirurgie 22:445–453, 1976.
13. Lora J, Long D: So-called facet joint denervation in the management of intractable back pain. Spine 1:121–126,1 976.
14. McCulluch J, Organ L: Percutaneous radio frequency lumbar rhizolysis. Can Med Assoc J 116:300–311, 1977.
15. Mooney V, Robertson J: The facet syndrome. Clin Orthop 115:149–156, 1976.
16. Oudenhoven R: Paraspinal electromyography following facet rhizotomy. Spine 2:299–304, 1977.
17. Ray CD: Percutaneous radio-frequency facet nerve blocks: Treatment of the mechanical low back syndrome [monograph]. Burlington, MA, Radionics, Inc., 1982.
18. Rees W: Multiple bilateral subcutaneous rhizolysis of segmental nerves in the treatment of the intervertebral disc syndrome. Ann Gen Pract 26:126–127, 1971.
19. Selby D, Paris S: Anatomy of facet joints and its clinical correlation with low back pain. Contemp Orthop 3:1097–1103, 1981.
20. Schuster G: The use of cryoanalgesia in the painful facet syndrome. J Neurol Orthop Surg 3:271–274, 1982.
21. Shealy C: Facet denervation in the management of back and sciatic pain. Clin Orthop 115:157–164, 1976.
22. Shealy C: Percutaneous radio frequency denervation of spinal facets. J Neurosurg 43:448–451, 1975.
23. Silvers R: Lumbar percutaneous facet rhizotomy. Spine 15:36–40, 1990.
24. Sluyter M: Percutaneous thermal lesions in the treatment of back and neck pain. Burlington, MA, Radionics, Inc., 1981.
25. Sluyter M: Radio frequency lesions in the treatment of cervical pain syndromes. Burlington, MA, Radionics, Inc., 1990.

Chapter 25

SACROILIAC JOINT INJECTION AND ARTHROGRAPHY WITH IMAGING CORRELATION

JOSEPH D. FORTIN, D.O.

Life is uncharted territory. It reveals its story one moment at a time.

Leo Buscaglia

Sacroiliac joint dysfunction as a primary source of low back pain is a resurgent topic. Metabolic, inflammatory, infectious, traumatic, degenerative, and structural sources of sacroiliac joint pain have all been described.[1,2,8,10–12,14,29,38,43,49,50] Still, the concept of mechanical pain of the sacroiliac joint has failed to gain widespread recognition in the differential diagnosis of low back pain.

One glance at a radionuclide scan shows that the sacroiliac joint is an area of high metabolic activity.[15] Like other synovial joints,[5,49] the sacroiliac joint moves,[7,9,13,20,30,39,42,44,46,52,53] is subject to certain mechanical stressors,[26,33,44,47,48,50] and is richly innervated.[45] Cognately, is the sacroiliac joint not an obvious putative source of mechanical low back pain? Why are clinicians reticent to diagnose and treat patients with sacroiliac joint dysfunction?

A host of factors has impeded modern scientific interest in validating the sacroiliac joint as a generator of mechanical low back pain. Paradoxically, at the turn of the century the sacroiliac joint was considered the most common cause of sciatica.[6,22] This theory fell from favor in 1934 when Mixter and Barr described the herniated nucleus pulposus.[36] The traditional philosophical approach to the soma in Western medicine has been a categorical one, as opposed to a holographic vantage. With a logarithmic trend toward subcategorization and subspecialization, it is no surprise that the pelvic girdle and lower extremities are routinely and myopically excluded in discussions on spinal disorders. Major medical texts fail to discuss the widespread neural innervation,[45] anatomic variability,[5,28,49] and unique biomechanical properties[3,11,23–25,40,47,50] of the sacroiliac joint. The

limited number of reports that provide basic science and clinical information pertinent to the sacroiliac joint are scattered among osteopathy, chiropractic, physiotherapy, biomechanics, radiology, and spine journals. Hence, even the scant information that is available has not been widely disseminated. Until recently, there were no studies to demonstrate that reproducible pain could be elicited upon stimulating a normal sacroiliac joint. True intra-articular injections were considered difficult, if not impossible,[4,28] and arthrography had not been described[27,34] except in cadavers.[28] Whether pain patterns exist that might be ascribed to the sacroiliac joint is also questionable. Therefore, the clinical presentation of sacroiliac joint dysfunction has remained obscure.

The author and coworkers have recently applied provocative injections and arthrography to (1) describe sacroiliac joint pain referral patterns in asymptomatic volunteers[16]; (2) predict symptomatic sacroiliac joints in patients with suspected lumbar discogenic or zygapophyseal joint pain[17]; and (3) describe morphologic features of the sacroiliac joint capsule.[19]

PATIENT SELECTION AND DIAGNOSTIC CONSIDERATIONS

While the discussion of sacroiliac joint syndrome is gaining acceptance, the steps toward its diagnosis remain enigmatic. The challenge for the clinician is to distinguish patients with sacroiliac joint dysfunction from those with other causes of low back pain.

Sacroiliac joint dysfunction is first suspected when a patient presents with a suggestive mechanism of injury. Common mechanisms include a direct fall on the buttocks; a rear-end motor vehicle accident, with the ipsilateral foot on the brake at the moment of impact; a broadside motor vehicle accident, with a blow to the lateral aspect of the pelvic ring; and a fall in a hole, with one leg in the hole and the other extended outside.[15] The diagnosis is readily established if the physician inquires where the pain emanates from and the patient is able to point directly to the involved joint. This exercise, known as the Fortin finger test, has a high correlation with provocation positive injections when other causes of low back pain have been excluded.[15,18] Pain diagrams, which document a predominant pain zone extending from the posterosuperior iliac spine to the caudal portion of the joint, can accurately predict which patients with suspected discogenic or posterior element pain have symptomatic sacroiliac joints upon provocative injection.[16,17] Tangentially, all patients with suspect presentations should have the necessary laboratory and radiological work-up to exclude spondyloarthropathy, metabolic, or infectious causes of sacroiliac joint pain.

Physical examination findings include a positive seated flexion, standing flexion test or Gillet test for aberrant sacroiliac motion,[4,35] positive Patrick's maneuver for ipsilateral sacroiliac joint pain,[4,18] and tenderness over the ipsilateral sacroiliac joint, sacrotuberous ligament, piriformis muscle, and pubic symphysis.[15]

Screening imaging modalities such as bone scan and CT may prove helpful[21,31,33,41,51]; however, a cost-effective clinical algorithm for their use has not been identified. A radionuclide scan may reflect misleading or indiscernible metabolic changes,[21] but asymmetric radioisotope uptake can sometimes be a credible clinical indicator.[15,32] One study suggests that bone scintigraphy has a viable role as a noninvasive method of diagnosing mechanical sacroiliac joint pain.[32] Mild degenerative changes of the sacroiliac joint on CT scan is a common sign in patients older than 30.[41]

Degenerative changes may be found earlier in athletes and workers who repetitively stress the joint: characteristic morphological changes develop in response to stress.[50] Subtle CT changes, such as asymmetric joint width or sacral torsion, in the overall clinical context may manifest a greater clinical significance.[15]

Diagnostic confirmation is attained when symptoms are reproduced upon distention of the joint capsule by provocative injection and subsequently abated with an analgesic block.[16,17] The ligamentous integrity of the joint is established arthrographically.[19]

Because diagnostic injections are invasive, the procedure should be reserved for patients who have the above profile for a potentially painful sacroiliac joint and have failed to respond to aggressive functional restoration or who have reached a plateau in the therapy process. In these cases, sacroiliac joint injection can be applied for diagnostic affirmation as well as for the therapeutic benefit of the intra-articular injection of anesthetic and long-acting corticosteroid.

The author has performed approximately 500 sacroiliac injections without complication. A low morbidity rate does not, however, obviate the need for preprocedural patient education and the same precautions and preparation for any spinal invasive technique. For details, see chapter 19.

RADIOLOGIC EQUIPMENT AND MATERIALS

Sacroiliac joint injections at or above the level of the posterosuperior sacroiliac spine (PSIS) are commonly performed as routine office procedures without the advantage of image intensifier control.[4] Due to the thickness of the dorsal sacroiliac and interosseous ligaments as well as the tortuous opposing surfaces of the medial iliac wing and dorsal sacrum, these injections most likely result in ligamentous or subligamentous deposit of solutions.[28] Even at the relatively accessible inferior portion of the joint, a "blind" injection is unlikely to find its way to the joint space because the needle is deflected by the irregular and convoluted joint surface or slips off the posterolateral margin of the iliac bone (deep to the gluteus muscle).

Hence, fluoroscopic control is essential to ensure an intra-articular injection. Suitable equipment options include (1) a routine fluoroscopy suite with an overhead tower or C-arm, (2) a special procedures suite with a C-arm or angio unit, or (3) an operating room with a C-arm.

Needle selection is easy since standard 25-gauge 3½-inch spinal needles without local infiltration can be used in most cases. Skin and subcutaneous anesthetization with 1% lidocaine (Xylocaine) is recommended for larger diameter needles. The tensile strength of a 22-gauge needle is necessary, on occasion, for narrow and tortuous joints. Rarely, a 6-inch needle is required.

Luer-Lok 3-ml syringes allow the greatest sensitivity to change in resistance at the needle hub. Larger syringes require substantially greater pressure to inject, even without obstruction.

Contrast medium is used for needle position verification, provocation, and arthrography. The author uses nonionic contrast agents routinely. Although nonionic contrast agents such as iohexol or iopamidol are more expensive, they are considered less allergenic and irritating than their ionic counterparts (e.g., methylgucamine-isothalamate). A concentration of 240–300 mg per ml is recommended.

THE PROCEDURE

The patient is sterilely prepared and draped in the prone position (Fig. 25-1). Under image intensifier

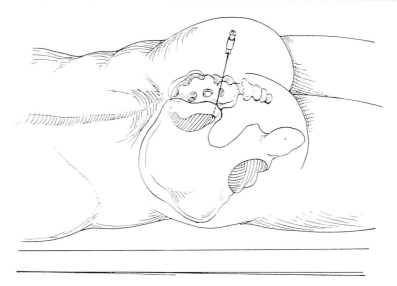

FIGURE 25-1. Sacroiliac joint injection. The patient is in a prone position and the needle has been guided into the inferior aspect of the joint using a direct posterior approach.

control, a 25- or 22-gauge 3½-inch spinal needle is directed into the inferior aspect of the sacroiliac joint using a posterior approach. The usual portal of entry is the inferior third of the joint. There is often a lucency in the inferior aspect of the joint that allows the least resistance upon needle passage (Fig. 25-2). There may be two or more "limbs" of the joint, because the joint is laterally divergent from its posterior to anterior borders and has interdigitations. In this instance, the medial or

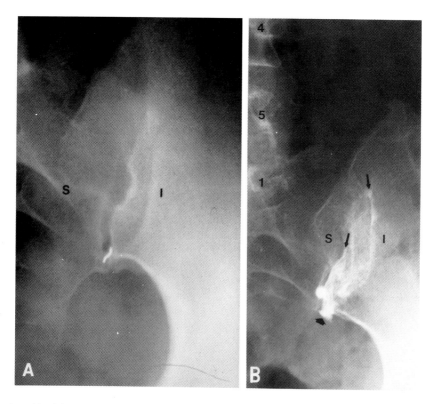

FIGURE 25-2. Sacroiliac joint arthrography. *A,* Preinjection spot film documents the needle, with a characteristic bend, within the inferior aspect of the joint. Note the lucent area around the needle. *B,* Anteroposterior arthrogram of the right sacroiliac joint. Divergent joint surfaces appear as distinct beads of contrast (*arrows*) or "separate" joint cavities. A 25-gauge 3½-inch spinal needle is in the inferior aspect of the joint. (Arrowhead: coin-shaped inferior recess; S: sacrum; I: ilium.) *(Continued on following page.)*

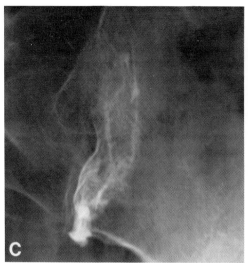
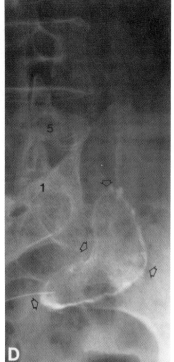

FIGURE 25-2 *(Continued)*. *C,* Magnified anteroposterior projection spot-film. *D,* Oblique view of the right sacroiliac joint (LAO). This "en-face" view delineates the auricular shape of the synovial joint (*arrowheads*). (4: pedicle of L4; 5: pedicle of L5; 1: pedicle of S1.)

(Continued on following page.)

posterior division is the most amenable to cannulation. Rolling the patient, obliquely, 5–10° from side to side will allow the technician a better three-dimensional perspective of the joint to select the "window" for optimal needle trajectory. With few exceptions, a direct posterior approach is used. Once the dorsal sacroiliac and interosseous ligaments are engaged, the needle often takes a characteristic bend as it conforms with the interdigitating contours of the diarthrodial joint (see Fig. 25-2). This phenomenon is often preceded by a subtle tactile sensation of a "giving way" at the needle hub as the needle has purchased and then penetrated through the ligaments entering the joint. If bony resistance is met after the ligaments are engaged and the needle is not yet within the joint margin, the needle should be withdrawn slightly without becoming disengaged from the ligaments. Subsequent needle advancement, while simultaneously rotating it around its own longitudinal axis, will allow it to deflect and conform to the joint margins. The initial instillation of a small amount of contrast material should outline the coin-shaped inferior recess of the joint. This landmark on the anteroposterior (AP) projection, together with the auricular shape of the diarthrodial joint (as noted on the oblique view), should allow definitive evaluation of proper needle position.

Following verification of initial needle position, further contrast is instilled to a volume commensurate with firm endpoint resilience or fluoroscopically visualized extravasation. Provocation responses are recorded at this time and anesthesia administered accordingly (see Codifying Provocation/Analgesia Responses, below). If arthrographic resolution is diluted by anesthesia, 0.2–0.4 ml of additional contrast material will serve to bolster the image.

Plain Film Evaluation

The AP view demonstrates the aforementioned inferior recess of the joint, contrast within the joint margins, and any subligamentous or inferior recess extension (see Fig. 25-2). The oblique (en-face) view is essential to delineate precisely where the contrast is in relation to the joint borders (see Fig. 25-2). This view will reveal diverticula and ventral capsular tears to vantage (Figs. 25-2 and 25-3). The lateral view also demonstrates posterior subligamentous or ligamentous extravasation, diverticulum or ventral tears (see Fig. 25-3). If bilateral arthrograms are obtained, an "offset" lateral (10–20° from a true lateral projection) will allow one to compare both capsular borders on one film (see Fig. 25-3). As a result of beam attenuation in the lateral projection, the ventral tears or diverticula are not as sharply resolved as on the en-face view. At times, the opposite oblique view can add additional information, including a clear view of the contrast within the superior joint space, superior recess extravasation, an outline of some diverticula, and reaffirmation of

FIGURE 25-2 *(Continued). E,* Opposite oblique arthrogram (RAO) contiguously demarcates the vertical extent of the joint space. Compare with Figure 25-2B. *F,* Lateral view of the right sacroiliac joint capsular margin. The ventral capsular border is outlined by contrast medium *(arrowhead).* (5: pedicle of L5; 1: pedicle of S1.)

any extravasation from the inferior recess or anteroinferior capsule (noted on other projections) (see Fig. 25-3).

CODIFYING PROVOCATION/ANALGESIA RESPONSES

Provocation

For the grading system, see chapter 19.

Fortin et al. arthrographically studied the sacroiliac joints of 10 asymptomatic volunteers. Upon direct intra-articular injection and under fluoroscopic visualization, these volunteers experienced unsustained, pressure type buttock discomfort—in contrast to intense buttock pain evoked upon stimulating a symptomatic sacroiliac joint. Hence, the disparity between an asymptomatic and symptomatic joint is easily distinguished by an experienced operator.

Analgesia

Following a provocation positive injection (0.6–1.0 ml of the long-acting anesthetic (0.75% bupivacaine) is instilled. This may be incorporated in a 2:1 mixture of a long-acting corticosteroid such as betamethasone (Celestone). Volumes are small (less than 2.0 ml of contrast material and anesthetic combined) commensurate with the joint's capacity. This ensures a focal anesthetic effect (i.e., limited

dispersal to adjacent structures). In a recent examination of 74 sacroiliac joint injections, the mean volume of contrast injected was 1.08 ml (standard deviation 0.29 ml).[19]

Some patients with a convincing mechanism of injury, pain diagram, physical examination, and provocative injection fail to respond favorably to anesthetization of the sacroiliac joint.[17] The reason for this is unclear but may involve supervening factors such as central neurogenic facilitation or psychosocial modifiers.

PLAIN FILM AND CT ARTHROGRAPHIC FINDINGS

Before ascribing morphologic capsular findings in the sacroiliac joint as "pathologic," the developmental and maturational changes of the normal sacroiliac joint must first be elucidated. The morphologic characteristics of 74 sacroiliac joint arthrograms were recently described by Fortin and Tolchin,[19] who classified and compared the findings of plain film arthrograms to their postarthrography/CT counterparts. After carefully scoring anterior, posterior, superior, and inferior aspects of the capsule, they found a significant direct correlation between data recorded from both modalities. Hence, they demonstrated that a detailed analysis of the sacroiliac joint capsule is possible by plain film arthrography or postarthrography CT, with excellent agreement between the two techniques.

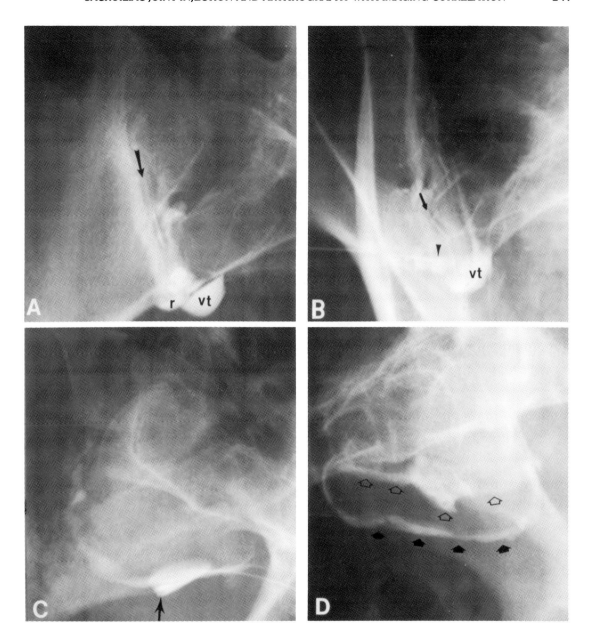

FIGURE 25-3. The patient is a 37-year-old housewife whose motor vehicle was hit in the rear while her left foot was planted firmly on the brake. She presented with left hip, thigh, and groin pain. With the lumbosacral plexus immediately anterior to the sacroiliac joint, these findings may help to explain the lower extremity symptoms in some patients with sacroiliac joint pain. *A,* An anteroposterior arthrogram. (r: inferior recess; vt: collection of contrast escaping through a ventral tear arrow-bead of contrast within joint margins.) *B,* Opposite oblique: confirms needle tip (*arrowhead*) is remote to ventral tear (vt). Arrow-bead of contrast is within joint space. *C,* Oblique view: smooth line of contrast medium outlining the capsular margins (*arrow*) is interrupted by an anterior capsular and anterior sacroiliac ligamentous rent. *D,* Offset lateral: bilateral arthrogram discloses an intact right ventral capsule (*closed arrowheads*) in contrast to disrupted left capsule (*open arrowheads*).   (*Continued on following page.*)

Moreover, each test has specific regional benefits—the plain film displaying diverticula to optimal advantage and postarthrography/CT superior in resolving anterior capsular "pathology."

Sacroiliac joint arthrographic findings are as diverse and fascinating as any other joint's arthrograms. An intriguing continuum of anterior capsular morphology has been disclosed from discrete attenuated areas and schisms to frank tears (Figs 25-3 and 25-4).[19] A vast array of diverticula varying in size, shape, and number have been isolated from all parts of the capsule (see Fig. 25-3).

Arthrographic findings reveal three potential pathways of communication between the sacroiliac

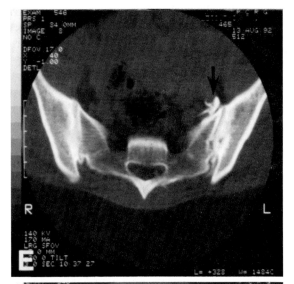

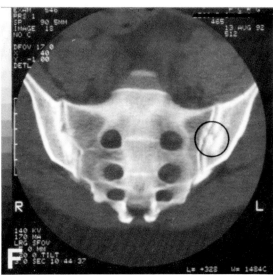

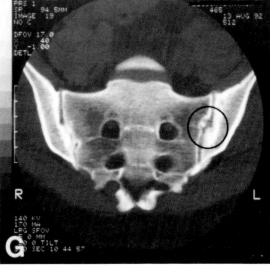

FIGURE 25-3 *(Continued)*. *E,* Postarthrography axial CT at the proximal S2 level (bone window/level settings). Contrast medium is present within both sacroiliac joints. A presacral collection of contrast medium is clearly noted, evidencing a ventral tear *(arrow)*. Contrast solution contacts the lumbosacral plexus elements. *F, G,* Two coronal views through the sacroiliac joint in the same patient. Note the area of joint margin cortical irregularity on the left. These changes are similar to osteochondritis dissecans commonly seen in appendicular joints. The opposing areas of bony prominence on the iliac (most remarkable) and sacral surfaces suggest a partially detached subchondral fragment with a surrounding lucent area and adjacent iliac sclerosis (areas encircled). This combination of eburnation, macroporosity, and sclerosis may be the osseous footprints of stress hardening as a result of trauma. Similar changes may be occurring on the right to a lesser extent.

joint and the neural elements.[19] These include (1) posterior subligamentous extension into the dorsal sacral foramina (Fig. 25-5), (2) superior recess extravasation at the alar level into the L5 epiradicular sheath (Fig. 25-6), and (3) leakage from a ventral tear to the lumbosacral plexus (see Fig. 25-3). Extravasation of inflammatory mediators from a dysfunctional sacroiliac joint to adjacent neural tissues may explain the radicular complaints of some patients. Electrodiagnostic correlation is needed; however, compelling anecdotal cases of impaired nerve function in patients with sacroiliac joint pain have been observed.[19]

The current combined information on sacroiliac joint injection and arthrography represents a mere first approximation. Most likely owing to a limited number of data points in any given category, no single arthrographic finding has been definitively correlated with pain provocation on injection.[19]

Accordingly, the relevance of all the arthrographic findings as they pertain to patient care is in question.

Presently we are resigned to extrapolate findings on sacroiliac joint arthrography to what is "normal" and "abnormal" in other joints. For instance, a full-thickness ligamentous tear often renders a joint unstable. In a weightbearing joint such instability is manifest as (1) intermittent and often "painful" sounds such as clicking, popping, grinding, or clunking, (2) sudden "giving way," (3) a sense of apprehension or being "off-balance," (4) an inability to fully bear weight on the affected side, or (5) the inability to load the joint in a manner that stresses the involved structure. Hence, like some patients with knee meniscal tears, these symptoms in a patient with a sacroiliac ventral capsular rent may be the result of instability. Conversely, some asymptomatic patients, or those whose knee pain is attributable to other causes, may have incidental meniscal tears[37];

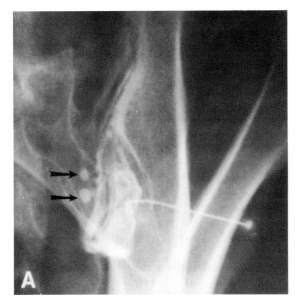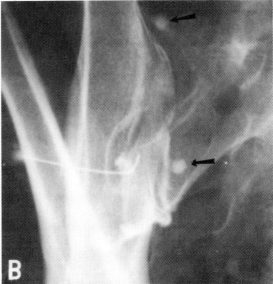

FIGURE 25-4. These figures demonstrate a spectrum of ventral sacroiliac capsular problems. *A* and *B* are bilateral opposite oblique view arthrograms. On the right, two diverticula project from the ventral capsule. Diverticula appear as "pearls" with pedunculated bases attached to the capsule. On the left, one diverticulum projects from the superior portion of the capsule and one from the midanterior region. *(Continued below.)*

some patients with or without back pain may have incidental ventral capsular tears of the sacroiliac joint.[19] Extrapolations must be made circumspectly since, when compared to other joints, the sacroiliac joint is unique in its configuration, mechanics, and histology. Arthrographic patterns aside, sacroiliac joint provocative injection remains the sole direct method to distinguish between a symptomatic and asymptomatic joint. Such tests are needed to predicate treatment on the correct diagnosis.

POSTPROCEDURE CARE

Patients are observed in a holding area following the procedure. Vital signs are obtained and the patient is given fluids. If an arthrography/CT is indicated, the patient is transported to the CT scan within 1–2 hours.

Postprocedural instructions include education on the application of ice to the affected area and information on the usual postprocedural symptoms such as increased local pain and/or stiffness. In one study, 48 hours after the sacroiliac joint injections of ten asymptomatic volunteers, none reported any residual pain.[16] On occasion, a 2-day supply of narcotic analgesics is judiciously dispensed. Driving, manual labor, and sports are discouraged the day of the procedure. Most patients resume their usual activities within 24 hours. An instruction sheet provides emergency phone numbers and details the warning signs of infection. Patients may be safely discharged 1–2 hours following the procedure.

SUMMARY

On the basic science front, future cadaveric studies will discern the natural maturational capsular changes thereby allowing a perspective for viewing arthrographic data. Neurophysiologic investigations promise to answer questions such as

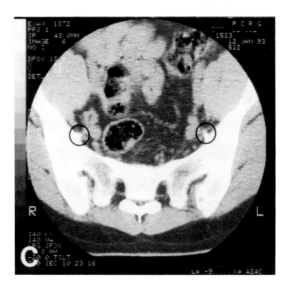

FIGURE 25-4 *(Continued)*. *C,* Same patient as in Figure 25-4A. Postarthrography axial CT at the proximal S1–2 level (soft tissue window/level settings). A right ventral diverticulum is intact. On the left, a markedly attenuated diverticulum allows seepage of contrast (areas encircled).

(Continued on following page.)

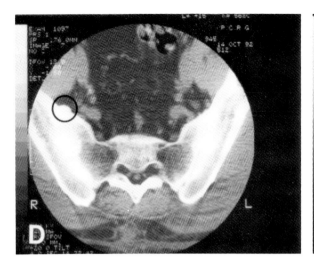
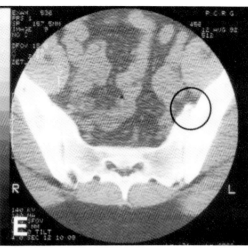

FIGURE 25-4 *(Continued)*. *D*, This is in the same series. A concentric area of ventral capsular attenuation is displayed at soft tissue settings (area encircled). This section is through the S2 level. *E*, A markedly attenuated area of the ventral capsule and sacroiliac ligament (i.e., a schism) allows seepage of contrast material in a feathery, wispy dispersal pattern into presacral region (area encircled) (transaxial CT, L = –21, W = 696). Compare this figure with the ventral tear demonstrated in Fig. 25-3. In contrast to a contained, attenuated area, schisms generally extend greater than a single 5-mm axial CT section. However, both contained attenuations and schisms are inconspicuous on plain film.

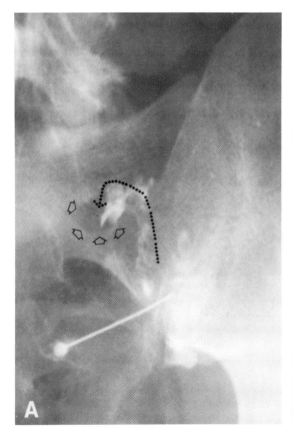
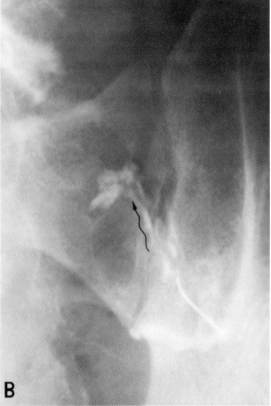

FIGURE 25-5. This case, involving a 33-year-old offshore worker with a prolonged right H-reflex (on electrodiagnostics), illustrates a third arthrographic link between the sacroiliac joint and neural elements. Posterior subligamentous extension of contrast medium into the S1 dorsal foramina *(arrowheads)* is shown on the right. *A*, Anteroposterior arthrogram. Contrast medium extends into the S1 dorsal foramina *(curved arrow)*. *B*, Opposite oblique view in same patient demonstrates pathway of contrast medium from the joint margins into the S1 dorsal foramina *(wavy arrow)*. *(Continued on following page.)*

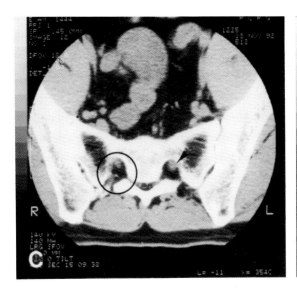
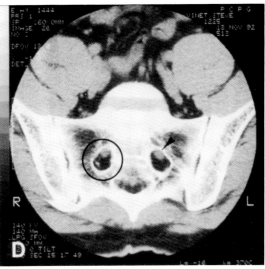

FIGURE 25-5 *(Continued)*. *C–D,* Axial and direct coronal postarthrography CT through the S1 dorsal foramina (soft tissue window settings). Contrast is visualized in the S1 dorsal foramina on both scans (areas encircled). (Arrowheads: contralateral S1 anterior ramus).

what inflammatory mediators are present within a dysfunctional sacroiliac joint and what type of nerve endings are present within the sacroiliac joint capsule. These findings will lend credence to the basis of provocative injections and help to explain referred pain.

It is hoped that MRI is on the horizon for the sacroiliac joint. Perhaps it will allow sophisticated, noninvasive, high resolution of the sacroiliac joint capsule and its ligaments as it has with appendicular joints. Upon cursory inspection, the capsular anatomy of the sacroiliac joint does not appear as

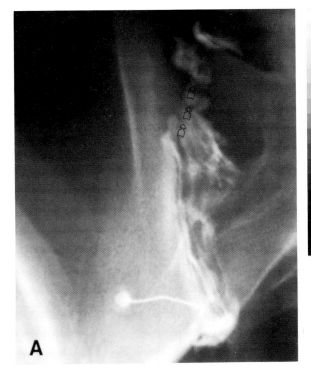
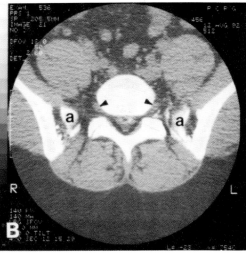

FIGURE 25-6. Another putative pathway between the sacroiliac joint and the neural elements is visualized in this case of a 19-year-old clerk with a pain diagram suggestive of a left L5 radiculopathy. *A,* Posteroanterior arthrogram demonstrates contrast medium extravasating from the superior recess *(arrows). B,* Postarthrography axial CT at the level of L5–S1. Contrast medium has extended from the superior recess to the L5 epiradicular sheath at the alar level (a: sacral ala; arrowheads: anterior rami of L5).

amenable to MR as to arthrography, but no studies have described the application of MR to the sacroiliac joint.

The statistical temperament of all diagnostic tests of the sacroiliac joint must be carefully investigated and assuaged against a more substantial basic science data base. This information, in turn, should be coalesced into a paradigm practical for clinical application.

However tenuous, this is an exciting time in the diagnostic realm of the sacroiliac joint. Scientists are deliberately piecing data together hoping to reach the inevitable "phase transition" in which an exponential, almost spontaneous coalition/cascade of all the necessary information will occur.

REFERENCES

1. Ahlstrom H, Feltelius N, Nyman R, Hallgren R: Magnetic resonance imaging of sacroiliac joint inflammation. Arthritis Rheum 33:1763–1769, 1990.
2. Bakalim G: Results of radical evacuation and arthrodesis in sacroiliac tuberculosis. Acta Orthop Scand 37:375–386, 1966.
3. Beal MC: The sacroiliac problem: Review of anatomy, mechanics, and diagnosis. J Am Osteopath Assoc 81:667–679, 1982.
4. Bernard PN, Cassidy JD: Sacroiliac joint syndrome: Pathophysiology, diagnosis and management. In Frymoyer JW (ed): The Adult Spine, vol. 2. New York, Raven Press, 1991, pp 2107–2131.
5. Bowen V, Cassidy JD: Macroscopic and microscopic anatomy of the sacroiliac joint from embryonic life until the eighth decade. Spine 66:620–628, 1981.
6. Brooke R: The sacroiliac joint. J Anat 58:299–305, 1924.
7. Brunner CH, Kissling RO, Jacob HAC: The effects of morphology and histopathology on the mobility of the sacroiliac joint. Spine 16:1111–1117, 1991.
8. Carrera GF, Foley WD, Kozin F, et al: CT of sacroiliitis. Am J Radiol 136:41–46, 1981.
9. Colachis SC, Worden RE, Bechtol CD, et al: Movement of the sacroiliac joint in the adult male. A preliminary report. Arch Phys Med Rehabil 44:491–498, 1985.
10. Coy JT, Wolf CR, Brower JD: Pyogenic arthritis of the sacroiliac joints. J Bone Joint Surg 5A:845–849, 1976.
11. DonTigny R: Function and pathomechanics of the sacroiliac joint. Phys Ther 65:35–44, 1985.
12. Dunn EJ, Byron DM, Nugent JT: Pyogenic infections of the sacroiliac joint. Clin Orthop 118:113–117, 1976.
13. Egun DN, Olsson TH, Schmid H, et al: Movements in the sacroiliac joint demonstrated with roentgenstereophotogrammetry. Acta Radiol Diagn 19:833–944, 1978.
14. Fortin JD: Enigmatic causes of spine pain in athletes. In Watkins RG (ed): The Spine and Sports. St. Louis, Mosby (in press).
15. Fortin JD: The sacroiliac joint: A new perspective. J Back Musculoskel Rehabil 3(3):31–43, 1993.
16. Fortin JD, Dwyer A, West S, Pier J: Sacroiliac joint pain referral patterns upon application of a new injection/arthrography technique. Part I: Asymptomatic volunteers. Spine 19(13):1475–1482, 1994.
17. Fortin JD, Dwyer A, Aprill C, Ponthieux B, Pier J: Sacroiliac joint pain referral patterns—Part II: Clinical evaluation. Spine 19(13):1483–1489, 1994.
18. Fortin JD, Falco F: The Fortin finger test: An indicator of sacroiliac joint pain (unpublished data).
19. Fortin JD, Tolchin R: Sacroiliac arthrograms and post-arthrography CT. Arch Phys Med Rehabil 74:1259, 1993.
20. Frigerio NA, Stowe RR, Howe JW: Movement of the sacroiliac joint. Clin Orthop 100:370–377, 1974.
21. Goldberg RP, et al: Applications and limitation of quantitative sacroiliac joint scintigraphy. Radiology 128:683–686, 1978.
22. Goldthwaite GE, Osgood RB: A consideration of the pelvic articulations from an anatomical, pathological, and clinical standpoint. Boston Med Surg J 152:593–601, 1905.
23. Greenman PE: Clinical aspects of sacroiliac function in walking. J Manual Med 5:125–129, 1990.
24. Grieve E: Lumbopelvic rhythm and mechanical dysfunction of the sacroiliac joint. Physiotherapy 67:171–173, 1981.
25. Grieve E: Mechanical dysfunction of the sacroiliac joint. Int Rehabil Med 5:46–52, 1982.
26. Gunterbert B, Romanus B, Stener B: Pelvic strength after major amputation of the sacrum. An experimental approach. Acta Orthop Scand 47:635–642, 1976.
27. Hendrix RW, Lin PP, Kane WJ: Simplified aspiration of injection technique for the sacroiliac joint. J Bone Joint Surg 64:1249–1252, 1982.
28. Kissling RO: Zur arthrographie des iliosacralgelenks. Z Rheumat 51:183–187, 1992.
29. Kuslich SD, Ulstrom CL, Michael CJ: The tissue origin of low back pain and sciatica. Orthop Clin North Am 22:181–187, 1991.
30. Lavignollc B, Vital JM, Senega S, et al: An approach to the functional anatomy of the sacroiliac joints in vivo. Anat Clin 5:169–176, 1982.
31. Lawson TL, et al: The sacroiliac joint: Anatomic plain roentgenographic and computed tomographic analysis. J Comput Assist Tomogr 6:307–314, 1982.
32. Mierau D: Scintigraphic analysis of sacroiliac pain. Scientific program of the 7th annual meeting of the North American Spine Society, 1992.
33. Miller JAA, Schultz AM, Anderson GBJ: Load-displacement behavior or sacroiliac joints. J Orthop Res 5:92–101, 1987.
34. Miskew DB, Block RA, Witt PF: Aspiration of infected sacroiliac joints. J Bone Joint Surg 32:1591–1597, 1979.
35. Mitchell SL, Moran PS, Pruzzo NA: An Evaluation and Treatment Manual of Osteopathic Muscle Energy Procedures. Manchester, MO, Mitchell, Moran and Pruzzo Assoc., 1979.
36. Mixter WJ, Barr JS: Rupture of the intervertebral disc with involvement of the spinal canal. N Engl J Med 211:210–215, 1934.
37. Negendank WG, Fernandez-Madrid FR, Heilbrom LK, et al: Magnetic resonance imaging of meniscal degeneration in asymptomatic knees. J Orthop Res 8:311–320, 1990.
38. Norman GF, May A: Sacroiliac conditions simulating intervertebral disc syndrome. West J Surg 64:461–462, 1956.
39. Pitkin HC, Pheasant HC: Sacrarthrogenetic telalgi II: A study of sacral mobility. J Bone Joint Surg 18:365–374, 1936.
40. Porterfield JA, Oerosu C: The sacroiliac joint. In Gould JA (ed): Orthopaedic and Sports Physical Therapy, 2nd ed. St. Louis, Mosby, 1990, pp 553–559.
41. Resnick E, Niwayama G, Georgen TG: Degenerative disease of the sacroiliac joint. Invest Radiol 10:608–621, 1975.
42. Reynolds HM: Three dimensional kinematics in the pelvic girdle. J Am Osteopath Assoc 80:277–280, 1980.
43. Roland MR, Morris RM: A study of the natural history of low back pain. Spine 8:145–150, 1983.
44. Scholten PJM, Schultz AB, Luchies CW, et al: Motions and loads within the human pelvis: A biomechanical model study. J Orthop Res 6:840–850, 1988.

45. Solonen KA: The sacroiliac joint in the light of anatomical, roentgenological and clinical studies. Acta Orthop Scand Suppl 27:1–127, 1957.

46. Sturesson B, Selvik G, Uden A: Movements of the sacroiliac joints: A roentgenstereophotogrammetric analysis. Spine 14:162–165, 1989.

47. Vleeming A, et al: Load application to the sacrotuberous ligaments. Influences on sacroiliac joint mechanics. Clin Biomech 4(4):204–209, 1989.

48. Vleeming A, Stoeckart TR, Snijders CJ: The sacrotuberous ligament: A conceptual approach to its dynamic role in stabilizing the sacroiliac joint. Clin Biomech 4(4):201–203, 1989.

49. Vleeming A, Stoeckart R, Volkers ACW, Snidjers CJ: Relation between form and function in the sacroiliac joint. Part I: Clinical anatomical aspects. Spine 15:130–132, 1990.

50. Vleeming A, Volkers ACW, Snidjers CJ, Stoeckart R: Relation between form and function in the sacroiliac joint. Part II: Biomechanical aspects. Spine 15:133–135, 1990.

51. Vogler JB, et al: The normal sacroiliac joint: A CT study of asymptomatic patients. Radiology 151:433–437, 1984.

52. Weisl H: The movements of the sacroiliac joint. Acta Anat 23:80–90, 1955.

53. Wilder DG, Pope MH, Frymoyer JW: The functional topography of the sacroiliac joint. Spine 5:575–579, 1980.

Chapter 26

CERVICOTHORACIC AND LUMBAR SYMPATHETIC BLOCKADE

ROBERT E. WINDSOR, M.D.
JONATHAN P. LESTER, M.D.
SUSAN J. DREYER, M.D.

The sympathetic nervous system is thought to play a role in many painful disorders involving the face and extremities, the most common of which are causalgia and reflex sympathetic dystrophy. Successful diagnosis and treatment of these conditions are best accomplished by an aggressive multimodal approach. Cervicothoracic (stellate ganglion) and lumbar sympathetic blocks play an integral role in the management of these conditions.[4,14,16,23] The physiatrist is encouraged to become familiar with the indications, techniques, and potential complications of these procedures.

Sympathetically maintained pain (SMP) may occur in response to or play a role in a wide spectrum of clinical disorders. These conditions include peripheral nerve injury, limb trauma or surgery, repetitive stress injury, central nervous system (CNS) insult (stroke or traumatic brain injury), myocardial infarction, phantom limb pain, herpes zoster, occlusive vascular disease, or Raynaud's syndrome.[3,4,14,16] Although the pathophysiology of SMP is not fully understood, several theories attempt to account for the clinical findings.[14,16,23] However, it is generally believed that either peripheral or central factors cause distorted information processing in the sympathetic neuronal pools of the dorsolateral spinal cord,[23] which leads to inappropriate response to afferent sensory input and overexcitation of efferent sympathetic outflow. SMP is classically described as a severe burning discomfort that may occur spontaneously or secondary to painful (hyperesthesia) or nonpainful (allodynia) stimuli. SMP is often associated with other signs of altered sympathetic tone, including erythema, edema, altered skin temperature, discoloration, and dystrophic changes of the skin, nails, and underlying bone and joints.[4,14,16,23,24]

SMP may be difficult to treat and requires early intervention. The condition may be suspected when common limb disorders have been excluded and patients complain of pain in association with signs or symptoms suggestive of altered sympathetic tone. However, SMP may be present without signs of autonomic disturbance and should also be suspected in any reliable patient who reports subjective pain out of proportion to objective pathology. The diagnosis may be supported or confirmed by the presence of characteristic findings on physical examination, plain radiographs, triple-phase bone scan, thermogram, or significant pain relief with sympathetic blockade.[4,13,14,21,23,24,27]

Aggressive treatment protocols are required to obtain successful lasting pain relief and prevent chronic dystrophic changes. Local or regional sympathetic blockade is the cornerstone of treatment for SMP and is thought to help by interrupting and disorganizing the inappropriate sympathetic activity.[16,23] However, treatment protocols should be multidimensional. Medications may be employed to decrease central and peripheral sympathetic tone.[19] Physical therapy may be beneficial for analgesic modalities, reduction of edema, and to promote active mobilization and reconditioning of involved extremities. Additionally, psychological support may be extremely helpful to assess and treat comorbid conditions such as anxiety, depression, and personality disorders. Recalcitrant cases unresponsive to traditional techniques may respond to stimulation of the dorsal column.[18] Surgical sympathectomy is reserved for confirmed SMP that has failed all other forms of treatment.[17]

CERVICOTHORACIC (STELLATE GANGLION) BLOCK

Stellate ganglion block (SGB) may be performed by the physiatrist in the outpatient setting for the diagnosis or treatment of SMP involving the face or upper extremity. A thorough understanding of the regional anatomy, injection techniques, and potential complications is required due to the high density of vital structures in the cervical region. SGB is contraindicated in patients taking heparin or coumadin and in patients with clinical blood dyscrasias associated with abnormal or prolonged bleeding.[14] Bilateral SGB should not be performed due to the increased risk of complications, including aspiration secondary to bilateral recurrent laryngeal nerve block or hypoventilation secondary to bilateral phrenic nerve block.

The sympathetic innervation to the head and upper extremity receives preganglionic fibers from the upper five to seven thoracic spinal segments.[8,11] These small myelinated fibers have their cell bodies in the gray matter of the dorsolateral spinal cord and exit the spinal canal with the anterior primary rami as white rami communicans. The fibers ascend along the anterolateral surface of the spinal column to synapse in one of the three cervical sympathetic chain ganglia (superior, middle, and inferior). The superior and middle ganglia lie just anterior to the prevertebral fascia covering the longus colli and longus capitus muscles, posterior to the carotid sheath, and medial to the vertebral artery at the levels of the C2 and C6 vertebrae respectively.[2,8,11] The inferior cervical sympathetic ganglion lies just superior to the dome of the pleura and anterior to the neck of the first rib where it is often fused with the first thoracic ganglia to form the stellate ganglion. Small unmyelinated postganglionic fibers exit the superior cervical ganglion as gray rami communicans and supply the first four cervical spinal nerve roots and the cardiac plexus before ascending to the head along the internal and external carotid arteries. Postganglionic fibers from the middle cervical ganglion supply the fifth and sixth cervical nerve roots with additional contributions to the cardiac plexus and thyroid gland. Postganglionic fibers from the stellate ganglion supply the C7, C8, and T1 nerve roots and the vertebral plexus. In some cases, preganglionic fiber will pass through the cervical ganglia to synapse with the posganglionic neurons at distant sites. However, local anesthetic blockade of the cervical sympathetic chain at the C6 or C7 level will disrupt the efferent and afferent sympathetic innervation to the head and upper extremity.[2,14]

SGB may be safely performed by a physician in an outpatient setting with or without the assistance of fluoroscopy. A variety of SGB techniques have been described; however, the most commonly performed and safest is the anterior paratracheal approach at the level of the C6 vertebra as modified by Carron, Litwiller, and others.[1,2,14,15] Intravenous access is recommended prior to the procedure to allow rapid management of potential complications and permit administration of preoperative intravenous sedation. Patients should be monitored for heart rate, blood pressure, and oxygen saturation. A full complement of resuscitative equipment and medications should be available, and the attending physician should be familiar with current advanced cardiac life support protocols.

Following informed consent, the patient is positioned supine with the neck slightly hyperextended and the jaw relaxed. The anterior cervical region is prepared with betadine and draped with sterile towels. Light sedation (1–4 mg of intravenous midazolam) may be given to increase patient comfort and promote patient compliance. Using a sterile technique, the carotid sheath is gently retracted laterally and the trachea retracted medially to allow the index fingertip to palpate for the bony protuberance at the base of the C6 transverse process (Chassaignac's tubercle) just lateral to the cricoid cartilage.[2,14] A skin wheal is raised with 1–3 ml of 1% zylocaine. A short, beveled 1.5-inch 22- or 23-gauge needle is inserted until body contact is made and then withdrawn 2–5 mm (Fig. 26-1). Following negative aspiration for CSF or blood in two quadrants, a small test dose of 0.2–0.5 ml of anesthetic solution is injected, and the patient is monitored closely for any signs of intravascular or intradural injection. If no signs of CNS toxicity, hypotension, or spinal block are observed, the remainder of local anesthetic is slowly injected.

Alternatively, the base of the C6 transverse process may be identified by direct fluoroscopic visualization. The needle is then inserted using a technique similar to retraction of the carotid sheath and trachea. Following negative aspiration and prior to injection of the test dose, a small amount of nonionic contrast material (iohexol 300) is injected. The resulting dye flow is observed to rule out occult intravascular injection and confirm fluid spread along the appropriate fascial planes (Figs. 26-2 and 26-3).

The recommended volume and content of anesthetic solution used for injection varies. Most authors recommend either 0.5–1.0% xylocaine (without epinephrine) or 0.25–0.5% bupivacaine (without epinephrine) in volumes ranging from 5–20 ml.[1,2,14,15,26] Smaller volumes and lower concentrations of anesthetic favor more selective sympathetic blockade and lower risk of complications but may be associated with a higher rate of incomplete or unsuccessful blockade.[15] In our practice, we routinely perform SGB with 5–10 ml of

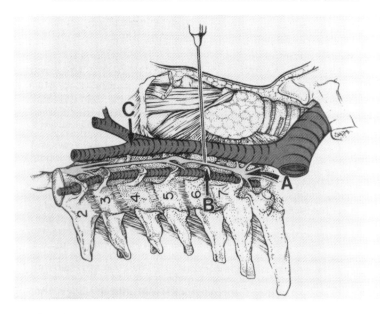

FIGURE 26-1. Lateral view of the neck demonstrates the relationship of the sympathetic chain and ganglia (A), anterior tubercle of C6 (Chassaignac's tubercle), (B), and the carotid artery (C). The needle tip is adjacent to Chassaignac's tubercle and sympathetic chain. (From: Sympathetic blocks. In Carron, Korbon, Rowlingson (eds): Regional Anesthesia, Techniques, and Clinical Applications. Harcourt Brace, 1984, p 133, with permission.)

0.25% bupivacaine without epinephrine. In extremely large individuals, the volume may be increased to 10–15 ml. In patients with a previously unsuccessful block, the concentration of bupivacaine may be increased to 0.5%. Additionally, smaller volumes (5 ml) may be recommended in individuals who have previously undergone anterior cervical surgery. In these patients, surgical dissection may cause permanent disruption of fascial planes, and anesthetic spread following SGB may be less predictable.

Following injections, patients should be observed for 1 hour to monitor their vital signs, observe for potential complications, and to assess block outcome. Successful sympathetic blockade is indicated by the development of an ipsilateral Horner's (ptosis, meiosis, and enophthalmos), conjunctival injection, and a temperature increase of the ipsilateral upper extremity of 2° C or an absolute temperature in excess of 34° C.[2,14,15]

Acute, potentially life-threatening complications may occur, including seizures, spinal block,

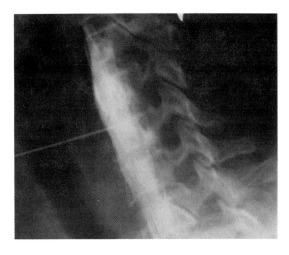

FIGURE 26-2. Lateral view of cervicothoracic (stellate ganglion) sympathetic block. Needle placement is anterior to the sixth cervical lamina and transverse process. Radiopaque dye confirms appropriate spread along the cervical and thoracic prevertebral fascial plane.

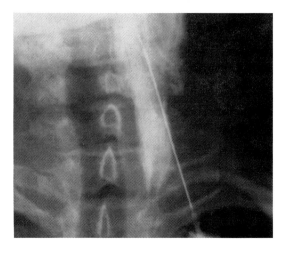

FIGURE 26-3. Posteroanterior view of a cervicothoracic (stellate ganglion) sympathetic block. Needle placement is lateral to the sixth cervical vertebral body and anterior to the lamina and transverse process. Radiopaque dye outlines the proper spread along the cervical and thoracic prevertebral fascial plane.

hypotension, or pneumothorax.[2,14,15,20,26] Additional complications including recurrent laryngeal nerve block, brachial plexus block, phrenic nerve block, or local hematoma may also occur. Following an uncomplicated postprocedure recovery, the patient is discharged to the care of a responsible friend or family member for transportation home. Patients should not be allowed to drive themselves home following SGB. Additionally, patients are counseled not to eat or drink for the expected duration of anesthetic blockade due to the increased risk of aspiration from clinical or occult blockade of the recurrent laryngeal nerve.

LUMBAR SYMPATHETIC BLOCK

The preganglionic sympathetic outlflow to the lower extremity originates in the neurons of the dorsolateral spinal cord corresponding to the lower thoracic and first two lumbar segments. From there, small myelinated fibers pass out of the spinal cord along with the anterior ventral rami as white rami communicans. These preganglionic fibers synapse with small unmyelinated fibers in the lumbar sympathetic chain ganglia. The lumbar sympathetic ganglia lie along the anterolateral surface of the lumbar vertebrae just anterior to the prevertebral fascia of the psoas muscle.[8,11,22] The number of lumbar sympathetic chain ganglia present varies considerably from one individual to another.[8,11] Postganglionic fibers exit the ganglia as gray rami communicans and supply one or more lumbar nerve roots. Deposition of local anesthetic along the sympathetic chain of the L2 or L3 levels will provide sympathetic denervation of the lower extremity.[25]

Fluoroscopically guided blockade of the lumbar sympathetic chain may also be safely performed in the outpatient setting. Techniques for "blind" injection are available but not recommended. Lumbar sympathetic blockade (LSB) is contraindicated in anticoagulated patients or in patients with blood dyscrasias as described for SGB. Bilateral blockade is not contraindicated but is not recommended due to the potential for significant hypotension. Intravenous access, preprocedure sedation, and cardiopulmonary monitoring are similar to those described earlier for SGB.

Following informed consent, the patient's upper lumbar region is prepared with betadine, and the patient is draped with sterile towels in either the prone or lateral decubitus position (block side up). The tip of the 12th rib is palpated, and a point 2–3 cm inferior is selected for skin entry.[22] Alternatively, the inferior margin of the L2 vertebra or the superior margin of the L3 vertebra is identified under direct fluoroscopic visualization and a point 10 cm lateral of midline is marked for skin entry.[14,25] Thin patients may benefit from a more medial point

of skin entry while obese patients may require a more lateral entry to provide the appropriate angle toward the vertebral column. A skin wheal is raised at the desired site of skin entry with 1–3 ml of 1% xylocaine. A 6-inch, 22-gauge spinal needle is inserted and angled medially and slightly ventral until contact is made with the vertebral body. The needle is then partially withdrawn and reinserted with a more ventral angle until it just slips by the vertebral body. Direct fluoroscopic visualization in the anteroposterior and lateral planes is used to direct and confirm accurate needle placement just anterolateral to the ventral surface of the lower third of L2 vertebral body or the upper third of L3 vertebral body.[14,22,25] Needle placement along the middle third of the vertebra is discouraged to avoid needle insertion into the penetrating nutrient blood vessels of the vertebral body. When appropriate needle tip placement is obtained, contrast injection is performed with 1–3 ml of nonionic contrast agent (iohexol 300) to rule out intravascular injection and to confirm flow in a inferolateral direction along the fascial plane of the psoas muscle (Figs. 26-4 and 26-5). If satisfactory contrast flow is seen, 15–20 ml of 0.25% or 0.5% bupivacaine is slowly injected.[4,14] Successful sympathetic blockade is indicated by a rise in lower extremity temperature of 3° C.[22]

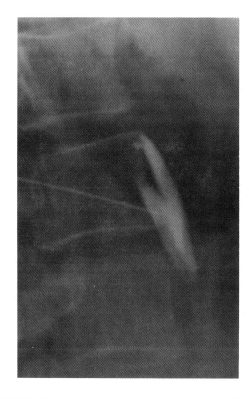

FIGURE 26-4. Lateral view of a lumbar sympathetic block. Needle placement is just anterolateral to the inferior margin of the second lumbar vertebral body. Radiopaque dye reveals the psoas fascial plan, confirming proper location of the needle.

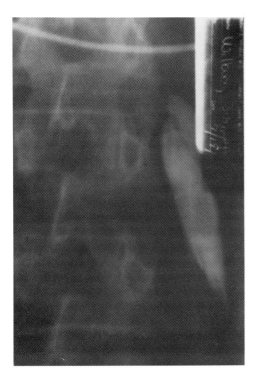

FIGURE 26-5. Posteroanterior view of the lumbar sympathetic block. Needle placement is just anterior and lateral to the inferior margin of the second lumbar vertebral body. Radiopaque dye displays the psoas fascial spread, verifyng correct needle placement.

Potential complications of LSB include intravascular injection, intradural injection with spinal anesthesia or postural headache, hypotension, lumbar plexus block, renal puncture, or genitofemoral neuralgia.[14,20,22] Postinjection monitoring is similar to that recommended for SGB, with the exception that patients are allowed to eat or drink when their intravenous sedation has worn off.

After successful SGB or LSB has been performed, it is important to carefully examine the involved extremity for resolution of pain or pain-producing stimuli. Significant reduction (greater than 50–75%) of pain or painful stimuli in the absence of somatic blockade indicates the presence of SMP. Serial diagnostic blocks may be required to rule out a placebo response.

Patients whose pain returns following a pain-free interval with SGB or LSB may be candidates for treatment with serial blocks. Additionally, arranging for the patient to participate in physical therapy for limb mobilization immediately following a successful block may greatly enhance the long-term treatment benefits of sympathetic blockade. Unfortunately, little controlled data exist to indicate the optimal frequency or ultimate number of serial blocks that are indicated in the management of SMP. Patients in whom the degree or duration of pain relief with serial single injection local sympathetic blocks is inadequate may benefit from techniques for continuous local sympathetic blockade or regional intavenous sympathetic blockade.[12]

CONCLUSION

Local anesthetic blockade of the cervicothoracic and lumbar sympathetic chains are valuable tools in the diagnosis and treatment of SMP. Physicians familiar with the regional anatomy, potential complications, critical care protocols, and experienced with the injection techniques may safely perform these procedures in the outpatient setting as part of the comprehensive management of SMP.

REFERENCES

1. Bruyne T, Devolder J, Vermeulen, et al: Possible inadvertent subdural block following attempted stellate ganglion blockade. Anesthesia 46:747, 1991.
2. Carron H, Litwiller R: Stellate ganglion block. Anesth Analg 54:567, 1975.
3. Carron H, Weller R: Treatment of post-traumatic sympathetic dystrophy. Adv Neurol 4:485, 1974.
4. Charlton J: Management of sympathetic pain. Br Med Bull 47:601, 1991.
5. Currey T, Dalsania J: Treatment for herpes zoster ophthalmicus: Stellate ganglion block as treatment for acute pain and prevention of postherpetic neuralgia. Ann Ophthalmol 23:188, 1991.
6. Ford S, Forrest W, Eltherington L: The treatment of reflex sympathetic dystrophy with regional bretylium. Anesthesiology 68:137, 1988.
7. Galer B, Lipton R, Kaplan R, et al: Bilateral burning foot pain: Monitoring of pain, sensation, and autonomic function during successful treatment with sympathetic blockade. J Pain Symptom Manage 6:92, 1991.
8. Gray H: The peripheral nervous system. In Clemente C (ed): Anatomy of the Human Body. Philadelphia, Lea & Febiger, 1985, p 1149.
9. Guntamukkala M, Hardy P: Spread of injectate after stellate ganglion block in man: An anatomical study. Br J Anesth 66:643, 1991.
10. Hatangi W, Boas R: Lumbar sympathectomy: A single needle technique. Br J Anesth 57:285, 1985.
11. Hollinshead H: The nervous system. In Textbook of Anatomy. Hagerstown, MD, Harper & Row, 1984, p 37.
12. Hord A, Rooks M, Stephens R, et al: Intravenous regional bretylium and lidocaine for treatment of reflex sympathetic dystrophy: A randomized double-blind study. Reg Anesth Analg 74:818, 1992.
13. Kozin F, Soin J, Ryan L, et al: Bone scintigraphy in the reflex sympathetic dystrophy syndrome. Radiology 138:437, 1981.
14. Lofstrom J, Cousins MJ: Sympathetic neural blockade of upper and lower extremity. In Cousins MJ, Bridenbaugh PO (eds): Neural Blockade in Clinical Anesthesia and Management of Pain, 2nd ed. Philadelphia, J.B. Lippincott, 1988, p 461.
15. Malmquist E, Bengtsson M, Sorenson J: Efficacy of stellate ganglion block: A clinical study with bupivacaine. Reg Anesth 17:340, 1992.
16. Mandel S, Rothrock R: Sympathetic dystrophies: Recognizing and managing a puzzling group of syndromes. Postgrad Med 87:213, 1990.

17. Olcott C, Eltherington L, Wilcosky B, et al: Reflex sympathetic dystrophy—the surgeon's role in management. J Vasc Surg 14:488, 1991.
18. Raj B, Lewis R, Laros G, et al: Electrical stimulation analgesia. In Raj P (ed): Practical Management of Pain, 2nd ed. St. Louis, Mosby, 1991, p 922.
19. Raja S, Davis K, Campbell J: The adrenergic pharmacology of sympathetically-maintained pain. J Reconstr Microsurg 8:63, 1992.
20. Schmidt S, Gibbons J: Postdural puncture headache after fluoroscopically guided lumbar paravertebral sympathetic block. Anesthesiology 78:198, 1993.
21. Smith F, Powe J: Effect of sympathetic blockade on bone imaging. Clin Nucl Med 1:665, 1992.
22. Sprague R, Rammamurthy S: Identification of the anterior psoas sheath as a landmark for lumbar sympathetic block. Reg Anesth 15:253, 1990.

23. Stanton-Hicks M: Upper and lower extremity pain. In Raj P (ed): Practical Management of Pain, 2nd ed. St. Louis, Mosby, 1991, p 312.
24. Tollison C, Satterthwaite: Reflex sympathetic dystrophy: Diagnosis and treatment. Phys Assist July:51, 1992.
25. Umeda S, Arani T, Hatano Y, et al: Cadaver anatomic analysis of the best site for chemical lumbar sympathectomy. Anesth Analg 66:643, 1987.
26. Wallace M, Milholland A: Contralateral spread of local anesthetic with stellate ganglion block. Reg Anesth 18:55, 1993.
27. Werner, Davidoff R, Jackson D, et al: Factors affecting the sensitivity and specificity of the three-phase technetium bone scan in the diagnosis of reflex sympathetic dystrophy syndrome in the upper extremity. J Hand Surg 14:520–523, 1989.

Chapter 27

EPIDURAL PROCEDURES
IN SPINE PAIN MANAGEMENT

JEFFREY L. WOODWARD, M.D.
STANLEY A. HERRING, M.D.
ROBERT E. WINDSOR, M.D.
SUSAN J. DREYER, M.D.
JONATHAN P. LESTER, M.D.
FRANCIS P. LAGATTUTA, M.D.

The use of epidural injections in the cervical, thoracic, and lumbosacral spine for both diagnostic and therapeutic purposes has developed as an important part of a comprehensive interdisciplinary approach to spinal pain. Diagnostic information garnered from epidural injections can be helpful in confirming hypotheses regarding the pain generators responsible for a patient's spine or extremity discomfort. It is well known that structural abnormalities seen on CT or MRI scans do not always cause pain, and diagnostic injections can often help correlate abnormalities on imaging studies with associated pain complaints. Therapeutically, epidural injections can provide significant pain relief, during which time recovery of disc and nerve root injuries can occur and patients can also progress their level of physical activity. Frequently, since the severe pain due to an acute disc injury with or without radiculopathy is often time-limited, therapeutic injections can help manage the patient's pain without reliance on oral analgesics. Epidural corticosteroid injections always are recommended in conjunction with a formal physical therapy program such as dynamic spine stabilization programs, which include spine mobility and strengthening exercises and postural and dynamic body mechanics training. A physiatrist knowledgeable in the appropriate spine exercise programs and also trained in diagnostic and therapeutic spine injections can often best manage the medical care of patients with spine pain.

Historically, the first published reports of epidural injections for low back pain and sciatica occurred in 1901 and involved the injection of cocaine.[42,135,160] Viner[177] injected mixtures of procaine, Ringer's solution, saline, and liquid petrolatum using a caudal approach. In 1930, Evans[75] published good results in 22 of 40 patients with unilateral sciatica treated by caudal epidural injection of procaine and saline. In 1955, Boudin et al.[27] became probably the first to inject corticosteroid into the subarachnoid space; this was followed in 1957 by Lievre[166] with the first published report of epidural corticosteroid injection with hydrocortisone for the treatment of low back pain. The literature contains many more reports on lumbar epidural injections than cervical epidural injections for pain management. Papers by Shulman et al.[159] and Catchlove and Braha[41] published in 1984 are the earliest references for cervical epidural injections. A review of the literature has revealed no historical information on thoracic epidural corticosteroid injections.

ANATOMY

The spine is often divided anatomically into the anterior (the vertebral body and intervertebral disc), neuroaxial (structures within the epidural space and neural pathways) and posterior (zygapophyseal joints and associated bony vertebral arch structures) compartments.[24] Epidural injections are used to diagnose and treat abnormalities in both the anterior and the neuroaxial compartments. The spinal anatomy that is pertinent to epidural injections is discussed below.

Posterior Compartment

A knowledge of spine surface and bony anatomy is helpful in performing epidural injections. Important surface bony landmarks include the vertebra prominens at C7, base of scapular spine at T3, inferior angle of scapula at T7, inferoposterior T12 rib margins 10 cm from midline at L1, line between iliac crests at about L5 (Tuffier's line), and the posterior superior iliac spine at S1. The C7 spinous process, the vertebra prominens, can be felt to move with flexion and extension of the cervical spine, but the T1 spinous process remains fixed during cervical motion.

The orientation of the vertebral spinous processes is important for midline epidural approaches (Fig. 27-1). In the middle and lower cervical spine, the spinous processes are often bifid and are angled inferiorly at about 45° to the spine axis except at C7, which is less acutely angled.[45] With the cervical spine in a flexed position, the tip of each spinous process roughly overlies its lamina.[139] The thoracic spinous processes angulate sharply downward, often covering the entire interlaminar space below, thereby making the paramedian approach easiest. Lumbar spinous processes have only a slight downward angulation with the inferior border of the spinous process directly above the widest part of the interlaminar space, making both the midline and paramedian approach relatively easy. The widest interlaminar space is typically at the L4–5 interspace just below the inferior border of the L4 spinous process.

The bony anatomy of the sacrum and its sacral hiatus has a direct effect on the performance and success of caudal epidural injections. The sacral hiatus is an inverted V-shaped bony defect in the posterior and inferior surface of the sacrum covered by the sacrococcygeal ligament. The edges of the hiatus are bony prominences called the sacral cornu, which are remnants of the S5 articular processes. Needle placement through the sacral hiatus allows percutaneous access to the sacral canal, which forms the distal extent of the epidural space. Numerous anatomic variations in the bony structure of the sacrum have been documented. Black and Holyoke[18] reported complete bony blockage of the sacral canal in 7.7% of cadaver specimens. They also noted other variations, such as a complete midline bony septum dividing the sacral canal into two small compartments or the presence of an extremely small sacral hiatus the size of pencil lead in a small percentage of subjects. An occasional extreme anteroposterior angulation in the sacrum was also reported. All of these variations would make a caudal epidural injection either more difficult or impossible. Moore[125] reported at least some anatomic abnormality in the bony structure of the sacrum in 20% of patients examined. Despite the presence of such bony abnormalities, Cousins and Bromage[49] reported successful caudal epidural anesthesia in 94% of their patients, which closely agrees with several more recent studies.

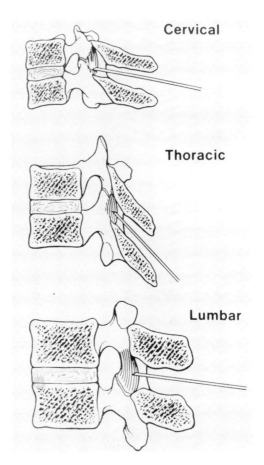

FIGURE 27-1. Spinous process and needle entry angle for cervical, thoracic, and lumbar spine midline epidural injection approaches. (From Cousins MJ, Bromage PR: Epidural Neural Blockade. In Cousins MJ, Bridenbaugh PO (eds): Neural Blockade in Clinical Anesthesia and Management of Pain. Philadelphia, J.B. Lippincott, 1988, with permission.)

Neuroaxial Compartment

The neuroaxial compartment includes all structures within the osseous and ligamentous boundaries of the spinal canal, including the posterior longitudinal ligament, the ligamentum flavum, and the epidural and epiradicular membranes (Fig. 27-2). Adequate knowledge of the cervicothoracic and lumbosacral epidural space is essential for proper epidural needle placement. The epidural space extends from the foramen magnum to the sacral hiatus and is located between the dura mater and the overlying ligamentum flavum and periosteum of the surrounding vertebral arches. No epidural space exists within the cranium due to the close adherence of the meningeal and endosteal dura, except where venous sinuses are present. At the foramen magnum, these two dural layers separate with the inner meningeal dura forming the spinal dura and the outer endosteal dura forming the periosteum of the bony spinal canal. Within the dural

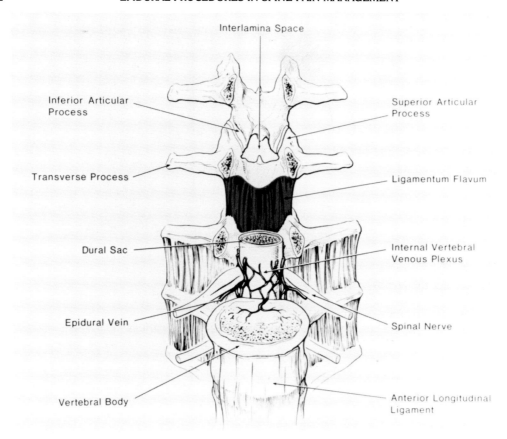

FIGURE 27-2. Lumbar spine anterior cutaway view with epidural structures and ligamentum flavum. (From Macintosh RR: Lumbar Puncture and Spinal Analgesia. Edinburgh, E & S Livingstone, 1957, with permission.)

covering resides the spinal cord and exiting nerve roots bathed in cerebrospinal fluid (CSF). In adults, the spinal cord generally extends inferiorly to the L1 or L2 level. The surrounding dural sac extends inferiorly in the sacrum to approximately the S2 level within the bony sacral canal and then terminates at the sacral hiatus at the S4 or S5 level. A sleeve of dura surrounds each nerve root as it exits through the neural foramen with a gradual thinning of the dural sleeve distally. Just distal to the dorsal root ganglion where the dorsal and ventral nerve roots join to form the spinal nerve, the dura adheres directly to the nerve, becoming continuous with the epineurium.

The width of the posterior epidural space beneath the neural arch at the midline varies throughout the length of the human spine. In the upper cervical region, the posterior epidural space is 1.5–2 mm wide and increases to 3–4 mm at the C7–T1 interspace, especially with spine flexion, but can become more narrow with neck extension. Cervical epidural injections in the midline at the C7–T1 interspace maximize the available epidural space and safety margin of the injection.[52] In the midthoracic region, the posterior epidural space is 3–5 mm wide and gradually expands to 5–6 mm at its greatest width in the midlumbar spine and then gradually decreases to about 2 mm at the S1 level.[44] At all levels, the triangular epidural space is widest in the midline underneath the junction of the lamina and narrows laterally beneath the zygapophyseal joints. The distance from the surface of the skin to the lumbar epidural space varies widely—from less than 3 cm to greater than 8 cm depending on the size and obesity of the patient.[50] The structures encountered during a midline epidural injection are skin, subcutaneous tissue, the supraspinous ligament, interspinous ligament, ligamentum flavum, and epidural space. The ligamentum flavum is a thick elastic fibrous band (3–5 mm in the midthoracic spine and 5–6 mm in the lumbar spine) running from the anteroinferior surface of the superior lamina to the posterosuperior edge of the lamina below (Fig. 27–3). The ligamentum flavum on each side of the vertebral arch usually join in the midline and taper in thickness laterally until connecting with the joint capsule of the adjacent zygapophyseal joint. The increased resistance to both needle advancement and injection afforded by the ligamentum flavum is an important indicator of needle depth, as is the subsequent loss of resistance with needle penetration into the epidural space. Due to the vertical overlapping pattern of the ligamentum flava, the epidural space at any interspace is wider just above the edge of the inferior lamina, and placement of the epidural needle in this location is recommended for the paramedian approach.

The intervertebral foramen are bordered superiorly and inferiorly by the pedicles of adjacent vertebrae, anteriorly by the vertebral body and disc, and posteriorly by the zygapophyseal joint capsule (Fig. 27–4). The course of the spinal nerve roots exiting through the neuroforamen vary considerably as they leave the spinal canal depending on the level of the spine. In the cervical spine, the nerve roots travel anteriorly and exit almost perpendicular to the long axis of the spine. In the thoracic and lumbar spine, the nerve roots travel more inferiorly and exit in a lateral plane without the anterior orientation seen in the cervical spine. The lumbar roots exit just under the pedicle with a downward course of 40–50° from horizontal and occupy the superior portion of each foramen. In order to safely inject medication as close to a lumbar nerve root as possible, the needle should be placed in the upper portion of the foramen just beneath the adjacent pedicle.

The sinuvertebral nerve is a branch of the somatic ventral nerve root and the sympathetic gray ramus communicans.[25] The sinuvertebral nerve originates just lateral to the neuroforamen and enters the spinal canal just anterior to the dorsal root ganglion. Within the vertebral canal, the sinuvertebral nerve innervates the outer annulus of the disc, posterior longitudinal ligament, epidural membranes, and dura at the same segmental level and adjacent levels. Branches of the sinuvertebral nerve form a dense plexus throughout the anterior and lateral dura and extend within the dural sheaths covering the spinal roots and dorsal root ganglion.[58] Neuroaxial compartment pain is caused by irritation of the tissues innervated by the sinuvertebral nerve or direct stimulation of adjacent nociceptive fibers. The complex multisegmental innervation pattern of the sinuvertebral nerve probably is responsible, at least in part, for the diffuse pain referral patterns characteristic of neuroaxial pain. Once an injury involves local nerve root tissue, extremity pain in a radicular pattern occurs.

In addition to neural structures, the epidural space also contains veins, arteries, and adipose and loose areolar tissues (Fig. 27-5). Epidural fat runs continuously throughout the epidural space and is most abundant in the dorsomedial region and less abundant in the ventromedial and lateral regions. Pads of loosely adherent epidural fat lie between the dural sac and the lamina or ligamentum flava and are apparently pushed aside by fluid injected into the epidural space. The presence of epidural fat can be important in the absorption and subsequent

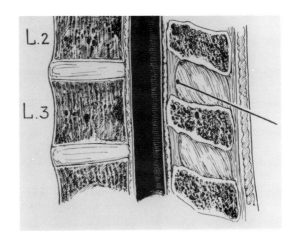

FIGURE 27-3. Lumbar spine sagittal view illustrating the ligamentum flavum and epidural space. (From Macintosh RR: Lumbar Puncture and Spinal Analgesia. Edinburgh, E & S Livingstone, 1957, with permission.)

slow release of various medications (most importantly, local anesthetics such as bupivacaine). Also, epidural fat is thought to decrease in compliance with aging and may contribute to the increased resistance to epidural injection often reported in elderly patients.[50] Within the epidural loose areolar tissue reside small invaginations in the dura known as arachnoid villi, which are most plentiful in the lateral recesses of the epidural space. Due to the profuse vascularity of these villi, a portion of any medication injected into the epidural space may diffuse

FIGURE 27-4. Lumbar spine sagittal view with exiting nerve roots. (From Macintosh RR: Lumbar Puncture and Spinal Analgesia. Edinburgh, E & S Livingstone, 1957, with permission.)

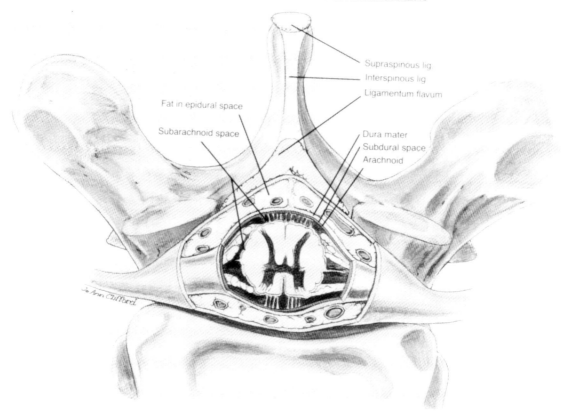

FIGURE 27-5. Lumbar spine axial view with epidural structures. (From Brown DL: Atlas of Regional Anesthesia. Philadelphia, W.B. Saunders, 1992, with permission.)

or be transported into the subarachnoid space and directly bathe the spinal cord and nerve roots.

Several other real or potential spaces within the dural sac are important when performing epidural injections. Just beneath the dura is the subdural space, which is a potential space between the dura and arachnoid mater containing only a small amount of serous fluid (Fig. 27-6). The subarachnoid space is between the arachnoid and pia mater and contains cerebrospinal fluid and blood vessels. The

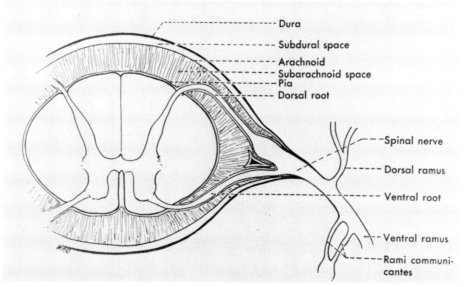

FIGURE 25-6. Schematic axial view of meningeal tissue layers. (From Hollingshead WH, Jenkins DB: Functional Anatomy of the Limbs and Back, 5th ed. Philadelphia, W.B. Saunders, 1981, with permission.)

pia mater is a very thin, highly vascularized membrane adhering closely to the spinal cord and nerve roots. Advancing a needle into the subarachnoid space will lead to a "wet tap" often with return of CSF through the needle. The injection of medications unknowingly into the subarachnoid space, especially local anesthetics and possibly corticosteroids, can lead to serious complications as described later. Inadvertent needle placement into the potential subdural space will not be associated with CSF return, but may also be associated with significant complications similar to a subarachnoid injection.

Vascular Anatomy

Venous drainage of the epidural space occurs through the relatively large and valveless epidural veins, which are most abundant in the anterolateral portions of the spinal canal.[29] The epidural veins are part of the vertebral venous plexus, which communicate directly with the basivertebral veins located within the vertebral bodies. Superiorly, the vertebral venous plexus communicates with the occipital, sigmoid, and basilar venous sinuses within the cranium. Inferiorly, the vertebral venous plexus drains through many segmental epidural veins that exit the spinal canal through the intervertebral foramen and allow venous return to the inferior vena cava and azygos vein via thoracic and abdominal veins. Maintaining epidural needle placement as medially as possible will decrease the risk of puncturing the large lateral epidural veins through which medications can be inadvertently delivered directly to intracranial veins, potentially causing CNS side effects.

The arterial blood supply to the epidural and subarachnoid space, including the spinal cord, is delivered through segmental radicular arteries entering the intervertebral foramen from the aorta, subclavian and iliac arteries, and from arterial vessels descending from the posterior inferior cerebellar arteries. The radicular arteries entering the spinal canal pass through the dura in the neuroforamen at the region of the thin dural cuff. The anterior spinal artery, which primarily supplies the ventral motor spinal cord, receives most of its blood via these segmental radicular arteries. Most of the radicular arteries are quite small and supply only a minimal portion of the total spinal cord arterial blood flow. In fact, most of the arterial blood reaching the anterior spinal artery does so primarily through only six or seven major radicular arteries. Damage to one of the larger radicular arteries from a needle in the neural foramen at or above L2 could cause significant arterial compromise of the cord at that level. The largest of these major radicular arteries enters in the lumbar region to supply the enlarged lumbar cord and is called the radicularis magna

(or artery of Adamkiewicz). The radicularis magna enters the spinal canal through a single intervertebral foramen between T8 and L3 and is located on the left side 78% of the time. Obviously, needle damage to this important arterial feeder could result in significant ischemic damage to the lumbosacral cord with primarily motor deficits.[32] A common variant of spinal arterial circulation as described above involves a smaller than usual radicularis magna and multiple large lumbar radicular arteries from the iliac artery traversing the lower lumbar neuroforamen, any of which could incur needle damage from a transforaminal approach.

CLINICAL KNOWLEDGE

Cervicothoracic Spine: Clinical Trials

Cervical epidural steroid injections (CESIs) have been used in the treatment of both acute and chronic neck, shoulder, and arm pain.[45,46,139,151,179] CESIs also have been reported in the treatment of reflex sympathetic dystrophy, postherpetic neuralgia, postlaminectomy cervical pain, acute viral brachial plexitis, and muscle contraction headaches, with at least some good responses reported anecdotally for each of these conditions.[45,119,139,151,159,179.181] Rowlingson and Kirschenbaum[151] studied 25 patients with neck and at least some radicular pain, but not necessarily with neurologic deficits, with each patient receiving 50 mg of triamcinolone diacetate epidurally and at least 6 months of follow-up. Six patients (24%) achieved excellent pain relief with full return to activities; all six had radicular pain and at least mild sensory deficits prior to the injection. Of the remaining patients, ten (40%) reported good relief (≥ 75% pain relief), six (24%) reported fair relief, and three (12%) reported little or no relief. Purkis[139] administered 113 CESIs to 58 patients with at least 6 months of neck pain; each injection contained 130 mg of methylprednisolone. A total of 38 (65%) of the patients reported at least 50% pain relief 3 weeks after the injection; 9 of these had no pain at all. In prolonged follow-up, three patients noted significant relief 12 months after corticosteroid injection. Shulman[159] studied 96 patients receiving 80–160 mg of methylprednisolone; 41% reported at least 50% pain relief several weeks after the injection; 35%, fair pain relief after several weeks; and 24%, poor or no relief.

More recently, Cicala et al.[45] treated 58 patients with CESIs using 1 mg/kg of methylprednisolone acetate; 24 (41%) had excellent relief (at least 90% pain relief for 6 months), 17 (~ 29%) noted good relief (50–90% pain relief for at least 6 months), and 17 (~ 29%) noted poor relief (no more than 50% or 6 weeks of pain relief). Cicala stated that excellent results were more likely in patients with cervical spondylosis, although some patients with subacute cervical strain also had excellent results; mostly poor results occurred with chronic cervical strains. Half of patients with pending litigation reported absolutely no pain relief. Mangar and Thomas[119] treated 40 patients with CESIs using 80 mg of methylprednisolone acetate; 15 (38%) of patients had excellent pain relief (greater than 70% relief); three (7%) had good relief (50–70%); nine (23%) had poor relief (1–50%); and 13 (32%) had no relief. Patients with cervical disc herniation had overall better responses with 75% noting at least 50% pain relief.

Finally, Ferrante[76] treated 100 patients with 235 CESIs, each containing 80 mg of methylprednisolone acetate; 40% of patients had at least 50% pain relief and at least partial return to activities. Patients with a true radiculopathy and associated neurologic deficits had a 62% probability of obtaining at least 50% pain relief. Also, 67% of all patients obtained at least some pain relief. The best results with CESIs occurred in patients with either a true radiculopathy (having symptoms and sensory and/or motor deficits at a specific root level) regardless of abnormalities on imaging studies or radicular pain only with structural abnormalities on imaging studies at the level corresponding to the symptoms. Better outcomes occurred in patients with cervical spondylosis or stenosis, without myofascial symptoms and with the presence of motor weakness.

According to the above studies, CESIs seem to work better in patients with cervical spondylosis, acute disc herniation, limited myofascial pain complaints, and significant radicular pain in a specific dermatomal distribution. No controlled blinded studies of CESIs including a placebo group or an accounting of associated treatments or therapies have been reported. For these reasons, further scientific study is needed to fully quantify the efficacy of CESIs.

Regarding thoracic epidural steroid injections (TESIs), due to the relatively low incidence of thoracic spine disease, few studies documented their efficacy for either thoracic spine or radicular pain. As in the cervical and lumbar spine, TESIs have been recommended for the treatment of thoracic disc disease. Thoracic disc herniations, however, account for less than 1% of all symptomatic disc herniations.[68,193] At least 11–13% of thoracic disc herniations are asymptomatic based on diagnosis by CT-myelography[9] and MRI.[188,190] Thoracic disc herniations that do not cause significant pain or neurologic deficits are thought to remain relatively asymptomatic in most cases and, therefore, require no preventive treatments.[9] The treatment of symptomatic thoracic disc herniations remains somewhat controversial. Brown[35] has stated "the thoracic herniated disc appears to follow a course similar to cervical or lumbar disc disease in that these herniations

frequently respond to a nonoperative therapy program." TESIs are known anecdotally to often provide pain relief in the treatment of painful thoracic disc herniations in patients without associated myelopathy.

TESIs also have been shown to provide pain relief from thoracic radiculopathies not only from disc disease, but also due to herpes zoster, trauma, or associated diabetes.[78,79] Degenerative scoliosis, generally seen in women, is the other condition most commonly associated with thoracic radiculopathies.[88] Reporting on the use of TESI in four cases of idiopathic thoracic neuralgia, Forrest[79] demonstrated nearly 50% pain relief lasting 12 months in one case and a similar level of relief lasting about three months in two other cases. The authors (REW, SJD, JPL) have also found TESIs to be helpful in the management of painful thoracic spondylosis and chronic inflammatory thoracic pain unresponsive to more conservative measures.

Lumbosacral Spine: Clinical Trials

According to Kepes and Duncalf,[109] about 100 reports on the use of subarachnoid and epidural spinal injections for low back pain were published worldwide from 1960–1985. Recent review articles on the efficacy of lumbosacral epidural steroid injections (LESIs) by Kepes and Duncalf,[109] Benzon,[13] Haddox,[88] and Bogduk et al.[24] are recommended. All of these articles mention the lack of well-controlled studies on LESIs and the variability between studies in the type and dosage of corticosteroid used, injection technique, patient diagnosis, length of follow-up, and quantitation of pain relief. The response rate obtained with LESIs in past studies has varied from 20–100%,[88,109] with an average response rate calculated from many studies at 60% by Kepes and Duncalf[109] and 75% by White.[186] A recent meta-analysis of literature concerning lumbosacral epidural corticosteroids published from 1966–1993 revealed an overall positive response with respect to pain relief from epidural corticosteroids.[93] A summary of the results from studies on LESIs including at least 100 patients is presented in Table 27-1. The majority of these studies involve no attempt to randomize treatments or provide a control group of patients and, although the studies do provide anecdotal information, no scientific conclusions regarding the efficacy of LESIs can be made from their data. The results of studies containing at least some control group of patients are presented in Table 27-2.

According to Bogduk,[24] more than 40 papers have been published on lumbar and caudal epidural corticosteroid injections involving a total of more than 4,000 patients. Only four of these papers have recommended against the use of lumbosacral epidural corticosteroids. Previous research has indicated that an epidural injection of saline or local anesthetic alone can be effective in relieving back and leg pain in some patients.[48,61,62,75] The occasional positive response to epidural saline or anesthetic questions the validity of these agents as experimental controls versus epidural corticosteroids. Numerous studies have, however, compared the efficacy of epidural injections using local anesthetic or saline compared to mixing these agents with corticosteroids. Beliveau[12] published one of the first such studies comparing patients with radicular pain injected by a caudal approach with procaine versus procaine plus 80 mg of methylprednisolone. He reported no significant difference in pain relief between these two groups. Snoek et al.[163] treated patients having unilateral radicular pain with lumbar epidural injections and used either 2 ml of saline or 80 mg of methylprednisolone (2 ml) and found no significant differences in pain relief between the two groups. Patients in both groups responded and reported pain relief ranging from 25–70%. Bush and Hillier[39] injected patients with either 25 ml of saline or 80 mg of triamcinolone plus 0.5% procaine up to a total of 25 ml. At 1 month of follow-up, patients treated with corticosteroid showed significant pain relief, mobility, and quality of life. At 1 year follow-up, this treatment group continued to have a tendency (although not statistically significant) of less pain and more mobility and significantly fewer patients with a positive straight leg raise test.

Cuckler et al.[59] also reported no significant difference in pain relief between an epidural injection of procaine versus corticosteroid; this 1985 study has been quoted frequently as evidence against the efficacy of epidural corticosteroids. However, since the authors examined the patients for pain relief only once 24 hours after epidural corticosteroid injection, a period of time considered too brief for epidural steroids to work effectively, the results are generally not considered valid. In addition, Cuckler's patients all received epidural corticosteroids at the L3–L4 level regardless of the level causing pain, and fluoroscopic guidance was not used. Several other well-known studies[31,39,168,196] compared various combinations of epidural saline and/or local anesthetic solutions against epidural corticosteroids and concluded that the steroid did provide better pain relief for back and radicular pain. However, according to Bogduk et al.,[24] no statistically valid conclusions can be drawn from the results of these studies due to small sample sizes or a poorly controlled study design.

Several controlled studies have compared the pain relief resulting from an epidural corticosteroid injection to a placebo injection involving needle placement into the interspinous ligament. In 1973, Dilke et al.[69] performed a randomized, prospective,

TABLE 27-1. Uncontrolled Epidural Steroid Studies Including at Least 100 Patients

Study	Number of Patients	Percentage of Patients Reporting Pain Relief	Volume Injected (ml)
Arnhoff, 1977	140	39	10
Burn & Langdon, 1979	138	78	40
Goebert et al., 1961	113	73	30
Heppner et al.	478	100	
Heyse-Moore, 1978	120	62	20
Ito, 1971	296	73	5–10
Jennings et al.	134	66	10–20
Mount	287	88	20
Sayle-Creer and Swerdlow, 1969	320	53	100
Swerdlow and Sayle-Creer, 1970	117	65	5
Warr et al., 1972	500	63	40

Adapted from Kepes ER, Duncalf D: Treatment of backache with spinal injections for local anesthetics, spinal and systemic steroids. A review. Pain 22:33–47, 1985.

double-blind study involving patients with radicular pain and comparing the efficacy of lumbar epidural injection using licocaine and 80 mg of methylprednisolone versus a 1-ml saline interspinous ligament injection. Compared with control patients, a significantly greater number of treated patients that reported pain being "clearly relieved," more treatment patients were pain-free at 3 months, and more had resumed work after 3 months. Ridley[147] evaluated epidural corticosteroid mixed with saline versus a control interspinous ligament injection of 2 ml saline and also reported a definite benefit from the epidural corticosteroid injection after 2 weeks. Klenerman et al.[111] studied patients who had radicular pain for less than 6 months and received an epidural injection of either 20 ml of saline, 80 mg

TABLE 27-2. Controlled Epidural Corticosteroid Studies

Study	Number of Patients	Approach	Follow-up	Steroid Benefit
Beliveau, 1971	48	caudal	1–3 mo	yes
Dilke, 1973	100	lumbar	2 wk & 3 mo	yes
Breivik, 1976	35	lumbar	3 wk	yes
Snoek, 1977	51	lumbar	48 hr	no
Yates, 1978	20	caudal	1 mo	yes
Klenerman, 1984	63	lumbar	2 wk & 2 mo	no
Helliwell, 1985	39	lumbar	1 mo & 3 mo	yes
Ridley, 1988	39	lumbar	2 wk	yes
Bush and Hillier, 1991	23	caudal	1 mo & 1 yr	yes

of methylprednisolone in 20 ml of saline, 20 ml of 0.25% bupivacaine or interspinous needling with a Touhy needle. These authors found no added benefit from the corticosteroid but did note a 75% response rate to epidural injection versus control patients. Finally, Helliwell et al.[95] injected patients having unilateral radicular pain with either 80 mg of methylprednisolone plus 10 ml of saline into the epidural space, or 5 ml of saline into the interspinous ligament. Follow-up was performed at 1 and 3 months and a significantly greater number of patients receiving the epidural corticosteroid had "definite improvement," loss of a positive straight leg raise test, and decreased pain with spine motion.

No previous studies have compared the efficacy of transforaminal epidural corticosteroid injection (also known as a selective epidural or selective nerve root block, all of which will be used in this chapter) versus midline or paramedian epidurals in the treatment of either back or radicular pain. According to Derby, Bogduk and Kline,[65] however, the transforaminal approach may more reliably place corticosteroid in the anterior epidural space where the most pain-sensitive structures are located. Many studies report the usefulness of selective nerve root blocks to identify or confirm a specific nerve root as a pain generator when such a diagnosis is not clear based on other clinical evidence.[71,94,97,114,165]

Previous studies have indicated that the majority of patients with substantial leg pain relief from a selective nerve root block, even if the relief is temporary, will benefit from surgery for the radicular pain when that nerve root injury is associated with a disc herniation or lateral bony stenosis.[71,97,114] It is thought that a single nerve root is almost always responsible for acute radicular symptoms. Kikuchi[110] treated patients diagnosed with acute radicular leg pain associated with intermittent claudication and was able to relieve the pain in 90% of the patients by blocking only one nerve root. Derby et al[65] showed the significant negative predictive value of transforaminal corticosteroid injections in relation to the surgical outcome for the treatment of chronic radiculopathy. Of 38 patients with radicular pain for at least 12 months and less than 80% pain relief 1 week after a selective nerve root block with corticosteroid, only 2 had significant relief following surgery for radicular pain. In addition, 11 of 13 patients with a positive response to the corticosteroid nerve root block had a positive surgical outcome. Therapeutically, one or two corticosteroid nerve root blocks have been shown to occasionally provide relief from radicular pain for more than 6 months, allowing adequate time for recovery and avoiding the need for surgery.[110]

Several important factors may have been addressed incompletely in studies regarding lumbosacral epidural corticosteroids. Most of these studies did not use fluoroscopy, and a significant incidence of improper needle placement without fluoroscopy has been documented, especially for a caudal approach, which has been used frequently in past studies.[12,31,39,186,196] In general, study participants receiving improper (not epidural) placement of corticosteroid due to the lack of fluoroscopic guidance and not responding because of this technical error are routinely grouped with patients in the same study receiving properly placed epidural corticosteroids, thereby lowering the apparent response rate. Also, the specific approach used for an epidural corticosteroid injection has often been uncontrolled in previous studies and sometimes appeared poorly matched to the patient's condition, especially for the many studies using a caudal approach. If localizing the corticosteroid in the epidural space as close to the pain generators as possible does strongly affect the response, then prior estimates of the efficacy of lumbosacral epidural corticosteroids may remain underestimated. For example, the response from a caudal epidural injection for an L4 radiculopathy, especially if a relatively small volume of injectate is used, is probably not as effective as a welll-placed selective transforaminal approach.

Various trends with epidural corticosteroid injections do seem apparent from previous research. First, patients with a more acute episode of back or leg pain generally respond better to epidural corticosteroids, particularly if the duration of pain is less than 3 months.[36,85,90] Unilateral radicular pain, especially when due to active nerve root inflammation from acute disc pathology rather than bony stenosis, tends to respond more favorably than strictly low back pain.[88,186] Patients also tend to have poor responses to epidural corticosteroids postoperatively unless a significant reinjury causing an acute disc or nerve root injury has occurred. The temporary nature of pain relief generally afforded by epidural corticosteroids has been well documented by White et al.,[186] who reported 82% of patients with pain relief one day after an LESI, 24% after 1 month, 16% after 2 months, and 7% for at least 6 months. However, since back or leg pain occurring from an acute disc injury often improves dramatically without surgery,[153] temporary pain relief from epidural injections can provide time during which disc or nerve recovery may occur. Also, a small but undetermined percentage of patients receiving epidural corticosteroids for back or leg pain obtain persisting pain relief and avoid potential surgery, thereby saving substantial medical costs and avoiding the iatrogenic risks of surgery. The benefits gained from epidural corticosteroids regarding patients' long-term functional status, not simply pain relief, also remain unclear, although one study has shown decreased return to work time in patients treated with epidural corticosteroids.[69]

Mechanism of Pain Relief

Prior to the use of corticosteroids, epidural injections were performed with large volumes of saline solution, and relief of back and leg pain was thought to be due to the disruption of scar tissue in the epidural space.[75] Such a mechanism is now disputed since large volumes of radiographic dye injected in the lumbar epidural space flow along a path of least resistance out of the epidural space through the neuroforamen.[184] More likely, mechanisms for pain relief seen after a saline epidural injection are an osmotic effect decreasing local epidural and nerve root tissue edema or dilution of inflammatory mediators.[88] Response to an epidural injection of local anesthetic may be due in part to the physical effects of the fluid itself, but also to the interruption of afferent nerve impulses, which is known to decrease the associated level of pain.[40]

Soon after Lindahl and Rexed[117] attributed sciatica to the persistent inflammation of lumbosacral nerve roots, the widespread use of corticosteroids in epidural and intrathecal injections began. Since that time, the key role that inflammatory mediators originating from the disc play in the production of local inflammation and resulting discogenic and neurogenic pain is well documented.[56,113,122,154,171] It has followed that the proposed primary mechanism of action of epidural corticosteroid injections is the potent anti-inflammatory properties of the corticosteroids.[77,168,180,184] Winnie[194] provided further evidence for an anti-inflammatory mechanism as compared to injectate volume alone by achieving significant long-term responses from LESI after injecting only 2 ml of corticosteroid. The marked pain relief often noted with epidural corticosteroid injection for an acute radiculopathy may also be due to the stabilization of nerve root membranes by the corticosteroid suppressing the ectopic neuronal discharges, which can cause pain and paresthesias.[67,183]

POTENTIAL COMPLICATIONS

Medications and Associated Risks

Local Anesthetics

Lidocaine and bupivacaine are the most common anesthetics used for epidural injection. The general characteristics and toxic effects of these two amide anesthetics have been presented earlier in this book. All local anesthetics injected into the epidural space must be preservative-free since the effect of preservatives in the epidural and subarachnoid spaces has not been evaluated satisfactorily. A major concern when administering anesthetics into the epidural space is systemic toxicity. The two most common systemic effects from epidural local anesthetics involve the central nervous system (CNS) and the

cardiovascular system. A rough estimate of the threshold plasma concentration in humans causing onset of CNS toxicity for lidocaine is 5–10 μg/ml (probably closer to 10 μg/ml), and for bupivacaine is 2–4 μg/ml (bupivacaine is about four times more toxic than lidocaine).[51] Braid and Scott[30] injected 400 mg of lidocaine epidurally in test subjects and recorded an average peak plasma concentration of about 4 μg/ml, slightly below the neurotoxic concentration given above. In order to give a total dose of 400 mg of lidocaine, 40 ml of 1% or 20 ml of 2% lidocaine would be required. Both of these doses are significantly above the usual dose of lidocaine used for epidural corticosteroid injections (generally 5–15 ml of 0.5 or 1% lidocaine for LESIs and less volume for selective nerve root blocks and CESIs). The maximum epidural dose recommended for a single injection is 500 mg for lidocaine and 225 mg for bupivacaine (90 ml of 0.25% bupivacaine).[51] These ranges for CNS toxicity are only estimates, however, and neurologic side effects have been reported at much lower doses. Higher concentrations of lidocaine (4 or 5%) can cause serious side effects at lower total dosages than cited above, requiring more cautious administration, but these concentrations are generally not used undiluted for standard epidural corticosteroid injections.[50] Peak plasma concentration of epidural anesthetics occurs 10–20 minutes after injection, so it is recommended that patients be monitored for at least 30 minutes following an epidural injection. Significant CNS toxicity caused by intravascular lidocaine is usually manifested by complaints of circumoral numbness, disorientation, light headedness, nystagmus, tinnitus, and muscle twitching in the face or distal extremities.

Cardiovascular toxicity can occur from the direct effect of the anesthetic on the sympathetic nerves, which help to regulate cardiac function and peripheral blood flow. The onset of sympathetic blockade is known to be more rapid from subarachnoid versus epidural injections, but both can be associated with serious cardiac side effects.[158] Sympathetic blockade develops with local anesthetics placed in the thoracic region and does not occur with these agents in the lumbar region unless a volume large enough to cause an ascending epidural block to the thoracic level is injected or inadvertent subarachnoid injection occurs. Studies using healthy adult patients have shown that anesthetic blockade to the T5 level caused only minimal cardiac changes provided that bradycardia was avoided.[81,162] Complete sympathetic blockade to the T1 level is associated with potentially more serious complications, including decreased cardiac output, decreased mean arterial pressure, and decreased peripheral resistance requiring cardiovascular support measures.[50]

Acute cardiac complications can result from an intravascular injection of lidocaine or bupivacaine, the most significant of which is decreased cardiac contractility. Previous studies have shown, however, that excellent cardiovascular function is maintained in humans with plasma lidocaine concentrations of 4–8 μg/ml.[108] Also, serious cardiac complications from lidocaine toxicity are thought to occur at plasma lidocaine concentrations which are about seven times higher than the concentration causing CNS seizure activity.[126] Large doses of bupivacaine in particular have been shown to have the potential to cause depression of both myocardial contractility and cardiac conduction resulting in resistant bradycardia and ventricular arrhythmias.[144] In human volunteers though, slow IV injection of bupivacaine to achieve plasma concentrations equivalent to those occurring during epidural anesthesia failed to cause any significant cardiovascular changes.[120]

Other than the use of excessive dosages, the most serious complications occur when local anesthetics to be given epidurally are inadvertently injected into the subdural or subarachnoid space or given intravascularly. Although many factors determine the spread and effect of a subarachnoid anesthetic injection, the level of the injection and the total dosage of the anesthetic are most important. Obviously, cervical and thoracic level blocks pose a greater risk for possible cardiac, autonomic, or central nervous system complications. For most LESIs done at the L3–L4 level or below, a typical single dose of 10 ml of 1% lidocaine or 0.25% bupivacaine inadvertently injected in the subarachnoid space may cause a complete sensory or even motor block (less likely with bupivacaine), but would typically be limited to the sacral and lumbar levels.[32] More superior levels of spinal anesthesia are possible from a lumbosacral approach, however, and all the appropriate equipment should be immediately available to manage any cardiovascular, neurological or respiratory sequelae. In fact, the maximum single dose recommended for a lidocaine subarachnoid injection is 100 mg, which is equivalent to 10 ml 1% lidocaine, a dosage frequently used with epidural corticosteroid injections.

Improper subarachnoid needle placement during an epidural injection can be identified with the use of fluoroscopy. In addition, a 3–5 ml test dose of local anesthetic prior to the injection of the total volume of anesthetic and corticosteroid can help prevent complications. The onset of significant sensory changes within 3–5 minutes of the test dose strongly suggests subarachnoid rather than epidural placement and can be used to prevent possible serious side effects occurring with improper needle placement. Accidental intravascular administration of local anesthetics is relatively common in epidural injections but can be virtually eliminated with the use of fluoroscopy.[186]

Corticosteroids

The corticosteroids most commonly used for epidural injection are methylprednisolone acetate, triamcinolone diacetate, and betamethasone (Celestone Soluspan). Andrade[7] presented a study of epidural corticosteroid side effects in 301 patients and listed the following possible effects: insomnia, mood swings, euphoria, depression, postinjection pain flare, facial erythema, fluid retention, hypertension, congestive heart failure, hyperglycemia, headache, gastritis, and menstrual irregularities. The study examined side effects occurring 5–7 days after patients received 3–12 mg of betamethasone. The most common problems were insomnia (39%), facial erythema (29%), nausea (21%), rash and pruritus (8%), and "fever" (10%, although no patient was found to have an oral temperature higher than 100° F). About 14 days after LESI, no persistent complaints were reported, and Andrade concluded that the majority of side effects after LESIs were temporary. Most of these side effects are clearly associated with the systemic absorption of corticosteroid and subsequent transient hypercorticism. Burn and Langdon[38] documented depressed plasma cortisol levels occurring for about 2 weeks after epidural methylprednisolone injection with a return to normal levels within 3 weeks. Raff et al.[141] reported chronic suppression of ACTH secretion and decreased plasma cortisol levels for 3 months in patients receiving 80 mg of triamcinolone at weekly intervals for 3 weeks. These corticosteroid effects constitute a valid reason for avoiding an arbitrarily scheduled series of epidural injections.

The development of Cushing's syndrome from epidural corticosteroid injections with more prolonged abnormalities is rare, but has also been documented. Cushing's syndrome was noted in four patients receiving 300–600 mg of epidural methylprednisolone over 3 days, although this represents a higher total corticosteroid dose than most recommendations suggest.[112] Tuel[173] reported a case of Cushing's syndrome with cushingoid appearance and an undetectable plasma cortisol level after one CESI of 60 mg of methylprednisolone. The patient's signs and symptoms developed over 1 month and resolved after about 4 months. Patients suffering from severe symptomatic adrenal suppression and decreased plasma cortisol after an epidural corticosteroid injection should be diagnosed, if possible, before being subjected to additional significant stressors in order to avoid a possible adrenal crisis. One such stressor could be spinal surgery. Our review revealed no published cases of an adrenal crisis occurring with a spine surgery following epidural corticosteroids. In diabetic patients, complications from epidural corticosteroids due to transient hyperglycemia must be monitored closely and can usually be managed satisfactorily with frequent checks of blood sugar and adjustments in medication. Finally, congestive heart failure developing in cardiac patients after epidural corticosteroids due to fluid retention must be considered, although only one such case has been documented.[83]

Concerns regarding the use of methylprednisolone acetate for spinal injections arose in the 1970s after reports of associated chemical arachnoiditis were published.[131] At that time, subarachnoid corticosteroid injections were being done and the causative agent of the arachnoiditis was thought to be the polyethylene glycol contained in methylprednisolone since years of similar injections with hydrocortisone did not seem to induce arachnoiditis. Animal studies have revealed no deleterious effect to neural tissue from repeated exposure to glucocorticosteroid alone.[64] Strict epidural without subarachnoid use of corticosteroid with polyethylene glycol has not been shown to cause arachnoiditis, but the potential always exists for accidental subarachnoid injection during an epidural procedure. Since no conclusive evidence has proven the cause and effect relationship between methylprednisolone with polyethylene glycol and arachnoiditis, some authors continue to approve the use of this corticosteroid preparation,[14,33] while many physicians recommend using other corticosteroid preparations.[16,128,130,150] Soluble corticosteroid preparations, such as the betamethasone solution that we recommend, does not contain polyethylene glycol or other potentially damaging preservatives. Betamethasone should not be mixed with lidocaine or any other local anesthetic containing preservatives such as methylparaben or propylparaben because these additives tend to cause flocculation of the corticosteroid.

Allergic and Anaphylactic Reactions

The medications injected during epidural blocks can lead to allergic or anaphylactic reactions. Pruess[137] reported that most allergic reactions to corticosteroids are not caused by the carrier vehicle but by the corticosteroid alone. An allergic or pseudoallergic reaction in a previously nonsensitized individual may be delayed up to 1 week after depot corticosteroid injection due to the gradual systemic uptake of these medications. However, anaphylactoid reactions (without a histologic immune response) or actual anaphylaxis (with a histologic immune response) occur most often within 2 hours after the epidural injection but have been known to develop up to 6 hours later.[161] Regardless of the cause, fatalities from anaphylactoid reactions and anaphylaxis are generally caused by respiratory-related complications involving mechanical airway obstruction.[82] We found no cases of fatal anaphylaxis following an epidural corticosteroid injection in the literature. Close patient monitoring after epidural injection is recommended for approximately 30 minutes, as well as direct patient access to an informed on-call physician after an injection in case of delayed but emergent complications.

Medical Complications

Systemic Complications

Relatively few serious complications occur in patients receiving epidural corticosteroid injection from well-trained and experienced clinicians. For CESIs, Waldman[179] performed 790 injections and reported three episodes of vasovagal syncope (two of which required treatment with IV fluids and ephedrine), one superficial infection at the injection site, and two unintentional dural punctures. Cicala et al.[45] did 204 CESIs and noted one instance of intermittent nausea and vomiting lasting 12 hours, one episode of transient upper extremity weakness, and two dural punctures without sequelae.

For LESIs, Brown[36] reported no serious side effects in 500 patients, and White[184] quoted a rate for significant complications of about 0.4% after lumbar epidural injections in 300 patients. Minor medical complications from LESIs include headache, dizziness, transient hypotension, nausea, and transient aggravation of back pain or leg pain.[12,62] Some of these minor complications are apparently due to the corticosteroid being injected into the epidural space.[17] Headache without dural puncture occurs occasionally, especially after injection of a large volume of epidural fluid. The incidence of such headaches has been estimated at 2%[90] and attributed to air injected into the epidural space, increased intrathecal pressure from the fluid injected around the dural sac, or possibly an undetected dural puncture.[4] A temporary increase in the patient's back or leg pain for 24–48 hours after epidural corticosteroid injection has been reported to occur 1–2% of the time either due to tissue irritation from the corticosteroid itself or from the rate or volume of the injectate and generally requires no treatment.[12,47,90]

Dural Puncture and Associated Headache

Unintentional dural punctures during epidural corticosteroid injections occur even in the hands of experienced physicians. The incidence of dural puncture during a cervical or lumbar epidural injection done by experienced physicians is estimated in the anesthesia literature as ranging from 0.5–1%,[57,139] 0–2%[132] and up to 5%.[23] The incidence of dural punctures with caudal epidural injection is much lower, as expected and reported by White[186] as two dural punctures out of 2,000 caudal injections. If needle advancement is not carefully controlled during an injection, a dural puncture can be associated with direct spinal cord trauma for any block at or above the L2 level. All documented reports of needle injuries to the spinal cord occurring during spinal injections state that patients complained immediately of severe lancinating pain at or below the dermatomal level of needle placement at the time of the injury.[50] Following laminectomy, midline or paramedian epidural injection at the level of the surgery is not recommended since the epidural space may be obliterated due to scarring leading to a subarachnoid injection; performing the block at a level above or below the surgery site or with a transforaminal approach is recommended.[191]

After accidental penetration of the dura, injection of even small volumes of local anesthetics may cause complete and ascending spinal anesthesia. Subarachnoid placement of the needle can usually be detected with fluoroscopy and a 3–5 ml test dose of 1% lidocaine before more anesthetic or corticosteroid is injected. However, a negative test dose does not guarantee epidural needle placement, and continued close observation is necessary.[50] Following an accidental dural puncture, White[186] suggests relocating the needle at a different interspace and injecting only corticosteroid with saline or sterile water to avoid possible complications from subarachnoid anesthetics.

The incidence of postdural puncture headaches in the anesthesia literature ranges from 7.5–75%[63] and depends significantly on needle size, with the highest estimates of 75% associated with 16- and 18-gauge epidural needles.[53,54] As mentioned, not all headaches developing after an epidural corticosteroid injection are due to dural punctures. The clinical features of a postdural puncture headache include delayed onset of several to about 48 hours, most severe pain with an upright position, and often total resolution in the supine or prone position. The most likely mechanism of postdural puncture headaches is loss of CSF through the puncture site with resultant tension on cranial meningeal vessels and nerves, as well as reflex vasodilatation, thereby causing pain.[37] Early conservative care involves 24–48 hours of bed rest, intake of oral fluid increased to 3 liters per day, oral analgesics as needed, and occasionally an abdominal binder.[32] Another treatment option involves the use of oral or intravenous caffeine, which has been shown to be safe and often effective, although the recurrence rate following caffeine treatment is significant.[129] If resolution of the headache is not achieved in 1–2 weeks with more conservative management, then an epidural blood patch may be needed, which has a success rate of 90–95% and can be repeated once as necessary.[2,129] The procedure for the administration of a blood patch is presented in the Technical Considerations section of this chapter.

Durocutaneous fistulae after epidural corticosteroid injections are rare but have been reported and usually occur after multiple attempts are made to enter the epidural space at the same level using large-bore needles or a series of repeated injections at the same level.[11,88,107] Contributing factors are a blunt perforation of the skin with a large epidural needle or the deposition of substances along the needle tract such as corticosteroid or blood, which then interferes with proper healing of the tract. Recommendations to avoid dural fistulae formation include flushing the corticosteroid solution out of the needle prior to withdrawal, cleaning the needle or using a new needle before attempting another injection, and puncturing the skin surface with a sharp introducer needle before pushing a blunt epidural needle through the skin.[107] Durocutaneous fistulas have been successfully treated with both blood patches and primary surgical closure of the dura and skin defect.[118]

Epidural Abscess and Hematoma

Epidural abscess or hematoma formation following an epidural injection is the most serious potential complication of this procedure. Epidural abscess formation following an injection of corticosteroids is extremely rare and is almost always associated with the use of an epidural catheter. Baker[10] reviewed reported cases of epidural abscesses, and only one case in the 39 reviewed was from a single-shot epidural corticosteroid injection. Most of the other cases followed the use of an epidural catheter for spinal anesthesia in patients with preexisting systemic infections. No apparent increase in epidural abscess formation was associated with the use of corticosteroids during epidural procedures done on patients without systemic disease. An epidural abscess following an injection usually includes complaints of severe back pain, fever, and often chills with a leukocytosis developing about 3 days after the injection.[43] Prompt clinical evaluation and diagnosis is required for successful treatment of the infection, which is usually caused by *Staphylococcus aureus*. Immediate surgical laminectomy and debridement are usually required.[10] Patients with diabetes mellitus are possibly more susceptible to epidural abscess formation, as well as patients with a significant local or systemic infection before the epidural injection.

Epidural bleeding during injections is generally caused by damage to an epidural vein during the procedure and usually leads to minimal problems without any serious sequelae. Epidural hematoma formation with associated neurologic damage following an epidural injection is extremely rare in patients with normal blood clotting mechanisms; only one such case has been reported to date, and that case was associated with numerous epidural injections.[115] Any medications causing abnormalities in the clotting mechanism taken prior to the epidural injection could potentially increase the risk of an epidural hematoma. Such medications include

Heparin, Coumadin, aspirin, and all nonsteroidal anti-inflammatory medications. Epidural injections should also be avoided in patients with a known platelet count of less than 100,000 platelets/ml.[1] Since epidural corticosteroid injection for pain management does not typically represent an emergency procedure, these procedures should be postponed until the clotting abnormalities can be corrected.

Serious concern regarding the presence of an epidural hematoma should be raised in patients complaining of severe neck or back pain associated with any significant neurologic complaints noted soon after receiving an epidural injection. Williams[188] reported a case of an epidural hematoma occurring after the seventh CESI performed in the same patient, all at the C7–T1 interspace; severe neck pain developed 20 minutes after the block and persistent sensory deficits within 2½ hours. An immediate physical exam followed by a CT or MRI scan if necessary is essential for patients thought to have an epidural hematoma since early surgical intervention can limit or even prevent permanent neurologic damage.[50]

TECHNICAL CONSIDERATIONS

Fluoroscopy

Most spine care specialists currently recommend fluoroscopy for diagnostic and therapeutic epidural injections for several reasons. Epidural injections performed without fluoroscopy are not always placed into the epidural space or at the desired interspace as intended.[73,166] White et al.[186] reported that experienced anesthesiologists misidentify the epidural space without the aid of fluoroscopy about 25% of the time during lumbar epidurals and about 30% of the time during caudal epidurals. After performing many caudal procedures, El-Khoury[79] and Renfrew[145] recommended fluoroscopy due to the many variations of the sacrum and subsequent difficulty assessing proper needle location during caudal injections. Renfrew[145] used fluoroscopy after needle placement to evaluate anesthesiologists performing blind caudal injections to document how many needles were initially placed in the epidural space. He found that for experienced physicians caudal epidural needle placement was achieved 62% of the time and, even when the sacral hiatus was easily palpated, initial epidural needle placement occurred in only 78% of patients. By definition epidurals done strictly for anesthesia involve a sensory and motor blockade, which helps confirm proper needle placement, while such signs are not obtained during most midline or paramedian epidural corticosteroid injections. During diagnostic selective epidural nerve root injections when a sensory block is routinely produced, fluoroscopy is essential for exact needle placement so only a small amount of local anesthetic can be placed as close to that specific nerve root as possible.

Epidural corticosteroids are thought to provide prolonged pain relief because of the gradual absorption of the depot corticosteroid in the vicinity of the pain-generating tissues. It follows that using fluoroscopic guidance to ensure corticosteroid placement as close as possible to the pain generator will probably yield the best results. The presence of significant anatomic anomalies such as a midline epidural septum[19] or multiple separate epidural compartments[101] can restrict the desired flow of the epidural injectants to the suspected pain generator and will remain undetected without fluoroscopy. If an epidural corticosteroid injection fails and fluoroscopy was not employed, the failure may be due to either a genuine poor response and/or to improperly placed medications. Important diagnostic information may then be lost.

Fluoroscopy also prevents accidental intravascular injections since the absence of blood return with needle aspiration prior to an injection is not a reliable indicator of intravascular needle placement. For caudal epidurals, White[184] reported a 6% incidence of intravascular needle placement documented by fluoroscopy following no blood return with needle aspiration, and Renfrew[145] noted the same in about 9% of his caudal injections. Repeated injections of nonionic contrast into the epidural space causes no apparent histological[68] or neurologic abnormalities.[100]

The various dye patterns seen with epidural injections must be recognized to avoid complications during these injections. The pattern typically seen with contrast injected into the epidural space is a fluffy spread of dye moving quickly away from the tip of the needle (Fig. 27-7). Other images indicating inappropriate needle placement include the rapid disappearance of dye in a vascular pattern (Fig. 27-8), the limited contained spread within a fascial plane, or the typical myelographic spread of a subarachnoid injection.

Needles and Equipment

Crawford and Tuohy needles are relatively blunt needles designed specifically for epidural injections. The blunt tip of these needles is ideal for less experienced physicians because it allows easier identification of the ligamentum flavum and less chance of puncturing the dura once the needle reaches the epidural space.[174] The curved tip of the Tuohy needle was initially designed to allow easier passage of a catheter through the needle into the epidural space. Winged needles or detachable wings for standard Tuohy needles are available for the hanging-drop technique to allow the needle to be held with the

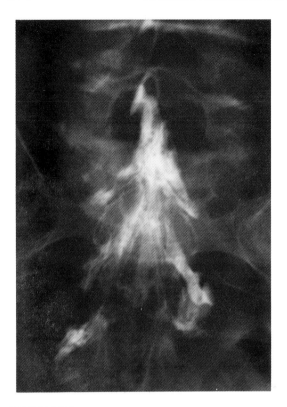

FIGURE 27-7. Caudal epidural injection contrast pattern or epidurogram.

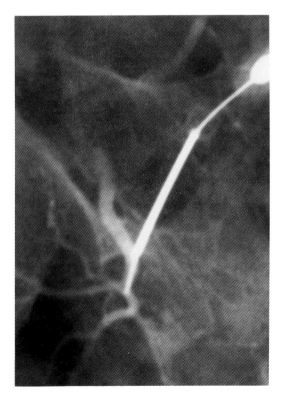

FIGURE 27-8. Vascular contrast pattern. (Courtesy of Ted Lennard, MD.)

fingers away from the fluid placed up to the needle hub during this technique.[50] Some experienced physicians prefer using needles designed for subarachnoid spinal procedures instead of an epidural needle for single-shot epidural injections. A 22-gauge standard spinal (Quincke-Babcock) needle is readily available and seems to be more comfortable for the patient than blunt epidural needles during an epidural injection. However, the risk of dural puncture is greater with a spinal needle because of the sharp point and medium-length cutting bevel. Most injectionists do choose the 22-gauge standard spinal needle for approaches that have less chance of a dural puncture, such as caudal approaches and single-needle selective nerve root blocks, and use epidural needles only for midline or paramedian approaches. Other spinal needles have rounded, noncutting bevels (Green or Whitacre needles), which may decrease the risk of dural puncture and headache after accidental dural puncture as compared to standard spinal needles benefitting less experienced physicians.[32]

Whichever needle is used, the incidence of headaches after dural puncture is known to be significantly less with smaller gauge needles.[140,172,176] The incidence of dural puncture headaches is also decreased when the needle bevel is aligned parallel to the spinal axis and the longitudinal dural fibers.[124] The bevel of the needle is always placed on the same side of the needle as the notch on the hub to allow proper needle orientation during an injection, which can decrease the incidence of headaches should accidental dural puncture occur.

The supplies needed for epidural injections can be obtained in pre-packaged trays (usually listed as myelogram trays), or the items can be opened separately as needed at the time of the injection. A list of essential equipment is presented in Table 27-3. One item not used for traditional anesthetic epidurals is a section of plastic IV tubing through which contrast can be injected under direct fluoroscopic view and significantly limit radiation exposure to the hands.

Identification of the Epidural Space

The standard technique used to identify needle tip advancement into the epidural space relies on the loss of resistance to the injection of air or fluids when the needle enters the epidural space as compared to the marked resistance to injection within the tough overlying ligamentum flavum and other adjacent dense soft tissues (Fig. 27-9).[50] Either the loss of resistance or the hanging drop technique can be used. The loss of resistance technique traditionally uses a lubricated glass syringe partially filled with air or fluid (or both), and the substantial resistance to injection is noted while the needle is advanced through the muscle, spinous ligaments, and ligamentum flavum. For epidural injections performed on patients in the prone position under fluoroscopy, the heel of the hand being used to advance the needle is rested on the patient's back for support and control. Constant gentle pressure is placed on the syringe plunger, and significant resistance to both needle advancement and injection is noted when the needle has entered the ligamentum flavum. A noticeable loss of resistance to injection occurs as the needle tip enters the epidural space. With fluoroscopy, the depth of the ligamentum flavum can be determined by first advancing the needle tip off the lamina and into the ligamentum flavum.

The hanging drop technique involves a similar process, except the needle is first filled with liquid to the top of the hub until the fluid meniscus is just visible. A winged-needle is used and advanced with a two-handed technique, and the epidural space is identified by the rapid disappearance of the fluid in the hub as it flows into the epidural space.[50] Two major disadvantages exist with the hanging drop technique. First, the increased resistance to injection characteristic of the ligamentum flavum is not experienced with the hanging drop technique, eliminating a useful landmark of needle depth. Also, a plug of epidermal or other tissues at the tip of the needle formed while advancing the needle through the skin will prevent the flow of fluid from the needle, signaling entrance into the epidural space.

Once the needle is thought to be in the epidural space, the hub should be observed for fluid dripping back from the needle, which could indicate a dural puncture with CSF drainage. Usubiaga[175] pointed out that a drip back of fluid (either dye or local anesthetic) just injected into the epidural space can occur possibly due to poor compliance of the epidural

TABLE 27-3. Equipment Needed for Epidural Corticosteroid Injections

Betadyne or other aseptic skin solution

Sterile drapes

Skin anesthetic: 1% lidocaine (for local anesthesia), 25- or 27-gauge 1½-inch needles

Epidural anesthetic: 1%, 2%, 4% lidocaine or 0.25%, 0.5%, 0.75% bupivacaine as needed without preservative approved for epidural use

Epidural injection needle: 18- or 20-gauge Crawford or Tuohy needles (for midline or paramedian approach), 23- or 26-gauge Chiba needles (for double needle transforaminal approach), 22- or 25-spinal needles as needed

Plastic IV tubing: 6–10 inches long

Glass syringes: 2 or 5 ml as needed

Fluoroscopy equipment

space and generally worsened by a rapid rate or increased volume of injection. Drip back of injected fluids, not CSF, usually ceases within 30 seconds as epidural pressure reequilibrates. In addition, a characteristic epidural dye flow pattern seen with fluoroscopy is most indicative of proper epidural needle position. The lack of fluid return with aspiration along with a negative test dose also indicates proper epidural needle placement.

Volume and Rate of Injection

Determining the most effective volume of injectate, especially for LESIs, has been considered since the onset of epidural injections. Large volumes of fluid, usually saline, have been recommended in the past for lumbar epidurals in the treatment of back and leg pain.[62] As the volume of injectate increases, however, gradually decreasing cephalad spread occurs as fluid spills out of the spinal canal through the paravertebral foramen. White[184] reported dye

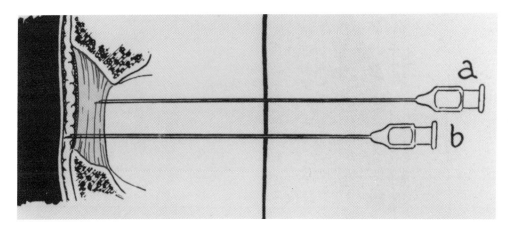

FIGURE 27-9. Needle A entering the ligamentum flavum; needle B entering the epidural space, at which time a loss of resistance to injection would be noted. (From Macintosh RR: Lumbar Puncture and Spinal Analgesia. Edinburgh, E & S Livingstone, 1957, with permission.)

flow from the lumbar epidural space through the neural foramen often at volumes as low as 5–10 ml. According to Harley,[90] 10 ml of dye injected at the L4–5 interspace usually spreads from the L1 to the S5 level and is a sufficient volume to bathe the areas involved in most lumbar disc derangements. For caudal epidurals, however, reliable spread is thought to occur up to the L4–5 level only, and injection at a more cephalad interspace should be used for disc lesions above the L4–5 level.[80] From these considerations, the most appropriate volume for lumbar midline, paramedian, and caudal epidural injections is 10–15 ml. There is no conclusive evidence that epidural corticosteroid injections using a greater volume provides more reliable pain relief. Smaller volumes are generally used for cervical epidurals ranging from 3–7 ml, although Cicala[45] used 10–15 ml without a noticeable increase in complications. Smaller volumes are needed for selective nerve root blocks, especially with local anesthetics, to maintain the diagnostic quality of the block. Bogduk[24] and Derby[65] recommend injecting only 1–2 ml of contrast and a 1–2 ml mixture of anesthetic and corticosteroid to limit injectate spread to a single nerve root as much as possible.

The rate of epidural injection does not appreciably change the ultimate spread of injectate.[38] Faster rates of injection are, however, thought to be associated with more pain during and after the epidural block.[69] The rate of epidural lidocaine injection causes only minimal changes in the maximum resulting lidocaine plasma concentation. Scott[155] reported an increase in the maximum plasma lidocaine concentration of just 16% when the anesthetic was injected within 15 seconds versus 60 seconds. The two most important reasons for injecting epidural solutions slowly over a 3–5 minute period are to decrease pain and to allow the best chance to identify complications from local anesthetics such as vasovagal reactions or accidental subarachnoid placement.

Patient Selection and Monitoring

The initial evaluation needed before a patient is scheduled for an epidural corticosteroid injection should include a review of any pertinent medical conditions. Each patient should be asked about conditions such as diabetes, past and present infections or immunocompromising conditions, blood clotting abnormalities or treatments, previous allergic reactions, previous injections, and the possibility of pregnancy. For cervical injections, the lack of controlled data makes informed selection of patients for CESI with respect to diagnosis and duration of symptoms difficult. As mentioned previously, the literature indicates perhaps better results in patients with spondylosis (cervical arthritis, disc

degeneration), cervical radiculopathy and radiculitis, cervical disc herniation, and spinal stenosis. Patients with radiculopathy and associated sensory or motor deficits generally respond well, at least temporarily, to CESIs.[76] According to Rowlingson and Kirschenbaum,[151] a negative EMG does not correlate with a poor response to CESI. Certainly, all patients receiving a CESI should receive conservative treatments (time for possible spontaneous recovery, oral medications, and therapy) and obtain only partial pain relief before being considered for a CESI due to the infrequent but potentially serious side effects of the injection.

No well documented guidelines exist for the timing of an initial CESI, although much of the published outcome data for CESI involved patients having neck pain for 6 months (but some up to 60 months) prior to receiving their first CESI.[76,139,151] Ferrante noted no correlation between outcome and duration of symptoms in his patients with a median duration of symptoms of 10.5 months (range 1–60 months). No thorough prospective studies have evaluated the necessity or the optimal time interval for repeat CESIs. Although some physicians employ a series of two or three CESIs spaced days or weeks apart, we recommend a more conservative approach. Patients who do not achieve significant pain relief (more than 50%) lasting for at least 2 weeks rarely have a significant component of inflammatory pain. More often, patients who do not respond significantly to CESI have residual neck pain of a mechanical origin, and a repeat CESI does not result in further pain relief. Any repeat injections should not be done sooner than 2 weeks since the anti-inflammatory effect of the first dose is still present at least up to 2 weeks after a CESI.[38] Another reason for not repeating CESIs on a scheduled 1- or 2-week interval is the significant number of patients with prolonged excellent pain relief from a single injection.[45] Probably no more than three CESIs are appropriate within 12 months due to possible cumulative side effects from the total dose of corticosteroids given.

Absolute contraindications for CESIs include significant local or systemic infection or any current anticoagulation treatments. Although no uniform guidelines exist, Cicala[45] discouraged CESI in patients with a "grossly" herniated disc or severe spinal canal stenosis. Obviously, extreme caution is needed for any CESI in a patient with a disc herniation or stenosis, especially in regard to the volume of injectate used.

Thoracic epidural corticosteroid injections can be used in patients with thoracic pain from intercostal neuralgia due to trauma or herpes,[78,79] thoracic disc herniation with or without radicular pain,[26] and chronic axial somatic pain.[123] It is imperative that viscerogenic sources of thoracic pain be excluded prior to performing a TESI. Timing of initial and repeat injections are performed as recommended in the previous section on CESIs.

For LESIs, no universally accepted guidelines exist regarding patient selection and timing of injections, although more informed choices are possible due to the larger base of clinical data versus cervicothoracic injections. According to Gamburd,[80] White et al.,[186] and Benzon,[13] LESIs are most effective in patients with pain of discogenic origin, especially if the condition is acute, involves a significant disc bulge or herniation, and is associated with significant radicular pain. Patients having internal disc disruption from an annular tear without significant disc degeneration or radicular pain respond less often to epidural corticosteroids.[80] Lumbar spinal stenosis is another diagnosis that will usually have a good, but often time-limited, response to LESI.[80,102,186] For any diagnosis, Jamison[106] listed the following factors associated with poor response to LESI: (1) numerous previous treatments for pain without any improvement, (2) current use of multiple medications, and (3) back pain that does not increase with activities.

Clinically, initial LESIs are often recommended and performed sooner than the first CESI, probably due to physicians having more experience with LESIs and the less severe potential iatrogenic sequelae. Approximately 85–90% of cases of acute low back pain resolve within 6–12 weeks, and allowing sufficient time for recovery without unnecessary treatments is important in patients showing gradual improvement.[6,17,187] However, several studies document better results for LESIs given within the first 3 months of low back or radicular pain.[90,136,185] Other factors must be considered when scheduling a patient's initial epidural injection, including (1) the failure of less invasive interventions, (2) the severity of the patient's pain and the need for pain control, (3) the use or misuse of oral analgesics, (4) the patient's ability to perform self-care activities, (5) the avoidance of hospitalization, (6) the facilitation of active rehabilitation, and (7) the allowance of an earlier return to work.[80] Routinely, the earliest an initial LESI is usually performed is about 6 weeks after the onset of back or radicular pain if other treatments are not effective. However, an LESI may be appropriate sooner if alternative pain management techniques are failing, especially in patients with severe radicular pain since there is a higher success rate from LESIs for this diagnosis. An experienced physician does not necessarily need a CT or MRI scan before giving an LESI, and the epidural injection can be done based on clinical judgment alone.[80] However, many physicians prefer to obtain a CT or MRI scan before performing a midline or paramedian epidural to assess the target epidural space.

No clear rationale exists for performing a series of LESIs at predetermined intervals since a positive response often lasts 4–8 weeks and sometimes longer. Also, a small percentage of patients with acute back with or without leg pain recover after one injection. It is generally accepted that if the initial epidural injection provides no relief, repeat injections are not recommended.[13,24,93,142,180] These authors also recommend a total of three LESIs per year due to possible cumulative side effects. Stambaugh[164] recommended the following absolute contraindications for LESIs: (1) cauda equina syndrome, (2) anticoagulation or bleeding disorder, and (3) suspected local or systemic infection.

Epidural corticosteroid injections at all levels of the spine are appropriate for an outpatient setting provided that all necessary resuscitative equipment is available, including oxygen, intubation equipment, and emergency drugs. For CESIs, Cicala[45] recommended always having IV access, monitoring pulse and blood pressure every 5 minutes during the injection, observing the patient for 45 minutes after the injection, and making a follow-up phone call 24 hours after the injection. Waldman[179] stated that IV access was not necessary for every patient receiving a CESI due to increased costs for the injection, risk of thrombophlebitis, and additional patient discomfort. He did suggest placing an IV in patients for which IV access might be difficult during an emergency, such as obese patients or patients receiving previous chemotherapy or having peripheral vascular disease. Waldman also recommended premedicating overly anxious patients to prevent complications secondary to movement or hypertension during the injection. If patients are to receive any IV sedatives during an epidural injection, continuous monitoring of pulse, blood pressure, and respiratory status is advisable. Patients receiving IV sedatives should not be allowed to drive after the injection, and transportation should be arranged before the procedure. We strongly recommend IV access in all patients undergoing CESI along with equipment to monitor blood pressure, pulse, and oxygen saturation. We also advise postinjection monitoring of pulse and blood pressure every 15 minutes for about 45 minutes before releasing the patient after a CESI.

Epidural injections in the lumbosacral spine are typically associated with fewer and less serious side effects. Routine IV access is not needed for lumbar or caudal epidurals done under fluoroscopy and using limited volumes of local anesthetics. Obviously, adequate resuscitative equipment for any potential complication should be readily available. Close observation of the patient's condition, which may include blood pressure and pulse checks every 15–20 minutes, should be provided for about 30–45 minutes after any lumbosacral injection. Careful assistance with ambulation immediately following an epidural injection should be provided for every patient, especially if any sensory changes are noted after the block.

All medications used in the ACLS protocols for emergency resuscitation must be readily available. Ephedrine can often be used effectively for the treatment of mild to moderate hypotension in addition to any IV fluids that may be needed. Also, atropine alone can often be used to successfully treat transient bradycardia associated with vasovagal reactions occurring during an injection. Finally, flumazenil (Mazicon), which is a benzodiazepine antagonist, should be available if any patients are to receive IV sedation with a benzodiazepine.

Careful evaluation of the patient's response to both the diagnostic anesthetic portion of the block and the more prolonged therapeutic steroid anti-inflammatory portion can provide useful clinical information about that patient's spine condition. For midline or paramedian CESIs, Cicala[45] noted that transient upper extremity warming with tingling paresthesias following injection of epidural lidocaine was an indication of a well-placed injection. Similar symptoms in the legs following a midline or paramedian LESI with either partial or complete sensory block, including the painful dermatomes, suggests appropriate placement of the injectate. During sensory blockade, more detailed information regarding the pain response can be obtained with postinjection pain diagrams or diaries and provocative maneuvers including spine mobilization, straight leg raising, and repetitive static or dynamic spine loading. An assessment of the patient's pain-coping abilities can also be gauged by the response to the pain and stress of the injection and the response to a common pain stimulus such as local subcutaneous lidocaine infiltration.

For selective nerve root blocks, the onset of decreased sensation in an extremity restricted to a single dermatome corresponding to the level of the injection indicates a successful technique. The relief of radicular pain and negative responses to provocative maneuvers after the anesthetic block helps document the pain being generated from that specific nerve root. Complete pain relief of both spine (either neck or low back) and extremity pain after a selective epidural confirms the epiradicular tissues or dural sleeve as the source of both the somatic and radicular pain.[65] Complete relief of extremity pain without significant relief of spine pain suggests that the radicular pain is generated by the nerve root at the injected level, but the spine pain may be of a different origin. Selective epidural injections providing only partial relief may be followed by zygapophyseal joint and medial branch blocks and occasionally by discography to further define the pain generators as clinically indicated.

Choosing the Injection Approach

Many authors with vast experience performing epidural corticosteroid injections advocate injecting the anesthetic and corticosteroid as close as possible to the suspected pain generator. The choice of approach to the epidural space in any specific patient should be made with such localization in mind. Nonradicular cervical pain is one exception in which particular levels (C6–C7, C7–T1) are used almost exclusively for epidural injection due to technical and safety factors. A paramedian approach is appropriate for the treatment of a corresponding paracentral disc herniation in either the cervical, thoracic, or lumbar spine. A transforaminal approach is typically used for patients having radicular pain secondary to a lateral or far lateral disc herniation or bony lateral stenosis from degenerative changes or spondylolisthesis.[65] Some physicians[24] feel that a transforaminal approach may also be more reliable than a midline or paramedian approach for delivering corticosteroid to the posterior annulus to treat midline and paracentral disc injuries. Significant flow of fluid to the anterior epidural space adjacent to the posterior disc region following an epidural injection with a translaminar approach has been documented, and similar studies are in progress for a transforaminal approach (personal communication, Stephen Andrade, MD) (Fig. 27-10). No specific studies have been completed to date to compare the efficacy of these different approaches. Occasionally, a transforaminal approach and a midline or paramedian approach is used in combination to ensure adequate spread of medication in the lateral foramen and central canal.[80] Midline or paramedian approaches should not be attempted routinely at postlaminectomy levels, and either an interspace just above or below the surgical scar should be chosen, or a caudal or transforaminal approach should be used. The caudal epidural approach is used routinely for patients having suspected L5–S1 discogenic pain without unilateral radicular pain and is usually not recommended for patients thought to have a significant pain generator above the L4–5 level.

EPIDURAL INJECTION TECHNIQUE

Cervical Epidural Injections

Paramedian Approach
Cervical epidural injections should routinely be done at the C7–T1 interspace unless previous posterior cervical spine surgery has been performed at this level, in which case the C6–C7 or T1–T2 level is substituted. The patient is placed in the prone position and the skin at the appropriate level is prepared and draped aseptically. Under fluoroscopic

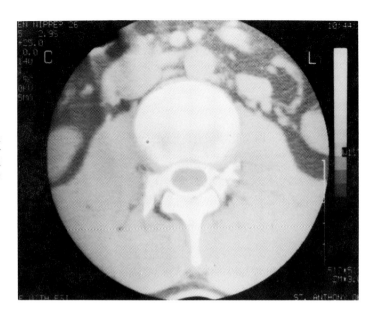

FIGURE 27-10. CT radiograph of contrast medium in the anterior and posterior lumbar epidural space following a translaminar epidural injection. (Courtesy of Stephen Andrade, MD.)

view, the lamina forming the inferior border of the target interspace is identified and marked 2–3 cm lateral to the midline. Using a 1.5 inch 25- or 27-gauge needle, a skin wheal is raised with 1% lidocaine, and the subcutaneous tissues are infiltrated down to the lamina under intermittent fluoroscopic control. A bicarbonate solution can be added to the lidocaine to reduce the burning sensation caused by the anesthetic. The skin needle is removed, and a nick is made in the skin with an 18-gauge needle prior to inserting the epidural needle down to the lamina under fluoroscopic control. The needle is then walked superiorly and medially off the edge of the lamina into the tough ligamentum flavum at or 1–2 mm lateral to the midline. The stylet is removed, and a syringe (often glass) filled with 2 ml of saline and 2 ml of air is attached to the epidural needle. Using a controlled grip with the hand holding the needle supported on the patient's back, the needle is slowly advanced while the other hand applies continuous pressure to the syringe. Loss of resistance should be felt within a few millimeters of needle advancement. Once loss of resistance is noted, aspiration to check for blood or CSF should be performed. If one is unsure if loss of resistance has been obtained, confirmation of position is critical by attempting aspiration followed by injection of a contrast agent. It is important to avoid the temptation to progress the needle deeper prior to documenting its location when a partial loss of resistance has been noted. Unless caution is exercised, inadvertent puncture of the dura and injury to the spinal cord may occur. After negative aspiration, a non-ionic contrast agent may be slowly injected under direct fluoroscopic visualization looking for the spread of the contrast agent in the epidural space. Once the epidural space has been identified and

confirmed radiographically (Fig. 27-11), a test dose of 1–2 ml of lidocaine is given. If there are no complaints of warmth, burning, significant paresthesias, or signs of apnea within 1–3 minutes, the corticosteroid preparation is slowly injected. After the injection, the needle is removed, the skin cleaned and a bandage is applied.

Some physicians perform cervical epidural injections with the patient in a sitting position with the head and chest supported and using C-arm fluoroscopy with a lateral view to document an epidural contrast pattern (personal communication, Paul H. Dreyfuss, MD).

Transforaminal Approach

The cervical transforaminal or selective nerve root block is started by identifying the target neuroforamen with the patient in either the prone or oblique position. In the oblique position, the C2–3 foramen is both the most superior and the largest of all the cervical foramen. The foramen and associated nerve root levels can be counted down from the C2–3 level. The injection is performed with the patient in an oblique position with the side to be treated elevated and supported with pillows under the shoulder and back. Using C-arm fluoroscopy, the x-ray beam can be angled to more easily obtain an adequate oblique view. The skin over the target foramen is prepared and draped aseptically, and a local anesthetic is injected carefully down to the level of the bony posterior edge of the neuroforamen. A 25-gauge spinal needle is then advanced down to the posteroinferior edge of the neuroforamen until bone is contacted. The needle is slowly walked off the bone into the foramen and advanced only a few millimeters and no further medial than the midpoint of the adjacent pedicle, as seen in an AP projection.

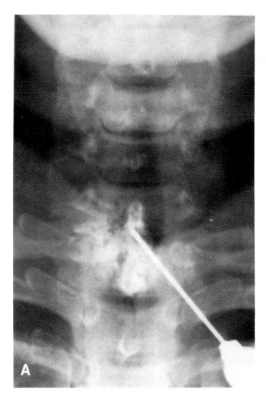

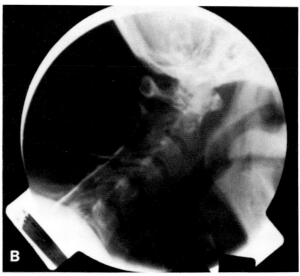

FIGURE 27-11. *A*, Anteroposterior view cervical epidurogram demonstrating a characteristic C7–T1 epidural contrast flow pattern. *B*, Lateral radiograph of a cervical epidurogram (Courtesy of Paul H. Dreyfuss, MD.)

Care must be taken not to advance the needle too far medial where the nerve root and epidural veins are located. Needle position can be evaluated by rotating the C-arm to an AP view and slowly injecting 0.5 ml of contrast material under direct fluoroscopic view. An acceptable dye pattern includes filling of the round neuroforamen and preferably contrast flow along the exiting nerve root (Fig. 27-12). The patient may often experience mild to moderate radiating arm pain during the injection of fluid into the foramen. Once an adequate dye pattern is achieved, about 2 ml of 1–2% lidocaine can be injected and the patient's response monitored for diagnostic purposes. Celestone can be mixed with the lidocaine or injected separately; a volume of 1–2 ml is recommended.

Thoracic Epidural Injections

Paramedian Approach

The paramedian approach is usually used in the thoracic spine due to the bony anatomy of the thoracic lamina. Patient preparation and equipment are similar to that employed for CESIs. The skin over the lamina at the target interspace is injected with 1% lidocaine, and local anesthetic is slowly injected down to the lamina. A small nick is made in the skin with an 18-gauge needle, and the epidural needle is introduced through the skin. The bevel of the epidural needle is oriented cephalad and the

needle is introduced at a 50–60° angle to the axis of the spine and a 15–30° angle toward midline (Fig. 22-13). With C-arm fluoroscopy, the x-ray beam can be tilted parallel to the lamina, which helps visualize the thoracic interspace and indicates the appropriate entry angle of the needle. Under fluoroscopy, the epidural needle is advanced down to the superior edge of the lamina and then walked off the edge into the ligamentum flavum at or just lateral to the midline. The loss of resistance technique is used to locate the epidural space. After negative aspiration for blood and CSF, epidural placement is confirmed by injecting 0.5–2 ml of contrast material and visualizing the appropriate dye flow pattern (Fig. 22-14). A test dose of 1–2 ml of 1% lidocaine without preservative is injected. If the test dose is negative, the corticosteroid preparation is slowly injected.

Transforaminal Approach

The thoracic transforaminal or selective nerve root block is performed with the patient in the prone position under fluoroscopy. The target neuroforamen and adjacent pedicle is marked, and the area is prepared and draped aseptically. Local anesthetic is applied to the skin and overlying soft tissues. A 22- or 25-gauge 3½-inch spinal needle is placed into the skin 1–2 inches lateral to the target pedicle and centered between the ribs located above and below the target neuroforamen. The needle is

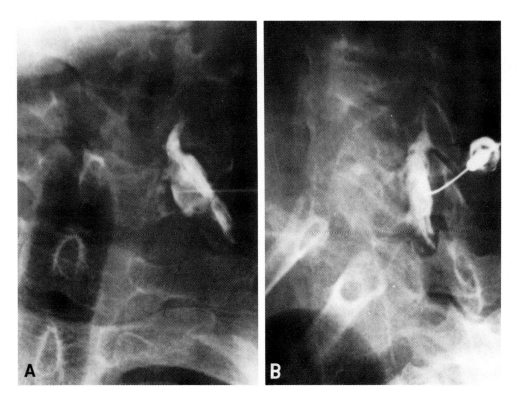

FIGURE 27-12. *A,* Anteroposterior view cervical selective nerve root injection contrast pattern. *B,* Oblique view cervical selective nerve root injection. (Courtesy of Paul H. Dreyfuss, MD.)

advanced toward the inferior border of the rib above the neuroforamen until the rib is contacted. The needle is then redirected inferiorly and medially

just under the pedicle, and a lateral view can be checked to verify an appropriate position in the neuroforamen. Care must be taken to redirect

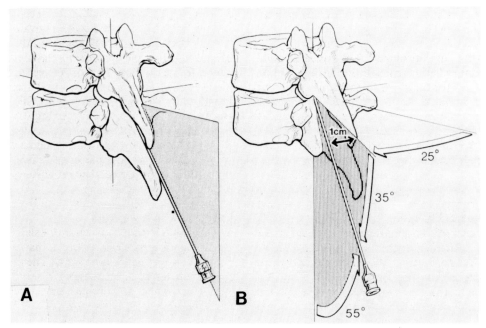

FIGURE 27-13. Thoracic spine midline (*A*) and paramedian (*B*) epidural injection needle position. (From Cousins MJ, Bromage PR: Epidural Neural Blockade. In Cousins MJ, Bridenbaugh PO (eds): Neural Blockade in Clinical Anesthesia and Management of Pain. Philadelphia, J.B. Lippincott, 1988, with permission.)

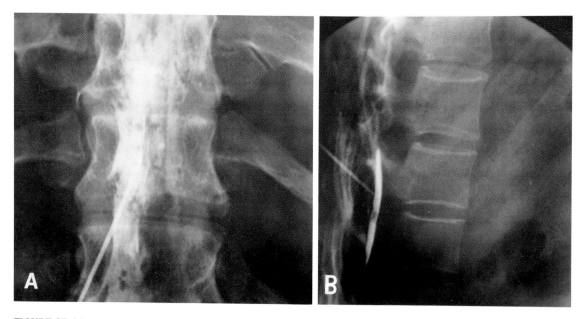

FIGURE 27-14. *A,* Anteroposterior thoracic epidurogram demonstrating a characteristic thoracic epidural contrast flow pattern. *B,* Lateral radiograph of a thoracic epidurogram. (Courtesy of Paul H. Dreyfuss, MD.)

the needle as medial as possible after contacting the rib to avoid a possible pneumothorax. Once the needle is placed under the pedicle and into the neuroforamen, contrast can be injected and the needle readjusted until an acceptable dye pattern with some flow medially into the lateral epidural space and preferably some flow along the exiting nerve root is observed. Lidocaine and corticosteroid solutions can be injected as described in the cervical transforaminal block section. If the patient does not have significant immediate pain relief from the local anesthetic, repeating the injection at the level above or below should be considered due to the difficulty of localizing the exact painful level in the thoracic spine.

Lumbosacral Epidural Injections

Caudal Approach

A caudal epidural injection is started by placing the patient prone on the fluoroscopy table. The sacral region is prepared aseptically, and a fenestrated drape is placed over the midsacral region. Palpation of the sacrum with the fingers starting at the coccyx will provide a reliable bony landmark; the sacrum is then palpated superiorly until the two horns of the sacral cornu are identified (Fig. 27-15A). The sacral hiatus, which is the entry point into the caudal epidural space, lies between the cornu. While holding a finger (usually easiest with the nondominant hand) in place over the hiatus to maintain proper position, local anesthetic can be applied to the skin and then deeper to the sacral bone between

the cornu. Using a 25- or 27-gauge 1½-inch needle to slowly inject the local anesthetic is usually less painful to the patient than larger needles. A 22-gauge spinal needle is directed between the cornu at about a 45° angle with the bevel facing ventrally until the sacrum is contacted. The needle is carefully redirected more cephalad as the bony anatomy requires in the midline or slightly to the side of the patient's pain to allow entry into the caudal epidural space through the sacrococcygeal ligament (Fig. 27-15B). Once the needle is thought to be in the caudal epidural space and a negative aspirate is achieved, nonionic contrast material is slowly injected under direct fluoroscopic view. Proper epidural placement is indicated by a typical epidural dye flow pattern (see Fig. 27-7). A dense well localized dye pattern indicates a subcutaneous position above the sacrum and is usually associated with increased resistance during injection. A lateral view of the sacrum with fluoroscopy can help determine both the initial and final needle placement using contrast to document adequate spread as needed. A vascular dye pattern necessitates careful withdrawal and repositioning of the needle. The volume of anesthetic and corticosteroid required to reach either the L4–5 or L5–S1 level can often be judged by the spread of dye, but at least 10 ml is generally required to reach the L5–S1 level and 15 ml to reach the L4–5 level.[22] The needle can also be carefully advanced more cephalad as superior as the S3 level to allow better flow of injectate as desired. Once appropriate needle placement is documented, the anesthetic and corticosteroid preparation can be slowly injected.

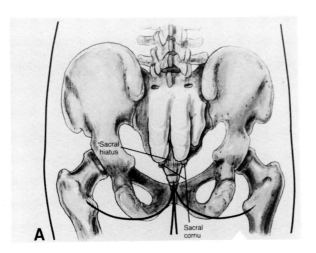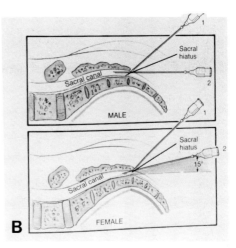

FIGURE 27-15. *A,* Schematic view of the sacrum and palpation of the sacral cornu. *B,* Needle 1 illustrates the initial angle of entry for a caudal epidural approach; needle 2 illustrates the redirected angle and advancement into the caudal epidural space (From Brown DL: Atlas of Regional Anesthesia. Philadelphia, W.B. Saunders, 1992, with permission.)

Lumbar Midline and Paramedian Approach

Lumbar epidural injections can be performed with either a midline or paramedian (also known as translaminar) approach (Fig. 27-16). Placing a pillow or cushion beneath the patient's abdomen to cause lumbar spine flexion can often facilitate lumbar epidural needle placement with the patient in a prone position. Some physicians prefer placing patients on their side and using a lateral view on fluoroscopy for a lumbar epidural injection. The midline approach is performed at the interspace most closely

located to the level of the suspected source of pain, with the needle placed just below the target level due to the cephalad flow of most fluids injected into the epidural space. Fluoroscopy is used to accurately identify the appropriate interspace, and the skin is prepared aseptically. A 25- or 27-gauge needle is used to anesthetize the skin over the target interspace midway between the adjacent spinous processes. A 22- or 25-gauge 1½-inch needle can be used to slowly anesthetize the interspinous ligament, being careful to constantly aspirate and check the

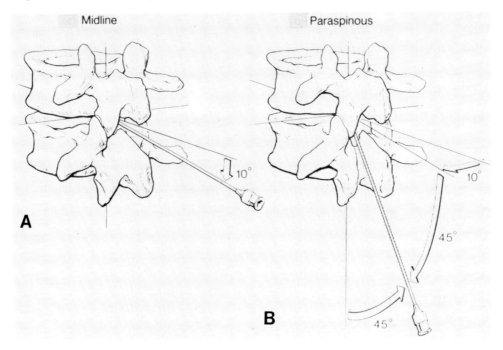

FIGURE 27-16. Lumbar spine midline (*A*) and paramedian (*B*) epidural injection needle position (From Cousins MJ, Bromage PR: Epidural Neural Blockade. In Cousins MJ, Bridenbaugh PO (eds): Neural Blockade in Clinical Anesthesia and Management of Pain. Philadelphia, J.B. Lippincott, 1988, with permission.)

resistance to injection since entry into the epidural space is possible. If an epidural needle is used, a nick in the skin is made with an 18-gauge needle and the 18- or 20-gauge epidural needle is placed through the skin. Alternatively, a 22-gauge spinal needle can be used for the injection. The needle is advanced at a slight upward angle (about 10° to horizontal) through the interspinous ligament. A 2-ml glass syringe can be used with the epidural needle to identify the epidural space by the loss of resistance technique. The hand used to advance the needle should be braced firmly against the patient's back at all times for controlled needle advancement. Proper midline needle placement during the injection can be assured by intermittent fluoroscopic imaging. Increased resistance to both needle advancement and injection with the glass syringe can usually be detected once the needle enters the ligamentum flavum. The epidural space is then identified using the loss of resistance technique. The glass syringe is removed and the needle observed for CSF drip back. If no drip back occurs and aspiration is negative, contrast dye is slowly injected under fluoroscopy. When an appropriate epidural pattern is noted, a test dose of 3–5 ml of preservative-free 1% lidocaine is given, and the patient is monitored for several minutes. After a negative test dose, a solution of 0.5 or 1% lidocaine and corticosteroid can be slowly injected.

The technique used for a paramedian approach is identical to the midline technique except for the specific injection site. After skin preparation and marking, an epidural or spinal needle is placed 1–2 cm lateral to the caudal tip of the inferior spinous process of the target interspace on the side of the patient's pain. A more lateral needle placement is to be avoided since such an approach increases the risk of encountering an epidural vein or adjacent nerve root. The needle is advanced under fluoroscopy until contacting the upper edge of the inferior lamina at the target interspace. The needle is walked superiorly into the ligamentum flavum, and the epidural space is identified by loss of resistance. After negative aspiration and no CSF drip back, contrast dye is slowly injected. If an acceptable epidural dye flow pattern is noted (Fig. 27-17) and a test dose is negative, the local anesthetic and corticosteroid solution can be injected.

Lumbar Transforaminal Approach

The patient is prepared in the prone position and fluoroscopy used to identify and mark the essential bony landmarks. Either an oblique or a posterior approach may be used with either a single or double needle technique. The most thorough presentation of transforaminal or selective nerve root blocks is by Derby, Bogduk and Kine,[65] and many of the

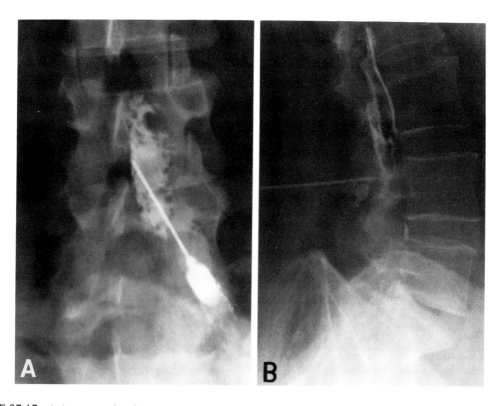

FIGURE 27-17. *A*, Anteroposterior view lumbar translaminar epidurogram demonstrating a characteristic contrast flow pattern. *B*, Lateral view lumbar translaminer epidurogram. (Courtesy of Paul H. Dreyfuss, MD.)

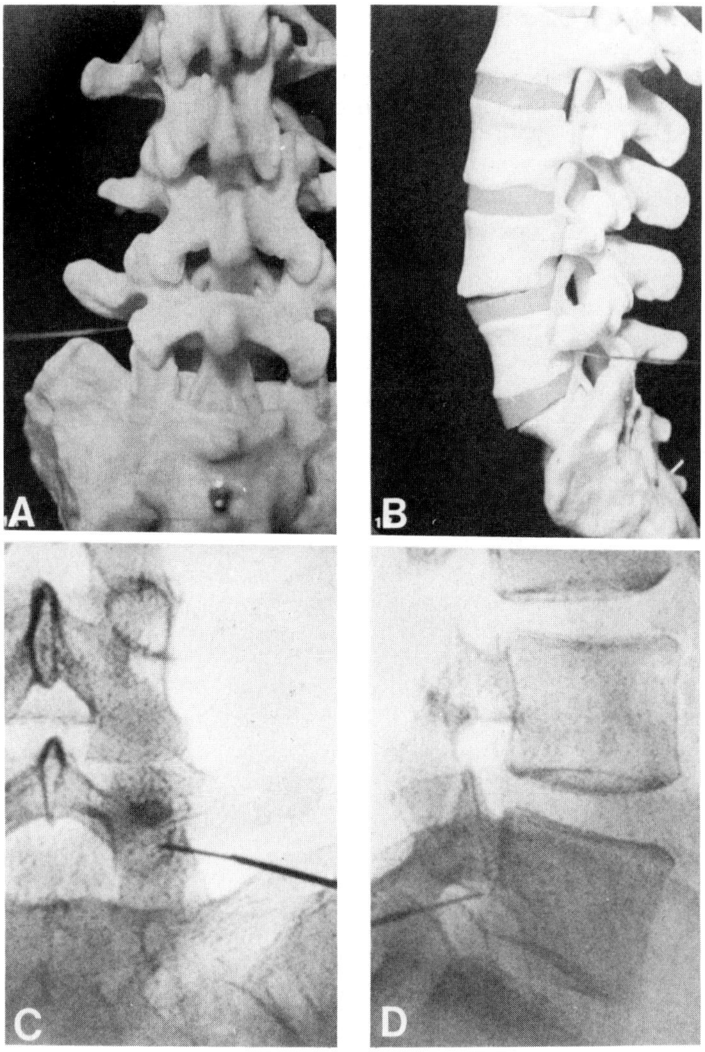

FIGURE 27-18. *A, B,* Spine model antero-posterior and lateral views, respectively, of appropriate needle position for left L5 selective nerve root injection. *C,* and *D,* Antero-posterior and lateral views, respectively, of appropriate needle position for right L5 selective epidural nerve root injection. (From Derby R, Bogduk N, Kine G: Precision percutaneous blocking procedures for localizing pain. Part 2. The lumbar neuroaxial compartment. Pain Digest 3:175–188, 1993, with permission.)

techniques described in this section were presented in their article. The bony landmark that is the target for transforaminal needle placement is just below the inferior aspect of the pedicle superior to the exiting nerve root or the "6 o'clock" position using the round pedicle as a clockface. Derby et al.[65] describe a "safe triangle" at this location with the three sides corresponding to the horizontal base of the pedicle, the outer vertical border of the intervertebral foramen, and the connecting diagonal nerve root and dorsal ganglion. A needle placed into the safe triangle will lie above and lateral to the nerve root (Fig. 27-18).

For the oblique approach, the patient and the fluoroscopy unit are rotated as needed to provide an oblique projection of the pedicle on the side of the affected nerve root. The fluoroscopic image is adjusted until the superior articulating process is seen between the anterior and posterior edge of the vertebral body and the base of the articular process

is in line with the pedicle above. After the skin and overlying tissues have been anesthetized, the needle is inserted just above the superior articulating process and directed toward the base of the pedicle. The needle is advanced slowly until bone is contacted just below the pedicle. Nonionic contrast dye can be injected very slowly and the dye pattern assessed (Fig. 27-19). If leg paresthesias are noted as the needle approaches the neuroforamen, the needle should be withdrawn slightly (about 1 mm) and dye injected.

The posterior approach is done with the patient in the prone position and begins with the needle inserted into the skin over the lateral border of and about halfway between the two adjacent transverse processes at the target interspace. The needle is advanced slowly toward the lower edge of the superior transverse process near its junction with the superior articular process. The needle is advanced until contacting the edge of the transverse process,

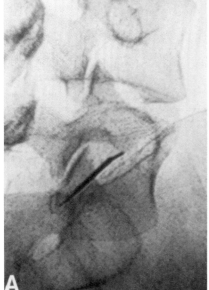

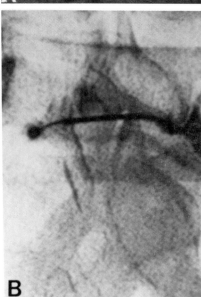

FIGURE 27-19. Lumbar spine oblique view of right L5 selective nerve root block using double-needle technique before (A) and after (B) contrast injection. (From Derby R, Bogduk N, Kine G: Precision percutaneous blocking procedures for localizing spine pain. Part 2. The lumbar neuroaxial compartment. Pain Digest 3:175–188, 1993, with permission.)

at which time the needle is retracted slightly (2–3 mm) and redirected toward the base of the appropriate pedicle and advanced very slowly to the final position. The fluoroscopic dye pattern is assessed.

The double needle technique is started by advancing an 18- or 20-gauge 3½-inch spinal needle to the lower edge of the transverse process as described above. A 23- or 25-gauge 6-inch Chiba needle is then placed through the introducer needle and redirected and advanced below the transverse

process. The stiffness of the introducer needle enables easier redirection of the thinner and more flexible inner needle, which is potentially less damaging to the nerve root if contact with the nerve is made. The inner needle can also be curved at the tip and directed with the curve pointing toward the pedicle to allow easier advancement in the medial direction necessary to pass under the pedicle and into the neuroforamen.

Once a needle has been placed at the 6 o'clock position of the pedicle, 0.5–1 ml of contast dye is injected slowly at a rate of about 1.0 ml per 20 seconds.[24] If the needle has penetrated the epiradicular membrane surrounding the nerve root, a positive image of the nerve root will be seen on fluoroscopy, indicating an acceptable needle position (Fig. 27-20). A more negative image of the nerve with flow of contrast in the region of the epidural fat indicates the need to carefully readjust the needle to localize the tip closer to the nerve root if possible. A classic dye pattern or neurogram is not always achieved due to the patient's level of cooperation and type of local spine problem. The dye pattern may reveal pathology in the area of the exiting nerve root such as an abnormal position and course of the nerve secondary to a compressive vertebral osteophyte or lateral disc herniation. Derby et al.[65] describe other abnormal dye patterns and their

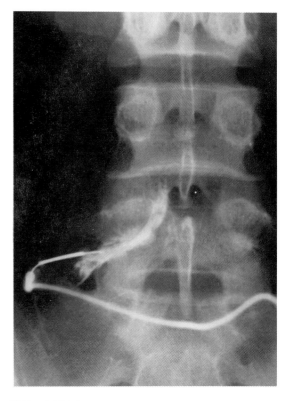

FIGURE 27-20. Left L5 selective nerve root injection contrast Pattern. (Courtesy of Ted Lennard, MD.)

possible clinical significance. After an adequate dye pattern is observed, an equal mixture of local anesthetic and corticosteroid is injected. A maximum volume of 2 ml of injectate is thought necessary to preserve the selectivity of the block to a single nerve root. Due to the small volume of local anesthetic injected, a higher concentration such as 4% lidocaine or 0.75% bupivacaine is recommended for this procedure.

The S1 nerve root can also be treated using a transforaminal approach, and a single needle technique is usually adequate. The patient is placed in a prone position, and the S1 foramen is visualized under fluoroscopy. The S1 foramen appears as a small radiolucent circle just below the oval S1 pedicle. Using C-arm fluoroscopy, the S1 foramen is often seen best by directing the x-ray beam in a cephalocaudad direction so that the anterior and posterior foramina align. The needle is inserted slightly lateral and inferior to the S1 pedicle and advanced slowly through the posterior foramen to the medial edge of the pedicle. Care must be taken to avoid advancing the needle through both the posterior and anterior S1 foramen and into the pelvis. The appropriate depth can be gauged by first striking posterior sacral bone just above the posterior S1 foramen before directing the needle tip into the S1 neural canal. Once the needle is properly located, the dye pattern is checked (Fig. 27-21) and the anesthetic and corticosteroid solution injected as with the lumbar selective nerve root blocks.

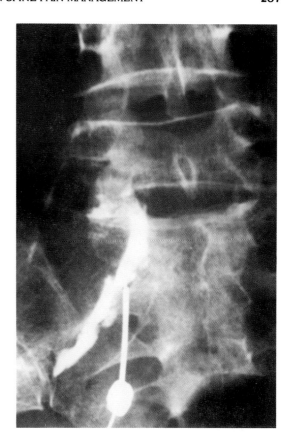

FIGURE 27-21. Left S1 selective nerve root injection contrast pattern.

Blood Patch Procedure

The patient is first placed in the lateral or prone position depending on the physician's preference. Using strict aseptic technique, an epidural needle is placed into the epidural space using the loss of resistance technique. The needle is inserted at the same level of the spine as the previous epidural procedure at which time the dural puncture occurred. If that specific interspace is not available, the interspace one level inferior is chosen since most epidural injectates flow in a more cephalad than caudad direction.[133] Once the needle is properly placed in the epidural space, about 10–20 ml of intravenous blood is drawn into a plastic syringe also using strict aseptic technique (plastic instead of glass is used because the clotting process occurs more slowly in a plastic container). The blood is injected slowly into the epidural space, and the injection is stopped immediately if any significant pain is reported by the patient. The needle is removed and the patient is kept in the supine position for 30 minutes before being released, with no other precautions necessary. If the headache is not markedly improved or the pain returns after a brief period of relief, the procedure should be repeated once more.[133] The most effective volume of blood to inject for a blood patch has been thoroughly evaluated, and 12–15 ml seems to be both safe and effective.[55] Also, 15 ml of radioisotope-labeled blood injected into the epidural space has been shown to spread an average of nine spinal segments, providing more than adequate coverage.[169] Contraindications for an epidural blood patch are septicemia, local infection of the back, or active neurologic disease.[134]

REFERENCES

1. Abboud TK, David S, Nagappola S, et al: Maternal, fetal and neonatal effects of lidocaine with and without epinephrine epidural anesthesia in obstetrics. Anesth Analg 63:973–979, 1984.
2. Abouleish E, de la Vega S, Blendinger L: Long-term follow-up of epidural blood patch. Anesth Analg 54:459–463, 1975.
3. Abram SE: Subarachnoid corticosteroid injection following inadequate response to epidural steroid for sciatica. Anesth Analg 57:313–315, 1978.
4. Abram SE, Cherwenka RW: Transient headache immediately following epidural steroid injection. Anesthesiology 50:461–462, 1979.

5. Abram SE, Hopwood MB: What factors contribute to outcome with lumbar epidural steroids. In Bond MR, Charlton JE, Wolf DJ (eds): Proceedings of the VIth World Congress on Pain. Amsterdam, Elsevier, 1991, pp 491–496.

6. Anderson GB: Epidemiologic aspects of low back pain in industry. Spine 6:53–60, 1981.

7. Andrade SA: Steroid side effects of epidurally administered celestone. International Spinal Injection Society [newsletter] 1(5):1993.

8. Auradio JP: Peripherally acting analgesics. Am J Med (Suppl):17–25, 1984.

9. Awwad EE, Martin DW, Smith KR Jr, et al: Asymptomatic versus symptomatic herniated thoracic discs: Their frequency and characteristics as detected by computed tomography after myelography. Neurosurgery 28:180–186, 1991.

10. Baker AS, Ojemann RG, Schwartz MN, et al: Spinal epidural abscess. N Engl J Med 293:463–468, 1975.

11. Ball CG, D'Alessandro FT, Rosenthal J, et al: Case history number 86: An unusual complication of lumbar puncture: A CSF cutaneous fistula. Anesth Anal 54:691–694, 1975.

12. Beliveau P: A comparison between epidural anesthesia with and without corticosteroid in the treatment of sciatica. Rheum Phys Med 11:40–43, 1971.

13. Benzon HT: Epidural steroid injections for low back pain and lumbosacral radiculopathy. Pain 24:277–295, 1986.

14. Benzon HT, Gissen AJ, Strichartz GR, et al: The effect of polyethylene glycol on mammalian nerve impulses. Anesth Analg 66:553–559, 1987.

15. Berman AT, Garbarino JL, Fisher S, et al: The effects of epidural injection of local anesthetics and corticosteroids on patients with lumbosciatic pain. Clin Orthop 188:144–150, 1984.

16. Bernat JL: Intraspinal steroid therapy. Neurology 31:168–171, 1981.

17. Berqquist-Ullman M, Larson U: Acute low back pain in industry. A controlled prospective study with special reference to therapy and confounding factors. Acta Orthop Scand 170(suppl):1–117, 1977.

18. Black MG, Holyoke MD: Anatomic reasons for caudal anesthesia failure. Anesth Analg 28:33–39, 1949.

19. Blomberg R: The dorsomedian connective tissue band in the lumbar epidural space in humans. Anesth Anal 65:747–752, 1986.

20. Boas RA, Cousins MJ: Diagnostic neural blockade. In Neural Blockade in Clinical Anesthesia and Management of Pain. Philadelphia, J.B. Lippincott, 1988, pp 885–898.

21. Bogduk N: The innervation of the lumbar spine. Spine 8:286–293, 1983.

22. Bogduk N, Aprill C, Derby R: Precise localization of low back pain and sciatica. International Spinal Injection Society Meeting [syllabus], San Diego, 1993.

23. Bogduk N, Cherry D: Epidural corticosteroid agents for sciatica. Med J Aust 143:402–406, 1985.

24. Bogduk N, Christophidis N, Cherry D, et al: Epidural steroids in the management of back pain and sciatica of spinal origin. Report of the Working Party on Epidural Use of Steroids in the Management of Back Pain. National Health and Medical Research Council, Canberra, Australia, 1993.

25. Bogduk N, Twomey LT: Clinical Anatomy of the Lumbar Spine, 2nd ed. New York, Churchill Livingstone, 1991.

26. Bonica JJ: Analgesic blocks for pain. In Bonica JJ, Procacci P, Pagin CA (eds): Recent Advances in Pain. Springfield, IL, Charles C Thomas, 1974, p 192.

27. Boudin G, Barbizet J, Guihard J: L'hydrocortisone intrarachniclienne ses applications cliniques en particular dans le traitement de la méningite tuberculouse. Bull Soc Med Hop (Paris) 21:817–821, 1955.

28. Bowman SJ, Wedderburn L, Whaley A, et al: Outcome assessment after epidural corticosteroid injection for low back pain and sciatica. Spine 18:1345–1350, 1993.

29. Bowsher D: A comparative study of the azygous venous system in man, monkey, dog, cat, rat and rabbit. J Anat 88:40, 1954.

30. Braid DP, Scott DB: The systemic absorption of local analgesic drugs. Br J Anesth 37:394, 1965.

31. Breivik H, Hesla PE, Molnar I, et al: Treatment of chronic low back pain and sciatica: Comparison of caudal epidural steroid injections of bupivacaine and methylprednisolone with bupivacaine followed by saline. In Bonica JJ, Alba D, Fessard O (eds): Advances in Pain Research and Therapy. New York, Raven Press, 1976, pp 927–932.

32. Bridenbaugh PO, Greene NM: Spinal (subarachnoid) neural blockade. In Cousins MJ, Bridenbaugh PO (eds): Neural Blockade in Clinical Anesthesia and Management of Pain. Philadelphia, J.B. Lippincott, 1988, pp 213–251.

33. Bromage PR: Epidural Analgesia. Philadelphia, W.B. Saunders, 1978.

34. Bromage PR: Physiology and pharmacology of epidural analgesia. Anesthesiology 28:592, 1967.

35. Brown CW, Deffer PA Jr, Akmakjian J, et al: The natural history of thoracic disc herniations. Spine 17:S97–102, 1992.

36. Brown FW: Management of discogenic pain using epidural and intrathecal steroids. Clin Orthop 129:72–78, 1977.

37. Brownridge P: The management of headache following accidental dural puncture in obstetric patients. Anaesth Intensive Care 11:4–15, 1983.

38. Burn JM, Langdon L: Duration of action of epidural methylprednisolone. Am J Phys Med 53:29–34, 1974.

39. Bush K, Hillier S: A controlled study of caudal epidural injections of triamcinolone plus procaine for the management of intractable sciatica. Spine 16:572–575, 1991.

40. Carr DB: Epidural steroids for radicualgia. Journées de club anesthésie-douleur 32:289–290, 1991.

41. Catchlove RF, Braha R: The use of cervical epidural nerve blocks in the management of chronic head and neck pain. Can Anesth Soc J 31:188–191, 1984.

42. Cathelin F: Mode d'action de la cocaine injecté dons l'espace epidural par le prócedá dee canal sacrè. C R Soc Biol 53:478, 1901.

43. Chan S, Lueng S: Spinal epidural abscess following steroid injection for sciatica. Spine 14:106–108, 1984.

44. Cheng PA: The anatomical and clinical aspects of epidural anesthesia. Curr Res Anesth Analg 42:398, 1963.

45. Cicala RS, Westbrook L, Angel JJ: Side effects and complications of cervical epidural steroid injections. J Pain Symptom Manage 4:64–66, 1989.

46. Cichini MS: Epidural corticosteroid injections. J Post Anesth Nurs 7:163–166, 1992.

47. Cohn ML, Huntington CT, Byrd SE, et al: Epidural morphine and methylprednisolone: New therapy for recurrent low back pain. Spine 11:960–963, 1986.

48. Coomes EN: A comparison between epidural anesth and bedrest in sciatica. BMJ 1:20–24, 1961.

49. Cousins MJ, Bromage PR: A comparison of the hydrochloride and carbonated salts of lignocaine for caudal analgesia in out-patients. Br J Anesth 43:1149–1154, 1971.

50. Cousins MJ, Bromage PR: Epidural neural blockade. In Cousins MJ, Bridenbaugh PO (eds): Neural Blockade in Clinical Anesthesia and Management of Pain. Philadelphia, J.B. Lippincott, 1988, pp 253–360.

51. Covino BG: Clinical pharmacology of local anesthetic agents. In Cousins MJ, Bridenbaugh PO (eds): Neural Blockade in Clinical Anesthesia and Management of Pain. Philadelphia, J.B. Lippincott, 1988, pp 111–144.

52. Covino BG, Scott DB: Handbook of Epidural Anesthesia and Analgesia. Orlando: Grune & Stratton, 1985.

53. Craft JB, Epstein BS, Coakley CS: Prophylaxis of dural-puncture headache with epidural saline. Anesth Analg 52:228–231, 1973.
54. Crawford JS: The prevention of headache consequent upon dural puncture. Br J Anesth 44:598–600, 1972.
55. Crawford JS: Epidural blood patch. Anaesthesia 4:381, 1985.
56. Crock HV: Internal disc disruption: A challenge to disc prolapse fifty years on. Spine 11:650–653, 1986.
57. Cronen MC, Waldman SD: Cervical steroid epidural nerve block in the palliation of pain secondary to intractable muscle contraction headache [abstract]. Headache 28:314–315, 1988.
58. Cuatico W, Parker JC Jr, Pappert E, et al: An anatomical and clinical investigation of spinal meningeal nerves. Acta Neurchir (Wien) 90:139–143, 1988.
59. Cuckler JM, Bernini PA, Wiesel SW, et al: The use of epidural steroids in the treatment of radicular pain. J Bone Joint Surg 67A:53–66, 1985.
60. Dallas TL, Lin RL, Wee W, et al: Epidural morphine and methylprednisolone for low back pain. Anesthesiology 67:408–411, 1987.
61. Daly P: Caudal epidural anesthesia in lumbosciatic pain. Anaesthesia 25:346–348, 1970.
62. Davidson JT, Robin GC: Epidural injections in the lumbosciatic syndrome. Br J Anesth 33:595–598, 1961.
63. Deisenhammer E: Clinical and experimental studies on headache after myelography. Neuroradiology 9:99–102, 1985.
64. Delaney T, Rowlingson RC, Carron H, et al: Epidural steroid effects on nerve and meninges. Anesth Analg 59:610–614, 1980.
65. Derby R, Bogduk N, Kine G: Precision percutaneous blocking procedures for localizing spinal pain. Part 2. The lumbar neuroaxial compartment. Pain Digest 3:175–188, 1993.
66. Derby R, Kine G, Saal J, et al: Response to steroid and duration of radicular pain as predictors of surgical outcome. Spine 17:5176–5183, 1992.
67. Devor M, Gourin-Lippmann R, Raber P: Corticosteroids suppress ectopic neural discharge originating in experimental neuromas. Pain 22:127–137, 1985.
68. Dietze DD, Fessler RG: Thoracic disc herniations. Neurosurg Clin North Am 4:75–90, 1993.
69. Dilke TFW, Burry HC, Grahame R: Extradural corticosteroid injection in the management of lumbar nerve root compression. BMJ 2:635–637, 1973.
70. Dirksen R, Rutgers MJ, Coolen JMW: Cervical epidural steroids in reflex sympathetic dystrophy. Anesthesiology 66:71–73, 1987.
71. Dooley JF, McBroom RJ, Taguchi T, et al: Nerve root infiltration in the diagnosis of radicular pain. Spine 13:79–83, 1988.
72. Dougherty JH, Fraser RAR: Complications following intraspinal injections of steroids; report of two cases. J Neurosurg 48:1023–1025, 1978.
73. Dreyfuss P: Epidural steroid injections: A procedure ideally performed with fluoroscopic control and contrast media. International Spinal Injection Society [newsletter] 1(5): 1993.
74. El-Khoury GY, Ehara S, Weinstein JN, et al: Epidural steroid injection: A procedure ideally performed with fluoroscopic control. Radiology 168:554–557, 1988.
75. Evans W: Intrasacral epidural injection in the treatment of sciatica. Lancet 2:1225–1229, 1930.
76. Ferrante FM, Wilson SP, Iacobo C, et al: Clinical classification as a predictor of therapeutic outcome after cervical epidural steroid injection. Spine 18:730–736, 1993.
77. Flower RJ, Blackwell GJ: Anti-inflammatory steroids induce biosynthesis of a phospholipase A2 inhibitor which prevents prostaglandin generation. Nature 278:456–459, 1979.
78. Forrest JB: Management of chronic dorsal root pain with epidural steroid. Can Anaesth Soc J 25:218–225, 1978.
79. Forrest JB: The response to epidural steroid injections in chronic dorsal root pain. Can Anaesth Soc J 27:40–46, 1980.
80. Gamburd RS: The use of selective injections in the lumbar spine. Phys Med Rehabil Clin North Am 2:79–96, 1991.
81. Germann PA, Roberts JG, Prys-Roberts C: The combination of general anesthesia and epidural block. I. The effects of sequence of induction on haemodynamic variables and blood gas measurements in healthy patients. Anaesth Intensive Care 7:229, 1979.
82. Giansiracers DF, Upchurch KS: Anaphylactic and anaphylactoid reactions. In Rippe JM, Irwin R, Alpert J, Dolen J (eds): Intensive Care Medicine. Boston, Little, Brown & Co., 1985, pp 1102–1112.
83. Goebert HW, Jallo ST, Gardner WJ, et al: Painful radiculopathy treated with epidural injections of procaine and hydrocortisone acetate: Results in 113 patients. Anesth Analg 40:130–134, 1961.
84. Green LN: Dexamethasone in the management of symptoms due to herniated lumbar disc. J Neurol Neurosurg Psychiatry 38:1211–1217, 1975.
85. Green PW, Burke AJ, Weiss CA, et al: The role of epidural cortisone injection in the treatment of discogenic low back pain. Clin Orthop 153:121–125, 1980.
86. Gupta RC, Gupta SC, Dubey RK: An experimental study of different contrast media in the epidural space. Spine 9:778–781, 1984.
87. Gustafssan H, Rutberg H, Bengtsson M: Spinal haematoma following epidural analgesia. Anaesthesia 43:220–222, 1988.
88. Haddox JD: Lumbar and cervical epidural steroid therapy. Anesth Clin North Am 10:179–203, 1992.
89. Hakelius A: Prognosis in sciatica. 129(suppl):1–76, 1970.
90. Harley C: Epidural corticosteroid infiltration. A follow-up study of 50 cases. Am Phys Med 9:22–28, 1967.
91. Harrison GR, Parkin IG, Shah JL: Resin injection studies of the lumbar extradural space. Br J Anesth 57:333–336, 1985.
92. Hartman JT, Winnie AP, Ramamurthy S: Intradural and extradural corticosteroids for sciatic pain. Orthop Rev 3:21–24, 1974.
93. Hasselkorn JK, Ciol MA, Rapp S, et al: Epidural steroid injections and the treatment of low back pain: A meta-analysis [abstract]. Back Pain Outcome Assessment Team, Fourth Annual Advisory Committee Meeting, Seattle, 1994.
94. Hasueisen DC, Smith BS, Myers SR, et al: The diagnostic accuracy of spinal nerve injection studies: Their role in the evaluation of recurrent sciatica. Clin Orthop 198:179–183, 1985.
95. Helliwell M, Robertson JC, Ellis RM: Outpatient treatment of low back pain and sciatica by a single epidural corticosteroid injection. Br J Clin Pract 39:228–231, 1985.
96. Herron LD: Selective nerve root block in patient selection for lumbar surgery. North American Spine Society Meeting [syllabus], Quebec, 1989, pp 28–29.
97. Herron LD: Selective nerve root block in patient selection for lumbar surgery—surgical results. J Spinal Disord 2:75–79, 1989.
98. Heyse-Moore G: A rational approach to the use of epidural medication in the treatment of sciatic pain. Acta Orthop Scand 49:366–370, 1978.
99. Hickey R: Outpatient epidural steroid injections for low back pain and lumbar sacral radiculopathy. N Z Med J 100:594–596, 1987.
100. Hindmarch T: Myelography with the non-ionic water-soluble contrast medium metrizamide. Acta Radiol 16:417–435, 1975.
101. Hogan GH: Lumbar epidural anatomy: A new look by cryomicrotome section. Anesthesiology 75:767–775, 1991.

102. Hoogmartens M, Morelle P: Epidural injection in the treatment of spinal stenosis. Acta Orthop Belg 53:409–411, 1987.
103. Hoppenstein R: A new approach to the foiled, failed back syndrome. Spine 5:371–379, 1980.
104. Howe JF, Loesser JD, Calvin WH: Mechanosensitivity of dorsal root ganglia and chronically injured axones—A physiological basis for the radicular pain of nerve root compression. Pain 3:25–41, 1977.
105. Irsigler FJ: Microscopic findings in spinal cord roots of patients with lumbar and lumbosacral disc prolapse. Acta Neurol 1:478–516, 1951.
106. Jamison RN, VadBoncouer T, Feriante FM: Low back pain patients unresponsive to an epidural steroid injection: Identifying predictive factors. Clin J Pain 7:311–317, 1991.
107. Jawalekar SR, Marx GF: Cutaneous cerebrospinal fluid leakage following attempted extradural block. Anesthesiology 54:348–349, 1981.
108. Jorfeldt L: The effect of local anesthetics on the central circulation and respiration in man and dog. Acta Anaesth Scand 12:153–169, 1968.
109. Kepes ER, Duncalf D: Treatment of backache with spinal injections for local anesthetics, spinal and systemic steroids. A review. Pain 22:33–47, 1985.
110. Kikuchi S, Hasue M, Nishiuama K, et al: Anatomic and clinical studies of radicular symptoms. Spine 9:23–40, 1984.
111. Klenerman L, Greenwood R, Davenport HT, et al: Lumbar epidural injections in the treatment of sciatica. Br J Rheumatol 23:35–38, 1984.
112. Knight CL, Burnell JC: Systemic side-effects of extradural steroids. Anesthesia 35:593–594, 1980.
113. Kornberg M: Discography and magnetic resonance imaging in the diagnosis of lumbar disc disruption. Spine 14:1368–1372, 1989.
114. Krempen JF, Smith BS: Nerve root injection: A method for evaluating the etiology of sciatica. J Bone Joint Surg 56A:1435–1444, 1974.
115. Lerner SM, Gutterman P, Jenkins F: Epidural hematoma and paraplegia after numerous lumbar punctures. Anesthesia 39:550–553, 1973.
116. Lievre JA, Bloch-Michel H, Pean G, et al: L'hydrocortisone en injection locale. Rheumatism 20:310–311, 1953.
117. Lindhal O, Rexed B: Histologic changes in spinal nerve roots of operated cases of sciatica. Acta Orthop Scand 20:215–225, 1951.
118. Longmire S, Joyce TH: Treatment of a duro-cutaneous fistula secondary to attempted epidural anesthesia with an epidural autologous blood patch. Anesthesiology 60:63–64, 1984.
119. Mangar D, Thomas PB: Epidural steroid injections in the treatment of cervical and lumbar pain syndromes. Reg Anesth 16:246, 1991.
120. Mather LE: Cardiovascular and subjective central nervous system effects of long-acting local anesthetics in man. Anaesth Intensive Care 7:215–221, 1979.
121. Matthews JA, Mills SB, Jenkins VM, et al: Back pain and sciatica: Controlled trials of manipulation, traction, sclerosant and epidural injections. Br J Rheumatol 26:416–423, 1987.
122. McCarron RF, Wimpee MW, Hudkins PG, et al: The inflammatory effect of nucleus pulposus: A possible element in the pathogenesis of low back pain. Spine 12:760–764, 1987.
123. Merwin JD: Chronic thoracic pain. In Ramamurthy S, Rogers JN (eds): Decision Making in Pain Management. St. Louis, B.C. Decker, 1993, p 112.
124. Mihic DN: Postspinal headache and relationship of the needle bevel to longitudinal dural fibers. Reg Anesth 10:76, 1985.
125. Moore DC: A surface marking for caudal block. Br J Anaesth 40:916, 1968.
126. Morishima HO, Peterson H, Finster M, et al: Is bupivacaine more cardiotoxic than lidocaine? Anesthesiology 59:A409, 1983.
127. Murphy RW: Nerve roots and spinal nerves in degenerative disc disease. Clin Orthop 129:46–60, 1977.
128. Murphy TM: Chronic pain. In Miller RD (ed): Anesthesia, 3rd ed. New York, Churchill Livingstone, 1990, p 360.
129. Neal JM: Management of postdural puncture headache. Clin Dialogues Reg Anesth 3:1–5, 1992.
130. Nelson DA: Dangers from methylprednisolone acetate therapy by intraspinal injection. Arch Neurol 45:804–806, 1988.
131. Nelson DA, Vates TS, Thomas RB: Complications from intrathecal steroid therapy in patients with multiple sclerosis. Acta Neurol Scand 49:176–188, 1973.
132. Okell RW, Sprigge JS: Unintentional dural puncture. A survey of recognition and management. Anaesthesia 42:1110–1113, 1987.
133. Olsen KS: Epidural blood patch in the treatment of post-lumbar puncture headache. Pain 30:293–301, 1987.
134. Ostheimer GW, Paluhniuk RJ, Schnider SM: Epidural blood patch for post-lumbar puncture headache. Anesthesiology 41:307–308, 1974.
135. Pasquier MM, Leri J: Injections intra et extra-durals de cocaine a dose minime dans la traitement de la sciatique. Bull Gen Therap 142:196, 1901.
136. Pearce J, Moll JMH: Conservative treatment and natural history of acute lumbar disc disease lesions. J Neurol Neurosurg Psychiatry 30:13–17, 1967.
137. Preuss L: Allergic reactions to systemic glucocorticoids: A review. Am Allergy 55:772–775, 1985.
138. Purcell-Jones G, Pitcher CE, Justins DM: Paravertebral somatic nerve block: A clinical radiographic and computed tomographic study in chronic pain patients. Anesth Analg 68:32–39, 1989.
139. Purkis IE: Cervical epidural steroids. Pain Clinic 1:3–7, 1986.
140. Quaynor H, Corbey M, Berg P: Spinal anesthesia in day-care surgery with a 26-gauge needle. Br J Anaesth 65:766–769, 1990.
141. Raff H, Nelson DK, Finding JW, et al: Acute and chronic suppression of ACTH and cortisol after epidural steroid administration in humans [abstract]. Program of the 73rd annual meeting of the Endocrine Society. Washington, DC, 1991.
142. Raj PP: Prognostic and therapeutic local anesthetic blockade. In Cousins MJ, Bridenbaugh PO (eds): Neural Blockade in Clinical Anesthesia and Management of Pain. Philadelphia, J.B. Lippincott, 1988, pp 899–934.
143. Ramsey HJ: Fat in the epidural space of young and adult cats. Am J Anat 104:345, 1959.
144. Reiz S, Nath S: Cardiotoxicity of local anesthetic agents. Br J Anaesth 58:736–746, 1986.
145. Renfrew DL, Moore TE, Kathol MH, et al: Correct placement of epidural steroid injections: Fluoroscopic guidance and contrast administration. AJNR 12:1003–1007, 1991.
146. Reynolds AF, Roberts PA, Pollay M, et al: Quantitative anatomy of the thoracolumbar epidural space. Neurosurgery 17:905–907, 1985.
147. Ridley MG, Kingsley GH, Gibson T, et al: Outpatient lumbar epidural corticosteroid injection in the management of sciatica. Br J Rheumatol 27:295–299, 1988.
148. Roberts M, Shepard GL, McCormick RC: Tuberculous meningitis after intrathecally administered methylprednisolone acetate. JAMA 200:894–896, 1967.
149. Rocco AG, Frank E, Kaul AF, et al: Epidural steroid, epidural morphine and epidural steroids combined with morphine in the treatment of post laminectomy syndrome. Pain 36:297–303, 1989.

150. Roche J: Steroid-induced arachnoiditis. Med J Aust 140: 281–284, 1984.
151. Rowlingson JC, Kirschenbaum LP: Epidural analgesic techniques in the management of cervical pain. Anesth Analg 65:938–942, 1986.
152. Ryan MD, Taylor TKF: Management of lumbar nerve root pain. Med J Aust 2:532–534, 1981.
153. Saal JA, Saal JS: Nonoperative treatment of herniated lumbar intervertebral disc with radiculopathy. An outcome study. Spine 14:431–437, 1989.
154. Saal JS, Transon RC, Dobrow R, et al: High levels of inflammatory phospholipase A2 activity in lumbar disc herniations. Spine 15:674–678, 1990.
155. Scott DB, Jebson PJ, Braid DP, et al: Factors effecting plasma levels of lignocaine and prilocaine. Br J Anaesth 44:1040–1049, 1972.
156. Shantha TR, Evans JA: The relationship of epidural anesthesia to neural membranes and arachnoid villi. Anesthesiology 37:543–557, 1972.
157. Shealy CN: Dangers of spinal injections without proper diagnosis. JAMA 197:1104–1106, 1966.
158. Shimasoto S, Etsten BE: The role of the venous system in cardiocirculatory dynamics during spinal and epidural anesthesia in man. Anesthesiology 30:619, 1969.
159. Shulman M: Treatment of neck pain with cervical epidural injection. Reg Anesth 11:92–94, 1986.
160. Sicard JA: Sur les injections epidurales sacrococcygienes. C R Soc Biol 53:479, 1901.
161. Simon DL, Kung RD, German JD, et al: Allergic or pseudoallergic reaction following epidural steroid deposition and skin testing. Reg Anesth 14:253–255, 1989.
162. Sjogren S, Wright B: Circulation, respiration and lidocaine concentration during continuous epidural blockade. Acta Anaesth Scand 16(suppl):5, 1972.
163. Snoek W, Weber H, Jorgenson B: Double blind evaluation of extradural methylprednisolone for herniated lumbar discs. Acta Orthop Scand 48:635–641, 1977.
164. Stambough JL, Booth RE Jr, Rothman RH: Transient hypercorticism after epidural steroid injection. A case report. J Bone Joint Surg 66A:1115–1116, 1984.
165. Stanley D, McLoren MI, Evinton HA, et al: A prospective study of nerve root infiltration in the diagnosis of sciatica: A comparison with radiculopathy, computed tomography and operative findings. Spine 15:540–543, 1990.
166. Stewart HD, Quinnel RC, Dann N: Epidurography in the management of sciatica. Br J Rheumatol 26:424–429, 1987.
167. Strong WE, Wesley R, Winnie AP: Epidural steroids are safe and effective when given appropriately [letter]. Arch Neurol 48:1012, 1991.
168. Swerdlow M, Sayle-Creer W: A study of extradural medication in the relief of the lumbosciatic syndrome. Anesthesiology 25:341–345, 1970.
169. Szeinfeld M, Ihmeidan IH, Moser MM, et al: Epidural blood patch: Evaluation of the volume and spread of blood injected into the epidural space. Anesthesiology 64:820–822, 1986.
170. Tajima T, Furukawa K, Kuramachi E: Selective lumbosacral radiculopathy and block. Spine 5:68–77, 1980.
171. Takata T, Inoue S, Takahashi K, et al: Swelling of the cauda equina in patients who have herniation of a lumbar disc: A possible pathogenesis of sciatica. J Bone Joint Surg 70A:361–368, 1988.
172. Tourtellotte WW, Henderson WG, Tucker RP, et al: A randomized, double-blind clinical trial comparing the 22 versus 26 gauge needle in the production of the postlumbar puncture syndrome in normal individuals. Headache 12:73–78, 1972.
173. Tuel SM, Meythaler JM, Cross LL: Cushing's syndrome from epidural methylprednisolone. Pain 40:81–84, 1990.
174. Tuohy ER: Continuous spinal anesthesia: A new method of utilizing a ureteral catheter. Surg Clin North Am 25:834, 1945.
175. Usubiaga JE, Wikinski JA, Usubiaga LE: Epidural pressure and its relation to spread of anesthetic solutions in epidural space. Anesth Analg 46:440–446, 1967.
176. Vandam LD, Dfipps RD: Long-term follow-up of patients who received 10,098 spinal anesthetics. JAMA 161:586–591, 1956.
177. Viner N: Intractable sciatica—the sacral epidural injection—An effective method of giving relief. Can Med Assoc J 15:630–634, 1925.
178. [Reference deleted.]
179. Waldman SD: Complications of cervical epidural nerve blocks with steroids: A prospective study of 790 consecutive blocks. Reg Anesth 14:149–151, 1989.
180. Warfield CA: Steroids and low back pain. Hosp Pract (Off Ed) 20:32J–32R, 1985.
181. Warfield CA, Biber MO, Crews IA, et al: Epidural steroid injection as a treatment for cervical radiculitis. Clin J Pain 4:201, 1988.
182. Warr AC, Wilkinson JA, Burn JMB, et al: Chronic lumbosciatic syndrome treated by epidural injection and manipulation. Practitioner 209:53–59, 1972.
183. Weinstein J: Mechanisms of spinal pain: The dorsal root ganglion and its role as a mediator of low-back pain. Spine 11:999–1001. 1986.
184. White AH: Injection techniques for the diagnosis and treatment of low back pain. Orthop Clin North Am 14:553–567, 1983.
185. White AH: Injections, where do they fit? In Aggressive Non-Surgical Rehabilitation of Lumbar Spine and Sports Injuries. San Francisco, 1989.
186. White AH, Derby R, Wynne G: Epidural injections for the diagnosis and treatment of low back pain. Spine 5:78–82, 1980.
187. White AWM: Low back pain in men receiving worker's compensation. Can Med Assoc J 95:50–56, 1966.
188. Williams KN, Jackowski A, Evans PJD: Epidural hematoma requiring surgical decompression following repeated cervical epidural steroid injections for chronic pain. Pain 42:197–199, 1990.
189. Williams MP, Cherryman GR: Thoracic disc herniation: MR imaging. Radiology 167:874–875, 1988.
190. Williams MP, Cherryman GR, Husband JE: Significance of thoracic disc herniation demonstrated by MR imaging. J Comput Assist Tomogr 13:211–214, 1989.
191. Williamson JA: Inadvertent spinal subdural injection during attempted spinal epidural steroid therapy. Anesth Intensive Care 18:406–408, 1990.
192. Willis RJ: Caudal epidural blockade. In Cousins MJ, Bridenbaugh PO (eds): Neural Blockade in Clinical Anesthesia and Management of Pain. Philadelphia, J.B. Lippincott, 1988, pp 361–386.
193. Wilson TA, Branch CL Jr: Thoracic disc herniation. Am Fam Phys 45:2162–2168, 1992.
194. Winnie AP, Hartmen JT, Meyers HL, et al: Pain clinic II. Intradural and extradural corticosteroids for sciatica. Anesth Analg 51:990–1003, 1972.
195. Yamazaka N: Intraspinal injection of hydrocortisone or prednisolone in the treatment of intervertebral disc herniation. Nippon Seikeigeka Gakkai Zasshi 33:689, 1959.
196. Yates DW: A comparison of the types of epidural injection commonly used in the treatment of low back pain and sciatica. Rheumatol Rehab 17:181–186, 1978.
197. Zimmerman M: Peripheral and central nervous system mechanisms of nociception, pain and pain therapy: Facts and hypotheses. In Bonica JJ, Liebeskind JC, Alber-Fessard T (eds): Advances in Pain Therapy. New York, Raven Press, 1979, pp 3–32.

INDEX

Entries in **boldface** type indicate complete chapters.